AREA MAPS

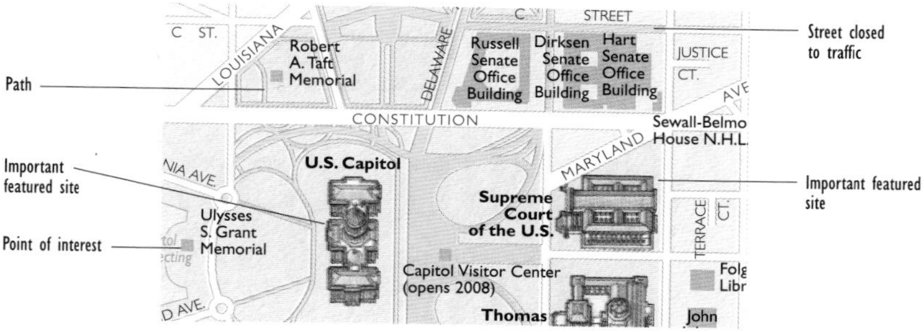

• A locator map accompanies each area map and shows the location of that area in the city.

WALKING TOURS

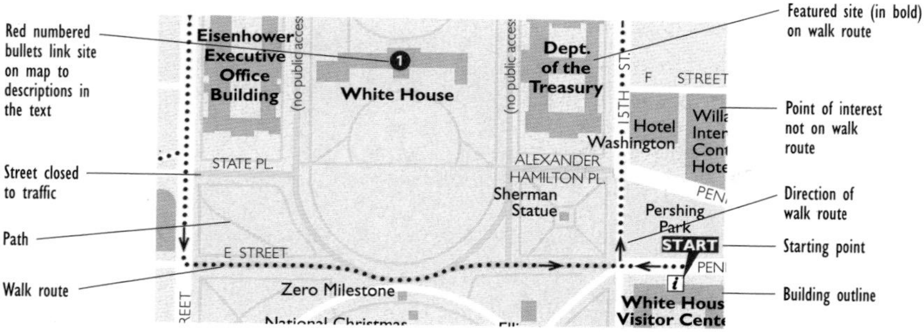

• An information box gives the starting and ending points, time and length of walk, and places not to be missed along the route.

REGIONAL/EXCURSION MAPS

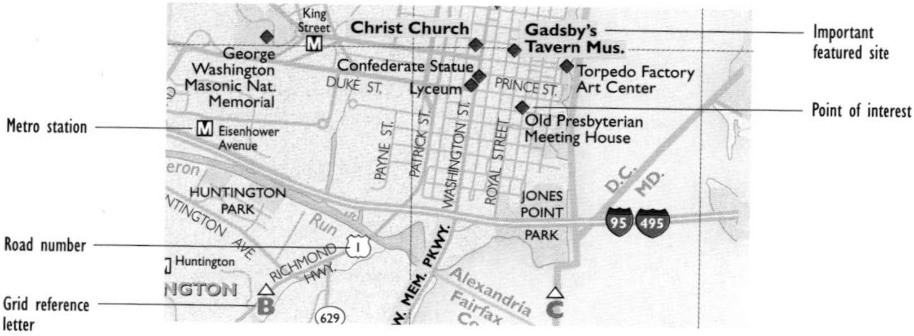

• Cities and sites described in the Across the Potomac and Excursions chapters (p. 201 & p. 215) are bolded and highlighted in yellow on the map. Other suggested places to visit are also bolded and are shown with a red diamond symbol.

NATIONAL GEOGRAPHIC

TRAVELER Washington D.C.

About the author & photographer

John Thompson has written or contributed to more than a dozen National Geographic books. His latest Society publications include *Wildlands of the Upper South* and *America's Western Edge*. A former resident of Washington, D.C., he now lives in Charlottesville, Virginia.

Richard Nowitz was a contract photographer for National Geographic *WORLD* (now *Kids*) magazine for 10 years and is now a contributing photographer to the National Geographic Image Collection. He has been the principal photographer of more than 20 large-format photo and travel guides; in 1968 he was honored by the Society of American Travel Writers as Travel Photographer of the Year. He lives in Maryland with his wife and three children.

Diana Parsell updated the 2008 edition.

With contributions by:
Sean Groom, author of "City on the river" feature on pp. 32–33
Thomas Head, former executive wine and food editor of *Washingtonian* magazine, author of the original Travelwise section
David Montgomery, reporter with the *Washington Post* Style section, author of "Washington today" on pp. 10–17
Barbara A. Noe, author of "It's a spooky little town" feature on pp. 120–121
Mark Rogers, author of "Politics at work" feature on pp. 58–59
James Yenckel, author of "Famous denizens of Georgetown" feature on pp. 158–159

NATIONAL GEOGRAPHIC

TRAVELER

Washington D.C.

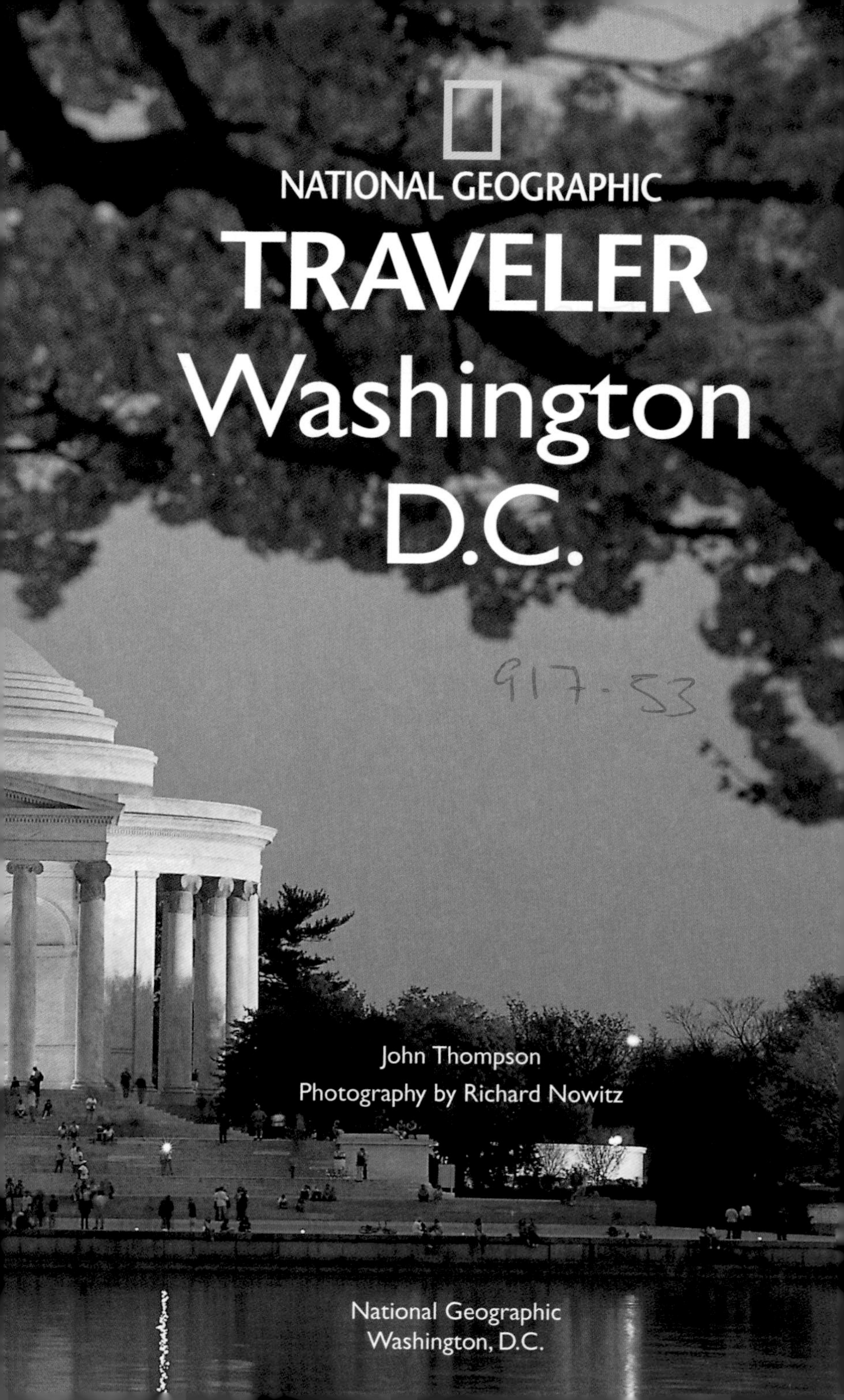

NATIONAL GEOGRAPHIC

TRAVELER Washington D.C.

John Thompson
Photography by Richard Nowitz

National Geographic
Washington, D.C.

Contents

Page 1: Snapshot of the Washington Monument and the Reflecting Pool
Pages 2–3: The Jefferson Memorial and cherry blossoms draw crowds on a spring evening.
Left: Colorful kayaks await their turn on the water beneath Key Bridge.

How to use this guide

See back flap for keys to text and map symbols.

The *National Geographic Traveler* brings you the best of Washington, D.C., in text, pictures, and maps. Divided into three main sections, the guide begins with an overview of history and culture.

Following are ten area chapters with featured sites selected by the author for their particular interest. Each chapter opens with its own contents list for easy reference. A map introduces the parameters covered in the chapter, highlighting the featured sites and locating other places of interest. Walks, plotted on their own maps, suggest routes for discovering the most about an area. Features and sidebars offer intriguing detail on history, culture, or contemporary life.

The final section, Travelwise, lists essential information for the traveler—pre-trip planning, special events, getting around, practical advice, and emergency contacts—plus provides a selection of hotels and restaurants arranged by area, shops, activities, and entertainment possibilities.

To the best of our knowledge, all information is accurate as of June 2007. However, it is always advisable to call ahead or check information online when possible to find out about any changes.

282

Color coding

Each area of the city is color coded for easy reference. Find the area you want on the map on the front flap, and look for the color flash at the top of the pages of the relevant chapter. Information in **Travelwise** is also color coded to each region.

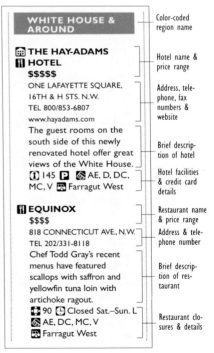

Corcoran Gallery of Art
www.corcoran.org
Map p. 106
500 17th St., N.W.,
202-639-1700
Closed Tues.
$$$
Metro: Farragut West; Bus: 80, S1

Visitor information

Practical information for most sites is given in the side column (see key to symbols on back flap). The map reference gives the page number of the map and grid reference. Other details are address, telephone number, days closed, entrance charge in a range from $ (under $5) to $$$$$ (over $25), and nearest Metro station and most important bus routes for sites in Washington. Other sites have information in italics and parentheses in the text.

TRAVELWISE

WHITE HOUSE & AROUND — Color-coded region name

THE HAY-ADAMS HOTEL
$$$$$ — Hotel name & price range

ONE LAFAYETTE SQUARE, 16TH & H STS. N.W.
TEL 800/853-6807
www.hayadams.com — Address, telephone, fax numbers & website

The guest rooms on the south side of this newly renovated hotel offer great views of the White House. — Brief description of hotel

145 AE, D, DC, MC, V Farragut West — Hotel facilities & credit card details

EQUINOX
$$$$ — Restaurant name & price range

818 CONNECTICUT AVE., N.W.
TEL 202/331-8118 — Address & telephone number

Chef Todd Gray's recent menus have featured scallops with saffron and yellowfin tuna loin with artichoke ragout. — Brief description of restaurant

90 Closed Sat.–Sun. L
AE, DC, MC, V
Farragut West — Restaurant closures & details

Hotel & restaurant prices

An explanation of the price bands used in entries is given in the Hotels & Restaurants section (beginning on p. 240).

History & culture

The gold-leaf eagle has landed—atop Union Station.

Washington today

A HEADY SELF-CONFIDENCE IS SWELLING IN WASHINGTON, D.C., AS THE CITY demonstrates it is a city, not some unclassifiable zone dubbed the District of Columbia—a phrase that appears in speeches but never in conversation.

To natives and long-time transplants, home is just Dee-Cee, thank you, or Wahr-shington in soft Southern-accented tones slightly edged by the oddly Elizabethan flint of dialects around the Chesapeake Bay. Washington never forgets that the government is the reason this once marshy lowland was reclaimed and the federal city was planted at a twinkling bend in the Potomac River. Yet the city defiantly transcends its role as a bland backdrop to the grandeur of the monuments, museums, and great American history hereabouts. Those things are why many people come—but not why they stay.

The map looks as if something took a ragged bite out of the once perfect 100-square-mile diamond-shaped District. That happened in 1846, when Virginia reclaimed its share of the land donated to create the capital. The remaining 68 square miles, originally part of Maryland, make an intimate city of 572,000 people.

The other physical dimension of the intimate city is up, and in Washington ambition soars higher than architecture. No building stands taller than the Capitol dome; in the densest part of town—the K Street canyon populated by lawyers and lobbyists—offices top out at the 12th floor. This architectural homage to the Capitol means the typical Washington street has one of the biggest skies in urban America. It makes walking a pleasure in a city designed with walkers in mind, with wide avenues and breathtaking sight lines anchored by Pierre Charles L'Enfant's ceremonial circles. Turn a corner and you might see the upper quarter of the Washington Monument peeking above the modest roofline of a modern office building—a juxtaposition of the monumental capital and the working city that is quintessentially Washington.

The dual nature of the city's soul is reflected in myriad ways as power Washington and workaday Washington mingle serendipitously. Spend time shopping on Connecticut Avenue, lunching on Wisconsin, or talking politics on Pennsylvania, and you'll be startled to see motorcycle police appear out of nowhere and block traffic. Next you'll hear the sirens and see the speeding motorcade: The President on his way to some engagement. Look through the limo's tinted glass and you might catch a wave in return. Then the police vanish—maestros of that Washington ballet, the rolling blockade.

Washingtonians always know when someone important has moved down the block. Suddenly fit-looking men and women in plain clothes wearing earpieces linger about. Several years ago, Capitol Hill residents reported that the U.S. attorney general, John Ashcroft, was an excellent piano player, after they heard his baby-grand renditions of show tunes and classical melodies floating out the windows of his row house. In Glover Park, trying to guess which neighbor's house conceals the entrance to a secret FBI tunnel under the old Soviet Embassy has been a favorite parlor game.

Not that the privilege of being the nation's capital isn't sometimes a burden. When that happens, Washington, ever the gracious Southern hostess, can also play the irreverent Northern wag. The lack of a vote in Congress is a sore point. Washingtonians pay 2.5 billion dollars a year in federal income taxes—more per capita than in 49 of the states—yet have no say in how the money is spent. The Constitution dictates that the District cannot be a state, but Congress could grant it a vote in the federal legislature. In 2000, the city's 200th anniversary as the capital, a resident came up with a new license plate motto, a cheeky civics lesson: "Taxation Without Representation."

As Washington strides into the future, its aspirations rise in glass and limestone amid the marble totems of its past. Construction cranes hover throughout the downtown like a new kind of Washington monument while layers of

A rosy dawn catches a mirror image of the U.S. Capitol and an equestrian statue of Ulysses S. Grant in the waters of the Capitol Reflecting Pool.

scaffolding signal exciting new uses of old spaces: a buzzing Seventh Street corridor, luxury hotel rooms inside the 19th-century Tariff Building, and welcome makeovers of august institutions such as the National Portrait Gallery and the National Archives.

Preservation guidelines are intended to ensure that development travesties don't mar the best of the old, but there's always a fear that shiny new facades and high rents will doom quirky neighborhood joints. A buttoned-down town like Washington needs as many of these places as it can get. People take infinite comfort that Ben's Chili Bowl on U Street continues to purvey the best chili dogs in the free world. All around Ben's, the street once known as the "Black Broadway," where Duke Ellington used to perform, is throbbing again with energy beneath the soulful gaze of Ellington himself—painted larger

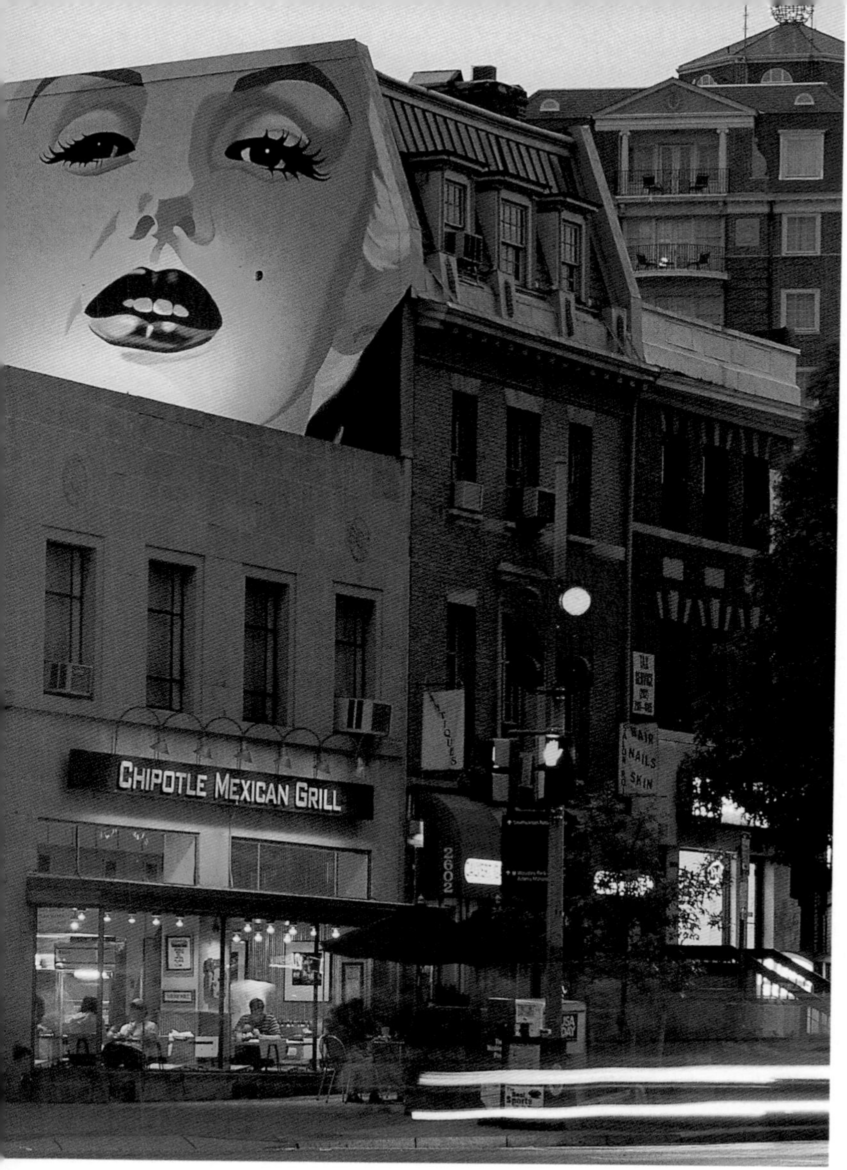

than life on the exposed side of a building.

Postcard Washington is a vision of famous buildings, but the people make the city. Contrary to reputation, this is not a population of transients, a capital of people from someplace else getting ready to leave. When a presidential administration changes, or a new Congress is seated, only a few thousand people arrive to replace the few thousand on their way out.

Most Washingtonians don't work for the government. Many settled here for opportunities in technology, education, public policy, international affairs, and journalism. A large core of native Washingtonians, particularly African-American families, moved here from the South generations ago when jobs in the

Marilyn Monroe is a regular on the busy corner of Calvert Street and Connecticut Avenue, popular for its ethnic restaurants.

federal government afforded one of the few avenues of advancement for blacks. Now about 60 percent of the population is black, 30 percent white. The growing Hispanic community is about 8 percent.

In the late 1990s Washingtonians began hearing real estate agents use an unaccustomed term for the city: "Hot!" Suburban traffic congestion, falling crime, and an improving economy merged to make city living fashionable again. Decades of population loss subsided, replaced by slight annual gains. The newcomers are busy restoring row houses in once neglected neighborhoods and discarding at least one of their two cars for sensible shoes and the clean comfort of the Metro.

Even longtime Washingtonians can afford to be choosy about how they savor monumental Washington. They stand at the top of the Capitol steps and try again to absorb the perfect

landscape geometry lesson that is the Mall. They visit their favorite Smithsonian exhibits religiously. They wait to see the Washington Monument at sundown, when the marble turns rose and gold. The Franklin Delano Roosevelt Memorial is popular for late-evening romantic interludes amid the mood-lit waterfalls.

But Washingtonians would just as soon leave the Mall and zip up to the National Arboretum in Northeast to study the exquisite bonsai tree

Downtown sidewalks such as this one on 17th Street fill with folks on lunchtime errands or simply taking a break from work.

exhibition. Or take the kids on an excursion to the remains of the Civil War forts that once ringed the city. Or catch a home baseball game, as the national pastime returned to the capital in 2005 after a 34-year hiatus. Or disappear into the wilds of Rock Creek Park, where you can

forget you are in a city. It is places like these—beyond the Mall—where the heart of the living city beats in four quadrants. The perfect coda to seeing the Lincoln Memorial is a visit to the Frederick Douglass house in Anacostia. During the Potomac springtime, when the perfume of Southern blooms intoxicates even the most hopeless workaholic, by all means see the cherry blossoms suspended like pink breath around the Tidal Basin—but also don't miss the less crowded and still spectacular blossom display at Dumbarton Oaks in Georgetown.

Spanish will get you as far as English in Adams Morgan, where club music blares until 2 a.m. and the cuisine runs from El Salvador to Afghanistan to Ethiopia to Lebanon. Hop a Metro to the southwest waterfront and find the latest Pulitzer Prize-winning play being presented at Arena Stage or the freshest catch from the Chesapeake

being sold on the Maine Avenue docks.

In the neighborhoods Washington comes most clearly into perspective. Climb the hill in Anacostia that John Wilkes Booth crossed when escaping after he assassinated Abraham Lincoln, and take in the view from the parking lot of Our Lady of Perpetual Help Church. Or find a perch on the Brookland heights occupied by the Basilica of the National Shrine of the Immaculate Conception. The bitten-off diamond city spreads before you—the low downtown skyline slipping into rings of row house neighborhoods stretched along the long lines of L'Enfant's broad boulevards.

And there, too, are the white dome and the obelisk—still grand at this distance, but not so dominating, and part of a larger picture. ■

Weekly jam sessions add a beat to beautifully landscaped Meridian Park.

History of Washington

GEORGE WASHINGTON, PIERRE CHARLES L'ENFANT, AND THE MANY OTHERS involved knew they were engaged in something momentous when they set out to design the capital of the United States. In an age when preplanned cities of this scale were unheard of, here was a chance to lay out a worldwide center of culture, commerce, and learning. Somewhat like the Constitution, the resulting city design was the product of a lively give-and-take among some of 18th-century America's greatest minds. Awkward and unattractive at first, the city has matured into a metropolis of unfinished grace and beauty—a reflection of the imperfect and ever evolving democracy it governs.

DOING IT ON PURPOSE

Seven years had passed since the Revolutionary War when, in July 1790, Congress agreed on the location of a new capital. Until that time, citizens of the new nation had identified primarily with their home state, thinking of themselves as Virginians or New Yorkers rather than Americans. Local ties would continue to command the loyalties of many, but it was clear that establishing the seat of a central government was essential to holding the loosely joined republic together.

One key was to avoid the mistakes of the European empires that had failed the very people who were here now. This was to be a government of the people, so the placement and design of the capital would set the tone for a federal government that aspired to be strong but not domineering. The capital, by extension, must be grand yet welcoming.

The first step in that tall order was to pick an appropriate place. With the 13 Colonies strewn the length of the eastern seaboard, it was logical to locate the capital about halfway down. In a classic display of democratic compromise, Secretary of the Treasury Alexander Hamilton agreed to urge northern states to vote for a southern capital if Virginia Representative James Madison would support federal assumption of state war debts (he did). So despite occupying the approximate midpoint of the coast, Washington was deemed a "Southern" town from the outset. This characterization had much to do with the fact that Washington lay (and lies) 60 miles south of the Mason-Dixon Line—the Maryland-Pennsylvania border that also divides the North from the South.

As for the precise size and site of the city, Congress left President Washington somewhat in the dark. The representatives decreed only that the capital was not to exceed 10 miles square, and that it must be positioned on the Potomac River somewhere between the mouth of the Eastern Branch (now the Anacostia River) and Conococheague Creek, some 70 miles upriver. The rest was up to Washington.

In January of 1791, Washington selected a swatch of land at the highest navigable point on the Potomac River, where it was joined by the Eastern Branch. The site was partly a marriage of convenience: The preexisting riverport towns of Alexandria, Virginia, and Georgetown, Maryland, could easily receive shipments of the lumber and foodstuffs the city would need to sustain construction.

Laid out in a square carved from Maryland (mostly) and Virginia, the capital was named "City of Washington" to honor America's first President. Surveyor Andrew Ellicott and Benjamin Banneker—his self-taught, freeborn black assistant—delimited a square 10 miles on a side, with the corners pointing in the cardinal directions.

Though President Washington had trained as a surveyor, like any good leader he was quick to recognize those moments when he needed expert advice. For his chief engineer he chose a well-connected young Frenchman who had fought against the British during the Revolutionary War and had gone on to design a temporary headquarters for the federal government in New York. The idea of creating an important city out of nothing appealed mightily to the brilliant Pierre Charles L'Enfant—and apparently daunted him not at all.

Charles Willson Peale's "George Washington" (1772) portrays the future president as a young colonel in a Virginia regiment.

Angling for the job, he wrote these words to President Washington in 1789: "No nation, perhaps, had ever before the opportunity offered them of deliberately deciding on the spot where their Capital City should be fixed."

L'Enfant got the job.

Throughout 1791, he could be seen standing high atop Jenkins Hill (now Capitol Hill) or striding the woods of Tiber Creek (modern-day Constitution Avenue), his surveying instruments in hand, measuring distances and elevations. By contrast, L'Enfant's motivation—a vision of a grand city of broad avenues, monumental government edifices, and stirring vistas—remained invisible to all but himself. "I see the capital city as something more than a place to live and work," he wrote. "I see it as a symbol.... [W]e should plan now with the realization that a great nation is going to rise on this continent.... Right now, we have a chance which no nation has ever given itself.... How can America plan for less than greatness?"

L'ENFANT TERRIBLE

L'Enfant's extraordinary prescience and pride were voiced at a time when the country's most populous city, Philadelphia, claimed only 28,522 residents. Yet here was L'Enfant, imagining a capital of 800,000 citizens—larger than many of the European cities such as Paris that had served as his models.

As it turned out, L'Enfant was dead on: At its population peak in 1950, Washington was home to 802,000 people. (That number is now about 570,000.)

Standing a mile apart but joined by Pennsylvania Avenue, the Capitol building and the President's House formed a barbell at the core of L'Enfant's design. (The presidential residence would not be officially named the White House until 1901.) Several broad streets would radiate from these two powerhouses, signifying their openness and accessibility. The avenues would unspool at length before ending at circular intersections atop existing hills, thus creating views of "magnificent distances."

The Capitol would divide the city into quadrants, while a grid of numbered and lettered streets would be superimposed on the radiating avenues. The Mall, extending about 1 mile west from the Capitol to the Potomac River, would be a grand esplanade similar to the one L'Enfant had beheld in Marly, near Versailles. The Frenchman foresaw fine baroque houses lining it on either side.

Within a year, L'Enfant had been fired by President Washington for insubordination and refusal to compromise. Even so, his plan was largely enacted: Trees and buildings may veil several of those hoped-for views of "magnificent distances," yet Dupont and Scott Circles, among others, still clearly display the beauty of the original design.

Despite its ambitious origin, the city hardly sprang up overnight. Congressmen arriving for the Inaugural session in 1800 looked out upon a dismal scene. The streets were muddy. Mosquitoes and snakes bred in abundance. Hogs and cattle roamed at will, while the unfinished Capitol and President's House had spawned attendant clusters of huts and shacks resembling refugee villages. One newly minted statesman dubbed this hardship post "a mudhole equal to the great Serbonian bog."

With no property tax on government buildings, the city relied on real estate speculation for funding. Yet buyers were scarce: By 1800, less than 10 percent of city lots had been sold. Washington grew from 8,208 people by 1810 to 18,826 by 1830, a rate far below the national average. Gazing upon these wide, uncluttered avenues going nowhere, Charles Dickens would dub Washington "the City of Magnificent Intentions."

WAR COMES TO WASHINGTON

The War of 1812 proved to be a turning point in the city's fortunes, which mirrored those of the country at large. In August 1814, with the British victory sealed, redcoats landed in Maryland and marched on Washington, where they torched the Capitol, the President's House, and all federal buildings except the old Blodgett's Hotel, which housed both the Post Office and the Patent Office at the time.

Afterward, Congress came close to voting that the capital be relocated. But with local bankers promising to help rebuild the city—and galvanized by the strong sense of community that often follows a disaster—Washington

Two years into the War of 1812, British soldiers gut the White House with fire in this undated Washington drawing.

"The Peacemakers" (1868) by George P. A. Healy depicts William Sherman, Ulysses S. Grant, President Lincoln, and David Porter discussing peace terms just before the Civil War's end.

dug in and bounced back. President Madison repaired to the Octagon (see p. 122), Congress moved to the Patent Office (and from there to a temporary building on the site of the present-day Supreme Court), and life went on.

The third of the District lying west and south of the river was ceded back to Virginia in 1846. Not only did the federal government have no need for the land on that side of the Potomac River, but Alexandria—having lost political advantages by its inclusion in the District—had petitioned the state to re-embrace it. This reduced Washington City to a parcel of land covering just 68 square miles.

A SECOND CITY

History's most bitter irony may be that this bastion of freedom was built on slave labor. Beginning in the 1790s, plantation owners in Maryland and Virginia were paid for the use of their slaves to supplement the meager supply of skilled workers constructing the capital.

In a parallel development, this city of solons became a magnet for the disenfranchised. Situated at the northern extreme of the upper South, Washington was a natural gateway for runaway slaves. Though slavery would not be outlawed in the city until 1862, by 1830 Washington contained more free blacks than slaves. A "second city"—one composed largely of African Americans—sprang to life within the federal city.

Lacking an entrenched society but rich with a transient mix of foreigners and congressmen, Washington was generally more tolerant of blacks than were other Southern cities. From 1807 to 1861, more than 15 private black schools flourished in the district.

Occasionally, however, race riots erupted. On the heels of the Nat Turner rebellion in 1831, the Snow Riot of 1835 was ignited by two unrelated events: A slave allegedly tried to murder the widow of the U.S. Capitol designer, William Thornton, and a white physician was arrested for possession of abolitionist tracts, whose publication or distribution was forbidden in D.C.

Rebuffed from lynching the doctor, a white mob turned its fury on Mr. Beverly Snow, the free black owner of a local restaurant. Though Snow escaped, roving bands attacked black churches, schools, restaurants, and tenements for the next week. Before long the city had tightened its black codes—discriminatory

Federal troops parade from the Capitol to the President's House to commemorate the end of the Civil War in April 1865.

laws governing the behavior of free blacks.

In the 1830s and '40s, Congress heard numerous petitions to banish slavery in Washington—the only place over which it exercised total control. Each time, shamefully, Georgetown's Southern-leaning aristocracy joined with the proslavery segment of Congress to keep the issue from being seriously debated.

In April 1848, 77 Washington slaves boarded the schooner *Pearl* at a city wharf and tried to escape to freedom down the Potomac River. Captured within a day, the slaves—many of them privileged house servants with only a few years' bondage remaining—were sold off to agents in Louisiana and Georgia. The deep passions stirred by the affair led the House of Representatives to pass a resolution that year calling for an end to the slave trade in Washington.

The resolution was nothing but paper. Slavery itself continued. Free blacks were only marginally better off. Black or white, poor neighborhoods were plagued by violent crime. The seedier areas of town included Swampoodle (now the area north of Massachusetts and New Jersey Avenues) and Murder Bay (today's Federal Triangle). The latter—located between President's Park (the Ellipse) and the fetid Washington City Canal (since covered by Constitution Avenue)—was especially notorious. "Crime, filth, and poverty seem to vie with each other in a career of degradation and death," a police superintendent characterized Murder Bay in 1866. "Whole families ... are crowded into mere apologies for shanties."

BROTHER AGAINST BROTHER

Monumental Washington started to take shape in the years leading up to the Civil War. Work began on the Washington Monument in 1848, but within six years funds had dried up, the monument was mired in political controversy, and construction was suspended with the building just 152 feet tall. By the time work resumed in 1880, white marble from the original quarry was no longer available; the white marble furnished by the second quarry has weathered differently from the base, yielding the two-tone tower in evidence today.

In 1855 the distinctive red-sandstone Smithsonian Castle rose beside the Mall, paving the way for several national museums. A forerunner to the National Theatre was in place on Pennsylvania Avenue by 1835. The

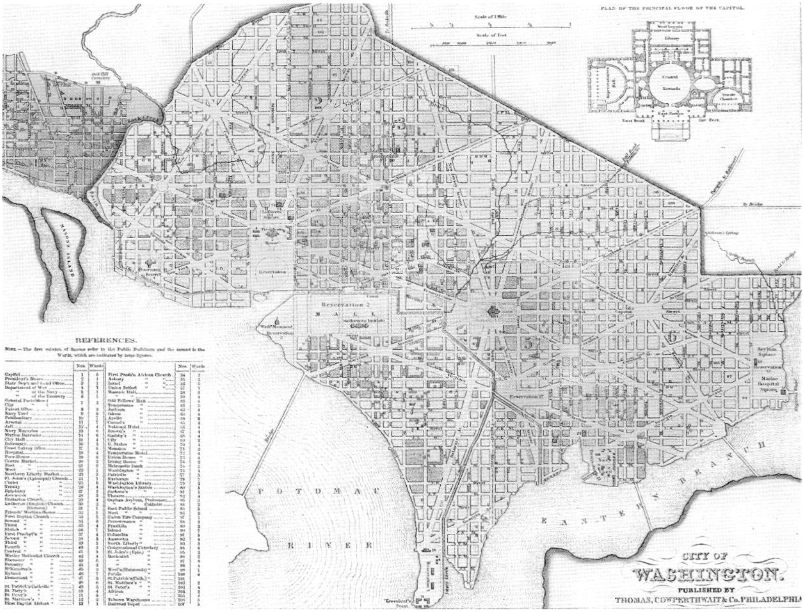

Willard and other fine hotels popped up in the neighborhood by the 1850s. Amid the statuary and posh town houses of Lafayette Square, the White House had settled into a state of manorial dignity, complete with greenhouses, flower gardens, and fruit trees.

Destined to tower above it all, the Capitol's cast-iron dome (replacing its wood dome of 1822) was under way by the Civil War's outbreak in April 1861. Despite an absence of building funds during that conflict, Lincoln ordered the Capitol's construction to go forward as a sign that the Union would endure.

Considered a remote and somewhat sleepy town before the war, Washington now entered the national consciousness as the staging ground for Union forces and the embattled capital of a divided nation. With the Confederate capital of Richmond just 100 miles distant, the war's major battles—Fredericksburg, Antietam, Gettysburg—formed an arc within easy striking distance of Washington. The first and second battles of Bull Run, for example, took place just 30 miles west of city limits.

To keep the Rebels at bay should they outflank the Union Army, a ring of 68 forts was hastily thrown up around Washington. These

installations proved their worth in July 1864, when a large Confederate force led by Gen. Jubal Early dashed through Maryland and reached the city's northern portal of Fort Stevens. Early's assault was repulsed within a day, but it gave the President a vivid taste of combat: Observing the skirmish from the fort's parapet, the 6-foot-4-inch top-hatted Lincoln made such a tempting target for enemy sharpshooters that a Union officer reprimanded him, "Get down, you damn fool, before you get shot!" The words were out of his mouth before the speaker—Lt. Col. (and future Supreme Court justice) Oliver Wendell Holmes, Jr.—realized he was upbraiding the President.

Washington was eventually overwhelmed—by its own troops. Bone-weary soldiers arrived by ship and rail, thronging the streets, falling asleep on vacant lots and sidewalks. Horse-drawn guns and caissons rutted the muddy streets; livestock grazed on the Mall; a bakery and barracks opened in the Capitol.

With more than 4,000 prostitutes in residence, a newspaper reported, the "majority of the women on the streets were openly disreputable." Troops under Gen. Joseph Hooker were such constant patrons of the red-light district southeast of the Treasury Department that the area was dubbed "Hooker's Division."

As battle casualties poured into Washington, the city scrambled to treat as many as 50,000 sick or injured soldiers at once. Practically every church, public building, and large private home in the city was pressed into service as military housing.

A time-lapse photograph of Dupont Circle on a winter's night (below) shows that L'Enfant's vision of central circles and radiating streets (opposite) is alive and well.

HAPPY DAYS AGAIN

The population explosion unleashed by the war—during which the city grew from 60,000 to 140,000 inhabitants, including 40,000 former slaves—continued to boom in peacetime. Freedmen's Village in Arlington and Barry Farm in Anacostia received federal aid to

Politics as unusual

If it is true that all politics is local, Washington seems more than happy to oblige. Native Washingtonians, fueled by the injustice of being deprived of full congressional-representation, often focus on the local political scene to the point of obsession.

Except for a brief flowering of self-governance from 1812 to 1871, Congress and the President have always controlled the city government and appointed its officials. In 1970, Washington was finally allowed to send a delegate to the House of Representatives, yet that deputy (in common with emissaries from Puerto Rico and other U.S. territories) could not vote, except in committees.

In 1973 Civil Rights and home rule activists won Washington the right to elect its own mayor and city council. Unwilling to cede power completely, Congress retained the right to interfere in local government whenever it deemed necessary.

That's exactly what happened in April 1995: With district finances in a shambles, Congress created a presidentially appointed D.C. financial control board to manage city spending. Two years later, Congress stripped Mayor Marion Barry of most of his authority and the control board took over the city reins.

After the 1998 mayoral election of Anthony Williams, previously the city's chief financial officer, the health of the city improved dramatically and the control board eventually released its grip. Adrian Fenty, who became mayor in 2007, has vowed to govern the city in a hands-on style. ■

house northward-migrating blacks.

With the help of radical Republicans bent on Reconstruction, black Washington enjoyed a sudden (if short-lived) heyday in the late 1860s and early 1870s. Howard University and the nation's first black high school—both staffed by top-notch instructors turning out well-educated graduates—were founded during this period. At the same time, blacks moved into jobs as officials and clerks, launched newspapers and other businesses, and mingled in white society.

Washington had elected its own mayors and aldermen since 1820. With the city in debt and apprehensive about the power of the newly granted black vote, Congress scrapped that system in 1871 and replaced it with a territorial government headed by a presidentially appointed governor. Other parts of the new city government included boards of public works and health; a nonvoting delegate to Congress; an elected house of delegates; and a president-appointed council, with Frederick Douglass one of three blacks among its 11 members.

President Ulysses S. Grant wanted to hand the governorship of this newborn political entity to his crony Alexander R. "Boss" Shepherd. He backed down when the city's conservative old guard protested his choice, but Shepherd wormed his way into power nonetheless: He was named vice president of public works, a post that allowed him to run the entire city.

"How is our new governor like a sheep?" went a riddle of the time.

"He is led by A. Shepherd" was the answer.

By hook but mostly by crook, Boss Shepherd led the way for the next three years. During his reign the city added miles of sewers, water lines, gas lines, sidewalks, and roads, as well as 60,000 trees and more than 1,000 houses and buildings. Most important, Shepherd saw to it that miles upon miles of streets were leveled and paved. Working people adored him for the jobs and civic improvements; blue bloods despised him for raising their taxes.

As it turned out, citizens were amply justified in feeling fleeced. Authorized to spend four million dollars on the city, Shepherd approved the expenditure of 20 million instead. This put the city in hock but landed Shepherd in a mansion on Farragut Square, two blocks from the White House.

Armed with Grant's tacit approval, Shepherd bullied the city into submission. When the Baltimore & Ohio Railroad delayed removing its tracks from the Capitol grounds, Shepherd loyalists materialized at midnight to rip up the offending ties and rails. He invited critics of such tactics to "git up and git."

Shepherd's undoing was the financial panic of 1873. The next year, Congress dissolved the territorial government and installed three presidentially appointed commissioners. The

Servicemen and friends form a conga line in front of the Red Cross Building on 17th Street to celebrate the end of World War II.

Organic Act of 1878 abolished home rule for good, giving the three commissioners "near-absolute power." It also set up the system, still in place today, whereby the district receives an annual operating subsidy from the federal government, compensating the district for the costs that the federal presence places on the city. (In 1997, however, that federal payment was suspended; in return, D.C. got tax breaks and a guarantee that the federal government would cover the district's substantial pension shortfall.)

INTO THE 20TH CENTURY

In Washington as in many other American cities, the final quarter of the 19th century was a fin-de-siècle free-for-all. Hotels, public buildings, and arriviste villas mushroomed along the city's main avenues. Though industry was confined to a handful of gristmills and breweries in Georgetown and Foggy Bottom, Washington's main employer—the federal government—provided thousands of jobs. In addition to the clerks needed to run the many newly born government agencies, construction workers were in demand to complete the long-delayed Washington Monument (1884), to construct the Library of Congress (1897), and to erect many other buildings that are city landmarks today. The National Zoological Park (1889) and Rock Creek Park (1890) were also created around this time, putting the pleasures of nature within easy reach of downtown museums and monuments.

Even as official Washington flourished, the city was nurturing seeds of discontent. Thousands of poor people had gravitated to the capital, lured by the simple notion that the President's adoptive home town would welcome them as well. Rarely was that the case. Washington's alleys, home to more than 17,000 residents, were notorious incubators of filth, crime, and disease. Most of these alleys would ultimately be torn down or gentrified, driving the poor underclass from one neighborhood to another.

To help the growing city realize the beauty envisioned by L'Enfant, in 1901 Senator James McMillan proposed a commission that would upgrade the Mall, expand the White House and the park system, and place judicial and congressional office buildings facing the Capitol. McMillan recruited four brilliant designers—architects Charles McKim and

Daniel Burnham, landscape architect Frederick Law Olmsted, and sculptor Augustus Saint-Gaudens—whose plans, drawn up free of charge, would be transformed into reality by the U.S. Army Corps of Engineers.

With Burnham leading the way, the city beautiful began to take shape. Railroad tracks crisscrossing the Mall were torn out. The Mall was extended to stretch all the way from the Capitol to the site of a planned memorial to Abraham Lincoln at its far west end. Gardens, fountains, and a reflecting pool were slated for the Mall as well. An opulent Union Station, designed by Burnham himself, rose north of the Capitol.

Not every aspect of the plan was enacted, yet it furnished a blueprint for future growth of the city core. It's fair to say that the McMillan Plan made possible the Mall's current status as a national showpiece.

STRUGGLES FOR FREEDOM

During the 1910s, the city's population swelled again as workers flooded in to support America's role in World War I. By decade's end, nearly 450,000 people called Washington home—a 32 percent increase since 1910. The Mall, which had begun to feel like a park, became a vast parking lot for hundreds of new automobiles that suddenly appeared in Washington.

With the proliferation of relief agencies during the Great Depression and President Franklin D. Roosevelt's New Deal, the number of workers on Washington's federal payroll rose from 70,261 in June 1933 to 108,673 in June 1935. Construction added many new facades to the cityscape: the Supreme Court building, the Federal Triangle buildings, the Library of Congress Annex (now called the John Adams Building), the Longworth House Office Building, and nearly 5,000 houses, apartment buildings, and office buildings.

As the city focused on winning World War II, the early 1940s brought yet another influx of new Washingtonians. Thousands of female office workers and servicemen descended on the city, and many of them stayed on after the war. By 1950, the district's population would peak at just over 800,000.

Once again, the Mall became a warehouse for the nation's needs. A beehive of "tempos"—temporary government office buildings made of cement and asbestos board—were built along both sides of the Mall, adding to those thrown up during World War I.

By war's end in 1945, Washington found itself the capital of the most powerful nation on Earth. It had evolved from a provincial Southern town to a world leader in little more than half a century. The city seemed to be flexing its new muscles, spearheading a Cold War against communism worldwide.

On a local level, however, the story of Washington was increasingly a tale of two cities. More and more, white and black Washingtonians led separate lives in separate

parts of town. Throughout the 1940s, D.C.'s schools, parks, playgrounds, restaurants, theaters, and water fountains remained as segregated as those in any Southern town.

Then, in 1954, came the U.S. Supreme Court ruling, in *Brown* v. *Board of Education,* that "separate but equal education facilities are inherently unequal." The ensuing rapid integration of D.C. public schools served as a model for the nation.

In the late 1950s, blacks outnumbered whites for the first time in Washington's history. The far reaches of the city's Northeast and Southeast quadrants had drawn a raft of new

Dr. Martin Luther King, Jr., salutes a crowd of Civil Rights activists during the August 28, 1963, March on Washington.

residents since World War II, most of them from rural backgrounds. Now, with whites leaving the severely overcrowded city for new housing in the suburbs, middle-class blacks moved en masse into such upper Northeast neighborhoods as Fort Totten and Brookland. From 1950 to 1975, the city's black population rose from 35 percent to more than 70.

With the appointment of Walter Washington as mayor-commissioner in 1967, black

Washington gained a degree of control over its affairs for the first time since the dissolution of the territorial government nearly 100 years earlier. Congress, however, retained final say over city governance—and it continues to wield that power today. This has created a troubling and inequitable political quirk: Washingtonians are the only modern Americans who suffer "taxation without representation," as some city vehicle licenses protest. D.C. voters can elect only nonvoting delegates (as opposed to representatives) to Congress, yet that body holds veto power over Washington's laws and budgets—a bone of lingering local contention and resentment.

THE PEOPLE'S PARADE GROUND

The Mall—the country's unofficial forum—has long been a rallying point for social causes. The women's suffrage movement, for example, demonstrated here in the 1910s; two decades later, thousands of Bonus Marchers descended on the Capitol to demand veterans' benefits, only to be run off by Gen. Douglas MacArthur's cavalry.

On August 28, 1963, more than 200,000 people marched on Washington to demand jobs and freedom for blacks. The event culminated in the rousing "I Have a Dream" speech delivered by Dr. Martin Luther King, Jr., on the steps of the Lincoln Memorial. Television cameras caught the historic moment on film, projecting it into living rooms and minds across the nation.

This progress was brought to a tragic end in April of 1968, when Dr. King fell to an assassin's bullet on a motel balcony in Memphis, Tennessee. Around the country, grief erupted in spasms of violence. In Washington, rioting and looting broke out near the intersection of 14th and U Streets and spread outward from there. Eventually the conflagration gutted 57 blocks in the heart of the city, crippling the once-thriving retail district downtown. Twelve people died and several hundred were injured amid the chaos.

It took 4,000 U.S. Army and National Guard troops three days to restore the peace. The scars lingered for years. Not until the late 1990s did some areas recover. The U Street corridor, for instance—once the epicenter of Washington nightlife—has been spruced up and now draws visitors from all backgrounds.

A FRESH START

The seeds of the city's rejuvenation had been planted several years before the 1968 riots. In 1961, President John F. Kennedy and his wife, Jackie, initiated improvements to the city core. They applied a mix of historic preservation and urban renewal to Lafayette Square and to the part of Pennsylvania Avenue from the White House to the Capitol. A few years later, the landscape received another official facelift from Lady Bird Johnson and her "Beautify America" campaign, which added tulips, daffodils, and flowering trees and shrubs to the banks of Rock Creek and the Potomac River.

1971 was a pivotal year in the city's growing emphasis on aesthetics. The Mall's tempos (see p. 28) were finally removed to make way for Constitution Gardens—a 50-acre park north of the Reflecting Pool—and the John F. Kennedy Center for the Performing Arts opened on the Potomac River just above the Theodore Roosevelt Memorial Bridge. Inscribed on a wall of the Kennedy Center are the words of arts patron JFK: "This country cannot afford to be materially rich and spiritually poor."

Yet poverty is still an ugly reality of Washington. As of 2004, per capita income for the District was $48,000, but the income gap between the city's poor and wealthy residents is one of the widest of major U.S. cities.

Poking fun at Washington politics has become a national pastime, yet the city possesses a beauty and grandeur that can win over the most hardened cynic. After Lincoln's assassination in 1865, Congressman James Garfield reportedly assured a mob in New York City: "Fellow citizens! God reigns, and the Government at Washington still lives!" Sixteen years later, Garfield, by then President himself, would be assassinated. But Washington's business went on, as it still does—through wars, deaths, financial crises, and administrations good and bad. As long as we have a United States, we will have a Washington, D.C. ■

A candlelit vigil held at the Lincoln Memorial soon after the September 11, 2001, terrorist strikes in the United States honors those who died.

Washingtonians soak up sunrays at Georgetown's Washington Harbour against a background of Watergate, the Kennedy Center, and Memorial Bridge.

City on the river

Most people don't think of Washington as a riverside city, yet the Potomac is the wildest watercourse running through any major metropolis. To experience this contradiction yourself, explore Washington by water. In the process you'll leave a world of traffic, concrete, and crowds for a realm where turtles bask on logs, an osprey wings low over the water with a fish flashing in its talons, and your only neighbor glides by in a scull.

The Potomac River has been the heart of Washington since Georgetown was founded as a shipping center in 1751. By the 1790s the harbor was exporting more tobacco than any other port in the country. Later, the Chesapeake & Ohio Canal (whose towpath you can still amble) connected Georgetown to villages inland, fueling both their growth and that of the capital city.

With affluence came effluence: The Potomac was declared unfit for bathing as early as 1894, and even touching the bacteria-laden water was deemed unwise as late as 1971. The 1970s brought a concerted, community-wide effort to clean up the river, with the result that today it has been reborn. The fish are back, the birds have returned, and the water bobs with all manner of recreational craft: canoes, kayaks, rowing shells, sailboats, and—alas—Jet Skis.

Washington's iconic landmarks appear grander and more intimate from the water. You can get especially close-up views of the Lincoln Memorial, Kennedy Center, and Jefferson Memorial. As you glide beneath one of the nine graceful arches of Memorial Bridge, Robert E. Lee's home, Arlington House, looms above Arlington Cemetery on the Virginia shore. Opposite Washington Harbour, heavily wooded, 88-acre Theodore Roosevelt Island makes a delightfully natural destination teeming with geese, snapping turtles, and beaver.

Many visitors take to the river aboard narrated cruises for a monumental view of the city or a leisurely trip to Mount Vernon. Brunch, lunch, dinner, and moonlight cruises are available, but schedules vary daily and seasonally. Options include Capitol River Cruises (301-460-7447); Potomac River Boat Company (703-548-9000); the *Spirit of Washington* (866-302-2469); and the luxury *Odyssey* (866-306-2469). For a quirky alternative, check out the land/sea tour of DC Ducks (800-213-2474), which carries you past the Mall and museums in a DUKW (an amphibious military personnel carrier in World War

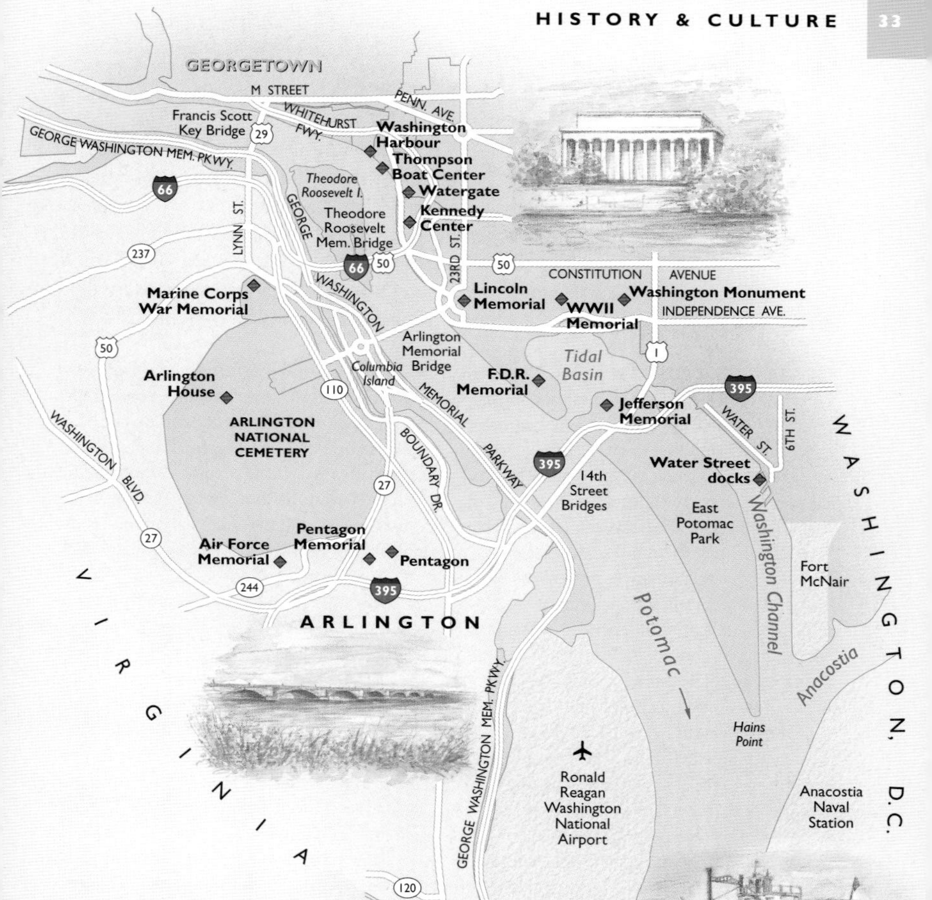

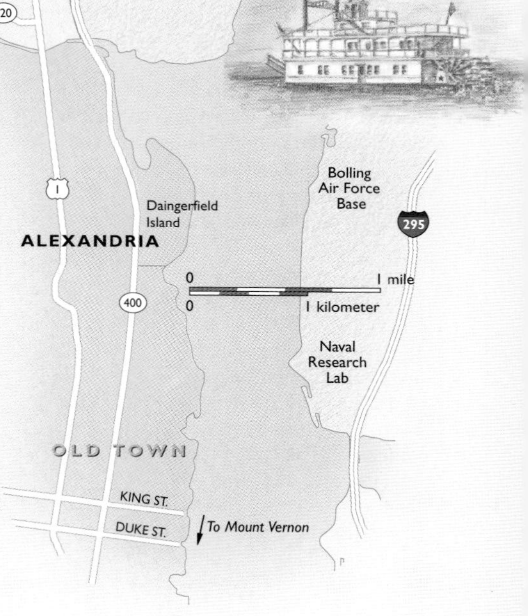

II), then splashes down in the Potomac before delivering you back to Union Station.

Probably the most intimate way to experience the river is by canoe or kayak. Quietly skimming across mirrorlike waters, you'll witness an abundance of wildlife appearing from the shadows. Near the shore a great blue heron freezes in midstride, waiting for a fish. In the safety of midriver, bass break the surface to feed on hatching bugs. Keen-eyed ospreys peer down from shaggy nests, screaming if you venture too close, while bald eagles soar high above. Rent canoes, kayaks, and rowing shells from Thompson Boat Center (Rock Creek Pkwy. & Virginia Ave., 202-333-9543) and Jack's (3500 K St., 202-337-9642). Atlantic Kayak (1201 N. Royal St., Alexandria, 703-838-9072 or 800-297-0066) offers rentals as well as instruction and guided tours. ■

The arts

WASHINGTON IS A RELATIVELY RECENT ARRIVAL ON THE BIG-LEAGUE ART scene. Despite the city's status as the birthplace of many gifted musicians and actors—among them John Philip Sousa, Duke Ellington, Helen Hayes, and Pearl Bailey—an artistic community of note did not really coalesce here until 1971, when the John F. Kennedy Center for the Performing Arts welcomed the first music and theater patrons to its riverside venue. Since then, Washington has distinguished itself in just about every field of artistic endeavor, making it a leading center of the arts worldwide.

CLASSICAL MUSIC

One of the nation's finest orchestral companies, the National Symphony Orchestra was officially incorporated in 1931. At the opening of the Kennedy Center 40 years later, the NSO premiered Leonard Bernstein's "Mass," a work commissioned for the occasion. The orchestra now has a busy year-round season that includes local performances in the Kennedy Center Concert Hall, tours in this country and abroad, televised Independence Day and Memorial Day concerts on the West Lawn of the U.S. Capitol, and programs for visiting heads of state and other occasions.

Leonard Slatkin has infused the NSO with new energy since assuming the role of music director in 1996. "The status of contemporary music is probably in better shape now than it's been in the last 25 years," says Slatkin. "What I think is coming in new compositions is a real infusion of the Americans from other cultures who are here—the Latino Americans, the Asian Americans."

From a regional company struggling to make its name in 1956, the Washington Opera has evolved into a world-class organization playing to sellout audiences in the Opera House at the Kennedy Center. In the early 1980s, the company scheduled 16 performances of four operas every year; it now stages up to eight operas a year. The Washington Opera has been under the artistic direction of Placido Domingo since 1996.

A commitment to staging new American operas, bringing out lesser known important works, and nurturing young talent keeps this company in the mainstream of the opera world. A 1984 innovation—projecting surtitles above the stage—helped attract a wider audience. The 1980s were also important growth years because of the enthusiastic support of local philanthropist David Lloyd Kreeger and the inventive direction of Martin Feinstein. Among the outstanding talents that have worked on Washington Opera productions are Gian Carlo Menotti, Franco Zeffirelli, Bruce Beresford, and Werner Herzog. Conductors have included Daniel Barenboim, Rafael Fruhbeck de Burgos, Mstislav Rostropovich, and Max Rudolf.

Washington music lovers can find a concert any night of the week, whether performed by a D.C.-based or visiting group. The Kennedy Center has hosted renowned companies from around the world, including the Berlin Philharmonic Orchestra, the Metropolitan Opera, and La Scala, while the Millennium Stage program brings free daily performances of all sorts of musical genres to the Kennedy Center's Grand Foyer.

Nor is the Kennedy Center the only game in town. Nearby Lisner Auditorium at George Washington University is a comfortable 1,490-seat hall, and other area universities feature classical music by local and guest artists. Downtown churches and museums often schedule musical events: Concerts at the National Gallery of Art, the Corcoran Gallery of Art, the Phillips Collection, and Dumbarton Oaks can be wonderfully intimate occasions. The 670-seat auditorium at the National Academy of Sciences, with its excellent acoustics, occasionally offers free concerts, often of new music. Another small venue, the Folger Shakespeare Library, presents medieval, Renaissance, and baroque music in an Elizabethan setting.

Many music aficionados consider the District of Columbia to be the nation's capital of

A ballerina performs the Washington Ballet's *Carmen* at the Kennedy Center, which presents touring companies and solo artists.

D.C. native and jazz maestro Duke Ellington gazes from a painting on sale at Eastern Market.

choral music. Prominent groups include the Master Chorale of Washington (formerly the Paul Hill Chorale) and the Choral Arts Society of Washington. Both frequently perform in concert with the National Symphony Orchestra and touring orchestras.

In the summer, the place to go with a picnic and a group of friends is Wolf Trap Farm Park, off the Dulles Toll Road or Va. 7. You can sit on the lawn or in the Filene Center—the open-air auditorium of this delightful park—and enjoy al fresco programs of the National Symphony Orchestra, touring opera companies, jazz, rock, or blues.

POPULAR MUSIC

Washington has historically excelled at military band music. The U.S. Marine Band received a great boost in 1868 when a local 13-year-old boy signed up as an apprentice. His name was John Philip Sousa, and within 12 years he would assume leadership of the band. Dismayed by the band's outdated and poorly arranged music, Sousa sent off to Europe for scores by Wagner, Berlioz, and other modern composers of the day. He also began writing music of his own. Demanding excellence from others as well as from himself, Sousa drilled the band into shape. Many members quit within a year, but those who stayed became a well-honed and disciplined unit. In 1892 Sousa formed his own band and toured the United States and abroad. His tuneful lifetime outpouring ultimately included 140 original military marches, among them "The Washington Post" march (1889) and "The Stars and Stripes Forever" (1896).

Heart-poundingly patriotic performances of the illustrious U.S. Marine Band and other military combos are staged free of charge on summer evenings at the Sylvan Theater (on the grounds of the Washington Monument) and on the West Terrace of the Capitol. Alternatively, you might enjoy an evening tattoo at the Marine Barracks on Capitol Hill.

Another local musician who made good was jazz legend Edward Kennedy "Duke"

Ellington. Born at 1217 22nd Street, N.W., in 1899 and raised in the Shaw neighborhood, Ellington studied classical music with a neighbor who taught music at Dunbar High School. At 24 he headed off to New York City—and thence into the Big Band and Jazz Hall of Fame. Washington jazz has enjoyed a devoted following ever since. When the Howard Theatre opened at 7th and T Streets in 1910, it marqueed such standouts as W. C. Handy, Fletcher Henderson, Bessie Smith, and Count Basie. Duke Ellington and Pearl Bailey were among the local talents who debuted at the Howard. Another star-studded black showcase, the 1922 Lincoln Theater on U Street, N.W., closed for a short while but reopened as a movie theater in the 1970s; renovated in 1994, the 1,250-seat theater today features a mixture of concerts, dance recitals, plays, and movies.

Blues Alley in Georgetown has long worn the crown as the best—sometimes the only—place in town to catch big-name jazz acts. This comfortable den has low ceilings, high cover charges, and a serious and sophisticated clientele. Other reliable spots for hearing live jazz include Columbia Station in Adams Morgan and Bohemian Caverns in the Shaw neighborhood.

Various venues host the occasional jazz concert. The most popular acts take the stage at DAR Constitution Hall, the Kennedy Center's Concert Hall, and Wolf Trap; others show up in smaller locales such as the Terrace Theater in the Kennedy Center or Baird Auditorium in the National Museum of Natural History.

If you get a chance to catch local piano virtuoso John Eaton in concert, don't pass it up. One of the country's leading exponents of classic jazz, Eaton played the piano bar circuit for years before graduating to his current trademark lecture-concerts. They are high-order entertainment.

An endless number of options exist for rock and other popular music. These range from headliner concerts at the 20,000-seat Verizon Center downtown to eclectic local acts (and some up-and-coming national ones) at popular hangouts such as the 9:30 Club on V Street and the Black Cat on 14th Street. On the east side of Rock Creek Park, Carter

Barron Amphitheatre is a fun summer weekend place for watching pop, rock, blues, and jazz. Acoustic folk and bluegrass have also carved out solid niches in the Washington area; the Birchmere in Alexandria, which nurtured Grammy-winner Mary Chapin Carpenter and bluegrass pioneers The Seldom Scene, is the top choice.

THEATER

Home to dozens of active theaters, the Washington metro area can boast more playhouses than any city besides New York. Whether the show is a classic drama, a local original, off-Broadway, pre-Broadway, or post-Broadway, the best of standard and contemporary theater captivates Washington audiences on a nightly basis.

Most prominent is the Kennedy Center, with two large theaters: The 1,100-seat Eisenhower Theater is a plush venue for touring productions of dramas and comedies, while the adjacent 2,300-seat Opera House presents elaborate musicals and performances of the Washington Ballet and other dance troupes.

Washington theater does not begin and end at the Kennedy Center, however. A theater has operated continuously on the Pennsylvania Avenue site of the National Theatre, rebuilt in the early 1920s, since 1835. In 1845 fire destroyed the building during a performance of *Beauty and the Beast*—the first of five such conflagrations in the theater's history.

Until 1873, blacks were confined to the balcony; after that, they were not admitted at all. Finally, in 1948, local Civil Rights activists campaigned to desegregate the National. They picketed the facility, and the actors playing at the time in a touring production of *Oklahoma!* voted to honor the picket lines; for the next four years, as a result, the theater staged only movies (it reopened as a live theater in 1952).

John Wilkes Booth, Jenny Lind, Helen Hayes, John Barrymore, Sarah Bernhardt, Vivien Leigh, and Katharine Hepburn have all trod the boards of the National, which has premiered such groundbreaking productions as *West Side Story, M. Butterfly,* and many other shows. The National also continues its

Putting on arias: Opera—in this case, a performance of "Figaro"—is just one of the musical offerings on tap at Wolf Trap Farm Park for the Performing Arts in Vienna, Virginia.

tradition of offering big glittery Broadway and pre-Broadway productions.

Half a block away on 13th Street, the Warner Theatre opened in 1924 as a silent-movie palace and vaudeville stage. From 1945 to the late 1960s, it presented movies only. It then deteriorated, as did much of downtown Washington, but stayed alive with a menu of porn films and rock concerts. After closing for three years, the Warner reopened in 1992 with its rococo finery intact. It now offers a mix of musical performances and live comedy.

About three blocks east of the Warner, Ford's Theatre on 10th Street had been in business for only four years when, in 1865, it became notorious as the scene of Lincoln's assassination. Restored to its 1860s appearance, it reopened in 1968 with a staging of *John Brown's Body.* Ford's Theatre now offers plays and musicals.

Probably the city's best program of serious and innovative drama is offered at the Arena Stage, on the waterfront in Southwest Washington. Since its 1950 founding by Zelda and Thomas C. Fichandler and Edward Mangum, the Arena has pioneered the resident theater movement; part of the fun is seeing your favorite local actors perform a wide variety of roles. Arena Stage also owns the distinction of being the first playhouse outside New York City to win a Tony award (the 1976 Regional Theatre Tony Award). James Earl Jones, Ned Beatty, Jane Alexander, and other notable actors cut their teeth here. Three theaters in one, the Arena holds the Fichandler Stage, a theater in the round with 816 seats sloping down to the stage; the 514-seat Kreeger Theater; and the 120-seat Old Vat Room, which presents works in progress.

After 20 praiseworthy years in its original home at the Folger Shakespeare Library, the Shakespeare Theatre moved in 1992 to a larger, 451-seat theater in the Lansburgh on Seventh Street, N.W. In 2007, the much-acclaimed company expanded further to include the 775-seat Sidney Harman Hall at Sixth and F Streets. The group also stages the "Shakespeare Free For All," a summer Shakespeare play at Carter Barron Amphitheatre that is presented free to the public.

Known for its bold and eclectic contemporary plays, the Studio Theatre at 14th and P Streets in the Logan Circle neighborhood has claimed many Helen Hayes awards in its three decades of existence. These homegrown awards for theatrical excellence recognize the formative contributions to local drama of Hayes, a Washington native who first appeared on a D.C. stage at the age of six and later won an Academy Award for her portrayal of the title character in 1932's *The Sin of Madelon Claudet.*

Perhaps seeking deliverance from the real-life hams on Capitol Hill, Washingtonians are flocking to comedy clubs. Two well-established companies spin out partially improvised political satire on a regular basis. The Capitol Steps, founded by congressional staffers, offer witty, well-polished songs and skits every Friday and Saturday night at the Ronald Reagan Building on Pennsylvania Avenue. On Saturday nights at the Warehouse Arts Complex on Seventh Street, N.W., the no-holds-barred duo Gross National Product lampoons politicos across the board, be they Democrats in "All the President's Women" or Republicans in "Son of a Bush." The Connecticut Avenue comedy club known as Improv features headliners as well as promising locals doing traditional stand-up.

FINE ARTS

In a city of monumental buildings and larger-than-life statuary created by some of the nation's finest architects and sculptors, D.C. art has tended to be powerful and realistic, depicting powerful people and real events. With a preponderance of these pieces being commissioned—and with many of them requiring committee approval—it's a wonder the city holds so many truly fine works of art.

The U.S. Capitol, for example, is a trove of officially sanctioned art. Its chief muralist, Italian artist Constantino Brumidi (1805–1880), was known as the Michelangelo of the Capitol; his 1865 "Apotheosis of George Washington" graces the ceiling of the Rotunda. Acclaimed artist John Trumbull (1756–1843) painted the eight large historical scenes hanging in the Rotunda.

Much of the city's great painting and sculpture is housed in established museums: the National Gallery of Art, the Corcoran Gallery of Art, the Phillips Collection. Significant works of art created on site in Washington have tended to be in portraiture and open-air sculpture (see pp. 44–45).

Early painting in Washington was documentary as well as aesthetic: Public figures, it was agreed, should have their portraits painted for posterity. Thus locals such as George Washington, James Madison, and the wife of Capitol designer William Thornton sat for eminent portrait painter Gilbert Stuart (1755–1828), who lived in Philadelphia and Boston.

Another leading portrait painter, Charles Willson Peale (1741–1827), completed seven life paintings of George Washington, as well as portraits of Benjamin Franklin, Thomas Jefferson, and John Adams. His son Rembrandt Peale (1778–1860) parlayed his family connections into a precocious start in painting: At age 17 he produced a life portrait of George Washington. The younger Peale studied under his father, whose sharply modeled neoclassic style exerted a strong influence; Rembrandt Peale's 1805 portrait of Jefferson, now owned by the New-York Historical Society, is considered his masterpiece—and our best likeness of the third President.

The White House, too, has a Rembrandt Peale oil of Jefferson, as well as other important portraits. The Reception Rooms of the Department of State hold several portraits by the Peales, Stuart, and Thomas Sully (1783–1872). Other places to look for early Washington faces include the National Portrait Gallery and the National Gallery of Art.

What did the city look like in its infancy? Thanks to the efforts of several minor artists, we have a fairly good idea. Sketches by surveyors and architects show the lay of the land around the Capitol, the White House, and other government buildings as they were going up. Views of Washington by painter George Jacob Beck depict the Georgetown waterfront in the 1790s as a Constable-style landscape, where a country lane stands sprinkled with little houses.

City views by August Kollner in the 1830s show a Potomac busy with sailboats and the new steamboats. The latter owed their existence to engineer and painter Robert Fulton (1765–1815), who in 1807 invented the first commercially successful steamboat; in the early 1800s Fulton had stayed with friends who owned a country estate that would become the Kalorama neighborhood, and he painted its pastoral scenes.

An 1832 lithograph of the west front of the Capitol by Hudson River artist Thomas Doughty (1793–1856) is a decidedly bucolic setting; the wooded hills and cultivated fields around Jenkins Hill (now Capitol Hill) make the government structure seem almost comically out of place. Washington's rural aspect would continue to be emphasized as late as the 1880s in the sketches and drawings of isolated cabins by DeLancey W. Gill (1859–1940), an illustrator for the Smithsonian Institution's Bureau of American Ethnology. Perhaps these were in wistful lament for a town changing into a city?

An artists' salon blossomed in Washington at the turn of the 20th century. It met at the studio-home of painter and playwright Alice Pike Barney (1857–1931), at 2306 Massachusetts Avenue, next to the current Turkish Embassy. Overlooking Sheridan Circle, Barney's Studio House became the venue for poetry readings, plays, art shows, and other creative undertakings of the sort now associated with a multitude of Dupont addresses. Barney helped establish the Sylvan Theatre on the Mall. Both George Bernard Shaw and Alice Roosevelt Longworth sat for portraits by her hand.

Nowadays the homes of the rich and au courant are graced by abstract art turned out by Washington Color School artists, who rose to prominence in the 1960s. Gene Davis (1920–1985), known for his boldly striped canvases, worked as a White House correspondent during the Truman years before settling down to abstract art. Sam Gilliam (1933–) stepped into the limelight with his "drape paintings" in the late 1960s—stained, unframed canvases thrown over sawhorses and furniture, hung from ceiling beams, or draped on walls. The *Washington Post* described a 1999 show of his glass-enclosed collages of acrylic on birch plywood as "cubist African kimono sculptures." Gilliam's work has been commissioned for the Washington Convention Center and Ronald Reagan National Airport. He has also been honored with solo exhibitions at the Corcoran Gallery of Art and other showcases.

LITERATURE

In more than two centuries as the nation's capital, Washington has embraced a succession of bards—writers who have succeeded in capturing this elusive power spot in prose or verse. The district's standout chroniclers have included Henry Adams, Allen Drury, and Gore Vidal.

Unlike literature set elsewhere, Washington novels often aspire to capitalize on their settings by tackling the city's major industry: politics. The first classic "Washington novel"—an insider's look at the political machinations of the federal government—was probably *The Gilded Age*, an 1873 satire of political and financial shenanigans coauthored by Mark Twain and newspaper editor Charles Dudley Warner. It was followed in 1880 by *Democracy, an American Novel*, a mysterious and anonymously authored exposé that became wildly popular for blowing the lid off corruption in the Grant Administration.

Leonardo da Vinci's portrait, "Ginerva de' Benci," (1474/1478) is part of the permanent collection at the National Gallery of Art.

Despite widespread public and private conjecture about the identity of the crusading novelist, not until the author's death in 1918 would it be revealed that *Democracy* had been written by Henry Adams.

Published more than 40 years ago but still relevant today, Allen Drury's *Advise and Consent* (1959) broke new ground for its startling portrayal of backroom politics. Focusing mainly on the U.S. Senate and a controversial nominee for secretary of state, the book won the former newspaper reporter a Pulitzer Prize in 1960; the 1962 movie version, starring Henry Fonda and Charles Laughton under the direction of Otto Preminger, remains one of Hollywood's more intelligent treatments of Washington.

Many consider Gore Vidal to be Washington's modern laureate, though the erudite author of *Washington, D.C.: a Novel* (1967) and more than 25 other books seems determined to flee that distinction; Vidal has lived in Ravello, Italy, since the early 1970s. Born in West Point, New York, in 1925, Vidal spent much of his childhood inhaling politics at the Rock Creek Park home of his grandfather, Thomas P. Gore, a populist senator from Oklahoma. Vidal himself ran for Congress (unsuccessfully) in 1960 and for the Senate (with identical results) in 1982. He was already a novelist by his first campaign, but his most popular work was still decades away: *Lincoln* (1984) painted a balanced and human portrait of a President who had been only canonized until then. Vidal's novel *1876* puts recent political history into perspective: In that year,

At Kramer Books & Afterwords café, a literary landmark just north of Dupont Circle, browsers converge to flip pages, sip coffee, enjoy a rich dessert, and listen to live music.

Republican Rutherford B. Hayes stole the election from Democrat Samuel J. Tilden, who had won the popular vote; one the states whose election returns were contested was Florida.

Edward P. Jones, who also grew up in Washington and still lives there, won the Pulitzer Prize in 2004 for his novel *The Known World,* based on the little-known story of free black people who owned slaves.

In a city of often secret doings, those who bring them to light can achieve near-mythic acclaim. Bob Woodward and Carl Bernstein, who broke the scandalous story of the Watergate break-in and burglary in the early 1970s, are but two of the many Washington reporters who have used journalism as a springboard to literary fame. The 1976 film version of their book *All the President's Men* was a real-life political thriller. Woodward riveted readers around the world in 2004 with the publication of his book *Plan of Attack,* a behind-the-scenes account of the White House's decision to wage war against Iraq.

Another scribe-turned-literary lion, Ward Just reported for the *Washington Post* until the late 1960s. While covering Richard Nixon's 1968 presidential campaign, Just concluded that fiction was the only medium capable of conveying the true nature of politics. His acclaimed work includes *The Congressman Who Loved Flaubert,* a 1973 collection of political short stories, and *Echo House,* a 1997 portrait of D.C. government that spans eight decades and three generations.

Newsweek columnist Joe Klein hit the jackpot with his first book, the 1996 best-seller *Primary Colors.* In common with Henry Adams's *Democracy* of a century earlier, Klein's book—a thinly veiled fictionalization of Bill Clinton's 1992 campaign—was first published anonymously.

Carrying a book by other leading local authors—satirical novelist Christopher Buckley, hard-boiled detective writer George P. Pelecanos, espionage master Charles McCarry, or journalist Stanley Karnow, to name just a few—should mark you instantly as a savvy Washingtonian.

Poets, too, have been pivotal in the city's literary life. Walt Whitman, who helped care for wounded soldiers in Washington during

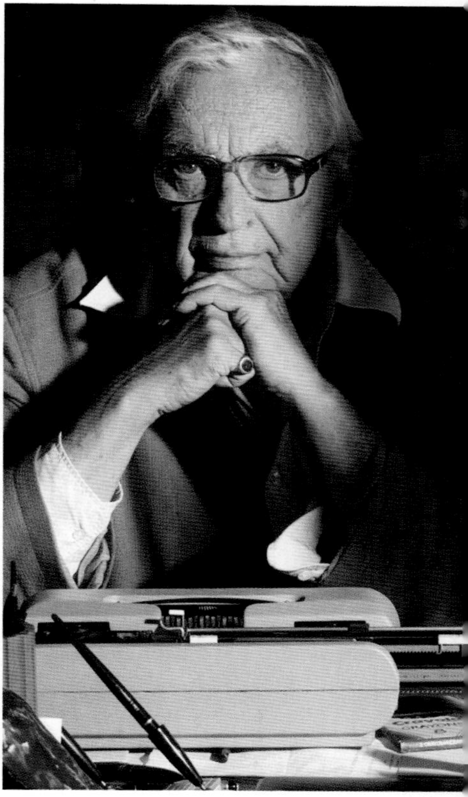

Novelist Gore Vidal has often based his fiction on events in Washington history.

the Civil War, wrote one of his greatest poems here: the moving elegy to Lincoln, "When Lilacs Last in the Dooryard Bloom'd." Its lines let the reader see the slain President's funeral cortege clatter by: "With the tolling tolling bells' perpetual clang, / Here, coffin that slowly passes, / I give you my sprig of lilac." Ironically, 1865 was the same year that Whitman was fired from his job as a clerk in the Indian Bureau. The charge: writing offensive poetry.

Another world-class poet served a Washington sojourn, but not by choice. Indicted for treason in 1945 for having broadcast Fascist propaganda during World War II, Ezra Pound was remanded to the care of St. Elizabeth's Hospital (formerly St. Elizabeth's Lunatic Asylum). Upon his release in 1958, Pound proclaimed:

Stories in stone

Filled with monumental architecture and heroic statuary, Washington is a city that can be read even by the illiterate. The pediment of the Supreme Court's west facade, for example, shows an enthroned Liberty holding the scales of justice. The busy scene depicted on the pediment of the National Archives uses winged horses, rams, and papyrus flowers as classical symbols of aspiration, parchment, and paper.

The more somber the structure, the less evident the signage. Nowhere on the outside of the Supreme Court is the building's function identified. Nor will you find the words "Abraham Lincoln" until you walk inside the Lincoln Memorial.

Yet building exteriors cannot narrate the welter of stories that Washington has to tell. As you walk around the district, you'll encounter more equestrian statues than in any other North American city. These sculptures—most of them depicting military men astride horses in various stances—came into vogue in the late 19th century, when the nation's compulsion to honor its Civil War heroes dovetailed with the rapid growth of its capital city. It's an urban myth, by the way, that a horse with one hoof raised denotes its rider was wounded in battle; nor is it true that both hooves in the air denote the rider died in battle.

Befitting its wartime role as the Federal capital, Washington bristles with Union generals in bronze. Only one Confederate officer is so honored: Even then, the statue of Brig. Gen. Albert Pike—at Third and D Sts., N.W.—recognizes his service not as a soldier but as a Mason. Otherwise you'll have to cross the river to Alexandria, Virginia, to find the nearest Confederate statue—the Rebel soldier who stands at Prince and South Washington Streets in Old Town, head downcast, arms crossed, back turned resolutely on the North.

Washington's late 19th-century renaissance in statuary also coincided with America's emergence as an environment favorable to artists. A nation of growing affluence and power demanded artists to document its glory. As a result, many world-renowned sculptors have work on display in Washington. One of them was Augustus Saint-Gaudens (1848–1907), a Dublin-born artist who grew up in New York City. His 1890 Adams Memorial (see p. 190), commissioned by author Henry Adams to honor his wife, Clover, is one of the most beautiful, moving, and remote pieces of sculpture in the city: It is tucked away in a grove of Japanese yews in Rock Creek Cemetery.

The most famous sculpture in Washington, if not the entire country, is Daniel Chester French's 1922 marble figure of Lincoln, who sits in brooding majesty 19 feet high inside the rectangular marble Lincoln Memorial at the

east end of Memorial Bridge. Lincoln clenches his left hand to show strength and resolve; his right lies open to signal compassion (it's another urban myth that he is signing "A. L.").

Thanks to the lobbying efforts of certain groups and the personal fortunes of certain individuals, tributes to elusive or lost causes dot the cityscape as well. The Temperance Fountain (ca 1880) at Pennsylvania Avenue and Seventh Street, for example, is a mini-temple surmounted by a long-legged crane; a San Francisco dentist and crusader in the temperance movement designed and donated the drinking fountain to advocate the salutary effects of water over spirits.

So what does it take to get yourself memorialized in the nation's capital? First, you must form a citizens' group to petition Congress. A vote must then be taken, a sculptor commissioned, an approval granted by the Commission of Fine Arts, and funds raised. Only a fraction of proposals make the long journey from paper to stone.

For a guide to more than 400 of the city's open-air sculptures, take a look at James M. Goode's *Outdoor Sculpture of Washington, D.C.* (Smithsonian Institution Press, 1974). ■

The 19-foot-high marble statue of Abraham Lincoln dominates the open-air Lincoln Memorial, built from 1914 to 1922 in the likeness of a Doric temple.

"All of America is an insane asylum."

The Willard Hotel on Pennsylvania Avenue provided nicer accommodations for the many writers who stayed there, among them Mark Twain, Emily Dickinson, and Charles Dickens. Julia Ward Howe wrote the "Battle Hymn of the Republic" during an 1861 stay. Martin Luther King, Jr., penned parts of his "I Have a Dream" speech here in August 1963.

The restrained symmetry of the Georgian Carlyle House (left) in Old Town Alexandria sets off the 1800 federal-style Octagon (right), a house museum and national historic landmark.

In the capital's quirkiest epistolary pattern, presidential progeny have written a host of murder mysteries with a Washington locale. FDR's son Elliott Roosevelt set a number of his books in the White House, where characters meet untimely ends in various locations. Margaret Truman, daughter of Harry S., likewise created a capital context for her capital crimes, strewing corpses around tourist sites from the Kennedy Center to the Smithsonian.

ARCHITECTURE

Conceived as a grand capital, Washington has attained a unifying look about its core. One of the main proponents of a neoclassic-style capital was architect-philosopher-statesman Thomas Jefferson. The great buildings and monuments, harking back to ancient Greek and Roman models, were designed to impress with their massiveness and their references to earlier democracies. Weighty columns of marble and pediments embellished with allegorical scenes are the general rule for these early (and many later) federal buildings.

Precious few 18th-century buildings remain. The White House and the Capitol were started in the early 1790s, but both were burned in 1814—and both have undergone many alterations and renovations since they were rebuilt. The Capitol recalls the Pantheon in Rome, begun in 27 B.C. as a temple for worshiping the gods. A less grandiose style was chosen for the executive mansion: Its Georgian format was popular in many manor houses of the day, among them Mount Vernon, Woodlawn, and Gunston Hall, all in Virginia. All three estates feature porticoes, cornices, steep roofs pierced by several chimneys, and almost perfect symmetry.

The federal style flourished in tandem with Washington's growth in the 19th century. Alexandria and Georgetown, already well established, built scores of elegant brick town houses and row houses for prosperous local merchants. Residences from the early 1800s tend to be unadorned, while those built after the Civil War betray unmistakable Victoriana: They sport rosettes, urns, swags, and decorative ironwork. The finest examples of the federal style in Washington are the 1800 Octagon at 1799 New York Avenue, N.W. and the 1816 Tudor Place at 1644 31st Street, N.W. The latter, despite its name, blends neoclassic and federal elements. Conceived as private homes by Capitol designer William Thornton, both are now national historic landmarks.

Other building styles began to appear later in the 1800s, but architects risked opprobrium if they strayed too far from the city's neoclassicism. Completed in 1887, the redbrick Pension Building (National Building Museum) has a breathtakingly cavernous interior. It was nearly razed in the 1960s.

Next to the West Wing of the White House, the Eisenhower Executive Office Building—the world's largest office building at the time of its 1888 construction—was ridiculed and likewise threatened with demolition. Harry S. Truman, for one, called it the "greatest monstrosity in America." But the Gilded Age building, with its mansard roofs and hundreds of window pediments and columns, is now recognized as an outstanding American example of French Second Empire-style architecture.

The Mediterranean façade of an 1868 Italianate villa (left) looms bright on Cooke's Row of Q Street in Georgetown; Victorian eclecticism reigns along a P Street block (right).

Daring and exuberant, the Old Post Office (1899) was likewise slated for obliteration until it was saved in the late 1970s and converted into a retail-office complex. Though it hunkers uneasily among its sedate neighbors on Pennsylvania Avenue, the castlelike building has become a beloved landmark.

Popular in the first half of the 20th century, the beaux arts style, with its use of columns and other classical elements, meshed well in Washington. Union Station (1908) by Daniel Burnham and John Russell Pope's National Archives (1935) and National Gallery of Art (1941) are grand without ostentation.

Many downtown buildings were razed in the mid-20th century and replaced with

concrete cubes, a few of them noteworthy. Though boxy, Edward Durell Stone's National Geographic Society 17th Street building (1964) and Kennedy Center (1971) have an interplay of columns and white stone well suited to Washington.

Other architectural styles have made their way onto Washington streets, but even these bear details of their forerunners. Architect I. M. Pei's radically modernist East Building (1978) of the National Gallery, for instance, is faced with the same pink marble as the West Building (1941). In general, no city building is allowed to rise more than 20 feet higher than the width of the street on which it stands. ■

Since its 1988 restoration, Union Station has been a hub of shopping, dining, partying, and transportation.

Grand marble halls of law, justice, and knowledge top Washington's most prominent hill. But here, too, you'll discover a more prosaic world of lively markets, soothing parks, and flower-filled gardens.

Capitol Hill

The Capitol Rotunda from below

Capitol Hill

"A PEDESTAL WAITING FOR A MONUMENT" CITY PLANNER PIERRE CHARLES L'Enfant called the swell of land then known as Jenkins Hill, on the city's southeastern side. Today beautiful monuments grace this hill, including the Capitol and the Supreme Court. Humanizing the grandeur of marble buildings and plazas are tree-lined residential streets. The heart of Washington, Capitol Hill is a good place to begin your tour.

For nearly one hundred years, the Capitol was the only building created for the use of the nation's legislature. To the east spread an orderly neighborhood of brick row houses. But by the end of the 19th century, the Library of Congress's Jefferson Building had risen across from the Capitol, followed shortly by architect Daniel H. Burnham's imposing Union Station and adjacent City Post Office. The early 1900s saw construction of the Cannon Building (1908) and Russell Building (1909), the first House and Senate office buildings. In the 1930s, the Supreme Court, the Folger Shakespeare Library, and the Adams Building of the Library of Congress added more density to Capitol Hill.

By the mid-20th century, much of the residential area was in decline as middle-class families abandoned the city for the suburbs. Then in the 1970s, urban pioneers, lured by low real estate values and the convenient location, began moving in and revitalizing the area. With the Eastern Market *(7th & C Sts., S.E.)* as an anchor, Capitol Hill became a vibrant neighborhood once again. Spruced up historic houses, shops, and restaurants from the Capitol to Lincoln Park make this a pleasant and lovely place to live in and visit.

You will need a full day to see all the sights here, two days to see them in detail. Union Station and Capitol South Metro stops are about equidistant from the Capitol. If you start from one, you can work your way to the other or do a leisurely loop back to your starting point. Either way, plan on getting some exercise—the area was designed on a grand scale. Walking gives you a chance to savor the magnificent architecture from various points.

As you walk, bear in mind that these buildings are both historical museums and working halls of democracy. Touring them gives you a sense of the great enterprise upon which the Founding Fathers embarked. If the free world has a geographical center, it is Capitol Hill. ■

Row houses cluster in the desirable Capitol Hill neighborhood.

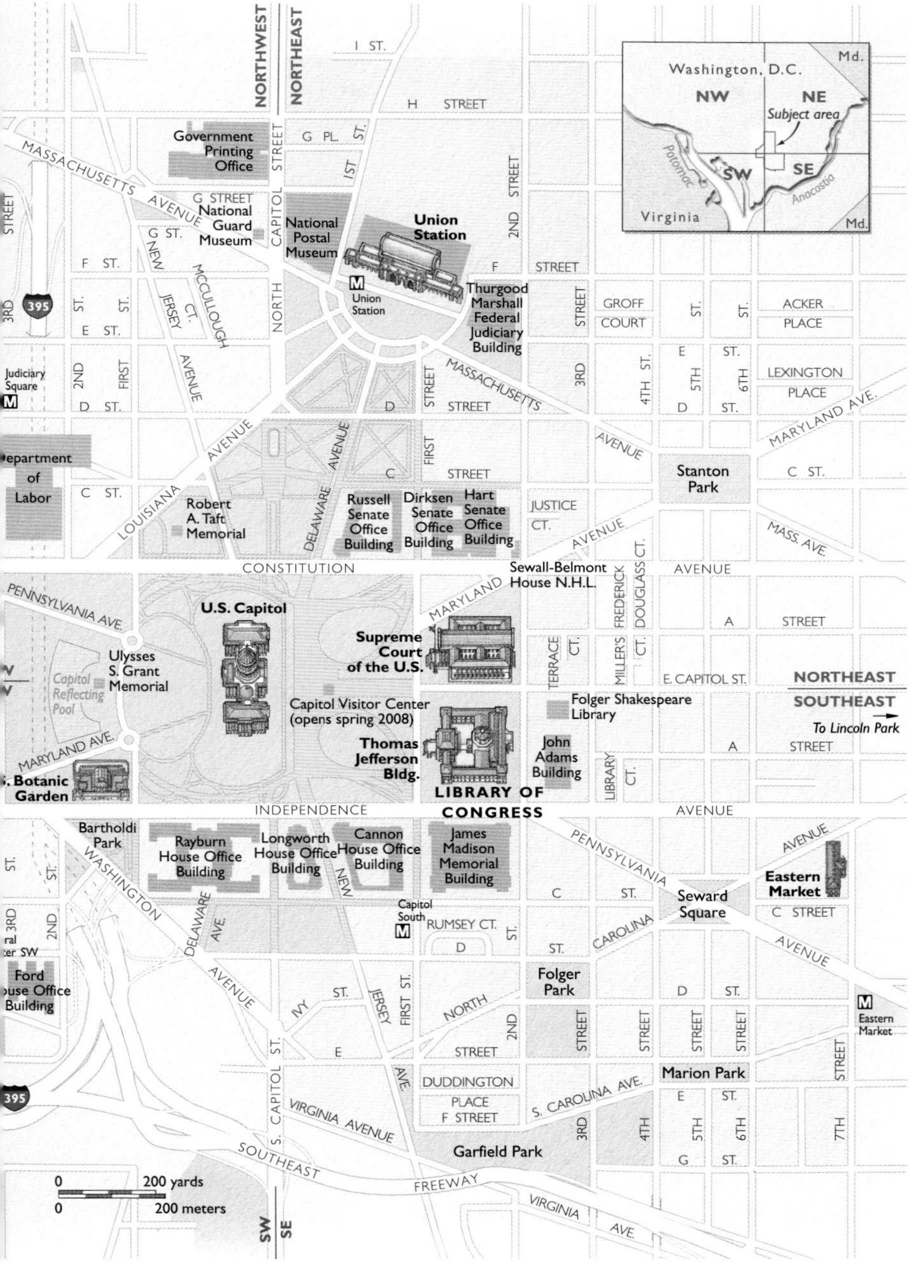
Washington, D.C.
NW
NE
SW
SE
Subject area
Potomac
Anacostia
Virginia
Md.
Md.
NORTHWEST
NORTHEAST
I ST.
H STREET
G PL.
1ST ST.
Government Printing Office
MASSACHUSETTS AVENUE
G STREET
National Guard Museum
National Postal Museum
Union Station
Union Station
G ST.
F ST.
F STREET
NEW JERSEY AVENUE
MCCULLOUGH CT.
NORTH CAPITOL STREET
2ND STREET
3RD STREET
395
Thurgood Marshall Federal Judiciary Building
GROFF COURT
ACKER PLACE
E ST.
LEXINGTON PLACE
Judiciary Square
2ND ST.
FIRST ST.
4TH ST.
5TH ST.
6TH ST.
D ST.
D STREET
MARYLAND AVE.
Department of Labor
LOUISIANA AVENUE
DELAWARE AVENUE
FIRST STREET
C STREET
C ST.
Stanton Park
Robert A. Taft Memorial
Russell Senate Office Building
Dirksen Senate Office Building
Hart Senate Office Building
JUSTICE CT.
MASS. AVE.
CONSTITUTION AVENUE
Sewall-Belmont House N.H.L.
PENNSYLVANIA AVE.
U.S. Capitol
MARYLAND AVENUE
Supreme Court of the U.S.
TERRACE CT.
MILLER'S CT.
FREDERICK DOUGLASS CT.
A STREET
E. CAPITOL ST.
NORTHEAST
SOUTHEAST
To Lincoln Park
Ulysses S. Grant Memorial
Capitol Reflecting Pool
Capitol Visitor Center (opens spring 2008)
Folger Shakespeare Library
MARYLAND AVE.
Thomas Jefferson Bldg.
John Adams Building
LIBRARY CT.
Botanic Garden
LIBRARY OF CONGRESS
INDEPENDENCE AVENUE
Bartholdi Park
WASHINGTON
Rayburn House Office Building
Longworth House Office Building
Cannon House Office Building
James Madison Memorial Building
PENNSYLVANIA AVENUE
Eastern Market
Seward Square
C STREET
C ST.
CAROLINA
3RD ST.
2ND ST.
Federal Center SW
Capitol South
RUMSEY CT.
D ST.
DELAWARE AVE.
Ford House Office Building
Folger Park
IVY ST.
NEW JERSEY AVE.
FIRST ST.
NORTH CAROLINA
D ST.
Eastern Market
E STREET
S. CAPITOL ST.
DUDDINGTON PLACE
Marion Park
7TH STREET
F STREET
S. CAROLINA AVE.
E ST.
VIRGINIA AVENUE
Garfield Park
G ST.
SOUTHEAST FREEWAY
VIRGINIA AVE.
0 200 yards
0 200 meters
SW
SE

U.S. Capitol

U.S. Capitol
www.aoc.gov
Map p. 51
Capitol Hill, between Independence & Constitution Aves.
202-225-6827
Metro: Capitol South or Union Station; Bus: 30-36, A11, J11-13, N22, 96-7

Paintings by John Trumbull (1756–1843) hang in the echoing cavern of the Capitol's Rotunda, depicting important moments in the American Revolution.

ONE OF THE MOST RECOGNIZED LANDMARKS IN THE world, the white marble U.S. Capitol, rising in domed and columned splendor at the Mall's east end, defines the center of Washington. South, East, and North Capitol Streets and the Mall radiate out from the Capitol in the cardinal directions, dividing the city into quadrants. In this vaulted location, Presidents are inaugurated, national issues debated, and new laws made.

EVOLUTION

The Capitol you see today looks almost nothing like its original conception. From the laying of the cornerstone by George Washington in 1793 to the placing of the statue of "Freedom" atop the dome in 1863, some half dozen major designers and architects put their visions and efforts into the final image. Erecting an edifice as important as the Capitol was about as easy as enacting a controversial new law. The egos of architects, engineers, and congressmen often clashed; funding grew scarce at times; and disputes drove major players into resigning their positions. Like the nation's early history, the history of the Capitol is one of false starts, compromises, and ultimate triumph.

Pierre Charles L'Enfant stubbornly refused to come up with an architectural plan for the Capitol, declaring that he had it "in his head." His dismissal in 1792 led to a national competition to design the building, the winning architect to receive $500 and a city lot. The 16 known entries were so poor that the contest had to be extended. An amateur architect named William Thornton finally came up with a winning design—a Pantheon-like dome flanked by symmetrical wings for the Senate and the House. Though greatly modifying and extending the design over the years, later architects generally followed

this basic layout; they also incorporated the Corinthian pilasters, seven-bay portico, balustrade, and other neoclassic details Thornton had envisioned. The beauty of his plan lay in the fact that it was both grand and simple, as George Washington said, yet also flexible enough to accommodate a growing nation.

In 1800 the government moved from Philadelphia to Washington, and President John Adams addressed the Congress in the Capitol's brick-and-sandstone north wing, the only completed part of the building. During these early years, Thornton resigned, and two out of the three other architects were fired over their attempted design alterations. Fortunately, in 1803 the government hired the brilliant British architect Benjamin Henry Latrobe, and his collaboration with President Thomas Jefferson, himself an amateur architect, made for substantial progress.

Then in August of 1814, British troops marched on Washington, and torched many buildings, including the Capitol. The fire destroyed much of the building's interior, though the walls remained standing. For the next few years, Latrobe worked at restoring the damage. Cost overruns and a dispute about vaulting the ceilings of the House and Senate Chambers finally led to his resignation. Boston architect Charles Bulfinch stepped in. Quieter and more conservative than Latrobe, Bulfinch ingratiated himself with Congress and President James Monroe. Bulfinch served until 1830, completing the building with a copper-covered wooden dome and an east portico.

By 1850, an expanding Congress had outgrown its chambers, necessitating the addition of new grand wings to the original building. The Capitol expansion project was still underway when the Civil War broke out. Construction went on, culminating in the addition of the current cast-iron dome, which replaced a leaky, wooden predecessor. On December 2, 1863, the magnificent nine-million-pound dome, rising from a circular portico, was crowned with "Freedom," the 19.5-foot-tall bronze figure of

Tulips highlight the beauty of the Capitol at night. The nation's leading landscape architect, Frederick Law Olmsted, designed the grounds in the 1870s.

a woman dressed in flowing robes. A 35-gun salute (for each of the states, including those that had seceded) greeted "Freedom's" ascent. An interesting historical footnote concerns her headgear. The original plan was that she would wear a liberty cap, worn by freed slaves in ancient Greece. Then Secretary of War Jefferson Davis—president of the Confederacy by the time the statue was placed atop the Capitol—objected, saying the cap was "inappropriate to a people who were born free." A helmet with eagle feathers was substituted.

In the 1870s, renowned landscape architect Frederick Law Olmsted designed and landscaped the grounds. Congress again outgrew the building in the early 20th century, scattering to the nearby Senate and House office buildings. A major addition in 1958–62 added 32 feet to the east front, leaving the sandstone west facade as the only original exterior not covered with a marble addition.

VISITING

At press time, a new Capitol Visitor Center, set for completion in 2008, was being built underground at the east front of the Capitol. Three levels of space will provide improved screening, orientation, and amenities for the thousands of visitors who line up early for tickets to enter the building. Until the project is complete, free timed-entry passes are issued beginning at 9 a.m. on a first-come, first-served basis at a kiosk on the southwest corner of the Capitol grounds (*1st St. & Independence Ave., S.W.*), opposite the Botanic Garden. Entry passes are not available in advance. Many members of Congress have tour information available on their websites; check with your representative or senator about the possibility of special tours. Keep in mind that Congress is usually in recess in August and in the fall during elections.

At the heart of the Capitol, the **Rotunda** soars 180 feet to a round ceiling fresco, "The Apotheosis of

Washington" (1865), by Italian-American artist Constantino Brumidi. A berobed George Washington stares down from on high, surrounded by a swirl of clouds and figures that represent the 13 Colonies and American democracy. Encircling the Rotunda, a 300-foot-long frieze begun by Brumidi but not completed until 1953 depicts more than 400 years of American history, from Columbus to the Wright brothers.

On the Rotunda's west side hang the four huge scenes from the American Revolution painted by Washington's aide-de-camp John Trumbull. Across from them, on the east side, are canvases portraying the discovery and settlement of the United States. A small white marble stone marks the center of the Rotunda's floor; here eminent Americans such as Abraham Lincoln and John F. Kennedy have lain in state.

One room south of the Rotunda is the **National Statuary Hall,** where the House of Representatives met from 1807 to 1857. In 1864 Congress first invited each state to send a bronze or marble statue of two prominent citizens. Some have been moved elsewhere, but among the notables on site are Henry Clay (Kentucky), Daniel Webster (New Hampshire), Robert E. Lee (Virginia), and King Kamehameha I (Hawaii).

North of the Rotunda is the **Old Senate Chamber,** which served the Senate from 1810 to 1859 (except between 1814 and 1819, when senators had to meet across the street after the British burned the Capitol). Here such famous men as Clay, Webster, and John C. Calhoun hotly debated the issues of slavery and economics prior to the Civil War. Today the Senate uses this chamber for closed-door conferences, including a 1999 session on the impeachment trial of Bill Clinton. Rembrandt Peale's famous portrait of George Washington (1823) hangs on the chamber's east wall, above the Vice President's dais.

On the first floor, directly beneath the Rotunda, awaits the **Crypt.** George and Martha Washington were to be entombed here, but family members objected, so the two remain at Mount Vernon, in Virginia. Ringing the room, 40 Doric sandstone columns help support the Rotunda. Gutzon Borglum, who carved Mount Rushmore, created the marble head of Lincoln displayed here. The statue's missing left ear symbolizes the slain President's incomplete life.

North of the Crypt, through the small Senate Rotunda and to the right, stands the **Old Supreme Court Chamber.** The Senate

Capitol views

One of the earliest travel books about America was written by Frances Trollope, mother of English writer Anthony Trollope and herself a prolific novelist. In her popular *Domestic Manners of the Americans* (1832), written after a three-year journey to the fledgling United States, she found much to disparage. But she was impressed by the Capitol:

"None of us, I believe, expected to see so imposing a structure on that side the Atlantic. I am ill at describing buildings, but the beauty and majesty of the American capitol might defy an abler pen than mine to do it justice. It stands so finely too, high, and alone. … The view from the capitol commands the city and many miles around, and it is itself an object of imposing beauty to the whole country adjoining." ■

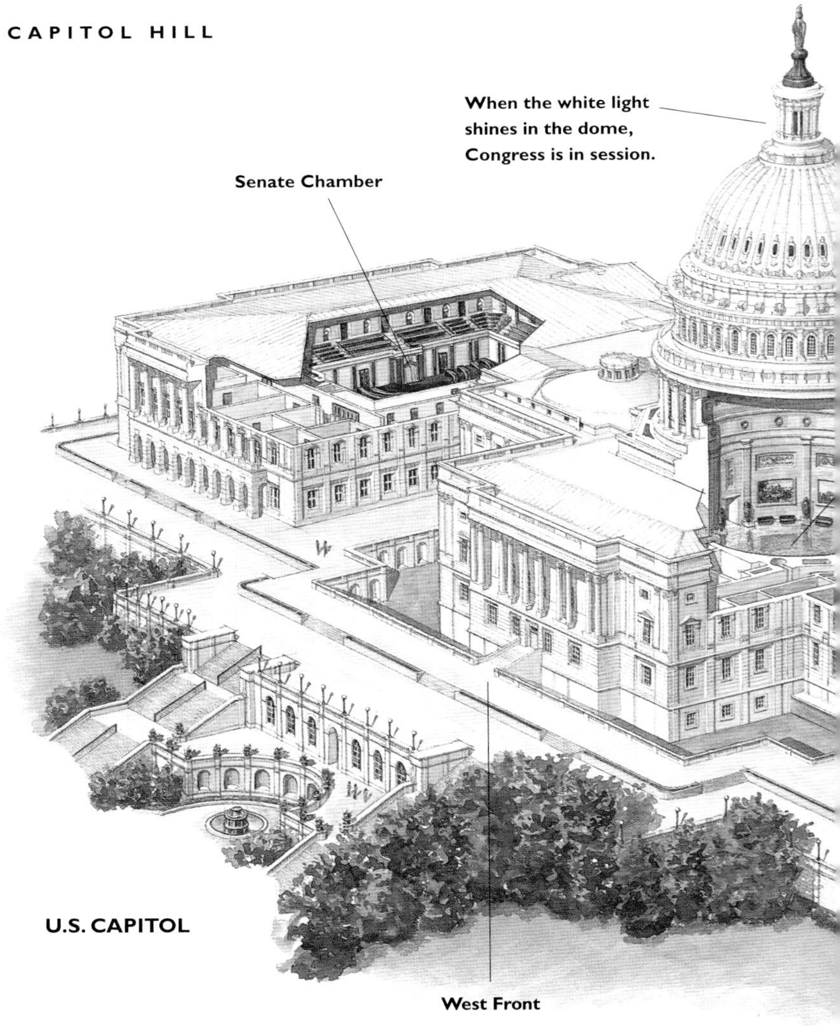
When the white light shines in the dome, Congress is in session.
Senate Chamber
U.S. CAPITOL
West Front

originally met in this vaulted room designed by Latrobe; the Supreme Court used it from 1810 to 1860. In the early 1970s, restorers armed with mid-19th-century descriptions returned the chamber to its earlier appearance. Half of the furnishings, including justices' desks and chairs, are original.

On the first floor of the north wing, the colorful Brumidi Corridors boast a wealth of frescoes and other paintings by Constantino Brumidi, who worked in the Capitol for 25 years in the late 1800s. Sometimes called the Michelangelo of the Capitol, Brumidi based his designs for the corridors on the Raphael loggia in the Vatican, where he had done some restoration work. The historical scenes and heroes, along with depictions of flora and fauna in trompe l'oeil frames, provide a rich summary of early

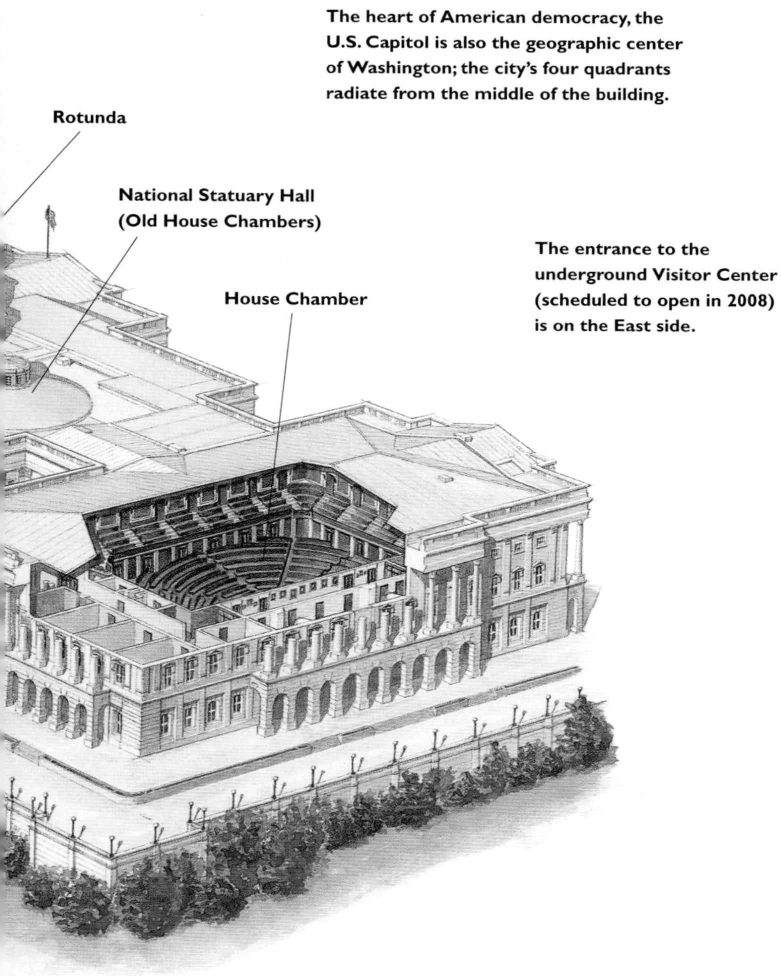
The heart of American democracy, the U.S. Capitol is also the geographic center of Washington; the city's four quadrants radiate from the middle of the building.
Rotunda
National Statuary Hall (Old House Chambers)
House Chamber
The entrance to the underground Visitor Center (scheduled to open in 2008) is on the East side.

America. Later paintings include scenes of the first moon landing and a tribute to the crew who died in the 1986 explosion of the *Challenger* space shuttle.

On the other side of the Crypt, in the south wing, are the **First Floor House Corridors** containing more statuary as well as murals by contemporary American artist Allyn Cox. Among the scenes are the Capitol in flames in 1814 and wounded Union soldiers lying in a makeshift hospital in the Rotunda.

The **Congressional Chambers** are in the Capitol's wings (the House south, the Senate north). The 435 House representatives are not assigned specific seats, though Democrats traditionally sit to the Speaker's right, Republicans to the left. The same arrangement holds for the more stately Senate, but here desks are based on seniority. ■

Politics at work

In the summer of 1787, following the successful rebellion of the 13 Colonies against England and the loosely structured "Confederation" period, 55 leaders from the newly independent states met in Philadelphia's State House (now Independence Hall) to revise the the Articles of Confederation, the country's first constitution. Trying to strike a delicate balance between sufficient government power to rule a nation yet guarantee adequate liberty for its citizens, the delegates decided to toss out the Articles and create a new document. The result: the Constitution of the United States of America—the fundamental law of the U.S. federal system and a landmark document of the Western world.

This constitution, having been the product of secret deals and silent compromises, could not become the law of the land by fiat, so the Founders asked that it be ratified by the people of the 13 independent states. There were many heated state conventions, some producing violence, other producing eloquent words, that have helped Supreme Court Justices determine the meaning of this concise blueprint for the government we have today—living up to its preamble: "We the People of the United States of America … ."

From the beginning Congress met to air differences and reach hard fought compromises. The reason the capital is in Washington, for instance, is because of the very public Compromise of 1790, in which northern congressmen and senators got their southern counterparts to approve funding our first national debt in return for placing the nation's capital in the south on the Potomac River, not far from George Washington's home. From the First Congress came the traditions of national debt and logrolling. And anyone who has tuned into C-SPAN knows that political debate and compromise continue to be integral ingredients in making laws.

You can see the fireworks firsthand in Washington several different ways. The most obvious is go to the Capitol, where it may be possible to hear your senator give a speech or watch a debate about a current issue on the floor of the House. Contact your representative or senator before leaving home to find out about access and making special arrangements, such as stopping in for a chat with your hometown legislator. Many congresspeople have information on their individual websites. Or call your politician's office *(202-224-3121)*.

"Senate Hearing" by William Gropper (1897–1977): Making fun of gasbag politicians is a 200-year-long tradition, but discord, as understood by James Madison, was effectively designed into our constitutional democracy to give voice to different groups.

While the work done on the Congress floor is well publicized, much of the real work goes on behind the scenes in committees and subcommittees—the first place where most bills being nominated as future laws are discussed and debated and picked apart. Committees and subcommittees—most of which are open to the public—meet on most days when the legislature is in session. You might be able to watch the future of high-definition television being decided, hear an EPA administrator grilled about pollution enforcement, listen to debates about space exploration, or attend the confirmation hearing for a newly nominated federal judge. To find out what committees your local elected officials are on, visit www.house.gov or www.senate.gov.

If a bill is good and has powerful friends on the committee, it will be recommended to the House or Senate for debate and vote. Of the thousands of bills introduced every year, only a small percentage make it to the floor of the House or Senate to be voted on.

If passed, the bill is sent to the other chamber, referred to committee, and so on. If the bill makes it through the tortured path to passage in that chamber, then a "Conference" committee is set up to settle differences between the two bills, if there are any. The Senate and House vote again on the revised bill, and if that compromise bill passes it goes to the President for his signature—or veto.

Regardless of how a bill turns out, the process is interesting and fun to watch. You will be observing how that blueprint for a government hashed out in a steamy room centuries ago works every day on issues great and small. ■

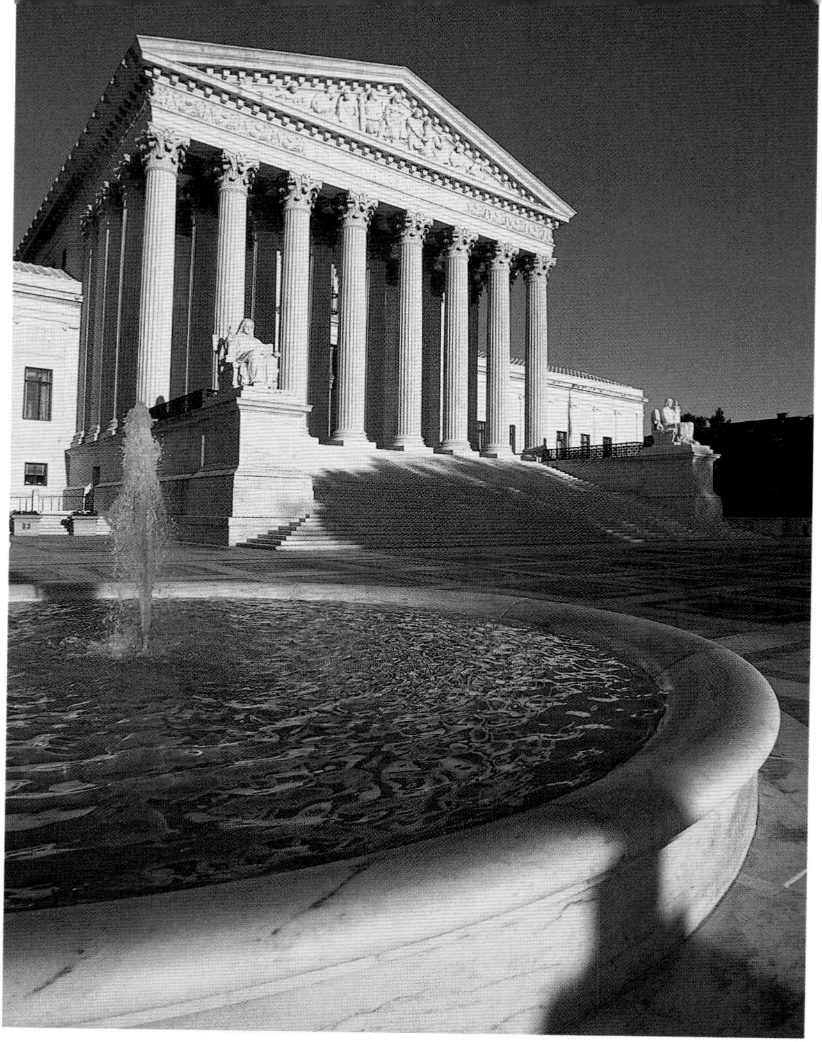

Supreme Court

Supreme Court
www.supremecourtus.gov
Map p. 51
1st & E. Capitol Sts., N.E.
202-479-3000 or 202-479-3211
Closed Sat.–Sun.
Metro: Capitol South, Union Station; Bus: 96-7, J11-13, A11, N22

THIS IMPOSING NEOCLASSIC BUILDING OPPOSITE THE Capitol makes a simple yet powerful statement with its wide marble stairway and its lofty portico rising on 32 Corinthian columns.

An architrave just below the pediment bears the inscription "Equal Justice Under Law," an echo of Justice John Marshall Harlan's famous dissenting opinion in 1896 in *Plessy* v. *Ferguson:* "In view of the Constitution, in the eye of the law, there is in this country no superior, dominant, ruling class of citizens. There is no caste here.... [A]ll citizens are equal before the law."

Here the nation's highest tribunal arbitrates cases involving the Constitution or the nation's laws. In this court of final appeal, decisions have been handed down that have profoundly influenced the country. In 2000 the Court showed its muscle again by effectively settling the controversial U.S. presidential race.

Surprisingly, the Supreme Court did not have its own building until 1935. Before then it sat in various places within the Capitol. In 1929 Chief Justice William Howard Taft, the only U.S. President (1909–1913) to serve on the Court (1921–1930), urged Congress to authorize the erection of a Supreme Court building. The neoclassic edifice designed by Cass Gilbert was constructed with 27,400 pieces of marble. Every feature lends a sense of gravity and dignity, from the 6.5-ton bronze doors to the seated marble giants out front—"Contemplation of Justice" (left) and "Guardian of Law" (right).

VISITING

You enter through the main (west) entrance on the building's second floor, which leads to the **Great Hall** and its long line of busts depicting former chief justices. At the end of the hall lies the actual **courtroom.** When the Court is not in session, you can visit the chamber, and learn about court procedure and the building's architecture, by attending a free lecture there, given on the half hour.

There is much for the eye to feast on in the nation's most important courtroom. Behind the raised mahogany bench stand the chairs of the nine justices, their height varying according to how tall the justice is (so that they all appear the same height when seated). Along the sides of the room rise 24 veined marble columns, above which sculpted marble panels depict such lawgivers as Moses, Confucius, and Napoleon. Above these friezes stretches the bright red and blue ceiling coffered with handcarved wood and plaster rosettes and lined with gold.

When the court is in session *(Oct.–April Mon.–Wed.)*, you can listen to oral arguments by lining up on the plaza in front of the building. Seating begins at 9:30 a.m., and at 12:30 when an afternoon case is scheduled. Some cases attract big crowds, with people even sleeping outside the court to ensure a place inside. You may have a better chance with the other line—for those who just want to hear a three-minute sample of the case. Seating begins at 10:00 a.m. and 1:00 p.m.

More than 8,000 petitions asking the Supreme Court to overturn a lower-court ruling arrive every year. Only 90 to 100 make it to the argument stage. Each side is given 30 minutes to argue its case; the justices then write their opinions. You can access these and other Court information via the internet.

Go down a flight of stairs to the ground level, where you'll find a small theater in the **Lower Great Hall;** a 24-minute film details the workings of the Court and includes interviews with current justices. The hall also has several exhibits on the Supreme Court. On the south side the famous Warren Court (1953–1969), presided over by Chief Justice Earl Warren, still sits in session, in a cast stone and aluminum sculpture. The Warren Court's progressive opinions included the outlawing of school segregation.

At the hall's east end is a statue of the great fourth Chief Justice, John Marshall, who served 1801–1835. He is considered responsible for our system of constitutional law, including the doctrine of judicial review (*Marbury* v. *Madison,* 1803), by which the Court can declare acts of Congress unconstitutional. Follow signs for a view of two amazing marble-and-bronze freestanding spiral staircases; the ascending ovals make the five-story building appear twice as tall as it really is. ■

Opposite: The neoclassic Supreme Court Building, with its open courtyard of Georgia marble, was completed in 1935.

Library of Congress

Library of Congress
www.loc.gov
Map p. 51
1st St. & Independence Ave., S.E.
202-707-8000 or 202-707-5000
Closed Sun.
Metro: Capitol South; Bus: 30-36, A11, J13, N22

AFTER EXTENSIVE RENOVATION FROM 1986 TO 1997, THE Library of Congress—the world's largest library—has emerged as one of the most breathtaking buildings in the city. Inside and out, the Italian Renaissance-style Thomas Jefferson Building (main building) dazzles the eye with its opulent yet tasteful cornucopia of sculpture, murals, mosaics, and architectural flourishes. Whether you come here for serious research or just to wander around, you'll leave understanding why this temple of learning was considered, at its opening in 1897, the most beautiful public building in America.

Originally housed in the U.S. Capitol, the Library began in 1800 as a reference collection for Congress. After the British burned the Capitol in 1814, destroying the books, Thomas Jefferson sold his personal library of 6,487 volumes—one of the country's most extensive—to Congress. Larger than the original collection, Jefferson's contained law books, as well as works of literature, history, science, architecture, and philosophy. As he wrote at the time, "There is, in fact, no subject to which a member of Congress may not have occasion to refer." His unbounded interest in everything has set the tone for the Library ever since.

The Library suffered a second devastating blow in 1851 when fire destroyed two-thirds of the collection. Though most titles have since been replaced, almost 900 remain missing. The Library is now conducting a worldwide search for copies of the books.

Ainsworth Rand Spofford, Librarian of Congress from 1864 to 1897, took Jefferson's eclectic philosophy seriously and began amassing a huge collection, including two copies of every copyrighted work in the country. The flood of material led to the construction of the Thomas Jefferson Building, the first of the Library's three buildings.

Though the Library does not hold every book published in the U.S., it does acquire some 10,000 of the 22,000 items received every day.

You can request books at the central desk, then read them at one of the tables in the octagonal Main Reading Room.

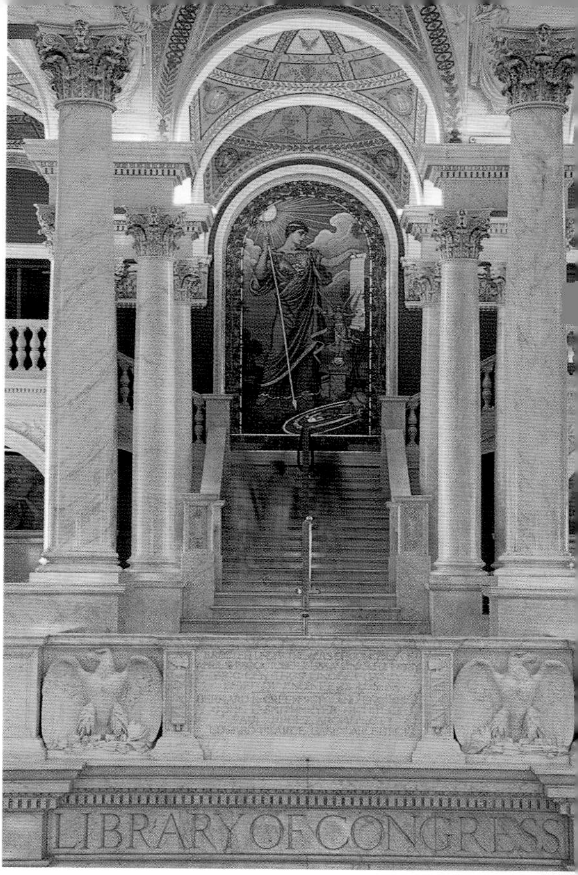

A grand marble staircase in the Library of Congress's exquisite Great Hall

The Library—an invaluable resource for legislators, students, scholars, and filmmakers—now holds 134 million items, including more than 20 million books, 5.3 million maps, and the papers of 23 U.S. Presidents, housed on 530 miles of shelves. The National Digital Library Program is putting much of the collection on the Internet *(www.loc.gov)*.

VISITING

You can take an organized tour of the **Jefferson Building** or pick up a self-guided tour brochure at the visitor center just inside the west side's ground level entrance. Several galleries in the building feature permanent and rotating exhibitions of American history and culture as well as important international materials from the Library's collection, such as a cuneiform tablet from 2400 B.C. and a copy of Ptolemy's *Geographica* (1480).

In the **Great Hall** on the first floor, you will feel as though you have entered a Mediterranean palazzo. Grand staircases lead up through carved marble arches; brilliant mosaics and paintings honor music, poetry, astronomy, and other disciplines; and columns and sculptures add to the vertical effect, as if to emphasize man's lofty aspirations. In the east corridor two Library treasures rest behind glass cases: the Giant Bible of Mainz and the Gutenberg Bible, both made in Germany in the mid-1450s.

On the second floor, an arcade makes a square around and above the Great Hall, offering unobstructed views of the first floor and the high ceiling. From the **Treasures Gallery,** a collection of exhibit halls at the south end, the east stairway leads up to the **Visitors' Gallery,** which has a wonderful view of the **Main Reading Room,** the sanctum sanctorum. A splendid coffered dome rises to a cupola 160 feet above the floor. Farther down, 16 bronze statues in balustrades represent luminaries such as Beethoven and Newton. Below, library patrons work at concentric circles of desks.

To use the library, you need a reader's pass. These are available at the **Madison Building,** across Independence Avenue. The Madison Building opened in 1980 and houses photos, prints, and a film archive; on the third floor, the **Mary Pickford Theater** *(202-707-5677)* screens free classic films. The 1939 deco-style **Adams Building,** behind the Jefferson on Second, has a business and science reading room. ■

Folger Shakespeare Library

Folger Shakespeare Library
www.folger.edu
Map p. 51
201 E. Capitol St., S.E., between 2nd & 3rd Sts.
202-544-4600
Closed Sun.
Metro: Capitol South; Bus: 96-7

THIS UNIQUE LIBRARY HOLDS THE WORLD'S LARGEST collection of William Shakespeare's works. Originating from a gift by Henry Clay Folger, the library opened in 1932 and now houses 310,000 books and manuscripts; 50,000 paintings, drawings, prints, and engravings; and many musical instruments, costumes, and films.

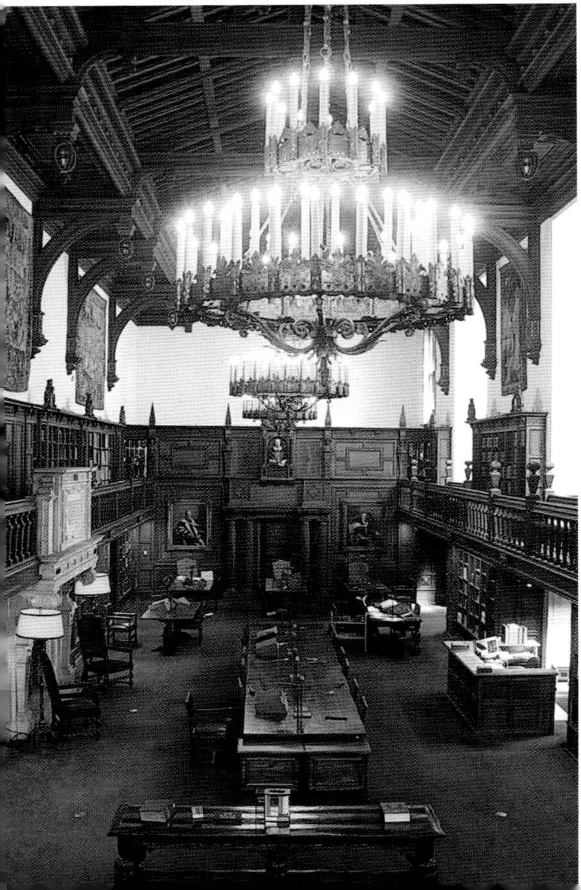

The Folger's Reading Room evokes an Elizabethan great hall.

In 1879 a lecture on the Bard by Ralph Waldo Emerson fired the interest of Folger, then a 22-year-old student at Amherst College. A decade later, he bought his first Shakespeare folio. With the money he made in the oil business (as president of the Standard Oil Company of New York), he went on to buy thousands of rare books, manuscripts, and paintings. In the early 1900s, he began casting about for a site to build a library; he finally chose one adjacent to the Library of Congress (see pp. 62–63). But just after the cornerstone was laid, in 1930, he died; his wife, Emily, saw the project to completion.

The bold lines of this art deco-inspired neoclassic marble building make it a fitting presence among its neighbors. Nine bas-reliefs on the north side depict scenes from the Bard's plays. A statue of Puck (from *A Midsummer Night's Dream*) graces a fountain on the west side. On the east lawn lies an **Elizabethan flower and herb garden.**

For more details on the Folger, take one of the daily tours, which start at the docent's desk directly inside the library's entrance. Or wander on your own through the wood-paneled 30-foot-high **Great Hall,** which displays a copy of the Bard's first folio and changing thematic exhibits from the library's collection. You may peer through an iron gate into the adjacent Tudor-style **Reading Room,** where a stained-glass window depicting the "Seven Ages of Man" *(As You Like It)* adorns the west end. A Shakespeare bust is mounted on the east wall. The room is open to scholars and graduate students for research.

At the building's eastern end, the **Folger Theatre** offers an intimate venue for the Bard's plays, or for lectures, readings, and education programs. The oak columns, tiered balconies, and sky canopy contribute to the atmosphere of an Elizabethan courtyard. ■

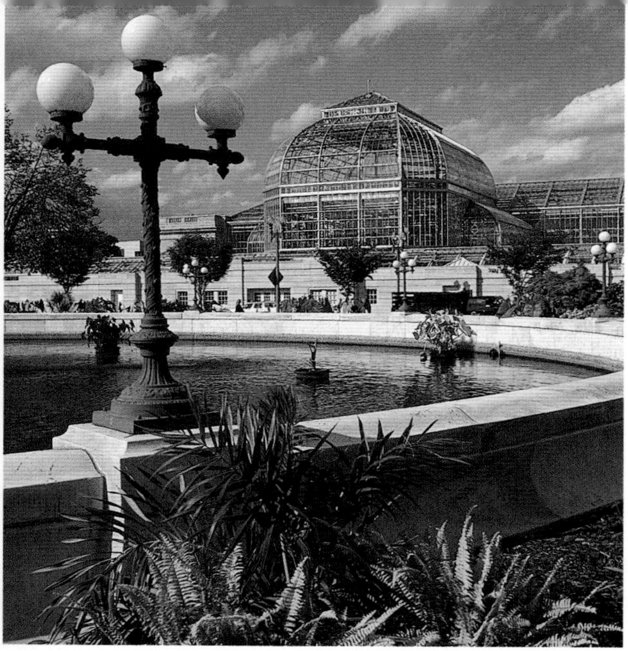

The renovated Conservatory as seen from across Independence Avenue

U.S. Botanic Garden

IF YOU'RE SURPRISED TO SUDDENLY FIND YOURSELF IN THE thick of a tropical rain forest or surrounded by a soothing oasis in the middle of downtown Washington, then you've stumbled onto the U.S. Botanic Garden in the shadow of the U.S. Capitol.

Congress established this garden in 1820 for the collection, growing, and distribution of important plants. Through the decades, numerous parts of the facility fell into disrepair. Eventually the site was closed for several years for repairs and restoration. In 1997 a 33.5-million-dollar renovation project was launched; the expanded and updated garden reopened in 2001 with a significantly enlarged—and spectacular—plant collection.

Today, more than 4,000 plants are on view at any one time in the glass-paneled **Conservatory.** They are selected from thousands of plants grown at a facility off-site. You can stroll through the various areas devoted to desert, jungle, and oasis flora, and explore exhibits on medicinal and economically useful plants, primeval vegetation, and plant exploration, among others. Don't miss climbing the stairs to the overhanging walkway in the large tropical atrium, where you can stroll through the outstanding collection of orchids and other epiphytes. The three-acre **National Garden,** adjacent to the Conservatory, opened in 2006

Across Independence Avenue is the garden's **Bartholdi Park.** Frédéric-Auguste Bartholdi, who created the Statue of Liberty, sculpted the park's 30-foot-high cast-iron fountain for the Centennial Exposition of 1876 in Philadelphia—the first world's fair. The sculpture's upper basin is borne by three upright sea nymphs, as water jets from the mouths of fish and turtles. ■

U.S. Botanic Garden

www.usbg.gov

Map p. 51

100 Maryland Ave., S.W.

202-225-8333

Metro: Federal Center S.W.; Bus: 30-36, P17-19, W13

More places to visit on Capitol Hill

EASTERN MARKET

A major fire in 2007 did significant damage to the interior of this much beloved Washington institution, which has operated as a public market since 1873. A concrete-and-steel structure has been erected across the street from the original marketplace and will serve as temporary home for the dozens of displaced vendors until the permanent building is restored. The rebuilt market is scheduled to be completed by the spring of 2009. The meat, produce, flower, and other

Vendor carts at Eastern Market in a picture taken in the 1880s

stalls are supplemented on weekends with extensive crafts and flea markets.
www.easternmarketdc.org Map p. 51
7th St.& North Carolina Avenue., S.E.
202-544-0083 Closed Mon. Metro: Eastern Market

NATIONAL POSTAL MUSEUM

The building that formerly housed the Washington City Post Office makes an elegant home for this interesting museum, near Union Station, which is part of the Smithsonian Institution complex. The galleries explore topics such as the history of mail delivery, stamp collecting, and the art of personal correspondence. Among the artifacts on display in the 90-foot-high atrium are prop planes and a railway car, modes of mail conveyance in the past. Half-hour guided tours for groups are available by calling in advance.
www.postalmuseum.si.edu Map p. 51
2 Massachusetts Ave., N.E. (just W of Union Station) 202-633-5555
Metro: Union Station

NATIONAL GUARD MUSEUM

Opened in February 2003, this small but engrossing museum at the National Guard Memorial uses memorabilia, light and sound effects, and dramatic narratives to chronicle the experiences of citizen soldiers who have served America at home and abroad for 370 years. The displays and interactive programs are especially poignant given the Guard's major role in homeland security and war in the Middle East following the September 11, 2001, terrorist attacks on the United States.
www.ngef.org Map p. 51
1 Massachusetts Ave, N.W. 202-789-0031
Closed Sat.–Sun. Metro: Union Station

SEWALL-BELMONT HOUSE

Robert Sewall built this two-story brick house in 1799–1800. In the 20th century, Alva Belmont helped purchase it for the National Woman's Party, headquartered here since 1929. Various collections document the movement to gain political rights for women. You can call to arrange a docent-led tour.
www.sewallbelmont.org Map p. 51
144 Constitution Ave., N.E. 202-546-1210 Closed Sun.–Mon. Metro: Union Station, Capitol South

UNION STATION

Completed in 1908 and beautifully restored in the 1980s, this grand beaux arts-style building is worth visiting just for its architecture. Faced in white Vermont granite, the station's huge Romanesque arches give way to a triumphal, echoing Main Hall where 36 larger-than-life Roman legionnaires preside on the gallery level. A barrel-vaulted ceiling with gold-leaf coffers soars 96 feet above the station's bustle. There are more than 100 shops and restaurants.
www.unionstationdc.com Map p. 51
40 Massachusetts Ave., N.E. 202-289-1908 Metro: Union Station ■

The vast expanse of the Mall, with its Smithsonian museums and stately monuments, is the Washington everyone comes to see. But this is also a laid-back place for picnicking, afterwork softball and soccer games, and just taking a stroll.

National Mall

Annual Smithsonian Folklife Festival, a summer highlight on the Mall

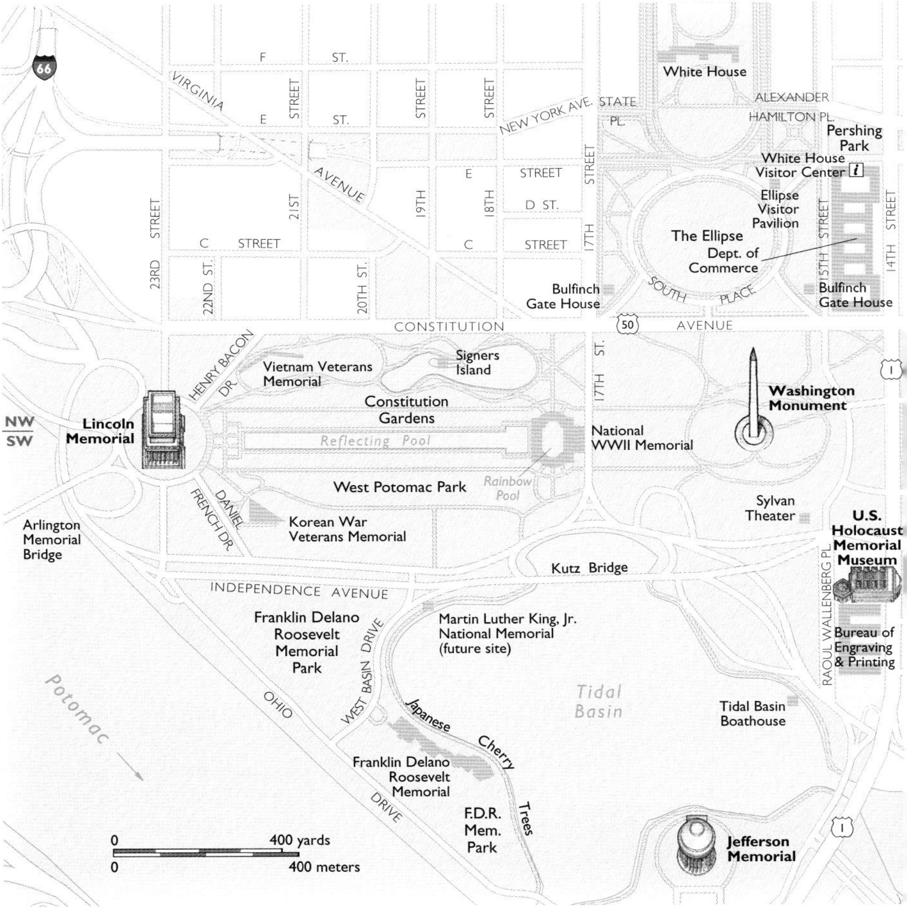

National Mall

LINED AND DOTTED WITH THE MOST SIGNIFICANT GROUP OF MUSEUMS AND monuments in the country, the National Mall is a long avenue of green grass edged by shade trees. You could spend a week, and more, visiting this world-famous tourist mecca.

One day hundreds of colorful kites are flying near the Washington Monument, on another a crowd is shouting and waving banners, and on yet another day the Mall is just a peaceful stretch of green. From the U.S. Capitol to the Lincoln Memorial, America's grand promenade extends for more than 2 miles between Constitution and Independence Avenues. Walkers, joggers, soccer players, and Frisbee throwers regularly take to the inviting lawns.

In summer, thousands flock to the Smithsonian Folklife Festival *(late June–early July)*, the Fourth of July celebration, and the Sylvan Theater's outdoor concerts. Numerous

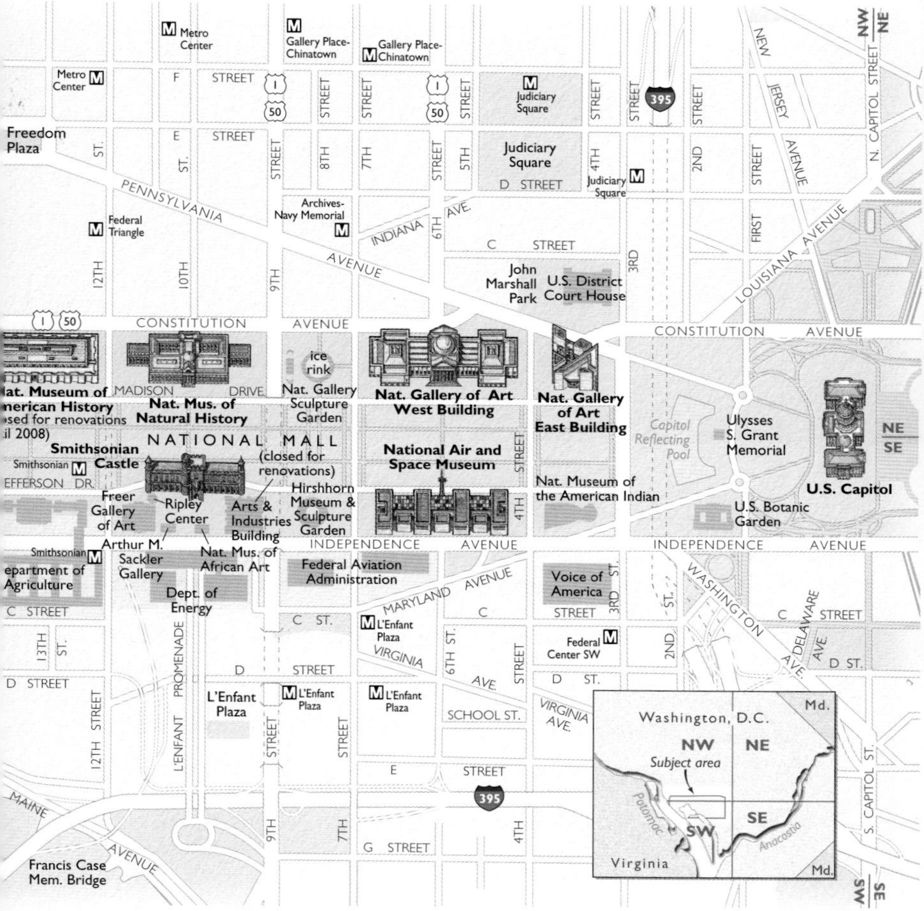

other events are held on the Mall, including a kite festival *(late March–early April)* and the Black Family Reunion *(Sept.)*. The Mall is also the stage for rallies by many national groups.

Pierre Charles L'Enfant's city plan of 1791 included a "vast esplanade" lined with magnificent residences. But by the end of the 1800s, the Mall was very different from his vision: Coal piles, sheds, tracks, and a railroad station made it less than appealing. In 1901 the MacMillan Commission recommended reviving L'Enfant's plan. Tracks and debris were removed, vistas were opened up, and marshy areas were filled. With the addition of the Lincoln Memorial, the Mall stretched to the Potomac River, making it the east-west axis of a memorial park area. The White House and Jefferson Memorial form the north-south axis, with the Washington Monument in the middle.

By the late 1980s, the Mall's eastern part held nine Smithsonian museums and two National Gallery of Art buildings. In 2004 the National Museum of the American Indian opened near the National Air and Space Museum, and the new World War II Memorial opened just west of the Washington Monument. ■

Freer Gallery of Art

Freer Gallery of Art
www.asia.si.edu
Map p. 69
Jefferson Dr. & 12th St., S.W.
202-633-4880
Metro: Smithsonian; Bus: 13A & G, 52-3

Artist James M. Whistler painted the sumptuous Peacock Room as though it were an enormous lacquer box.

DATING FROM THE FOURTH MILLENNIUM B.C. TO MODERN times, the objects in the Freer make a comprehensive sweep of Asian art. The collection, donated by Detroit businessman Charles Lang Freer (1856–1919), now numbers more than 24,000 individual works and is considered among the finest in the world. It is complemented by a large collection of 19th- and 20th-century American pieces, including many works by James McNeill Whistler.

Opened in 1923, the Italian Renaissance-style building has a pink granite exterior and polished white marble floors. Its galleries surround a hallway where large windows look out onto a refreshing inner courtyard. The lighting and exhibit space combine to lend a refined, contemplative atmosphere.

Of the 19 galleries, 16 are devoted to Asian art, including Indian sculpture, Japanese lacquerware, Chinese paintings, Korean and Vietnamese ceramics, and Islamic metalware. The Freer does not host traveling exhibitions or lend its objects; but rotates pieces from its collection.

Among the Asian works are the 10th-century Indian bronze "Queen Sembiyan Mahadevi as the Goddess Parvati" and a 12th-century wood sculpture, "Bosatsu," from the late Heian period of Japan.

American treasures include the exquisite **Peacock Room,** which is a must-see. Whistler painted the room, called "Harmony in Blue and Gold," for a rich London shipowner. Recently restored to its original elegance, the room features antique gilded leather walls, a metal ceiling painted in a feather pattern, and a painting known as "The Princess in the Land of Porcelain." The opposite wall has a painting of two peacocks, a reference to a quarrel between Whistler and his patron over the fee. Freer bought the room intact from a London dealer and installed it in his Detroit home; it was moved to Washington in 1919.

The Freer's lower level connects to the Arthur M. Sackler Gallery. ■

Arthur M. Sackler Gallery

HOUSED ALMOST ENTIRELY BELOW THE GROUND, THIS 1987 museum has at its core the Asian collection of research physician and medical publisher Arthur M. Sackler. Among its nearly 9,000 treasures are Chinese bronzes and jades, Persian manuscripts, ancient Iranian silver, and works from Tibet and Japan. The museum exhibits items from its growing permanent collection as well as from other collections in the United States and elsewhere. Visiting the Sackler and the Freer, which are administered jointly, gives you a comprehensive overview of traditional and modern Asian art.

Arthur M. Sackler Gallery
www.asia.si.edu
Map p. 69
1050 Independence Ave., S.W.
202-633-4880
Metro: Smithsonian; Bus: 13A & G, 52-3

The **first level**—one level below ground—contains works from a variety of cultures. The treasures are artfully displayed, enhancing their beauty and viewers' appreciation. Many of the rooms feature only half a dozen or so objects in glass cases, with subtle lighting and just enough information to keep you interested but not overwhelmed. Drawing on a recently donated collection, "Taking Shape: Ceramics in Southeast Asia" features about 200 pots and jars used in daily life and trade over four millennia.

In the **Arts of China galleries,** also on the first level, the Ancient Chinese Art section displays 12th- to 13th-century B.C. jade knives crafted by artisans with meticulous care and great skill—not attributes often associated with pieces from the Neolithic period. Another section, the Arts of Six Dynasties and Tang in China, holds Tang dynasty tomb guardians adorned with brilliant horns and flames. The guardians look as fierce and imposing as they must have 13 centuries ago.

The **second level** of the gallery is composed mainly of administrative offices. Be sure not to overlook the **third level** of the Sackler, where displays of contemporary Japanese bowls and vases, colorfully glazed, are complemented by a small pool and bubbling fountains.

From the third level, visitors can make their way to the **S. Dillon Ripley Center,** which features temporary exhibits. ■

Shindo Susumu's (1952–) porcelain bowl (above) was created in 1992 using iron and cobalt pigments and platinum, gold, and silver enamels. It is one of many master works at the Arthur M. Sackler Gallery (left).

National Museum of African Art

National Museum of African Art
www.nmafa.si.edu
Map p. 69
950 Independence Ave., S.W.
202-633-4600
Metro: Smithsonian or L'Enfant Plaza; Bus: 13A & G, 52-3

THIS MUSEUM TRACES ITS ROOTS TO A TOWNHOUSE ON Capitol Hill once owned by Frederick Douglas, a former slave who became a noted abolitionist. In 1964 Warren M. Robbins founded the Museum of African Art there as a private educational institution that mainly displayed some Douglas memorabilia.

The museum's early holdings also included a donated collection of 19th-century paintings by African-American artists, but for exhibitions of African works Robbins had to rely on loaned objects.

In 1979 the museum became part of the Smithsonian Institution. Three years later it was officially renamed the National Museum of African Art, and in 1987 the steadily growing institution moved to its present location on the Mall. Its permanent collection has grown to include more than 7,000 objects. They represent 900 cultures across the continent and a vast range of materials and art forms—textiles, sculpture, pottery, paintings, jewelry, masks, musical instruments, furniture, tools, and religious and household objects. Together they show the degree to which art permeates African culture and how great a bearing it has on African life. Changing exhibitions highlight treasures from the museum's collection along with pieces from public and private collections, dating from the 14th to the 20th centuries.

Face mask from Democratic Republic of Congo (early to mid-1900s)

The displays are designed to illuminate the high aesthetic and technical craftsmanship that is not always readily apparent in African art. They show, for example, how Africans often fashion all kinds of materials—from simple household utensils to ceremonial objects to monumental sculpture honoring the living and the dead—in ways meant to embody expressions of an "ideal" that reflects standards of beauty, moral behavior, leadership, intelligence, and fertility.

A long-running exhibit of contemporary traditional handcrafted **African ceramics** shows the dexterity and artistry of the continent's master potters—mainly women.

The museum recently added 525 outstanding pieces to its holdings with the Walt Disney Company's donation of a collection assembled by real estate developer Paul Tishman and his wife, Ruth. Many of the items, which represent most of Africa's major artistic traditions, are historically important.

The museum also houses a major library and research center and offers a variety of cultural programs. Its **Eliot Elisofon Photographic Archives,** named for the famous *Life* magazine photographer, has an expanding collection of 300,000 photo prints and transparencies and 120,000 feet of unedited film footage. ■

Hirshhorn Museum & Sculpture Garden

A STRIKING TOUCH OF MODERNITY ON THE MALL, THE Hirshhorn houses the Smithsonian's preeminent works of international modern and contemporary art. The museum opened in 1974, after American entrepreneur and philanthropist Joseph H. Hirshhorn (1899–1981) donated his art collection to the Smithsonian. An elevated drum-shaped building five stories high, this eye-catching landmark has 60,000 square feet for interior exhibitions and a bi-level sculpture garden and plaza of nearly four acres, with spaces designed to encourage intimate, contemplative viewing of the art works.

Hirshhorn Museum and Sculpture Garden
www.hirshhorn.si.edu
Map p. 69
Independence Ave. & 7th St., S.W.
202-633-1000
Metro: L'Enfant Plaza; Bus: 30-36, 54, 13B & F

Architect Gordon Bunshaft designed the museum, which has a permanent collection of more than 11,500 works by leading artists from the late 19th century to the present. Paintings, mixed media pieces, photography, works on paper, videos, and films are among the holdings, along with an outstanding modern sculpture collection that's regarded as one of the most comprehensive in the world.

A piece that is hard to miss is Roy Lichtenstein's towering "Brushstroke" (1996), recently installed on the plaza. Among the 60 pieces in the sculpture garden are traditional figures by artists such as Auguste Rodin and Aristide Maillol, biomorphic figures by Henry Moore and Barbara Hepworth, and abstract and kinetic works by Alexander Calder and Mark di Suvero.

Other major artists represented in the museum's wide-ranging collection of paintings and sculpture include Willem de Kooning, Alberto Giacometti, Jackson Pollack, Pablo Picasso, Clyfford Still, Gerhard Richter, Ana Mendieta, Georgia O'Keeffe,

The Hirshhorn's circular courtyard often serves as a setting for receptions.

What was there before

Before the Hirshhorn took shape on the Mall, the U.S. Army Medical Museum (now the National Museum of Health & Medicine; see p. 190) occupied the site from 1887 to 1968. The museum was established during the Civil War to help advance medical treatment. More than 25,000 specimens of diseased or wounded flesh and bones were kept here, and morbidly fascinated tourists could see preserved gunshot wounds, a vertebra from John Wilkes Booth, and disfigured and diseased organs. Over the years the tastes of the public changed, and the museum was moved to the Walter Reed Army Medical Center at 6900 Georgia Avenue, N.W. ■

Ernesto Neto, Hiroshi Sugimoto, Lorna Simpson, Robert Lazzarini, Ann Hamilton, Yoko Ono, and many others.

In an effort to continually expand its holdings and showcase modern works, the Hirshhorn works closely with practicing artists. To present pieces from its collection in fresh, new ways, the museum recently introduced a program series, titled **Ways of Seeing,** in which working artists, filmmakers, and other creative thinkers are invited to organize exhibitions using objects from the museum's holdings. In one such installation, for example, artist John Baldessari incorporated paintings by Milton Avery, Philip Guston, and Thomas Eakins, photographs by Eakins, and sculpture by Emily Kaufman.

A series titled **Directions** explores new work by emerging and established artists, while the **Black Box** series presents recent film and video works.

Other programs include "Meet the Artist" lectures, gallery talks, and art-related activities for children. Several times a year the Hirshhorn hosts "After Hours" events that offer inviting social environments in which to enjoy the exhibits.

In addition, a renowned film program—one of the first in the United States to focus on independent cinema—presents narrative and experimental features, documentaries, and shorts in the museum's 272-seat auditorium. ■

An angular ode to modern art: "Are Years What? (for Marianne Moore)" (1967), composed of industrial I-beams with a suspended, moving V element, is considered one of Mark di Suvero's greatest works.

National Air and Space Museum

THE EXCITEMENT OF AERONAUTICAL AND SPACEFLIGHT technology has made the National Air and Space Museum the most-visited museum in the world. Every year millions of people roam its flagship building on the Mall, where the exhibits feature only 10 percent of the Smithsonian's aviation and space collection. Most of the remaining artifacts are on display at a huge additional facility in suburban Virginia (see Steven F. Udvar-Hazy Center, pp. 220–221).

The Smithsonian's involvement in air and space goes back to 1857, when it began using balloons to collect weather data. Later, during the Civil War, the first secretary of the Smithsonian, Joseph Henry, won President Abraham Lincoln's support for making military observations from balloons. The third secretary, Samuel Pierpont Langley (1887–1906), was an astronomer and airplane pioneer. He experimented successfully with heavier-than-air craft on the Potomac in the 1890s, but the first actual manned, controlled flight was made by the Wright brothers in 1903.

During the first half of the 20th century, the Smithsonian participated in and funded major rocket research and astrophysical observation projects. In 1971, Apollo astronaut Michael Collins

National Air and Space Museum

www.nasm.si.edu

Map p. 69

Independence Ave. & 7th St., S.W.

202-633-1000

Metro: L'Enfant Plaza; Bus: 30-36, 54, P1-6

A mural showing the Milky Way galaxy highlights the "Explore the Universe" exhibit.

Lindbergh

Perhaps more than any other aviator, Charles Lindbergh (1902–1974) captured the public's admiration. Son of a Minnesota congressman, he spent many of his early years in Washington, D.C. Later he attended a Wisconsin college but dropped out to enroll in a Nebraska flying school. For a few years he was a stunt flyer and an airmail pilot. Then he competed for a $25,000 prize offered to the first person to fly from New York to Paris nonstop.

Charles A. Lindbergh (1902–1974), with the *Spirit of St. Louis*

On May 20, 1927, the aviator took off in the *Spirit of St. Louis,* named for the city where he received financial backing. Because the large fuel tank partially blocked his view, Lindbergh relied on a periscope or tilted the plane to see forward. He flew for 33.5 exhausting hours before landing at Le Bourget Field near Paris and receiving a warm welcome by a cheering crowd of 100,000.

Back in Washington, Lindbergh stayed a few days at the Patterson House on Dupont Circle with President Coolidge, who lived there while the White House was being renovated. Later that year the U.S. Congress awarded him a Medal of Honor. The following year he gave his plane to the Smithsonian, where it is prominently displayed.

In 1929, Lindbergh wed Anne Morrow, and together they made several flights to chart airline routes. When their son was kidnapped and killed in 1932, the unending publicity drove them abroad. Lindbergh advocated neutrality at the outbreak of World War II, leading to criticism by President Roosevelt, yet he quietly served as an aircraft consultant and flew on combat missions over the Pacific. He described his famous transatlantic flight in thrilling detail in *We* (1927) and *The Spirit of St. Louis* (1953), the latter winning a Pulitzer Prize. ■

was appointed director of the new National Air and Space Museum, and construction began the next year. The Wright Flyer and other aircraft that had been on display in the Arts and Industries Building, another Smithsonian facility on the Mall, were moved to the new museum, which opened to the public in 1976.

Opposite: The Milestones of Flight gallery contains some of the most iconic air- and spacecraft in the museum's collection.

VISITING

With so much to see at this museum and such large distances to cover, it's best to map out a plan for your visit, especially if you're with children or others who tire easily (see the floor plan on pp. 78–79). If you want to see any of the shows in the IMAX theater or the Planetarium, it's a good idea to purchase the tickets at the start of your visit, because tickets often sell out. Then tour the galleries that interest you until the show starts.

In a half-day visit, it's best to choose one tactic: either aim for a quick overview of the entire museum, or take a close look at just a few galleries. Moving around in this wildly popular museum can be a challenge during peak visiting times because of the huge crowds, so pace yourself—and agree on a place to meet others in your party if you get separated. At lunchtime, you can grab a bite to eat at the museum's large cafeteria.

USAF

In general, the layout of the museum is arranged so that airplanes and aviation are in the west end of the building, while rockets and spaceflight are in the east end. Almost all the artifacts on display are the real thing, though in some cases backups, test vehicles, or authentic reproductions are shown instead. Labels indicate the difference.

FIRST FLOOR

Just inside the Mall entrance, the **Milestones of Flight** gallery highlights aviation's "greatest hits," with artifacts such as the *Spirit of St. Louis,* in which Charles Lindbergh made the first solo, non-stop flight across the Atlantic in May 1927; the Apollo II command module *Columbia,* which carried astronauts home from the first moon landing in 1969; a replica of Sputnik 1; and John Glenn's Mercury Friendship 7 capsule. One of the gallery's newest additions is SpaceShipOne, the first privately built and piloted vehicle to reach space.

Proceeding to the right, you'll come to the museum's gift shop and toy store. Beyond that is a new gallery, **America by Air,** with attractions that include a giant nose cone section from a Boeing 747 and interactive programs. The gallery next door features flight simulators.

Across the hall, in the far corner gallery, is the exhibit **Golden Age of Flight.** Scratchy recordings of old torch songs set the tone for this exhibit of the glamour days of aviation in the period between the two World Wars. A small theater features historic footage, including information about the life of famed pilot Jimmy Doolittle.

In the adjacent **Jet Aviation** gallery, you'll take a leap forward in time to focus on the development of jet technology. The display includes a German WWII fighter, the Messerschmitt Me 262. Then wander next door to the **Early Flight** gallery to experience the time when flight was still a novelty. Among the featured artifacts are the world's first military plane, the 1909 Wright Military Flyer, and an 1894 Lilienthal glider with bat-like ribbed wings.

As you cross the hall, moving past the Welcome Center at the Independence Avenue entrance, take a few minutes to view the two impressive murals. Robert T. McCall's 1976 "The Space

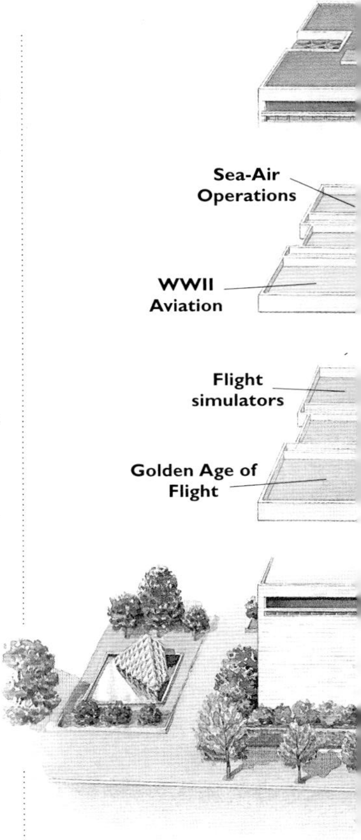

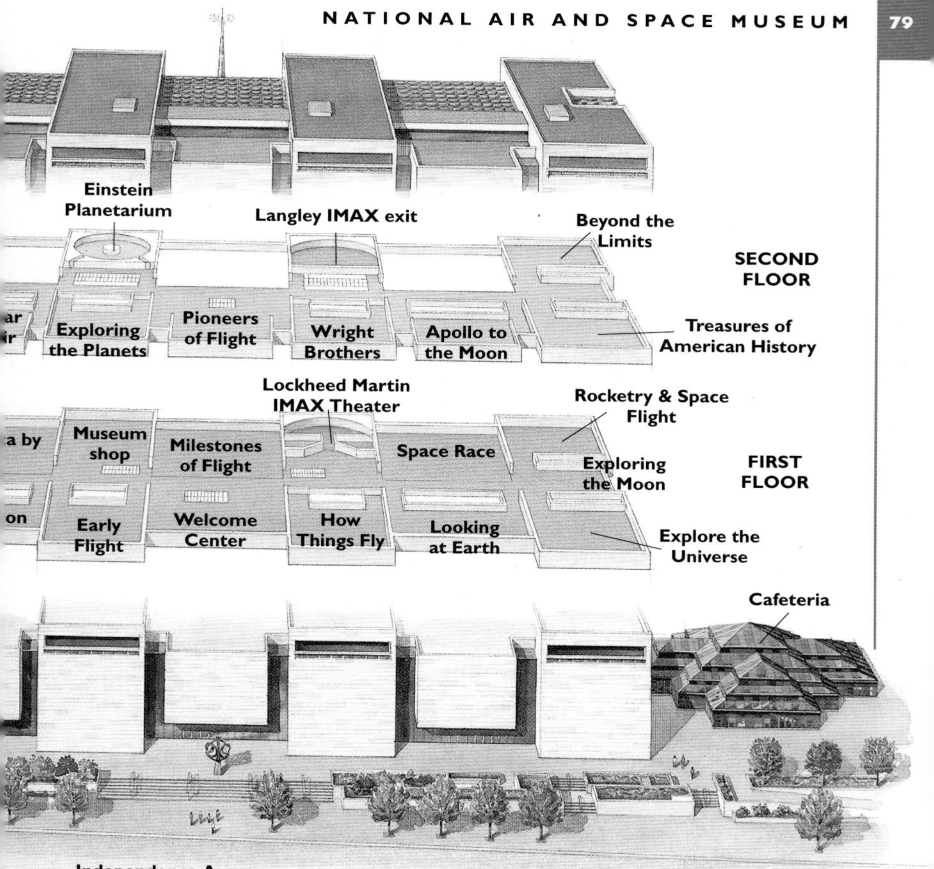

Mural: A Cosmic View" traces space history from the Big Bang to lunar exploration and beyond. On the opposite wall, Eric Sloan's "Earthflight Environment" (1976) shows a western landscape beneath a sky filled with the kinds of weather pilots must fly through.

A favorite of children, the **How Things Fly** gallery, adjacent to the Welcome Center, has 50 hands-on exhibits with gadgets that explain principles such as lift, drag, air pressure, and wave action. Depending on the time of your visit, you may have a chance to enjoy—or even participate in—some of the regularly scheduled science demonstrations.

Next door, the **Looking at Earth** gallery shows how views of the planet obtained from the sky through Landsat and other means aid our understanding of Earth. Several surrounding galleries continue the space theme in this wing of the building. Hard-to-miss artifacts on display include a giant black-and-white V-2 rocket in the two-story **Space Race** gallery and a shiny lunar module featured in the **Exploring the Moon** gallery. Displays in the nearby **Rocketry and Space Flight** gallery trace the development of spaceflight from fantasy to reality, with a fanciful space capsule based on the ideas of

The 1975 Apollo-Soyuz mission (Apollo on left, Soyuz on right) was the first human spaceflight managed jointly by two nations. Conceived during the era of détente, it signified the end of the space race between the United States and the Soviet Union.

19th-century science fiction writer Jules Vern. Directly across the hall, past the lunar exhibit, **Explore the Universe** showcases some of the many tools that astronomers have used for centuries in studying the universe.

Also on this level, between the Space Race and Milestones of Flight galleries, is the **Lockheed Martin IMAX Theater** *(fee)*. Its several films—including the long-running classic "To Fly!"—are projected on a screen that's five stories high.

SECOND FLOOR

Escalators in the Milestones of Flight gallery carry you to the second floor, where you can visit the **Einstein Planetarium** *(fee)* and see multimedia presentations on the planets and stars.

Across the hall from the planetarium, a full-scale model of a Mars rover is on display in the **Exploring the Planets** gallery, along with spacecraft, telescopes, and other tools used to acquire an understanding of the universe. The displays, designed to be easy enough for children to understand, include highlights of recent planetary discoveries.

Also in the west end of the second floor, several galleries focus on various aspects of aviation during the World Wars: the **Sea-Air Operations** gallery, which includes a simulated aircraft carrier; **World War II Aviation;** and **Great War in the Air,** which offers an unromanticized view of aerial combat in World War I.

Once you leave this end of the second floor and head in the other direction, you'll come to the **Pioneers of Flight** gallery which is devoted to individual feats in aviation history. Among the famous aircraft you'll find here is Amelia Earhart's Lockheed Vega, in which she became the first woman to fly solo across the Atlantic in 1932. Next door, the **Wright Brothers & the Invention of the Aerial Age**

offers an eye-level view of the famous wood-and-fabric Wright Flyer that was flown at Kitty Hawk, North Carolina, in 1903, marking the dawn of modern aviation. This gallery was established in 2003 during the centennial of that momentous event.

Apollo to the Moon, the adjacent gallery, examines the heady years of manned spaceflight, and in particular the challenges of putting humans on the Moon. Featured artifacts range from food, clothing, and personal items of astronauts such as Neil Armstrong, Buzz Aldrin, and Gene Cernan to a sample of moon dust. Just outside the gallery stands a mockup of Skylab, which you can enter to find out how everyday activities were performed aboard the international space station, which was launched in 1973.

The gallery across the hall in the far corner, **Beyond the Limits,** emphasizes the critical importance of digital computers to flight. The featured attractions include a theater devoted to the use of computers for training pilots and astronauts, along with a full-size cockpit simulator that you can command in order to get a feel for what it's like to pilot a space shuttle.

To view yet another of the National Air and Space Museum's exhibits, you'll have to return to the first floor and step outside, through the Mall entrance. There, **Voyage: A Journey Through Our Solar System** depicts the solar system—at one-ten-billionth of its actual size—in an arrangement that depicts the relative size of the planets and the great distances between them. The planets are represented by porcelain balls mounted atop stainless steel posts; the sun is about the size of a large grapefruit; Earth is the size of the head of a pin. The installation runs along the Mall, extending all the way from the Air and Space Museum to the front of the Smithsonian Castle. ■

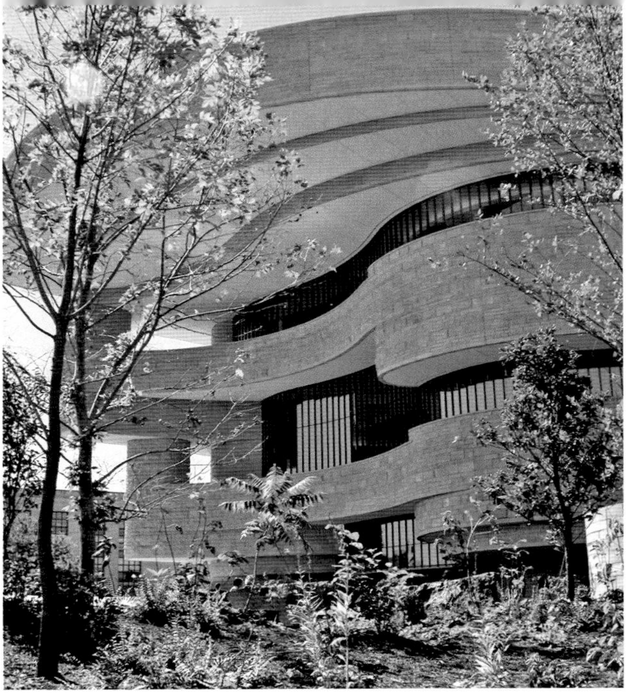

The museum's exterior has undulating curves and deep window ledges, giving it the appearance of a stratified stone mass that has been carved by wind and water.

National Museum of the American Indian

National Museum of the American Indian
www.nmai.si.edu
Map p. 69
Fourth St. & Independence Ave., S.W.
202-633-1000
Metro: L'Enfant Plaza; Bus: 30-36, 54, P1-6

STRIKING IN ITS ARCHITECTURE, WHICH WAS INSPIRED BY the rocky mesa cliffs of the American Southwest, the National Museum of the American Indian opened in September 2004 after 15 years of planning. It gives the nation a vibrant center for Native American events and educational programs as well as a showcase for outstanding Indian art and artifacts.

The museum got its start at the turn of the 20th century when a wealthy New York banker, George Gustav Heye, needed a place to house the objects he had obtained from North and South American Native cultures in a buying frenzy from 1903 to 1954—an astonishing collection of almost a million pieces spanning 10,000 years. He established a museum in what is now the restored Alexander Hamilton U.S. Custom House in lower Manhattan.

In 1989 Heye's collection was transferred to the Smithsonian Institution. Among the artifacts were human remains that had to be repatriated and buried in Native grounds. As the Smithsonian's Native American collection swelled to some 400,000 objects, a campaign began to build a major museum for Indian art and culture. The original location in New York City is now a branch of this new 4.25-acre museum on the Mall, along with a 200,000-square-foot Cultural Resources Center in Suitland, Maryland, where a large bulk of the collection is preserved, documented, and researched.

Among the museum's treasures are intricate carvings and masks from Pacific Northwest coastal tribes; embellished hides and feather bonnets from North American Plains Indians; pottery and basketry from the southwestern United States; 18th-century materials from the Great Lakes region; and early Navajo weavings. Artifacts from Mexico, Central and South America, and the Caribbean include jade carved by the Olmec and Maya and elaborate Amazonian feather works.

VISITING

As you wander about the five-story museum, observe the many symbolic references to the cultures it honors. The curvy outside façade of Kasota limestone was made to appear like an ancient slab of stratified stone. Crystal prisms embedded in the south-facing wall create "light shows" when reflecting the mid-day sun, while the main doors bear Native sun symbols.

Inside, you first reach a central space called the **Potomac,** a Piscataway word for a place "where the goods are brought in." The overhead dome, 120 feet high and 120 feet wide, has an oculus offering views of the sky and celestial bodies—critical reference points in Native cultures. In the floor is an abstract fire design, and rings of black and red granite that map the solstices and equinoxes. A wall of copper bands woven to suggest Native baskets and textiles encircles the room.

Near the information desk, a **Welcome Wall** projects hundreds of Native American words for "welcome" onto a 23-foot screen. A theater on the ground floor features storytelling, music, dance, and other programs. An inaugural temporary exhibit in the Potomac area spotlights boatbuilding traditions of Native peoples.

Take the elevators to the exhibition areas on the upper levels. The 120-seat **Lewali Theater** on the fourth floor offers a short orientation program explaining the themes and messages emphasized throughout the exhibits.

The museum has four permanent exhibits. **Our Universes: Traditional Knowledge Shapes Our World** looks at the primary role of cosmology in the myths and everyday life of Native peoples, and their reverence for the spiritual relationship between mankind and the natural world. The galleries show how various tribes interpret the order of the world and its meaning for harmony in their lives.

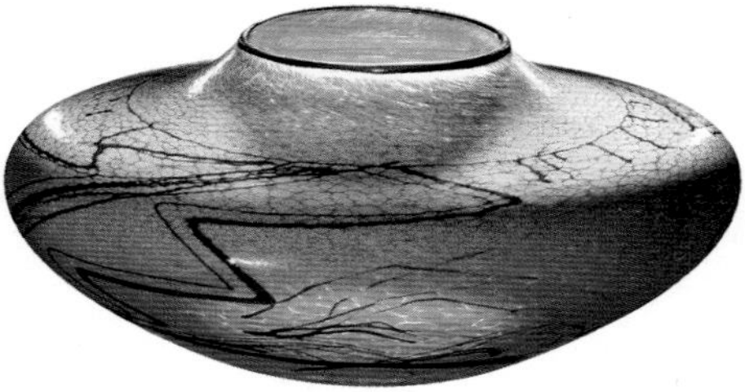

"Lightning Strikes," a blown glass vase by Tom Jojola (Isleta Pueblo), New Mexico, circa 1990

The exhibit **Our Peoples: Giving Voice to Our Histories** conveys events that have shaped the lives and outlook of American Indians from 1491 to the present. **Our Lives: Contemporary Life and Identities** examines how American Indians work to preserve and define their identities amid the challenges of the 21st century.

On the second floor, **Return to a Native Place: Algonquian Peoples of the Chesapeake** features displays that highlight events affecting the Nanticoke, Powhatan, and Piscataway tribes.

On the third and fourth levels, more than 3,500 objects from the museum's magnificent and wide-ranging collection are on display, arranged by categories in drawers and glass-fronted cases. ■

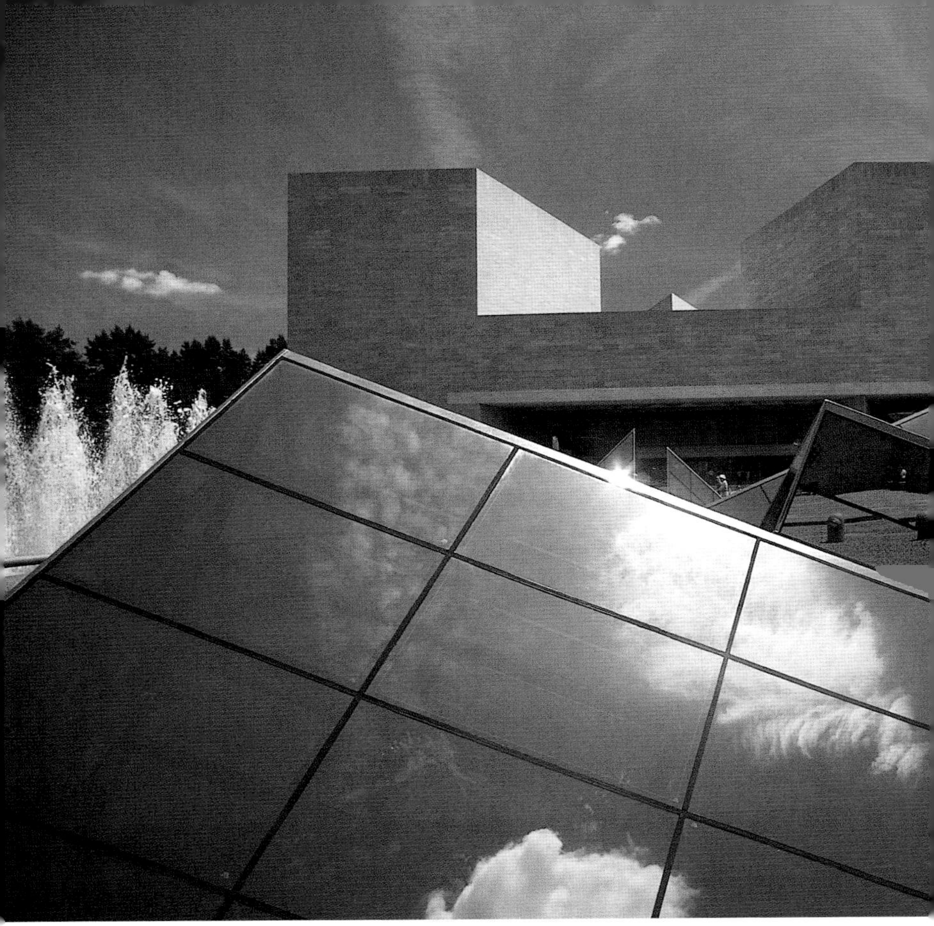

National Gallery of Art

National Gallery of Art
www.nga.gov
Map p. 69
Constitution Ave. between 3rd & 9th Sts., N.W.
202-737-4215
Metro: Archives, Smithsonian; Bus: 30-36, 54, 13A & G

ONE OF THE COUNTRY'S TOP ART MUSEUMS, THE NATIONAL Gallery of Art holds a comprehensive collection of Western masterpieces. The West Building exhibits European painting and sculpture from the 13th to 19th centuries; American art; and prints, drawings, photography, and decorative arts. The East Building contains modern and contemporary art. Both buildings also present temporary exhibits.

In the 1920s, financier and Secretary of the Treasury Andrew Mellon began planning to establish a museum in Washington. In 1931 he completed a purchase of 21 paintings from Russia's Hermitage Museum, including Raphael's "Alba Madonna." Mellon died in 1937, the same year that construction began for the new museum designed by John Russell Pope and funded by the A. W. Mellon Educational and Charitable Trust. In March 1941, President Roosevelt presided over a dedication ceremony attended by nearly 9,000 guests.

The holdings grew rapidly, thanks to many generous donations,

Rising from the plaza between the East and West Buildings, glass tetrahedrons act as skylights for a lower concourse.

and in the late 1960s, architect I. M. Pei was hired to create a plan for a new building to accommodate the collection. Opened in 1978, the East Building had to fit a trapezoidal site, mesh with the neoclassic West Building, and be an appropriate receptacle for modern art. The resulting marble-faced monolithic surfaces, acute angles, and glass hyphens make it not only visually arresting but also a fitting counterpart to the nearby 1970s buildings—the Hirshhorn and the Air and Space Museum. An underground concourse connects the two buildings.

Under phased renovation plans, various galleries in the two buildings close temporarily and some works may be moved to different locations in the museum, so check the website before your visit if there's a particular masterpiece you want to see.

Also check for special exhibitions and new acquisitions. In 2004, for example, art scholar and collector John Wilmerding donated 51 notable works of 19th-century American art, such as George Caleb Bingham's "Mississippi Boatman" (1850). In recent years 22 new galleries were added on the ground floor of the West Building, featuring 900 works of art such as sculpture masterpieces from the Middle Ages through the late 19th and early 20th centuries, including a major group of works by Edgar Degas. New galleries for photos and works on paper opened in 2004.

WEST BUILDING

All entrances other than on the Mall put you on the ground floor. One level up is the **main floor,** where European art from the 13th to 19th centuries and American painting and sculpture from colonial times to the early 20th century are displayed. The spectacular **Rotunda,** ringed by Tuscan marble pillars, rises to a high oculus above a central fountain graced by a statue of Mercury. The dome is strongly reminiscent of John Russell Pope's other great Washington structure, the Jefferson Memorial.

Extending from either side of the Rotunda, the **West Sculpture Hall** contains works in bronze, while the **East Sculpture Hall** has works in marble. Each hall ends in a garden court, where free concerts are often held. Several cafés and coffee bars throughout the National Gallery facilities offer light fare.

The halls and courts are surrounded by galleries that are numbered 1 to 93 and generally proceed

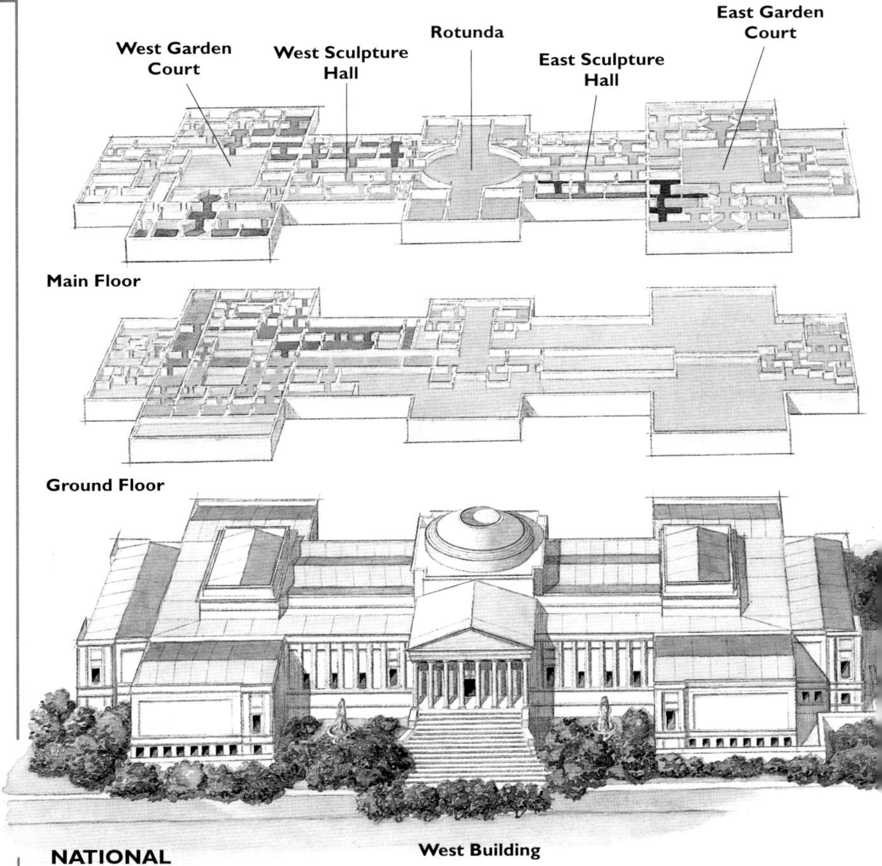

NATIONAL GALLERY OF ART

in chronological order, with nationalities grouped together.

Galleries 1–13 hold **13th- to 15th-century Italian paintings.** Representing the early Florentine and central Italian Renaissance, these works range from Byzantine iconography to the beginnings of the high Renaissance. Masterpieces include Giotto's "Madonna and Child" (ca 1320–1330); Fra Filippo Lippi's "Adoration of the Magi" (ca 1445); Leonardo da Vinci's "Ginevra de' Benci" (1474); and Botticelli's "Giuliano de' Medici" (ca 1478).

You'll find **16th-century Italian and Spanish works** in Galleries 13–28. Here is art from the northern Italian Renaissance, distinguished by allegorical and religious scenes within a colorful, sensual, pastoral setting. Especially outstanding are paintings by the Venetian master Tiziano Vecelli, or Titian, whose lovely "Venus with a Mirror" (1555) is vibrant with life. Raphael's "Alba Madonna" (1510) hangs here, as do works by Tintoretto, one of the great Venetian painters. Don't fail to pause in Gallery 26 for Bernardino Luini's "Fresco Cycle," with the "Story of Procris and Cephalus" (1520–22). America's only Italian Renaissance fresco series recounts a

WEST BUILDING GALLERIES

- **12th- to 15th-century Italian**
- **16th-century Italian and Spanish**
- **17th- and 18th-century Italian, Spanish, and French**
- **15th- to 16th-century Netherlands and German**
- **17th-century Dutch and Flemish**
- **18th- and 19th-century Spanish**
- **18th- and early 19th-century French**
- **19th-century French**
- **British**
- **American**
- **Special Exhibitions**
- **Drawings from the Armand Hammer Collection**
- **Non-Exhibition Space**
- **Sculpture**

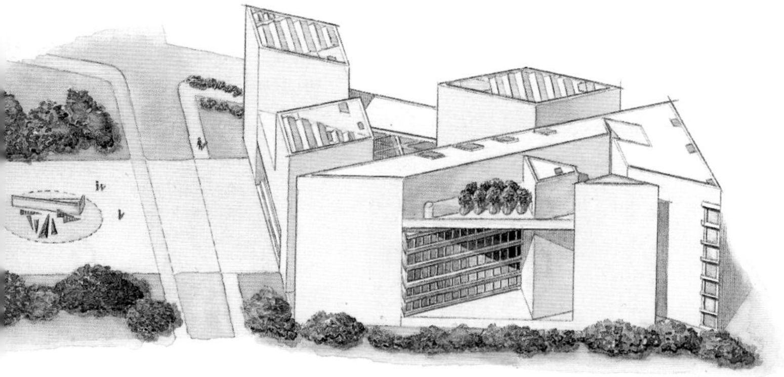

East Building

myth in nine pastoral scenes around a villa-like room that's floored with mosaic tiles from third-century Tunisia. Gallery 28 has several works by El Greco.

Galleries 29–34 and 36–37 display **17th-century Italian, Spanish, and French Baroque** paintings. Among the artists are Canaletto, a Venetian master known for his views of Venice, and Tiepelo, another Venetian, who painted in an exuberant and colorful style. Look for Georges de la Tour's "The Repentant Magdalene" (1640) and Procaccin's sensuous "Ecstasy of the Magadalen" (ca 1620).

In Galleries 35, 35A, and 38–41A, **15th- to 16th-century Netherlands and German** painters include Albrecht Dürer and Matthias Grunewald, whose relatively few works, mostly of religious subjects, such as "The Crucifixion" (ca 1520) were enough to secure his reputation as one of the greats of his time.

Among the most popular areas of the museum, Galleries 42–51 feature **17th-century Flemish and Dutch** paintings. The large collection of Van Dyck portraits is among the finest in the world. Here also is Ruben's monumental

Self-portrait by Vincent van Gogh

"Daniel in the Lions' Den," a favorite of viewers. Dutch realism can be found in portraits by Frans Hals, landscapes by Jacob van Ruisdael, and still lifes by Ambrosius Bosschaert. Great treasures on display include the luminous paintings of Johannes Vermeer (among them "Girl with the Red Hat") and the forceful images of Rembrandt van Rijn, including his brooding "Self-Portrait" of 1659 and his landscape "The Mill," with its powerful chiaroscuro effects.

Walk now to the east side of the rotunda, where Gallery 52 contains **18th- and 19th-century Spanish** paintings, notably by Francisco de Goya. **French art** from the **18th and early 19th centuries** lines the walls of Galleries 53–56, much of it in a florid style depicting lighthearted sophistication in French society. Among the treasures are Antoine Watteau's "Italian Comedians" (1720), Boucher's "Madame Bergeret" (1746), and Fragonard's "A Young Girl Reading" (1776).

British works fill Galleries 57–59, 61, and 63. Painters represented here include Hogarth, Reynolds, Romney, Gainsborough, Constable, and Turner. The landscapes of Constable and seascapes of Turner are particularly worth noting. **American** paintings are on view in Galleries 60A–B, 62, and 64–71. Gilbert Stuart's portraits of early U.S. Presidents vie for attention with the big mid-19th-century landscapes of Bierstadt, Cole, and Church. Other works are by Homer, Whistler, Bellows, Ryder, Sargent, and Cropsey. Galleries 72–79 are reserved for **special exhibitions.**

Impressionist and other 19th-century French painting is on exhibit in Galleries 80–93. These rooms are filled with the light and color of leading exponents Renoir and Monet, and the idiosyncratic styles of Cézanne and van Gogh.

Also on display are Parisian nightlife scenes by Degas and Toulouse-Lautrec. Among the great works are Renoir's "Girl with a Watering Can" (1876), Manet's "The Railway" (1873), and Monet's "Woman with a Parasol—Madame Monet and her Son" (1875).

The ground floor showcases **photography and sculpture,** as well as **prints and drawings** by luminaries such as Michelangelo, Leonardo, Manet, and Cézanne. From here you can reach the East Building via a below ground concourse, or enter it from Fourth Street.

EAST BUILDING

The walls and angles of the East Building (or East Wing) are marvels in themselves. Gracing the entrance, Henry Moore's curvy bronze "Knife Edge Mirror Two Piece" (1977–78) mimics the shape of the building. The building itself consists of two triangular shapes; the one on the north exhibits works of modern art, while the other one has offices.

At the ground-floor information desk, you can check on current exhibits and the tour schedule. This floor opens to an atrium that features an untitled mobile by Calder. Other art is usually on view as well, such as small French paintings by masters of Impressionism and Postimpressionism. The **mezzanine** and **upper levels** hold several large rooms for permanent and temporary exhibits. On display are works that trace the evolution of modernism, and the artists include Picasso, Braque, Miró, Mondrian, Arp, Magritte, Stella, O'Keeffe, Lichtenstein, Kandinsky, Brancusi, and Giacometti.

Take the winding staircase to the **tower level** to view the Matisse cutouts (1950s), huge colorful paper collages the artist created near the end of his life. The **concourse level** also has exhibit space for large canvases and installations.

SCULPTURE GARDEN

Opened in 1999, the 6-acre Sculpture Garden is across Seventh Street from the West Building. Its 17 works include "Puellae" (1992), featuring 30 headless, shriveled, 3-foot-tall girls—Polish-born sculptor Magdalena Abakanowicz's chilling depiction of a Holocaust story. You can't miss Louise Bourgeois's 9-foot-tall "Spider" (1997), part of her series exploring childhood memory and loss. Another large piece, "Aurora" (1992–93) by Mark Di Suvero, illustrates elegance and balance on a massive scale.

An attractive glass-sided café in the garden serves sandwiches, salads, and drinks. It is a pleasant spot for free "Jazz in the Garden" concerts held on Friday evenings from Memorial Day to Labor Day. Nearby is an outdoor ice-skating rink that is open from November to March. ■

Opposite: Jan van Eyck's "The Annunciation" (1434–36, oil on wood transferred to canvas) was probably once the left wing of a triptych.

Below: Claes Oldenburg and Coosje van Bruggen's "Typewriter Eraser, Scale X" (1999, stainless steel and fiberglass), found in the Sculpture Garden, depicts one of Oldenburg's favorite childhood playthings from his father's office.

National Museum of Natural History

National Museum of Natural History

www.mnh.si.edu

Map p. 69

10th St. & Constitution Ave., N.W.

202-633-1000

Metro: Federal Triangle, Smithsonian; Bus: 13A-B & F-G, P1-2, A42-48

DINOSAUR FOSSILS, SPARKLING GEMS, MAMMALS, AN insect zoo, and rare Native American artifacts—these are the kinds of things that make this such a popular museum. The Smithsonian's National Museum of Natural History explores in wondrous detail the natural world and our place in it. Housed in a green-domed beaux arts building from 1910, this was the third Smithsonian building, erected to hold the institution's bursting collection.

The teeming variety of nature continues to assert its importance: More than 90 percent of the Smithsonian's entire collection of artifacts, specimens, and works of art belongs to this museum alone. That's more than 126 million individual specimens and artifacts. Though most people won't see these specimens, researchers from around the world use the collection —much of it stored off-site—to carry out various systematic studies. Think of all the millions of beetles, butterflies, mosquitoes, sponges, mollusks, mineralogical samples, birds' eggs, microscopic organisms, and Native American baskets stored in drawers and on shelves.

VISITING

You can easily spend a day wandering through the museum, getting sidetracked from whatever it was you had set out to see. If you have only a few hours, pinpoint a couple exhibits and plot your route (maps available at information desks at

Crowds pass in and out of the Rotunda on their way to galleries, often pausing to view the mounted African elephant, on view since 1959.

both entrances). Entering from the Constitution Avenue side puts you on the **ground floor,** which has a **highlights** exhibit, a sampler of the treasures awaiting you within. Before you head up to the two exhibit floors, walk to the back of this floor, past the Atrium Café and Museum Shop, to the **Birds of D.C.** exhibit. Many people miss this compendium of taxidermed eastern birds, on display since the 1920s. Along with bald and golden eagles, swans, and warblers, the extinct Carolina parakeet and passenger pigeon are represented.

The museum features a number of special exhibitions. One new program, for example, examines the physical, biological, and cultural interactions that shape our world. Called **Forces of Change,** it shows connections between seemingly remote forces such as gas bubbles inside the Antarctic ice cap and famines in tropical Africa.

First floor

If you enter the museum from the Mall side, you'll step into the grand **Rotunda,** one of the city's great interior spaces. The eight-sided Rotunda rises to a dome 125 feet from the floor; columned galleries offer splendid views from above. But the sight in the middle of the Rotunda is what grabs most people's attention: Standing 13 feet 2 inches at the shoulder, the **African bush elephant** weighed 12 tons when it was killed in 1954. It is the largest mounted specimen of Earth's largest land animal, and its grassy savanna display has sound effects and other mounted animals.

You may want to begin your visit in the building's recently restored west wing, which features an exciting new attraction: the **Kenneth E. Behring Family Hall of Mammals.** The 25,000-square-foot permanent exhibition, which tells the story of mammal evolution through adaptation to

A model of a salt crystal, enlarged nearly 1.5 billion times, bedazzles visitors to the Hall of Geology, Gems, and Minerals.

changing habitats, features 274 taxidermied specimens artfully posed in a variety of environments—from polar to desert, dry to humid. Interactive features enhance the displays by explaining aspects of the incredible diversity of mammals, including humans, and the processes by which they arose and continue to adapt. A short film traces mammal evolution.

Just to the right of the Mall entrance, the **Early Life** exhibit contains one of the oldest known fossils—a mass of fossilized microbes 3.5 billion years old—and presents a short animated film that outlines the origins of life. The rare fossils of 530-million-year-old soft-bodied animals, among the museum's most important finds, were discovered in 1909 by geologist Charles Walcott, the Smithsonian's fourth secretary.

The adjacent **Dinosaur Hall** exhibit showcases the skeleton of an 80-foot-long *Diplodocus*, a family member of the largest land animals ever. **Life in the Ancient Seas** displays the curving, partially reconstructed skeleton of a 30-foot whale that swam the ocean about 39 million years ago. Before moving on to the next area, watch scientists and artists at work in the glassed-off **FossiLab.**

Just around the corner, the **Ice Age Hall** explores the beginnings of human influence on the world of animals and plants. Casts and composite skeletons of a woolly mammoth, mastodon, and giant ground sloth illustrate the large creatures that went extinct more than 10,000 years ago. Pleistocene survivors include a mounted wolverine, musk ox, and badger. You can't help pausing before the diorama of a Neanderthal burial, a re-creation of a ritual performed 70,000 years ago. In a compelling, intimate scene, the deceased lies bound in the fetal position while his family and a shaman look on.

The other exhibits on this floor explore various cultures. The **African Voices** exhibit sports a jazzy look with world-beat music and touch terminals.

In the far corner, the **Discovery Room** *(closed Mon.)* holds a number of animals, fossils, shells, and minerals that visitors can handle. Also in this part of the museum, a 400-seat **IMAX Theater** *(fee)* shows large-format 2-D and 3-D films on a screen six stories high.

Second floor

On the second floor, many people head directly for the **Janet Annenberg Hooker Hall of Geology, Gems, and Minerals.** Here you can learn how a meteorite impact may have wiped out the dinosaurs, build a virtual volcano, touch a piece of limestone scarred by Ice Age glaciers, see fluorescent minerals, view a mock-up vertical mine shaft, and watch a film on plate tectonics. You will definitely want to ogle the dazzling **National Gem Collection,** starring the 45.52-carat Hope Diamond, the largest blue diamond in the world. Other outstanding riches include a thousand-diamond diadem given by Napoleon I to his wife Empress Marie Louise; a pair of Marie Antoinette's earrings; and the world's largest perfect quartz sphere, a magically clear 107-pound globe from China. Just beyond lies a hall of sparkling crystals in a myriad of colors, shapes, and sizes, including such oddities as twinned and twisted crystal formations.

The next-door **Western Cultures** exhibit covers the rise of Western civilization from the end of the Ice Age to about A.D. 500. Helping to tell the story of the emergence and spread of Western culture are a reconstructed Ice Age cave with flint tools; early Egyptian pottery; reconstructed Bronze Age tombs from Jordan's Bab-edh-Dhra, the City of the Dead (3000 B.C.); an Egyptian coffin; and a mummified bull.

Walk on to the **Hall of Bones and Reptiles,** where you can see mammal skeletons varying in size from the pocket mouse to the huge, extinct Steller's sea cow. The adjoining **O. Orkin Insect Zoo** is a storehouse of delights for anyone who appreciates the most abundant animals on Earth. Live exhibits, animated by buzzing and chirping sounds, give this exhibit an edge. Watch live bees, water striders, darkling beetles, centipedes, tarantulas, and whip scorpions. Labels indicate which species, such as scorpions and tarantulas, are "insect relatives." Here, you can add a bit of excitement to your life by walking through a simulated rain forest with leaf-cutter ants and cave arthropods. ■

Perhaps the world's most famous precious stone, the dazzling 45.52-carat Hope Diamond is a highlight of the museum's National Gem Collection.

National Museum of American History

National Museum of American History
www.americanhistory.si.edu

Map p. 69
14th St. & Constitution Ave., N.W.
202-633-1000
Metro: Federal Triangle, Smithsonian; Bus: 13A-B & F-G, 52-3, 11Y

Closed for renovation until summer 2008

A museum visitor delivers an impromptu Inaugural presidential address.

THE SMITHSONIAN INSTITUTION, WITH 19 SEPARATE museums and galleries, has been called "the nation's attic," and the National Museum of American History is particularly rich in treasures that document American history and culture. At any one time, only about 3 to 5 percent of the 3 million artifacts in the museum's collections are on display.

When it opened in 1964, the building was called the National Museum of History and Technology. That name was changed in 1980 to reflect the museum's changing focus.

In recent years the museum has been redesigning its exhibits to present various artifacts in the context of broad themes relevant to U.S. life, from colonial to modern times. The museum closed down in late 2006 for the first phase of major renovations; once it reopens in the summer of 2008, additional changes to the building and displays will be ongoing. The recent improvements included adding a state-of-the-art gallery for safeguarding one of the country's most beloved artifacts: the original Star-Spangled Banner, which inspired the poem that became the national anthem.

During the temporary closure, more than 150 of the most popular artifacts from the museum's vast collection are on display at the nearby Air and Space Museum. Among them are Dorothy's ruby slippers and the Scarecrow costume from "The Wizard of Oz"; President Abraham Lincoln's top hat; a compass used by Lewis and Clark during their journey across the Louisiana Territory; the

Woolworth lunch counter from Greensboro, North Carolina, where four African-American students staged a six-month "sit-in" to protest segregation; Thomas Jefferson's Bible; and Kermit the Frog.

VISITING

Because the new floor layout wasn't complete at press time, visitors should check the museum's website for the latest information on the various displays and where they are located inside the building.

If you enter the museum from Constitution Avenue, you'll be on the first floor; the Mall entrance puts you on the second floor, where there's a new **Welcome Center.** Maps and information are available at both entrances. The museum has stores on both the first and second floors, and food services on the building's lower level. Described here (by floor location but not necessarily in the order of their layout) are some of the exhibits you can expect to see in the refurbished museum.

First floor

A large exhibition called **America on the Move** anchors the Hall of Transportation. More than 300 vehicles and other artifacts are showcased in period settings that offer a chronological look at how transportation has shaped American lives and landscapes. The journey takes you, for example, along 40 feet of Route 66's pavement in Oklahoma and aboard a commuter car of a Chicago "L" train in the 1950s.

Be sure also to check the impressive ***John Bull* Locomotive**. The oldest operable self-propelled locomotive and a striking symbol of the industrial revolution, it was built in England and brought to America in 1831 for use on one of the first public U.S. railroads, which carried passengers from Philadelphia and New York City.

Set to open in 2009 is **On the Water,** an exhibit on the country's maritime history and culture. Maritime trade and transportation fueled the establishment of major cities and was vital to America's development, connecting people and places across the continent.

For the highly popular exhibit **Bon Appétit! Julia Child's Kitchen,** museum staff catalogued and packed 1,200 items from the late chef's custom-designed home kitchen in Cambridge, Massachusetts, where many of her TV shows were taped. They then reassembled everything in the museum. Objects in the 14-by-20-foot kitchen include Child's personal cookbooks, utensils, kitchen sink, and six-burner commercial range.

Magazine photographs and campaign buttons in the museum's political history collection

Electricity & Lighting: A Revolution highlights the development of electrical inventions and shows how that process has changed from Thomas Edison's era to modern times. The major exhibit **Science in American Life** looks at scientific developments since 1876 that have had a profound impact on society, from the building of the atomic bomb to the increasing role of genetics in human health. More than a thousand pieces

A primer on the nation's leaders from an American Presidents exhibit.

of scientific equipment are featured, along with interactive video presentations. A related **Hands-on Science Center** enables children ages 5 and up (accompanied by parents) to experience the excitement of scientific practice and discovery. Participants can, for example, solve crimes using DNA fingerprinting methods and test for food additives and water purity.

Second floor

The exhibit **Explore American History,** which opens in 2010, gives museum-goers an overview of American history focusing on key events and people that have shaped the national experience and pursuit of the "American dream."

The new **Star-Spangled Banner Gallery** on this floor enhances the museum's important mission of preserving the Star-Spangled Banner. The exhibit was designed to evoke the conditions under which Francis Scott Key saw the flag flying during wartime, on the morning of September 14, 1814 (see sidebar p. 97).

Within These Walls conveys the history of a house at 16 Elm Street in Ipswich, Massachusetts, and looks at the everyday life of five of the many families who occupied it from the mid-1760s through 1945. Historically important activities the house "witnessed" include American colonists working to spark a revolution, African Americans struggling for freedom, community activists organizing an end to slavery, immigrants striving to build new lives for themselves, and a grandmother and her grandson serving on the home front during World War II.

Similarly, in **Communities in a Changing Nation: The Promise of 19th-Century America,** you can experience the rapidly changing nature of U.S. life in the 1880s through the lens of the industrial era in Bridgeport, Connecticut; Jewish immigration in Cincinnati, Ohio; and the transition from slavery to freedom among African Americans in Charleston, South Carolina.

Among the special artifacts on display on this floor is a famous

marble **statue of George Washington,** which was commissioned by the U.S. government in 1932 and sculpted by Horatio Greenough. He had in mind as a model for his design Phidias' "Olympian Zeus." The very popular display of **First Ladies' Ball Gowns,** splendid garments worn to presidential Inaugurations, also can be found on this level.

Third floor

A major new multimedia exhibition, **The Price of Freedom: Americans at War,** looks at how the United States has shaped its destiny, protected its values, and maintained its leadership in world affairs through engagement in wars, from the colonial era to the present.

The featured objects include a rare Revolutionary War uniform, furniture used during the surrender ceremony that ended the Civil War, a restored Huey helicopter that was used in the Vietnam War, and the uniform worn by Gen. Colin Powell during Operation Desert Storm.

A separate exhibit, **Gunboat Philadelphia,** illustrates events in October 1776 when American troops with only a ragtag collection of boats faced an advancing line of British ships on Lake Champlain in New York. The Americans, under the command of Benedict Arnold, were forced to retreat, but not before they fought the British to a standstill. The American vessel *Philadelphia* sank during the battle, but was retrieved from the lake in 1935 and has been part of the museum's holdings since 1964.

The American Presidency: A Glorious Burden highlights aspects of presidential leadership and life in the White House. ■

"What So Proudly We Hail'd"

The 30-by-34-foot flag known as the Star-Spangled Banner is fragile despite its size. Woven loosely to fly on a 90-foot flagpole, its expected life span was only two years. Flying over Fort McHenry, it incurred much damage. When the British attacked Baltimore in 1814, amateur poet Francis Scott Key was on a ship in the Chesapeake. Moved by the sight of the enormous flag still flying in "the dawn's early light" after a 25-hour bombardment, he scribbled the words that became the lyrics for a popular patriotic song; Congress made it the national anthem in 1931.

As part of conservation efforts, specialists at the Smithsonian recently removed a cloth backing (and 1.7 million stitches) added decades ago for support. Photo images documented the original flag's condition close-up, guiding work to ensure the flag's survival for future generations. ■

A wreath adorns the black-granite wall of names at the Vietnam Veterans Memorial.

A walk around the monuments

The western end of the Mall, where you'll find the city's most significant monuments and memorials, is a delightful place for walking. A 3-mile loop taking you past a half dozen major memorials makes for a wonderful morning or afternoon; benches along the way offer rest stops. About two blocks from the start is the Smithsonian Metro stop. Parking during cherry blossom season *(late March–early April)* is nearly impossible.

Begin at the **Washington Monument ❶,** off 15th Street between Constitution and Independence Avenues. Set on a slight rise, this 555-foot marble obelisk is surrounded by flags from every state in the nation.

Begun in 1848, the monument rose slowly but steadily for five years to 152 feet; at that point funding ran out and building ceased for almost 25 years. Look about a third of the way up to see where the work stopped. Though taken from a nearby Maryland quarry, the more recent marble is of a darker color. The monument recently underwent a comprehensive restoration. You can ride the elevator to the 500-foot level for one of the best views of the city. You can descend the 897 steps only on group tours led by rangers. Visit the ticket kiosk near the monument for free same-day tickets, but go early—the kiosk opens at 8:30 a.m.—because tickets usually go quickly. Or visit the National Park Service website for information on reserving in advance *(www.nps.gov/wamo)*.

From the grounds of the Washington Monument, you can see the Lincoln Memorial directly to the west and the Jefferson Memorial across the Tidal Basin, but your next destination is hidden among the trees of **Constitution Gardens,** a memorial to the founders of this nation. Walk down the hill, cross 17th Street, and take the sinuous trail through lovely landscaping just north of the **Reflecting Pool.** On small **Signers Island,** a memorial honors the 56 signers of the Declaration of Independence.

On the pool's east end is the newest attraction, the **National World War II Memorial ❷.** Thousands of veterans were on hand for the Memorial Day 2004 dedication of the $174 million, privately funded memorial, which has drawn much criticism for its massive design and overwhelming presence amid the Mall's more graceful monuments. Around a fountain-spouting pool are two facing arcs of granite columns, each bearing two bronze wreaths; the 56 pillars represent U.S. states and territories during the war and the District of Columbia. The columns are anchored by a pair of 43-foot-

The FDR Memorial also remembers the Depression-era President's lovable dog, Fala.

high arches—one for the war's Atlantic theater and one for the Pacific. Two dozen bronze panels depict scenes from the war, and a Freedom Wall with 4,000 gold stars honors the 400,000 Americans who were killed during World War II.

See area map pp. 68–69
➤ Washington Monument
3 miles
2 hours
➤ Jefferson Memorial

NOT TO BE MISSED

- Vietnam Veterans Memorial
- Lincoln Memorial
- Jefferson Memorial
- World War II Memorial

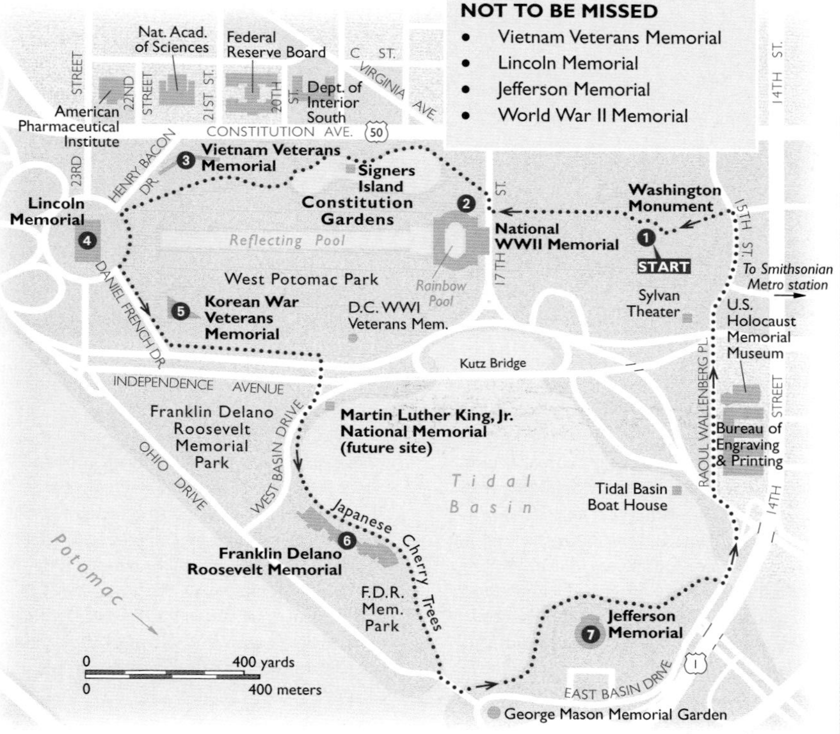

The World War II Memorial honors the 16 million who served in the U.S. armed forces during World War II and the more than 400,000 who died.

Just west, architect Maya Lin's stunning **Vietnam Veterans Memorial** ❸ presents a moving contrast to the classical-style monuments all about. A tremendous black-granite wedge, bermed into the earth instead of standing above it, is inscribed with the names of all the 58,209 Americans who died or were missing in action in the Vietnam War. Polished to a reflective sheen, the walls of the wedge seem to project life as much as honor death. As you walk the path beside the memorial, the names of the dead increase dramatically as the walls reach their high point at 10.1 feet. The nearby bronze group of three soldiers, by Washington sculptor Frederick Hart, adds a dose of gritty realism. Dedicated in 1982, the memorial was supplemented in 1993 by another bronze group, the **Vietnam Women's**

Memorial, in tribute to the women who took part in the war.

Continue on to the magnificent **Lincoln Memorial** ❹ built from 1914 to 1922 to honor Abraham Lincoln, President during the Civil War. The 36 Doric columns represent the number of states at the time of Lincoln's death. Inside, facing the Mall, the 19-foot-tall statue of a seated Lincoln was carved from 28 blocks of white Georgia marble. The walls of the memorial are inscribed with words from the Gettysburg Address and Lincoln's second inaugural speech.

Just to the southeast is the **Korean War Veterans Memorial** ❺. Dedicated in 1995, it features 19 gray soldiers warily crossing a field of scrubby junipers. Next to this riveting stainless-steel group, a black-granite wall is etched with a mural of those who served, while another wall bears the simple message: "Freedom Is Not Free." Beside a "pool of remembrance" stands a stone carved with the war's toll—the numbers of killed, wounded, missing, and captured.

Walk east toward the **Tidal Basin** and cross West Basin Drive at the second traffic light, in front of the nearly hidden **D.C. WWI Veterans Memorial,** honoring the District's veterans.

Amid the trees of West Potomac Park on the Tidal Basin's west side is the **Franklin Delano Roosevelt Memorial** ❻, honoring the 32nd President. Four unroofed, granite-walled alcoves—one for each of his four terms—spread along the water's edge, surrounded by landscaped plazas, statuary, and waterfalls. After the memorial was dedicated in 1997, disability advocacy groups criticized the design for failing to publicly recognize FDR's regular use of a wheelchair, which he was confined to from age 39 when paralyzed by polio. Finally, in 2001, a statue of Roosevelt in a wheelchair was added.

On the south side of the Tidal Basin stands the impressive **Jefferson Memorial** ❼. The view from here, across the Tidal Basin with its gulls and paddleboats and springtime cherry blossoms, is not to be missed. Dedicated to the author of the Declaration of Independence and third U.S. President, the structure was designed by John Russell Pope in the style of the ancient Roman Pantheon and completed in 1943. Inside the colonnaded building a 19-foot bronze of Jefferson stands beneath a towering dome. Among the quotes on the wall is one from a letter written in 1800: "I have sworn upon the altar of God eternal hostility against every form of tyranny over the mind of man." A lower lobby has exhibits, a gift shop, and a bookstore.

Behind the monument on Ohio Drive is the **George Mason Memorial Garden,** which opened in spring 2002. In keeping with the quiet patriot's love of his garden at Gunston Hall (see p. 222), the setting is a classical landscape designed as a peaceful, contemplative place. ■

More to see

As the Mall continues to fill up with monuments and museums, there is growing concern about overbuilding on the grounds. Yet plans for more projects are in the works, including a memorial to Martin Luther King, Jr.

While the National Mall is the most obvious place to find memorials, it isn't the only one. Across the river in Arlington, Virginia, there are two new landmarks worth visiting. One is the soaring U.S. Air Force Memorial, consisting of three elegant stainless steel spires that are visible from downtown Washington (see p. 208) The second is the Pentagon Memorial (see p. 207), which honors the 184 people who died when American Airlines Flight 77 was hijacked and flown into the Pentagon on September 11, 2001.

D.C. itself has many memorials celebrating U.S. armed forces, but if you're interested in a museum that provides an in-depth look at a branch of the military, visit the National Museum of the Marine Corps, in Triangle, Virginia, which opened to the public in November 2006. Situated on a 135-acre site near the Quantico Marine Corps base (36 miles south of Washington on Interstate 95), it has galleries and interactive exhibits that tell the 230-year-old Marine story and feature artifacts from Marine missions. The museum is open daily, with tours available and free admission and parking (www.usmcmuseum.org). ■

U.S. Holocaust Memorial Museum

U.S. Holocaust Memorial Museum
www.ushmm.org
Map p. 69
100 Raoul Wallenberg Pl. (15th St.), S.W., just S of Independence Ave.
202-488-0400
Metro: Smithsonian; Bus: 52-3, 11Y, 13A-B & F-G, V7-9

The Holocaust Museum's first floor sets a somber tone for a visit to the galleries above.

OPENED IN 1993, THIS MUSEUM SERVES AS A MEMORIAL TO the millions of people murdered during Nazi rule in Germany from 1933 to 1945. The architecture—windowless recesses, brickwork guard towers, and obscured windows—suggests some of the themes and images documented within. Inside, the skylit first-floor atrium is overshadowed by heavy steel trusses. A factory-like brick wall on one side is where visitors enter and ascend, via a cargo-style elevator, to see the permanent exhibition, starting on the fourth floor.

VISITING

Pick up timed passes at the museum on the day of your visit, or call 800-400-9373 for advance passes (*service fee*). The exhibition is self-guided and takes two to three hours. Because there are several films, audio programs, and a lot of text on the three-floor exhibit, you may want to make a selective tour. Most of the exhibits are not recommended for children under 11; it's also a good idea to prepare older children for what they are about to see.

On the **fourth floor,** which covers the spread of Nazism from 1933 to 1939, visitors are funneled through hallways from one exhibit area to the next. The dim, quiet halls reflect the museum's somber content. A theater, grim photographs, and monitors displaying silent footage bespeak the early years of the Third Reich and the start of its sanctioned violence toward Jews, Poles, Gypsies, homosexuals, political dissidents, the handicapped, and others.

Also on the fourth floor, walk-through tower is lined with family photos from a shtetl, a Jewish village; you later learn that this entire village of 4,000 was destroyed in 1941, bringing 900 years of continuous history to an abrupt and complete end. Perhaps most telling are the shelfloads of victims' belongings—rusty scissors, can openers, graters, razors, toothbrushes—and the huge piles of old shoes. There are bunks from Auschwitz and a scale model that shows how the gas chambers and crematoria worked. Video monitors show unsettling images such as medical experiments, executions, and malnourished children. The monitors are shielded by walls so young children cannot see them; adults can elect not to watch.

On the **third floor,** the years 1940–45 are examined in detail through displays on ghettos, deportations, slave labor, and extermination camps. Among the powerful artifacts are cobblestones from a street in a Warsaw ghetto, clothing, and a cemetery gate from Karnow where Jews were routinely shot.

Efforts at resistance and the ultimate liberation of survivors are documented on the **second floor.** In the **Hall of Remembrance,** an eternal flame honors victims of the Holocaust; visitors may light candles in their memory.

On the **ground floor,** an exhibit called **Remember the Children, Daniel's Story** is targeted to families, including children eight years and older. It recounts the Holocaust from a child's perspective. The **concourse level** has changing exhibits and a **Wall of Remembrance** honoring the estimated 1.5 million children who died. Outside the museum, it's a relief to look across the Tidal Basin to the Jefferson and FDR Memorials and remember those who stood against tyranny and won. As one FDR Memorial donor put it, a man in a wheelchair beat Hitler. ■

More places to visit around the National Mall

DISCOVERY THEATER IN SMITHSONIAN'S RIPLEY CENTER

The Smithsonian's Discovery Theater recently relocated to this building after its former home, the nearby Arts and Industries Building, closed down for renovations. The theater presents a wide range of performances for children on a specially built stage. Visit the website for ticket and program information.
www.discoverytheater.org Map p. 69
1100 Jefferson Dr., S.W. 202-633-1000
Metro: Smithsonian, L'Enfant Plaza

BUREAU OF ENGRAVING & PRINTING

One of the popular standards of Washington tourism, the bureau is the place to see a lot of money—up to 38 million dollars—being printed daily. To replace worn-out bills and keep up with economic growth, this facility and a similar one in Fort Worth, Texas, churn out about 7 billion notes a year in denominations from $1 to $100. The 24 high-speed presses run 24 hours a day, 5 days a week, turning out mainly $1 bills, which have a shelf life of only 18 months. You can see 32-note currency sheets rolling through production and 4,000-note "bricks" being prepared for distribution to the 12 Federal Reserve Banks around the country. You'll also learn about the latest techniques to prevent counterfeiting.
www.moneyfactory.gov Map p. 69
14th & C Sts., S.W. 866-875-2330
Call for summer and winter tour hours; obtain free tickets from booth on west side of the building Metro: Smithsonian, L'Enfant Plaza

VOICE OF AMERICA

This government-run news service has operated continuously since it went on the air in February 1942, soon after America entered World War II. Today, the service broadcasts news and educational and cultural programs in nearly four dozen languages to millions of people in other countries. It's transmitted by radio, satellite television, and the Internet. On 45-minute tours you can see 1940s murals by Ben Shahn and observe production.
www.voa.gov Map p. 69
330 Independence Ave., S.W. 202-203-4990 Tours Mon.–Fri. noon and 3 p.m., except for federal holidays Metro: Federal Center, S.W. ■

Visitors can tour streets near the National Mall in old-fashioned style.

Although a certain famous residence at 1600 Pennsylvania Avenue gets most of the attention, the neighborhood around the White House overflows with art galleries, historic houses and hotels, churches, museums, and other stops of note.

White House & around

The south portico of the White House

White House & around

A LOCUS OF POLITICAL POWER THAT IS ALSO A MAJOR TOURIST ATTRACTION, the home of the Chief Executive is a living museum of the Presidency in downtown Washington. The immediate environs are rich in history, culture, and political excitement.

In 1791 a surveyor and an engineer picked the site for a presidential "palace," as the latter called it. The surveyor was George Washington, the engineer was Pierre Charles L'Enfant, and the site was a cornfield above a tidal marsh where hunters shot ducks and geese. Just a mile from the site of the future Capitol, the manse they envisioned would be about four times the size of the current White House.

Thomas Jefferson, Secretary of State at the time, persuaded Washington to hold a competition for the design. Unimpressed by the

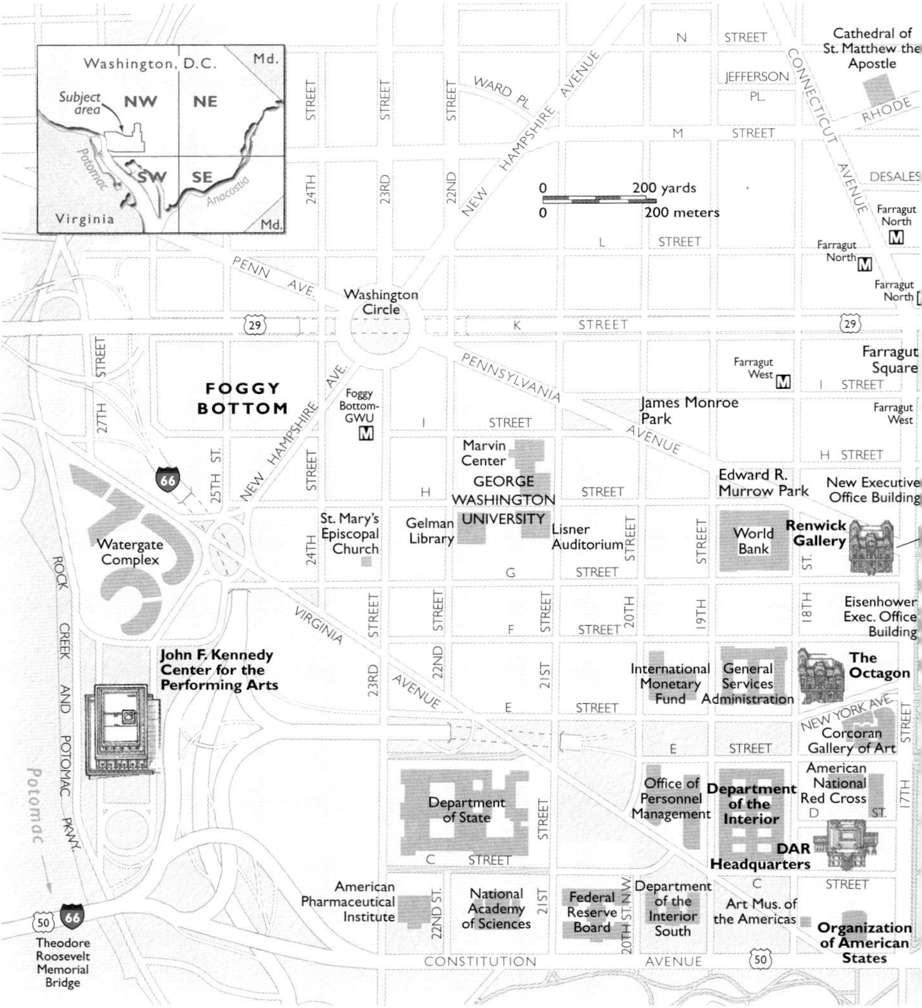

mundane entries that resulted, Washington urged Irish-born architect James Hoban to have a go. Hoban's entry, selected in 1792, was an adaptation of the Duke of Leinster's palace near Dublin. Regrettably, Washington—then on the verge of his second term as President—would not live to see the structure completed.

The next President, John Adams, moved into the partially completed mansion on November 1, 1800, only to lose his reelection bid less than a month later. Jefferson, his successor, spent the next eight years in the

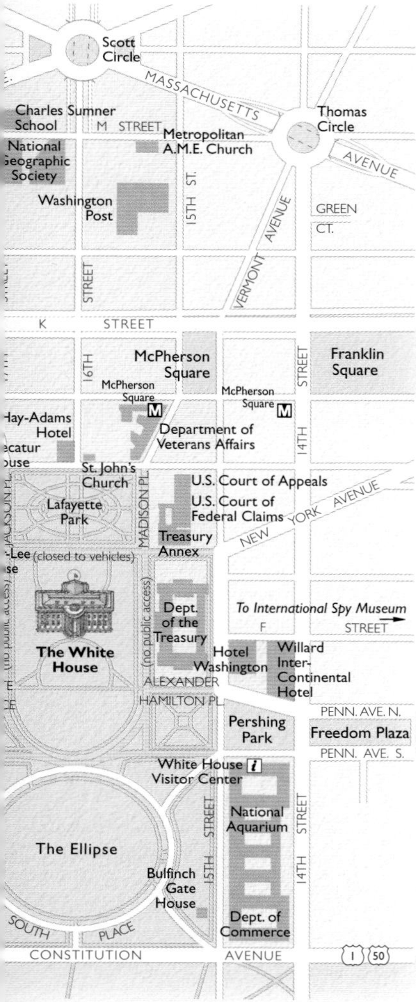

President's House (it was not called the White House until 1901), opening it to the public and establishing it as a national symbol. President James Madison enjoyed no such stability: The British burned the building to the ground in 1814, forcing Madison to abandon the President's House for temporary quarters nearby.

After Abraham Lincoln's assassination in 1865, some lobbied to move the President to a more secluded location, in Rock Creek Park. President Ulysses S. Grant, who had served as Lincoln's commanding officer, nixed that idea.

By the turn of the 20th century, it was clear that the White House—Theodore Roosevelt's designation for it—enshrined the American presidential legacy. Indeed, each President has left his stamp on the place: Rutherford B. Hayes put in the first telephone, Benjamin Harrison installed electric lights, and Theodore Roosevelt hung a moose head above the fireplace in the State Dining Room.

The presidential neighborhood grew in tandem with the White House. In the 1810s, St. John's Church, Decatur House, and a number of posh, federal-style residences were built around President's Park (renamed Lafayette Square in 1824). By 1900—when the Treasury Building, Old Executive Office Building (now officially the Eisenhower Executive Office Building), Corcoran Gallery, Renwick building, Blair House, the Octagon, and Willard Hotel had all gone up around 1600 Pennsylvania Avenue—the area was a thriving mix of government buildings, art galleries, hotels, and residences.

From west of 20th Street to the Potomac River, the Foggy Bottom neighborhood is a busy mix of 19th-century row houses, apartment buildings, and major institutions: the State Department, World Bank, Kennedy Center, and George Washington University. The breweries and gasworks that once filled this bottomland with foggy vapors were gone by the mid-20th century, when the area began to morph into a middle-class neighborhood.

The White House area maintains and inspires a polished decorum. Until World War II, you could walk to the front door of the White House and leave your calling card. Security then moved outward to the fence line, and in 1995 Pennsylvania Avenue in front of the building was closed to traffic. ■

White House

White House
www.whitehouse.gov
- Map p. 107
- 1600 Pennsylvania Ave., N.W.
- 202-456-1414
- Closed Sun.–Mon.
- Metro: Federal Triangle, McPherson Square or Metro Center; Bus: 30-36, S2-4, 11Y, X2, 42, 68

The dignified north portico basks in the glow of early evening.

THE OLDEST PUBLIC BUILDING IN THE DISTRICT OF Columbia, the White House has been the home of every U.S. President except George Washington. In this most famous of residences, the President signs bills into law, meets with national and international leaders, entertains guests, and does his best to lead a private family life. Despite more than 200 years of expansions and renovations, the White House has kept its essential appearance and design.

Washington's designers intended the executive mansion to be one of two focal points of the new Federal City (the Capitol would be the other). Nine blueprints were submitted to a competitive design panel; among those rejected was a plan put forward anonymously by Thomas Jefferson.

The winning design—the work of Irish-born architect James Hoban—honored the stately symmetries of Georgian manor houses in the British Isles. Not that it lacked detractors: Benjamin Henry Latrobe, who worked on the White House in the early 1800s and is considered the country's first professional architect, assailed Hoban's concept as "a mutilated copy of a badly designed original near Dublin."

Nonetheless, the cornerstone of the President's House (George Washington's preferred term for it) was laid in October 1792, a year before work began on the Capitol. The pale sandstone for the white-painted walls came from Aquia Creek, on the Virginia side of the Potomac. Eight years later, with President John Adams nearing the end of his term, the house was finally ready for occupation.

Jefferson, the third President, held the first Inaugural open house in 1805 and forged the tradition of throwing the house open to public tours. The custom got out of hand in 1829, when some 20,000 well-wishers tromped through the White House, muddy boots and all; while President Jackson slipped away to a nearby hotel, his aides filled tubs with juice and whiskey and set them on the lawn to coax the crowds outside. The Inaugural open houses continued until 1869, when Ulysses Grant replaced them with a parade, which he watched from the relative safety of a grandstand in front of the White House.

During the War of 1812, the British retaliated for the American burning of public buildings in Canada by burning down the President's House and other city landmarks in 1814. When British soldiers arrived at the hastily vacated executive mansion on the night of August 24, 1814, they found Dolley Madison's dinner still on the table (a few of them sat down and polished it off). Shortly after midnight, the soldiers threw flaming javelins into the mansion. By morning it was a smoldering shell. The house was rebuilt within its original walls over the next few years.

By the mid-20th century, the White House had reached a truly concerning state of structural decline: The walls and floors could no longer support the alterations and additions of previous decades. From 1948 to 1952, Harry and Bess Truman lived in Blair House, across Pennsylvania Avenue, while the White House was gutted. Everything from furniture to paneling was taken out; a new basement was dug, new foundations were laid, and a steel framework was installed. The basic house was still there, but it was now much safer. Since then, each First Family has added its own decorative touch: The Kennedys redesigned the Rose Garden, while the Reagans contributed a new set of Lenox china.

VISITING

Free public tours of the White House are available for groups of 10 or more people. Requests must

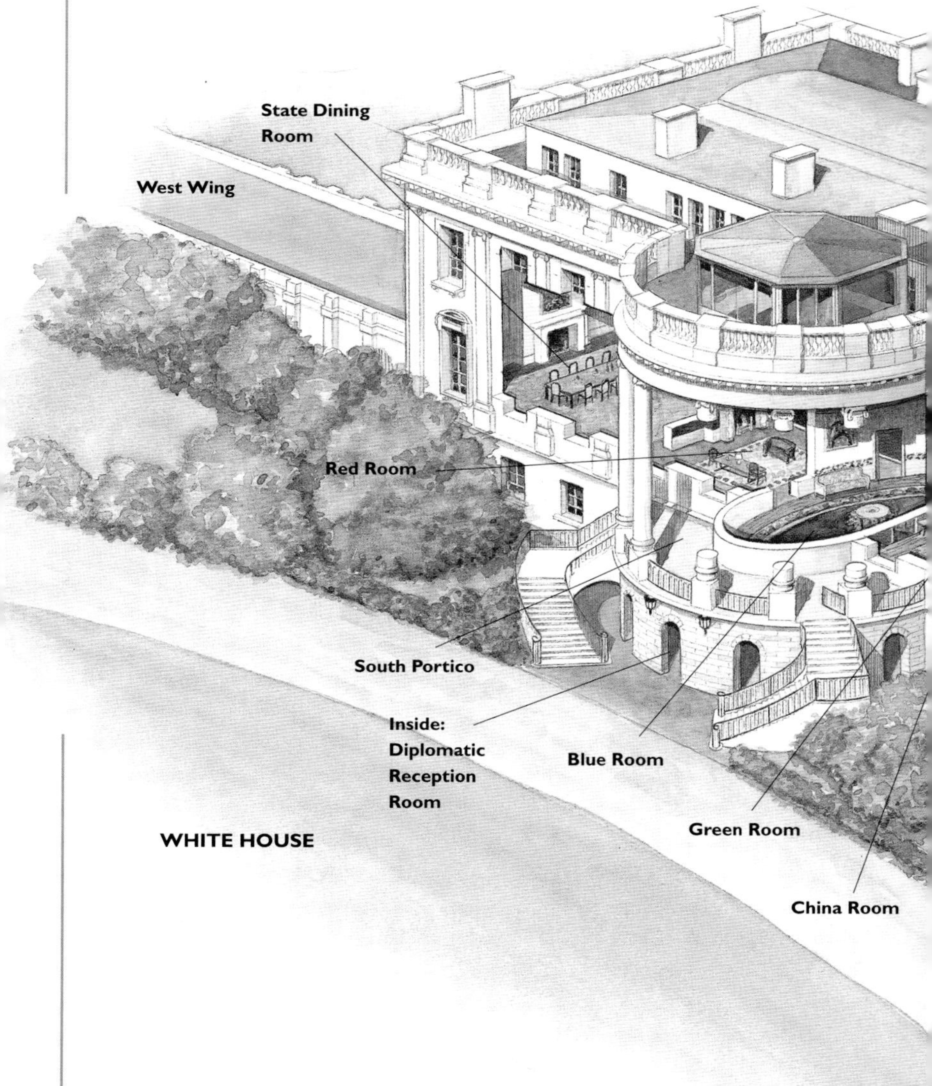

be submitted through your member of Congress and are accepted up to six months in advance. The self-guided group tours are scheduled from 7:30 a.m. to 12:30 p.m. Tuesday through Saturday, excluding federal holidays; they're scheduled on a first-come, first-served basis about one month in advance of the requested date. The number of tours is limited so submit your request early. Call the 24-hour line *(202-456-7041)* for current tour information. (All tours are subject to last-minute cancellation.)

Another option is to forgo a tour of the interior altogether and, instead stop by the White House

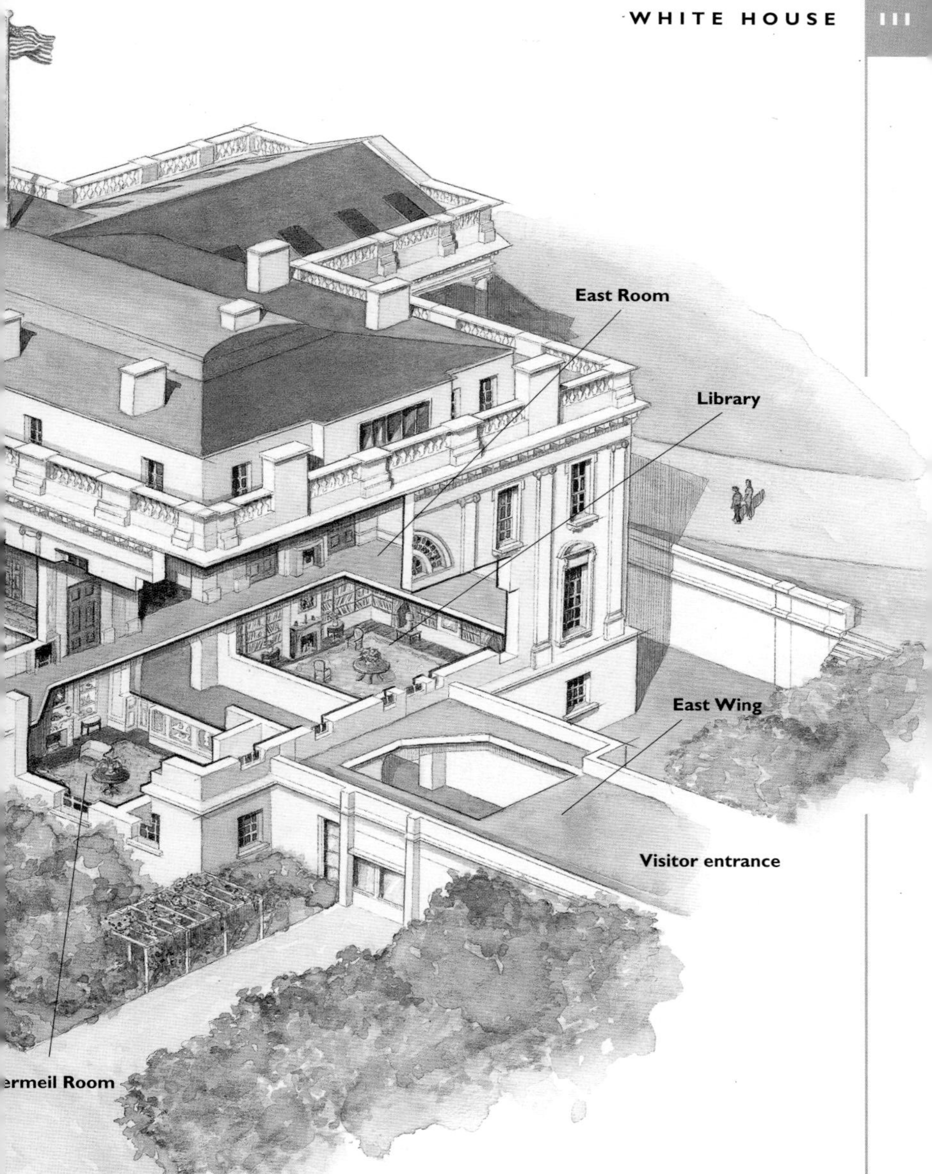

Visitor Center in the lobby of the Commerce Department building (*SE corner of 15th & E Sts., 202-456-7041*). Open every day from 7:30 a.m. until 4:00 p.m., it features displays on many aspects of the White House, including its architecture, furnishings, First Families, and social events, as well as a 30-minute video. Allow yourself up to an hour to view the exhibits. The White House Historical Association sponsors a gift and souvenir area in the center, but no restrooms or food services are available.

If you do plan your visit to Washington well in advance and

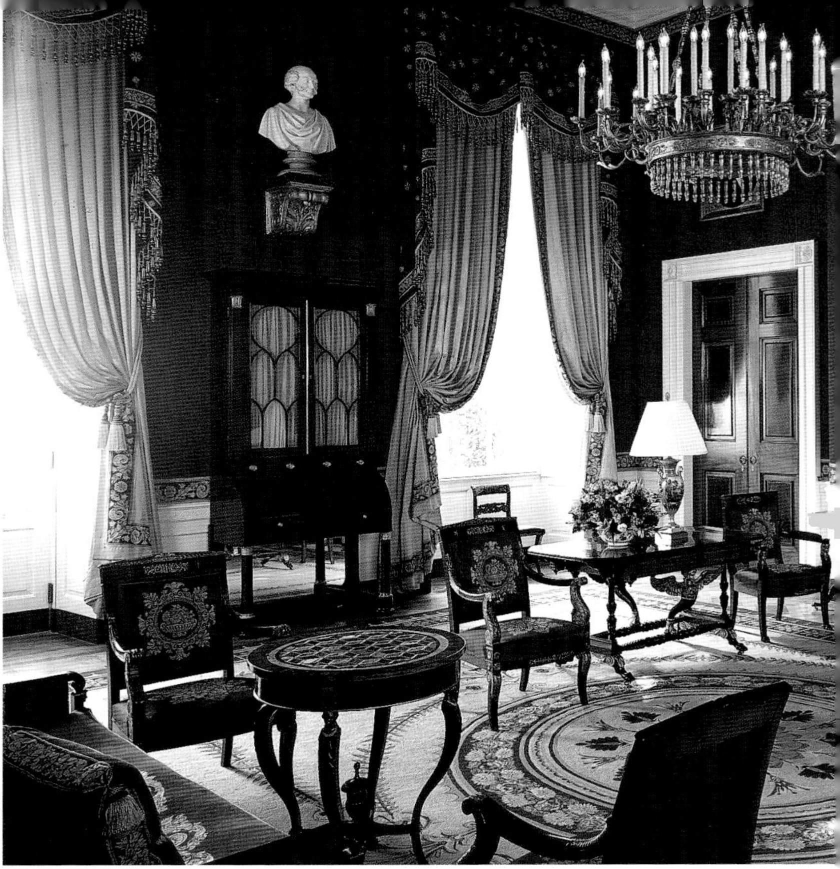

The Red Room's French Empire-style furniture dates back to the early 1800s.

succeed in arranging to join a scheduled group tour, you will enter the grounds from a visitors entrance around the corner from Pennsylvania Avenue on 15th Street, next to the Treasury building and across the street from the Hotel Washington. When you arrive for your visit, look through the gate to see part of the mansion's lovely 18-acre grounds. Once you get inside, expect to spend 20 minutes to half an hour viewing the rooms.

After being cleared by security, you enter a corridor on the ground floor that has photo displays on White House life and glass-walled views of the carefully manicured **Jacqueline Kennedy Garden.** Next, peer into the roped-off **Library,** filled with federal-style furniture. Across the hall, the **Vermeil Room** has portraits of recent First Ladies and a collection of gilded silver known as vermeil.

The rooms you can actually walk through are up on the State Floor. The first one you enter—the expansive **East Room—**is also the largest in the house: It hosts press conferences, award ceremonies, and concerts. Among the weddings held here were those of Nellie Grant, Alice Roosevelt, and Lynda Bird Johnson. Imagine skid marks on this floor; the energetic children of Theodore Roosevelt are said to have roller-skated across it.

Continue around to the **Green Room,** used by Jefferson as a dining room but now functioning as a

President and Mrs. Bush hosted Queen Elizabeth II and her husband, Prince Philip, at a white-tie State Dinner on May 7, 2007.

reception parlor. The window affords a great view beyond the Ellipse (an open greensward just north of Constitution Avenue) to the Jefferson Memorial. Much of the Green Room's furniture came from the workshop of Duncan Phyfe in the early 1800s. The green watered-silk wall coverings were chosen by Mrs. Kennedy.

The elegant and oval **Blue Room** contains several pieces of furniture bought by James Monroe, who refurbished the room after the 1814 fire. Presidents still receive guests here. First Ladies frequently entertain in the adjacent **Red Room,** furnished as an American Empire parlor of 1810 to 1830.

Some 130 guests can be seated in the gracious **State Dining Room,** which boasts painted oak paneling from a 1902 renovation. In the **Cross Hall** and **Entrance Hall** the floors are made out of Tennessee marble. The furnishings include a decorated concert grand piano, a 1938 gift from the Steinway company.

A carpeted marble staircase leads to the second and third floors, open only to the First Family and their guests. Famous rooms there include the Lincoln Bedroom and the Queen's Bedroom. The West Wing *(not open to public)* holds the Cabinet Room, numerous staff and reception rooms, and the President's Oval Office (built in 1909) and its adjoining Rose Garden. The White House also contains a jogging track, swimming pool, movie theater, bowling lane, and billiard room. The total number of rooms in the house: 132.

Your tour will exit the front door beneath a columned portico, then follow the walkway to the front gate. As photos are forbidden inside, many people pause here before leaving to get a shot. Through the viewfinder you may discover that the White House looks not at all palatial—a mansion, yes, but at heart just a home. ■

A stroll around the White House

Walking in the area around the White House will give you a concentrated taste of Washington's core. Yet the knots of tourists, security officers, and limousines that buzz around the executive mansion like drones around a queen bee are only part of the picture. Because local laws bar skyscrapers, you can enjoy long, green views across the Ellipse and the Mall. The area is also dotted with house museums, art galleries, benches for idling, and restaurants for both tourists and power brokers.

Once you've viewed or visited the White House, you tend to forget it's there, as do the locals who go about their business in the area, regarding the structure mainly as an attractive backdrop. Since virtually no one sees the First Family come and go, it's easy to forget that the President of the United States is living in splendid isolation in that beautiful historic house. The isolation is heightened by the restricted areas and physical barriers added in recent years for greater security. The occasional presence of TV crews and reporters is a reminder that "presidential privacy" is something of an oxymoron.

The Eisenhower Executive Office Building's ornate style shocked the public at its 1888 unveiling.

The section of Pennsylvania Avenue in front of the **White House** ❶ (see pp. 108–113) is closed to traffic, so it offers good photo opportunities if you aren't hampered at the time of your visit by security constraints and construction fences. The park just north of the White House, **Lafayette Square** ❷**,** is a perfect place to sit with a sandwich and people-watch. As a public park in full view of the White House, the square has been strategically ideal for demonstrating for or against something. Activists for nuclear disarmament and other causes have mounted peaceful vigils here. In the middle of the square is Clark Mills's statue of Andrew Jackson on a rearing horse. Statues of foreign-born Revolutionary War heroes occupy the four corners: Marquis de Lafayette, Baron

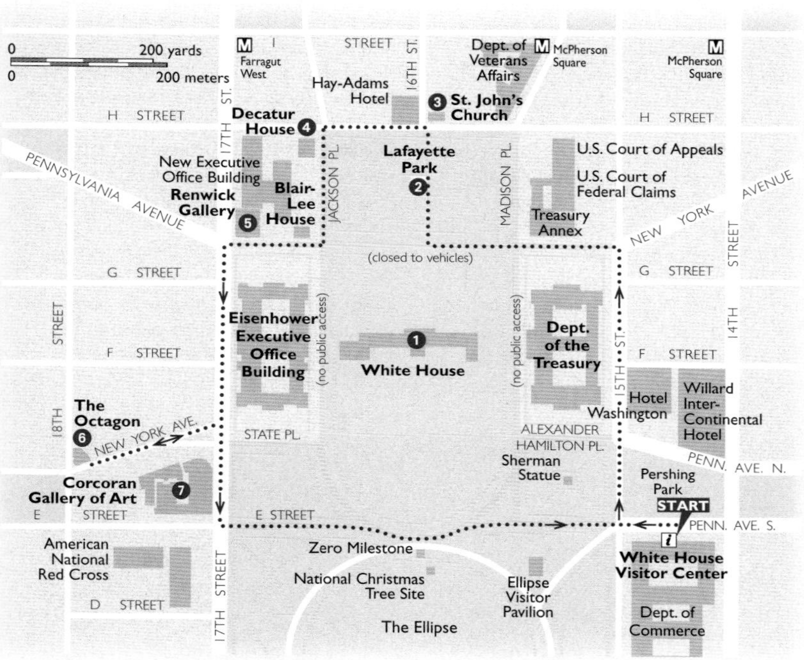

Friedrich von Steuben, Thaddeus Kosciusko, and Comte de Rochambeau. Many of the federal-style row houses along the square are White House offices, saved from the wrecking ball by Jackie Kennedy's determination to preserve the historical character of the square.

Across H Street from the square stands the gold-domed **St. John's Church** ❸ (see p. 128), known as the "church of the Presidents." Diagonally across the corner from here, at Jackson Place and H Street, is **Decatur House** ❹ (see p. 127), which was built in 1818 for naval hero Stephen Decatur.

Next, head south and turn right on Pennsylvania Avenue to see the 1810 white brick **Blair House,** where foreign dignitaries often stay; Robert E. Lee was offered command of the Federal Army here in 1861. On November 1, 1950—about midway through the Trumans' four-year stay at Blair House while the White House was being renovated—a policeman was killed on the street defending the President from an assassination attempt.

In that block, the **Renwick Gallery** ❺ (see p. 117), a Smithsonian museum, shows off its mansard roof and redbrick-and-sandstone exterior opposite the even more flamboyant **Eisenhower Executive Office Building.** A massive piece of architecture originally named the Old Executive Office Building, the EEOB is one of the country's finest Second Empire-style structures. Built from 1871 to 1888 (just after the Renwick), the granite pile shocked locals who had expected a neoclassic temple to house the State, War, and Navy departments. It now holds

- See area map pp. 106–107
- White House Visitor Center
- 1.5 miles
- 3 hours
- Corcoran Gallery of Art

NOT TO BE MISSED

- White House
- Lafayette Square
- Corcoran Gallery of Art
- Renwick Gallery

offices of White House staff members, the Office of Management and Budget, and the Office of the Vice President.

Head south on 17th Street and turn right on New York Avenue. The historic **Octagon** ❻ (see p. 122) stands on the corner of 18th Street. Go back to 17th and turn right; on your right is the **Corcoran Gallery of Art** ❼ (see pp. 118–19), housed in an attractive beaux arts building. From here, walk east on E Street, between the South Lawn of the White House and the Ellipse. *Marine One,* the President's helicopter, lands on the South Lawn, site of the annual Easter Egg Roll. The National Christmas Tree, planted during the Carter Administration, stands on the Ellipse near the Zero Milestone, whence city distances are measured. On the corner of E and 15th Streets, a bronze William Tecumseh Sherman sits astride a horse, its tail raised toward the South, on the spot where he reviewed victorious Union troops. He faces the Greek Revival **Department of the Treasury** and its statue of Alexander Hamilton; sadly, the building blocks the view from the White House to the Capitol.

Cap the day with a drink in the rooftop Sky Terrace Restaurant of the 1918 Hotel Washington *(15th & F, May–Oct.).* On clear days, it offers a great panoramic view of the White House, Mall, and abundant treetops in parts of the city and neighboring Virginia. ■

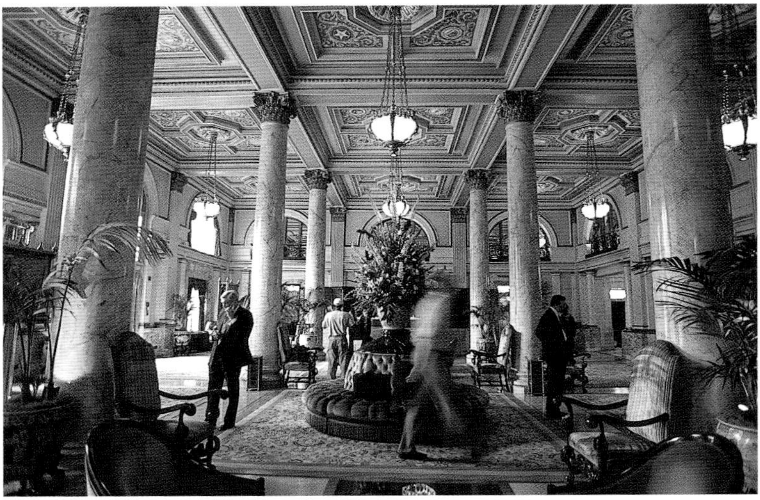

The Willard

While you're in the vicinity of the White House, peek inside the Willard Hotel *(202-628-9100),* a Washington landmark since the 1850s at 1401 Pennsylvania Avenue. Nathaniel Hawthorne called the Willard the "center of Washington" for its role as the heart of political lobbying in the 19th century. The hotel has hosted Presidents, foreign heads of state, and a gaggle of celebrities from Mark Twain to Harry Houdini to Mae West.

In 1901 the venerable hostelry was rebuilt as a 12-story beaux arts hotel under the guidance of Henry Hardenbergh, architect of New York's famous Plaza Hotel. Closed in 1968 when much of Pennsylvania Avenue hit the skids, the Willard reopened in grand style in 1986, a crowning achievement of the Congressionally created Pennsylvania Avenue Development Corporation.

The restored Willard boasts scagliola marble columns, polished wood paneling, glittering chandeliers, and other trappings of opulence. Shops, a bar, a café, and an elegant restaurant provide multiple opportunities to splurge. ■

Renwick Gallery

THE ARCHITECTURALLY DISTINCTIVE RENWICK GALLERY has housed the Smithsonian American Art Museum's contemporary craft program since 1972. Designed in 1858 by James Renwick, Jr., architect of the Smithsonian's Castle, the Second Empire-style building features sandstone pilasters and garlands gracing the redbrick and decorative ironwork crowning the tripartite mansard roof.

During the Civil War, the building functioned as a military warehouse. Beginning in 1874, the Renwick served as the original Corcoran Gallery. After that collection moved to a new building nearby, the U.S. Court of Claims was located here, from 1899 until 1964.

Slated for demolition, the building instead came under the aegis of the Smithsonian Institution in 1965, and now features 20th- and 21st-century American crafts and decorative arts. Objects from the museum's permanent collection are on display, along with objects from changing exhibitions. Work by master artists such as Larry Fuente, Anni Albers, Dale Chihuly, Albert Paley, Wendell Castle, James Cederquist, Lia Cook, and Claire Zeisler has been featured.

The museum's sumptuous centerpiece, the **Grand Salon,** awaits you at the top of a red-carpeted staircase. Dark rose walls covered with 19th-century paintings confer the air of a Victorian collector's picture gallery. Three monumental landscapes of the Grand Canyon and the Colorado River by Thomas Moran are hard to miss. They inspired Congress to establish Yellowstone as the first national park in 1872.

The smaller **Octagon Room,** opposite the Grand Salon, holds works by such iconic American painters as George P. A. Healy, Winslow Homer, and others. Flanking the Grand Salon and the Octagon Room are permanent collection galleries that contain fun, daring contemporary works in fiber, clay, wood, metal, glass, and mixed media. The **first floor** features galleries for short-term exhibitions of contemporary crafts and decorative arts. Special exhibitions open in the early spring and in the fall. ■

Renwick Gallery
www.americanart.si.edu/renwick
Map pp. 106–107
17th St. & Pennsylvania Ave., N.W.
202-633-1000
Metro: Farragut West; Bus: 30-36, P17 & 19, W13, 42, 11Y, X2

Grand indeed is the Renwick's 90-foot-long Grand Salon.

Corcoran Gallery of Art

Corcoran Gallery of Art
www.corcoran.org
Map p. 106
500 17th St., N.W.
202-639-1700
Closed Tues.
$$$
Metro: Farragut West; Bus: 80, S1

WASHINGTON'S OLDEST ART MUSEUM (AND THE THIRD oldest in the country), the Corcoran Gallery holds a distinguished collection of American and European artworks. It is the largest non-federal art museum in Washington, D.C.

The Corcoran started out three blocks north, in the building that now houses the Smithsonian's Renwick Gallery (see p. 117). The stately mansion was built to hold the collection of banker-philanthropist William Wilson Corcoran (1798–1888).

An enthusiastic patron of contemporary American art at a time when most collectors favored European works, Corcoran was a personal friend to several of the artists whose work now hangs in the gallery, including Albert Bierstadt, Frederic Church, Thomas Doughty, and George Inness. Corcoran's holdings came to include American and European landscapes and genre paintings, as well as sculpture.

When Corcoran's collection outgrew its available space, an architectural competition was held, which resulted in the hiring of New York architect Ernest Flagg. His stately beaux arts-style building, the first of its kind in the city, was completed in 1897. Bronze lions flank the entrance to the symmetrical white marble building; the green copper roof caps an architrave inscribed with the names of Rembrandt and other great artists.

Today, treasures of the museum's permanent collection include Frederic Edwin Church's "Niagara Falls" (1857), Mary Cassatt's "Young Girl at a Window" (1883), Winslow Homer's "A Light on the Sea" (1897), John Singer Sargent's "Madame Eduoard Pailleron" (1879), Thomas Cole's "The Departure" and "The Return"

Philanthropist William Corcoran founded his art gallery "for the purpose of encouraging American genius."

(both 1837), and Edward Hopper's "Ground Swell" (1939). Don't miss Albert Bierstadt's splendid "The Last of the Buffalo" (1889), which captures vividly the impending end of the American West: It shows an Indian on horseback spearing an attacking buffalo.

Also showcased is the gold-and-white **Salon Doré,** an 18th-century room from Paris's St.-Germain quarter. Part of an extensive donation of European art works and objects from industrialist and U.S. senator William A. Clark (1839–1925) of Montana, the gilded room glitters with Corinthian pilasters, huge framed mirrors, and a ceiling mural.

In addition to its excellent historic American and British art, the Corcoran has sizable collections of contemporary art, photography, and decorative arts. In 2006, under new director Paul Greenhalgh, the museum began devoting more of its gallery space to exhibits of modern work. In spring 2007, the Corcoran held a modestly successful modernism exhibition, presenting a new direction for the museum. This exhibit was the first major evidence of Greenhalgh's taste, and was the third most popular in recent history. It was also the most expensive, costing $2 million. The exhibit, "Modernism: Designing a New World 1914–1939," was the largest modern art show in the United States.

The Corcoran devotes particular attention to artists in the Washington area, and its on-site college of art and design, **The Corcoran School of Art,** offers an extensive program of classes, workshops, and lectures. The school (which has another campus in Georgetown) is Washington's only four-year accredited fine-arts institution. Its BFA program includes concentrations in fine art, photography, graphic design, and photojournalism.

Special exhibitions at the Corcoran run for several months at a time and have featured well-known contemporary artists and photographers such as Annie Leibovitz and Ansel Adams. Tickets for the temporary shows are $14. Private tours can be arranged for adult groups of 15 or more, and usually last about 45 minutes. These tours must be reserved at least one month in advance through the Corcoran's Education Department. ■

Albert Bierstadt's "The Last of the Buffalo" is one of the Corcoran's finest works.

It's a spooky little town

Intrigue. Mystery. Romance. Spies and spy catchers have captured the imagination of the moviegoing public for years, but in Washington—home of the CIA, the FBI, and the Pentagon—such cinematic proxies are redundant: The streets are alive with secret agents seeking or supplying classified information in nonstandard ways. Every now and then an agent is nabbed, exposing an underworld in which backyard barbecuers such as Aldrich Ames or Robert Hanssen turn out to have led lives of treachery and deceit.

"Rebel Rose" Greenhow and daughter

Spying caught on in Washington during the Civil War, when amateur agents on both sides of the Mason-Dixon Line scoured the capital city for war-related information. Thomas Nelson Conrad, a former Georgetown College headmaster, sat in Lafayette Park across from the White House for hours, meticulously noting President Lincoln's comings and goings. Conrad hoped to kidnap the President, then exchange him for prisoners of war. The Confederacy rejected his plan as infeasible.

The most romantic figure in Washington's espionage history may be the Rebel Rose. Intelligent, beautiful, and duplicitous, Rose O'Neal Greenhow (1815–1864) haunted Washington's loftiest social circles before the Civil War, befriending Presidents, senators, and tycoons. When war broke out and men left for battle, spying became women's work. None was more deft than Greenhow. Inside her modest house at 398 16th Street, N.W. (it's no longer standing), she plied unsuspecting targets with oysters, wild turkey, and champagne, pumping them for information all the while.

At one dinner party, Greenhow learned that the Federals were planning to move into Virginia. By quickly passing a coded message to Confederate Gen. Pierre G. T. Beauregard inside a woman's hair bun, she enabled him to reposition some of his troops—and, ultimately, to win the First Battle of Bull Run.

Soviet KGB colonel Vitaly Yurchenko made world headlines when he strolled into the U.S. Embassy in Rome in August 1985 and stated he wished to defect. Among the tidbits he had to share: NSA analyst Ronald Pelton had served as a double agent since 1980 and CIA officer Edward Lee Howard since 1984.

But Yurchenko was not a happy decamper. His ex-girlfriend, who married a Russian diplomat stationed in Montreal, had no plans to leave her husband. Worse, the good colonel was relegated to a prisonlike existence in the United States, where his CIA case officers insisted on escorting him everywhere.

On November 2, 1985, Yurchenko and his CIA handler repaired to a popular neighborhood restaurant in Georgetown that is now defunct. At some point Yurchenko stepped out for a breath of fresh air—and grabbed a cab to the Soviet embassy, where he rescinded his defection. Four days later he was on a plane to the Soviet Union, leaving the intelligence community to debate whether he had been a legitimate defector or a KGB plant.

Following in the forked footsteps of Greenhow and Yurchenko came career CIA officer Aldrich Ames, who in 1994 was accused of exposing U.S. intelligence assets inside the former Soviet Union. The info swap occurred at Chadwick's, at 3205 K Street in Georgetown; Ames chalkmarked a blue mailbox on R Street at 37th as a dead-drop signal. For his tip-offs, Ames received more than 2.7 million dollars from the Soviets—and from the Americans, a lifelong prison sentence.

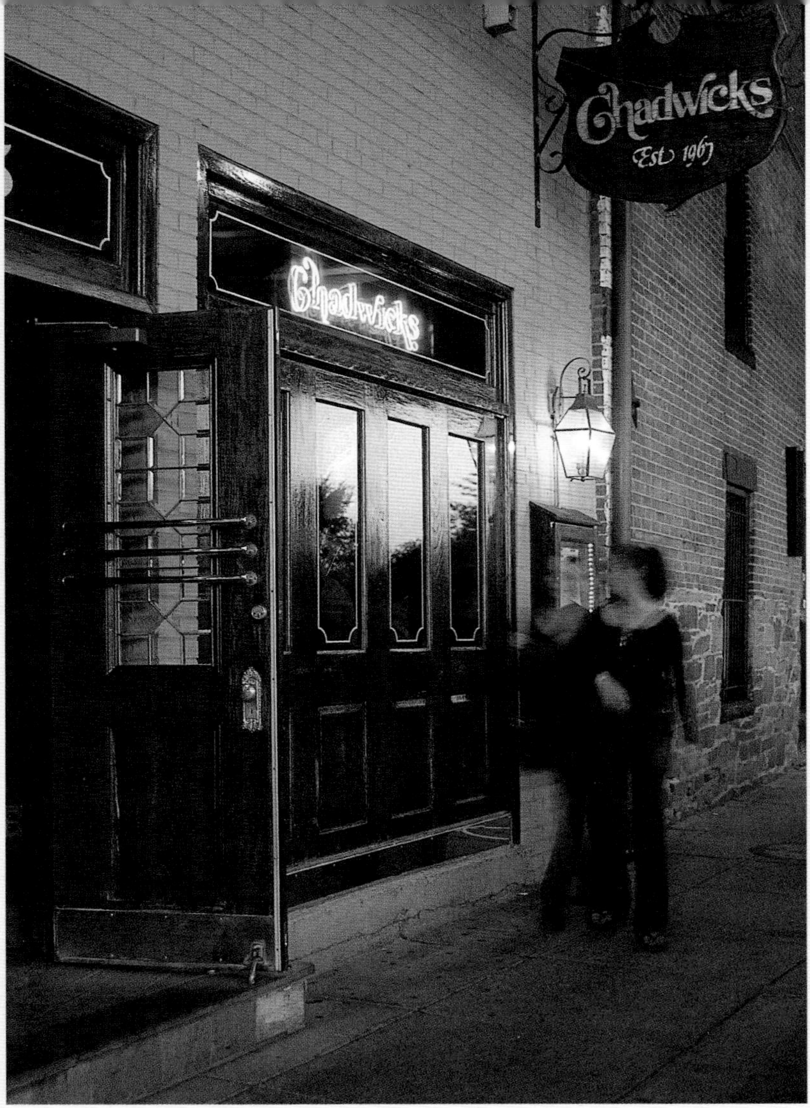

At this chummy beer-and-burger joint on Georgetown's K Street, the traitorous Aldrich Ames revealed to Russian agents the names of 20 CIA operatives working within the Soviet bloc; 10 were executed as spies.

TO WATCH A SPY

The Clandestine Capital emerges from the shadows in several formal ways. An unlikely team of former FBI, CIA, and KGB agents offers a **SpyDrive tour** of espionage sites for large groups, only by advance arrangement *(866-779-8735, www.spytrek.com)*. Another spy tour is offered through reservation by the **Cold War Museum** *(www.coldwar.org)*. Founded in 1996 to preserve Cold War history, this traveling exhibit is in search of a permanent home. The city's popular new **International Spy Museum** (see p. 138) houses one of the world's largest collections of espionage paraphernalia, plus interactive exhibits and a store. Or go to the source: The CIA's headquarters *(www.cia.gov)* in Langley, Virginia, has a museum and store. ■

The Octagon
www.archfoundation.org/octagon
Map p. 106
1799 New York Ave., N.W.
202-638-3221
Prearranged group tours only
$
Metro: Farragut West, Farragut North; Bus: 80, H1, L1, S1

The Octagon

A gem of early Washington history, the redbrick Octagon stands bravely in the shadow of austere modern buildings. The neighborhood's first private residence, it was built about the same time as the White House. Its longevity owes much to its designer, William Thornton, also the first architect of the Capitol (see pp. 52–57).

The house was completed in 1801 for entrepreneur/political aspirant/urban pioneer John Tayloe III. The location and stylish architecture paid off when the British burned the President's House in 1814 and the Madisons took shelter in the Octagon, just a five-minute walk from the executive mansion. Less than six months later, Madison signed the war-ending Treaty of Ghent in an upstairs parlor.

The Tayloes moved back in and made good use of the space—they raised 15 children. After Mrs. Tayloe's death in 1855, the Octagon was rented out as a girls' school, then a naval office, then a tenement house. The American Institute of Architects bought and restored the building in 1902. It now houses a museum operated by the American Architectural Foundation.

Reserved **group tours** are the only way to visit the Octagon, which, despite its name, only has six sides. ■

The Octagon was not named for the shape of its staircase.

DAR Headquarters

Daughters of the American Revolution
www.dar.org
Map p. 106
1776 D St., N.W.
202-628-1776
Closed Sun. & 2 weeks in June, July
Metro: Farragut West; Bus: 80, H1, L1, S1

This robust beaux arts building was built between 1905 and 1929 to serve as the headquarters of the Daughters of the American Revolution. Visitors may tour 33 **period rooms** that showcase early American decorative arts.

Highlights include an 18th-century Georgia tavern, an 1850s California whaling station, and a parlor furnished with pieces from the White House of James and Elizabeth Monroe. A museum displays exhibits drawn from the DAR's collection of 33,000 pieces of textile, ceramic, silver, glass, and furniture.

Built in the 1920s on the building's west side, **Constitution Hall** is a 3,800-seat horseshoe-shaped auditorium designed by John Russell Pope (the hand behind the National Gallery of Art, Jefferson Memorial, and National Archives). All kinds of concerts and lectures are held here, but Constitution Hall is best (or worst) known for the one that never took place: After the DAR's 1939 refusal to let black contralto Marian Anderson perform, Eleanor Roosevelt bravely stepped in, and Anderson sang at the Lincoln Memorial instead. ■

Organization of American States

The OAS courtyard offers a whiff of the tropics.

BLENDING CLASSICAL AND SPANISH COLONIAL ELEMENTS this striking white building is the headquarters of the Organization of American States, a regional alliance of 35 nations promoting peace and economic cooperation among its member countries from the Americas and the Caribbean.

Dedicated in 1910, the building was the work of architects Paul Cret (designer of the Folger Shakespeare Library; see p. 64) and Albert Kelsey. Just inside the elaborate triple-arched entry, a lush villa-like courtyard boasts an octagonal Aztec-style fountain and overflows with tropical plants. Upstairs, the large **Hall of the Americas** auditorium is graced by Tiffany stained-glass windows and a vaulted ceiling.

In the back, a walkway through an Aztec garden leads to the **Art Museum of the Americas,** roofed in red tile (the museum must be entered from 201 18th St.). Several attractive galleries host exhibits from the museum's permanent collection, plus traveling shows of Latin American and Caribbean art and photography.

After your visit, head for the triangular park across 18th Street to view the raised-sword equestrian statue of Simón Bolívar the Liberator, a gift to the United States in 1958 from Venezuela. ■

Organization of American States & Art Museum of the Americas

www.oas.org

www.museum.oas.org

Map p. 106

17th St. & Constitution Ave., N.W.

202-458-3000; museum, 202-458-6016

Closed Sat.–Sun. and federal holidays; museum closed Mon.

Metro: Farragut West; Bus: 80, H1, L1, S1

John F. Kennedy Center for the Performing Arts

John F. Kennedy Center for the Performing Arts
www.kennedy-center.org
Map p. 106
2700 F St., N.W.
202-467-4600
Metro: Foggy Bottom–GWU; Bus: 80

ONCE MALIGNED AS AN UNSIGHTLY PILLBOX SITTING BY the Potomac, the Kennedy Center has since earned the affection of Washingtonians as the city's premier bastion of culture. The center was designed by architect Edward Durrell Stone and its 1971 opening elevated the city from a cultural backwater to a leader in the live arts. The world's foremost opera singers, pianists, jazz musicians, dancers, and actors have performed on the stages of the Kennedy Center. The National Symphony Orchestra and the Washington Opera, both based here, have achieved recognition. Among the many groups that have performed at the center are the Metropolitan Opera, La Scala opera company, the Bolshoi ballet, and the Berlin Philharmonic.

The center is the "national living memorial" to a fallen president, John F. Kennedy. A presidentially appointed board of trustees oversees the operation of the center, which is supported both by ticket sales and by private donations.

VISITING

Free guided tours are offered daily; call for times. You may also wander about on your own, but some theaters are closed to the public during rehearsals. Tickets *(purchase at box office or call 202-467-4600 or 800-444-1324)* must be purchased for most performances. The Millennium Stage program, however, offers free daily performances at 6 p.m. in the Grand Foyer.

The Kennedy Center is at its best at night, when floodlights envelop its white Carrara marble in a vibrant glow. The north entrance opens into the **Hall of States,** its soaring ceiling lined with state flags; at the south entrance the **Hall of Nations** contains the flags of countries with diplomatic ties to the United States. Both halls lead

The Kennedy Center (left) sits serenely beside the Potomac River. Inside (below), patrons hurry to a performance of the Washington Ballet.

to the **Grand Foyer—**at 630 feet one of the longest rooms in the world. This royal, red-carpeted space is outfitted with floor-to-ceiling mirrors and 18 crystal chandeliers donated by Sweden. Halfway down the hall you'll find Robert Berks's big, emotive bronze bust of Kennedy.

Seeing a performance is the reason to come here—and the best way to take in the auditoriums. The 2,450-seat **Concert Hall,** renovated in 1997, is home to the National Symphony; the 1,100-seat **Eisenhower Theater** is named for the President who signed legislation for a National Cultural Center; and the spectacular 2,300-seat **Opera House** completes the trio of big performance spaces. Just inside the north entrance, off the Hall of States, the 320-seat **Family Theater** presents performances for young audiences.

On the Roof Terrace level, the 500-seat **Terrace Theater** is a delightful venue for jazz combos, solo recitals, chamber music, and dramatic performances. For a cozier setting, take in an experimental or family show at the 350-seat **Theater Lab.** The **Jazz Club** on this level offers live jazz in a cabaret setting.

Up on the **Roof Terrace,** walk out onto the patio for a view of the memorials, the Potomac, Arlington high-rises across the river, and the distant form of the hilltop Washington National Cathedral. There are also many restaurants and cafés in the area at which to dine. ■

Robert Peary, Louis Leakey, Jacques Cousteau, and Jane Goodall are some of the explorers and scientists who have been supported by National Geographic, founded in Washington in 1888.

More places to visit around the White House

NATIONAL GEOGRAPHIC SOCIETY

The National Geographic Society's magazines, books and guidebooks (including this one), maps, TV programs, and classroom materials—all aimed at "the increase and diffusion of geographic knowledge"—are produced here at the organization's headquarters. A variety of events, exhibits, and slide-illustrated lectures are available for visitors. **Explorers Hall** often exhibits the work of National Geographic photographers, researchers, and explorers, including conservationist Mike Fay—whose grueling 2-year, 2,000-mile trek across the heart of Africa inspired the country of Gabon to set aside 10 percent of its land as national park—and paleontologist Paul Sereno with his newest dinosaur discoveries. Explorers Hall also houses the National Geographic Store, which offers a wide array of maps, books, magazines, international music CDs, as well as a variety of other educational, entertainment, and decorative products from around the world.

www.nationalgeographic.com Map p. 107
17th & M Sts., N.W. 800-647-5463
Metro: Farragut North, Farragut West

B'NAI B'RITH KLUTZNICK NATIONAL JEWISH MUSEUM

This museum of Jewish art, history, and culture documents the life and festival cycles of Judaism. Named for the B'nai B'rith service organization and Chicago attorney Philip Klutznick, the collection includes 18th-century German and Italian berith knives, a silver phylactery (ca 1800) from Poland, 18th-century bronze Sabbath lamps, and a case of shining silver Torah finials and crowns. A 1790 letter from George Washington to Moses Seixas, a sexton of the Touro Synagogue in Newport, Rhode Island, promises that the U.S. government "gives to bigotry no sanction; to persecution no assistance."

2020 K St., N.W. (temporary location)
202-857-6583 Call for appointment; closed Sat.–Sun. Metro: Farragut West, Foggy Bottom–GWU

CATHEDRAL OF ST. MATTHEW THE APOSTLE

This redbrick 1890s cathedral, with its ribbed copper dome, is a commanding downtown presence. The funeral Mass of John F. Kennedy was held here in 1963; outside, three-year-old John Jr. bravely saluted his father's casket,

creating an indelible image. A cavernous interior, embellished with mosaics, a skylit dome, flickering votive candles, and paintings and statues, forms a haven for prayer or meditation.
www.stmatthewscathedral.org Map p. 106 1725 Rhode Island Ave., N.W. 202-347-3215 Metro: Dupont Circle, Farragut North

CHARLES SUMNER SCHOOL

Its handsome M Street exterior rivets the gaze on this redbrick building, opened in 1872 as a school for African-American children (and named for the abolitionist senator from Massachusetts). Now an archive and museum of the District's public schools, the Sumner School also hosts concerts, lectures, films, and art exhibitions.
Map p. 107 1201 17th St., N.W. 202-442-6060 Closed Sun. & July–Aug. Metro: Farragut North, Dupont Circle

DECATUR HOUSE

For his triumphs in the War of 1812, Commodore Stephen Decatur earned enough to build this three-story federal-style house on Lafayette Square. Benjamin Henry Latrobe designed the redbrick town house, completed in 1818, but Decatur never really got to enjoy the place: He was killed in a duel with a fellow officer 14 months after moving in. His wife rented the house to the likes of Henry Clay and Martin Van Buren. Guided tours cover the period-furnished rooms of the first floor and the lavish Victorian rooms of the second, which still seem to pulse with the vibrant presence of a later owner, Mrs. Truxtun Beale, who presided over a salon for ambassadors and politicians in these quarters.
www.decaturhouse.org Map p. 107 1610 H St., N.W. 202-842-0920 No tours Mon. $ Metro: Farragut West

The Decatur House dining room contains period furnishings and table settings.

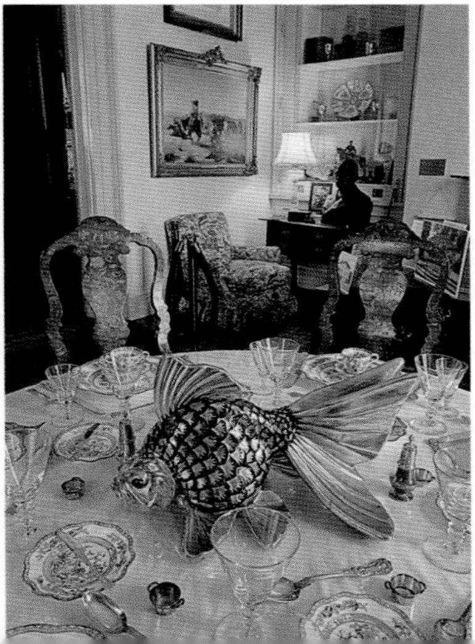

DEPARTMENT OF STATE

What must foreign heads of state think when they arrive at the door of this drab 1961 building to meet with the or secretary of state? Most of them aren't given the time to form a negative opinion; they are whisked to the eighth floor, where they step into a sparkling geode of elegance.

The designers of the **Diplomatic Reception Rooms** may have calculated this dismay-cum-delight effect on visiting dignitaries. The suite of rooms is decorated with one of the country's finest collections of early American furnishings. A 45-minute tour reveals such surprises as Paul Revere silver and George Washington's Chinese porcelain *(advance reservations are required, usually several months ahead)*. Elsewhere you'll come across portraits of George and Martha Washington by Rembrandt Peale, paintings by Gilbert Stuart and John Singleton Copley, and Chippendale furniture from Philadelphia, New York, and Boston. The rooms on the south side—among them the breathtakingly grand State Dining Room—give impressive views of the Mall and its monuments.
www.receptiontours.state.gov Map p. 106 23rd & C Streets, N.W. 202-647-3241 Closed Sat.–Sun. & federal holidays $ Metro: Farragut West

DEPARTMENT OF THE INTERIOR MUSEUM

Tucked inside the Department of the Interior, this small, quiet museum chronicles the Interior Department's 1930s origins, when it comprised the National Park Service, U.S. Fish and Wildlife Service, U.S. Geological Survey, and the Bureaus of Mines, Indian Affairs, Reclamation, and Land Management. Drawings, homestead claims, handmade

maps, exploration tools, and videos tell the story of the country's settlement.
Map p. 106 1849 C St., N.W. 202-208-4743 Closed Sun., open third Sat. afternoon each month Metro: Farragut West, Foggy Bottom–GWU

HAY–ADAMS HOTEL

The elegant Italian Renaissance-style Hay-Adams, one of Washington's finest small hotels, fronts the north side of Lafayette Square, offering a good view of the White House. Built in the 1920s, the hotel occupies the site of residences owned by statesman John Hay and historian Henry Adams. Stop in for afternoon tea, fine dining, or the nighttime piano bar.
www.hayadams.com Map p. 107
16th & H Sts., N.W. 202-638-6600
Metro: Farragut West, McPherson Square

A bronze Albert Einstein at the National Academy of Sciences holds the three mathematical equations summarizing his most important scientific contributions.

NATIONAL ACADEMY OF SCIENCES

Free concerts are often performed and art exhibits showcased in this think tank. Otherwise, it is most well known to visitors for its impressive outdoor bronze statue of Albert Einstein, seated on white granite amid a cool glade of elms and hollies. Robert Berks, who sculpted the similarly mudpie-style JFK bust in the Kennedy Center, uses proportion to emphasize his subject's striking head. A 28-foot-wide sky map swirls at Einstein's feet.
www.nationalacademies.org Map p. 106
2101 Constitution Ave., N.W. 202-334-2000 Metro: Foggy Bottom–GWU

ST. JOHN'S CHURCH

Presidents since James Madison have worshiped at this Episcopal church on occasion. The yellow stucco building, with its white wood bell tower and bright gold dome, was completed in 1816 after Benjamin Henry Latrobe, who also helped conceptualize the Capitol, the White House, and neighboring Decatur House, submitted an acceptable design. A national historic landmark, the church is open weekdays from 10 a.m. to 2:30 p.m. for meditation and prayer. A skylit dome and stained-glass windows brighten the interior; a brass plate marks the President's Pew—No. 54.
www.stjohns-dc.org Map p. 107
1525 H St., N.W. 202-347-8766
Metro: Farragut West, McPherson Square

ST. MARY'S EPISCOPAL CHURCH

Originally St. Mary's Church for Colored People, this building was the city's first house of worship for black Episcopalians. The congregation pooled its money to hire famous architect James Renwick to build this simple yet lovely church; the first services were held in 1887. The altar triptych depicts two saints of African descent; the center window is Tiffany stained glass. A national historic landmark, the church boasts working gas lights and iron radiators.
www.stmarysfoggybottom.org Map p. 106
730 23rd St., N.W. 202-333-3985
Closed Sat. Metro: Foggy Bottom–GWU ■

With its eclectic mix of entertainment venues, hotels, historic structures, museums, retail establishments, and federal and private office buildings, downtown offers something for everyone.

Downtown

Detail at the entrance to the National Building Museum

Downtown

WASHINGTON'S DOWNTOWN HAS BEEN LOCATED JUST NORTH OF THE MALL since the city's founding in 1791. Sprung from the intersection of Pennsylvania Avenue and Seventh Street, where the city's main street met the main northern thoroughfare, the area has since sprawled to 14th Street and Louisiana and Massachusetts Avenues. Booming with new vitality, downtown buzzes with new restaurants, shops, theaters, and galleries, making all the more reason to come visit its clutch of long-established museums.

Throughout the 1800s, boutiques, hotels, and theaters thrived downtown, catering to the area's residents. The turn of the 20th century, however, brought the exodus of affluent merchants and residents to the suburbs, thereby opening up the downtown area to successive groups of lower income citizens. Then came the assassination of Martin Luther King, Jr., in 1968, instigating riots and the large-scale abandonment of commercial ventures. As buildings fell into miserable disrepair and the crime rate exploded, the area became one to avoid.

The outlook soon changed. In 1972, Congress created the Pennsylvania Avenue Development Corporation to plan the revitalization of Pennsylvania Avenue—the neglected

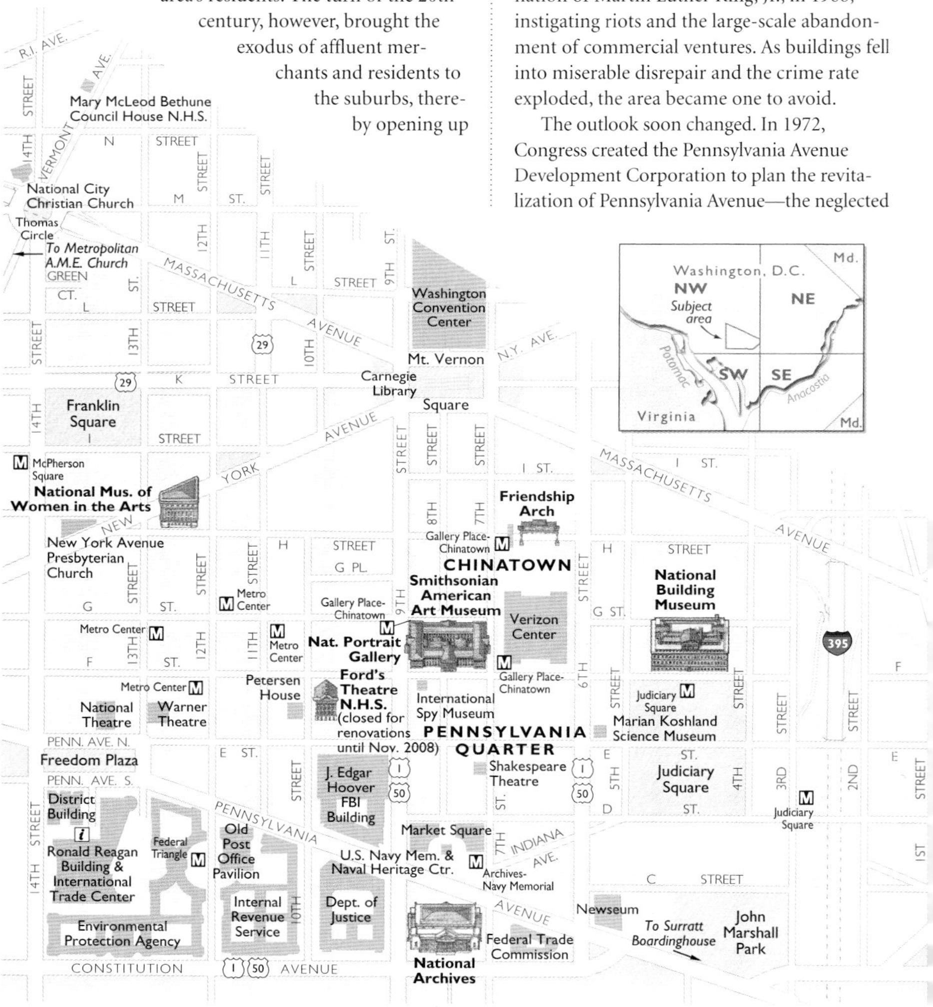

Vendors and courting couples are often spotted on downtown sidewalks.

streetscape was unbefitting what many consider to be America's Main Street. Initially, the PADC focused on renovating Pennsylvania Avenue's historic buildings: the Old Post Office, the Willard Hotel, and the National and Warner Theatres. Each successful venture encouraged the next, as city planners and developers saw the possibility of returning downtown into a dynamic commercial district and residential neighborhood.

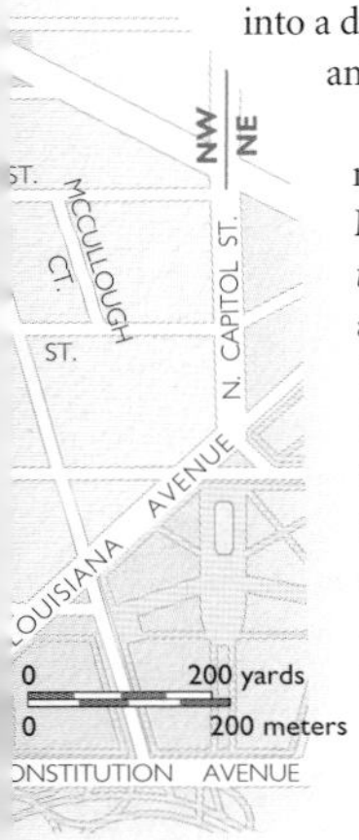

Coupled with renovation, new construction brought Market Square (1984, *N of the Archives*), with offices and apartments; the Lansburgh (1992, *8th & E Sts.*), a residential/retail/cultural arts venue complex; and in 2003 the new convention center *(N of Mt. Vernon Sq.)*. In the last few years, billions of dollars have been invested in the area's development, including many new restaurants.

The most important development, however, was the arrival of the MCI Center in 1997 (since renamed the Verizon Center). This entertainment and sports arena showcases basketball, hockey, concerts, and other special events, hugely increasing annual downtown visitation.

All this new life complements several museums that often have been overshadowed by those on the nearby Mall, including the National Museum of Women in the Arts, the Smithsonian American Art Museum, the National Portrait Gallery, and the National Building Museum. The area's newest attraction is the Newseum at Sixth Street and Pennsylvania Avenue.

Amid the modernization rush, tiny Chinatown clings to its heritage. Clustered on the north side of Pennsylvania Avenue in the 1880s, the enclave established its distinctive appearance after moving to the H Street area in the 1930s, where it remains today. The area features Cantonese, Szechuan, and Hunan restaurants, as well as Chinese pharmacies selling all kinds of traditional remedies. ■

Ford's Theatre National Historic Site

Ford's Theatre National Historic Site
www.fordstheatre.org
Map p. 130
511 10th St., N.W.
202-426-6924
Metro: Metro Center; Bus: D1-6

Closed for renovation until November 2008

A WORKING THEATER AND A MUSEUM TO ONE OF THE nation's most tragic dramas, Ford's Theatre has a morbidly compelling quality. John Wilkes Booth shot President Abraham Lincoln here on April 14, 1865, five days after Lee's surrender at Appomattox. Lincoln's untimely death pushed to legendary heights the historical greatness he had achieved by keeping the Union from falling apart.

The theater closed shortly thereafter, serving as an office building and later as a storage facility. Acquired by the National Park Service in 1933, it was restored to its original 1865 splendor and reopened to the public in 1968. The theater now hosts a full program of contemporary American plays.

Scene of the crime: The Presidential Box is on permanent display at Ford's.

The ornate interior boasts the authentically re-created **Presidential Box** with American flags, lace curtains, red velvet wallpaper, plush seats, and the original settee. You can walk up to the balcony for a look. No one sits there anymore—which is just as well, since it's apparently the only bad seat in the house.

When the theater is not in use, Park Service officials offer short informative talks on the night's events. Booth, a disgruntled actor and Confederate sympathizer, shot Lincoln in the head and then jumped down to the stage, breaking a small leg bone; he supposedly shouted "*Sic semper tyrannis*—Thus always to tyrants" and hobbled off. He fled on horseback through the southern Maryland countryside, only to be caught 12 days later and shot dead.

The **museum** downstairs contains several noteworthy artifacts, including the .44-caliber derringer Booth used in the shooting, the hunting knife he used to stab one of Lincoln's box companions, and the clothes Lincoln was wearing.

Continue following the night's events across the street at the **Petersen House** *(516 10th St., N.W.)*, where Lincoln was taken. Never regaining consciousness, the President died the next day. Peek into the parlor where Mary Todd Lincoln waited through the night, the back parlor where Lincoln's secretary of war began investigating the murder, and the period-furnished bedroom in which Lincoln died. A weary sadness pervades these cramped quarters, the empty boots and jacket evocative of the owner that will never return. ■

National Museum of Women in the Arts

THIS WELL-DESIGNED MUSEUM FOCUSES SOLELY ON THE work of women artists. Founder and art collector Wilhelmina Cole Holladay felt that women were often completely overlooked in standard art history texts. Determined to correct the imbalance, her resulting museum, which opened in 1987, showcases and promotes the talent of women artists from the Renaissance to the present.

National Museum of Women in the Arts

www.nmwa.org

Map p. 130

1250 New York Ave., N.W.

202-783-5000

$$

Metro: Metro Center; Bus: 80, S2 & 4, G8

Notable in itself, the Renaissance revival building began as a Masonic temple in 1907, served as a movie theater in the 1960s, and, after being threatened with demolition in the early 1980s, was purchased by Holladay in 1983. Restored to its former glory, the grand hall shines with polished marble floors and decorative plasterwork. On the mezzanine level's north side, added during the restoration, you can still see a Masonic cartouche with the letter *M* worked in.

Works in the permanent collection, on view in the **Great Hall, Mezzanine,** and **third floor** chronicle women's artistic achievements from the 16th century to modern times. Look for Lavinia Fontana's 1580 "Portrait of a Noblewoman"; Fontana was the first widely known woman to sustain a career as an artist. Other treasures include "Sheep by the Sea" (1869) and other works by Rosa Bonheur (1822–1899), famous for her straightforward depictions of animals, as well as "The Bath" (1891) and others by Impressionist Mary Cassatt (1844–1926). Georgia O'Keeffe, Helen Frankenthaler, Lee Krasner, Judy Chicago, Imogen Cunningham, and Louise Nevelson are among the artists represented. And this museum is the only place in Washington where you can see work by Frida Kahlo. Her "Self-Portrait–Dedicated to Leon Trotsky" (1939), also known as "Between the Curtains," is now part of the museum's permanent collection; another of her works is on loan.

Special exhibits are found on the second floor, while the fourth floor has an 18,500-volume library and research center. ■

"Self-Portrait–Dedicated to Leon Trotsky" (1939), by Frida Kahlo

Pennsylvania Quarter

Pennsylvania Quarter

- Map p. 130
- 5th to 8th & G to I Sts.
- Metro: Gallery Place–Chinatown; Bus: 80, P6, 70-71, X2, G8

THE SHINING STAR OF DOWNTOWN'S REVITALIZATION, the Pennsylvania Quarter neighborhood, also called the Seventh Street corridor, is quickly becoming Washington's hippest hangout. With an explosion of luxury apartment complexes, trendy restaurants, theaters, and galleries joining a panoply of established and future museums, the once neglected area teems with life both night and day.

The real success story of the Pennsylvania Quarter begins with the abandoned Lansburgh department store. In 1992 this imposing building was rehabilitated into a mixed-use complex housing 385 luxury residential units, retail space, and a cultural arts venue. The combination of location, amenities, and cultural flavor attracted people (former attorney general Janet Reno and actor Harry Hamlin have been among its residents); and new businesses moved into the commercial spaces.

The Lansburgh's reigning tenant, the nationally renowned **Shakespeare Theatre** *(450 7th St., 202-547-1122)* moved to Seventh Street from its Capitol Hill quarters in 1992. Devoted to presenting the Bard's works—as well as those of his contemporaries and of the playwrights he influenced—the theater is considered one of the nation's most prestigious. The theater expanded dramatically in October, 2007, when the new Harman Center for the Arts opened. The Center's **Sidney Harman Hall** added 775 seats and a second venue to the theater's performance

Chinese influences along Seventh Street

capacity. The well-established repertory **Woolly Mammoth Theatre** is located nearby *(641 D St., 202-393-3939).*

A major contributor to revitalization is the colossal **Verizon Center** *(601 F St., 202-628-3200),* which draws thousands of visitors on any given day. Opened in 1997, the 20,000-seat arena hosts circuses, ice skating performances, concerts, and other special events. It's also home to the Washington Wizards and Mystics professional basketball teams (men and women, respectively), the Georgetown Hoyas college basketball team, and the Washington Capitals hockey team.

An even bigger addition to downtown is the **Washington Convention Center** *(www.dcconvention.com)* at 801 Mount Vernon Place, which opened in 2003. With 2.3 million square feet of space—covering 6 city blocks on 17 acres—the behemoth is more than double the size of the old convention center that was just blocks away.

Keeping in step with the quarter's new face, many of its museums—including the **National Portrait Gallery** (see p. 137)and the **Smithsonian American Art Museum**—have been renovated.

And more museums are adding to the area's appeal. The highly popular **International Spy Museum** (see p. 138) opened in 2002 at 800 F Street. The Historical Society of Washington and the National Music Center are bringing new life to the beautiful 1903 beaux arts-styleformer **Carnegie Library** (see p. 143) on Mt. Vernon Square at Eighth and K Streets. Formerly located in Virginia, the **Newseum** (see p. 142), an interactive museum on newsmaking, is relocating to this area in 2008. And, the latest outpost of the **Madame Tussauds** franchise opened at 1025 F Street in October, 2007.

Sandwiched amid all this growth is Washington's small but distinctive **Chinatown** *(6th to 8th Sts. & G to H Sts.),* which has thrived since it was established here in the 1930s. Its shops cater to a heavily Chinese clientele, and the many restaurants offer a wide range of tasty Szechuan and Cantonese dishes. ■

The Friendship Arch (above) recalls the quarter's Chinese legacy, while the Shakespeare Theatre (below) offers quality thespian fare.

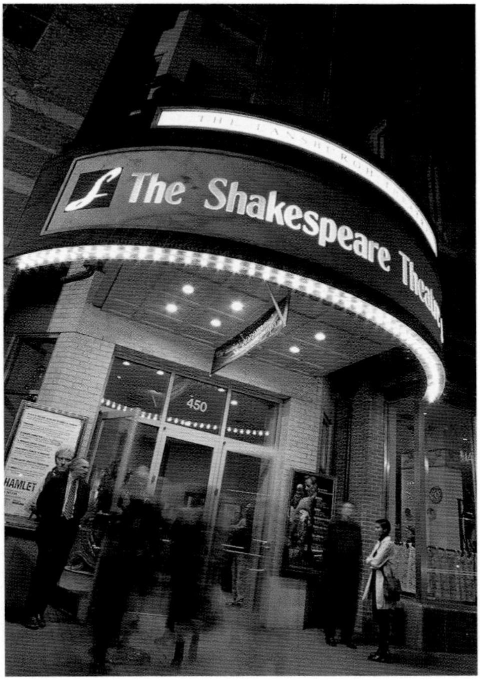

Smithsonian American Art Museum

Smithsonian American Art Museum
www.americanart.si.edu
Map p. 130
8th & F Sts., N.W.
202-633-1000
Metro: Gallery Place–Chinatown; Bus: 42

HOUSED IN A HISTORIC LANDMARK THAT WALT WHITMAN called the "noblest of Washington buildings" is the nation's oldest federal art collection. Here and at its Renwick Gallery (see p. 117), the museum features works in every media—all by American artists and spanning more than three centuries. The National Portrait Gallery shares the impressive building, which recently reopened after a major overhaul.

One of the finest examples of Greek Revival public architecture in the United States, this stunning building has porticos modeled on the Parthenon in Athens, a curving double staircase, colonnades, and vaulted galleries. Construction began in 1836 under the direction of Robert Mills, then architect of public buildings.

Pierre L'Enfant's original plan for the capital called for putting a national nondenominational church or a pantheon for the nation's heroes on this site. Instead, Congress claimed it for a patent office, which moved into the south wing in 1840 while construction continued. The building was used as a hospital and barracks during the Civil War, and President Abraham Lincoln held his second Inaugural ball here in March 1865. After a fire in 1877, much of the third floor was restored in the ornate Victorian style of the time. Scheduled for demolition in the 1950s, the building was championed by historic preservationists and later donated to the Smithsonian.

The collection features colonial portraits, 19th-century landscapes, American Impressionism, 20th-century realism and abstraction, sculpture, photography, prints and drawings, African-American art, Latino art, and folk art. Well-known 19th-century painters and sculptors such as Albert Pinkham Ryder, Mary Cassatt, Daniel Chester French, and Augustus Saint-Gaudens are represented; 20th-century works include Edward Hopper's "Cape Cod Morning" (1950) and Georgia O'Keeffe's "Yellow Calla" (1926).

The recent renovations have enabled the museum to quadruple the number of artworks on display from its permanent collections. A new 346-seat auditorium on the building's lower level accommodates lectures, films, and performances. ■

Self-taught artist Malcah Zeldis (1931–) created the inspirational "Miss Liberty Celebration" in 1987 while recovering from cancer.

The National Portrait Gallery contains the only complete collection of presidential portraits outside the White House.

National Portrait Gallery

CELEBRATING THE NATION'S HEROES, INTELLECTS, ROGUES, and famous personalities, this gallery reveals America's history through portraiture and sculpture. After a major renovation of the historic building, the gallery recently welcomed home many of its celebrated treasures.

The idea of a national portrait gallery dates back to 1857, when Congress commissioned George P. A. Healy to paint official portraits of all the Presidents for the White House. After World War I, a national portrait gallery was proposed as part of a general art collection within the Smithsonian Institution. Yet this gallery didn't officially open until 1968.

The collection consists of more than 18,000 objects in a wide range of media, including marble, oil on canvas, drawing, and photography. Among the formal portraits of all the Presidents is Gilbert Stuart's famous "Lansdowne" portrait of George Washington.

Opening onto the magnificent third-floor **Great Hall** are four galleries that feature 20th-century Americans who were significant in politics, culture, and science. "Champions" salutes figures whose impact has extended beyond their achievement in American sports. "Bravo!" showcases composers and performers from the beginning of the 20th century to the present, with video clips of performances by such legends as John Wayne, Katherine Hepburn, Leonard Bernstein, and Aaron Copland.

Other notable personalities unfold in these works, from the first meeting of Native Americans and European explorers, through the onset of the Gilded Age. The Civil War galleries have selections from the museum's outstanding daguerreotypes.

Caricatures by Al Hirschfeld, *Time* magazine portrait covers, David Geary's photographs of Marilyn singing to troops in Korea, sculptor Jo Davidson's striking bronze and terra-cotta portraits of famous Americans such as Franklin D. Roosevelt and Gertrude Stein—all this provides an engaging museum experience. ■

National Portrait Gallery
www.npg.si.edu
Map p. 130
8th & F Sts., N.W.
202-633-8300
Metro: Gallery Place–Chinatown; Bus: 42

International Spy Museum

International Spy Museum
www.spymuseum.org
Map p. 130
800 F St., N.W.
202-393-7798
$$$
Metro: Gallery Place/Chinatown; Bus 42

ONE OF THE HOTTEST ATTRACTIONS IN WASHINGTON these days lies in the shadow of the city's grand monuments—fitting, perhaps, given the shadowy world it illuminates. The International Spy Museum takes you inside the world of espionage through engrossing exhibits and programs designed with the help of real agents and spy-catchers such as CIA masters of disguise.

The privately developed museum opened in 2002 in the shell of five historic buildings dating from 1875 to 1892. The American Communist Party had offices here during World War II. In the refurbished space, the museum's state-of-the-art exhibits highlight the people, tools, and techniques of espionage tradecraft around the world.

A not-so-secret entrance to the International Spy Museum

The displays are built around a collection of more than 600 objects ranging from popular G-Man toys from the 1930s and 1940s ("G" for "government") to spying devices such as a KGB pistol encased in a lipstick tube. Espionage from biblical times to the present is represented. One item on display is a 1777 letter by George Washington authorizing creation of a spy network.

Among the fascinating stories highlighted in the exhibits are those of women who traveled undercover as spies during the Civil War. In fact, an entire room is devoted to women agents through the first decades of the 20th century.

VISITING

There is often a waiting line on weekends and holidays for same-day admission. To avoid long waits and disappointment, it's a good idea to reserve in advance *(800-551-7328, TicketMaster.com)*. Inside, most visitors spend about two hours; add an hour to see simulated U.S. intelligence work in **Operation Spy.**

You begin the self-guided tour by adopting an alias. The role-playing continues through scenarios that test your skill at analyzing situations and maintaining your cover, as real agents must do. Find out in **School for Spies** whether you have what it takes for this risky business. The exhibits include 200 of the spying gadgets developed by agencies from the OSS to the KGB, some still in use today.

In **Secret History of History,** you'll learn how important secret intelligence has been to many notable leaders throughout history, from Elizabeth I to Joseph Stalin. **Spies Among Us** spotlights spy rings and intelligence gathering in the climate of World War II, such as the Allies' top-secret code-breaking success (named Ultra) and the brilliant work of Navajo code-talkers.

War of the Spies and **The 21st Century** bring espionage into the present, showing how spies from Kim Philby to Robert Hanssen have operated. ■

National Building Museum

THE GARGANTUAN REDBRICK PENSION BUILDING IS ONE of Washington's architectural treasures. Designed by civil engineer Gen. Montgomery C. Meigs, the 1887 building was modeled after the 18th century Palazzo Farnese in Rome, but was referred to as Meig's Old Barn by critics in the U.S. Though it had deteriorated by the 1960s, a study highlighting its potential as a museum space saved it from proposed demolition. Congress called for its restoration in 1980 to house a museum about architecture, urban planning, and design.

National Building Museum

www.nbm.org

Map p. 130

401 F St., N.W.

202-272-2448

Metro: Judiciary Square; Bus: D1-6

Girdling the entire building, the most striking exterior feature is the 3-foot-high terra-cotta frieze designed by Bohemian-born sculptor Caspar Buberl (1834–1899). Depicting a procession of Civil War infantry, artillery, cavalry, and other units, it is emblematic of the building's original purpose: serving the needs of Union veterans.

The interior is just as impressive. The spectacular **Great Hall** will take your breath away. Standing in the middle of this immense, light-filled, open space, bordered on all sides with four tiers of arcades and high clerestory windows, you feel as if you've stepped into an Italian gallery. Eight Corinthian columns, made of brick but plastered and painted to resemble marble, rise 75 feet high on either side of a central fountain. Meigs modeled aspects of this room after several classical and Renaissance palaces and churches.

The museum galleries, which feature a variety of changing exhibits on the building arts, are on the Great Hall's first two levels. The long-term exhibit **Washington: Symbol and City** presents a good overview of D.C.'s development and role as a national symbol and evolving municipality. A push-button map of L'Enfant's original city plan, models of the evolving Mall, and a short video of citizens talking about Washington provide insight into the city. Artifacts include the five rejected designs for the U.S. Capitol and a copy of the 1792 letter signed by Jefferson dismissing city planner L'Enfant for refusing to take orders from the District Commissioners.

The museum offers lectures, films, and even outings to the area's architectural and construction sites. Check the website for information. The first floor has a cafe and a museum shop twice rated the "best museum shop in Washington" by the *Washington Post.* ■

Elegant arcaded galleries and marbleized columns define the cavernous Great Hall, which measures 116 by 316 feet.

National Archives

National Archives
www.archives.gov
Map p. 130
Constitution Ave. between 7th & 9th Sts. N.W.
202-357-5000
Metro: Archives—Navy Memorial; Bus: P1-2, 13A-B & F-G, X1, V8, 70-71

The somber Rotunda room is where America's Charters of Freedom are displayed for all to see.

SERVING AS THE NATION'S MEMORY BANK, THE NATIONAL Archives contains several billion pages of documents, including the original parchment copies of the Declaration of Independence, the U.S. Constitution, and the Bill of Rights. John Russell Pope, architect of the Jefferson Memorial, designed the distinguished 1935 building expressly for the purpose of housing these all-important manifestos. In fact it was Jefferson, author of the Declaration, who first voiced concern about the deterioration of the national records.

Ringed with 72 massive Corinthian columns, Pope's grand neoclassic edifice takes up a whole city block. Bas-reliefs decorate the pediments atop the north and south porticos. The 39 limestone steps that front the south portico on Constitution Avenue represent the 39 signers of the Constitution. The foot-thick bronze doors at the top of the stairs soar 40 feet high.

Inside, the echoing, semicircular **Rotunda,** which recently underwent major renovation, rises to a 75-foot-high dome. New York artist Barry Faulkner painted the two large 1930s murals decorating the Rotunda. "The Constitution," on the right side, depicts James Madison presenting the document to George Washington. "The Declaration of Independence," on the left, shows Thomas Jefferson submitting the proclamation to John Hancock, presiding officer of the Continental Congress.

VISITING

The low-lit Rotunda is where you can view the United States' most important documents: the **Charters of Freedom.** Each sheet of the Declaration of Independence, the U.S. Constitution, and the Bill of Rights lies in a new state-of-the-art case that fiercely protects the document against air and moisture. The cases allow all four pages of the Constitution to be shown at the same time. At night, and in the event of an emergency, the documents are retracted into a deep vault for safekeeping.

In cases flanking the Charters of Freedom, a changing selection of other milestone documents related to the creation of the United States is presented along with information about their origin and impact. **Special documents** such as the Magna Carta and the Emancipation Proclamation also are on display, some rotated throughout the year.

The interactive exhibit **Public Vaults** presents stories of how various kinds of records in the National Archives "stacks"—documents, maps, photos, and films—are used by the federal government, organizations, and individual citizens to clarify historical events, investigate mysteries, make documentaries, and pursue family history and genealogy.

Every few months, the Archives presents fresh exhibits in a new space called the **O'Brien Gallery**. The focus ranges from themed photographic displays to selected holdings from the Presidential libraries and other museums. The **McGowan Theater** screens short films about the Archives, produced by the Discovery Channel and NOVA, every 20 minutes throughout the day. The **Boeing Learning Center** offers a variety of programs that introduce children, teachers, and other adults to the methods of document-based research *(closed Sun. & federal holidays)*.

The Archives preserve for posterity more than 18 million maps, aerial photographs, and charts; 9 million still photos; hundreds of thousands of films, videos, and sound recordings; and many other files and artifacts. The National

ETERNAL VIGILANCE
IS THE PRICE OF LIBERTY

In search of guidance outside the National Archives

Archives and Records Administration, established in 1934 to oversee what to save, deems less than 2 percent of the federal records worthy of permanent storage.

Representing more than 200 years of history, the repository is creating a rich paper trail. Among the original treasures are the Louisiana Purchase Treaty, the Emancipation Proclamation, Mathew Brady's Civil War photographs, Robert Peary's polar expedition journals, Dust Bowl photographs, Indian treaties, recordings of FDR's fireside chats, captured German records and Japanese surrender documents from World War II, and Nixon's letter of resignation.

The Archives is popular among scholars, historians, and researchers, who are welcome to use the research facilities here and in College Park, Maryland. Alex Haley used slave ship manifests in researching his novel *Roots*. Opened in 1994, the Maryland branch is the largest archival facility in the world. ■

Newseum

Newseum
www.newseum.org
Map p. 130
555 Pennsylvania Ave., N.W.
888-639-7386
Metro: Archives–Navy Memorial; Bus: P1-6, 13B & F, X1

THE NEWSEUM, AN ARRAY OF FAST-PACED EXHIBITS THAT convey the nature of modern journalism, has brought a new energy to Pennsylvania Avenue in the shape of an elaborate building that lies near the U.S. Capitol, amid the buildings of "official" Washington.

The original Newseum, a project of the Freedom Forum, opened in 1997 in Rosslyn, Virginia. It became such a hit—drawing more than 2 million visitors in its first five years—that planning soon began to build a bigger facility in downtown Washington. The new Newseum, opening in early 2008, shares the block-long building with apartments, a conference center, and a three-level restaurant, "The Source," featuring the cuisine of noted chef Wolfgang Puck. The **terrace** offers panoramic views of the Capitol and the National Mall.

Emblazoned on the outside of the building is a 74-foot-high marble engraving of the First Amendment, which guarantees press freedom. As you enter the 90-foot-high **Great Hall of News,** images of historical and current news events are projected on a wall-size screen.

The museum has 14 galleries of exhibits on the history of the press; news traditions in more than 90 countries; milestones in the growth of radio, television, and Internet news; photojournalism; and behind-the-scenes looks at how the media have reported major events such as the fall of the Berlin Wall and the September 11 terrorist attacks on the U. S. One gallery draws from the museum's collection of more than 30,000 newspapers spanning five centuries.

The interactive displays and other programs allow visitors to cast themselves in the various roles of news producers or serve as audience members for news programs hosted in the Newseum's **TV studio and theaters.** ■

An artist's rendering of the exterior of the Newseum, scheduled to be completed in early 2008

More places to visit downtown

FREEDOM PLAZA

The frequent venue of free concerts, popular rallies, and ethnic festivals, this granite plaza is anchored by an equestrian statue of Casimir Pulaski, the Polish nobleman who fought for America in the Revolutionary War and was mortally wounded at the siege of Savannah. The plaza offers a sweeping view down Pennsylvania Avenue to the U.S. Capitol. Inlaid in bronze on the ground are L'Enfant's 1791 city plan, as are outlines for the Congress House and President's Palace.

Map p. 130 Pennsylvania Ave. between 13th & 14th Sts., N.W. Metro: Metro Center

MARY MCLEOD BETHUNE COUNCIL HOUSE

Now a national historic site, this former residence of educator Bethune (1875–1955), who founded Bethune-Cookman College in Daytona Beach, Florida, and the National Council of Negro Women, stores and displays artifacts pertaining to African American women's history. In addition, the house museum is decorated with Bethune's original furnishings and photographs.

www.nps.gov/mamc Map p. 130 1318 Vermont Ave., N.W. 202-673-2402 Closed Sun. Metro: McPherson Square

NATIONAL THEATRE

The sixth theater erected on this site since 1835, the National Theatre can claim to be Washington's oldest continuously operating theater. The current theater replaced an ornate five-story structure in 1922. The sumptuous decor includes dazzling chandeliers and the satin brocaded stage curtain. Unlike most large modern theaters, the mezzanine and balcony are close to the stage, giving the space an intimate feel for theatergoers. Lavish Broadway and pre-Broadway shows and other presentations are staged here, many starring well known actors of stage and screen.

www.nationaltheatre.org Map p. 130 1321 Pennsylvania Ave., N.W. 202-628-6161 Metro: Federal Triangle, Metro Center

OLD POST OFFICE

This castlelike building was erected in the 1890s as headquarters for the U.S. Post Office. A group of preservationists prevented its demolition in the 1970s, and after several years of renovation it reopened as a spacious pavilion of government offices, retail stores, and eateries. For one of the best views in the downtown area, take the elevator to the ninth-floor exhibit room, then follow the signs to an elevator that takes you to the top of the tower.

www.nps.gov/opot Map p. 130 Pennsylvania Ave. & 12th St., N.W. 202-606-8691 Metro: Federal Triangle

CARNEGIE LIBRARY

In 1899 Andrew Carnegie donated $682,000 to build this main library and three additional branches in Washington. The classic white marble beaux arts-style structure was completed in 1903 and served as the city's central library until 1972. Today it houses the Historical Society of Washington, which operates a research

Performers entertain the lunchtime crowd at the Old Post Office Pavilion.

Around the world in more than 80 steps: A 100-foot-diameter map of the world graces the U. S. Navy Memorial plaza.

library. The building is also used for performances, exhibits, classes, and various special events organized by the National Music Center, aimed at showcasing both national and local acts.
www.historydc.org Map p. 130 801 K St., N.W., at Mount Vernon Square 202-383-1850 Metro: Mt. Vernon Square/7th St., Gallery Place/Chinatown

MARIAN KOSHLAND SCIENCE MUSEUM OF THE NATIONAL ACADEMY OF SCIENCES

This 5,700 square-foot museum that opened in April 2004 provides insight into scientific issues at the core of many of the nation's public policy decisions. Interactive exhibits explore global warming, the wonders of science, and the universe, and emerging health threats from infectious diseases.
www.koshland-science-museum.org Map p. 130 500 E St., N.W. 202-334-1201 $ Closed Tues. Metro: Gallery Place/Chinatown, Judiciary Square

U.S. NAVY MEMORIAL & NAVAL HERITAGE CENTER

Situated directly behind the National Archives, this small center contains artifacts, photographs, a gift shop, and changing exhibits that highlight U.S. naval history and compiles data on sea service veterans. A 242-seat theater screens the films *At Sea* and *A Day in the Life of the Blue Angels.* Outside, the circular memorial features a 7-foot bronze statue of "The Lone Sailor" and a correctly oriented granite map of the world. Bronze relief sculptures of famous events in naval history ring the perimeter of the memorial.
www.lonesailor.org Map p. 130 701 Pennsylvania Ave., N.W. 202-737-2300 Closed Sun. March–Oct., Sun.–Mon. Nov.–Feb. Metro: Archives–Navy Memorial

WARNER THEATRE

A block east of the National Theatre, the Warner Theatre started life in 1924 as a silent-movie palace and vaudeville stage. From the mid-1940s to the late 1960s, it only presented movies. Thereafter it functioned mainly as a rock concert venue until eventually being shut down completely. It finally reopened in 1992, after being refurbished with dazzling crystal, red velvet, and gold leaf. The theater now hosts a varied program of established dance and theater companies.
www.warnertheatre.com Map p. 130 13th & E Sts. 202-783-4000 Metro: Federal Triangle, Metro Center ■

Cobbled streets, redbrick row houses, and mule-drawn canal boats elicit Georgetown's historic past. Come evening, the city's young and trendy flock to the neighborhood's buzzing bars, clubs, and restaurants.

Georgetown

Cobblestones of Georgetown

Georgetown

WASHINGTON'S POSHEST SQUARE MILE IS A HIGH-OCTANE COCKTAIL OF cultural refinement and giddy nightlife. While side streets exhibit elegant federal and Victorian architecture, Wisconsin Avenue and M Street inject excitement with boutiques, bars, and restaurants.

The PNC Bank at the corner of Wisconsin and M marks Georgetown's center.

Georgetown began life as a tobacco inspection and shipment port at the confluence of Rock Creek and the Potomac, the highest navigable point on the river, on a 795-acre tract acquired by Scottish immigrant Ninian Beall in 1703. The Maryland Assembly established a town there in the 1750s and named it for George II. After independence, when the country was planning its federal city, Georgetown had become a thriving trade center, with lordly merchants' houses rising on the hill and artisans' houses and warehouses dotting the riverside. The new city proved a boon to Georgetown's silversmiths, cabinetmakers, and other craftspeople, who did a brisk business fitting the White House and other federal buildings. During the Civil War, Georgetown's significant black community made it an important Underground Railroad stop.

In 1871 the city of Washington annexed Georgetown. By then the little town needed the capital more than the reverse. The advent

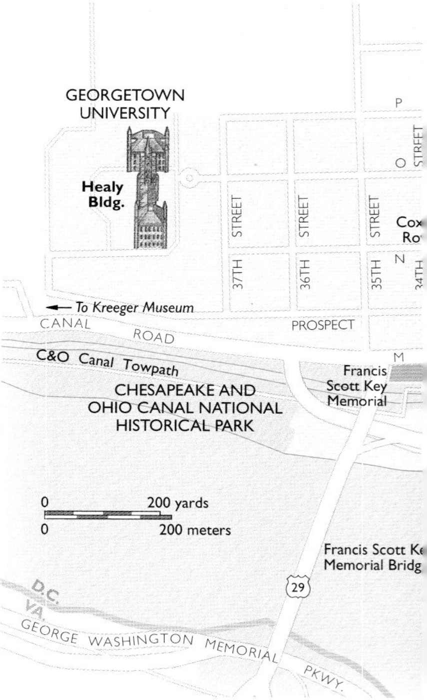

of the railroad and steam power had greatly diminished the importance of the C&O canal and thus Georgetown at its eastern end. In the first half of the 20th century, Georgetown lost the cachet of its early years; it functioned primarily as industrial muscle for Washington, its foundry and mills supplying iron, paper, and coal. During Roosevelt's administration, white-collar workers began moving back into Georgetown; then, in 1950, Congress declared it a national historic district, speeding its restoration and return to fashion.

Rock Creek and the Potomac River form Georgetown's eastern and southern borders; to the west lies Georgetown University and north the hill on which Dumbarton Oaks sits. In these blocks have lived members of such clans as the Washingtons, Lees, and Kennedys. Today diplomats, politicians, journalists, and socialites walk shady brick sidewalks and party in book- and art-filled houses, lubricating the wheels of government, business, and culture. ■

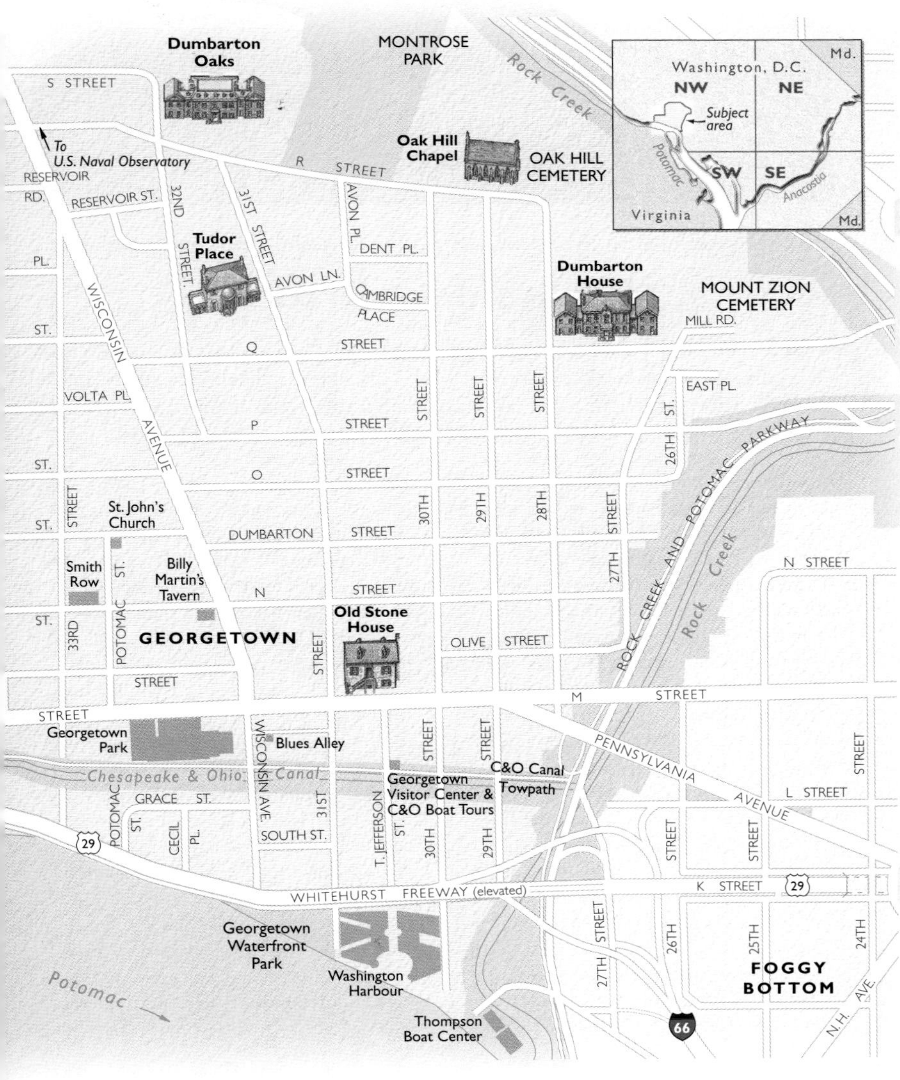

The federal-style town houses of Cox's Row typify the neighborhood's elegant architecture.

Brick sidewalk tour

With its inviting brick sidewalks, tree-lined streets, and historic architecture, Georgetown was made for the leisurely stroller. You can try seeing the city's oldest neighborhood by car, but traffic moves slowly on the narrow streets, some of which are still cobbled and veined with trolley tracks. Better to leave the car behind.

If you drive in, you can find street parking, but it may take a while, especially on the weekends. The network of streets north of M Street is your best bet for parking, though you should pay attention to the signs—most streets are zoned for two-hour parking from 7 a.m. to 9 p.m. (except Sunday). There are several parking lots along M Street and below the canal. Metro buses service M Street and Wisconsin Avenue. You can also walk from the Foggy Bottom–GWU Metro—just over a half mile to the eastern edge of Georgetown.

If you do start from the Metro, you'll head west on Pennsylvania Avenue. Across the bridge, Pennsylvania feeds into M Street, Georgetown's main avenue for shopping, dining, and partying. Spring and summer evenings, the ten-block stretch from here to the Francis Scott Key Bridge is a steady parade of the chic, the casual, and the grungy. While the shops tend to be upscale, the bars, dance floors, and some restaurants cater to a young crowd, liberally supplied by Georgetown and George Washington Universities. A longstanding favorite restaurant on the east end of M, **La Chaumière** *(2813 M St., 202-338-1784)* features French provincial cuisine; hanging brass pans and a central fireplace give a rural ambience, nicely contrasting with the busyness outside.

Continue west on M to the **Old Stone House** ❶ *(3051 M St., 202-895-6070, closed Mon.–Tues.)*, one of the oldest structures in the city. A craftsman named Christopher Layman built the first floor of the three-story house of local fieldstones in 1765, probably as both home and shop. A legend, later disproved, that George Washington had a headquarters here helped preserve the house. In 1953 the National Park Service acquired the property, restored it, and opened it to the public in 1960. The ground floor has a shop with replicas of 18th-century tools and a kitchen with cast-iron stove. On the second floor, built

Casual posh: Georgetowners relax on shady sidewalks.

by the next owner, you'll find an oak-paneled dining room, a parlor, and bedrooms.

Cross M Street and head downhill on Thomas Jefferson Street to the eastern terminus of the **C&O Canal ❷,** a muddy-bottomed, shallow waterway, bordered by a towpath, that served as a key shipping link in the 19th century. Originally slated to stretch 460 miles to Pittsburgh and connect with the

See area map pp. 146–47
- M and 29th Sts. (Metro: Foggy Bottom–GWU)
- 2 miles
- 2 hours
- St. John's Church

NOT TO BE MISSED
- Old Stone House
- Washington Harbour
- Cox's Row

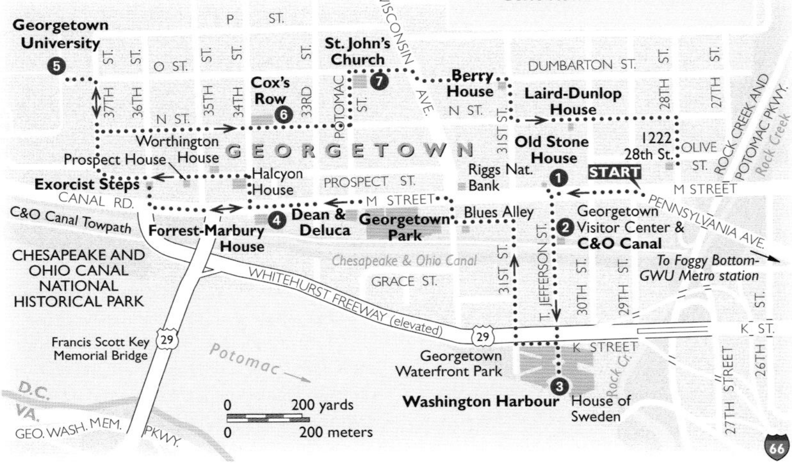

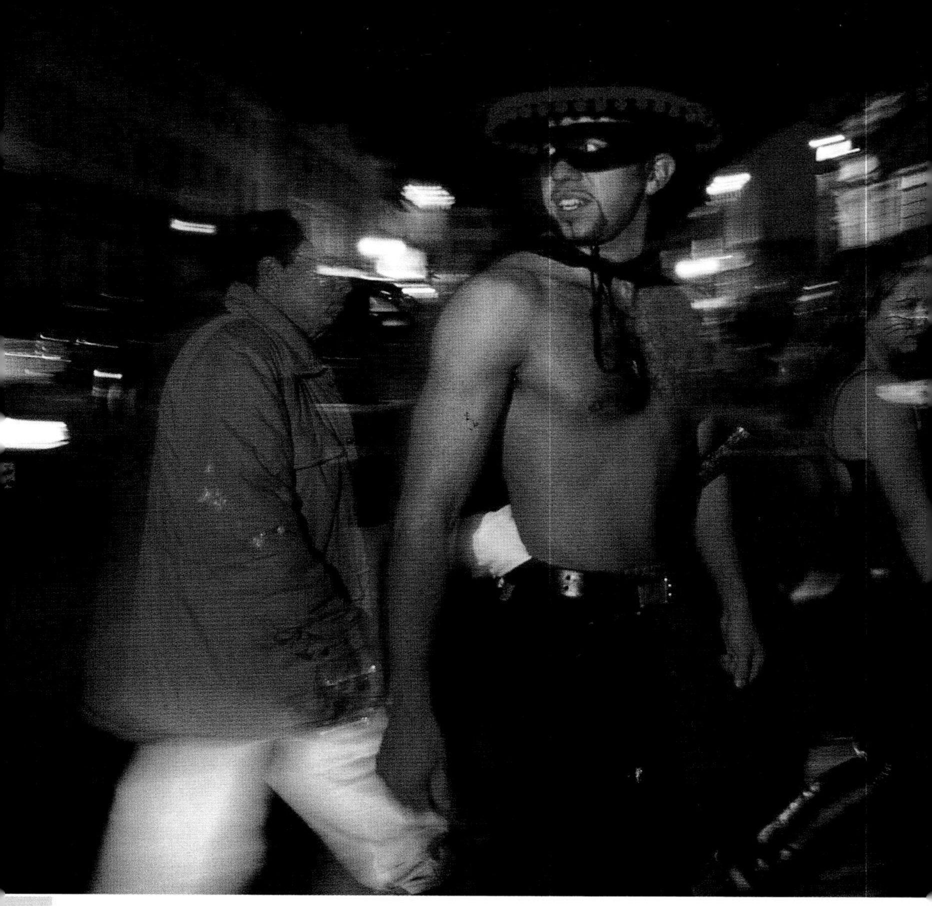

Ohio River, the Chesapeake and Ohio Canal, begun in 1828, made it only 185 miles up the Potomac to Cumberland, Maryland, where work stopped in 1850. From April through October you can take a scenic ride *(fare)* on a replica 19th-century canalboat, starting from the Georgetown Visitor Center *(1057 Thomas Jefferson St., 202-653-5190)*. A mule-drawn ride is a nice way to while away an hour.

Don't miss the small brick row houses that run along the canal just off Thomas Jefferson Street; they were built after the Civil War as homes for laborers. A few are now Asian take-out restaurants.

Go from the old to the new at the bottom of the hill by crossing K Street under the Whitehurst Freeway; in front of you spreads **Washington Harbour ❸,** a 1980s complex of offices, apartments, shops, and restaurants. At the entrance stands J. Seward Johnson's realistic sculpture, "Let's Just Skip the Meeting." The Harbour offers views of the Potomac, Roosevelt Island, the Kennedy Center, Watergate, and the high rises of Rosslyn, Virginia, across the river.

The sleek glass box neighboring the Harbour is the **House of Sweden** *(901 30th St., N.W.)*. Opened in 2006, it houses Sweden's embassy and business interests, with tours available *(closed Mon.–Tues.)*.

Next head up 31st Street. On your right, just below M, **Cannon's Seafood** has supplied locals with fresh fish since 1937. The alleyway across the street from Cannon's leads to **Blues Alley** *(1073 Wisconsin Ave., 202-337-4141)*, which may look like a dive outside but is actually Washington's swankiest jazz joint. On nights when a big name is in town, you might see 50 people lined up just hoping for no-shows on the reservation list. Definitely

Zorro and other revelers make the streets of Georgetown the place to be and be seen on Halloween.

call ahead, and expect to pay a hefty cover charge—well worth it for the intimate setting.

Turn right from the alley onto Wisconsin Avenue and walk back up to M Street. This intersection is the area's busiest; the gold dome on the ornate old Farmers and Mechanics Branch of the PNC Bank serves as a landmark. Turn left heading west on M to the nearly block-long glitzy mall called **Georgetown Park** *(3222 M St.);* it has upmarket shops and restaurants on three levels, with skylit courtyards and chuckling fountains.

Continue west on M until you reach No. 3276, **Dean and Deluca,** a gourmet food shop where you can pick up lunch. Erected in 1865, the building sits on a site that also held markets in the 18th century.

A little farther down the street, just before Key Bridge, you'll come to the 1788 **Forrest-Marbury House** ❹ (now the Embassy of Ukraine). Here George Washington met with local landowners in 1791 to work out the agreement on the sale of their land to create the new federal city. Gen. Uriah Forrest owned the house then; in 1800–1835 it belonged to William Marbury of the landmark *Marbury* v. *Madison* case, in which the Supreme Court established the doctrine of judicial review.

For a small detour into cinematic history, cross to the north side of M Street and walk west a short distance. Tucked away near a gas station, an eerily familiar 75-step stone stairway stretches upward. Known as the **Exorcist Steps,** the stairs played a prominent role in the 1973 horror classic, *The Exorcist.*

Prospect Street has some of Georgetown's oldest and most impressive houses. For an easier ascent to Prospect, go back east on M and turn left onto 34th Street. At the corner of 34th and Prospect stands the classic Georgian-style **Halcyon House** (1786), built by Benjamin Stoddert, the first secretary of the Navy and an important Georgetown landowner. A few buildings away is **Worthington House,** No. 3425, built in 1798 by prominent lawyer John Thomson Mason. Note the 24-paned windows lining both main floors. Just past 35th Street look for **Prospect House** (1788), No. 3508, another imposing Georgian, home of a 19th-century shipping merchant. Much of its structure and impressive gardens lie hidden behind a brick wall.

Prospect Street ends at 37th Street, the eastern edge of **Georgetown University** ❺, whose main entrance is at 37th and O. The Gothic-spired university is best known for its schools of medicine, law, and foreign service, and its basketball team.

From 37th, turn back east on N; across 34th on the north side runs a line of five stately brick town houses known as **Cox's Row** ❻, built in 1805 by John Cox, Mayor of Georgetown. Down the block, in 1957–1961, Sen. John F. Kennedy and his wife, Jacqueline, lived at 3307 N Street, a three-story house with a fanlight and black shutters. On the corner of Potomac and O, Anglican services are still held at **St. John's Church** ❼, opened in 1804, and designed by William Thornton, first architect of the Capitol.

East of Wisconsin Avenue lie several more blocks of elegant 19th-century houses. Bare brick alternates with stucco facades painted in muted shades of blue, gray, red, and yellow. Victorian bay windows and turrets are much in evidence. At the corner of Dumbarton and 31st Streets look for **Berry House,** built in 1810 when the street level was several feet higher. As a result, the front door stands unusually far above the street.

Walk one block south to N Street and turn left to see a noteworthy block. On your right is No. 3038, built in 1805, the longtime home of statesman Averell Harriman and his wife, Pamela. The large brick town house has a lovely arched doorway and odd, shingled dormers.

In No. 3017 across the street, Jackie Kennedy lived for several months after the assassination of President Kennedy. Almost directly facing it stands the 40-room **Laird-Dunlop House,** No. 3014, built in 1799. Robert Todd Lincoln, the only son of Abraham Lincoln to survive into adulthood, lived here from 1918 to 1926. Especially notable is the raised fanlight doorway.

If you stroll on to 28th and Olive Streets, you'll come upon one of Georgetown's oldest and smallest houses. The tiny wooden cottage at 1222 28th St. was built sometime before the Revolution, though the date is uncertain. Very little has changed in its basic structure. ■

Glitzy Washington Harbour, a splash both day and night

Georgetown crawl

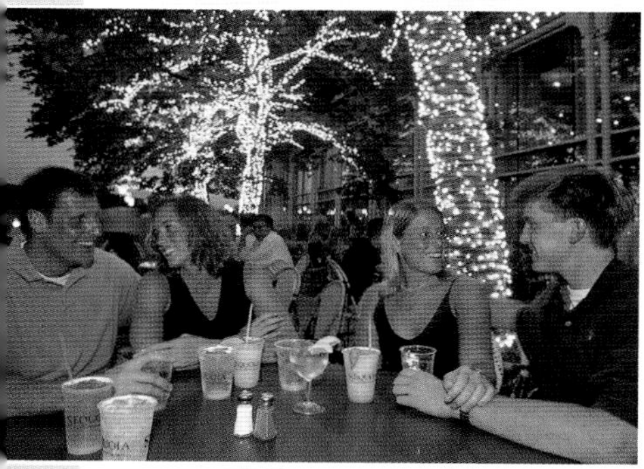

Before Adams Morgan and U Street became hip, anyone seeking nightlife went to Georgetown. Though club options have now spread to those and other locations in the city and suburbs, Georgetown still reigns supreme as party central. If you've a mind to join the fun, be aware that the revelry can be excessive at times, particularly on Halloween and the rare occasions the Redskins win the Superbowl. Traffic woes—Key Bridge, the main feeder from Virginia, is a solid jam on weekend evenings—and parking problems don't deter the crowds along M Street. Cabbing here makes the most sense; the fare for two from downtown costs about as much as a single movie ticket.

There are many options to choose from. A sampler: The first thing you may notice when you enter **J. Paul's** (3218 M St., 202-333-3450) restaurant and tavern is the oyster shucking at the street-side raw bar. J. Paul's also features crab cakes and steaks and a 100-year-old mahogany bar. Down the street, **Clyde's of Georgetown** (3236 M St., 202-333-9180), with its interesting daily specials, old stone fireplace, vintage model planes, and gold record commemorating the 1976 hit song "Afternoon Delight"—inspired by Clyde's afternoon appetizers—offers a delicious dining experience. For simpler fare such as pizza, locals and students hit **The Tombs** (1226 36th St., 202-337-6668), a block from Georgetown University, beneath the upscale restaurant **1789.**

Mr. Smith's (3104 M St., 202-333-3104) has a piano bar, a garden patio, and a devoted crowd of regular patrons. **Nathan's** (3150 M St., 202-338-2000) offers a bar in the front and quieter dining in the back room. Its weekly "Q&A Café" lunches (reservations required) bring in well-known journalists, political analysts, and others for interviews.

If you want to find a table on the weekend at Georgetown's hot spots, arrive early. ■

The Pebble Garden

Dumbarton Oaks

Dumbarton Oaks
www.doaks.org
- Map p. 147
- Garden entrance, 31st & R Sts., N.W.; museum, on 32nd bet. R & S
- 202-339-6401
- Closed Mon., federal holidays, & in inclement weather
- Gardens: $$ March–Oct., free in winter
- Metro: Dupont Circle, Foggy Bottom; Bus: 30-36, D1-6,

AN ANTIQUE PROVENÇAL FOUNTAIN, A MINIATURE ROMAN amphitheater, and a 16th-century French-style arbor are among the many treasures awaiting you in Dumbarton Oaks's terraced gardens. Spring to fall, the gardens offer an ever changing display that includes early blooming dogwoods, magnolia blossoms, and cherries, peonies and roses, day lilies and chrysanthemums.

Presiding over the gardens is a federal-style house acquired in 1920 by Mildred and Robert Woods Bliss, stepsiblings and antiquities collectors who married and traveled widely in the Foreign Service. They hired the architectural firm McKim, Mead and White to renovate and enlarge the house for their extensive library and collection of Byzantine and pre-Columbian art. In 1940 they conveyed the property and museum to Harvard University, though they remained actively involved in Dumbarton Oaks until their deaths (Robert in 1962, Mildred in 1969). In 1944 a series of informal conferences held here laid the foundation for the establishment of the United Nations.

Today the main part of the house functions as Harvard's center for Byzantine studies and is not open to the public. Visitors are allowed into the gardens, which have only afternoon hours. The museum and music room, along

with a museum shop, are usually open to the public but were closed temporarily for renovation of the main building. Check the website for updates, and if you visit once they have reopened, use the entrance on 32nd Street.

VISITING

The 10-acre formal gardens, designed by landscape architect Beatrix Farrand, spread across a gentle hill and down to a wooded valley. Ornate ironwork and stonework—in the form of gates and balconies, fountains and urns, pillars and stairways—adorn the grounds. Brick paths lined by boxwoods and perennial borders lead from one garden to the next, and little trellised bowers offer places to sit and admire the sound of birdsong, scent of flowers, and garden aesthetics.

A self-guided tour brochure, available at the entrance, highlights the gardens and plantings. Inside the gates to the right stands an old Katsura tree, its limbs almost touching the ground. Head up the path to the early 19th-century **Orangery;** a pre-Civil War fig tree climbs its walls. Through here you access the main gardens. Outside, to the right, a tremendous beech presides over the **Beech Terrace.** Next, steps take you down to the **Rose Garden,** planted with nearly 1,000 varieties of roses. Just below are gardens with fountains and a wisteria-draped arbor based on a 16th-century French design. At the property's edge, a winding walkway skirts the reflecting pool of Lovers' Lane and its small amphitheater. Farther north the garden becomes less formal, with flowering cherry trees, a hillside of golden forsythia, and views of Dumbarton Oaks Park, given by the Blisses to the National Park Service and now part of Rock Creek Park.

Head back uphill to the **Ellipse,** an oval formed by a double ring of hornbeams, pruned to a uniform 16 feet, enclosing a Provençal fountain. Up the steps lies another landscaping masterpiece: **The Pebble Garden** is composed of rounded stones embedded on edge to create a terrace of varying textures; espaliered magnolias and wisteria vines bedeck the walls. Walk on past the pool to the grassy sweep of the **North Vista,** behind the main part of the house.

Filled with natural light, the museum galleries display Byzantine and pre-Columbian art objects. The Byzantine collection includes 6th-century ecclesiastical silver and beautiful 13th-century mosaic icons. ■

Tudor Place Historic House and Garden

Tudor Place
www.tudorplace.org
Map p. 147
Visitor entrance, 1644 31st St., N.W.
202-965-0400
House closed Mon.
House tour $$, garden tour $
Metro: Dupont Circle, Foggy Bottom; Bus: D1-6, G2

SIX GENERATIONS OF THE PETER FAMILY, RELATIVES TO George Washington and Robert E. Lee, lived in this handsome neoclassic house. During those years (1805–1984), the country passed through many wars, two of them waged just outside the Peters' door.

Martha Custis, daughter of George Washington's stepdaughter, married Thomas Peter, son of Georgetown's first mayor. In 1805 the Peters purchased an 8.5-acre city block in Georgetown Heights; to design a home there, they hired William Thornton, architect of the Capitol—the building Martha would watch burn from a window of the house in 1814. The Peters' daughter Britannia inherited Tudor Place in 1854. A Southern sympathizer during the Civil War, she allowed Union officers to board at the house to prevent its becoming a hospital. In 1984 the house was transferred to the Tudor Place Foundation.

The one-hour guided tours of Tudor Place begin with a look at Thornton's design. On the south lawn, a domed "temple" portico projects from the two-story stuccoed main building, while one-story hyphens connect the two wings, lending a pleasing symmetry. The curving portico creates a convex wall of windows, which can be lifted to allow a breeze to circulate. All the furniture, silver, porcelain, and decorative objects are original, some pieces acquired from an auction at Mount Vernon in the early 19th century. Not limited to one period, the furnishings reflect 180 years of family continuity. The restored Pierce-Arrow automobile out in the garage, for example, was maintained by Armistead Peter III from 1919 until his death in 1983.

The 5.5 acres of gardens include a sweeping south lawn, woodlands, and a formal federal-style garden on the house's north side. Among highlights are trees and roses planted in the early 19th century, and an old-fashioned "flower knot" pattern of English boxwoods and pathways. ■

The south-facing temple portico presides over a serene sweep of lawn, set apart from the hubbub of Georgetown.

Dumbarton House

Dumbarton House was built on a hill high above Rock Creek in the first years of the 19th century, when only a few large houses dotted the port of Georgetown. Originally called Cedar Hill, the federal-style brick house's second owner, Charles Carroll, changed its name in 1813 to Belle Vue; he sheltered Dolley Madison here the following year, after she fled the burning White House. In 1915, to make way for the extension of Q Street into Georgetown, the house had to be put on rollers and moved approximately 100 feet north, to its current location.

In 1928, the National Society of the Colonial Dames bought the house (which would become its headquarters), and renamed it Dumbarton House after the Rock of Dumbarton, the tract that originally encompassed much of present-day Georgetown. With great attention to detail, the Colonial Dames—one of the world's largest private historical preservation societies—restored the house to its early 1800s appearance.

The guided 45-minute tour here covers the parlor, dining room, library, music room, and three bedrooms, with furnishings primarily from the federal period, including furniture such as a mahogany sewing work table, silver, ceramics, textiles (including a carriage cloak belonging to Martha Washington's granddaughter), and paintings by artists such as Charles Willson Peale. Out back, the small formal courtyard and garden add a grace note to the estate. ■

Dumbarton House
www.dumbartonhouse.org
Map p. 147
2715 Q St., N.W.
202-337-2288
Closed. Sun.–Mon.; and federal holidays
$
Metro: Dupont Circle, Foggy Bottom; Bus: D1-6, G2

Oak Hill Cemetery

Occupying some of the city's finest real estate, this 1849 cemetery rambles over a hill above Rock Creek Park. William Wilson Corcoran, founder of the Corcoran Gallery, bought 15 acres from George Corbin Washington, a great nephew of the first President. The following year he gave the parcel to the new congressionally established cemetery company, and James Renwick, architect of the Smithsonian Castle, designed the iron entrance gates and the English Gothic-style chapel.

At the attractive brick and sandstone gatehouse, you can buy a map showing the locations of 68 graves and mausoleums, including those of W. W. Corcoran, John Marbury, Edwin Stanton (Lincoln's secretary of war), Dean Acheson (Truman's secretary of state), and members of the Peter family from nearby Tudor Place. Also buried here is Philip Graham, publisher of the *Washington Post,* as is his widow Katharine, his successor at the *Post* until her death in 2001.

A murky overcast day makes a good time for wandering through this crowded village of the dead, with its elaborate Victorian monuments and obelisks. Winding paths circle knolls that offer views of adjoining Montrose Park, Rock Creek, and the parkway. Hiding behind trees and high walls, the property at the corner of 28th and R Streets is another Georgetown mansion with a long past: Evermay was built in the 1790s by Scotsman Samuel Davidson with funds acquired from selling some of his extensive property to the new federal city. Family members lie buried in Oak Hill. ■

Oak Hill Cemetery
Map p. 147
3001 R St., N.W.
202-337-2835
Closed Sat., holidays, & in inclement weather
Metro: Dupont Circle, Foggy Bottom; Bus: D1-6, G2

Famous denizens of Georgetown

By day, the power of national government is exercised in the monumental edifices clustered around Washington's Mall and at both ends of Pennsylvania Avenue. At night, some of the action moves to Georgetown, residence down the decades of political leaders, media heavies, diplomats, legal minds, writers, and society doyennes—names in the news past and present. In elegant 19th-century houses, the House or Senate bill that seemed doomed by day may be quietly revived over cocktails or at a formal dinner party, where fine wines and informed conversation are equally savored.

Even Hollywood celebrities have found their way to Georgetown, though at times reluctantly. Elizabeth Taylor, married briefly to Virginia Sen. John Warner, has said she thought the couple would live on his hunt country estate, near Middleburg, where the talk centered on horses. Instead, she found herself in Warner's Georgetown house at 3240 S Street, where dinnertime chat explored the ins and outs of arms control and tax bills.

As a bachelor, Sen. John F. Kennedy lived in a Victorian town house at 1528 31st Street. In fact, John and Jackie first met at a Georgetown dinner party in 1951. He later claimed that he made up his mind at that party that she was "the one," though they dated only sporadically over the next year. He finally proposed, and a year later, he and his bride moved to 3271 P Street. President-elect Kennedy purchased the three-story brick town house at 3307 N Street in 1957, while Jackie was in the hospital giving birth to their first child, Caroline. Tastefully austere, the 1811 house occupies an especially handsome street of classic federal-style homes.

After her husband's death, Jackie Kennedy and her children moved temporarily to 3038 N Street at the invitation of statesman W. Averell Harriman. (His widow, Pamela, a celebrated hostess and Democratic party activist, later became President Clinton's Ambassador to France.) The former First Lady soon bought the house across the street at 3017 N Street, but departed for New York after only a few months to escape the busloads of gawkers.

Just up the street at 3014 N Street stands another grand federal-style mansion with a presidential link. Built in 1799, it was the home of Robert Todd Lincoln, the 16th President's oldest son, a railroad lawyer who served as secretary of war and minister to Great Britain. He lived here until his death in 1926. The current owners, a prominent newspaper couple, consider themselves "caretakers" of the 40-room property.

The top ranks of government have always been well represented in Georgetown. Dean Acheson, President Truman's secretary of state, lived in the Georgian town house at 2805 P Street. Here Acheson hosted a farewell luncheon for the president on his last day in office. A four-story town house at 3018 Dumbarton Street is the one-time home of Supreme Court Justice Felix Frankfurter. Later Henry Kissinger, secretary of state under Presidents Nixon and Ford, briefly rented it.

Washington Post owner Katharine Graham, once called "the most powerful woman in America," lived in the mansion at 2920 R Street. Set well back from the street, it is approached by a semicircular gravel drive—a real Georgetown luxury—that gives it the look of a French country estate.

Writers, too, have found Georgetown's vibrant society congenial. In 1922 Sinclair Lewis moved to Washington from his Minnesota hometown, calling it the perfect place to write, "with neither the country nor lake tempting one out to play, as in Minnesota, nor the noise and phone calls of New York." As soon as he made his fortune with *Main Street,* which later won him the Nobel Prize in literature, he moved to a stately Georgetown house, at 3028 Q Street. In the early 1960s, Katherine Anne Porter reportedly completed her acclaimed novel *Ship of Fools* while a boarder at 3106 P Street; with the money it made her she bought her dream house complete with lawns and a rose garden—outside of Georgetown. ■

Washington Post owner Katharine Graham lived in the above house (R & 30th Sts., N.W.) from 1947 until her death in July 2001. Sen. John F. Kennedy and his wife, Jackie, lived for a brief time at 3321 Dent Place (below) in 1954; Kennedy bought the house at 3307 N Street (right) in 1957.

More places to visit in & around Georgetown

Tending bar at Martin's

BILLY MARTIN'S TAVERN

Opened by William G. Martin, a Georgetown University sports star who also played professional baseball in the early part of the 20th century, Billy Martin's Tavern has been operating at the southwest corner of N Street and Wisconsin Avenue since 1933. Four generations of Martins have managed the restaurant, and many of the staff have been here for years. Stop in for a draft or a meal and imbibe this Georgetown tradition.

Wood floors, dark paneling, and a friendly bar create the ambience of a European pub. Among menu offerings are crab cakes, Delmonico steaks, linguine with clam sauce, and daily home specials such as meatloaf and corned beef with cabbage. The back of the menu lists some of the politicos and celebrities that have visited or been regulars, including former Secretary of State Madeleine Albright, actress Elizabeth Taylor, and the Kennedys. Martin's serves three meals a day, with a good brunch on weekends, at moderate prices.

✉ 1264 Wisconsin Ave., N.W. ☎ 202-333-7370 🚌 Metro: Foggy Bottom, Rosslyn, then bus

KREEGER MUSEUM

Designed by Philip Johnson and Richard Foster and completed in 1967, the modernist travertine house of late philanthropist David Lloyd Kreeger and his wife, Carmen, opened in 1994 as an art museum showcasing the Kreegers' collection of 19th- and 20th-century paintings and sculptures. A chairman of GEICO insurance company, Kreeger was famous for his contributions to the city's cultural life, at various times serving as president of the National Symphony, the Washington Opera, and the Corcoran Gallery of Art.

The art collection, which the Kreegers began acquiring in 1959, includes more than 180 works by artists such as Monet, Cézanne, van Gogh, Rodin, Picasso, Miró, Munch, Kandinsky, and Chagall; among Washington artists represented are Gene Davis, Sam Gilliam, and Thomas Downing. Also on display are pieces of traditional African and Indian art. The building's spectacular **Great Hall,** with its 25-foot-high domed ceiling, was often the scene of concerts; an amateur violinist, Kreeger played his Stradivarius with such greats as Pablo Casals, Isaac Stern, and Pinchas Zukerman.

www.kreegermuseum.org ✉ 2401 Foxhall Rd., N.W., 1.5 miles N of Georgetown ☎ 202-338-3552 🕒 Closed Sun.–Mon.; visit Tues.–Fri. by tours only, reservations req.; Sat., open visits $ Donation

MOUNT ZION CEMETERY

When Mount Zion Methodist Episcopal Church realized in 1879 that it needed a place to bury its members, it leased a parcel of land on the edge of the Dumbarton Cemetery. On this site had already been buried several generations of slaves and freed blacks. The resulting Mount Zion Cemetery, now showing its age with toppled and crumbling gravestones, is Washington's oldest black burial ground. The last burial occurred here in the 1950s, and in 1975 it was designated a national historic landmark. At the back is a brick vault where slaves escaping to the North via the Underground Railroad are said to have hid.

Map p. 147 ✉ Q St., between 27th St. & the Buffalo Bridge ☎ 202-234-0148 🚌 Foggy Bottom, Dupont Circle, then bus ■

A lively mix of cultures, cuisines, lifestyles, and music awaits in the neighborhoods beyond downtown, while stately mansions preserved as embassies and museums recall 20th-century glamour days.

Dupont Circle & Adams Morgan

A local artist at work in Dupont Circle

Dupont Circle & Adams Morgan

AT THE INTERSECTION OF THREE MAJOR THOROUGHFARES, DUPONT CIRCLE anchors the city's buzzing residential neighborhoods, replete with row houses, cafés, bookstores, restaurants, and galleries.

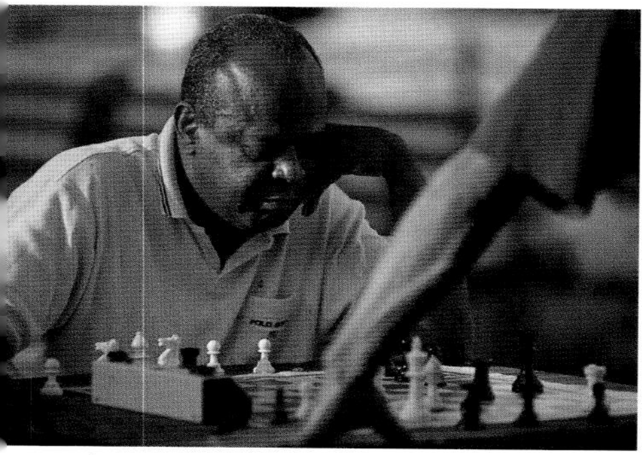

Chess match at Dupont Circle

Dupont Circle sits at the crossroads of New Hampshire, Massachusetts, and Connecticut Avenues, marking a key interface between business and residential Washington. The circle itself, centered on a marble fountain, is in constant motion, with pedestrians passing through and traffic circling around. Yet it is also a place for casual picnics, jackets-off meetings, people-watching, and general loafing. Bicycle messengers form little impromptu gatherings, chess players study their next moves, joggers pound through. In 15 minutes the scene has changed, and a new series of small dramas has begun to unfold.

Starting in the 1870s, the area, then called Pacific Circle, began developing into the most elite neighborhood in Washington. New millionaires with fortunes from mining, steel, railroads, and shipping started putting up ornate beaux arts mansions and attending receptions and musicals in one another's houses, every hostess seemingly intent on outdoing her neighbor. A newspaper reporter in the 1880s wrote that going to lavish parties at Senator William M. Stewart's "Castle" (torn down in 1901) made him feel like Marco Polo at the court of Kublai Khan. This belle epoque lasted only until the 1930s, when the stock market crash and Depression forced many of the wealthy to scale back.

Some mansions were razed, though many were sold to private clubs, organizations, and embassies; surrounding row houses became boarding establishments and apartments. In the 1960s, the area was a haven for hippies and other counterculturalists, and the circle became a focal point for marches and rallies. Development threatened many of the area's old "palaces" in the 1970s, but the efforts of preservation groups to save the neighborhood resulted in its designation as a historic district that stretches all the way to T Street.

Over the ensuing years Dupont Circle became the core of Washington's young gay community. Today the bars, restaurants, shops, and museums along the neighborhood streets attract a stimulating heterogeny of intellectuals, café-society devotees, and experimentalists of all stripes.

A residential zone of about ten blocks lies between the Dupont Circle neighborhood and the Latino enclave to the north—Adams Morgan, which centers on the intersection of Columbia Road and 18th Street, N.W. Adams Morgan has become a magnet for immigrants, artists, and young professionals, who now fill enormous apartment buildings or old brick houses and frequent the neighborhood's many restaurants and popular nightspots.

Running eastward from Adams Morgan into the Shaw neighborhood is the U Street corridor, where the black community was drawn beginning in the 1880s. This area possesses a rich legacy of music and culture—Pearl Bailey, Duke Ellington, and other greats once performed at its various theaters and clubs. Deteriorated after the 1968 riots, U Street has in recent years made a comeback, with restored theaters and new clubs, restaurants, and shops. ■

Washington, D.C.
NW
NE
SW
SE
Md.
Subject area
Potomac
Anacostia
Virginia
MOUNT PLEASANT
ADAMS MORGAN
KALORAMA
SHAW
HARVARD ST.
Mexican Cultural Institute
ADAMS MILL RD.
ONTARIO PLACE
LANIER PLACE
COLUMBIA ROAD
FULLER ST.
MOZART PL.
CALVERT ST.
EUCLID ST.
Duke Ellington Memorial Bridge
18th Street
BILTMORE ST.
District of Columbia Arts Center
MINTWOOD PLACE
Rock Cr.
16TH STREET
15TH STREET
17TH ST.
ONTARIO ROAD
CHAMPLAIN ST.
KALORAMA ROAD
CRESCENT PL.
Meridian Hill Park
Meridian International Center
W ST.
CONNECTICUT AVENUE
BELMONT ROAD
BELMONT PL.
20TH STREET
19TH STREET
18TH STREET
ASHMEAD PLACE
WYOMING AVE.
FLORIDA AVENUE
V ST.
KALORAMA ROAD
CALIFORNIA ST.
U STREET
VERNON ST.
WILLARD STREET
T STREET
To African American Civil War Memorial, Howard University, Lincoln Theatre, Mary Church Terrell House
CALIFORNIA ST.
LEROY PL.
23RD ST.
BANCROFT PLACE
SWANN ST.
NEW HAMPSHIRE AVENUE
S STREET
DECATUR PLACE
RIGGS PLACE
Conner Contemporary Art and Gallery
Scottish Rite Headquarters
R STREET
Sheridan Circle
Cosmos Club
The Phillips Collection
CORCORAN STREET
Q STREET
Anderson House
MASSACHUSETTS AVENUE
Dupont Circle
CHURCH ST.
Washington Club
P STREET
Wadsworth House
Burton Marinkovich Fine Art
O STREET
Rock Creek
22ND STREET
21ST ST.
Heurich House Museum
CONN. AVE.
N STREET
Scott Circle
RHODE ISLAND AVE.
MASS. AVE.
N ST.
0 200 yards
0 200 meters
To Metropolitan Club
M STREET
Thomas Circle

The Phillips Collection

The Phillips Collection
www.phillipscollection.org
Map p. 163
1600 21st St., N.W. (corner of 21st & Q Sts.)
202-387-2151
Closed Mon. & federal holidays
Admission to permanent collection included in fee for special exhibits ($$$) but is free on weekdays
Metro: Dupont Circle; Bus: D1-6, N2-6, L4

VISIT THE PHILLIPS COLLECTION AND YOU'LL UNDERSTAND why it's the favorite museum of many Washingtonians and regarded as one of the best small museums in the world. It has an outstanding collection of works by masters of Impressionism and American and European modern art, is situated in an intimate setting in the lively arts and residential neighborhood of Dupont Circle, and carries out a busy program of cultural and educational activities. And the attractions keep getting better. In 2006, this nongovernmental museum completed a major expansion that added galleries and other amenities to better serve visitors, students, and scholars

Begun in the 1920s by founder Duncan Phillips (1886–1966), The Phillips Collection was the first modern art museum in the United States. Its permanent holdings now include nearly 2,500 carefully chosen pieces of art from the late 19th century to the present.

One of the most charming things about the Phillips Collection is the feeling you get of touring a private home as you walk around the museum, which is still located in Phillips' 1897 Georgian

Renoir's "The Luncheon of the Boating Party" (1881) remains a highlight of the Phillips Collection.

Revival brownstone and has been expanded by compatibly scaled additions. The house gives off a comfortable, informal aura, and that effect is exactly what Phillips had in mind when, in a memorial to his recently deceased brother (James Laughlin Phillips) and father (Maj. D. Clinch Phillips), he opened up two rooms of his home in 1921 so that other art lovers could enjoy the works he and his brother had collected. After Phillips—himself an heir to the Jones and Laughlin steel fortune—married artist Marjorie Acker that same year, the couple began assembling an outstanding collection of Impressionist, Postimpressionist, and Cubist art.

In 1930, Phillips and his family moved to a new home on Foxhall Road and opened up their entire former home to the expanding collection. A new wing was added to the north side in 1960, and in the late 1980s it was renovated again. Phillip's son, Laughlin, a founder of *Washingtonian* magazine, helped guide the growth of the museum through the renovations of the 1980s.

The museum's best-known piece is Pierre-Auguste Renoir's dazzling work of impressionism, "The Luncheon of the Boating Party." It captures a moment of

Collect your own

If the Phillips stirs your desire for an original Picasso of your own, Dupont Circle, with more than two dozen galleries, is the place to shop. In recent years one gallery offered a Toulouse-Lautrec lithograph for $70,000, a Picasso painting for a mere $16,000, and a piece by Miró for under $5,000. Stop in Burton Marinkovich Fine Art (1506 21st St.), for example, and you can purchase prints and works on paper by the likes of Frankenthaler, Hockney, Motherwell, and Diebenkorn. Or check out the Kathleen Ewing Gallery (1767 P St., second floor) for vintage and contemporary photography as well as paintings and drawings. Some of the galleries specialize in African art, Inuit sculpture, and English and American crafts. To find your way around, pick up a free guide, available in any of the galleries. A consortium of 25 galleries in the area holds opening receptions on the first Friday of every month, from 5 to 8 p.m. ■

Master of color and light: Henri Matisse's "Interior with Egyptian Curtain" (1948)

Opposite: The Phillips Collection houses several larger works of post-1950s art.

leisure on the banks of the river Seine, and features a colorful mix of Renoir's friends from all walks of life.

The permanent collection also includes works by Paul Cézanne, Edgar Degas, Paul Klee, Henri Matisse, Claude Monet, Pablo Picasso, Maurice Prendergast, Paul Gauguin, Vincent van Gogh, James Abbott McNeill Whistler, Richard Diebenkorn, Elizabeth Murray, and Sean Scully.

A strong patron of emerging modern artists, Phillips collected works of many artists who had not yet become widely recognized, including Georgia O'Keeffe, Arthur Dove, John Marin, and Milton Avery. The **Rothko Room,** designed in accordance with both Mark Rothko's and Phillips' aesthetic preferences, represents a rare bond between artist and patron.

Phillips felt that artists were strongly influenced by their predecessors, and he sought to illustrate that in the museum's collection. A key link between impressionism and expressionism, he believed, was Pierre Bonnard, and today the museum has one of the largest collections of works by this artist. Phillips also acquired pieces by such 18th-century masters as El Greco, Francisco Goya, and Jean-Baptiste-Simeon Chardin to show how they affected later painters of modern art.

The latest renovation, completed in 2006, almost doubled the size of the Phillips; two-thirds of the new space is below ground, thereby preserving the character of the neighborhood.

In conjunction with the recent renovation, the museum launched The Phillips Collection Center for the Study of Modern Art, which brings together scholars from across academic fields to engage in discussion, research, and publishing of modern art.

VISITING

Some of the museum's galleries offer special exhibitions that change regularly, but selections from the permanent collection are always on display. On the first floor, take time to visit the **Music Room,** a perennial favorite, with its dark oak paneling, decorative ceiling, and carved stone and wood mantelpiece. Since 1941, Sunday afternoon concerts *(Oct.–May, free with admission)* here have been a Washington favorite.

A café and museum shop are located on the main level near the entrance. Behind the café is an **Outdoor Courtyard,** which features a sculpture by Barbara Hepworth and a specially commissioned work by Ellsworth Kelly. The museum has extended hours on Thursday evenings, when gallery talks and other special events are scheduled. ■

The Indonesian Embassy boasts 60 rooms and four stories behind its beaux arts facade.

A walk down Embassy Row

Walking west from Dupont Circle along Massachusetts Avenue takes you past the affluence and glamour of the early 1900s, when this was the fashionable neighborhood for Washington tycoons. After the Great Depression, many of the grand residences were sold to foreign delegations. Today the triangle formed by Massachusetts and Connecticut Avenues and Rock Creek holds more than 50 embassies, or about one-third of the city's total. It's about a mile from Dupont Circle to the Islamic Center, at the end of the walk, but you'll probably spend at least a good half day here if you stop for the museums. For a coffee or lunch break, you need to return to the circle; Connecticut Avenue on either side of Dupont has several good cafés and restaurants.

Start your walk a block east of Dupont Circle and take a look at the kind of structure wealthy people had in mind when they thought of the term "apartment building." On the northeast corner of 18th Street and Massachusetts Avenue stands the **National Trust for Historic Preservation ❶**, a beaux arts palace originally built in 1915 as the McCormick apartment building. The first floor contained two apartments, while five floors above each held an 11,000-square-foot apartment with six bedrooms and 14.5-foot ceilings. The most famous tenant, Andrew W. Mellon, founder of the National Gallery of Art and a U.S. secretary of the treasury, lived on the top floor from 1921 to 1937. In 1936 he paid 21 million dollars for paintings and sculptures owned by Sir Joseph Duveen, an art dealer leasing the apartment below; at the time, it was the largest art transaction on record. Robert Woods Bliss, owner of Dumbarton Oaks, also lived here in the 1920s.

Head west to the circle, where you can see more fine examples of turn-of-the-20th-century mansions that never became embassies. Now housing the Sulgrave Club *(private)*, a stalwart sorority of socially prominent Washington ladies, the circa 1900 **Wadsworth House** *(1801 Massachusetts Ave., N.W.)* was the winter residence of landowners Herbert and Martha Wadsworth of upstate New York. With a bow window facing the circle like the prow of a ship, the house is an early illustration of how a large building could be designed to fit the triangular lots around the circle.

Taking a different approach to the same problem, the Wadsworth's neighbor to the north, the ornate **Washington Club** *(private)*, fits into its wedge at 15 Dupont Circle with symmetrical wings and a concave front. Now a women's social club, the 1903 house was designed by Stanford White for Robert W. Patterson, publisher of the *Chicago Tribune*.

Standing in **Dupont Circle ②,** you can see a striking example of how L'Enfant's city plan works, with grand avenues vectoring out from the central green. In the middle of the circle is a marble fountain designed in 1921 by Daniel Chester French, who is also known for the giant statue of Lincoln in the memorial. Spilling into a large pool, an upper basin is supported by a central column surrounded by three allegorical figures representing the sea, wind, and stars—elements that Civil War naval hero Samuel Francis du Pont would have known well. Benches around the circle and grassy plots under trees are constantly in use for lounging and informal lunching. Tables with built-in chessboards draw an egalitarian cross section of suits, uniforms, jeans, and cutoffs for serious games.

A block southwest, at 1307 New Hampshire Avenue, the **Heurich House Museum ③** (see p. 176) is one of the country's best remaining examples of an intact late-Victorian home.

Now head north 1.5 blocks to 2000 Massachusetts Avenue. This brick Victorian mansion was built in 1881 for Republican presidential candidate James Blaine, who lost in 1884 to Grover Cleveland. Shops occupy its first floor, with offices above.

On the same side of the street, the curving sweep of the **Indonesian Embassy ④** *(2020 Massachusetts Ave.)* makes an impressive sight. Featuring marble columns, arched windows, and a red-tiled mansard roof, the mansion was built at the turn of the 20th century by Irishman Tom Walsh, who struck gold in a Colorado mine. He moved to Washington, built his dream house, and became part of the

See area map p. 163
- National Trust
- 1 mile
- 3–4 hours
- Islamic Center

NOT TO BE MISSED

- Textile Museum
- The Phillips Collection
- Islamic Center

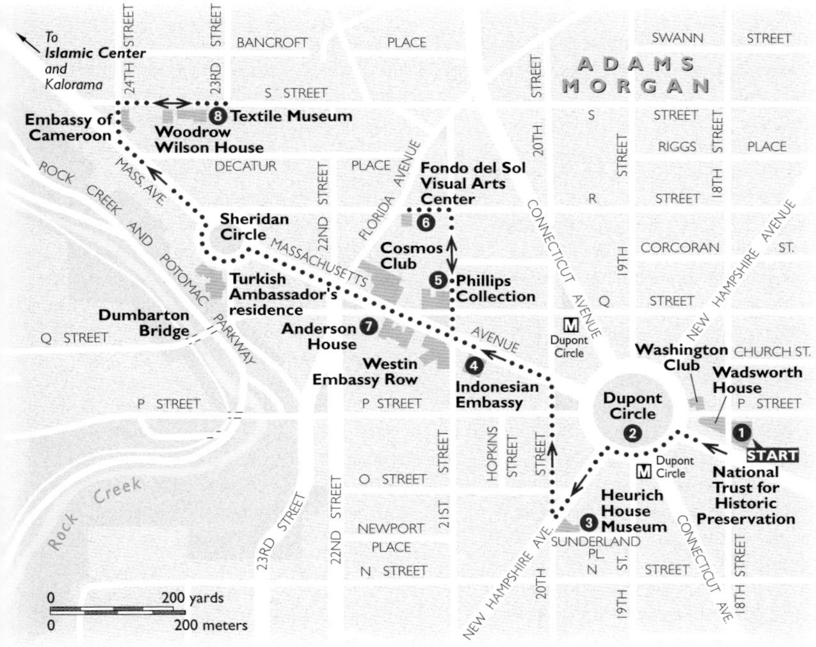

new moneyed class. His daughter, prominent hostess Evalyn Walsh McLean, was the last private owner of the Hope Diamond (now in the National Museum of Natural History; see p. 94); in 1951 she sold the mansion to the Republic of Indonesia.

At 2100 Massachusetts Avenue, the building housing the **Westin Embassy Row,** dating from 1927, exudes the flair of a European-style hotel. Al Gore lived here when his father was a U. S. senator. Across Massachusetts, a statue of Mahatma Gandhi stands in front of the Embassy of India. A block north on 21st Street, the **Phillips Collection** ❺ (see pp. 164–67) is one of Washington's most cherished museums.

If Latin American art interests you, continue north another block to **Fondo del Sol Visual Arts Center** ❻ *(2112 R St., 202-483-2777, open afternoons, closed Sun.–Mon., donation),* which helps preserve and promote the cultural heritage of the Americas with exhibits, concerts, poetry readings, and lectures, as well as pre-Columbian and folk art.

Back on Massachusetts, the double-winged mansion at 2118 Massachusetts Avenue is the **Anderson House** ❼ (see p. 176), headquarters of the Society of the Cincinnati. Across the avenue, at 2121 Massachusetts, stands the exclusive **Cosmos Club** *(private),* completed in 1902 as the home of Richard Townsend, president of the Erie & Pittsburgh Railroad. The fabulous limestone mansion was sold in 1950 to the club, whose members have earned recognition in the arts and sciences.

A number of embassies edge **Sheridan Circle,** named for Union general Philip H. Sheridan; the 1908 equestrian bronze in the center is by Gutzon Borglum, sculptor of Mount Rushmore. Among the impressive buildings nearby is the **Turkish Ambassador's residence** *(1606 23rd St.),* built in the 1910s for industrialist Edward Everett. A block south, the 1914 **Dumbarton Bridge—**often called the Buffalo Bridge for its bronze bison—carries Q Street over Rock Creek into Georgetown.

Back on Massachusetts, at the corner of Massachusetts and 24th, is the château-style **Embassy of Cameroon.** It was built in 1907 to house Norway's ambassador and legation, but it was never used as such because the ambassador died.

The Islamic Center's lofty minaret

Turn up 24th Street, then go east on S Street. Compared to many area houses, the **Woodrow Wilson House** *(2340 S St., 202-387-4062, closed Mon., $$),* designed in 1915 by Waddy B. Wood, has a modest appearance. The president spent the last three years of his life in this Georgian Revival brick town house after leaving the White House in 1921; his wife stayed until her death in 1961.

Next door, the **Textile Museum** ❽ *(2320 S St., 202-667-0441, donation)* was founded in 1925 by President Wilson's neighbor, George Hewitt Myers, to house a collection of rugs and other textiles. The museum incorporates Myers's residence and the adjoining house he bought as his collection grew; John Russell Pope designed the latter house in 1913. The collection numbers over 18,000 carpets and textiles, dating from 3000 B.C. to the present.

About four blocks away is the **Islamic Center** *(2551 Massachusetts Ave., 202-332-8343),* a mosque richly embellished with tilework, arches, and pillars; in the carpeted sanctuary, shoes and shorts are not allowed, and women must cover their heads. The network of streets to the east is the prestigious Kalorama neighborhood, which holds several embassies and large houses. ■

Adams Morgan

THE CITY'S TRADITIONALLY HISPANIC NEIGHBORHOOD, Adams Morgan became in the 1980s and '90s the top apartment-and-nightlife nexus for artists and hip young professionals alike. With its international restaurants, funky shops, and rocking nightclubs, the little neighborhood sprang to life with a personality all its own, an enclave of bohemian flair in the center of staid Washington. Never mind that all this popularity meant there was no longer any place to park—especially on weekend evenings.

Adams Morgan

Map p. 163

Between Columbia Rd., 16th St., & Florida Ave., N.W.

Metro: Dupont Circle (1.5 miles S) or Woodley Park–Zoo/Adams Morgan (0.75 mile NW); Bus: 90-93, L1-4

The name itself alludes to the neighborhood's cultural mix: By combining the names of two schools—the mostly white Adams School and the predominantly black Morgan School—local citizens coined the term Adams Morgan in the 1950s for an area that had been part of four neighborhoods. In that same decade, the Spanish-speaking population swelled as an influx of students from Latin America and Mexican professionals added to the existing community of embassy workers. The early 1960s saw an increase in Cuban immigration, followed by large numbers from South and Central America through the next few decades. The ethnic influence still tends toward Latin—Spanish is heard on the streets as often as English; but in the smorgasbord of restaurants and shops, you'll find many other cultures, including Ethiopian, Chinese, Thai, Indian, and Vietnamese.

The heart of Adams Morgan is the intersection of **Columbia Road** and **18th Street.** On the northeast corner a kiosk provides lists of upcoming cultural events. At the intersection's southwest corner is a plaza where vendors set up shop on weekends and sell fresh produce and breads. Most of the area's action—eating, drinking, and dancing—takes place south of the intersection on 18th Street between Columbia Road and Florida Avenue, and along a little branch west on Columbia Road to Belmont Road. That's pretty much it. Although the few attractions are worth seeing, they do not draw crowds.

VISITING

The three-story, brightly painted brick buildings lining the blocks of 18th Street south of the

Local Peruvians celebrate Our Lord of Miracles Day in Adams Morgan.

Shoppers examine local wares at a street fair on 18th Street—the heart of Adams Morgan.

Columbia Road–18th Street intersection hold most of the ethnic restaurants, bohemian bars, and boutiques. On sultry summer evenings, the sidewalks buzz with people strolling, walking dogs, or sipping cool drinks at sidewalk cafés and bars. Ethiopian seems to be the most sought-after cuisine here; among a number of places to give it a try is Meskerem *(2434 18th St., 202-462-4100),* where diners scoop up communal stews with pieces of spongy sourdough bread.

The **District of Columbia Arts Center** *(2438 18th St., 202-462-7833, open afternoons, closed Mon.),* features the work of emerging artists and holds live performances at night.

Columbia Road on either side of 18th also has several good restaurants—including Perry's *(1811 Columbia Rd., 202-234-6218), the* place to be and be seen; its rooftop dining is one of the city's most pleasant experiences. Along Columbia you'll also find Latino grocery stores, outdoor jewelry stands, and vintage clothing and sundries shops.

Daytime Adams Morgan offers different sights to see. For grand interiors, walk down **16th Street.** Just below Columbia, the **Mexican Cultural Institute** *(2829 16th St., 202-728-1647, closed weekends),* in a 1911 Italianate house, holds a huge tile-covered solarium, a lively stairwell mural, and ornately furnished salons; rotating exhibits are presented on two floors.

A few blocks farther, opposite Meridian Hill Park, **Meridian International Center** *(1624 & 1630 Crescent Pl., 202-667-6800, closed Mon.–Tues.)* promotes international understanding through cultural exchanges. The adjoining houses, with free art exhibits, were designed by John Russell Pope in 1911 and 1921; the 1630 address boasts antique French furnishings and a courtyard with 40 linden trees.

Pope also designed the glorious 1911 **Scottish Rite Headquarters** *(1733 16th St., 202-232-3579, closed weekends)*, just beyond Adams Morgan at S Street; he modeled the building after the Mausoleum at Halicarnassus in Turkey.

The northwest portion of Adams Morgan, up 18th and onto Adams Mill Road and Calvert Street, is quieter and more residential, with closely packed town houses. Just off Adams Mill, on the right, is one of the neighborhood's many colorful wall murals, this one dating from the 1970s and depicting life in Washington's barrio. If you follow Calvert, you'll come to the **Duke Ellington Memorial Bridge** over Rock Creek *(toward Woodley Park–Zoo/Adams Morgan Metro station)*. ■

Chuck Brown

Since its birth some 25 years ago, go-go music appeared to be an indigenous creation that was not exportable beyond the Beltway. It's finally beginning to gain broader attention. The "godfather" of go-go, Chuck Brown (1934–) cobbled the style by combining Latin and soul rhythms, jazz progressions, and gospel-style call-and-response lyrics. The result is a very funky sound that is more melodic and less aggressive than its rap and hip-hop cousins. Distinguishing features include long songs, heavy use of horns, cowbells, and congos, and undeniably danceable rhythms. For an introduction, try his *Greatest Hits* release, with "Bustin' Loose," "Back It On Up (Sho' Ya Right)," and "It Don't Mean a Thing (If It Don't Have the Go Go Swing)." A local legend in Washington, Brown still performs live and in ad campaigns. ■

A chanteuse performs at U-topia on U Street.

U Street

ONCE HOME TO CIVIL WAR CAMPS, THE U STREET CORRIDOR in the Shaw neighborhood—named for Robert Gould Shaw, the white colonel of the Civil War's first black regiment—was home to leading black intellectuals and professionals in the second half of the 20th century. People donned their finest attire to frequent the restaurants, movie theaters, pool halls, and dance halls of this "Black Broadway."

The baroque 1910 **Howard Theatre** *(620 T St.)* was the country's first legitimate theater built for black audiences and entertainers. Hosting vaudeville acts, musicals, road shows, and concerts, the Howard commanded center stage: All the big names in entertainment played its boards. In 1922 the opulent **Lincoln Theatre** opened at 1215 U Street. Both a movie palace and live-performance venue, it was designed to have the look and feel of a great opera house. Big bands played at its Colonnade dance hall.

At both theaters, the level of performance was so great that racial segregation was often ignored. Many white people also would come to see luminary performances by Duke Ellington, Cab Calloway, Ella Fitzgerald, Sarah Vaughan, and many more.

Ironically, desegregation in the 1950s led to the eventual decline of U Street's venues. The 1968 riots (which fanned out from 14th and U) led to further deterioration,

Washingtonian, singer, and film star Pearl Bailey (1918–1990), strikes a seductive pose.

and by the early '70s, both the Howard and the Lincoln had closed. In recent years, however, U Street has been revitalizing, with an eclectic mix of cafés, restaurants, shops, and nightclubs attracting a diverse crowd.

The Lincoln Theatre has been restored, and **Bohemian Caverns** *(11th & U Sts., 202-299-0800),* formerly known as Crystal Caverns, has returned after 30 years with live jazz; it was a haunt of Pearl Bailey, Miles Davis, John Coltrane, and others back in the 1960s. Other hot clubs in this neighborhood include Republic Gardens, State of the Union, and the 9:30 Club.

At 1816 12th St., the **Thurgood Marshall Center** offers exhibits on the neighborhood in a 1912 building designed by W. Sidney Pittman, one of the country's first black architects. Another way to get to know this area's legacy is to take the U Street Heritage Trail, a self-guided, 90-minute walk past historical buildings relating to the once thriving black community. Pick up information from merchants along the trail.

For a taste of yesterday, stop by **Ben's Chili Bowl** *(1213 U St.).* Opened in 1958, it still serves up half smokes and burgers beneath a press-tin ceiling. ■

Left: Edward Kennedy "Duke" Ellington (1899–1974) returned to his native Washington many times as a preeminent jazz bandleader and composer.

More places to visit in Dupont Circle & beyond

ANDERSON HOUSE

This spectacular 1905 mansion serves as the headquarters and museum of the **Society of the Cincinnati,** a patriotic organization whose first president general was George Washington. The house was once the winter residence of diplomat Larz Anderson III, whose wife, Isabel Weld Perkins, inherited $17,000,000 from her grandfather's shipping fortune. After Anderson died in 1937, his widow turned the mansion over to the society, of which Anderson was a member.

A bulwark of fraternal tradition dating from 1783, the society's 3,500 members descend from officers in the Continental Army or Navy. Its name comes from the Roman senator Cincinnatus.

Among the first-floor treasures are walnut choir stalls from 16th-century Italy, decorative Japanese screens, and a ballroom with Verona marble columns. Off the ballroom, a sun-drenched winter garden room opens onto a Japanese garden. A billiard room holds society members' portraits by Gilbert Stuart and John Trumbull. On the second floor are English furniture, Belgian tapestries, Italian paintings, and Chinese jades and porcelains. A 42,000-title research library focuses on the military history of the American Revolution.

www.thesocietyofthecincinnati.org Map p. 163 2118 Massachusetts Ave., N.W. 202-785-2040 Closed Sun.–Mon. Metro: Dupont Circle

HEURICH HOUSE MUSEUM

Built in 1895 for brewer Christian Heurich, this Romanesque castle is now a landmark building on the National Register of Historic Places. Heurich, a poor German immigrant, came to the U.S. in 1872. Within seven years he had gotten married and purchased this property just off Dupont Circle. He lived in this castle and ran a brewery on what is now the site of The Kennedy Center. In 1956 his descendants deeded the house to the organization that became the Historical Society of Washington (which has since relocated).

A self-guided tour takes you through 11 rooms on three levels. Sumptuous decorations include a marble mosaic floor in the main hall and elaborately carved furniture in the dining room.

www.brewmasterscastle.com Map p. 163 1307 New Hampshire Ave., N.W. 202-429-1894 Midday tours offered Wed.–Sat. $ Metro: Dupont Circle

MARY CHURCH TERRELL HOUSE

The LeDroit Park neighborhood *(S of Howard University)* has been the home of many prominent African Americans since the 1890s. Civic leader Mary Church Terrell, wife of the city's first black municipal judge, lived a long, active life, but is now remembered for the work she did in her later years. In 1950, at age 86, she spearheaded a campaign to reinstate antidiscrimination laws that had been written in the 1870s. Her three-story brick house *(not open to the public)* is located at 326 T Street, N.W. Other blacks who have lived in this area include poet Paul Laurence Dunbar and Walter Washington, the city's first elected mayor. ■

Howard University

Gen. Oliver Otis Howard (1830–1909) came to Washington after the Civil War and took charge of the new Bureau of Refugees, Freedmen, and Abandoned Lands (better known as the Freedmen's Bureau). Under Howard's leadership, the bureau bought the Barry Farm near what would become the Anacostia neighborhood, in southeast Washington, and sold off parcels to black families. The Freedmen's Bureau also helped fund and establish educational programs for freed people. In 1867 Howard University was founded (named for the general against his wishes) on land that was purchased by the bureau. The institution, located at Seventh and Bryant Streets, N.W., is now the country's leading black university, with an enrollment of more than 10,000. ■

With inducements ranging from the bucolic (Rock Creek Park) to the divine (Washington National Cathedral), this city-center enclave is a pleasing paradox: a tourist destination that provides a respite from touring.

Cleveland Park & beyond

Soaring arches inside National Cathedral

Noodleheads spill onto the sidewalk of a Thai restaurant on Connecticut Avenue.

Cleveland Park & beyond

BY FOOT, METRO, OR BICYCLE, THE LEAFY NEIGHBORHOOD OF CLEVELAND Park offers a pleasant afternoon of relaxed sight-seeing or lounging in cafés. Higher elevations and the nearness of Rock Creek Park provide relief from the heat of downtown.

Tourists who venture this far from the Mall generally come for the zoo. That's a great reason for a visit, made easy by the Metro's Red Line to Cleveland Park or Woodley Park–Zoo/Adams Morgan stations. And any of the outstanding sites nearby may land on your list of D.C. favorites.

The tony neighborhood of Cleveland Park is named for President Grover Cleveland, who spent the summers of his second administration (1893–97) at Woodley, a Georgian mansion built about 1800 at 3000 Cathedral Avenue. President Cleveland preferred the cool breezes that buffeted Woodley to the miasmas of the marshy lowlands around the White House about 2.5 miles away. Woodley is now part of the private Maret School.

When the city's trolley tracks were extended across Rock Creek valley at Calvert Street in the 1890s and thence up Connecticut Avenue, the area took on a fashionable cachet. Today Connecticut Avenue is still lined with big apartment buildings (the more ornate ones from the 1920s and '30s), behind which stand fine old houses with wide front porches and trim gardens. Indeed, the city's largest hotel, the Marriott Wardman Park *(Woodley Rd. & Conn. Ave.)*, got its start in 1928 as a luxury apartment building called the Wardman Tower. The tower's residents have included Herbert Hoover, Earl Warren, and Clare Booth Luce. Across Calvert Street, the 1930 Omni Shoreham has hosted inaugural balls since Franklin Delano Roosevelt took office in 1933.

Farther up Connecticut Avenue is one of the city's top attractions: the almost pastoral, 163-acre Smithsonian's National Zoo. It abuts Rock Creek Park, a delightful preserve of trees, meadows, and cycling paths.

A mile west of the zoo, Washington National Cathedral towers gloriously on its high hill. Scores of stonemasons labored 83 years to complete this national architectural masterpiece. Unknown to many locals, the Hillwood estate to the north is a jewel box of Russian and French antiques. Afterward, reward yourself with a Frappuccino or some Thai food at one of the many establishments clustered near the Metro stops along Connecticut Avenue. ■

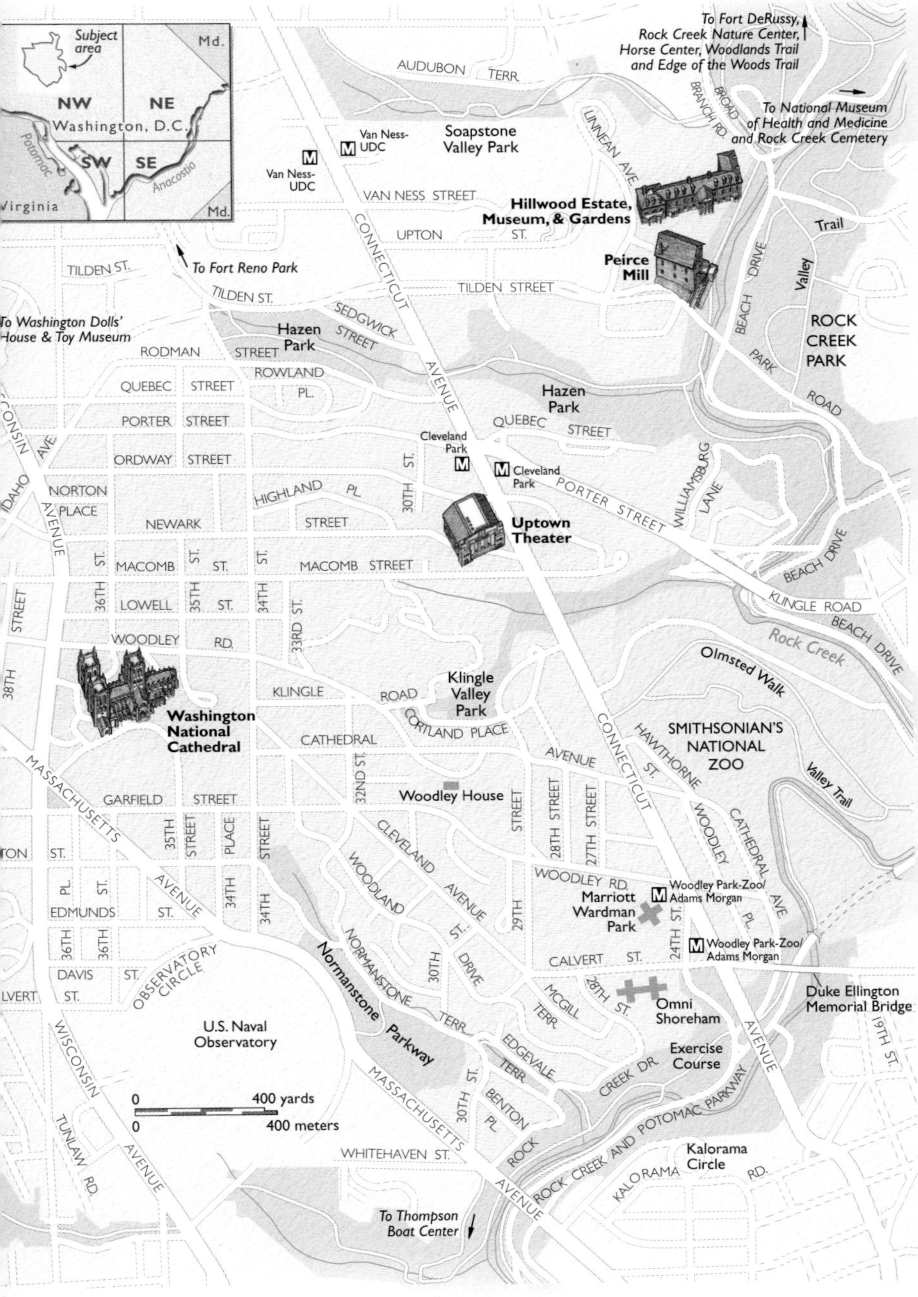
Subject area
Md.
NW
NE
Washington, D.C.
Potomac
SW
SE
Anacostia
Virginia
Md.
To Fort DeRussy, Rock Creek Nature Center, Horse Center, Woodlands Trail and Edge of the Woods Trail
To National Museum of Health and Medicine and Rock Creek Cemetery
AUDUBON TERR.
Van Ness-UDC
Van Ness-UDC
Soapstone Valley Park
VAN NESS STREET
Hillwood Estate, Museum, & Gardens
UPTON ST.
Peirce Mill
LINNEAN AVE.
BRANCH RD.
BROAD
Trail
BEACH DRIVE
Valley
TILDEN ST.
To Fort Reno Park
TILDEN ST.
TILDEN STREET
SEDGWICK STREET
To Washington Dolls' House & Toy Museum
Hazen Park
RODMAN STREET
ROWLAND PL.
QUEBEC STREET
PORTER STREET
ORDWAY STREET
ROCK CREEK PARK
PARK ROAD
Hazen Park
QUEBEC STREET
Cleveland Park
Cleveland Park
WISCONSIN AVE.
IDAHO AVENUE
NORTON PLACE
NEWARK STREET
HIGHLAND PL.
30TH ST.
PORTER STREET
WILLIAMSBURG LANE
Uptown Theater
MACOMB ST.
MACOMB STREET
36TH ST.
35TH ST.
34TH ST.
LOWELL ST.
33RD ST.
38TH STREET
BEACH DRIVE
KLINGLE ROAD
BEACH DRIVE
Rock Creek
WOODLEY RD.
Olmsted Walk
KLINGLE ROAD
Klingle Valley Park
Washington National Cathedral
CORTLAND PLACE
CATHEDRAL AVENUE
SMITHSONIAN'S NATIONAL ZOO
CONNECTICUT AVENUE
HAWTHORNE ST.
Valley Trail
32ND ST.
Woodley House
MASSACHUSETTS AVENUE
GARFIELD STREET
35TH STREET
PLACE
STREET
29TH STREET
28TH STREET
27TH STREET
WOODLEY PL.
CATHEDRAL AVE.
CLEVELAND AVENUE
WOODLAND DRIVE
WOODLEY RD.
Woodley Park-Zoo/Adams Morgan
Marriott Wardman Park
ST.
EDMUNDS ST.
36TH PL.
36TH ST.
34TH
34TH
30TH ST.
24TH ST.
Woodley Park-Zoo/Adams Morgan
DAVIS ST.
OBSERVATORY CIRCLE
CALVERT ST.
CALVERT ST.
NORMANSTONE TERR.
Normanstone Parkway
28TH ST.
MCGILL TERR.
Omni Shoreham
Duke Ellington Memorial Bridge
19TH ST.
U.S. Naval Observatory
WISCONSIN AVENUE
EDGEVALE TERR.
Exercise Course
CREEK DR.
AVENUE
0 400 yards
0 400 meters
30TH ST.
BENTON PL.
MASSACHUSETTS AVENUE
ROCK CREEK AND POTOMAC PARKWAY
TUNLAW RD.
WHITEHAVEN ST.
ROCK
Kalorama Circle
KALORAMA RD.
To Thompson Boat Center

Smithsonian's National Zoo

Smithsonian's National Zoo
www.si.edu/natzoo
Map p. 179
3001 Connecticut Ave., N.W.
202-633-4800
Parking up to $16 per day
Metro: Cleveland Park, Woodley Park–Zoo/Adams Morgan; Bus: L1-4, H5 & 7

THE NATIONAL ZOO WAS CONCEIVED AS "A HOME AND A city of refuge for the vanishing races of the continent." In 1887, Smithsonian taxidermist William T. Hornaday corralled some of North America's vanishing bison and a few other animals in a small zoo on the Mall. Two years later, Congress set aside acreage along a bend in Rock Creek to create the National Zoo "for the advancement of science and the instruction and recreation of the people."

Part of the Smithsonian Institution, the 163-acre biological park opened in 1891 and is now home to more than 2,700 animals representing 435 species. Nearly a third of the species—including Asian elephants,

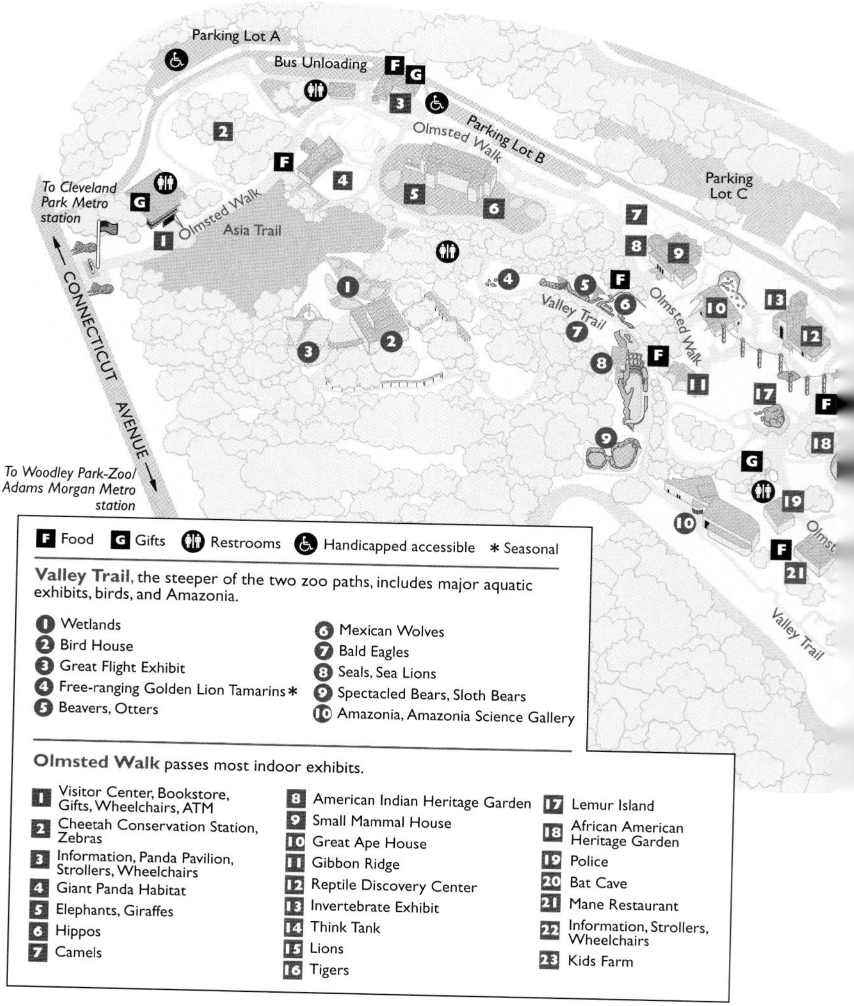

Pandas at play: Tian Tian ("more and more") and Mei Xiang ("beautiful fragrance"), born in Wolong, China, are star attractions at the zoo.

cheetahs, Sumatran tigers, giant pandas, western lowland gorillas, and Komodo dragons—are endangered. The animal enclosures aim to re-create natural habitats. Meanwhile, at the zoo's 3,000-acre Conservation and Research Center near Front Royal, Virginia, zookeepers have bred golden lion tamarins, red wolves, and black-footed ferrets for reintroduction to the wild.

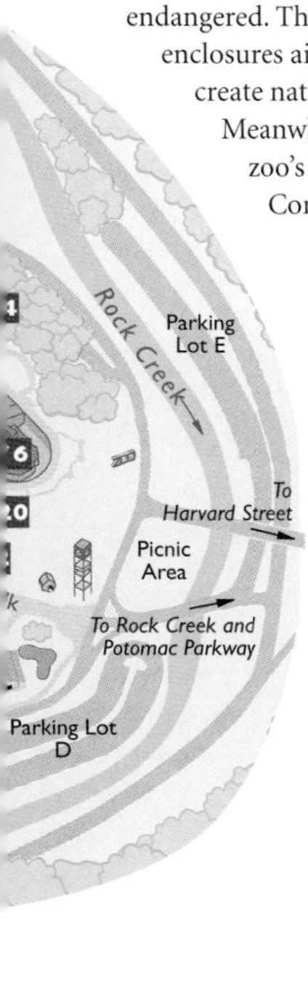

VISITING

Given the zoo's 5 miles of hilly paths, it's hard to avoid at least some uphill walking. To minimize your efforts, pick up a map at one of the information stations at either end of the zoo's main east-west thoroughfare, the Olmsted Walk (landscape architect Frederick Law Olmsted designed the zoo's original layout). With more than 30 exhibit areas to choose from, you may want to hit a few highlights and save the rest for another day. Fall and winter are the least crowded seasons, but the buildings close early from November 1 to April 2.

If you begin at the visitor center inside the Connecticut Avenue entrance, the **Olmsted Walk** will lead you past the cheetahs, zebras, and other enclosures to the **Giant Panda Exhibit.** This indoor-outdoor area features Tian Tian and Mei Xiang, a pair of pandas on long-term loan from China. Within days of arriving in December 2000, the pandas had adapted so well that they were literally chewing up the scenery, devouring the decorative plantings of ornamental bamboo. The exhibit outlines efforts to save the panda, whose numbers have dwindled to about 1,000 in the wild and 140 in captivity.

Continue downhill and east past the Elephant House to reach the **Small Mammal House,** where the challenge is to spot the golden lion tamarins, pygmy marmosets, two-toed sloths, and three-banded armadillos that occupy the glassed-in jungle. The **Great Ape House** next door is home to gorillas and orangutans. The latter can climb over an aerial pathway called the O Line to Think Tank, swinging on vinelike cables attached to a set of towers. A popular stop nearby, the **Reptile Discovery Center** features Komodo dragons, huge Aldabra tortoises, spiky matamata turtles, and hands-on exhibits.

Behind the center lies the fascinating **Invertebrate Exhibit.** Here you'll find giant octopuses, anemones, and spiders; an adjoining greenhouse thrums with pollinators such as butterflies, hummingbirds, and honeybees. Beyond you'll find the Bat Cave, the Great Cats, and Monkey Island.

Recently added to this area, near Parking Lot D, is a 2-acre **Kids' Farm** that was designed to introduce young children to farm animals and the basics of animal care.

Head back to Connecticut Avenue on the **Valley Trail,** south of the Olmsted Walk. Your first stop will be the warm, humid **Amazonia** exhibit, which simulates a journey through a rain forest; here parrots and other tropical birds flit through kapok and mahogany trees beneath a domed 50-foot-high ceiling.

Next on the Valley Trail is a delightful outdoor exhibit housing seals and sea lions, followed by enclosures for red wolves, beavers, otters, and free-ranging golden lion tamarins. Farther up the trail, the raucous **Bird House and Flight Exhibit** offers a walk-through aviary and a boardwalk spanning a wetland. ■

Feeding time for the sea lions is one of the zoo's most popular spectacles.

Rock Creek Park

WHEN YOU NEED TO GET AWAY FROM THE HURLY-BURLY OF urban living (or touring, for that matter), a peaceful Washington park awaits nearby. Rock Creek Park runs in a long strand of hilly woods and meadows from the National Zoo to the Maryland border 4 miles north, with tendrils of green branching off the main park into other parts of the city. At 1,739 acres—more than twice the size of New York's Central Park—Rock Creek is one of the nation's largest urban parks. Visitors and residents seek solace and rejuvenation in the park's 18-hole golf course, tennis courts, picnic areas, playing fields, nature center and planetarium, and more than 35 miles of trails for jogging, hiking, biking, and horseback riding.

Rock Creek Park
www.nps.gov/rocr
Map p. 179
Rock Creek Nature Center & Planetarium
5200 Glover Rd., S of Military Rd.
202-895-6070

For some 5,000 years, Algonquin Indians camped in the woods around Rock Creek above its run-in with the Potomac. There they gathered fruits and nuts and hunted deer, bear, and elk. They also quarried the Rock Creek valley, extracting quartz for tools and soapstone for bowls and other implements.

By the early 1700s, however, the Indians were gone, displaced by white settlers who cleared out more of the forest and built mills along Rock Creek. The only one remaining is the 19th-century **Peirce Mill** *(Tilden St. & Beach Dr.)*. The barn adjacent to it is open several hours on weekends.

During the Civil War, Washington erected a ring of 68 forts to protect itself from Confederate attack. You can see some earthworks remaining from **Fort DeRussy,** half a mile north of the nature center. Other nearby fort sites—most of them long since reduced to fields for picnicking or playing ball—include **Fort Bayard Park** *(River Rd. & Western Ave.);* **Fort Reno Park** *(Chesapeake St. & Belt Rd.),* occupying the highest point of land in Washington; and partially

Bridges, trails, and autumn glory are among the enticements of this sprawling urban sanctuary.

reconstructed **Fort Stevens Park** *(13th St., N of Military Rd.)*, the only Washington-area battlement that came under enemy fire.

Set aside in 1890, Rock Creek Park is today the city's playground, administered by the National Park Service. About 85 percent of the park is forested; the remainder is wildflower-dotted meadows and fields. Over the years, Theodore Roosevelt, Ronald Reagan, and other Presidents have availed themselves of the park's walking and bridle trails. Unlike them, the average citizen will need no bodyguards; the park is generally safe by day.

Just spin 'em: Rock Creek Park's 10 miles of bike paths link to a Washington-wide web of other trails.

VISITING

Start your visit at the **Rock Creek Nature Center** *(closed Mon.–Tues. & major holidays)*. Here you can learn about the park's flora and fauna that fill this urban wildlife mecca, scope out its cycling and running paths, and pick up a trail map. The center's excellent displays include a bee colony, dioramas, and several hands-on exhibits; astronomy programs are staged in a planetarium.

Outside, two short nature loops—the **Woodlands Trail** and the wheelchair-accessible **Edge of the Woods Trail**—help you identify local trees and plants. Towering oaks, hickories, and beeches are much in evidence; come spring the dogwoods, redbuds, and azaleas emerge in a gaudy show of blossoms.

From the nature center, you can also access the park's larger trail network. Some pathways are open to bikes and horses; others allow only foot traffic. One bike trail heads north from the nature center to the Maryland border and 14 miles beyond that to Lake Needwood. You can return the same way and pick up **Beach Drive;** normally a pulsing commuter artery, it has certain sections closed on weekends, allowing cyclists a traffic-free ride from the Maryland border all the way to its intersection with Broad Branch Road. From there, a paved **bike trail** extends south beyond the park boundary, running alongside the Rock Creek and Potomac Parkway until it hits Memorial Bridge. About halfway along this trail, near Calvert Street and Connecticut Avenue, you'll find a 1.5-mile **exercise course** with fitness-apparatus.

Hikers should seek out the moderate, blue-blazed, 5.6-mile **Valley Trail,** which winds along the east side of Rock Creek all the way from Boundary Bridge on the Maryland line down to Bluff Bridge at the park's southern end. Its analogue on the park's western edge is the strenuous, green-blazed, 4.6-mile **Western Ridge Trail.**

Just south of the nature center, sign up for a trail ride or lesson at the **Rock Creek Horse Center** *(202-362-0117)*, an NPS concessioner amid a 13-mile web of bridle trails. Much farther south, where Rock Creek joins the Potomac, **Thompson Boat Center** *(202-333-9543)* rents canoes and kayaks for exploring the river and Theodore Roosevelt Island (see p. 208); it also rents bicycles. ■

Frank O. Salisbury painted Marjorie Merriweather Post in 1934, when she was 47.

Hillwood Estate, Museum, & Gardens

A HIDDEN GEM, HILLWOOD WAS THE FINAL HOME OF heiress Marjorie Merriweather Post (1887–1973). With her fabulous collection of Imperial Russian and 18th-century French decorative arts, she furnished the house with the idea that it would become a museum after her death. The site opened to the public in 1977, and Hillwood is now one of the top art collector's house museums in the country. Objects on display include Romanov family treasures, Fabergé eggs and other objets d'art, Russian religious icons, French tapestries, and Sèvres porcelain. The 12 acres of formal gardens enhance the museum experience, while family photos and memorabilia remind visitors that Hillwood was once a home.

Hillwood Estate, Museum, & Gardens

www.hillwoodmuseum.org

Map p. 179

4155 Linnean Ave., N.W.

202-686-5807

Closed Sun.–Mon. & all Jan.

$$$

Metro: Van Ness–UDC; Bus: L1-4

As the only child of cereal magnate C. W. Post, Marjorie inherited a fortune at age 27 when her father died (just two years after her mother). She and her husband bought a mansion on Fifth Avenue in New York and began furnishing it with the help of renowned art dealer Sir Joseph Duveen, who became Post's mentor. She also educated herself by taking classes on tapestries, porcelain, and furniture at the Metropolitan Museum of Art.

In the course of a long and extraordinary life, Post married and divorced four times and amassed a tremendous collection of European artwork. An astute businesswoman, she also donated millions of dollars to charities and other organizations, including $100,000 to help build the Kennedy Center (see pp. 124–25).

Post's treasures include the French Drawing Room (top) and Russian imperial Easter eggs created by Fabergé.

It was after her third divorce, in 1955, that Post purchased Hillwood—a 1926 Georgian house on the woodsy edge of Rock Creek Park. She spent two years renovating and enlarging the house, transforming it into a residence where she could entertain in legendary style. Hillwood parties routinely exceeded 200 guests, the politicians mixing with celebrities in the gardens. At formal dinners, guests ate off Post's antique porcelain and silver; informal dinners sometimes ended with square dancing in the Pavilion.

In the interstices between soirées, Post expanded her art collection, eventually turning Hillwood into a stunning showcase of decorative and fine arts. Today the museum is best known for its collection of 18th- and 19th-century Russian imperial art—the most comprehensive outside Russia—and for its distinctive array of French decorative art.

VISITING

Get oriented to the museum and gardens with a 15-minute film at the visitor center. You can take a one-hour guided tour of the house, usually offered several times a day, or a self-guided audio tour, and you can stroll the gardens. There's a café on site which serves lunch and royal tea; for reservations, call 202-243-3920.

The imposing exterior of the brick house and the inside customarily prompt a chorus of oohs and aahs. One highlight, the **Russian Porcelain Room,** contains Imperial Glassworks pieces from the 1730s.

More tsarist treasures are on display in the outstanding **Icon Room,** where you can feast your eyes on the diamond wedding crown worn in 1894 by Russia's last empress, Alexandra Fedorovona; two Fabergé Easter eggs (one dates from 1914 and is studded with gold, diamonds, and pearls); and Russian Orthodox icons from the 16th century. Post discovered her love of Russian decorative and liturgical art while living in the Soviet Union from 1937 to 1938 with her third husband, U.S. Ambassador Joseph E. Davies.

The elegant **French Drawing Room** is furnished in the style of Louis XVI, with 18th-century tapestries designed by painter François Boucher and furniture by David Roentgen. Upstairs, Post's bedroom is likewise decorated in Louis XVI style; a display of her clothing and jewelry adds life and personality to the collection.

Almost as impressive as the house are the lush 12 acres of lawns and formal gardens and 13 acres of native woodlands. A French parterre with a fountain, a circular rose garden, a lunar lawn, a Japanese-style garden, a cutting garden, and an orchid-filled greenhouse round out the gardens. It all makes strolling through Hillwood a delight in any season. ■

Washington National Cathedral

DOMINATING THE CITYSCAPE, WASHINGTON NATIONAL Cathedral is visible from points all over the district. Conversely, its lofty perch on Mount St. Alban gives cathedral visitors a commanding vista of the urban skyline. Officially known as the Cathedral Church of St. Peter and St. Paul, this towering Gothic church is one of Washington's most magnificent architectural achievements.

The idea of a national church featured in Pierre Charles L'Enfant's planning of the Federal City. He envisioned a house of prayer that would be used for national services and open to all rather than reserved for the special use of a particular denomination. It took nearly a century for the idea to gain adequate support. In 1893 the Protestant Episcopal Cathedral Foundation obtained a charter allowing the church to be established.

After the 57-acre site atop Mount St. Albans was selected and public donations were obtained, President Theodore Roosevelt and a crowd of ten thousand were on hand in 1907 for the laying of the foundation stone. The Bethlehem Chapel, named for one of its stones that came from a field near Bethlehem, opened in 1912. Services have been held since then at the cathedral, although construction of the entire building lasted for 83 years. President George H. W. Bush dedicated the west towers, the final section to be added, in 1990.

For half a century, construction of the cathedral was guided by Philip Hubert Frohman, who had dreamed of becoming its architect; he got the job after the two initial designers died in 1917. Obsessed with detail, Frohman once ordered that all the molding on the central tower be shifted by one-eighth of an inch. He died in 1972, at the age of 85, after being struck by car while walking to work from his home nearby.

Others who dedicated their lives to the cathedral were the many masons, stone carvers, and stained-glass artisans who applied 14th-century skills to modern times. Their legacy includes more than 200 stained-glass windows, 3,000 stone sculptures, and many other artfully crafted works. Most of the building was constructed of grey Indiana limestone, selected for its ability to endure without the need for major restoration over many centuries.

VISITING

Half-hour docent-led tours are offered several times at mid-day *(donation)*, beginning at the west end of the nave. For groups, reservations are required *(202-364-6616)*. You can also wander on your own with an audio tour ($5 rental). Tours may be unavailable, however, if the cathedral is being used for a special event, so check the website before you visit. It also provides the schedules of Sunday and weekday services, and musical events that include pipe-organ recitals, concerts, festivals, and bell peals.

Stroll outside to admire the flying buttresses, the arches, and some of the 112 **gargoyles** whose expressions range from silly to fiendish. In addition to warding off evil, the gargoyles repel rainwater; in storms they spout water away from the building. The figures are carved in various shapes: wild boars, mythical

Washington National Cathedral
www.cathedral.org/cathedral
Map p. 179
Massachusetts & Wisconsin Aves., N.W.
202-537-6200
Bus: N2-8, 30-36

Stained-glass "History of the Baptism" in the south transept.

beasts, cats, dogs, even caricatures of people who were central to the construction of the cathedral. Binoculars are handy for inspecting the higher ones.

Outside is also the best place to absorb the immensity of the sixth largest cathedral in the world, and the second largest in the U.S. (only New York's St. John the Divine is bigger). The central Gloria in Excelsis Deo tower rises 300 feet, while the nave runs one-tenth of a mile.

The west-entrance central portal features Frederick Hart's spellbinding tympanum sculpture, "Ex Nihilo," in which the act of divine creation is expressed through half-formed men and women.

Faithful to its Gothic style, the church was built in a cruciform shape. Stand at the crossing and look up; the massive piers rise 98 feet to the vaulting overhead. The arches are held in place by a keystone and supported by buttresses.

The intricate pulpit, from which Dr. Martin Luther King, Jr., delivered his final sermon on March 31, 1968, was carved from stone donated by England's Canterbury Cathedral. The 10,500 pieces of glass in the spectacular **West Rose Window** cast a late-afternoon rainbow on the floor.

Running along the nave are memorial alcoves, or bays. The **Woodrow Wilson Bay** honors the life of the 28th President, the only U.S. President whose final resting place is Washington, D.C. The floor of the **Lincoln Bay** is inset with 33 Lincoln-head pennies—one for each state in the Union at the time of the Great Emancipator's assassination. About halfway down on the right (south) side, the modernistic **Space Window** has a moon rock embedded in the center lancet.

Scattered throughout, nine chapels vary from the tiny **Good Shepherd Chapel** to the church-size **Bethlehem Chapel** on the crypt level. Especially appealing is the intimate **Children's Chapel,** where every item has been scaled to the size of a six-year-old. Also on the crypt level is a store offering books, tapes, cards, and snacks.

For a closer look at the cathedral's towers and gargoyles (and a panoramic view of the city), take an elevator to the **Pilgrim Observation Gallery** on the seventh floor of the St. Peter and St. Paul towers. When the weather is nice, stroll in the beautifully landscaped **Bishop's Garden**, which was designed by Frederick Law Olmsted. ■

Bell appeal

National Cathedral's central tower holds ten peal bells and a 53-bell carillon. It is the world's only cathedral blessed with both kinds of bells in one tower.

Each peal bell is mounted on a wheel, from which a rope hangs down to the ringers' chamber. The pull must be smooth and even, so one ringer is assigned to each bell. Weighing 600 to nearly 3,600 pounds apiece, the bells cannot be rung fast enough to play a melody; instead, sequences of notes called "changes" are played.

Change ringing is difficult and dangerous: Lose your concentration and you not only sabotage the change but risk injury when the bell's momentum jerks you high off the floor. Peals *(Sun. after a.m. service)* can last from several minutes to the rare "full peal," a three-hour extravaganza of 5,000 changes. The joyous noise can be heard at the White House, 3 miles distant. ■

Opposite: The St. Peter and St. Paul towers on the west facade of Washington National Cathedral bask in the golden sunrays of late afternoon.

More places to visit in Cleveland Park & beyond

NATIONAL MUSEUM OF HEALTH & MEDICINE

Though it now stresses science over spectacle, this museum is not for the squeamish: Exhibits range from preserved human fetuses and a stomach-shaped hairball to a leg swollen by elephantiasis and a hands-on brain. The collection was begun during the Civil War as a research tool for military medicine and surgery. Today the museum's vast collection of skeletal specimens, organs, and models is used for research on human anatomy.
http://nmhm.washingtondc.museum/
Walter Reed Army Medical Center, 6900 Georgia Ave., N.W. 202-782-2200
Donation Metro: Takoma Park

The last picture palace: The Uptown theater anchors upper Connecticut Avenue.

ROCK CREEK CEMETERY

A mile and a half east of Rock Creek Park in the Petworth neighborhood, this 86-acre site exudes the feel of an old country parish. Set amid this pastoral glebe, St. Paul's Episcopal (or "Rock Creek") Church is the city's sole surviving colonial church. It was founded in 1719, long before Washington was a city; the current building dates from 1775, though only the walls are original.

Some of the city's finest cemetery memorials reside here. They honor crusading novelist Upton Sinclair, Cabinet members, Supreme Court justices, and National Geographic Society founder Gilbert H. Grosvenor. The cemetery also houses one of the finest works by one of America's greatest sculptors: The Adams Memorial (1890) by Augustus Saint-Gaudens was commissioned by historian Henry Adams to honor his wife, Clover. It depicts a seated figure wearing a heavy cloak, the face obscured by shadows. Mark Twain remarked that the sculpture embodied all of human grief, while Saint-Gaudens himself called his work "The Mystery of the Hereafter" and "The Peace of God that Passeth Understanding."
www.rockcreekparish.org/cemetery
Map p. 179 Rock Creek Church Rd. & Webster St., N.W. 202-829-0585

UPTOWN THEATER

Opened in 1936, the art deco Uptown is Washington's premier movie palace. Its 830 seats, including a balcony, make it the city's largest remaining cinema theater. A curved screen, 72 feet long and 32 feet high, wraps viewers in movie magic, while a Dolby digital sound system keeps the illusion up-to-date. Though the Uptown offers only one film at a time, almost anything looks great in a house this big.
Map p. 179 3426 Connecticut Ave., N.W. 202-966-8805 Metro: Cleveland Park ■

A lesser known niche away from the tourist center, the land east of the Capitol holds a few charms of its own, including a museum honoring African Americans, a dazzling basilica, and gardens galore.

East of the Capitol

Stokes' aster at the National Arboretum

Rev. Willie Wilson plays washboard at Union Temple Baptist Church in Anacostia.

East of the Capitol

MORE THAN HALF THE CITY LIES EAST OF THE CAPITOL, AN AREA RICH IN AFRICAN American and military history, as well as gardens, marshes, and woods. Architecture lovers will find one of the city's most awe-inspiring buildings here, the nation's largest Catholic church.

The history of the eastern part of the city is tied to its river, the Anacostia, first seen by a European, explorer John Smith, nearly 400 years ago. Back then the Nacotchtank Indians (whose corrupted name, Anacostan, would be given to this East Branch of the Potomac) lived here, harvesting shad, catfish, and yellow perch. The arrival of white settlers meant the Indians' demise and the spread of tobacco plantations. In 1790 the lower Anacostia became part of the new capital. Soon developments arose on the northwest riverfront—the Washington Navy Yard (1799) and the U.S. Arsenal (1803).

Across the river from the Navy Yard, the city laid out its first planned, whites-only suburb, Uniontown, in 1854. During the Civil War, the military erected several forts east of the river. After the war, the Freedman's Bureau bought nearby, 375-acre Barry farm and sold lots to 500 black families. Still the community, renamed Anacostia in 1886, remained mostly white until the 1950s. That changed with the migration of whites to the suburbs, and by 1970, Anacostia had become 86 percent black.

While the area along Martin Luther King Jr. Avenue (formerly Asylum Avenue) supports take-out restaurants, auto shops, and several other small businesses, the neighborhoods on U, V, and W Streets possess many early working-class row houses. The District government and private corporations have recently committed nearly a billion dollars to this area, hoping to improve neglected neighborhoods and enhance the waterfront. In the past decade, a rise in new housing and the arrival of the Metro have brought new residents, tourists, and life.

On the other side of the river, one of the last areas of the city to develop, the Northeast quadrant is anchored by the glorious grounds

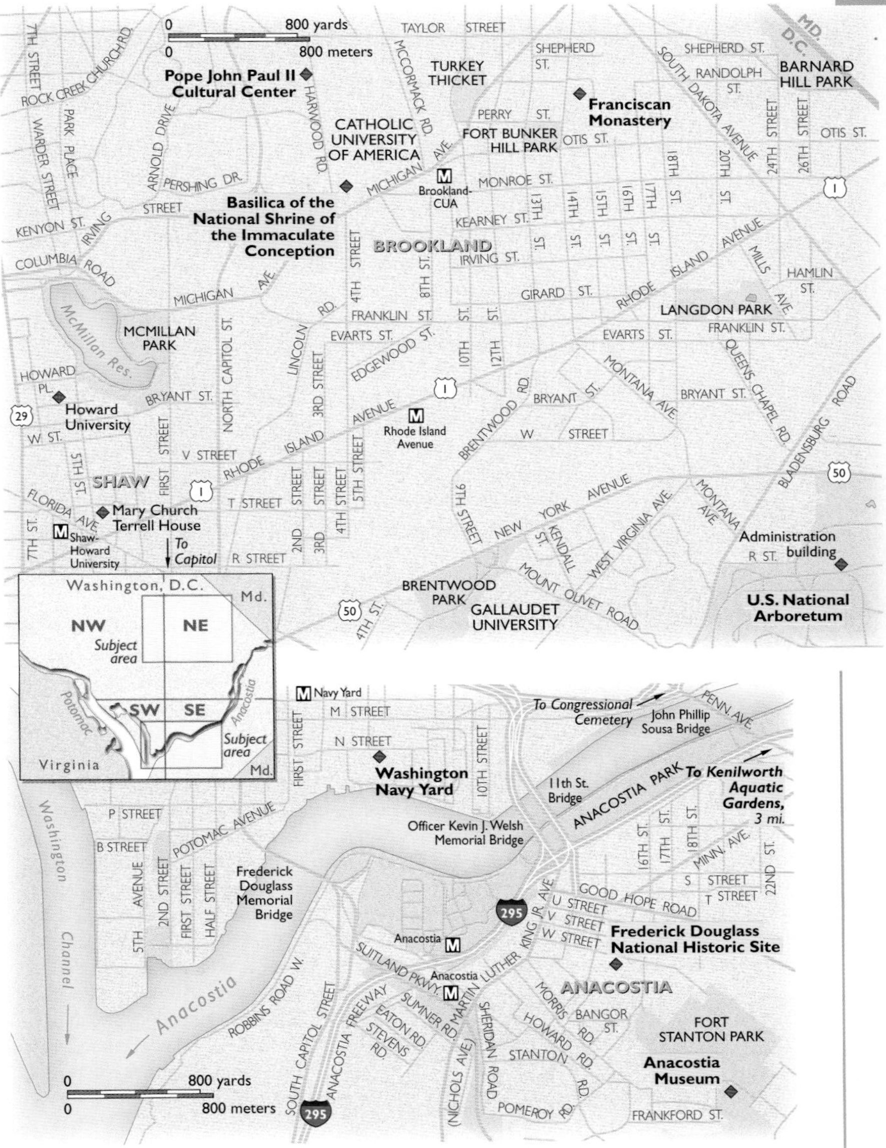

of the U.S. National Arboretum and by the Catholic University of America, home of the Shrine of the Immaculate Conception. Also in this area is Gallaudet University, the country's premier school for the deaf.

Sports fans know the area east of the Capitol as the site of Langston Golf Course (*202-397-8638*) and RFK Stadium (*2400 East Capitol St., S.E.*). Opened in 1961, the stadium was once home to the Washington Redskins football team and the now defunct Washington Senators baseball team. In 2005 it also began hosting the city's Nationals baseball team (formerly the Montreal Expos), while the building of a new stadium in the Southeast commenced. ■

Frederick Douglass NHS
www.nps.gov/frdo
Map p. 193
1411 W St., S.E.
202-426-5961 or 877-444-6777 for tour reservations
Metro: Anacostia, then Bus B2, U2, or W6-8 & transfer

Frederick Douglass National Historic Site

SITUATED AMONG THE ROW HOUSES OF ANACOSTIA, Cedar Hill—former home of abolitionist Frederick Douglass—was built in the 1850s atop a grassy knoll. The 21-room tan brick house, which recently reopened after a major face-lift, offers a commanding view of Washington from its gracious front porch. A visit to this National Park Service site provides a fascinating glimpse into the life and work of the "sage of Anacostia," the most prominent African-American orator of the 19th century.

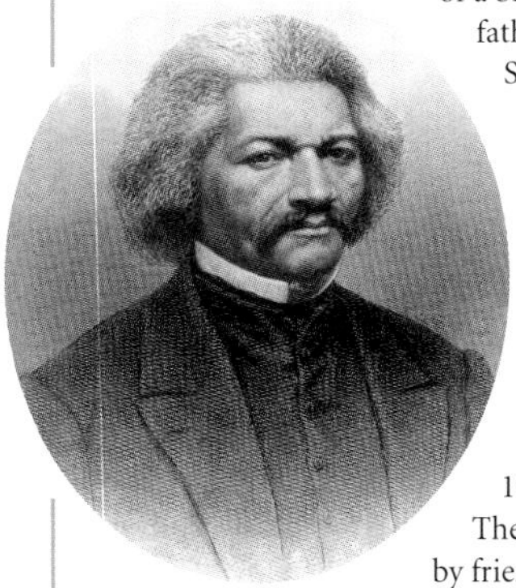

Douglass was born a slave in Maryland's Talbot County in 1818, son of a black mother and a white father, possibly his owner. Sent to Baltimore as a servant, he taught himself to read; at 20 he escaped to New York, then Massachussetts, where he lectured for the Massachusetts Anti-Slavery Society. To elude slave hunters after publishing his autobiography, in 1845, he fled to Europe. The purchase of his freedom by friends allowed him to return two years later. He began the *North Star* newspaper and kept working for the rights of blacks and women.

After the Civil War, he moved to Washington, D.C. Appointed U.S. marshal of the District in 1877, he bought 9-acre Cedar Hill. He expanded it to 15 acres and enlarged the house by seven rooms. After his 1895 death, his widow, Helen, preserved Cedar Hill and organized the Frederick Douglass Memorial and Historical Association. The house was later turned over to the National Park Service.

The guided 30-minute tour begins in the **visitor center** with a 17-minute orientation film. Among items on display is a Lincoln cane given to Douglass by the President's widow. After the video, you climb the steps to the **Victorian house.** Inside, the tastefully appointed parlors, library, and dining room look much as they did in Douglass's time—some 90 percent of the furnishings are original. The kitchen, with its coal and wood-burning stove, and the adjoining washroom are reminders of the days before electricity and indoor plumbing. Upstairs, Douglass's bedroom has a 19th-century bootjack and pair of shoes tucked by a chair. To see the different styles of his two wives, peek into their separate bedrooms.

Outside, you'll find the **Growlery** (a reconstruction), the private study to which Douglass often escaped. Cedar Hill was originally a farm estate with chicken coops, barn, and carriage house; Hurricane Hazel destroyed all but two of the outbuildings in 1967. ■

The Douglass house contains many of the early civil rights leader's personal effects.

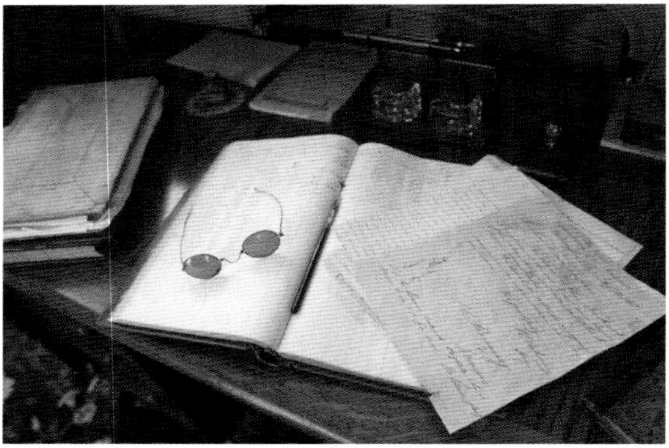

Kenilworth Aquatic Gardens

A cool feast of water lilies and lotuses floats on the waters of the Kenilworth Aquatic Gardens, on the east bank of the Anacostia. Started in 1880 by Civil War veteran Walter B. Shaw, this lovely 14-acre sanctuary, now managed by the National Park Service, is in full bloom in midsummer. Garden tours are offered mornings on weekends during summer months.

A **visitor center** near the gardens' parking lot has exhibits on the area. With 40 ponds and a 335-yard boardwalk extending into marshes, the gardens offer excellent opportunities for viewing birds and other wildlife, such as osprey, snapping turtles, and muskrats.

The 0.7-mile (one way) **River Walk** offers a closer look at 77-acre Kenilworth Marsh, which borders the gardens. A city dump in the 1950s and '60s, the fill area is now rich in bird and plant life. Here American bittern, long billed marsh wrens, and spotted salamanders live in a cattail-fringed wetland.

The best time for seeing wildlife and catching night-blooming lilies is early morning. The gardens open at 7 a.m. ■

Kenilworth Aquatic Gardens
www.nps.gov/keaq
Map p. 193
1550 Anacostia Ave., N.E.
202-426-6905
Bus: V7 & 8

An aquatic perennial indigenous to Asia, the sacred lotus flower opens in the early morning.

Anacostia Community Museum

Located in Fort Stanton Park, site of a Civil War fortification, this Anacostia museum opened in 1967 as a neighborhood museum devoted to the interpretation of the African American experience, particularly in Washington, D.C.

Now part of the Smithsonian Institution, the museum offers a changing program of exhibits, music, art, dance, storytelling, and poetry. The exhibit "East of the River," for example, focuses on daily life and activities in Anacostia neighborhoods, spanning the time between the 1940s and 1990s.

Other exhibits have included retrospectives on black photographers, such as New Orleans's Jules Lion, who began producing daguerreotypes in 1840, and inventors such as Benjamin Banneker, who helped plan the capital city. In addition, the museum has staged exhibits covering topics as diverse as African-American quilts, black churches, the antebellum South, the civil rights movement, Malcolm X, the 1920s renaissance, and the meaning and celebration of the Kwanzaa and Juneteenth holidays. There's always something interesting on display. ■

Anacostia Community Museum
www.si.edu/anacostia
Map p. 193
1901 Fort Pl., S.E.
202-633-4820
Metro: Anacostia, then Bus W2-3

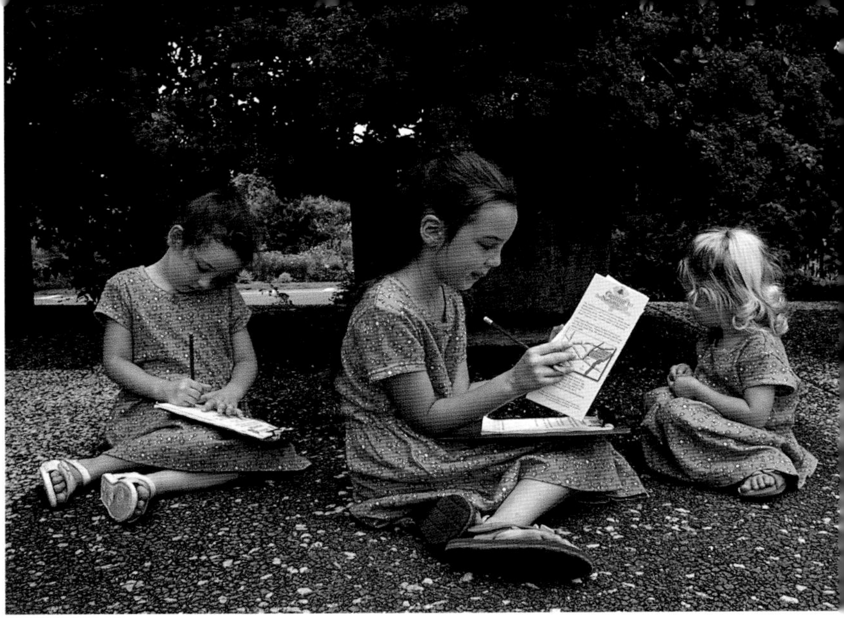

U.S. National Arboretum

U.S. National Arboretum
www.usna.usda.gov
Map p. 193
24th & R Sts., N.E., or 3501 New York Ave., N.E.
202-245-2726
Bus: X6 & B2

A BIT OFF THE BEATEN TOURIST TRACK, THIS WHOLLY delightful oasis of fields, ponds, fountains, gardens, and flowering trees is just the tonic for those in need of some outdoor beauty. Established by an act of Congress in 1927, the National Arboretum is run by the Department of Agriculture as a living museum and a research and education facility. The arboretum's 446 acres include 9.5 miles of gentle roadways that wind past a dozen garden areas.

A pleasure any time, the arboretum is especially beautiful in spring, with 15,000 multicolored azaleas and blossoming dogwoods, cherries, and crabapples blushing on the hillsides. The sweet fragrances of magnolias and roses blend with those of woodland wildflowers.

In summer, the delicate flowers of high grasses stipple meadows, while daylilies and crape myrtles take to the heat with ease, and water lilies bloom in the koi pool that surrounds one wing of the administration building. Fall enriches the color palette with the vivid yellows of hickory and tulip poplar and the wine reds of sweet gum and dogwood. The late flowers of witch hazel and spider lilies fan the flames.

In the cold quiet days of winter, the bright red berries of holly glisten like little beads, and dwarf conifers and other evergreens are often rimed with ice. Ornamental grasses and dry leaves chatter in the winds that sweep through the open fields.

VISITING

On the way to the administration building from the New York Ave-nue entrance, you'll notice beehive-shaped **brick kilns.** When the brickyard, dating from 1909, shut down in 1972, the acreage and buildings were sold to the arboretum.

At the administration building, you'll find maps and a list of gardens currently in bloom. Next to

Children create their own floral tableaus beneath a flowering "Tonto" crape myrtle at the arboretum.

this building, the recently redone **National Bonsai and Penjing Museum** has an outstanding collection of miniature trees from Japan, China, and America. Breezes lilt through feathery Japanese maples and gravel paths meander among bonsai pavilions.

Across the drive, the 2.5-acre **National Herb Garden** features some 800 varieties of herbs in ten themed gardens. Standing like ruins in a nearby field are 22 sandstone Corinthian columns, removed from the Capitol's east central portico in 1958 when the Senate side of the Capitol building was enlarged. To see other gardens, take the guided 35-minute open-air tram tour *(weekends mid-April–mid-Oct., $)* starting near the R Street entrance. Or drive or bike to most by looping the outer roads.

Heading southwest from the administration building, you come first to the **National Boxwood Collection—**more than a hundred species on 5 acres. Adjoining perennials include irises, peonies, and daylilies. Continue to the **azalea collections,** which peak in late April. To the east, on Crabtree Road, pull over for **Fern Valley** and its native plants of the eastern United States; a half-mile wooded path traipses past wildflowers, a meadow, prairie, and a stream. Plants are grouped by region—piedmont, southern mountains, coastal plain, and prairie.

At the arboretum's far eastern end, the **Asian collections** are one of the city's highlights. Flora from Japan, Korea, and China have been planted on a hillside so that from strategically placed benches you have glimpses of a pagoda through the trees and views down to the Anacostia River. Ginkgos and bamboo bend in gentle breezes, and in spring Japanese wisteria and other flowers scent the air. To the north, the **Gotelli Collection of dwarf and slow-growing conifers** is considered to be among the world's best. The 1,500 specimens include juniper, cedar, spruce, fir, hemlock, and arborvitae.

The setting of the **dogwood collections** nearby offers a spectacular view of the Anacostia River. South of the Asian collections, the glossy **hollies and magnolias** are striking in all seasons. ■

Anacostia River

Since the arrival of Europeans nearly 400 years ago, the Anacostia watershed has been used, overused, and abused. Runoffs from big farms in the 18th century silted the river, and urban growth has troubled the waters ever since. In the early 20th century, efforts to reshape the waterway and "reclaim" the adjoining swamps for development nearly killed the Anacostia.

Fortunately, the tide is turning. Government agencies as well as citizen groups, such as the Anacostia Watershed Society, are working to protect this valuable ecosystem, a vital part of the country's largest estuary—the Chesapeake Bay. Over the past decade, hundreds of tons of debris have been cleaned up, and some 12,000 trees have been planted. In the city, the river's watershed is essentially sidewalk and street drains, which means that unfiltered trash too often finds its way into the river. With an eye on the future, the Anacostia Watershed Society has enlisted the help of thousands of city youths to help clean up this river. ■

Basilica of the National Shrine of the Immaculate Conception

THE BLUE DOME AND 329-FOOT-TALL CAMPANILE OF THE National Shrine preside over the skyline of Northeast Washington. Built along Byzantine and Romanesque lines, the National Shrine is the country's largest—and the world's tenth largest—Roman Catholic church and one of the most beautiful and impressive pieces of architecture in a city renowned for its monuments.

Basilica of the National Shrine of the Immaculate Conception
www.nationalshrine.com
Map p. 193
Michigan Ave. & 4th St., N.E.
202-526-8300
Metro: Brookland–CUA; Bus: 80, H1-4

In 1913, while rector of the Catholic University of America, Bishop Thomas J. Shahan (1857–1932) presented Pope Pius X with plans for building a shrine to the Blessed Virgin Mary on the campus. With the Pope's support, work began in 1920; the building was dedicated four decades later, in 1959. In 1990, John Paul II designated the shrine a basilica because of its significance as a national center of worship.

You can arrange a free tour on the website, or pick up a floor plan near the entrance and wander on your own. More than 75 chapels and oratories, many funded by American ethnic groups, circle the perimeter of the crypt level and upper church. You should enter on the upstairs level, where the grandiose **Great Upper Church,** its vaulted ceilings soaring to a height of 100 feet, takes your breath away. Natural light floods the vast interior, stained glass casts color on walls and floors, and mosaics and candles sparkle in almost every niche and dome. Notice the swirling cosmos and the Creation depicted above the east transept and, in the west transept, the people rising toward a cloud-enthroned Jesus. The chancel dome holds a huge mosaic titled "Christ in Majesty." A soothing contrast can be see in the green marble walls and trickling fountain of the **Mary Queen of Ireland chapel.**

Stairs lead down to the **crypt level,** where black and white marble walls and pillars adorn **Memorial Hall,** honoring the shrine's donors. Also noteworthy here is the **Crypt Church,** modeled on the Roman catacombs. It holds services six times a day during the week. In **Our Mother of Africa Chapel,** sculpture groups depict African American history from slavery to freedom. ■

Pope John Paul II Cultural Center

Up the street from the Romanesque National Shrine is this modernistic limestone and granite multimedia museum (3900 Harewood Rd., N.E., 202-635-5400, closed Mon., $). Visitors watch a short orientation video about the center, then take a self-guided tour through galleries exploring such themes as church and papal history, community, and the life of Christ. Computer terminals offer background information and activities such as designing a stained-glass window. One room is devoted to the teachings of Pope John Paul II; another—equipped with bell ropes—offers an opportunity for "virtual" change ringing. ■

Opposite: The National Shrine's tiled dome and soaring bell tower punctuate the city's skyline.

More places to visit east of the Capitol

CONGRESSIONAL CEMETERY

Originally intended to contain the graves of congressmen and officials who died in office, the Congressional Cemetery, established in 1807, is the oldest national cemetery and the final resting place of many Washington notables. Beginning in 1839, sandstone monuments were created for every member of Congress, though only 90 are actually occupied (the others are empty memorials to people buried elsewhere). Congress stopped the practice in 1877 after a furious debate, in which Senator George Hoar of Massachusetts argued that being buried under one of the massive monuments added "a new terror to death."

Among the cemetery's famous residents are Capitol architect William Thornton (1828), Civil War photographer Mathew Brady (1916), Marine Corps bandmaster John Philip Sousa (1932), and J. Edgar Hoover (1972), director of the FBI. Visitors can stroll the grounds; a map is located at the entrance.

www.congressionalcemetery.org
Map p. 193 1801 E St., S.E.
202-543-0539 Metro: Stadium Armory

FRANCISCAN MONASTERY

If you can't afford a trip to the Holy Land, this working monastery near the National Shrine of the Immaculate Conception offers a good facsimile. Tours are offered hourly. Built in 1899 to educate missionaries, it contains full-scale reproductions of such sacred places as the Grotto of Lourdes, the Grotto of Gethsemane, the Tomb of the Virgin Mary, and the Holy Sepulchre of Christ. The Byzantine-style church is laid out in the shape of a Crusader's cross, with chapels in the four corners. Especially memorable are the Roman-style catacombs downstairs. In spring the gardens grace the monastery with flowering rosebushes, dogwoods, and cherry trees. You'll almost forget you're in the middle of a 21st-century city.

www.myfranciscan.org Map p. 193
1400 Quincy St., N.E. 202-526-6800
Metro: Brookland–CUA

A monk leads a tour down into the catacombs of the Franciscan Monastery.

WASHINGTON NAVY YARD

On a plot of land set aside by George Washington is this ceremonial "Quarterdeck of the Navy." Kids enjoy clambering through the passages and up and down the ladders of the decommissioned destroyer **U.S.S. *Barry*,** permanently moored here *(closed Sun.)*. The 424-foot-long ship took part in the 1962 Cuban missile crisis and in the Vietnam War. You can walk through the wardroom, bunk room, sick bay, galley and mess deck, and pilothouse.

Just across the parking lot from the ship stands the **Navy Museum,** which houses thousands of artifacts dating from the Revolutionary War *(reservations required for weekend visits; 202-433-6897)*. Among these are working periscopes, a fighter plane, hands-on antiaircraft guns, and more than a hundred model ships. Other facilities on the site include parade grounds, art galleries, and a historical research center. To the north are the Greek Revival arched gate and guardhouses designed in 1804 by Benjamin Henry Latrobe, one of the Capitol's architects.

www.history.navy.mil Map p. 193
9th & M Sts., S.E. 202-433-4882 (Navy Museum), 202-433-3377 (U.S.S. *Barry*)
Hours and access for branches varies
Metro: Eastern Market, Navy Yard ■

Only on the Virginia side of the Potomac can you complete the story of the country's past, including colonial Alexandria and its early associations with the Revolutionary War, and Arlington, famous for its national cemetery.

Across the Potomac

Pineapple door knocker, symbolizing hospitality

Across the Potomac

GRACEFULLY ARCHING ACROSS THE POTOMAC RIVER, CONNECTING Washington to Virginia, Arlington Memorial Bridge makes a powerful visual statement by linking memorials dedicated to Union Commander in Chief Abraham Lincoln and Confederate Gen. Robert E. Lee—a symbolic joining of North and South. Overlooking Lincoln's templelike memorial on the Mall is Lee's Arlington House, high on a hill in what is now Arlington National Cemetery, surrounded by the somber white graves of Civil War veterans from both North and South, as well as servicepeople from all succeeding wars.

The Northern Virginia region just outside Washington proper is a suburban mix of historic sites, residential neighborhoods, and shopping malls. Arlington and Alexandria especially have much to offer. Separated by the Crystal City high-rises around Ronald Reagan Washington National Airport, the two heavily populated and developed communities are connected by the Metro system and highly scenic George Washington Memorial Parkway.

Both of these suburban areas originally belonged to the District of Columbia, then a diamond-shaped city straddling the river. But in 1846, Virginia took back its part, the returned land equaling about one-third of the entire city. The fortunes of the two areas have been tied to Washington ever since.

Already a tobacco port, Alexandria got its official start in 1749 as a 60-acre townsite. George Washington, who lived 9 miles south at Mount Vernon, and Robert E. Lee, both considered Alexandria their hometown. Falling on hard times after the Civil War, the town has prospered in recent years with the sprucing up of its waterfront and the restoration of 18th-century town houses. Now a fashionable residential area, the town draws a steady stream of tourists to its bars, boutiques, restaurants, and riverside craft shops. Historical sites give insight into the lives of Washington, Lee, and other prominent locals.

One of the nation's smallest counties, and containing no incorporated cities or towns within its boundaries, Arlington did not exist as its own separate entity until after 1846, when the land was returned from Washington to Virginia. Today it is home to Arlington National Cemetery and the Pentagon. The moving Marine Corps War Memorial, Theodore Roosevelt Island and its tribute to the 26th President, and the string of Potomac River parks along the parkway are other good reasons for venturing to the Virginia side of the river. ■

Theodore Roosevelt Memorial Bridge connects Washington with the burbs.

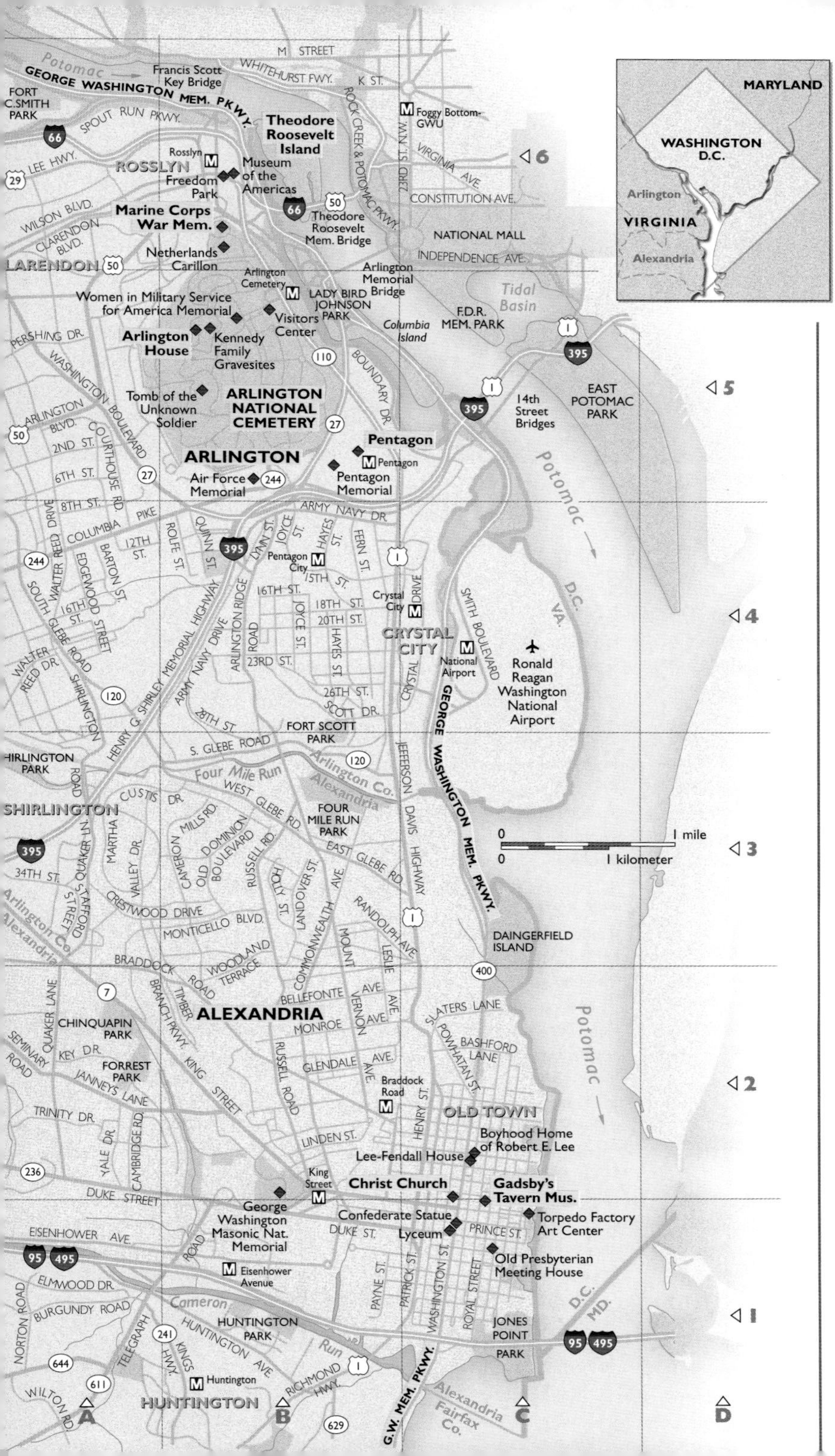

MARYLAND
WASHINGTON D.C.
Arlington
VIRGINIA
Alexandria
M STREET
WHITEHURST FWY.
K ST.
Potomac
Francis Scott Key Bridge
GEORGE WASHINGTON MEM. PKWY.
FORT C.SMITH PARK
SPOUT RUN PKWY.
Theodore Roosevelt Island
Foggy Bottom-GWU
ROCK CREEK & POTOMAC PKWY.
23RD ST. N.W.
VIRGINIA AVE.
6
LEE HWY.
Rosslyn
ROSSLYN
Freedom Park
Museum of the Americas
CONSTITUTION AVE.
WILSON BLVD.
Marine Corps War Mem.
Theodore Roosevelt Mem. Bridge
NATIONAL MALL
CLARENDON BLVD.
Netherlands Carillon
INDEPENDENCE AVE.
LARENDON
Arlington Cemetery
Arlington Memorial Bridge
Tidal Basin
LADY BIRD JOHNSON PARK
Women in Military Service for America Memorial
Visitors Center
F.D.R. MEM. PARK
Columbia Island
PERSHING DR.
Arlington House
Kennedy Family Gravesites
BOUNDARY DR.
WASHINGTON BOULEVARD
Tomb of the Unknown Soldier
ARLINGTON NATIONAL CEMETERY
14th Street Bridges
EAST POTOMAC PARK
5
ARLINGTON BLVD.
2ND ST.
COURTHOUSE RD.
Pentagon
ARLINGTON
6TH ST.
Air Force Memorial
Pentagon Memorial
8TH ST.
ARMY NAVY DR.
COLUMBIA PIKE
12TH ST.
ROLFE ST.
QUINN ST.
LYNN ST.
JOYCE ST.
HAYES ST.
FERN ST.
Pentagon City
15TH ST.
WALTER REED DRIVE
EDGEWOOD STREET
BARTON ST.
16TH ST.
18TH ST.
20TH ST.
Crystal City
CRYSTAL DRIVE
SOUTH GLEBE ROAD
HENRY G. SHIRLEY MEMORIAL HIGHWAY
ARMY NAVY DRIVE
ARLINGTON RIDGE ROAD
23RD ST.
CRYSTAL CITY
National Airport
SMITH BOULEVARD
D.C.
VA.
4
Ronald Reagan Washington National Airport
WALTER REED DR.
SHIRLINGTON
26TH ST.
SCOTT DR.
28TH ST.
FORT SCOTT PARK
S. GLEBE ROAD
HIRLINGTON PARK
ROAD
Four Mile Run
Arlington Co.
Alexandria
JEFFERSON DAVIS HIGHWAY
GEORGE WASHINGTON MEM. PKWY.
CUSTIS DR.
WEST GLEBE RD.
FOUR MILE RUN PARK
SHIRLINGTON
MILLS RD.
DOMINION BOULEVARD
CAMERON
OLD
RUSSELL RD.
MARTHA
N. QUAKER
VALLEY DR.
EAST GLEBE RD.
0
1 mile
1 kilometer
3
34TH ST.
STAFFORD STREET
HOLLY ST.
LANDOVER ST.
COMMONWEALTH AVE.
RANDOLPH AVE.
CRESTWOOD DRIVE
MONTICELLO BLVD.
MOUNT VERNON AVE.
LESLIE AVE.
DAINGERFIELD ISLAND
Arlington Co.
Alexandria
BRADDOCK ROAD
WOODLAND TERRACE
TIMBER
BRANCH PKWY.
BELLEFONTE AVE.
QUAKER LANE
ALEXANDRIA
SLATERS LANE
CHINQUAPIN PARK
MONROE AVE.
POWHATAN ST.
BASHFORD LANE
Potomac
SEMINARY ROAD
KEY DR.
FORREST PARK
KING STREET
RUSSELL ROAD
GLENDALE AVE.
JANNEYS LANE
Braddock Road
HENRY ST.
2
TRINITY DR.
OLD TOWN
YALE DR.
CAMBRIDGE RD.
LINDEN ST.
Boyhood Home of Robert E. Lee
Lee-Fendall House
King Street
Christ Church
Gadsby's Tavern Mus.
DUKE STREET
George Washington Masonic Nat. Memorial
Confederate Statue
Torpedo Factory Art Center
DUKE ST.
Lyceum
PRINCE ST.
EISENHOWER AVE.
ROAD
Old Presbyterian Meeting House
Eisenhower Avenue
ELMWOOD DR.
PAYNE ST.
PATRICK ST.
WASHINGTON ST.
ROYAL STREET
NORTON ROAD
BURGUNDY ROAD
Cameron
D.C.
MD.
HUNTINGTON PARK
JONES POINT PARK
1
TELEGRAPH
HUNTINGTON AVE.
KINGS HWY.
Run
RICHMOND HWY.
G.W. MEM. PKWY.
WILTON RD.
Huntington
HUNTINGTON
Alexandria Fairfax Co.
A
B
C
D

Arlington National Cemetery

Arlington National Cemetery
www.arlingtoncemetery.org
203 B5
Virginia side of Arlington Memorial Bridge, off Va. 110
703-607-8000
Changing of the Guard, every hour Oct.–March, every half hour April–Sept.
$ (parking fee)
$$ tourmobile
Metro: Arlington Cemetery; Bus: 5A & B, 13A-B & F-G

ROWS OF WHITE HEADSTONES ON ROLLING HILLS, THE Changing of the Guard at the Tomb of the Unknowns, the eternal flame at John F. Kennedy's grave: These enduring images immediately bring to mind the nation's most famous national cemetery.

The nearby mansion atop the hill is Arlington House, once the home of Robert E. Lee and his wife, Mary. Lee's father-in-law—George Washington Parke Custis, the first president's adopted grandson—built the Greek Revival mansion in 1802–1817; it anchored a 1,100-acre plantation. Lee and his wife lived here on and off for 30 years while traveling between U.S. Army posts.

Soon after Lee left to fight for the Confederacy in 1861, the federal government confiscated the estate. In 1864, the mansion and 200 acres were set aside for a national cemetery at the urging of Union Quartermaster Gen. Montgomery Meigs. Later that year, his son was killed in the war; a high-relief tomb effigy of him lying slain by the side is one of the cemetery's most distinctive memorials.

Despite the objection of Meigs, Confederate soldiers were allowed burial in Arlington, but without any official observances. In 1900 Congress finally designated a Confederate section of the cemetery, and in 1914 the **Confederate Memorial** was dedicated by President Woodrow Wilson.

As for the Lee family's fate, Lee's son, G. W. C. Lee, sued the government after the Civil War for confiscating the land. The Supreme Court ruled that he should be paid the market value, $150,000.

The 612-acre cemetery is now the final resting place for more than 290,000 service people. With 100 funerals conducted every week, the cemetery is expected to be filled by 2025, at which time it may expand onto other government-owned land. For burial here, a service person must have died on active duty or been awarded a high military decoration; the cremated remains of any veteran with an honorable discharge can be entombed in the Columbarium. For a funeral with

Hundreds of thousands of servicemen and women lie buried beneath Arlington's green expanses.

full military honors, a flag-draped coffin is accompanied by an honor guard. After three rifle volleys, the coffin is lowered, while "Taps" is played. The guards then present the folded flag to the next of kin.

VISITING

Entering the cemetery via Memorial Drive, you'll see the semicircular building of the **Women in Military Service for America Memorial.** Dedicated in 1997, it honors the nearly two million women who have served since 1776. Begin your tour in the visitor center, which has exhibits, a 12-minute film, and a map of the cemetery. You can stroll on your own among the quiet, tree-shaded pathways or hop aboard a tourmobile *(fare)*, which stops at major points of interest.

From behind the visitor center, head up the pathway to find the **gravesite of President John F. Kennedy.** At his funeral in 1963, his widow, Jacqueline, lit an eternal flame that continues to flicker even in the rain. She and their two infant children also are interred here. The site offers a grand view of familiar monuments across the river in Washington. Nearby, a white wooden cross marks the **grave of Senator Robert F. Kennedy.**

The best view of Washington, however, is further up the hill at **Arlington House.** The Union Army used the house as a defense post headquarters. After the war, the cemetery superintendent lived and worked here for many years. In 1955 it was officially designated the Robert E. Lee Memorial.

Restored to its antebellum appearance, the high-ceilinged house looks much as it did during the Lee years. Though many heirlooms in the 15 rooms were looted, about a third of the furnishings are original. (In 2007, however, the furnishings were removed for a major restoration of the mansion that will continue through 2010.) In the slaves' quarters and museum out back are exhibits on the Lee and Custis families.

About a half-mile walk south of the house, adjacent to the amphitheater, the **Tomb of the Unknowns** holds the remains of unidentified servicemen, one each from the World Wars and Korea (the Vietnam veteran's remains were removed in 1998 when they were identified). A 24-hour guard patrols this symbolic

A horse-drawn caisson and flag-draped coffin are standard at a full military funeral.

site, carrying an M-14 rifle with a ceremonial bayonet. The sentinel takes 21 steps on the plaza (symbolic of a 21-gun salute), then turns to face the tomb for 21 seconds.

Among those buried at Arlington are polar explorer Richard Byrd, boxer Joe Louis, 229 sailors from the U.S.S. *Maine* (sunk in Havana harbor in 1898), and the city designer of Washington, Pierre Charles L'Enfant, whose grave lies in front of the mansion. Another is Gen. John J. Pershing, commander of the American Expeditionary Forces in World War I, who lies buried among those with whom he served. Section 60 contains the biggest concentration of new graves, those of military men and women killed in Iraq and Afghanistan. ■

Arlington House
www.nps.gov/arho
Map 203 B5
Tel 703-235-1530

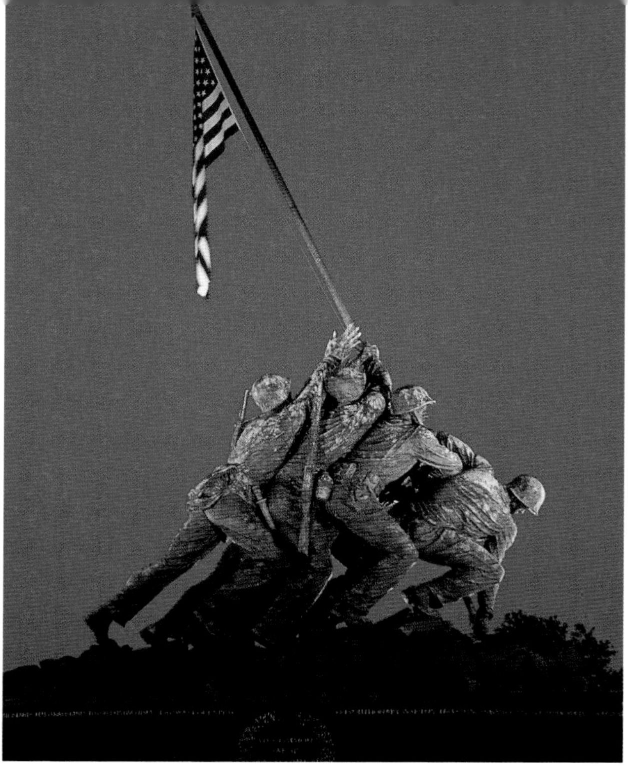

Only three of the six men depicted in the memorial survived the war.

Marine Corps War Memorial

Marine Corps War Memorial
www.nps.gov/gwmp/usmc.htm
203 B6
N. Meade St., just N of Arlington Cemetery
703-289-2500
Metro: Arlington Cemetery or Rosslyn; Bus: 4A

KNOWN AS THE IWO JIMA MEMORIAL, ONE OF THE NATION'S most famous war monuments sits in a grassy park adjacent to Arlington Cemetery. Its larger-than-life realism rests on the fact that the figures are nearly six times life size, and the event they depict really happened.

There were, however, actually two flag raisings. On Feb. 23, 1945, four days into a vicious struggle for control of Iwo Jima, a detachment of U.S. Marines made it to the top of Mount Suribachi, the island's highest point, and raised a small American flag. Later that afternoon, after the slopes had been cleared of enemy resistance, five Marines and a Navy hospital corpsmen raised a larger flag. It was this second flag raising that news photographer Joseph Rosenthal captured in the famous image that won him a Pulitzer Prize. The Marines' capture of the island three weeks later was a crucial victory in the Pacific campaign.

Sculptor Felix de Weldon, then on duty with the U.S. Navy, was so moved by the image that he cast it in bronze. Dedicated in 1954, the 78-foot-high sculpture depicts the soldiers standing atop a chunk of jagged black granite that resembles the island's volcanic rock, their cloth flag flying 24 hours a day. On Tuesday evenings in summer, the Marine Corps presents a spirited parade here.

Nearby rises the **Netherlands Carillon,** with 49 bells, presented by the Dutch in 1960 in thanks for American aid during the war. ■

The Pentagon and Memorial

No one today can look at this massive fortress without recalling the tragedy of September 11, 2001, when a hijacked jetliner crashed into the building's south side, now rebuilt. Millions of dollars in donations were collected to construct a memorial park honoring the 184 civilian and military victims of that incident.

One of the world's largest office buildings, the 6.5-million-square-foot Pentagon was built in 16 months during World War II to combine the offices of the War Department under one roof. The number five has no particular significance; the building originally conformed to a five-sided site, and since President Roosevelt liked the unique shape, it was kept.

Today the Pentagon is a city unto itself, housing 23,000 military, civilian, and support personnel working to protect national interests. On weekdays, volunteers from the military services conduct 60-minute tours along more than a mile of corridors, where military art, model planes, and portraits of military leaders are on view. Out of sight are the top-secret War Room and other situation rooms. Reservations are mandatory for tours and should be made online at least two weeks in advance.

The adjacent two-acre memorial occupies a site near where American Airlines Flight 77 hit the Pentagon. In an open competition, the winning design for the memorial was submitted by a pair of young architects in Manhattan, Julie Beckman and Keith Kaseman. It features reflecting pools, maple trees, and rows of lighted concrete benches—one for each of the victims.

The 125 benches of the Pentagon victims face the building; those of the 59 airline passengers are oriented toward the flight path. The benches bear numbers corresponding to the individual names of the victims and are organized according to their ages (ranging from 3 to 71).

The site can be approached from the Pentagon' south parking lot and nearby Metro station or from public parking lots at Pentagon City. ■

The Pentagon and Memorial

http://pentagon.afis.osd.mil

203 B5

I-395 and Jefferson Davis Hwy. (Va. 110)

703-697-1776

Closed Sat.–Sun. & federal holidays

$ for parking at Pentagon City

Metro: Pentagon; Bus: 5A & B, 16, 13A-B & F-G, Art73SH 4

The Pentagon Memorial is located on the West Lawn of the building, within 200 feet of the September 11, 2001, impact site.

Air Force Memorial

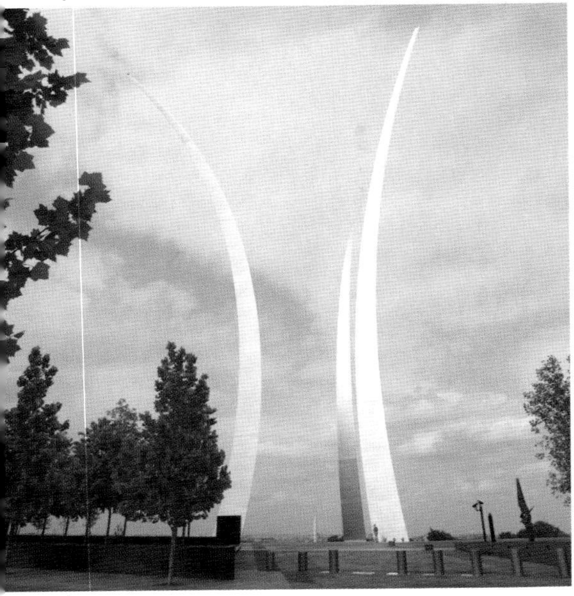

The soaring Air Force Memorial

www.airforcememorial.org
203 B5

Visible across the Washington skyline, the sleek stainless steel spires of the Air Force Memorial soar skyward from a promontory near the Pentagon and Arlington Cemetery. The new landmark opened in October 2006.

The novel design is by architect James Ingo Freed, whose other local credits include the U.S. Holocaust Memorial Museum (see pp. 102–103) and the Ronald Reagan Building on Pennsylvania Avenue. He drew his inspiration from the "bomb burst" formation of Air Force jet maneuvers. The tallest spire reaches to 270 feet. Three spires were used to represent the three core values of the Air Force (integrity, service before self, and excellence) and its three divisions (active, guard, and reserve). In granite beneath each spire is the Air Force star.

The memorial also has a bronze honor guard statue, by renowned sculptor Zenos Frudakis, and an engraved glass wall in honor of those who died serving in the Air Force and its predecessor services, which date back to the U.S. Army Air Corps of the early 1900s. Plans call for adding a park and parade ground. ■

Theodore Roosevelt Island

Theodore Roosevelt Island

www.nps.gov/gwmp/tri.htm
203 B6
Potomac River, 0.25 mile N of Theodore Roosevelt Bridge via George Washington Memorial Pkwy. north (no vehicle access southbound)
703-289-2550
Metro: Rosslyn

An arcadia of wooded paths and bird-filled marshes, this 91-acre island opposite the Kennedy Center is a favorite lunchtime retreat for office workers. Some 2.5 miles of trails are just right for walking, running, bird-watching, and general relaxing from city life stresses.

In 1967 the island was turned into a memorial to the charismatic, conservation-minded U.S. President. Many people heading over the footbridge for a walk are surprised to find, tucked in the middle of the woods, a rather grandiose **memorial** featuring a 17-foot-high bronze of Roosevelt, fountains, and several enormous granite tablets inscribed with his words.

After a look at the memorial, you can choose between wooded or river-edged paths. One of the most delightful areas is the **boardwalk** through the swamp and marsh on the island's east side. Along here, herons stalk prey among cattails and pickerelweed, while bald cypresses and gnarled oaks suggest a pre-Washington landscape. ■

George Washington Memorial Parkway

OFFERING PEERLESS VIEWS OF THE CAPITAL CITY, THIS stunning roadway lends the perfect excuse for a leisurely drive. Ambling along the Potomac River between Mount Vernon and the American Legion Bridge, it links historic sites, riverside parks, and overlooks.

George Washington Memorial Parkway

www.nps.gov/gwmp

203 A6, B5–B6, C1–C5

703-289-2500

Beginning south of Alexandria at **Mount Vernon** (see pp. 222–224), the parkway winds north through maples, oaks, beeches, and tulip polars, chosen when the parkway was designed in the 1930s to give it the look of the Virginia countryside. Two miles beyond Mount Vernon sprawls **Fort Hunt Park,** preserving batteries that guarded the river approach to the city from 1898 to 1918. Look across the river to see its mate, **Fort Washington** (1824).

Ahead, a right turnoff leads to **River Farm** *(703-768-5700, closed Sun.),* once part of George Washington's estate. Beyond **Belle Haven Marina** spreads a wide-sweeping upriver view—birders congregate along here to scan the water and sky for migrating geese and songbirds. For a closer look, take a stroll at **Dyke Marsh** *(Belle Haven Marina),* a 240-acre bird haven.

Within **Old Town Alexandria** (see pp. 212–214), the parkway becomes Washington Street. Two blocks beyond King Street rises **Christ Church** (see p. 211), on the left. Beyond town you'll spot **Daingerfield Island,** site of a small marina and restaurant with a view.

Just north of Reagan Washington National Airport comes the most breathtaking stretch—the **Washington skyline** and its parade of monuments: the Capitol, Jefferson Memorial, Washington Monument, and Lincoln Memorial. The grassy riverbank here is ideal for picnicking. Beyond the 14th Street Bridges rises the **Navy and Marine Memorial.** Farther, you'll pass through the **LBJ Memorial Grove** and **Lady Bird Johnson Park,** abundant with flowers.

About a quarter mile beyond Roosevelt Bridge, you'll spy the turnout for **Theodore Roosevelt Island** (see opposite). The road passes beneath Key Bridge, with **Georgetown University's** spire looming across the river. The drive then climbs above the Potomac, offering overlooks of the increasingly wild and rocky river. About 1.5 miles beyond Turkey Run Park, the parkway ends at I-495 and the American Legion Bridge. ■

The parkway in springtime splendor

Alexandria

With its brick sidewalks, federal town houses, and quaint shops and restaurants, Alexandria's Old Town reminds many people of Georgetown. No coincidence here, since both arose as tobacco ports in the mid-1700s a mere 8 river miles from one another.

Scotsman John Alexander, for whom Alexandria is named, purchased much of present-day Alexandria in 1669 from an English ship captain for 6,000 pounds of tobacco. Incorporated in 1749, the town blossomed as a foreign port of entry. Strolling along Old Town's beautifully preserved wharf today, it's easy to visualize how Alexandria must have looked, when tall-masted brigs and schooners docked at the piers, mariners bustled between brick warehouses, and captains strutted cobbled lanes. Slaves and grain as well as tobacco added to the early prosperity of this genteel Southern town.

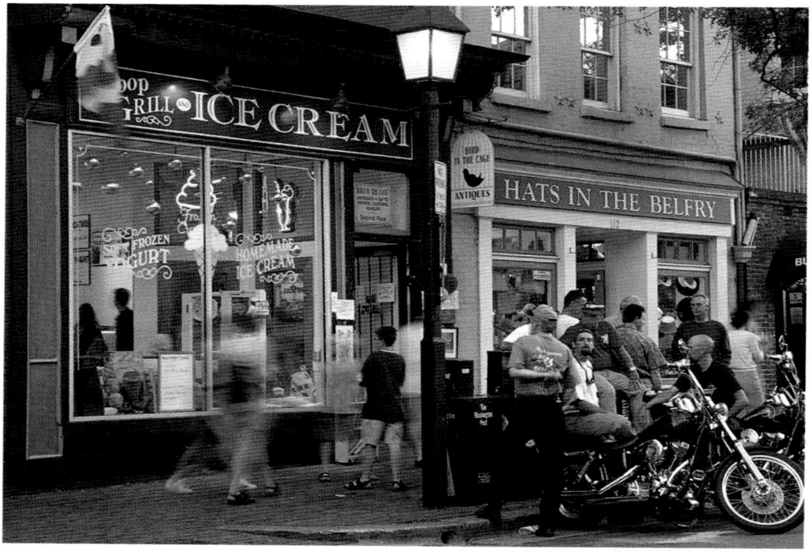

King Street's panoply of shops and restaurants is housed in centuries'-old row houses.

The Civil War, however, changed all that. As a buffer for Washington, only 100 miles north of the Confederate capital of Richmond, Alexandria was immediately occupied and soon overrun with Union forces. The fortified town became a crossroads for men and supplies—hundreds of thousands of soldiers tramped through on their way to postings and battles, and train after train rolled in with the wounded. Warehouses, churches, hotels, even large houses were requisitioned for use as military stations and hospitals.

After the war, the small-town atmosphere was all but gone, and as Washington grew Alexandria sprawled and deteriorated. In 1946 the City Council stepped in to protect the splendid 18th- and 19th-century row houses, making Old Town the nation's third officially designated historic district.

Today, Old Town is a delightful place to spend a sunny afternoon, poking into shops, eating ice cream, watching boats glide by on the river. Especially on weekend evenings, crowds pack a spate of restaurants and pubs, enjoying the vibrant nightlife against its historical backdrop. ■

Christ Church

Historic Christ Church has sat behind its iron-gated fence on Washington Street since before Alexandria was established. Completed in 1773 in simple Georgian country style, it features a typical brick exterior and whitewashed interior. The fine Palladian chancel window is unusual ornamentation for a church of its time.

George Washington was one of the first to buy a pew here, now marked by a silver plaque (No. 60). Tradition says that on the lawn he first declared to friends his intent to fight the war of American independence. Robert E. Lee was confirmed here on July 17, 1853 (a fact marked by another silver plaque, on the chancel), and he worshiped here with his family.

The tree-shaded **burying ground** was used for Alexandrians until 1808; the earliest tombstone is dated March 20, 1791. Look for one of the latest tombstones, for Anne Warren, a popular actress in her day. Her 1808 epitaph reads in part: "The unrivaled excellence of theatrical talents was surpassed by the mighty virtues ... which adorned her private life. In her were contained the affectionate wife and mother and the sincere friend."

Docents lead **tours** daily; meet at the church's front door. ■

Christ Church
www.historicchristchurch.org
203 C2
118 N. Washington St.
703-549-1450
Metro: King St.; Bus: 10A

Gadsby's Tavern Museum

Consisting of a 1785 tavern and a 1792 hotel, Gadsby's Tavern was colonial Alexandria's center of social, political, and business life. Festive balls, patriotic meetings, theatrical performances, and presidential receptions once enlivened its rooms, earning it praise as the finest public house in America. Restored as a museum and operating restaurant, the tavern appears just as George Washington (a frequent visitor) might have seen it, complete with colonial decor and fare served on candlelit tables.

A 30-minute **guided tour** of the museum shows the taproom where patrons dined on whatever the tavern happened to be serving that night—perhaps ham and cheese "pye" or cream of County Surrey peanut soup. You learn that the drink of choice was rum, sometimes mixed with fruit juice and imported sugar to make a punch. You also see the dining room; ballroom; assembly room, where the Masonic Orders, the Alexandria Dragoons, and other local groups convened; and the third-floor communal bedchambers—the beds and floors were shared by as many travelers as could fit the space. ■

Gadsby's Tavern Museum
www.gadsbystavern.org
203 C1
134 N. Royal St.
703-838-4242
$
Closed Mon.–Tues. Nov.–March
Metro: King St.; Bus: AT2-7

Setting up for lunch

Old Town by foot

Strolling is the best way to enjoy Old Town's colonial ambience, allowing you plenty of time to study the architectural details of historical row houses, admire postage-stamp gardens filled with peonies and begonias, visit the many historic buildings once frequented by Thomas Jefferson, George Washington, and Robert E. Lee, poke into specialty shops, and simply see what there is to see. The walk outlined here can be done in a couple of hours, but, depending on how many sites you stop by, you could easily spend a day.

Begin in the heart of the historic core at the two-story, yellow-frame **Ramsay House Visitors Center** ❶ *(221 King St., 703-838-4200)*, a reconstruction of the 1724 home of town founder William Ramsay. Across Fairfax Street, **Market Square** holds a Saturday morning market that dates from 1753, making it one of the country's oldest.

From the visitor center, walk south on Fairfax Street. About half a block down on the right, the **Stabler-Leadbeater Apothecary Museum** ❷ *(105-107 S. Fairfax St., 703-838-3852; closed Mon.–Tues. Nov.–March; $)* operated from 1792 to 1933. George Washington, James Monroe, and Robert E. Lee all knew these walls, stocked with all kinds of goods including medical supplies. Preserved intact, the shop contains original potions, herbs, mortars, and journals.

Now go back to King Street and turn right. Situated along the river, the **Torpedo Factory Art Center** ❸ *(105 N. Union St., 703-838-4565, www.torpedofactory.org)* holds 80-odd studios where you can watch artisans sculpt, paint, weave, and make stained glass. A museum of local archaeological artifacts is on

The wharf (above) offers pleasant waterfront views. Dating from 1792, the Stabler–Leadbeater Apothecary Museum (left) was George Washington's pharmacy.

the third floor. Built in 1918, the factory turned out torpedo shell casings and other weaponry for both World Wars (look for the torpedo on view on the ground floor); the federal government used the spacious building for storage until the city of Alexandria bought it in 1969. The art center opened in 1974, and it was incorporated into a major waterfront development a decade later. Out back, you can stroll along the boat docks, or park yourself on a bench and enjoy the fresh air.

Walk south on Union and make a right on Prince Street. Known as **Captain's Row,** this cobblestoned block is lined with sturdy federal town houses, many of which were owned by ship captains in the 18th century. Cross Lee Street, and on the right stands the 1851 pink stucco Greek Revival **Athenaeum** *(201 Prince St., 703-548-0035),* which once functioned as a bank; with the onset of the Civil War, the bank closed and documents were hidden until after the war, when customers were reimbursed. Now owned by the Northern Virginia Fine Arts Association, the Athenaeum features a contemporary art gallery. A little farther up the block, William Fairfax, an original trustee of Alexandria, lived at **207 Prince**

See area map p. 203
- Ramsay House visitor center
- 2 miles
- 3 hours, without stops
- Carlyle House

NOT TO BE MISSED
- Torpedo Factory Art Center
- Christ Church
- Gadsby's Tavern Museum

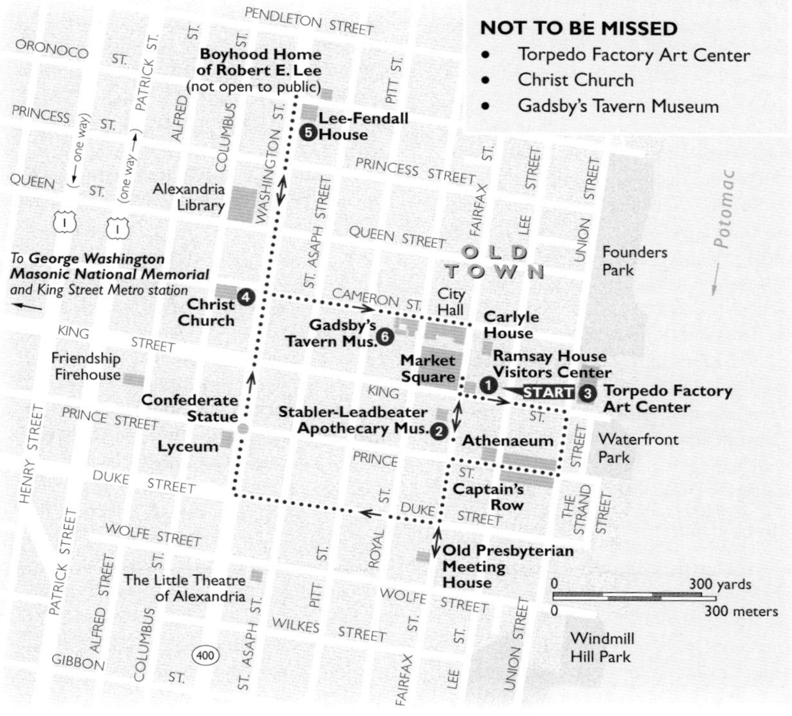

Green Christmas boughs adorn town houses on historic Queen Street.

Street, and next door at **209 Prince** lived Dr. James Craik, the surgeon-general who was with George Washington throughout the Revolutionary War, and who attended him at his death at nearby Mount Vernon.

At Fairfax Street, turn left and head south across Duke Street to the **Old Presbyterian Meeting House** *(321 S. Fairfax St., 703-549-6670, www.opmh.org)*. Built in 1774, the church has a large unadorned interior with wood floors and clear windows; in the churchyard lies the Tomb of the Unknown Soldier of the American Revolution.

Proceed back up Duke Street to Washington Street, the main north-south thoroughfare, and head north. On the street's west side, the Greek Revival-style **Lyceum** *(201 S. Washington St., 703-838-4994)* was built in 1839 as a cultural center and library. It now maintains permanent and temporary exhibits on Alexandria's history.

At the intersection of Washington and Prince stands the bronze **Confederate Statue,** a memorial to the town's Confederate dead. Created by Casper Buberl and erected in 1889, the defeated-looking veteran faces south, head bowed, arms folded. A block north you're back at **King Street,** Old Town's main commercial avenue. Along here you can find a busy assortment of restaurants, bars, and boutiques. Antique shops pack the stretch to the west.

The monument rising on the hill a mile or so west is the grandiose **George Washington Masonic National Memorial** *(King St. & Callahan Dr., 703-683-2007, www.gwmemorial.org)*, with sprawling views of Alexandria and Washington from the ninth-floor observation deck. The free one-hour tour lingers a bit much on Masonic history, but it is worthwhile for the good collection of Washington memorabilia, including his family Bible and leather field trunk. If you don't want to walk from Washington Street, it's an easy drive and there's plenty of parking.

Back at Washington and King Streets, the next block north holds historic **Christ Church** ❹ (see p. 211). Three blocks farther north on Washington, the **Lee-Fendall House** ❺ *(614 Oronoco St., 703-548-1789, closed Mon., $, www.leefendallhouse.org)* was built in 1785 by lawyer Philip Fendall, who married an aunt of Robert E. Lee. Family heirlooms are on display, including portraits, letters, and books. Across Oronoco Street, at No. 607, the **Boyhood Home of Robert E. Lee** was recently bought by private owners. Although the house is no longer open to the public, you can "visit" it through a virtual tour online *(http://leeboyhoodhome.com)*.

Head back down Washington and make a left on Cameron. To get a feel for how early Alexandrians dined out, stop by the **Gadsby's Tavern Museum** ❻ (see p. 211). Then walk east to Cameron and Fairfax Streets and end your stroll at the Georgian Palladian-style **Carlyle House** *(121 N. Fairfax St., 703-549-2997, closed Mon., $, www.carlylehouse.org)*, built in 1753 by Scottish merchant John Carlyle. British Gen. Edward Braddock convened a meeting here in 1755 with five colonial governors to discuss the financing of the French and Indian War. Interesting tours showcase the lifestyle of an 18th-century Virginia family and their servants and slaves. ■

Buzzing with life before Washington, D.C., was there, the land beyond the Beltway is laced with a wealth of historic sites that would be worth a peek even without the capital city nearby.

Excursions

Standing in formation at the U.S. Naval Academy, Annapolis

Excursions

WITH RIVERSIDE PARKLANDS AND COBBLE-LANED VILLAGES, COLONIAL plantations and busy harborfronts, Washington is blessed with an abundance of easy escapes within an hour's drive away.

Among the most accessible is the Chesapeake & Ohio National Historical Park, which preserves the ruins of a 19th-century canal and its towpath. Beginning in Georgetown and paralleling the Potomac River for more than 180 miles north, it's especially popular with walkers, bikers, and campers. Great Falls—its most distinctive feature and probably the most spectacular natural attraction anywhere between the Blue Ridge and the Chesapeake Bay—is only 5 miles beyond the Beltway (I-495). Great Falls Park on the Virginia side of the river is also a popular place to view the falls.

One of the area's newest additions is the National Air and Space Museum annex, near Washington Dulles International Airport in northern Virginia. The hangarlike facility houses notable aircraft too large to fit in the downtown museum, including the *Enola Gay* and a supersonic Concord.

You'll find history that goes even further back on the Potomac River south of Washington. More than 250 years ago, Virginia colonists established vast plantations and manor houses, including Washington's Mount Vernon and Gunston Hall. Built by the slaves of early citizens, these historic houses, and the younger Woodlawn, stand today as tributes to the quality workmanship and to the tireless efforts of preservationists.

Annapolis, poised some 30 miles east of Washington at the point where the Severn River spills into the Chesapeake Bay, is equally well preserved. You couldn't ask for a more charming, history-saturated, seafood-proud water town. It's easy to fill a day—or two, if you're lucky—exploring the town's lively colonial historic center and admiring the sailboats.

To the north, Baltimore, with its vibrant Inner Harbor, sits on the Patapsco River off the Chesapeake Bay. Boasting a world-class aquarium, stellar museums, and the only Civil War-era vessel still afloat today, this popular, newly revitalized city makes for another good waterside excursion. ■

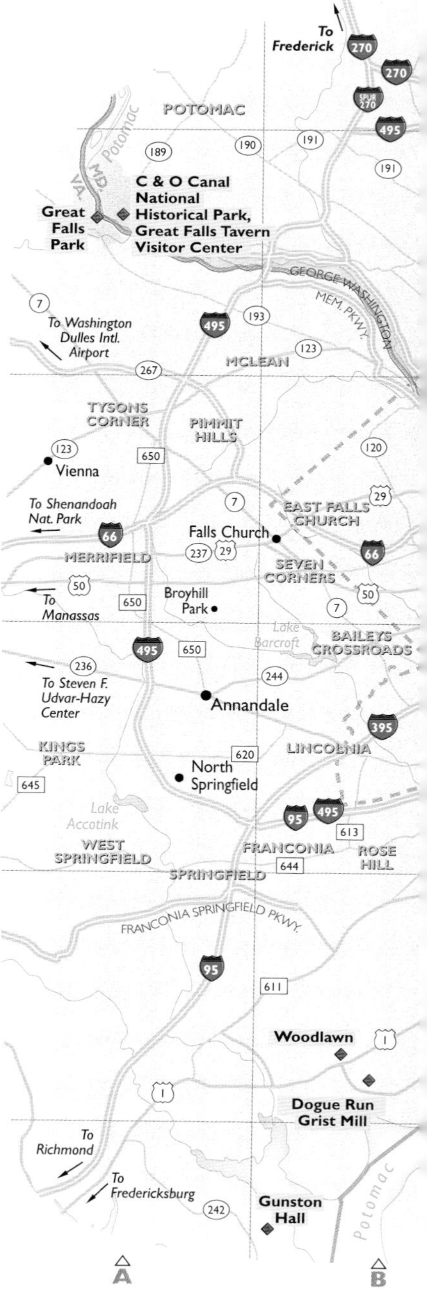

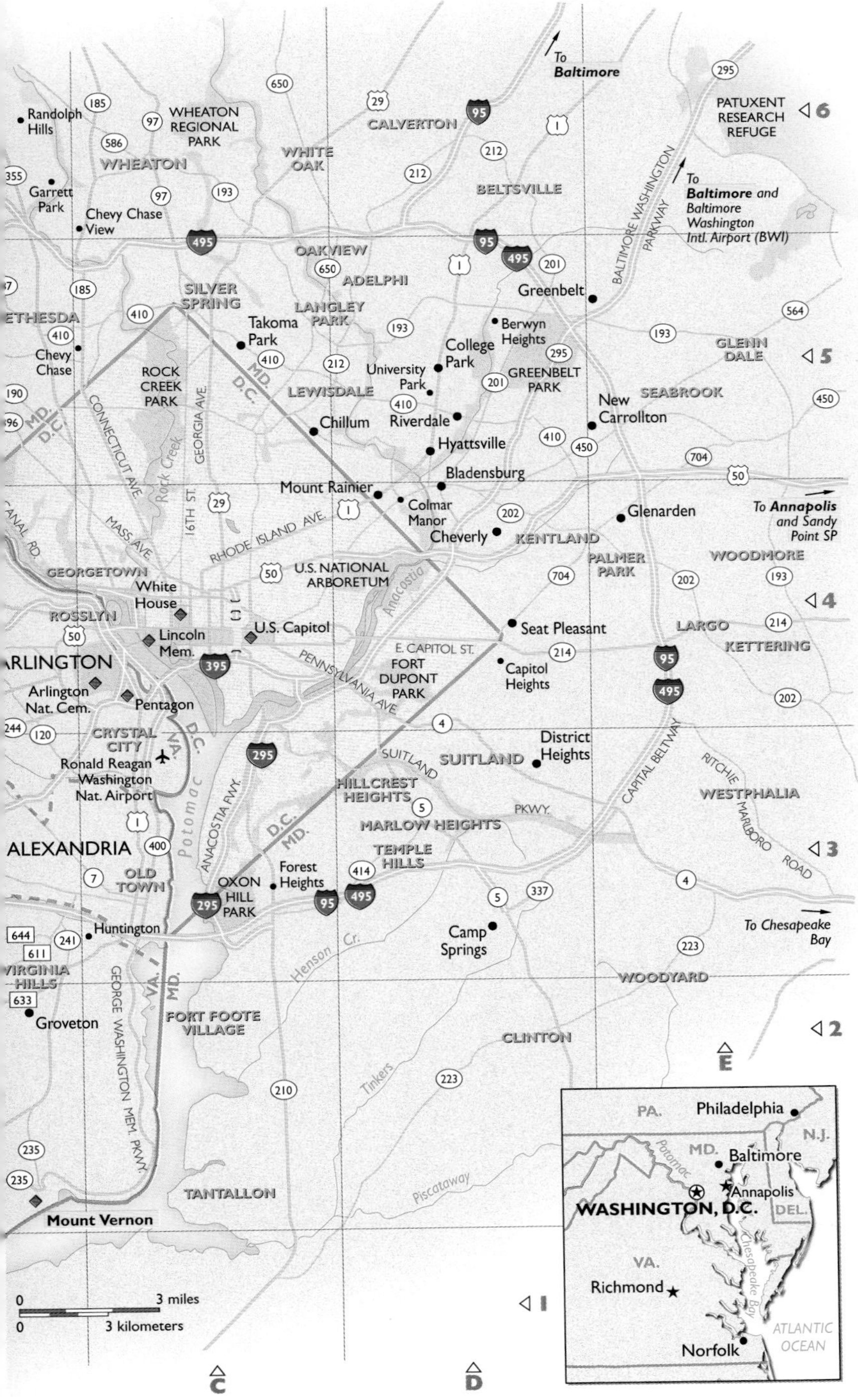
To Baltimore
Randolph Hills
WHEATON REGIONAL PARK
WHEATON
WHITE OAK
CALVERTON
PATUXENT RESEARCH REFUGE
6
BELTSVILLE
Garrett Park
Chevy Chase View
To Baltimore and Baltimore Washington Intl. Airport (BWI)
BALTIMORE WASHINGTON PARKWAY
OAKVIEW
ADELPHI
Greenbelt
SILVER SPRING
BETHESDA
LANGLEY PARK
Takoma Park
Berwyn Heights
College Park
GLENN DALE
5
Chevy Chase
ROCK CREEK PARK
University Park
GREENBELT PARK
New Carrollton
SEABROOK
LEWISDALE
MD. D.C.
CONNECTICUT AVE.
GEORGIA AVE.
Rock Creek
Chillum
Riverdale
Hyattsville
Bladensburg
Mount Rainier
Colmar Manor
Glenarden
To Annapolis and Sandy Point SP
CANAL RD.
MASS AVE
16TH ST.
RHODE ISLAND AVE.
Cheverly
KENTLAND
PALMER PARK
WOODMORE
GEORGETOWN
White House
U.S. NATIONAL ARBORETUM
Anacostia
4
ROSSLYN
Lincoln Mem.
U.S. Capitol
Seat Pleasant
LARGO
KETTERING
ARLINGTON
E. CAPITOL ST.
FORT DUPONT PARK
PENNSYLVANIA AVE
Capitol Heights
Arlington Nat. Cem.
Pentagon
CRYSTAL CITY
D.C. VA.
Ronald Reagan Washington Nat. Airport
District Heights
SUITLAND
SUITLAND PKWY.
CAPITAL BELTWAY
RITCHIE MARLBORO ROAD
WESTPHALIA
HILLCREST HEIGHTS
Potomac
ANACOSTIA FWY.
MARLOW HEIGHTS
ALEXANDRIA
TEMPLE HILLS
3
OLD TOWN
OXON HILL PARK
Forest Heights
Camp Springs
To Chesapeake Bay
Huntington
Henson Cr.
VIRGINIA HILLS
WOODYARD
Groveton
GEORGE WASHINGTON MEM. PKWY.
VA. MD.
FORT FOOTE VILLAGE
CLINTON
2
Tinkers
Piscataway
TANTALLON
Mount Vernon
0 3 miles
0 3 kilometers
1
C
D
E
PA.
Philadelphia
N.J.
MD.
Potomac
Baltimore
Annapolis
WASHINGTON, D.C.
DEL.
VA.
Richmond
Chesapeake Bay
ATLANTIC OCEAN
Norfolk

Chesapeake & Ohio Canal and Great Falls

C&O Canal National Historic Park
www.nps.gov/choh
216 A5
Georgetown Visitor Center, 1057 Thomas Jefferson St., N.W.
202-653-5190
Great Falls Tavern Visitor Center, 11710 MacArthur Blvd., Potomac, MD
301-767-3714
$

A kayaker hones his technique in the holes and waves below Great Falls.

SNAKING 184.5 MILES NORTHWEST FROM GEORGETOWN to Cumberland, Maryland, the Chesapeake & Ohio Canal National Historical Park has to be one of the longest, skinniest parks in the system. The most dramatic section is certainly the Great Falls area, just north of Washington, where the Potomac River hurls over steep, ragged rocks in a spectacular series of thundering falls before flowing through narrow Mather Gorge.

President John Quincy Adams broke ground for the C & O Canal on July 4, 1828. At that time, it was considered a Great National Project that would link Georgetown in Washington with Pittsburgh on the Ohio River, thus connecting the Atlantic Ocean with the Mississippi River. Plagued with problems from the start, however, including stiff competition by the new Baltimore & Ohio Railroad, the canal only made it as far as Cumberland.

Thousands of laborers—using hand tools, mule scoops, and black powder—toiled for 22 years to carve the trench, sometimes out of pure rock. A feat of engineering, its 74 lift locks raise it 605 feet in elevation from beginning to end.

The mule-drawn canal barges hauled coal, hay, fertilizer, and cement from the Appalachian Mountains to the city until 1924. Today, you can hop aboard a mule-powered canal boat in Georgetown for a ride through a working lock *(April–Sept., $$)*.

In the early 1950s, Supreme Court Justice William O. Douglas led a movement to preserve the abandoned canal. The C & O was designated a national historical park in 1971.

VISITING

If you have the stamina, bike or hike the 14-mile towpath stretch from Georgetown to Great Falls, a lovely trek offering pretty river views; otherwise, you can drive, via MacArthur Boulevard, to the Great Falls Tavern section of the national historical park.

The big white stucco building overlooking the canal houses the **visitor center.** Built in 1831, the structure served as a lodge for travelers and boatmen for nearly a century. Exhibits tell about the area and the canal's history.

To see the falls, and perhaps bald eagles, head a short distance downstream on the towpath to the quarter-mile trail leading to **Great Falls Overlook.** A combination of boardwalk and bridges, the trail links the two sections of Olmsted Island, ending at a close-up look at frothing, roaring Great Falls as it narrows and tumbles 76 vertical feet over craggy boulders into swirling eddies.

Back on the towpath, continue downstream a little way. Before the stop-lock bridge, pick up the **Billy Goat Trail,** a wild, 2-mile romp over jagged rocks high on the river's edge and along Mather Gorge. In spring, trout lilies, jack-in-the-pulpits, and bluebells sprinkle the forest floor, and goose honks and songbird trills fill the air. On nice days kayakers play in the rapids below the falls and rock climbers scale the opposite gorge wall. The blue-blazed trail ends farther down on the towpath, allowing an easy 1.25-mile walk back to the visitor center.

Away from the water, the 4.2-mile **Gold Mine Loop** behind the visitor center winds through post oaks and river birches to the Maryland Mine. This little known outfit, now in ruins, operated from 1867 to 1939.

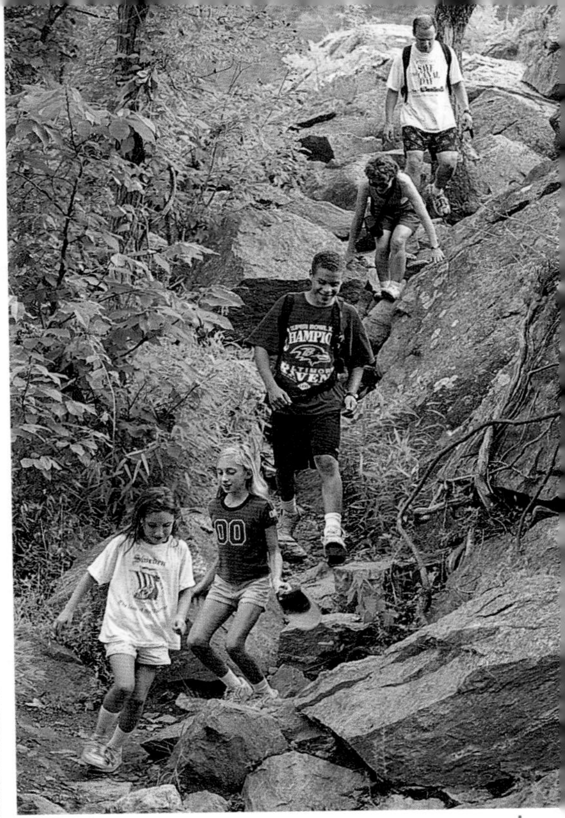

On the Virginia side of the falls, a short distance as the crow flies but about 12 miles by car, lies 800-acre **Great Falls Park.** Learn about local flora and fauna, kayaking and rock climbing at the **visitor center.** Nearby overlooks provide splendid views of the wide river. The popular, blue-blazed **River Trail** ambles downstream from here for about a mile and a half, edging the bluff high above Mather Gorge.

Here, too, you'll find the ruins of the **Patowmack Canal,** started by George Washington in 1786 and closed in 1830 after work on the C & O had begun; five locks raised or lowered boats the height of the falls. A 2.2-mile trail runs alongside the canal's shallow ditch, taking you past the ruins of **Matildaville,** a town that served the needs of the canal industry. ■

Great Falls Park

www.nps.gov/grfa

216 A5

Intersection of Georgetown Pike (Rte. 193) and Old Dominion Dr. in Mclean, VA

703-285-2965

$

Clambering along the Billy Goat Trail provides a chance to exercise and commune with nature.

Steven F. Udvar-Hazy Center

Steven F. Udvar-Hazy Center
http://www.nasm.si.edu/museum/udvarhazy
14390 Air & Space Museum Parkway, Chantilly, Va. (S of main terminal at Dulles Airport, near Rtes. 28 & 50)
202-633-1000 (Closed Christmas Day)
Parking, $$

Aircraft is displayed high and low at the Smithsonian National Air and Space Museum's new facility.

THIS ANNEX OF THE NATIONAL AIR AND SPACE MUSEUM (see pp. 75–81), located near Washington Dulles International Airport in Northern Virginia, was built to house additional aircraft and space artifacts too large and numerous to fit into the downtown building. But the splendid hangarlike facility, named the Steven F. Udvar-Hazy Center for its major donor, hardly plays second string to the more established museum when it comes to attractions.

Planning for the annex began in the early 1980s. In 1998, the Smithsonian and the Metropolitan Washington Airports Authority signed a long-term lease for the center's 176-acre site, which lies south of the Dulles airport's main terminal, in Chantilly, Virginia. The doors to the new facility opened in December 2003, timed to coincide with the 100th anniversary of the Wright brothers' first powered flight.

The center continues adding to the items on display, which have grown to some 270 aircraft and large space objects and more than 1,500 smaller artifacts. When the entire 760,057-square-foot facility is completed, it will include, among other things, a hangar where it will be possible to observe restoration of historic artifacts related to flight.

VISITING

Visitors enter on the second level of the museum. Pick up a map inside

the entrance to see the layout of the building, which is arranged according to different types, eras, and uses of flight, such as military, sport, general, and commercial. Begin your tour in the far western corner of the building, with a display on helicopters and vertical flight.

The cavernous **Boeing Aviation Hangar** that makes up the core of the Udvar-Hazy Center rises 10 stories high and extends as long as three football fields. The objects are displayed on three levels, with elevated walkways allowing a closer look at suspended aircraft.

Among the featured aircraft are the Boeing B-29 Superfortress *Enola Gay,* which dropped the first atomic bomb; an Air France Concorde, the first supersonic airliner; a sleek, black Lockheed SR-71A Blackbird, the fastest airplane in the world; the Boeing "Dash 80" prototype of the 707, America's first commercial jet airliner; and the de Havilland Chipmunk aerobatic airplane.

Other objects in this hangar include engines, hang gliders and ultralights, and experimental flying machines. The exhibit on sport aviation, for example, explains how designers of homebuilt aircraft often used the most advanced ideas in aerodynamics, propulsion, and structures. Check out the flight suits and other artifacts of giants in aviation such as Charles Lindbergh, Amelia Earhart, James Doolittle, Roscoe Turner, and "Hap" Arnold. Displays of aircraft models, aerial cameras, and "balloonamania"—popular culture items from the 18th century—add further interest.

After you've covered the immense space in the aviation hangar, head to the adjoining building, which houses the **James S. McDonnell Space Hangar.** The centerpiece here is the restored space shuttle *Enterprise.* You can also view displays on satellites, missiles, rockets, Mars probe equipment, space capsules, and other equipment used in human space flight, such as the mobile quarantine unit used by the returning crew of the *Apollo 11.*

Circling back to the entrance area, visit the nearby **observation tower** to watch overhead traffic at the Dulles airport. Also in this area is an IMAX theater *(fee).* Near the main stairs in the aviation hangar, you can climb inside a simulator to ride on a variety of history's greatest flying machines—from the Sopwith Camel to the F-5 Tiger—or take a 3-D journey around the International Space Station *(fee).*

On your way out, take a closer look at the **Wall of Honor,** running along the entryway to the building. The memorial bears the names of hundreds of people who have contributed to aviation and space exploration. ■

Potomac River plantations

Mount Vernon
www.mountvernon.org
217 B2
S end of George Washington Memorial Pkwy., Mt. Vernon, VA
703-780-2000
$$$

IN THE 18TH AND EARLY 19TH CENTURIES, LANDOWNERS built magnificent plantation houses along the Potomac south of present-day Washington, D.C. Three—Mount Vernon, Woodlawn, and Gunston Hall—lie within easy reach of the city. A visit to any one of these mansions, each carefully preserved in period detail, immerses you in the early slaveholding aristocratic life.

MOUNT VERNON

The stately Georgian-style home of George Washington sits on 500 acres of smartly kept grounds overlooking the Potomac, about a half hour from Washington by car. This estate richly deserves its ranking as the country's second most visited historic home; only the White House (see pp. 108–113) edges it out.

George Washington moved to Mount Vernon, home of his elder half-brother Lawrence, when he was in his teens; he acquired the estate from Lawrence's widow in 1754 at the age of 22. As commander in chief of the Continental forces, Washington rarely saw his home between 1775 and 1783. He then spent the next six years farming, expanding the plantation to nearly 8,000 acres. After serving as the country's first President (1789–97), he had only a couple of years left to enjoy his beloved home before his death.

The Mount Vernon Ladies' Association purchased the estate from a Washington relative in 1858 and continues to own and operate it. Both the Confederate and Union Armies considered the estate neutral ground during the Civil War.

Washington enlarged Mount Vernon—once a modest 1.5-story farmhouse—to its present appearance.

Visiting

Even if you've been to Mount Vernon before, a return visit is a must, after a large-scale expansion of educational facilities that was completed in October 2006. Today, you could easily spend an entire day here learning about Washington

during every stage of his life, through a dizzying array of films, museum displays, tours, and interactive programs.

Visitors now must enter the estate through a new **Orientation Center.** Audio-tour equipment is available if you want to get more information while wandering the 45-acre grounds on your own. A 20-minute film depicts pivotal moments in Washington's life as a citizen, soldier, and statesman.

The biggest attraction remains the famous red-roofed mansion and its gardens, pasture, and woodlands. The wood exterior of the mansion looks like stone; sand thrown onto wet paint created this impression. All details of the house's appearance, down to the exact color of the interior, are authentic.

Inside, many of the furnishings are original to the house; others, 18th-century duplicates. Docents are on hand to provide information about each of the 12 rooms. The large two-story green dining room, which appears much as it did in the Washingtons' lifetime, was used for many different functions; it held chairs and sideboards, but formal tables were installed only when the family entertained. Washington's study sits at the other end of the house. Various personal artifacts displayed here, including a telescope and an 884-volume library, reflect his varied interests.

A small staircase connects the study to the master bedroom on the second floor. This simply decorated bedroom contains the four-poster bed in which Washington died in 1799. After his death, his wife, Martha, could not bear to stay in the room; she moved to another one on the third floor.

Back on the first floor, before you step onto the piazza, note the framed key hanging on a wall in the passageway. It's the key to the Bastille's west portal, which the Marquis de Lafayette sent to Washington as a gift in 1790. The piazza, looking east over a lawn that dips toward a deer park, offers a grand view of the Potomac River.

On the house's west side, explore the formal grounds and **outbuildings.** The smokehouse, kitchen, wash-house, servant's hall, and other buildings suggest how much work it took to run a large, profitable 18th-century estate. Walled upper and lower gardens flank the bowling green.

Circle around the fruit garden and nursery to the iron-gated brick **tomb** that holds the remains of George, Martha, and other family members. A nearby memorial marks the estate's slave burial ground. Downhill is the site of a wharf where Washington used to transport his goods to Alexandria.

Most of Mount Vernon's historic artifacts are now housed in a new **Museum and Education Center** that's five times larger than the estate's previous museum. The new complex is tucked beneath a

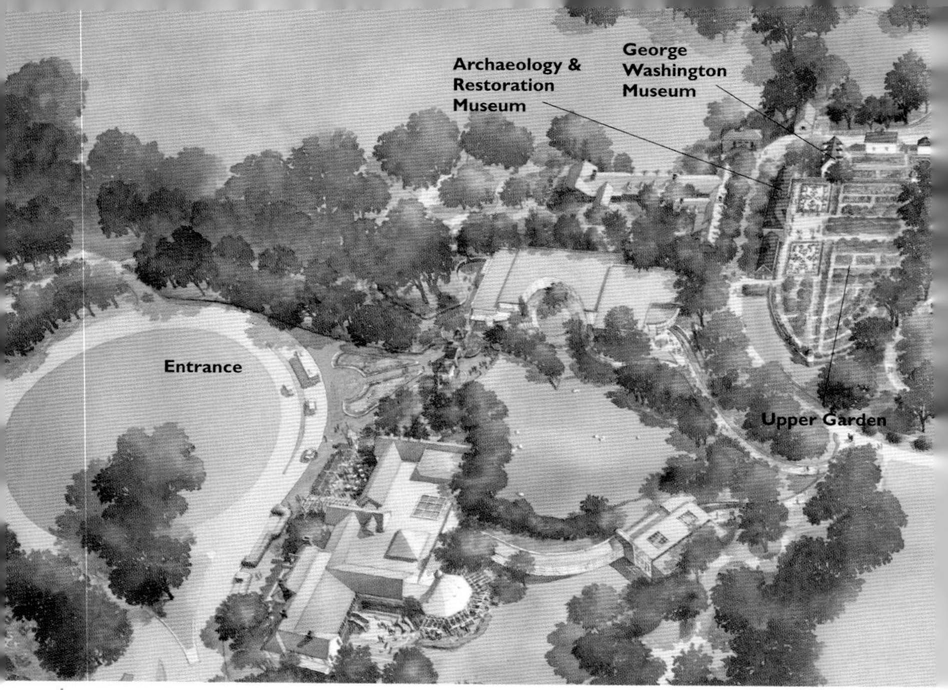

pasture, just inside the main gate, to preserve the estate's pastoral character. Two dozen galleries and related activities offer insight into numerous aspects of Washington's family and professional life. You can see, for example, a scenario of the dinners Washington held every Thursday at 4 p.m. for invited members of Congress and other government officials.

The greatest treasure in the museum is the 1785 terra-cotta bust of Washington that French sculptor J. A. Houdon made from a life mask. The center also has three life-size figures of Washington—at ages 19, 45, and 57—that were based on forensic research.

On-site dining facilities and shops at Mount Vernon have been expanded. And if time allows, stroll over to the 4-acre demonstration farm that depicts Washington's crop and planting experiments.

Distillery and gristmill

George Washington had the largest distillery in early America, which provided revenue for Mount Vernon. It was built in 1771 to grind corn and wheat into meal. From April through October, you can watch demonstrations of how whiskey was made. Adjacent to the distillery is a water-powered mill where wheat was ground into flour for export. The site lies three miles south of Mount Vernon, on Route 235. ■

WOODLAWN

George Washington gave Nelly Custis, his step-granddaughter, and Maj. Lawrence Lewis, his nephew, 2,000 acres of his estate in 1799 as their wedding present and asked William Thornton, first architect of the U.S. Capitol, to design a house for them. Thornton completed the late Georgian/early federal-era two-story

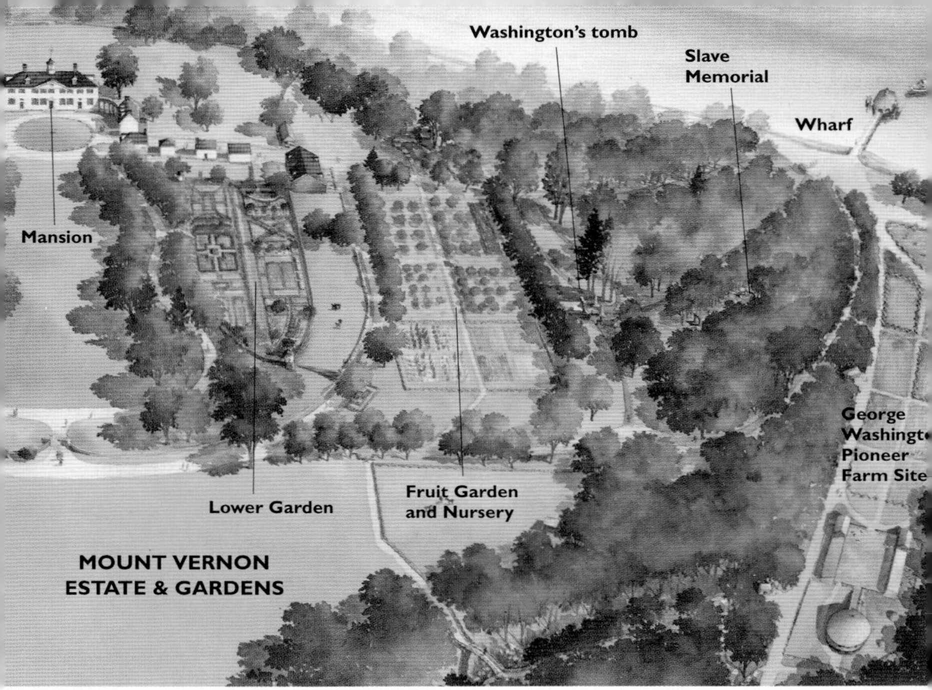

mansion in 1805. Typical of the period, the house is arranged symmetrically according to a five-part Palladian plan. There is no "front" or "back," rather two formal facades for approach by land or river.

The Lewis family and over 90 slaves lived on the estate for more than 40 years. The family sold the estate in 1846 to a Quaker community, which used the house as a nucleus for their growing abolitionist organization. The National Trust for Historic Preservation acquired the house and some of the land in 1951; the estate now comprises about 120 acres. The house is furnished much as it was during the Lewises' occupation, with some furnishings that the Lewises brought from Mount Vernon.

The refined **first-floor interior** includes a dining room, a family sitting room, and a parlor, where formal entertaining took place. The ceilings soar 13.5 feet high—the parlor excepted, which is a foot higher, in keeping with the grand proportions of the space. The second floor is divided into four graciously appointed chambers. In honor of its first patron, Woodlawn's **reception area** features a bust of George Washington commissioned by Nelly Custis Lewis; it stands on a pedestal at 6 feet 2 inches, the general's actual height.

Outside in the **formal garden** bloom lilacs, azaleas, and roses. From the riverside portico you can make out the Potomac, although silting over the past two centuries has pushed the river back. On the eastern horizon, tall trees block your view of Mount Vernon.

Before leaving Woodlawn, you can also walk over to view the 1940 **Pope-Leighey House** *(703-780-4000)*. This Frank Lloyd Wright-designed house was moved here in 1964 from Falls Church, Virginia, to save it from destruction. The small, low-ceilinged, flat-roofed dwelling is a classic example of Wright's Usonian style.

Woodlawn

www.woodlawn1805.org

- Map: 216 B2
- 9000 Richmond Hwy. (US 1), 3 miles W of Mount Vernon
- 703-780-4000
- Closed Mon., & Jan.–Feb.
- $$

Gunston Hall
www.gunstonhall.org
216 B1
10709 Gunston Rd., Mason Neck, VA, 20 miles S of Washington, off I-95 and U.S. 1
703-550-9220
$$

GUNSTON HALL

The farthest south of the three plantation houses, Gunston Hall anchors 550 magnificently lush acres, with tree-lined lanes, formal gardens, and farm animals. Its owner was Virginian George Mason (1725–1792), a lesser known but brilliant patriot and statesman.

Mason tried to quit public life after his wife's death in 1773, but the fledgling country would need him in the years ahead. Mason penned the 1776 Virginia Declaration of Rights, advocating religious tolerance and freedom of the press. Thomas Jefferson picked up, in some cases almost word for word, the same sentiments for the Declaration of Independence. Mason holds distinction as one of three delegates who refused to sign the Constitution in 1787. His passionate orations objecting that the Constitution gave the government too much power helped pave the way for the Bill of Rights.

Begin your tour at the **visitor center,** which holds several interesting exhibits, including family objects; a 12-minute film presents Mason as a paradoxical man. Although an ardent supporter of human rights and intellectually opposed to slavery, Mason's 5,500 acres were tended by up to 90 slaves. He could not reconcile his desire to end slavery with a means to ensure the continued prosperity of his plantation.

Then head over to the two-story Georgian **brick house.** Designed in 1755 by indentured servant and soon-to-be-prominent architect William Buckland, each room has its own distinctive style. The Chinese-style formal parlor and the neoclassic, Palladian-style dining room, with arches and painstaking embellishments, are works of art. The rooms are furnished with family and period pieces.

In the **gardens,** a boxwood allée, likely dating from Mason's time, runs between formal plantings to the brow of a hill that provides a glimpse of the distant Potomac. You can take a 1-mile trail through coastal plain woods to the river, perhaps spotting deer, herons, and geese along the way. ■

A rudimentary curtsying lesson at Gunston Hall

Annapolis

YACHTS, MIDSHIPMEN IN CRISP UNIFORMS, STREETS LINED with colonial architecture, and restaurants serving world-famous crabcakes: The colorful port of Annapolis, less than an hour's drive east of Washington, offers big-time history in a small-town setting.

Puritans escaping persecution first settled at the strategic mouth of the Severn River, just off the Chesapeake Bay, in 1649. Named the Capital of the Proprietary of Maryland in 1694, the settlement grew to become one of the Colonies' most sophisticated towns by the eve of the American Revolution. As tobacco flowed out of its port, in flowed European luxuries to adorn beautiful Georgian homes and their elegant inhabitants.

Annapolis's political high point occurred between November 1783 and August 1784, when it served as the fledgling nation's working capital. After the capital was moved to Trenton, New Jersey, in 1784, however, the city dozed for two centuries.

The U.S. Naval Academy came in 1845, turning Annapolis into a sort of company town that catered to its guest institution. In the 1960s, interest in historic preservation brought about new life, as taverns, shops, restaurants, and museums moved into restored structures.

Today Annapolis showcases more than a dozen architectural styles spanning three centuries; some 1,300 buildings—all meticulously maintained—predate 1900. Much of the small city's charm owes to the fact that it preserves its 1695 radial street plan, which gives the highest elevations for the church (St. Anne's) and state (State House)—and offers many vistas of the picturesque waterfront. ■

Annapolis

217 E4

Visitor information

www.visitannapolis.org

Annapolis & Anne Arundel County Conference & Visitors Bureau, 26 West St.

888-302-2852

Ego Alley in the heart of Annapolis is the place to show off your yacht.

The Maryland State House (1779) anchors Annapolis's 18th-century downtown.

Walking around Annapolis

The narrow streets and brick sidewalks in the historic center of Annapolis will enchant you. Plan to spend at least half a day strolling around and visiting its sights. With limited street parking available, your best bet is to park in one of the garages near the visitor center.

Start your stroll at the friendly, information-packed **visitor center** ❶ *(Annapolis & Anne Arundel County Conference & Visitors Bureau, 26 West St., 888-302-2852).* Just to the east, Church Circle features the Romanesque **St. Anne's Episcopal Church** ❷ *(410-267-9333),* built in 1858–59 as the third church on this site. The church still has the communion silver set sent by King William III in 1696. Standing at the intersection of Church Circle and Main Street, the venerable 1772 **Maryland Inn** *(410-263-2641)* features wood balconies and a posh, award-winning restaurant, the Treaty of Paris. Proceed six blocks down Main Street, attractively lined with two-story brick and wood buildings harboring boutiques, restaurants, galleries, and bars.

At end of the street awaits Market Space and its busy waterfront, the **City Dock** ❸. No longer a thriving working dock, it's still the heart of the city, bustling with cafés, shops, and restaurants. The number of yachts moored here year-round attests to Annapolis's standing as one of the East Coast's great sailing centers; visiting boaters often cruise down the narrow, alleylike waterway fronting the dock to show off their boats (hence its local name, Ego Alley). Stop by the dockside **Market House** for a sandwich and join a life-size bronze of *Roots* author Alex Haley by the water's edge, where he sits telling a story to a group of children on the same spot where his ancestor, Kunta Kinte, arrived in 1767 on a slave ship. For another dining option, head across Market Space to **Middleton Tavern** *(410-263-3323),* a cozy, dark-paneled establishment dating from 1750 that has welcomed the likes of George Washington, Thomas Jefferson, and Benjamin Franklin.

Just up Pinkney Street, step into the **Waterfront Warehouse** (ca 1815) and take a look at the scale model of the waterfront as it appeared in the 1700s. A few doors up, **Shiplap House** ❹ *(18 Pinkney St.)* dates from 1715; an exhibit inside details worldwide trade of slaves, china, linens, and cotton.

Now go back down Pinkney and turn left on Randall; in two blocks turn right for the gates to the **U.S. Naval Academy** ❺ *(410-263-6933, tours available by reservation, $$)* and follow signs to the visitor center. Established in 1845, the academy is now a 338-acre, four-year coed college attended by 4,000 midshipmen. Flanking the tree-dotted central green to the southeast is the enormous beaux arts **Bancroft Hall,** one of the world's largest

See area map pp. 216–17
- Visitor center
- 1.8 miles
- 4 hours
- Maryland State House

NOT TO BE MISSED
- City Dock
- U.S. Naval Academy Chapel
- Hammond-Harwood House

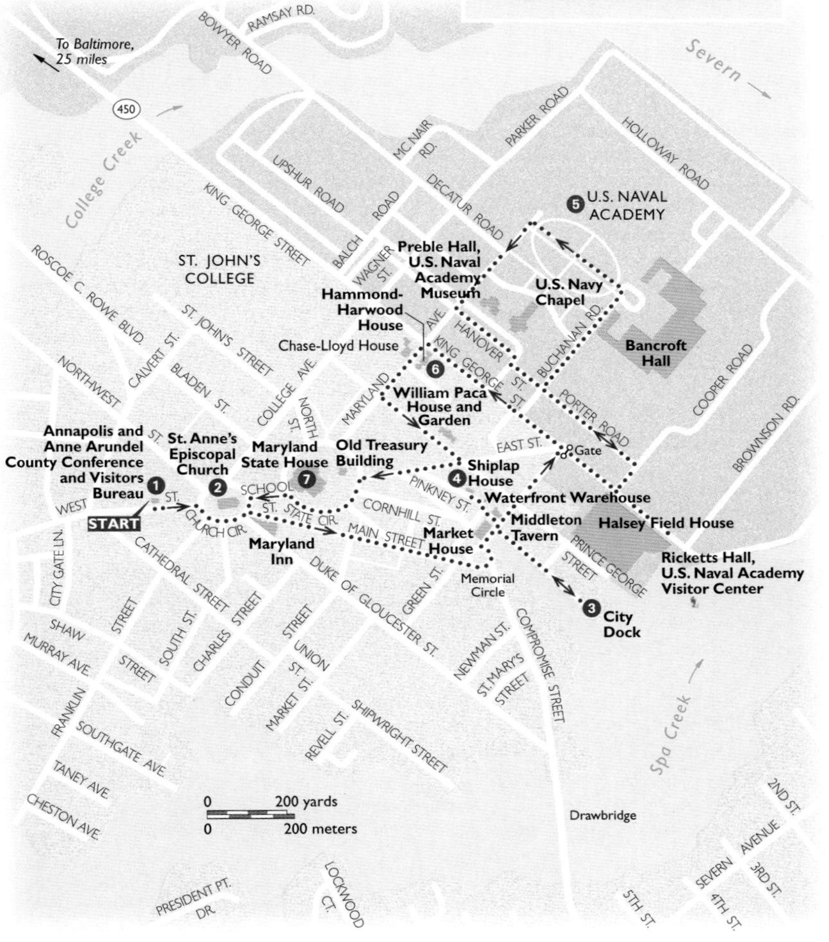

Sandy Point State Park

For a change of scenery, drive out to this Chesapeake Bay park *(9 miles E of Annapolis on US 50, 410-974-2149, $)*. A sandy beach is great for swimming, as well as for views of the Bay Bridge and of freighters far out on the bay. Rowboats and motorboats are available for rent, and 5 miles of trails wind through woods and marshes. ■

dormitories. All of the midshipmen live and eat here. Step inside the palatial entrance hall to see paintings of historic sea battles. The nearby copper-domed **Navy Chapel** features a long, shiplike nave; don't miss the lavishly displayed marble tomb of Revolutionary War naval hero John Paul Jones in the chapel's crypt. Just to the northwest, Preble Hall houses the **Naval Academy Museum,** containing one of the world's finest collections of model warships. (Note: Visitors are allowed within the academy only on foot and must show a photo ID at the entrance gate.)

Back at the entrance gate turn northwest on King George Street, then southwest on Maryland Avenue. The 1774–75 **Hammond-Harwood House** ❻ *(19 Maryland Ave., 410-263-4683, closed Jan.–Feb., $$)* stands on the left, just beyond King George Street. This national historic landmark house was the last project of architect William Buckland, once an indentured servant, who also designed Gunston Hall in Northern Virginia (see p. 226) and the interiors of the Chase-Lloyd House across the street. Many consider this house to be the finest example of Georgian architecture in colonial America. The furnishings date from the mid-18th and early 19th centuries.

Continue down Maryland Avenue to Prince George Street and turn left to the Georgian **William Paca House and Garden** *(186 Prince George St., 410-267-7619, $)*, built in 1765. Paca was a signer of the Declaration of Independence and a three-term governor of Maryland. Inside and out, the house has been meticulously restored to its colonial appearance. Two acres of gardens have also been returned to their former glory, down to the terraced rose beds, brick canal, and Chinese Chippendale bridge.

Walking a block west on East Street brings you to State Circle, upon which sits the **Old Treasury Building** and the **Maryland State House** ❼ *(State Circle, 410-974-3400)*. Completed in 1779, the state house is the nation's oldest continuously used capitol building. Two events of national importance took place in its old Senate Chamber during the nine months when Annapolis served as the new country's working capital: George Washington resigned his commission as commander in chief of the Continental Army on December 23, 1783, and, three weeks later, Congress ratified the Treaty of Paris, officially ending the Revolutionary War. Return to your starting point via School Street and Church Circle. ■

The U.S. Naval Academy Band stays crisply in line and in tune.

Baltimore

ONLY AN HOUR AWAY, BALTIMORE SEEMS LIKE AN ALTOgether different place than Washington, its brick buildings, puffing factories, older ethnic neighborhoods, and active ship traffic giving it more of a "real city" feel. But it also has its share of world-class museums, including the Baltimore Museum of Art and the Walters Art Museum. And the Inner Harbor, a showcase of urban revitalization, ranks as one of the East Coast's top tourist destinations.

Baltimore
217 D6
Visitor information
www.baltimore.org
Baltimore Area Convention & Visitors Association, 100 Light St.
888-BALTIMORE

Strategically placed at the mouth of the Patapsco River at Chesapeake Bay, the Inner Harbor has long been a major port for coal and grain. Also considered an urban eyesore, it was targeted for demolition and renewal as far back as 1963. Buildings began coming down in the late 1960s, and the first skyscrapers appeared in the early '70s. Restaurants, tourist attractions, and Oriole Park at Camden Yards followed thereafter, contributing to the harbor's vitality.

A wide promenade lined with shops and restaurants edges the waterfront and offers a delightful stroll past the harbor's various museums. Water taxis will ferry you from sight to sight if you'd rather ride than walk.

On the harbor's north side, at Pier 3, the seven-story **National Aquarium** *(410-576-3800, $$$$)* is Baltimore's biggest tourist draw. Inside, bottlenose dolphins perform feats in a 1.2-million-gallon oceanarium; an Atlantic coral reef teems with colorful tropical fish; and sharks and manta rays glide effortlessly through a pool that you cross on bridges.

The submarine U.S.S. *Torsk* and the lightship *Chesapeake* are moored alongside the aquarium. They, along with the Coast Guard cutter *Taney* and Seven Foot Knoll Lighthouse on Pier 5, form the **Baltimore Maritime Museum** *(410-396-3453, $$)*. Exhibits aboard World War II veterans *Taney* and *Torsk* tell about U.S. naval history; the other two focus on local maritime history.

Led by the Inner Harbor, Baltimore has stepped into the limelight of urban revitalization.

The wonderful world of fish eyes at Baltimore's National Aquarium

Baltimore Museum of Art
www.artbma.org
10 Art Museum Dr.
443-573-1700
Closed Mon.–Tues.

Walters Art Museum
www.thewalters.org
600 N. Charles St.
410-547-9000
Closed Mon.–Tues.

Fort McHenry National Monument and Historic Shrine
www.nps.gov/fomc
2400 East Fort Ave.
410-962-4290
$$

The last Civil War-era vessel still afloat, the **U.S.S. *Constellation*** is moored at Pier 1 *(410-539-1797, $$)*. Climb aboard to learn about her many commissions. Launched in 1854, she has caught slave traders off the coast of Africa, blockaded ports during the Civil War, and served as a relief flagship of the U.S. Atlantic Fleet in World War II.

Walk past the cruise ship docks toward the harbor's south side and the **Maryland Science Center** *(601 Light St., 410-685-5225, $$$)*. You can easily spend half a day here exploring three floors of hands-on exhibits, seeing an IMAX film, and picking out constellations in the planetarium.

Located inland, on the harbor's north side, is the interactive **Port Discovery** *(35 Market Pl., 410-727-8120, closed Mon. in winter, $$$)*. Exhibits let you decipher hieroglyphics, create musical instruments, and make chewing gum; the highlight is a three-story "urban treehouse," in which kids climb and crawl like monkeys. For breathtaking views of the city and harbor, ride in the swaying gondola of a helium balloon, anchored by a steel cable.

Within a short driving distance of the harbor are a number of other sights. Impressionist lovers will not want to miss the Cone Collection—works by Henri Matisse, Pablo Picasso, and others—on display at the **Baltimore Museum of Art.** The fascinating **Walters Art Museum** offers a broad look at over 55 centuries of world art, including Roman sarcophagi, Asian ceramics, Old Master paintings, and art deco jewelry.

Fort McHenry sits southeast of the harbor. During the War of 1812, as American forces valiantly defended the fort against the British, a young lawyer named Francis Scott Key felt inspired to pen some words as he saw its flag still waving in the early dawn light; later, these words became our national anthem. A tour of this restored monument to American freedom is illuminating.

At the end of the day, consider a jaunt to historic **Fells Point,** where the city took root in the early 1700s. Located east of the Inner Harbor, this salty waterfront district's brick row houses, congenial pubs, and snug restaurants have an enduring charm. ■

Travelwise

The soaring lines of Eero Saarinen's Dulles International Airport

TRAVELWISE INFORMATION

PLANNING YOUR TRIP

WHEN TO GO/ CLIMATE

Until well into the 20th century, Washington was, because of its reputation for heat and humidity, classified as a hardship post for British diplomats. It is true that July and August in the capital are frequently hot and steamy, but Washington has relatively brief winters and often long and lovely springs and falls. Rain is fairly evenly divided throughout the year (an average of 3.21 inches per month), but afternoon thundershowers in June, July, and August make rain more likely during those months.

The busy season for tourism starts in April with school spring vacation, when busloads of schoolchildren visit the museums, monuments, and U.S. Capitol. Spring is also the time of the annual cherry blossoms display around the Tidal Basin, and when the blossoms are at their peak, the area around the monuments is packed with sightseers. Summer, despite the heat, is family vacation time.

The average high and low temperatures are as follows:

January—44°F/30°F
February—46°F/29°F
March—54°F/36°F
April—66°F/46°F
May—76°F/56°F
June—83°F/65°F
July—87°F/69°F
August—85°F/68°F
September—79°F/61°F
October—68°F/50°F
November—57°F/39°F
December—46°F/32°F

WHAT TO BRING

Heavy winter coats are usually essential only in December, January, and February, but a light coat or jacket can come in handy in the cooler spring or fall months. Government buildings and museums have miles of corridors with marble floors—comfortable shoes are a good idea.

TRAVELING TO WASHINGTON, D.C.

BY PLANE

Washington is served by three major airports: **Ronald Reagan Washington National Airport** (DCA), in Virginia about 4 miles from the city center; **Washington Dulles International Airport** (IAD), 26 miles west of Washington; and **Baltimore/Washington International Thurgood Marshall Airport** (BWI), 25 miles northeast of Washington.

Ronald Reagan Washington National Airport is the closest to the city and the most convenient to reach, because Washington's state-of-the-art Metro system has a station located there, adjacent to terminals B and C. (A shuttle bus connects terminal A to the Metro station.) Taxi fare to downtown Washington is about $12 to $14. Reagan National is also served by SuperShuttle, which picks up from and delivers passengers to their homes, hotels, and offices. Call 800/BLUEVAN or 202/296-6662 for reservations.

Dulles International Airport is served by its own Washington Flyer taxi fleet, which provides 24-hour service to and from the airport. For information, call 703/661-6655. Taxi fare to downtown Washington is approximately $50 to $55. Washington Flyer also operates a coach service (888/WASHFLY) connecting Dulles to the West Falls Church Metro station for $9 one way. An express bus, operated by the Washington Metropolitan Area Transit Authority (www.wmata.org), connects Dulles to L'Enfant Plaza downtown for $3. SuperShuttle also serves the airport (800/BLUEVAN).

BWI Airport is served by SuperShuttle (800/BLUEVAN), by taxi 410/859-1100 (about $63 to downtown Washington), or by train. Both MARC's Penn Line (800/325-RAIL) and Amtrak (800/872-7245) provide frequent service between Union Station in downtown Washington and BWI's own rail station; a free shuttlebus connects the station and the airport terminal.

AIRPORT INFORMATION

For airport information (not information about specific flights), for Reagan National airport, call 703/417-8000; for Dulles airport, 703/572-2700; and for Baltimore/Washington airport, 410/859-7100. Their combined website is www.metwashairports.com.

AIRLINES

The Washington, D.C., metropolitan area is served by the following airlines. They fly into DCA, IAD, and BWI unless otherwise indicated.

Aeroflot 888/340-6000, www.aeroflot.com (IAD only)
Air Canada 888/247-2262, www.aircanada.com
Air France 800/321-4538, www.airfrance.com
Air Tran 800/247-8726, www.airtran.com
Alaska Airlines 800/252-7522, www.alaskaair.com (DCA & IAD only)
Alitalia 800/223-5730, www.alitalia.com (IAD only)
American Airlines 800/433-7300, www.aa.com
ANA 800/235-9262, www.fly-ana.com (IAD only)
British Airways 800/247-9297, www.britishairways.com (IAD & BWI only)
Continental 800/525-0280, www.continental.com

Delta Air Lines 800/221-1212, www.delta.com
Frontier Airlines 800/432-1359, www.frontierairlines.com
Icelandair 800/223-5500, www.icelandair.com (BWI only)
JetBlue Airways 800/538-2583, www.jetblueairways.com (IAD only)
KLM 800/225-2525, www.klm.com (IAD only)
Korean Air 800/438-5000, www.koreanair.com (IAD only)
Lufthansa 800/645-3880, www.lufthansa.com (IAD only)
Midwest Express 800/452-2022 www.midwestairlines.com (DCA & IAD)
Northwest Airlines 800/225-2525, www.nwa.com
SAS 800/221-2350, www.flysas.com (IAD only)
Saudi Arabian Airlines 800/472-8342 www.saudiairlines.com (IAD only)
South African Airlines 800/722-9675 www.flysaa.com (IAD only)
Southwest Airlines 800/ 435-9792, www.southwest.com (BWI only)
Spirit Airlines 800/772-7117 www.spiritair.com (DCA only)
Swiss 877/359-7947, www.swiss.com (IAD only)
Taca 800/535-8780 www.taca.com (IAD only)
Ted 800/225-5833, www.flyted.com
United Airlines 800/241-6522, www.united.com
US Airways 800/428-4322, www.usairways.com
Virgin Atlantic 800/862-8621, www.virgin-atlantic.com (IAD only)

BY TRAIN

Amtrak (800/872-7245) trains arrive at Washington's spectacularly refurbished Union Station on Capitol Hill. The station, which has a variety of shops and restaurants, and a downstairs food court, is worth a visit for its own sake.

Although locals use the train mostly as a fast, convenient way to get to New York on the Acela and Metroliner trains, Washington is a major rail hub, and it is connected by train to most U.S. destinations with rail service. The Metro station at Union Station provides easy access to the rest of the city.

GETTING AROUND

BY PUBLIC TRANSPORTATION

METRO

The Washington Metropolitan Area Transit Authority operates the bus and subway systems in the metropolitan area. The impressively clean and efficient system was designed primarily to enable commuters to travel easily to the downtown area. Metrorail stations are marked by large brown columns with colored stripes that indicate the lines served by the station.

Metro farecards are purchased at vending machines in the stations. The minimum fare is $1.35, the maximum is $3.90, based on the distance traveled and time of day. Fare information is available near the ticket machines. Metrorail opens at 5 a.m. on weekdays and 7 a.m. on weekends. It closes at midnight Sunday through Thursday. On Friday and Saturday nights, it runs until 3 a.m.

Route information: Call 202/637-7000 or log onto www.metroopensdoors.com

BUS

Metrobus service covers the city and the suburbs, with some lines running 24 hours. The fare for any destination within Washington is $1.25 or $3 for express service. Exact fare is required. For route and fare information, call 202/637-7000. For just $1 per ride, the DC Circulator bus service operates daily in central Washington, with frequent stops. The three routes extend from the Washington Convention Center to the Southwest waterfront (7 a.m. to 9 p.m.); from Union Station to Georgetown (7 a.m. to 9 p.m.); and around the National Mall (9:30 a.m. to 6 p.m.). You can pay with exact change, a Metro SmarTrip pass, or tickets obtained from designated meters.

METRO TIPS

Plan your trip before arriving at the station by visiting www.metroopensdoors.com. The farecard machines bear step-by-step illustrated explanations of how to buy a farecard. Ask the station manager (usually stationed in the glass kiosk near the farecard machines) for help if you have difficulty.

Carry plenty of one-dollar bills for the farecard machines. If not, you will likely be saddled with a Vegas-style payoff, since the machines give change—up to $6.25—in coins only. If making numerous trips after 9:30 a.m., consider buying a One Day Pass—at $6.50 an excellent bargain.

On the escalators, stand right, walk left. Otherwise you risk being trampled by others in a hurry.

BY TAXICAB

Washington's taxi fleet may not be the most modern in the country, and the fares are determined by a mysterious—to visitors and sometimes to locals as well—zone system, but cabs are plentiful and fairly inexpensive. It's usually possible to hail a cab on major streets.

The fare is $6.50 in the central zone, which covers the downtown from the Capitol on the east to 23rd Street on the west. There are frequent surcharges—$1.50 for each extra passenger, $1 for rush hour, $2 for radio dispatch. The driver may pick up extra passengers if it does not take the original passenger more than five blocks out of his or her way.

BY CAR

Visitors should consider the possibility that a car will be more an annoyance than a convenience. Parking is difficult, parking garages are expensive, and the most efficient branch of the city government is the one that gives parking tickets.

Should you find on-street parking, check the signs, since many streets become no parking zones during rush hour. If your car is not where you left it, call 202/541-6078 for information on its location.

Some streets are two-way most of the time, but during rush hour become one-way—including Rock Creek and Potomac Parkway and 17th Street, N.W.

CAR RENTALS

Washington's airports are served by the following national car rental companies:

Alamo	800/462-5266
Avis	800/331-1212
Budget	800/527-0700
Dollar	800/800-4000
Enterprise	800/264-6350
Hertz	800/654-3131
National	800/227-7368
Thrifty	800/847-4389

BY TOUR

Old Town Trolley Tours, 202/832-9800. This two-hour tour allows you to visit the sights at your own pace, by simply getting off the bus to see what you want for as long as you want, and reboarding at will.

Tourmobile, 202/554-5100. Narrated shuttlebus tours of major monuments, museums, and attractions. You can get off the bus to visit any of these, and simply get on the next bus when it comes along.

DC Ducks: The Boats On Wheels, 202/832-9800. DC Ducks' amphibious vehicles allow you to tour the Mall by land, then splash into the Potomac River on the boats with wheels. Fully narrated 90-minute tours depart regularly 10 a.m.–4 p.m. from Union Station.

See more specialty tours, at www.thedistrict.com

NEGOTIATING THE CITY

When seeking a site, first check the quadrant address, which indicates where it lies vis-a-vis the Capitol. Are you looking for N.W., N.E., S.W., or S.E.? The city is laid out in these four quadrants, with the Capitol building in the center. North Capitol, South Capitol, and East Capitol Streets radiate from this nucleus, separating the quadrants (the Mall runs west from the Capitol building).

Beware that many addresses can be found in more than one quadrant, and therefore are not the same place (for instance, there is a 400 M St. in N.E., S.E., S.W., and N.W.).

After locating the quadrant, note that there are three types of streets in Washington. First are the numbered streets—those that run in a north-south direction from the Capitol. First Street, for instance, is located one block east or west of North or South Capitol Street, respectively.

The second street type is the lettered or named streets laid out in an east-west direction. Starting from East Capitol Street or the Mall, the streets run through the alphabet (with the exceptions of J, X, and Z). The ones nearest the Capitol are one-syllable words; when the alphabet has been run through, they become two syllables, then three. As such, you can tell how far a certain street is from the Capitol by the letter with which it begins and how many syllables it contains.

Finally, the avenues that are named after states run diagonally across the grid.

PRACTICAL ADVICE

COMMUNICATIONS

NEWSPAPERS

Washington, D.C., is a city of news. Most national and international news agencies have Washington bureaus. The Washington-based daily newspapers are the *Washington Post* and the *Washington Times*.

For upcoming local events, check the Weekend section of the *Washington Post*, published on Fridays, and the Washington Weekend section of the *Washington Times*. Both provide excellent suggestions for making plans. Also of interest is the free weekly publication, the *Washington CityPaper*, published on Thursdays. It provides an up-to-date listing of what's happening in the clubs and theaters around town.

RADIO

WTOP (AM 1500 and FM 103.5) News, talk
WACA (AM 1540) Spanish
WAMU (FM 88.5) National Public Radio
WPFW (89.3) Pacifica, non-commercial jazz
WCSP (FM 90.1) CSPAN/Public affairs
WETA (FM 90.9) Classical
WKYS (FM 93.9) Urban
WARW (FM 94.7) Classic rock

WPGC (FM 95.5), Urban hits
WHUR (FM 96.3) Hip hop
WASH (FM 97.1) Soft rock
WMZQ (FM 98.7) Country
WIHT (FM 99.5) Top 40
WBIG (FM 100.3) Oldies
WMMJ (FM 102.3) R&B
WJZW (FM 105.9) Pop, jazz

TELEPHONE

Local and long-distance information, 411
Toll-free directory information, 800/555-1212
Public telephones are located in all hotels, at tourist attractions and other public places, at most restaurants, and along some city streets. Local calls cost 50 cents. Long-distance calls are easier and cheaper if you use your home carrier's telephone calling card or purchase a prepaid calling card (available at post offices and larger drug-stores).

Area codes: The area code of Washington, D.C., is 202; for Maryland it's 240, 301, 410, and 443; and for Northern Virginia it's 703 and 571. When in Virginia, you must always dial the area code with the number, even for local calls.

CRIME

Washington has a reputation as a dangerous city, but crimes of all sorts have been on the decrease in the last few years. Reduce your risk by following a few common-sense rules:

Don't wander onto deserted or ill-lighted streets or parks, particularly at night. If a neighborhood looks dangerous, it probably is. Stay with the crowds. There's safety in numbers.

If someone tries to rob you, give the robber whatever he or she asks. Your life is more valuable than your belongings.

Keep your wallet in a front trouser pocket—they're less vulnerable to pickpockets than rear pockets or breast pockets. Women should keep their purses close and not wear expensive jewelry. Don't carry large amounts of cash. Leave credit cards you don't plan to use at home.

Don't leave valuables in your car. The trunk is more secure than the space under the seats.

MONEY MATTERS

ATM LOCATIONS

Cirrus, 800/424-7787
Plus, 800/843-7587

Banks and automatic tellers (ATMs) are located throughout the city, and most major attractions and shopping centers also have them. Check with your home bank to find out which system accepts your card. Credit cards, debit cards, and traveler's checks are accepted almost everywhere; make sure you have an official I.D. on you as some places require it before you can make a transaction.

NATIONAL HOLIDAYS

New Year's Day; Martin Luther King, Jr., Day (3rd Mon. in Jan.); President's Day (3rd Mon. in Feb.); Easter Sunday; Memorial Day (last Mon. in May); Fourth of July; Labor Day (1st Mon. in Sept.); Thanksgiving Day (4th Thurs. in Nov.); Christmas Day.

PLACES OF WORSHIP

The citizens and churches in Washington welcome people of all faiths and practices. With more than 2,000 established churches in the area, you will be able to find a service of your choice. Check with your hotel concierge or the local yellow pages for a listing of times and locations. The *Washington Post* and the *Washington Times* also publish listings of services in the religion sections in their Saturday editions.

SALES TAX

Taxes will increase your cost of purchased goods by 5.75 percent, hotel bill by 14.5 percent, restaurant bill by 10 percent, and rental car bill by 10 percent.

SECURITY

Security has become a major issue in many places worldwide, but is especially a concern in and around Washington's public areas and main buildings. Sreets sometimes close with or without notice, and may be blocked by concrete barriers.

Government buildings are generally open to the public, but they may close for security reasons with little or no notice. Be flexible, and call ahead.

Metal detectors are standard equipment in most public buildings. Be prepared for searches. If you have a pacemaker or other medical device that might be affected, let the guards know. And do not carry anything that could be considered a weapon and might be confiscated—e.g. Grandpa's pocketknife.

TIPPING

Leave at least 15 percent of the bill at restaurants (20 percent at upscale places). Taxi drivers should receive 10-15 percent, bartenders 10 percent, hairdressers 15 percent, porters at least a dollar a bag, valet parking attendees $2 or more, parking attendees $2 or more, and doormen a couple of dollars every time they whistle you a cab. Tip the hotel concierge or restaurant maitre d' at your discretion, depending upon services performed.

TRAVELERS WITH DISABILITIES

Washington is a very accessible city for travelers with disabilities.

The Washington, D.C. Convention & Tourism Corporation (www.washington.org) publishes a fact sheet detailing general accessibility of Washington hotels, restaurants, shopping malls, and attractions. For a free copy, call 301/528-8664.

The Washington Metropolitan Area Transit Authority also publishes a free pamphlet on Metro's bus and rail system accessibility for the elderly and physically disabled. Call 202/637-7000 to order the guide, or visit the Metro's Web site at www.wmata.com.

Smithsonian museum buildings are accessible to wheelchair visitors. A comprehensive free publication called "Smithsonian Access" lists all services available to visitors with disabilities, including parking, building access, sign language interpreters, and more. To obtain a copy, call 202/357-2700.

VISITOR INFORMATION

The best source of visitor information is the **Washington, D.C. Visitor Information Center,** located in the Ronald Reagan International Trade Center at 1300 Pennsylvania Ave., N.W. (202/328-4748; www.dcvisit.com). Here you can obtain tickets, tour information, and maps. For details on events, pick up the weekly *Washington CityPaper,* free, or the *Washington Post or Washington Times.*

EMERGENCIES & HEALTH CARE

USEFUL NUMBERS

- Emergencies (police/fire/ambulance) 911
- Washington, D.C., Police (non-emergency) 311
- Metro Transit Police (emergency) 202/962-2121
- U.S. Park Police (emergency) 202/619-7300
- Travelers Aid 202/371-1937
- International Visitors Information Desk (offers multilingual information and assistance; located at Dulles) 703/572-2536

LOST CREDIT CARDS

American Express, 800/327-2177
Diners Club, 800/234-6377
Discover Card, 800/347-2683
MasterCard, 800/307-7309
Visa, 800/847-2911

ANNUAL EVENTS

JANUARY

Martin Luther King Jr.'s Birthday Mid-January. Lincoln Memorial, 202/619-7222. A military color guard salute at the site where King delivered his famous "I have a dream" speech.

Presidential Inauguration January 20, every fourth year. After the swearing-in on the Capitol steps, a parade follows down Pennsylvania Avenue to the White House.

FEBRUARY

Chinese New Year Parade 703/851-8777. Late January or early February, depending on the moon. Chinatown, H St., N.W., between 5th and 8th Sts. Colorful parade with firecrackers and dragons.

Abraham Lincoln's Birthday February 12. Lincoln Memorial, 202/619-7222. A reading of the Gettysburg Address and a wreath-laying ceremony at the memorial.

George Washington's Birthday February 22. Wreath-laying ceremonies at Mount Vernon (703/780-2000) and at the Washington Monument (202/619-7222).

MARCH

Smithsonian Kite Festival Late March or early April. 202/357-3030, kitefestival@si.edu. Professional and amateur kitemakers and kite flyers compete for prizes at a contest on the Washington Monument grounds.

APRIL

National Cherry Blossom Festival Late March or early April. 202/547-1500. The annual display of blossoms around the Tidal Basin doesn't always coincide with the festival, but the city celebrates with two weeks of performances, exhibitions, and activities. The Cherry Blossom Parade is usually held on the first Saturday in April. For up-to-date information on when the blossoms will peak, consult the National Park Service at www.nps.gov/nacc/cherry.

Filmfest DC 202/628-FILM, www.filmfestdc.org. Two weeks of international and American films, shown at local theaters and other auditoriums.

White House Easter Egg Roll Monday after Easter. 202/456-7041. This annual event dates back to 1878 during the Rutherford B. Hayes Administration. Children, ages seven and under, have a chance to play on the South Lawn of the White House. The event includes storytelling, music, and costumed characters.

White House Spring Garden and House Tour April. 202/456-7041. A chance to tour the lovely spring gardens of the White House's South Lawn.

MAY

Georgetown Garden Day 2nd Sat. in May. 202/965-1950, www.georgetowngardentour.com. Visit the private gardens of some beautiful, historic homes.

Evening Parade Friday nights, May–Aug. U. S. Marine Barracks, 8th and I Sts., S.E., 202/433-6060, www.wmb.usmc.mil. The evening begins with a concert by the United States Marine Band, followed by a demonstration of precision marching by Marine Drum and Bugle Corps, and the Marine Corps Silent Drill Platoon.

Memorial Day Celebrations Events on Memorial Day weekend include ceremonies at the Vietnam Veteran's Memorial (703/393-0090), the Tomb of the Unknowns at Arlington National Cemetery (703/607-8000), President, and a concert by the National Symphony Orchestra on the West Lawn of the Capitol (202/619-7222).

Washington National Cathedral Flower Mart Early May. Massachusetts and Wisconsin Aves., N.W., 202/537-3185. An annual flower and crafts show and sale on the cathedral grounds.

JUNE

Dupont-Kalorama Museum Walk Weekend 1st weekend in June. Dupont Circle neighborhood, 202/785-2040, www.dkmuseums.com. Visit museums and enjoy textile-weaving demonstrations, interactive tours, hands-on workshops, and concerts.

Capital Pride Festival In Dupont Circle area, 202/797-3510, www.capitalpride.org. A week-long celebration of the area's gay, lesbian, bisexual, and transgender residents, culminating in a parade through Washington.

JULY

Smithsonian Folklife Festival Late June/early July. On the Mall, 202/633-6440, www.folklife.si.edu. An annual two-week celebration of folk cultures, American and foreign, with music, food, and handicraft demonstrations.

Fourth of July Celebrations The National Independence Day Parade takes place at 11:45 a.m. on Constitution Ave. between 7th and 17th Sts., N.W. The National Symphony Orchestra, with guest stars and soloists, performs at 8 p.m. on the West Lawn of the Capitol.
The **Fourth of July fireworks** show starts at about 9:30 p.m. over the Washington Monument grounds (202/619-7222).

AUGUST

Virginia Wine Festival Mid-Aug. weekend. Leesburg area, 866/877-3343, www.virginiawinefestival.org. A chance to sample the wares of Virginia's emerging wine industry with music, food, and entertainment.

SEPTEMBER

Labor Day Concert 202/619-7222. The National Symphony Orchestra closes its summer season with a concert on the West Lawn of the Capitol.

Kalorama House and Embassy Tour 202/387-4062. Get inside looks at some of the mansions and stately homes in this distinguished neighborhood.

Washington National Cathedral Open House Massachusetts and Wisconsin Aves., N.W., 202/537-6200. Washington National Cathedral holds its annual open house, with special tours, tower climbs, and entertainment.

OCTOBER

Marine Corps Marathon 800/RUN-USMC, www.marinemarathon.com. Thousands of runners take part in this annual marathon. It starts at 8:00 at the Iwo Jima memorial in Arlington and follows a course in Washington past monuments on the Mall.

NOVEMBER

Veterans Day Celebrations Events honoring the service of the U.S. military veterans occur November 11 at Arlington National Cemetery (703/607-8000) and various memorials throughout the area.

Washington Craft Show Washington Convention Center, 203/254-0486. A juried show of American crafts, including basketry, ceramics, fiber decorative and wearables, furniture, glass, jewelry, leather, metal, mixed media, paper, and wood.

DECEMBER

Pageant of Peace/Lighting of the National Christmas Tree On the Ellipse south of the White House, 202/208-1631. The official kickoff of the Christmas season in Washington, with concerts and a Christmas tree from each of the states.

Washington National Cathedral Christmas Services Massachusetts and Wisconsin Aves., N.W., 202/537-6200. Holds Christmas Eve services; passes are required.

FURTHER READING

The best book on Washington architecture is E. J. Applewhite's *Washington Itself.* Applewhite, a former CIA officer, has a keen eye for buildings and an ear for the details of history that make his opinions come alive.

Fiction lovers should check out one of Margaret Truman's many murder mysteries set in and around Washington, D.C.

HOTELS & RESTAURANTS

Where you sleep and eat can make all the difference between a good visit and bad. Washington offers a panoply of hotel and restaurant selections in all price categories and styles—something for every taste.

HOTELS

Washington hotels vary from the luxurious and very expensive—the Four Seasons in Georgetown and the Mandarin Oriental near the Mall being good examples—to the basic and still fairly expensive, such as the large downtown hotels that cater mostly to the convention and meeting trade. Small and charming is harder to find, but the new boutique hotels being opened in Washington by the Kempton Group are a hopeful sign.

Because every major business in the country is affected by government legislation and regulations, Washington hotels cater to business travelers on expense accounts. That means high prices during the week, when businesses are paying the tab, but it also means weekend bargains for the leisure and family traveler. Similarly, prices are higher in the winter, when Congress is in session, and lower in the summer, when much of official Washington takes vacation time and flees the city for cooler climes.

Because hotels in the city are expensive, many visitors prefer to stay in less expensive places in suburban Virginia and travel into the city each day. It's always worth asking a hotel "Is this the best rate you can give me?"

Many hotels routinely offer rates cheaper than their posted rack rates, and many offer discounts through organizations such as AAA or AARP. All know that a room rented for a discounted price is income, but an unrented room is income lost forever.

RESTAURANTS

For many years, Washington was thought to hold little interest as a restaurant city. It's a city obsessed by power, the popular wisdom had it, and people cared more about whom they were eating with than what they were eating. Well, things have changed in the last decade. There's still plenty of meat-and-potatoes power dining—since the late '90s an unprecedented number of steakhouses have opened in the city and the suburbs. But a number of distinguished chefs running national-class restaurants now make Washington their home. Roberto Donna at Galileo, Michel Richard at Citronelle, and Gerard Pangaud at Gerard's Place are at the top of the class, but their students, many of whom have stayed in Washington and opened their own restaurants, continue to enrich Washington dining.

In addition to this wonderful but pricey dining, the Washington area has long been an attractive place for exiles from their own countries to locate, and they have brought their food with them. It is said that any upheaval in a foreign country enriches Washington dining. Refugees from Vietnam opened fine restaurants in the Virginia suburbs. Washington has more Ethiopian restaurants than any other city in the country. Thailand, India, Pakistan, and Malaysia have all given the city fine restaurants.

Unless otherwise noted, all restaurants are open daily and air-conditioned.

As of January, 2007, smoking is prohibited in all bars and restaurants.

PRICES

HOTELS

An indication of the cost of a double room in high season, excluding tax, is given by **$** signs.

$$$$$	$225+
$$$$	$175–$225
$$$	$125–$175
$$	$85–$125
$	Under $85

RESTAURANTS

An indication of the cost of a three-course dinner without drinks, tax, or tip is given by $ signs.

$$$$	Over $50
$$$	$35–$50
$$	$15–$35
$	Under $15

L=lunch
D=dinner

CREDIT CARDS

Many hotels and restaurants accept all major credit cards. Smaller ones may accept some or none, as shown in their entry. Abbreviations used are: AE American Express, D Discover, DC Diners Club, MC MasterCard, and V Visa.

ORGANIZATION

Hotels and restaurants are listed first by chapter area, then by price category, then alphabetically.

Hotel restaurants of note have been bolded in the hotel entries and indicated by a restaurant icon beneath the hotel icon (if they're unusually special, they are treated in a separate entry within the restaurant section).

CAPITOL HILL

HOTELS

THE HOTEL GEORGE
$$$$$
15 E ST., N.W.
TEL 202/347-4200 OR
800/576-8331
FAX 202/347-0359
www.hotelgeorge.com
A completely renovated building originally built in 1928, the George is convenient to Capitol Hill offices and attractions. The decor is striking and modern. The restaurant **Bistro Bis** (see below) offers quality updated French bistro fare. Cigar-friendly Billiard Room.
139 AE, D, DC, MC, V Union Station

HYATT REGENCY WASHINGTON ON CAPITOL HILL
$$$$
400 NEW JERSEY AVE., N.W.
TEL 202/737-1234
FAX 202/737-5773
washingtonregency.hyatt.com
This large convention hotel occupies a full city block on Capitol Hill. The hotel is centrally located to offer access to museums, monuments, and government buildings.
834 AE, D, DC, MC, V Union Station

PHOENIX PARK HOTEL
$$$$
520 N. CAPITOL ST., N.W.
TEL 202/638-6900 OR
800/824-5419
FAX 202/393-3236
www.phoenixparkhotel.com
Named after the park in Dublin, this newly renovated hotel has a European ambience. The adjoining **Dubliner Pub** offers good pub cooking and Irish entertainment.
149 AE, D, DC, MC, V Union Station

CAPITOL HILL SUITES
$$$
200 C ST., S.E.
TEL 202/543-6000
FAX 202/547-2608
www.capitolhillsuites.com
Tucked behind the Library of Congress on the House side of the hill, Capitol Hill Suites offers kitchenettes in every suite. The hotel was refurbished in 2000.
152 AE, D, DC, MC, V Union Station, South Capitol

WASHINGTON COURT HOTEL
$$$$
525 NEW JERSEY AVE., N.W.
TEL 202/628-2100
OR 800/321-3010
FAX 202/ 879 7918
www.washingtoncourthotel.com
The Washington Court has a dramatic four-story atrium lobby with leather furniture. Billiards and cigars offered in the Club Room.
264 AE, D, DC, MC, V Union Station

HOLIDAY INN ON THE HILL
$$$$
415 NEW JERSEY AVE., N.W.
TEL 202/638-1616
OR 800/638-1116
FAX 202/638-0707
www.hionthehilldc.com
This recently renovated hotel offers many family-oriented amenities. The rooftop pool overlooks Washington's skyline.
343 AE, D, DC, MC, V Union Station

RESTAURANTS

B. SMITH'S
$$$$
UNION STATION
50 MASSACHUSETTS AVE., N.E.
TEL 202/289-6188
This gracious restaurant, owned by former supermodel B. Smith, occupies the former presidential reception room at Union Station, perhaps the grandest dining room in Washington. The menu is a combination of traditional Southern, New Orleans-style, and Mid-atlantic seafood dishes.
300 In rear of station AE, D, DC, MC, V Union Station

BISTRO BIS
$$$$
THE HOTEL GEORGE,
15 E ST., N.W.
TEL 202/661-2700
Chef owner Jeffrey Buben serves traditional bistro fare and intelligently updated versions of it in this sleek, modern Capitol Hill hangout that is a favorite of many who work and do business in the neighborhood. Start with a terrine of duck liver, and for a main course try the monkfish with mussels and clams.
115 AE, D, DC, MC, V Union Station

JOHNNY'S HALF SHELL
$$$
400 N. CAPITOL ST., N.W.
TEL 202/737-0400
Until recently a beloved neighborhood seafood bar in Dupont Circle, Johnny's has a sleek new setting to spotlight Ann Cashion's southern-accented seafood. Also open for breakfast and lunch.
270 Closed Sun. AE, D, DC, MC, V Union Station

DUBLINER
$$
520 N. CAPITOL, N.W.
TEL 202/737-3773
There are many things to eat at this lively Irish pub—fish and chips, shepherd's pie, even a burger—but the only thing to drink, particularly if you're Irish, is Guinness on tap, or maybe Irish whiskey. It all goes well with the Irish entertainment, every night after 9 p.m.
136 AE, DC, MC, V Union Station

THE MONOCLE

$$$

107 D ST., N.E.

TEL 202/546-4488

Its position as the closest restaurant to the Senate side of the Capitol means that there's no better place in town for sighting politicos, either eating a meal or arriving for one of the frequent political fund-raisers in the private rooms upstairs. Run by the Valanos family for 40 years, the Monocle serves an all-American menu of burgers, steaks, and seafood.

110 Closed Sat.–Sun. AE, DC, MC, V Union Station

TWO QUAIL

$$$

320 MASSACHUSETTS AVE., N.E.

TEL 202/543-8030

A quirky but romantic place located in three town houses near Union Station, Two Quail draws its flea-market decor and its menu from eclectic sources. The cooking is basically Modern American—portobello mushrooms or duck and orange salad to start, pasta and grilled meats for main courses.

80 Closed all Sat., & Sun. L AE, DC, MC, V Union Station

BANANA CAFÉ

$$

500 8TH ST., S.E.

TEL 202/543-5906

This cheerful Latin American and Cuban restaurant has a bar and dining room on the main level and a piano bar above. Order from a small selection of tapas to start, but then dive into the Cuban specialties—*ropa vieja* (shredded flank steak cooked with tomato and spices), *carnitas Cubanas* (pork roasted with bitter oranges), and stuffed plantains. Don't miss the mango margaritas, a house specialty.

100 AE, D, DC, MC, V Eastern Market

SOMETHING SPECIAL

MONTMARTRE

A welcome addition to the Capitol Hill neighborhood, this charming bistro offers consistently good French fare in a simple, inviting space. The braised rabbit is a signature dish, and other menu selections might include truffle-perfumed pasta, veal kidneys, and monkfish. Outdoor patio is popular in warm weather.

$$$

EASTERN MARKET

327 7TH ST., S.E.

TEL 202/544-1244

50 Closed Mon. AE, DC, MC, V Eastern Market

THE MALL

HOTELS

LOEWS L'ENFANT PLAZA

$$$$$

480 L'ENFANT PLAZA, S.W.

TEL 202-484-1000

FAX 202/646-5060

www.lenfantplazahotel.com

Close to the Smithsonian museums, Loew's L'Enfant Plaza is attractive to both business and leisure travelers. Dining options include a seafood-dominated brasserie and a brew pub.

370 AE, D, DC, MC, V L'Enfant Plaza

MANDARIN ORIENTAL

$$$$$

1330 MARYLAND AVE., S.W.

TEL 202/554-8588

FAX 202/554-8999

www.mandarinoriental.com/washington

This super-luxury hotel opened in 2004 near the southeastern end of the Mall, overlooking the Potomac Tidal Basin and the Jefferson Memorial. The lush carpets, marble baths, lacquered furniture, silk furnishings, and extensive spa services make for a soothing stay. Chef Eric Ziebold of the hotel's Asian-inspired **Cafe Zen** has been named one of America's "best new chefs."

400 P AE, D, DC, MC, V L'Enfant Plaza

RESTAURANTS

LES HALLES

$$$$

1201 PENNSYLVANIA AVE., N.W.

TEL 202/347-6848

No restaurant in Washington feels more like Paris than this bustling French steakhouse. Washingtonians throng here to eat the flavorful *onglet,* hearty *cassoulet,* heaping platters of *choucroute garnie,* and the best French fries in town. The wine list is well-chosen and inexpensive.

186 P Valet AE, D, DC, MC, V Metro Center, Federal Triangle

TENPENH

$$$

1001 PENNSYLVANIA AVE., N.W.

TEL 202/393-4500

Asian-American fusion cooking is everywhere these days, but few places do it more intelligently than this strikingly attractive downtown place. Chefs Jeff Tunks and Cliff Wharton have put together a menu that ranges from Vietnam to the Philippines, from Hong Kong to Thailand. Tunks's specialty, a Chinese-style smoked lobster, is a delicious marriage of East and West.

166 P Valet Closed Sat. L, & all Sun. AE, D, DC, MC, V Metro Center

CAFÉ ATLANTICO
$$
405 8TH ST., N.W.
TEL 202/393-0812
With an attractive three-level dining space tucked into an old power plant, Café Atlantico serves a fascinating menu of nuevo Latino dishes and other cuisines, including an interesting take on feijoada, Brazil's national dish. The tiny minibar offers a prix fixe menu of about 30 tiny courses and other innovative food. At the bar here, you'll find the best caipirinhas in town, and the wine list offers well-chosen South American wines at fair prices.
105 Valet Closed Sun. L AE, DC, MC, V Archives/Navy Memorial

MITSITAM NATIVE FOODS CAFE
$$
NATIONAL MUSEUM OF THE AMERICAN INDIAN
4TH ST. AND INDEPENDENCE AVE., SW.
TEL 202/ 633-1000
The best food court on the Mall is in the Smithsonian's National Museum of the American Indian (Mitsitam means "Let's eat!"). Far from typical cafeteria fare, the selections are tasty and diverse, based on the cuisines of various Native American regions—empanadas and pork tamales, fried bread dipped in honey, nutty grains. There's something for everybody.
365 AE, D, DC, MC, V Smithsonian

NATIONAL GALLERY OF ART CAFES
$
6TH ST. & CONSTITUTION AVE.
TEL 202/737-4215
The **Garden Café** offers a light lunch fare, while the large **Cascade Café,** in the concourse between the two buildings, has a varied cafeteria menu. The **Sculpture Garden Pavilion Café** seres pizzas, sandwiches, desserts, wine, and beer. Check out the weekend jazz brunches, and for a treat, don't miss the great gelato at the **Espresso Bar.**
Archives/Navy Memorial or Smithsonian

WHITE HOUSE & AROUND

HOTELS

THE HAY-ADAMS HOTEL
$$$$$
ONE LAFAYETTE SQUARE, 16TH & H STS. N.W.
TEL 202/638-6600 OR 800/853-6807
FAX 202/638-2716
www.hayadams.com
Built on the site where, alternately, President Lincoln's secretary John Hay and John Adams's grandson Henry Adams lived. The newly renovated hotel is just across Lafayette Park from the White House. The **Lafayette Dining Room** and guest rooms on the south side offer great views of the Executive Mansion.
145 AE, D, DC, MC, V Farragut West or McPherson Square

PARK HYATT
$$$$$
24TH AT M ST., N.W.
TEL 202/789-1234
FAX 202/419-6795
www.washington.hyatt.com
Located in Washington's West End, just three blocks from Georgetown, the Park Hyatt is comfortably but strikingly modern. The lobby is decorated with an impressive collection of modern art. Rooms are large and luxurious. The distinguished restaurant **Blue Duck Tavern** serves chef Brian McBride's accomplished Modern American cooking and a lavish brunch on weekends.
223 AE, D, DC, MC, V Foggy Bottom

THE ST. REGIS
$$$$$
923 16TH ST. AT K ST., N.W.
TEL 202/638-2626 OR 800/562-5661
FAX 202/638-4231
www.stregis.com
The posh St. Regis, well located near the White House and museums, is built in Italian Renaissance style with elaborate plasterwork ceilings, European antiques, and ornate chandeliers. In fall 2007 the hotel reopened after an extensive renovation.
193 AE, D, DC, MC, V Farragut North

HOTEL LOMBARDY
$$$$
2019 PENNSYLVANIA AVE., N.W.
TEL 202/828-2600 OR 800/424-5486
FAX 202/872-0503
www.hotellombardy.com
This low-key but well-located hotel recently underwent a stylish renovation to reflect the spirit of the1926 building. The rooms now showcase imported Italian and German fabrics, oriental rugs, local art, stainless steel kitchenettes, and fine bedding. **Café Lombardy** is a cozy neighborhood bistro with European-inspired cuisine.
136 AE, D, DC, MC, V Foggy Bottom

WILLARD INTER-CONTINENTAL HOTEL
$$$$$
1401 PENNSYLVANIA AVE., N.W.
TEL 202/628-9100 OR 800/327-0200
FAX 202/637-7326
washington.intercontinental.com
A Willard Hotel has been located on this site since

1850. Abraham Lincoln stayed here before his inauguration; Julia Ward Howe wrote the "Battle Hymn of the Republic" here. The hotel has been luxuriously updated. The **Willard Room** is perhaps the grandest dining room in the city. The **Round Robin Bar** is one of the city's most popular gathering places.
332 P AE, D, DC, MC, V Metro Center

SOFITEL LAFAYETTE SQUARE
$$$$$
806 15TH ST, N.W.
TEL 202/730-8800 OR 866/397-8800
FAX 202/730-8500
www.sofitel.com
This new hotel at the corner of Lafayette Square, near the White House, is convenient to museums, monuments, and government buildings. Housed in a 12-story 1880s building, the hotel has the restrained elegance characteristic of its parent, the French Accor chain. **Cafe´ 15**, the hotel's restaurant serves star-quality French cuisine and **Le Bar** lounge is a popular meeting place for its great location.
237 P AE, D, DC, MC, V McPherson Square

JW MARRIOTT HOTEL
$$$$$
1331 PENNSYLVANIA AVE., N.W.
TEL 202/393-2000
FAX 202/626-6991
www.mariott.com
Large, centrally located, and connected to the shops and boutiques of National Place, the JW Marriott is a convenient hub for explorations of the city.
738 P AE, DC, MC, V Metro Center

FAIRMONT HOTEL
$$$$$
2401 M ST., N.W.
TEL 202/429-2400 OR 888/257-7544
FAX 202/457-5010
www.fairmont.com/washington
Built around an attractive garden courtyard, the Fairmont is in the West End of town near Georgetown. Rooms are luxurious, service is attentive. The fitness center, with pool, is one of the most complete in the city. **Juniper** offers good Modern American cooking, while the **Collonade** offers an elaborate Sunday brunch that's popular.
415 P AE, D, DC, MC, V Foggy Bottom

ONE WASHINGTON CIRCLE HOTEL
$$$$
ONE WASHINGTON CIRCLE, N.W.
TEL 202/872-1680 OR 800/424-9671
FAX 202/887-4989
www.thecirclehotel.com
Near the Kennedy Center and George Washington University, this small hotel houses suites popular with business travelers. Circle Bistro does innovative takes on classics.
151 P AE, D, DC, MC, V Foggy Bottom

THE WESTIN GRAND
$$$$$
2350 M ST., N.W.
TEL 202/429-0100
FAX 202/429-9759
www.westin.com/washingtondc
This low-key hotel, located between Georgetown and the White House, is known for its friendly, attentive service. Comfortable rooms and great location offer good value.
263 P Valet AE, D, DC, MC, V Foggy Bottom

PRICES

HOTELS
An indication of the cost of a double room in high season, excluding tax, is given by **$** signs.

$$$$$	$225+
$$$$	$175–$225
$$$	$125–$175
$$	$85–$125
$	Under $85

RESTAURANTS
An indication of the cost of a three-course dinner without drinks, tax, or tip is given by $ signs.

$$$$	Over $50
$$$	$35–$50
$$	$15–$35
$	Under $15

HOTEL WASHINGTON
$$$$
15TH ST. & PENNSYLVANIA AVE., N.W.
TEL 202/638-5900 OR 800/424-9540
FAX 202/638-4275
www.hotelwashington.com
Near the White House and the Treasury Department, the Hotel Washington is popular with locals and visitors for its seasonal rooftop bar, Sky Terrace, offering great views (see p. 246).
345 AE, D, DC, MC, V Metro Center

WASHINGTON SUITES GEORGETOWN
$$$$
2500 PENNSYLVANIA AVE., N.W.
TEL 202/333-8060 OR 877/736-2500
FAX 202/338-3818
www.washingtonsuites georgetown.com
Located just over Rock Creek from Georgetown, thi hotel has fully equipped suites that feel like private apartments, in a great location for walking.
124 P AE, D, DC, MC, V Foggy Bottom

RESTAURANTS

EQUINOX
$$$$
818 CONNECTICUT AVE., N.W.
TEL 202/331-8118
Chef Todd Gray is fascinated by, but never limited by, the food of the Chesapeake Bay region. Many restaurants claim to use the freshest local ingredients, but few have taken the trouble, as Gray has, to research historical recipes and to update them for contemporary tastes while respecting their basic tastes. Gray's recent menus have featured scallops with saffron and yellowfin tuna loin with artichoke ragout.
90 Closed Sat.–Sun. L
AE, DC, MC, V
Farragut West

SOMETHING SPECIAL

KINKEAD'S
The popularity of this Foggy Bottom seafood restaurant makes reservations a must. Like most Modern American chefs, Robert Kinkead offers a repertoire that includes dishes from a wide range of international cuisines and American regions: pepita-crusted salmon, roasted cod with crab imperial, rockfish with red curry and coconut-milk broth. His cooking is also impressive when he returns to his New England roots—Kinkead's has the best fried clams in town.
$$$$
2000 PENNSYLVANIA AVE., N.W.
TEL 202/296-7700
190 Valet AE, D, MC, V Foggy Bottom

GALILEO
$$$$
1110 21ST ST., N.W.
TEL 202/293-7191
The flagship restaurant of one of Washington's most popular and inventive chefs, Galileo offers a number of ways of dining. For a quick lunch or snack, the bar menu of sandwiches and salads is a great bargain. The main dining room has a large selection of dishes from chef Roberto Donna's native Piedmont, but for a real treat (and splurge), make reservations for Donna's Laboratorio, where the chef himself cooks a ten-course tasting menu based on what is available in the market.
175 Valet Closed Sat.–Sun. L AE, DC, MC, V Foggy Bottom or Farragut West

MARCEL'S
$$$$
2401 PENNSYLVANIA AVE., N.W.
TEL 202/296-1166
Chef Robert Wiedmaier's Belgian-influenced French cooking is both sophisticated and robust. Start a meal with his wonderfully light *boudin blanc*; continue with a game dish, perhaps loin of venison in a subtle sauce of beats and blackberries. The wine list is particularly strong in red Burgundies and wines from the Côtes du Rhone.
120 Valet Closed L AE, DC, MC, V Foggy Bottom

CENTRAL MICHEL RICHARD
$$$
1001 PENNSYLVANIA AVE., N.W.
TEL 202/626-0015
This lovely and low-key new restaurant near the White House has Washingtonians flocking to its affordable takes on the innovative mastery of celebrated chef Michel Richard of Citronelle. The fare is French bistro with a twist. An onion tart translates to a sort of pizza with bacon and caramelized onions. There's a classic hamburger served in a brioche bun, but also a version made with lobster meat and scallop mousse.
140 Valet Closed Sat. L & all Sun. AE, D, MC, V Metro Center or Archives/Navy Memorial

OVAL ROOM AT LAFAYETTE SQUARE
$$$$
800 CONNECTICUT AVE., N.W.
TEL 202/463-8700
Just across Lafayette Square from the White House, the Oval Room is a favorite lunch spot for senior executive branch staffers, drawn by the innovative cooking. Try the seared sea scallops with chorizo and squid, the loin of pork served with root vegetables, and finish with a selection of the perfectly kept cheeses.
125 Valet Closed Sat. L & all Sun. AE, DC, MC, V Farragut West

TABERNA DEL ALABARDERO
$$$$
1776 I ST., N.W.
TEL 202/429-2200
The small tapas bar at the entrance is a good first stop at this distinguished Spanish restaurant, perhaps for a glass of dry sherry and a plate of Serrano ham to whet the appetite. The main-course selections demonstrate that there is much more to Spanish cooking than paella—maybe lovely garlic soup or stuffed squid to start and a main course of a hearty rabbit stew.
162 Valet Closed Sat. L & all Sun. AE, D, DC, MC, V Farragut West

OLD EBBITT GRILL
$$$
675 15TH ST., N.W.
TEL 202/347-4801
Large, casual, and always crowded, the Old Ebbitt Grill feeds Washingtonians and out-of-towners with a large menu that ranges from burgers to grilled fish and meat. There's no better place in town for oysters.

The grill always has a large assortment of varieties from waters that are certified safe, and a crew of able shuckers to open them.
500 Valet
AE, D, DC, MC, V
Metro Center

SKY TERRACE
$$
15TH ST. & PENNSYLVANIA AVE., N.W.
TEL 202/638-5900
The Hotel Washington's Sky Terrace, open from May through October, has spectacular views of Washington toward the south and the monuments and toward the west and the White House. It's a favorite summer place for drinks and also serves light American fare such as sandwiches, salads, and fish.
200 Closed Nov.–April AE, D, DC, MC, V Metro Center

BREAD LINE
$
1751 PENNSYLVANIA AVE., N.W.
TEL 202/822-8900
Owner Mark Furstenburg's popular lunch spot near the White House specializes in bread and sandwiches. If you're lucky enough to be in Washington in tomato season, try the BLT on brioche—but you can also find wonderful pizzas, emapanadas, pirogis, and soups. It's also a great place to buy bread for a summer picnic. Hours are 7 a.m. to 7 p.m. weekdays.
100 Closed Sat.–Sun. AE, D, MC, V Farragut West

MALAYSIA KOPITIAM
$
1827 M ST., N.W.
TEL 202/833-6232
Owners Penny and Leslie Phoon are hospitable guides to the food of Malaysia, which is less well known than it ought to be. The menu thoughtfully provides photos of the dishes, but the Phoons are glad to make recommendations—maybe appetizers of fish balls or a spicy lamb satay followed by Malaysian chili shrimp or a Chinese noodle dish.
110 AE, D, DC, MC, V
Dupont Circle

DOWNTOWN

HOTELS

JEFFERSON HOTEL
$$$$$
1200 16TH ST., N.W.
TEL 202/347-2200
FAX 202/331-7982
www.thejeffersonwashington.dc
Small boutique residential-type hotel, with every room unique. First an apartment house, in 1955 it was converted into a hotel. Oliver North resided here during the Iran Contra trials. During the '80s the Larry King radio program was broadcast from here. A major renovation was set for completion in fall 2008.
100 P AE, D, DC, MC, V Farragut West

THE MADISON
$$$$$
1177 15TH ST., N.W.
TEL 202/862-1600
FAX 202/785-1255
www.madisonhoteldc.com
The Madison, which opened in 1963, is filled with works of art and antiques. Federal-period decor is designed to be reminiscent of James and Dolly Madison's stately Virginia home, Montpelier.
353 P AE, D, DC, MC, V McPherson Square

MORRISON CLARK INN
$$$$
MASSACHUSETTS AVE. & 11TH ST., N.W.
TEL 202/898-1200
OR 800/222-8474
FAX 202/289-8576
www.morrisonclark.com
This stately Victorian mansion was built as two town homes in 1864. Chefs of the **Morrison Clark Restaurant,** have won many awards for their New American cuisine.
54 P AE, D, DC, MC, V Mt. Vernon Sq.

GRAND HYATT WASHINGTON
$$$$$
1000 H ST., N.W.
TEL 202/582-1234
FAX 202/637-4781
www.grandwashington.hyatt.com
Located near the Washington Convention Center and the Verizon Center, this large hotel features a parklike atrium, cigar bar, and six dining options, including a martini lounge.
888 P
AE, D, DC, MC, V
Metro Center

HENLEY PARK HOTEL
$$$$
926 MASSACHUSETTS AVE., N.W.
TEL 202/638-5200 OR 800/222-8474
FAX 202/638-6740
www.henleypark.com
Quaint, Tudor-style hotel in the tradition of Europe's finest mall hotels—one of Washington's most charming. One hundred eighteen gargoyles and real lead windows decorate its exterior. The **Coeur de Lion** restaurant offers very good New American cooking.
96 P AE, D, DC, MC, V Mount Vernon Square or Gallery Place/Chinatown

SOMETHING SPECIAL

HOTEL MONACO

This luxury Kimpton boutique hotel is housed in the architecturally stately 1839 Tariff Building in the Penn Quarter, within steps of Verizon Center, Washington Convention Center, downtown monuments, and the Seventh Street arts scene. The distinctive rooms with 15-foot ceilings feature neoclassic furnishings and vivid contemporary colors. The **Poste** restaurant is a brasserie offering modern American cuisine.

$$$$$
700 F ST., N.W.
TEL 202/628-7177 OR 800/649-1202
FAX 202/628-7277
www.monaco-dc.com
184 AE, D, MC, V Gallery Place/Chinatown

RENAISSANCE MAYFLOWER HOTEL

$$$$$
1127 CONNECTICUT AVE., N.W.
TEL 202/347-3000 OR 800/228-7697
FAX 202/776-9182
www.renaissancehotels.com

Once the home to many members of Congress, the historic Mayflower has been the site of an inaugural ball for every President since its opening in 1925. J. Edgar Hoover had breakfast here every morning. The gracious lobby runs an entire city block from Connecticut Avenue to 17th Street. The **Lounge** is a favorite gathering spot.

657 AE, D, DC, MC, V Farragut North

MARRIOTT AT METRO CENTER

$$$$$
775 12TH ST., N.W.
TEL 202/737-2200
FAX 202/347-5886
www.marriott.com

Conveniently located at the flagship station of the city's Metro system, the Marriott at Metro Center is attentive to both business and vacation guests.

451 AE, D, DC, MC, V Metro Center

HOTEL HARRINGTON

$$
436 11TH ST., N.W.
TEL 202/628-8140 OR 800/424-8532
FAX 202/347-3924
www.hotel-harrington.com

Low prices, a prime location, and very plain, clean rooms, make the Hotel Harrington popular with bus groups of students and other travelers on a tight budget. Its **Harry's** restaurant has one of the best burgers in town.

242 AE, D, DC, MC, V Metro Center

RESTAURANTS

GERARD'S PLACE

$$$$
915 15TH ST., N.W.
TEL 202/737-4445

Although Michelin two-star chef Gerard Pangaud has left the kitchen for a teaching career, this popular and comforting restaurant continues producing its exquisite takes on French cuisine. Whether sautéed fois gras, lobster in Sauternes, or veal sweetbreads, the results are memorable.

55 Closed Sat. L & all Sun. AE, DC, MC, V McPherson Square

INDEBLEU

$$$$
707 G ST., N.W.
TEL 202/333-2538

This high-concept restaurant fuses modern cuisine with Indian accents in a sleek and sensual setting of deep spicey colors. Appetizers might include lobster and crabmeat paired with mango, pine nuts, and curry oil, while recent entrees featured veal shank roganjosh and tandoori rack of lamb with green lentil ragout. Dining is also available at a chef's table or in the Tantra Lounge.

150 Valet Closed Sat. L AE, D, MC, V Gallery Place/Chinatown

TOSCA

$$$$
1112 F ST., N.W.
TEL 202/367-1990

Chef Cesare Lanfranconi spent five years in the kitchen at Galileo before starting his own restaurant with a menu based on the food of his native Lake Como region. The sophisticated modern setting with widely spaced tables is designed for privacy and conversation. Signature dishes include the ravioli, roast meats and stews, and a wonderful tiramisu that makes you understand why this dish was popular.

120 Valet Closed Sat. L. & all Sun. AE, DC, MC, V Metro Center

LE PARADOU

$$$$
678 INDIANA AVE., N.W.
TEL 202/347-6780

Yannick Cam, who helped introduce Washingtonians to nouvelle cuisine a generation ago, is back with this elegant French restaurant that opened in April 2004. The de´cor is awash in lovely honey tones, and the food is equally sophisticated: lobster and mascarpone cheese in ravioli packets dressed with carrot and ginger sauce, roasted pigeon breast served on red cabbage with foie gras. A three-course prix fixe menu and a chef's tasting menu are options.

70 Valet Closed Sat. L & all Sun. AE, D, DC, MC, V Archives/ Navy Memorial

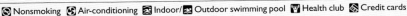

JALEO

$$

480 7TH ST., N.W.

TEL 202/628-7949

There are main courses at Jaleo, but most diners choose to make a meal of the large selection of tapas—wonderful Spanish cheeses and cold cuts, eggplant flan, spicy octopus, sausages and beans. It's a great place for a light dinner before a performance at the nearby Shakespeare Theatre.

145 Valet parking AE, D, DC, MC, V Gallery Place/Chinatown

GEORGETOWN

HOTELS

SOMETHING SPECIAL

FOUR SEASONS HOTEL

Located on the very eastern edge of Georgetown, this luxurious hotel provides a nice link into the rest of the city. Seasons restaurant, overlooking the C&O Canal, is a favorite power breakfast spot. The three-level fitness center with an adjoining spa is one of the most opulent in town.

$$$$$

2800 PENNSYLVANIA AVE., N.W.

TEL 202/342-0444

FAX 202/944-2076

www.fourseasons.com/washington

259 AE, DC, MC, V Foggy Bottom

RITZ CARLTON GEORGETOWN

$$$$$

3100 SOUTH ST., N.W.

TEL 202/912-4100 OR 800/241-3333

FAX 202/912-4199

www.ritzcarlton.com

Built on the former site of a historic brick incinerator building, complete with a 130-foot-high smokestack, this hotel offers views of the Potomac waterfront. The rooms and suites offer luxury and soothing retreat. The top-floor **Fahrenheit Restaurant** features new American cuisine while **Degrees Bar and Lounge** offers classic cocktails and tasting menus.

86 AE, DC, MC, V Foggy Bottom

HOTEL MONTICELLO

$$$$$

1075 THOMAS JEFFERSON ST., N.W.

TEL 202/337-0900 OR 800/388-2410

FAX 202/333-6526

Completely remodeled in 2000, this all-suite hotel is located in the center of Georgetown and is popular with international guests. Rooms are bright, cheery, and spacious, and all have wet bars, microwaves, and refrigerators. It is close to the historic C&O Canal.

47 AE, D, MC, V Foggy Bottom

THE GEORGETOWN INN

$$$$$

1310 WISCONSIN AVE., N.W.

TEL 202/333-8900 OR 800/368-5922

FAX 202/333-8308

www.georgetowncollection.com

Opened in 1961, this pleasant red brick hotel has colonial decor, large rooms, and marble bathrooms. It's conveniently located for Georgetown shopping and entertainment. The **Daily Grill** is reminiscent of the great American grills of the 1920s.

96 AE, D, MC, V Foggy Bottom

THE LATHAM HOTEL

$$$$$

3000 M ST., N.W.

TEL 202/726-5000 OR 800/368-5922

FAX 202/337-4250

www.georgetowncollection.com

This well located hotel has a variety of rooms and suites. The nearby C & O Canal towpath is convenient for jogging and bicycling. Michel Richard's **Citronelle** restaurant and cocktail lounge (see below) offers exceptional food.

143 AE, DC, MC, V Foggy Bottom

RESTAURANTS

CITRONELLE

$$$$

LATHAM HOTEL

3000 M ST., N.W.

TEL 202/625-2150

There's no more imaginative French cook at work in America today than Michel Richard. The open kitchen at Citronelle, with banks of tables rising above it, is a fitting stage for his art. The menu changes frequently, according to the availability of ingredients and the chef's whims. For a sampling, order one of his fixed-price menus, and don't forget dessert—he started as a pastry chef.

PRICES

HOTELS

An indication of the cost of a double room in high season, excluding tax, is given by $ signs.

$$$$$	$225+
$$$$	$175–$225
$$$	$125–$175
$$	$85–$125
$	Under $85

RESTAURANTS

An indication of the cost of a three-course dinner without drinks, tax, or tip is given by $ signs.

$$$$	Over $50
$$$	$35–$50
$$	$15–$35
$	Under $15

---

100 Valet Closed all L & Sun. July–Aug. AE, D, DC, MC, V Foggy Bottom, then 15-min. walk

1789
$$$$
1226 36TH ST., N.W.
TEL 202/965-1789
One of Washington's loveliest and most beloved restaurants, housed in a federal town house. Chef Nathan Beauchamp has infused the traditional menu—long known for its rack of lamb—with new energy in such surprising offerings as tongue salad and escargot tart. Downstairs you'll find the **Tombs,** where generations of Georgetown students have drunk countless pitchers of beer.
300 Valet Closed L AE, D, DC, MC, V Foggy Bottom, Rosslyn, then bus

SEA CATCH
$$$$
1054 31ST ST., N.W.
TEL 202/337-8855
The Carrera marble oyster bar at the entrance to this dependable seafood restaurant overlooking the C & O Canal hints at what to order first—a selection of oysters and clams on the half-shell. The seafood selection, always perfectly fresh, is based on market availability. Try the steamed shellfish platter, seared sea scallops or grilled rainbow trout with jumbo lump crab.
200 Closed Sun. AE, D, DC, MC, V Foggy Bottom

BISTRO FRANCAIS
$$
3128 M ST., N.W.
TEL 202/338-3830
In a city where restaurants close early, this lively French bistro serves until 3 a.m. on weekdays and 4 a.m. on weekends. The classics of bistro cooking are dependably done: roast chicken with *pommes frites;* a hearty *cassoulet;* rabbit in mustard sauce.
150 AE, DC, MC, V Foggy Bottom, then walk

CLYDE'S
$$
3236 M ST., N.W.
TEL 202/333-9180
The founder of the Clyde's group of restaurants had the idea that he'd "rather eat in a bar than drink in a restaurant." This Georgetown original of the chain is built around a bar business, but offers an impressive menu of bar food, particularly in the summer when Clyde's makes a point of sending trucks to local farms for fresh produce. It's a good place for a restorative drink and light meal while shopping in Georgetown.
188 Georgetown Park Mall lot AE, D, DC, MC, V Foggy Bottom, Rosslyn, then bus

PATISSERIE POUPON
$
1645 WISCONSIN AVE., N.W.
TEL 202/342-3248
Primarily a bakery that makes wonderful fruit tarts, cakes, and Washington's best croissants, Patisserie Poupon has a small dining area and a small menu of sandwiches, soups, and salads.
26 Closed Mon. L & all D AE, MC, V Tenleytown–AU, then bus

DUPONT CIRCLE & ADAMS MORGAN

HOTELS

THE CHURCHILL
$$$$$
1914 CONNECTICUT AVE., N.W.
TEL 202/797-2000
FAX 202/462-0944
www.thechurchillhotel.com
Located just north of the vibrant Dupont Circle area in Kalorama, an area known for its stately residences and embassies, the Churchill offers a variety of suites and room with separate studies. The **Chartwell Grill** offers elegant dining.
144 AE, D, DC, MC, V Dupont Circle

JURYS WASHINGTON HOTEL
$$$$$
1500 NEW HAMPSHIRE AVE., N.W.
TEL 202/483-6000
FAX 202/328-3265
www.jurysdoyle.com
Owned and operated by Ireland's Jurys Doyle Hotels, this recently remodeled hotel on Dupont Circle is one of the city's liveliest areas. Dine in the hotel's Irish pub or **Dupont Grille.**
309 AE, D, DC, MC, V Dupont Circle

PALOMAR HOTEL
$$$$$
2121 P ST., N.W.
TEL 202/448-1800
FAX 202/448-4801
www.hotelpalomar-dc.com
Sophistication and personalized service are the hallmarks of this sleek Kimpton hotel inspired by 1930s French Moderne style. Exotic woods, bold artwork, and geometric touches abound. Urbana restaurant features northern Italian cuisine.
335 AE, D, DC, MC, V Dupont Circle

HOTEL HELIX
$$$$
1430 RHODE ISLAND AVE., N.W.
TEL 202/462-9001
FAX 202/332-3519
www.hotelhelix.com
Pop-art is the decorating theme here, with a Magritte-like mural welcoming you and lots of cherry red, royal blue, lime green, pink, orange, and purple inside.

An example of the amenities designed to create an atmosphere of fun are "bunk beds" for grown-up slumber parties: a sofa-cum-twin-bed that converts to a regular-sized double bed. **Helix Lounge** features politically inspired cocktails.

(i) 178 P [ ] AE, D, MC, V Dupont Circle

🏨 TOPAZ HOTEL
$$$$
1733 N ST., N.W.
TEL 202/393-3000 OR
800/424-2950
FAX 202/785-9581
www.topazhotel.com
This Kimpton boutique hotel promises "cosmic energy and good karma." A yoga exercise room provides instruction videos, and you can even get an energy drink on your way out in the morning. The **Topaz Bar** is open for meals and drinks.

(i) 99 P AE, D, MC, V Dupont Circle

🏨 WASHINGTON 🍴 COURTYARD MARRIOTT
$$$$
1900 CONNECTICUT AVE., N.W.
TEL 202/332-9300 OR
800/842-4211
FAX 202/328-7039
www.jurysdoyle.com
This pleasant Dupont Circle hotel is popular with conventioneers, and business- and vacation travelers. **Claret** restaurant serves American cuisine.

(i) 147 P [ ] [ ] AE, D, DC, MC, V Dupont Circle

🏨 WESTIN 🍴 EMBASSY ROW
$$$$$
2100 MASSACHUSETTS AVE., N.W.
TEL 202/293-2100
FAX 202/293-0641
Opened in 1924 as the Fairfax Hotel, it was for many years the residential hotel favored by members of

Congress. Former Vice President Al Gore grew up here. Guest rooms are luxurious, as one would expect from a hotel on Massachusetts Avenue's Embassy Row. The **Fairfax Lounge** restaurant offers American bistro cuisine.

(i) 206 P [ ] [ ] AE, D, MC, V Dupont Circle

🏨 HOTEL MADERA 🍴
$$$$
1310 NEW HAMPSHIRE AVE., N.W.
TEL 202/296-7600 OR
800/430-1202
FAX 202/293-2476
www.hotelmadera.com
This pampering metro hideaway is like a B&B tucked in a quiet location near downtown office buildings and embassies. Part of the Kimpton chain, it has a sophisticated decor and the amenities of a big hotel. **Firefly** restaurant offers American bistro fare.

(i) 82 P AE, D, DC, MC, V Dupont Circle

🏨 TABARD INN 🍴
$$$
1739 N ST., N.W.
TEL 202/785-1277
FAX 202/785-6173
www.tabardinn.com
This small hotel is greatly loved by those who consider it quaint and love the Victorian clutter. Others hate it for the same reason. Locals love the hotel's restaurant (see p. 251), which has a charming outdoor garden and imaginateive food. The rooms vary widely in size, so look before you commit.

(i) 40 P AE, D, MC, V Dupont Circle

🏨 HOTEL ROUGE
$$$$
1315 15TH ST., N.W.
TEL 202/232--8000
800/368-5689
FAX 202/667-9827
www.rougehotel.com
Quirky red accents—from

Bloody Marys to wax lips—dominate this hip Kimpton hotel within walking distance of Dupont Circle.

(i) 137 [ ] AE, D, MC, V Dupont Circle or McPherson Square

RESTAURANTS

🍴 THE PALM
$$$$
1225 19TH ST., N.W.
TEL 202/293-9091
The downtown branch of this steakhouse chain is the epicenter of Washington power dining. You'll see political figures, faces familiar from the news talk shows, and a flock of lesser Washington lights who like to be seen there. The main attractions are the Palm's steaks and five-pound lobsters, served by an efficient and irreverent crew of wisecracking waiters, but the Italian food is also very good.

🪑 185 P Valet 🕐 Closed Sat.–Sun. L AE, DC, MC, V Dupont Circle

🍴 VIDALIA
$$$$
1990 M ST., N.W.
TEL 202/659-1990
Named after the sweet Georgia onion, Vidalia is one of the city's leading exponents of Southern cooking. In season, there's a large variety of Vidalia onion dishes. At other times of the year, onion offerings are likely to be limited to a dish of onion relish with your bread and the wonderful five-onion soup. The shrimp and grits is a signature dish, as is gravy-smothered chicken-fried steak. For dessert, don't miss lemon chess pie.

🪑 115 P Valet 🕐 Closed Sat.–Sun. L AE, D, DC, MC, V Farragut West

CASHION'S EAT PLACE
$$$$
1819 COLUMBIA RD., N.W.
TEL 202/797-1819
Chef Ann Cashion's Adams Morgan restaurant offers distinguished Modern American cooking in a setting that's casual enough for a weeknight dinner and attractive enough for a special occasion. The menus change frequently, but you'll usually find a perfectly roasted free range chicken, and if you're lucky, roast leg of pork with creamed collard greens, or a *fritto misto* of crisply fried seafood. Desserts are a treat, particularly the chocolate cake and the frozen lemon tart.
100 P Valet Closed Mon. MC, AE, V
Woodley Park/Zoo–Adams Morgan or Dupont Circle plus 15-minute walk

MONTSOURIS
$$$
2002 P ST., N.W.
TEL 202/833-4180
After the popularity of Montmartre on Capitol Hill, chef Stephane Lezla has brought his French bistro cuisine to Dupont Circle in this new restaurant—named for a park in Paris—that's bathed in red and dusky gold. Here he focuses on simple and homey fare such as chestnut soup, beet salad, and steaks. The kitchen does an especially good job with fish and desserts.
76 Closed Sun. AE, MC, V Dupont Circle

SETTE OSTERIA
$$
1666 CONNECTICUT AVE., N.W.
TEL 202/483-3070
A companion restaurant of Washington's popular Café Milano, this casual eatery was fashioned on traditional trattorias of Napoli. Pizzas from a wood-burning oven are the star attraction, along with homemade pastas, a range of appetizers, and a few grilled entrees. Tile floor and crowded tables make it noisy here. Patio dining in season
75 P Valet Dupont Circle

RESTAURANT NORA
$$$$
2132 FLORIDA AVE., N.W.
TEL 202/462-5143
Chef Nora Pouillon was a pioneer advocate of organic farming, and her restaurant is the first locally to be certified organic by Oregon Tilth, an organization that promulgates standards for organic growers. This means that 95 percent of the ingredients at the restaurant comes from certified organic sources. But the handsome appearance and polished service at Restaurant Nora belie our '60s preconceptions of what an organic restaurant might be. The menu changes daily, but you will find wonderful first course salads, beautifully cooked organic chicken, fresh seafood, and spectacular pies for dessert.
135 P Valet Closed L & all Sun. AE, MC, V
Dupont Circle

OBELISK
$$$$
2029 P ST., N.W.
TEL 202/872-1180
At Obelisk, everything is small in scale except flavor. This tiny Italian restaurant holds fewer than 40 people, which makes it one of the hardest-to-get reservations in town. The $65 fixed-price menu, which changes too often to recommend specific dishes, offers two or three choices of antipasto, pasta, main course, and dessert. Chef Peter Pastan's cooking is simple but never precious and is likely to be a memorable culinary experience, based on fresh ingredients in the hands of a skilled chef.
30 Closed L, & all Sun.–Mon. DC, MC, V
Dupont Circle

TABARD INN
$$$
1739 N ST., N.W.
TEL 202/331-8528
The restaurant of this quaint hotel south of Dupont Circle serves New American cuisine in a well-worn dining room that's a popular lunch spot for the offices nearby. Sunday brunch is a favorite with the neighborhood, and the pleasant brick-walled garden is a good place for a drink and dinner on a spring evening. Similary, the fireplace-cozy lounge with creaky wood floors is cozy on winter evenings.
80 (30 summer patio)
P Valet Fri. & Sat. AE, MC, V Dupont Circle

BISTROT DU COIN
$$$
1738 CONNECTICUT AVE., N.W.
TEL 202/234-6969
It's not a place for quiet conversation, particularly in the evenings when locals from the neighborhood crowd around the zinc-topped bar and fill the trestle tables, but Bistrot du Coin is a lot of fun. Owner Michel Verdon and chef Yannis Felix strike a good balance between good cheer and good cooking. Mussels are a good way to start a meal here, particularly the curried *mouclade de Charantes*. For a main course, it's hard to go wrong with *steak frites*, but the more adventurous can order *tripes à la Niçoise* or a delicious stew of rabbit and mushrooms. The house wines—a Beaujolais, a Rhone, and an Alsatian white—are good value.
150 AE, D, MC, V
Dupont Circle

LAURIOL PLAZA
$$
1835 18TH ST., N.W.
TEL 202/387-0035
There's almost always a wait to get into this well-run Tex-Mex restaurant, but there are good margaritas and baskets of chips and salsa to help you while away the time. The Mexican side of the menu is more interesting than the selection of international dishes—great fajitas, good enchiladas and burritos. The roof deck is a wonderful place to spend a summer evening over a pitcher of sangria or a few bottles of Dos Equis.
330 P AE, D, DC, MC, V Dupont Circle

SOMETHING SPECIAL

IRON GATE INN
There's no more charming spot in Washington for outdoor dining than the terrace at the Iron Gate Inn, a former stable built after the Civil War. The menu is Mediterranean-inspired and the kitchen does a good job on Middle Eastern dishes—stuffed grape leaves, braised lamb shank and grilled fish.
$$$
1734 N ST., N.W.
TEL 202/737-1370
120 Closed Sun., & Sat. L Dupont Circle

HANK'S OYSTER BAR
$$
1624 Q ST., N.W.
TEL 202/462-4265
After laboring in several Washington restaurants, chef Jamie Leeds opened this intimate restaurant in her own neighborhood near Dupont Circle to offer the kind of New England beach seafood cherished by her fisherman father, Hank. The crowded tables and eclectic décor were designed for joviality. Lobster rolls, clam chowder, steamed mussels, fish and chips, oysters, and ceviche are on offer, along with signature dishes from Leeds's former cooking days, such as molasses-braised short ribs. A few wines and microbrews are available to wash it all down.
65 Closed Tues. & Mon.–Fri. L AE, MC, V Dupont Circle

MESKEREM
$$
2434 18TH ST., N.W.
TEL 202/462-4100
Washington has one of the largest concentrations of Ethiopian restaurants outside Addis Ababa, and Meskerem is a good place for an introduction to this appealing culture and cuisine. *Alechas* and *wats,* and spicy stews of meats, vegetables, and pulses form the center of this cooking. Eat with your hands, picking up small bites with pieces of *injera,* a large, floppy pancake. It's inexpensive and an unusual treat.
200 AE, DC, MC, V Woodley Park/Zoo–Adams Morgan or Dupont Circle

PERRY'S
$$$
1811 COLUMBIA RD., N.W.
TEL 202/234-6218
Despite its meat-and-potatoes name, Perry's serves sushi and new takes on familiar fare such as scallops and soft-shell crabs. The Sunday drag brunch, with lip-synched entertainment by glamorous drag queens, is an Adams Morgan institution. The roof deck is pleasant for dinner.
90 outdoors, 90 indoors P Valet Closed Mon.–Sat. L AE, D, DC, MC, V Woodley Park/Zoo–Adams Morgan or Dupont Circle

PRICES

HOTELS
An indication of the cost of a double room in high season, excluding tax, is given by **$** signs.

$$$$$	$225+
$$$$	$175–$225
$$$	$125–$175
$$	$85–$125
$	Under $85

RESTAURANTS
An indication of the cost of a three-course dinner without drinks, tax, or tip is given by $ signs.

$$$$	Over $50
$$$	$35–$50
$$	$15–$35
$	Under $15

SKEWERS
$$
1633 P ST., N.W.
TEL 202/387-7400
The food at this small Dupont Circle eatery, popular with the locals, is Middle Eastern with an overlay of pastas, salads, and sandwiches. Kebobs, both meat and vegetable, are very well done here and are available as an entrée or atop a salad, making for a light, healthy meal.
65 AE, MC, V Dupont Circle

COPPI'S ORGANIC
$$
1414 U ST., N.W.
TEL 202/319-7773
Long a neighborhood favorite for its pizzas from a wood-burning oven, this modest restaurant also offers an excellent selection of Italian fare made from the best ingredients chef Elizabeth Bright can find. There's also a good selection of inexpensive Italian wines.
50 Closed L AE, D, MC, V U Street–Cardozo

BEN'S CHILI BOWL
$
1213 U ST, N.W.
TEL 202/667-0909
A fixture on the U Street corridor since 1958, Ben's has served chili dogs, chili burgers, and chili half-smokes to a generation of Washingtonians and visitors. Bill Cosby, a frequent visitor when he's in town, loves the chili half-smokes.
60 Cash only
U Street–Cardozo

PIZZERIA PARADISO
$
2029 P ST., N.W.
TEL 202/223-1245
This small pizza parlor, which you will be able to recognize by the line reaching out the front door and down the steps, makes simply the best pizza in Washington, maybe in the country. The crust, which tastes like good bread, is thin but supports the sparely applied toppings. This is not the place for a sweep-the-kitchen pizza. Order one of the set toppings—the spicy Atomica, the potato-and-pesto Genovese, or the delicious five-cheese combination. If you don't want pizza, there are also superb panini, Italian sandwiches, and salads.
35 DC, MC, V
Dupont Circle

CLEVELAND PARK & BEYOND

HOTELS

MARRIOTT WARDMAN PARK HOTEL
$$$$$
2660 WOODLEY RD., N.W.
TEL 202/328-2000 OR 800/228-9290
FAX 202/234-0015
www.mariotthotels.com
Washington's largest hotel, the Wardman Park is set on 16 acres of flower-planted gardens within walking distance of the National Zoo. There are several on-site dining options.
1340
AE, D, DC, MC, V
Woodley Park/Zoo–Adams Morgan

OMNI SHOREHAM HOTEL
$$$$
2500 CALVERT ST., N.W.
TEL 202/234-0700
FAX 202/265-7972
www.omnishorehamhotel.com
Opened in 1930 on 11 landscaped acres near Rock Creek, the Shoreham is a frequent convention site and location for large events. Its location gives it convenient access to the jogging trails and paths of Rock Creek Park.
835 AE, D, DC, MC, V Woodley Park/Zoo–Adams Morgan

KALORAMA GUEST HOUSE
$$
2700 CATHEDRAL AVE., N.W.
TEL 202/328-0860 OR 800/974-9101
FAX 202/328-8730
www.kaloramaguesthouse.com
This and a companion guest house in Adams Morgan offer B&B-style accommodation in the European tradition, with some shared baths and continental breakfast, afternoon lemonade, and sherry in the evening. The many repeat customers can help attest to its comfortable atmosphere.
19 AE, D, DC, MC, V
Woodley Park/Zoo–Adams Morgan or Dupont Circle

RESTAURANTS

DINO
$$$$
3435 CONNECTICUT AVE., N.W.
TEL 202/686-2966
This elegantly designed restaurant provides rustic Italian-style cooking at its best. New Executive Chef Stephan Boillon prepares traditional meals harkening from Venice to southern Tuscany, including wild boar pasta and roasted whole fish. Dino also boasts fresh vegetable salads, all-natural steaks, and an award-winning wine list of over three hundred labels.
104 Valet Closed L
AE, DC, MC, V
Cleveland Park

NEW HEIGHTS
$$$$
2317 CALVERT ST., N.W.
TEL 202/234-4110
A gracious second-floor dining room with large windows overlooking Rock Creek and a menu of creative New American cooking make this restaurant a perennial favorite. Sunday brunch, the only time the restaurant is open during the day, is particularly pleasant—almost, in the spring and summer, like eating in a tree house.
92 Valet Closed Mon.–Sat. L, Sun. D AE, D, DC, MC, V Woodley Park/Zoo–Adams Morgan

PALENA
$$$$
3529 CONNECTICUT AVE., N.W.
TEL 202/537-9250
Chef Frank Ruta and pastry chef Ann Americk met when both were working in the White House kitchen. Ruta's style is a combination of French, Italian, and Modern American. You might find tiny ravioli stuffed with oxtail almonds, raisins, and spinach, or veal cheeks paired with sweetbreads.

The menu changes frequently, and the prix fixe menus of three, four, or five courses are good value. Amernick's homey desserts are legendary. The newly upgraded bar room offers a light café menu.
68 Closed Sun., Mon., & L AE, D, DC, MC, V Cleveland Park

ARDEO
$$$
3311 CONNECTICUT AVE., N.W.
TEL 202/244-6750
This sophisticated neighborhood restaurant, with its warm woods, white tablecloths, and lively bar is the creation of restaurant entrepreneur Ashok Bajoj, who also owns the wine bar Bardeo next door. The kitchen starts with top-quality ingredients, and when it stumbles, it's because of bad combinations or faulty execution. So it's best to order simply—diver scallops, fresh fish, braised lamb shanks—and you'll eat well.
40 Valet Closed Mon.–Sat. L, open Sun. brunch AE, D, DC, MC, V Cleveland Park

LAVANDOU
$$$
3321 CONNECTICUT AVE., N.W.
TEL 202/966-3002
A sunny, cheerful bistro with a loyal neighborhood following, Lavandou features Provençal cooking. Soups are a good beginning here, the *soupe au pistou* with vegetables, basil, and garlic, or a country soup of leeks and beans. For a main course, try the daube of beef, cooked in wine to a melting tenderness, or the *carbounado* of lamb, a deeply flavorful stew of lamb, artichokes, and beans.
80 Closed Sat. L AE, DC, MC, V Cleveland Park

CACTUS CANTINA
$$
3300 WISCONSIN AVE., N.W.
TEL 202/686-7222
This many-chambered cantina, usually noisy and crowded, serves very good Tex-Mex food, both large combination platters and specialties from its mesquite-grill. The tamales are a terrific way to begin, but for a main course, order from the grill: crispy quail, great grilled shrimp, or full-flavored spareribs.
130 inside, 30 outside P AE, D, DC, MC, V Tenleytown–AU

SOMETHING SPECIAL

LEBANESE TAVERNA
There's no better place in Washington to experience the legendary hospitality of the Middle East—and its wonderful cooking—than at this busy Lebanese restaurant. It's possible to order a traditional three-course meal here, but you'll get to try a larger variety of dishes if your party makes a meal from mezze, the small appetizer plates that precede a Middle Eastern meal: spicy beef sausages, stuffed vine leaves, tart hummous, babaganoush, Lebanese "pizzas"—count on about three dishes per person.
$$
2641 CONNECTICUT AVE., N.W.
TEL 202/265-8681
100 P Closed Sun. L AE, DC, MC, V Woodley Park/Zoo–Adams Morgan

TESORO
$$
4400 CONNECTICUT AVE., N.W.
TEL 202/363-6766
This friendly neighborhood restaurant serves authentic and delicious Italian fare at reasonable prices. The pastas and pizza dough are made fresh in-house, and the quality shines through. Intriguing weekly specials cap off the fine menu, while a front patio offers alfresco dining in nice weather. Tesoro's lively bar is a popular meeting place for locals as well as visitors from the adjoining Days Inn hotel.
75 P Valet Closed Sat. L AE, D, MC, V Van Ness–UDC

EAST OF THE CAPITOL

RESTAURANT

COL. BROOKS' TAVERN
$
901 MONROE ST., N.E.
TEL 202/529-4002
A good place for a casual meal while visiting the nearby Shrine of the Immaculate Conception, Col. Brooks' Tavern has a Southern-inspired menu of steak and chicken dishes, burgers, and other sandwiches, all complemented by a large selection of beers. Live Dixieland Jazz on Tuesday nights.
100 P AE, D, MC, V Brookland–CUA

ACROSS THE POTOMAC

HOTELS

ALEXANDRIA, VA

HAMPTON INN OLD TOWN
$$$
1616 KING ST.
TEL 703/299-9900
FAX 703/299-9937
www.hamptoninn.com
Located in the heart of historic Old Town and near Metro, this well-run hotel combines comfort and value with convenience. Walk to many restaurants in the area.
80 AE, D, MC, V King Street

MORRISON HOUSE
$$$$$
116 S. ALFRED ST.
TEL 703/838-8000 OR 866/834-6628
FAX 703/684-6283
www.morrisonhouse.com
A Kimpton hotel designed to evoke the atmosphere of Old Alexandria, the Morrison resembles an 18th-century manor house. Guest rooms are furnished in federal-period reproductions. Dinner offered at the hotel's very good **Grille** restaurant.
45 P AE, MC, V
King Street, then bus to Old Town

ARLINGTON, VA

RITZ-CARLTON PENTAGON CITY
$$$$$
1250 S. HAYES ST.
TEL 703/415-5000 OR 800/241-3333
FAX 703/415-5061
www.ritzcarlton.com
A part of the Fashion Centre mall, this hotel offers luxury with the added advantage of shopping. It is minutes from Reagan National airport. Dinner is offered in the club-like atmosphere of the **Grill**. Afternoon tea is popular.
366 P AE, D, DC, MC, V
Pentagon City

CRYSTAL CITY MARRIOTT
$$$$
1999 JEFFERSON DAVIS HWY.
TEL 703/413-5500
FAX 703/413-0192
www.mariott.com
Located a mile from Reagan National Airport, this hotel connects to the Crystal City Metro stop, so access to the memorials and Smithsonian museums is easy.
343 AE, D, DC, MC, V Crystal City

KEY BRIDGE MARRIOTT
$$$$
1401 LEE HWY.
TEL 703/524-6400
FAX 703/524-8964
www.mariott.com
Just across the river from Georgetown, the Key Bridge Marriott offers easy access by Metro to downtown and its sites. The recently renovated **Capital View Ballroom** offers an indulgent Sunday brunch with stunning views of Washington.
582 AE, D, DC, MC, V Rosslyn

RESIDENCE INN BY MARRIOTT PENTAGON CITY
$$$$
550 ARMY NAVY DR.
TEL 703/413-6630 OR 800/331-3131
FAX 703/418-1751
All rooms are suites with fully equipped kitchens and other amenities for extended stay.
299 AE, D, DC, MC, V Pentagon City

DAYS INN CRYSTAL CITY
$$$
2020 JEFFERSON DAVIS HWY.
TEL 703/920-8600
FAX 703/920-2840
www.daysinn.com
A mile from downtown Washington, this Days Inn is within walking distance of the Crystal City Metro stop, two shopping malls, and many restaurants.
247 AE, D, DC, MC, V Crystal City

HOLIDAY INN ROSSLYN
$$$$
1900 N. FORT MYER DR.
TEL 703/807-2000 OR 800/465-4329
FAX 703/522-8864
www.ichotelsgroup.com
This hotel is located in Rosslyn, just across the Key Bridge from Georgetown. Enjoy dinner in Rosslyn, Georgetown, or the hotel's **Vantage Point** Restaurant.
306 AE, D, DC, MC, V Rosslyn

BEST WESTERN PENTAGON
$$
2480 S. GLEBE RD.
TEL 703/979-4400 OR 800/780-7234
FAX 703/979-0189
www.bestwestern.com
This newly renovated Best Western provides a courtesy shuttle to Reagan National airport, Pentagon City Metro station, and the Fashion Centre Mall. The restaurant **Monuments** serves breakfast and dinner.
206 P AE, D, DC, MC, V
Pentagon City, then courtesy shuttle

AMERICANA HOTEL
$
1400 JEFFERSON DAVIS HWY.
TEL 703/979-3772 OR 800/548-6261
www.americanahotel.com
This modest but well maintained hotel offers good value and a great location for easy access to Washington and many restaurants in Arlington.
102 AE, D, MC, V
Crystal City

RESTAURANTS

ALEXANDRIA, VA

LA BERGERIE
$$$$
218 N. LEE ST.
TEL 703/683-1007
This dependable French-cum-Belgian restaurant has long been Old Town Alexandria's favorite place for special occasions. Start perhaps with lobster-studded corn soup and move on to pheasant breast with foie gras or veal sweetbreads with smoked bacon. La

Bergerie is one of the few restaurants that still go to the trouble to make dessert soufflés (order at th beginning of the meal). Hazelnut is the best.
70 Closed Sun. L
AE, D, DC, MC, V King Street, then bus

BLUE POINT GRILL
$$$$
600 FRANKLIN ST.
TEL 703/739-0404
The casually elegant dining room at Blue Point Grill, attached to a Balducci's gourmet market, is a wonderful place for a dozen oysters and a glass of wine, a shopping lunch on weekends, or a full-scale special occasion dinner. The prime draw is immaculately fresh fish and shellfish. You have to pass the impressive raw bar to get to your table, so let that be a clue to the best first courses. Main course selections depend on availability, but good picks have included sea bass margherita with black beans, tomato-corn relish, and cilantro; and seared halibut with creamy polenta. A Sunday brunch is popular.
66 P AE, D, MC, V
King Street, then bus

MAJESTIC CAFÉ
$$$
911 KING ST.
TEL 703/837-9117
Chef Susan Lindeborg reopened this landmark Alexandria restaurant, which had been standing vacant for many years, and the result is impressive. The place has been modernized and many of its art deco elements preserved. Lindeborg's forte is Southern-inspired home cooking—moist chicken breast served with cornbread dressing; a simple gratin of oysters, Virginia ham, and cracker crumbs; richly satisfying spoonbread. And don't leave without a piece of the fabulous buttermilk pie.
72 Closed Mon.
AE, D, DC, MC, V King Street, then DASH bus or Metro shuttle

EVENING STAR CAFÉ
$$$
2000 MT. VERNON AVE.
TEL 703/549-5051
An ambitious American comfort-food menu and an impressive wine program raise this appealing eatery out of the neighborhood restaurant category. A new bar offers wines by the glass and small plates for snacking. In fair weather, there's outdoor seating.
70 Closed Mon. L
AE, D, DC, MC, V
Braddock Road

LE GAULOIS
$$$
1106 KING ST.
TEL 703/739-9494
Loyal diners have followed this popular French restaurant from its former home in Washington to its present one in Alexandria. What keeps them coming back is a menu of familiar classics of French bourgeois cooking, all done very well. You can get a comforting *pot-au-feu* in cool weather, a well-made omelet at lunch, and dinner specials such as chicken fricassée Normandy-style with a sauce made from apples, mushrooms, calvados, and cream.
100 AE, D, DC, MC, V
King Street, then walk six blocks

TYSONS CORNER, VA

MAESTRO
$$$$
RITZ-CARLTON HOTEL, 1700 TYSONS BLVD.,
TEL 703/821-1515
Maestro is one of the most ambitious restaurants to open in Northern Virginia in the last few years, the successful collaboration of a team that includes chef Fabio Trabocchi and wine steward Vincent Feraud. Trabucchi divides his Italian menu in traditional and contemporary sections. The setting is sumptuous, the food is frequently dazzling, and the experience is worth the charge on the credit card. Where else might you be served sea urchin in its shell; lobster-and-black-truffle pasta; and three different preparations of lamb in the same meal?
86 P Valet Closed all Sun., Mon., & L AE, D, DC, MC, V

ARLINGTON, VA

BEBO TRATTORIA
$$$
2550-B CRYSTAL DR.
TEL 703/412-5076
When inventive Washington chef Roberto Donna's celebrated Galileo closed down in 2007 for extensive renovation, he decamped across the Potomac River to open this casual Italian eatery. The name "Bebo" comes from his boyhood nickname, and the simple cooking gets its inspiration from favorites of his native Piedmont region. A wood-

PRICES

HOTELS
An indication of the cost of a double room in high season, excluding tax, is given by **$** signs.

$$$$$	$225+
$$$$	$175–$225
$$$	$125–$175
$$	$85–$125
$	Under $85

RESTAURANTS
An indication of the cost of a three-course dinner without drinks, tax, or tip is given by $ signs.

$$$$	Over $50
$$$	$35–$50
$$	$15–$35
$	Under $15

burning oven turns out pizzas and panini sandwiches, while other entrees include a variety of antipasti, pastas, and grilled meats. The overall effect is family-friendly and affordable.
140 AE, D, DC, MC, V
Crystal City

EXCURSIONS

RESTAURANTS

ANNAPOLIS, MD

TREATY OF PARIS
$$$$
16 CHURCH CIRCLE
TEL 410/216-6340
The menu at this historic inn in the heart of Old Annapolis is not groundbreaking, but it's well prepared. Crab is king here. Crab Louis with a Cajun remoulade sauce is a good starter, as are the fried crab cakes. If you haven't had your fill of crab in the first course, the Crab Imperial is traditional and good. There is also a good selection of meat dishes—beef Wellington, rack of lamb, prime rib. Fixed-price menu available.
75 Valet AE, DC, MC, V

CANTLER'S RIVERSIDE INN
$$
458 FOREST BEACH RD.
TEL 410/757-1467
A short drive from downtown Annapolis, Cantler's—owned by a family of watermen—is one of the city's most popular seafood restaurants. You eat at benches at communal tables, or at picnic tables on the deck, overlooking the docks and beautiful creek. Begin with a Styrofoam cup of she-crab soup. There are meat and chicken dishes, but the best main courses feature seafood from Maryland waters—crab cakes, softshell crabs, and rockfish.
318 AE, D, DC, MC, V

BALTIMORE, MD

CHARLESTON
$$$$
1000 LANCASTER ST.
TEL 410/332-7373
Chef Cindy Wolf's Charleston place on the Inner Harbor is Baltimore's most praised restaurant. As the name suggests, the specialty is low-country Southern cooking. Starters have included Charleston she-crab soup, cornmeal-crusted oysters, and fried green tomatoes with lobster and crab hash. Wolf frequently features traditional Carolina dishes such as seafood Perlau, or southern improvisations such as venison medallions with spoonbread or duck breasts with Madeira-poached pears and pecan rice. The wine selection is well chosen and well priced.
130 Valet Closed Sun. & all L AE, D, DC, MC, V

SOMETHING SPECIAL

OBRYCKI'S CRAB HOUSE
Don't leave Baltimore without eating at one of the city's traditional crab houses. Tables are covered with paper; steamed crabs coated with Old Bay Seasoning are dumped in the middle; and if you don't know how to eat them, your friendly server gives you a quick lesson in the art of opening crabs with a knife and wooden mallet. Obrycki's is closed for the winter and opens with crab season about the middle of March. You can also order crab cakes or softshell crabs, or crabmeat sautéed in butter, which require less work to eat.
$$$
1727 EAST PRATT ST.
TEL 410/732-6399
Closed Dec.–Feb.

SHOPPING

Washington is the place to pick up that perfect political souvenir—from campaign buttons to White House Easter eggs to Presidential seal mousepads. But just as there is more to the city than what goes on atop Capitol Hill, there is more to Washington shopping than political paraphernalia. The museum stores, for starters, have wonderful inventories of unique books, arts and crafts, jewelry, and artifact reproductions. It's natural that in such a highly educated city you'll find countless excellent bookstores. And local markets feature interesting bric-a-brac.

For a real shopping experience, however, wander into the neighborhoods, which harbor neat little one-of-a-kind shops and boutiques. Georgetown's two main arteries—M Street and Wisconsin Avenue—have many fashionable boutiques, bookstores, art galleries, antique stores, and contemporary clothing stores. Dupont Circle is much funkier, with its eclectic boutiques, vintage clothing stores, antique furniture shops, plus stores catering to the neighborhood's gay population. Adams Morgan resembles Berkeley, California, more than anything found on the East Coast, with its down-to-earth selection of African goods and curious New Age paraphernalia. Across the river, Old Town Alexandria's historic core along King Street showcases a slew of antique shops, galleries, and carpet stores in 18th-century buildings.

This listing covers some of the more unique shopping experiences in the Washington, D.C., area.

ANTIQUES

Georgetown overflows with antique shops, especially on Wisconsin Avenue between P and S Streets, and along M and O Streets. Store after store features gorgeous furniture and such accessories as grandfather clocks, 19th-century paintings, and sterling tableware. **Adams Morgan** and **Dupont Circle** also offer a good selection of antiques. In **Kensington, Maryland,** Howard Avenue is one of the foremost antique districts in the mid-Atlantic, with prices being better than those in Georgetown. Head to the lower, warehouse end of the street for serious antique shopping. The downtown Antique Row has cute, smaller shops full of collectibles. **Old Town Alexandria** has dozens of antique shops, purveying real Persian rugs, as well as French, English, and American period furniture.

ARTS & CRAFTS, GALLERIES

The best places to look for handmade works of art are Adams Morgan, Georgetown, Dupont Circle, and Old Town Alexandria. Seventh Street, N.W., between D Street and the Verizon Center, has become a mecca of galleries.

Addison/Ripley Fine Art, 1670 Wisconsin Ave., N.W. (Georgetown), 202/338-5180. One of Washington's foremost galleries, established in 1981, featuring painting, sculpture, photography, and fine arts prints.

Appalachian Spring, 1415 Wisconsin Ave., N.W. (Georgetown), 202/337-5780; & Union Station (Capitol Hill), 202/682-0505. Traditional and contemporary crafts, including jewelry, gorgeous pottery, quilts, and woodcarvings.

Canal Square, 31st & M Sts. (Georgetown) Art galleries galore.

Torpedo Factory Art Center, 105 N. Union St., Alexandria (Across the Potomac), 703/838-4565. 82 working artists' studios (each one selling their works) and six galleries showcase sculpture, pottery, paintings in watercolor, acrylic, and oil, plus much more.

BOOKS

Chapters, 445 11th St, N.W. (White House & around), 202/737-5553. Metro: Metro Center. Independent literary bookstore with current events, contemporary fiction, classics, and poetry.

Government Printing Office Bookstore, 710 N. Capitol St., N.W. (between G and H Sts.), 202/512-0132, closed weekends. Metro: Union Station. The largest general printing plant in the world, the GPO serves the printing needs of Congress. With nearly 16,000 titles (books and pamphlets) covering every conceivable area, from Cardiac Rehabilitation to the Dictionary of American Naval Fighting Ships, you should be able to find something that relates to any new hobby, interest, or activity. Also photography books, CD-ROMS and diskettes, prints, lithographs, and posters.

Kramerbooks & Afterwords Café, 1517 Connecticut Ave., N.W., (Dupont Circle & Adams Morgan), 202/387-1400, open 24 hours on weekends. www.kramers.com. Metro: Dupont Circle. Small but good selection of books. Late-night dining and entertainment at the café.

Olsson's Books & Records, 1307 19th St., N.W., 202/785-1133; 418 7th St., N.W., 202/638-7610; www.olssons.com. Large and varied collection of books and a good selection of classical and folk records and CDs.

Politics and Prose Bookstore & Coffeehouse, 5015 Connecticut Ave., N.W., (Cleveland Park & beyond), 202/364-1919. Metro: Friendship Heights. www.politics-prose.com. Popular with Washington's intelligentsia. Frequent author readings. Café.

Second Story Books, 2000 P St., N.W. (Dupont Circle & Adams Morgan), 202/659-8884. Metro: Dupont Circle. Used and rare books, including first editions, fine bound volumes, and just plain used. Stays open late.

DEPARTMENT STORES & MALLS

The Shops at Chevy Chase Pavilion, 5335 Wisconsin Ave., N.W., 202/686-5335. Metro: Friendship Heights. Stores at this popular mall include Pottery Barn, Joan and David, and Talbots. Food court.

Crystal City Shops, Crystal Dr. between 15th & 23rd Sts., Arlington (Across the Potomac), 703/922-4636. Metro: Crystal City. More than 200 stores, shops, and eateries.

Fashion Centre at Pentagon City, 1100 S. Hayes St., Arlington (Across the Potomac), 703/415-2400. Metro: Pentagon City. Four-story mall with 130 shops, including Macy's and Nordstrom. Dining and cinema as well.

Mazza Gallerie, 5330 Wisconsin Ave., N.W., 202/966-6114. Metro: Friendship Heights. This complex of exclusive shops, restaurants, and theaters showcases Neiman Marcus, Saks Fifth Avenue Men's Store, and Filene's Basement.

Old Post Office Pavilion, 1100 Pennsylvania Ave., N.W. (Downtown), 202/289-4224. Metro: Federal Triangle. Clothing, souvenirs, gifts in a historic 19th-century building. Dining. Entertainment.

Potomac Mills Outlet Mall, 2700 Potomac Mills Circle, Woodbridge, VA (Excursions), 703/490-5948. Off I-95 about 30 miles south of Washington. Said to be Virginia's number one tourist attraction, the 152-acre shoppers' paradise has some 250 discount and outlet stores, including Nordstrom Rack, Ralph Lauren, Laura Ashley, Coach, and L.L. Bean. IKEA, a popular Swedish furniture store, has recently expanded to twice its original enormous space.

Shops at Georgetown Park, 3222 M St., N.W. (Georgetown), 202/342-8190. More than 75 upscale shops and boutiques in a restored tobacco warehouse.

Shops at National Place, 13th & F Sts., N.W. (Downtown), 202/638-4412. Metro: Metro Center. Three levels of shops, including men's and women's clothing, jewelry, gifts, shoes, and an enormous food court.

Tyson's Corner Center, 1961 Chain Bridge Rd., McLean, VA (Excursions), 703/893-9400. Washington's largest mall, with more than 300 shops and boutiques, including Nordstrom, Bloomingdale's, and Lord & Taylor's. Dining.

Union Station, 50 Massachusetts Ave., N.E. (Capitol Hill), 202/289-1908. Metro: Union Station. 100-plus stores on 3 levels, plus a food court and cinema multi-plex, in an active train station.

FARMER & FLEA MARKETS

Alexandria Farmer's Market, 301 King St., Alexandria (Across the Potomac), Sat. a.m. only. Traditional farmer's market with the freshest fruit and vegetables, preserves, pastries, and flowers.

Eastern Market, 225 7th St., S.E. (Capitol Hill), closed Mon. Damaged by a major fire in 2007, Washington's last remaining public market, dating from 1870, is operating at a temporary site nearby until rebuilding is complete. The location also features a farmers' market and flea market (Sat. & Sun.). Popular breakfast grill.

Georgetown Flea Market, Arlington County Courthouse Metro Parking Lot (across Key Bridge), Sat. & Sun. Now at a new location, vendors offer a museum's worth of antique musical instruments, rugs, clothes, furniture, new jewelry and sunglasses, old cameras and books, and much more.

Maine Avenue Seafood Market, Washington Channel, S.W. Canopied dockside barges hold beautiful, gleaming piles of the recently swimming rockfish, bluefish, shad, catfish, swordfish, pompano, crabs, clams, and just about any other catch you can name. A couple of stands sell hot cooked crabs, for those who can't wait.

GOURMET FOODS & WINE

Dean & Deluca, 3276 M St., N.W. (Georgetown), 202/342-2500. Gourmet foods in the historic Markethouse building, plus kitchen accessories and gifts. Its café is a wonderful place to pick up a quick bite, including sandwiches, sushi, and salads.

Marvelous Market, 5035 Connecticut Ave., N.W., 202/686-4040; 1511 Connecticut Ave., N.W., 202/332-3690; 1800 K St., N.W. , 202/828-0944; 3217 P St., N.W., 202/333-2591; 1510 19th St., N.W., 202/332-9525; 303 Seventh St., S.E., 202/544-7127. Inventive sandwiches, small yet impressive selection of prepared foods, and wonderfully crusty bread.

Balducci's,
4 locations in the Washington area, including 3201 New Mexico Ave., N.W., 202/363-5800. Modeled on European markets, featuring specialty foods and wines.

MUSEUM SHOPS

Bureau of Engraving & Printing, 14th and C Sts., S.W. (The Mall), 800/456-3408, closed weekends. Metro: Smithsonian. Engravings of Presidents, Washington landscapes, and government seals. Buy sheets of uncut $1 and $2 bills.

Decatur House museum shop, 1610 H Street, N.W. (White House & around), 202/842-1856. Reproductions of home accessories from the 18th and 19th centuries, including Presidential china. Books, jewelry, and children selections.

Hillwood Museum, 4155 Linnean Ave., N.W. (Cleveland Park & beyond), 202/686-8510 The former residence of Marjorie Merriweather Post, cereal heiress, includes a gift shop purveying French and Russian decorative arts and reproductions.

Hirshhorn Museum, 950 Independence Ave., S.W. (The Mall) 202/357-1429. Metro: Smithsonian.Contemporary jewelry that's fun and quirky.

John F. Kennedy Center for the Performing Arts, Rock Creek and Potomac Pkwy. & New Hampshire Ave., N.W. (White House & around), 800/444-1325, Metro: Foggy Bottom. Good selection of gifts with music, dance, theater, and opera themes.

Mount Vernon Estate, George Washington Memorial Pkwy., Alexandria (Across the Potomac), 703/799-6301. Reproductions of the Washingtons' belongings, including china and silver, as well as toys and souvenirs.

National Air and Space Museum, 7th St. & Constitution Ave., N.W. (The Mall), 202/633-1000. Freeze-dried ice cream (like what the astronauts eat), kites, books, and videos for aspiring pilots and astronauts.

National Archives Museum Store, 7th St. & Constitution Ave., N.W. (Downtown), 800/357-5000. Replicas of the Charters of Freedom, posters, and postcards.

National Building Museum, 401 F St., N.W. (Downtown), 202/272-7706. Architecture-related books, prints, posters, toys, and gifts.

National Gallery of Art, 600 Constitution Ave., N.W., (The Mall), 800/697-9350 or 202/842-6002. Metro: Archives, Judiciary Square. Several shops in the museum feature quality prints and posters, art reproductions, gifts, and art books.

National Geographic Society, 1145 17th St., N.W. (White House & around), 800/857-7588. Metro: Farragut North, Farragut West. Wall maps, books, globes, and educational children's toys.

National Museum of African Art, 950 Independence Ave., S.W. (The Mall), 202/786-2147. Books for adults and children on African culture and history. Also African crafts, posters, dolls, jewelry, records, and tapes.

National Museum of Women in the Arts, 1250 New York Ave., N.W. (Downtown), 202/226-5294. Unique jewelry, decorative objects, books, and other gifts.

Phillips Collection, 1600 21st St., N.W. (Dupont Circle & Adams Morgan), 202/387-2151. Jewelry, ceramics, glassware, and other objects by contemporary artists, plus hand-painted scarves, reproductions, books, and more.

Renwick Gallery, Pennsylvania Ave. at 17th St., N.W. (White House & around).Features contemporary crafts of fiber, metal, ceramic, and wood, plus books, toys, posters, and more.

Textile Museum, 2320 S St., N.W., 202/546-1210 (Dupont Circle). Exquisite tapestries, clothing, gift items, and books related to fiber arts.

White House Gift Shop, National Press Bldg., 529 14th St., N.W. (Downtown), 202/662-7280, closed Sun. Gifts and collectibles, including glassware, jewelry, and clothing.

OTHER

The Map Store, 1636 I St., N.W. (White House & around), 202/628-2608, closed Sun. Metro: Farragut West. More than 5,000 maps from around the world, plus guidebooks, narratives, and globes.

Counter Spy Shop, 1027 Connecticut Ave., N.W. (White House & around), 202/887-1717, closed Sun. Metro: Farragut North. Gadgets for spies & aspiring 007s.

Washington National Cathedral, 3101 Wisconsin Ave., N.W., 202/537-6267. Gothic- and Medieval-inspired ware, including window decorations, scarves, and stuffed gargoyles. Don't miss the Herb Cottage on the grounds.

ENTERTAINMENT

After traipsing around all day from site to site, be sure to save some energy for Washington after dark. Your choices are many: theater, a movie, dancing, or just hanging out at one of the local bars. Check the Friday Weekend section of the *Washington Post* for goings-on; as well as the weekly *Washington CityPaper. Washingtonian* magazine is another good source of information.

DANCE

Dance Place, 3225 8th St., N.E., 202/269-1600. Metro: Brookland. Dance Place presents programs of modern and ethnic dance most weekends.

Washington Ballet, 202/362-3606. The nationally recognized Washington Ballet presents a full season between September and May at the Kennedy Center and also presents the *Nutcracker* each Christmas at the Warner Theater.

FILM

American Film Institute, The AFI (www.afi.com) screens hundreds of films every years at its AFI Silver Theatre and Cultural Center at 8633 Colesville Rd., Silver Spring, Md. (301/495-6720). Actors and directors often discuss their work at these showings.

Filmfest DC, 202/628-FILM; www.filmfestdc.org. The DC International Film Festival, held in late April and early May, screens American and international films in a variety of local theaters and auditoriums.

National Gallery of Art East Building, 4th St. and Constitution Ave., N.W., 202/842-6799. The National Gallery shows free classic films and films relating to exhibitions in the galleries.

Reel Affirmations, 202/986-1119. D.C.'s gay and lesbian film festival, held in October each year, shows films of gay and lesbian interest at various Washington area theaters. Between festivals, films are screened at the E Street Cinema (555 11th St., N.W.) and other locations.

MUSIC

CHAMBER MUSIC

Corcoran Gallery of Art, 17th St. and New York Ave., N.W., 202/639-1700. Metro: Farragut West. Well known groups appear in the Corcoran's musical evenings series from October to May.

Library of Congress, 1st St. and Independence Ave., S.E., 202/707-5502. Metro: Union Station, Capitol South. Both the Julliard String Quartet and the Beaux Arts Trio are in residence at the Library of Congress and present frequent free concerts.

Phillips Collection, 1600 21st St., N.W., 202/387-2151. Metro: Dupont Circle. Free Sunday-afternoon concerts in the Phillips mansion's wood-paneled music room from October to May.

CHORAL MUSIC

Choral Arts Society of Washington, 202/244-3669. Between September and May, this 200-voice ensemble, directed by Norman Scribner, presents frequent classical programs in the Kennedy Center Concert Hall.

OPERA

Washington Opera, Kennedy Center Opera House, 202/295-2400. Metro: Foggy Bottom. During its lengthy season, the Washington Opera, directed by Placido Domingo, produces up to eight operas, sung in their original languages with English subtitles.

ORCHESTRA

National Symphony Orchestra, Kennedy Center Concert Hall, 202/416-8100. Metro: Foggy Bottom. From September to June, the NSO performs at the Kennedy Center. In the summer, there are concerts at Wolf Trap (703/255-1900), Carter Barron Amphitheatre, and other locations.

NIGHTLIFE

The Birchmere, 3701 Mount Vernon Ave., Alexandria, 703/549-7500; www.birchmere.com. The Birchmere takes music very seriously—the club's no-talking policy is strictly enforced. But the performers and the sound are terrific; the food, from Alexandria's King Street Blues, is very good; and there's also a pool hall, a brewery, and a large bar.

Blue Gin, 1206 Wisconsin Ave., N.W., 202/965-5555; www.bluegindc.com. Metro: Foggy Bottom, then walk or bus. This two-story lounge and club space has a stylish bar with fancy drinks and features dance sounds ranging from disco and '90s pop to R&B and hip-hop.

Blues Alley, 1073 Wisconsin Ave., N.W., 202/337-4141; www.bluesalley.com. Metro: Foggy Bottom, then walk or bus. All the legends of blues have played at this small club—Dizzy Gillespie, Wynton Marsalis, Nancy Wilson, Charlie Byrd. Tickets are $18 to $60—and there's a $10 minimum plus a $2.50 per-person surcharge for the Blues Alley Music Society. There are usually 8 and 10 p.m. shows, and sometimes on weekends a midnight set. Reservations are essential.

Bohemian Caverns, 2001 11th St., N.W., 202/299-0800; www.bohemiancaverns.com. Metro: U Street–Cardozo. Bohemian Caverns was once a Washington institution, hosting Duke Ellington, Billie Holiday, Louis Armstrong, Jelly Roll Morton, Thelonious Monk, and others.

HR-57 Center for the Preservation of Jazz and Blues, 1610 14th St., N.W., 202/667-3700; www.hr57.org. Named for the House of Representatives resolution that honored jazz as a national treasure, this nonprofit music cultural center holds jazz jam sessions and performances several evenings a week. The Riot Act on the lower level is a comedy club (202/625-5160).

IOTA Club & Cafe, 2832 Wilson Blvd., Arlington, 703/522-8340. Metro: Clarendon. Iota consistently books some of the best folk, alternative country, and rock music in the area, and the food's good, too. Live music offered every night.

Kramerbooks & Afterwords café, 1517 Connecticut Ave., N.W., 202/387-1462; www.kramers.com. Metro: Dupont Circle. Serving latte´ to the literati, this bookstore with attached café is the informal community center for the Dupont Circle neighborhood. It's open all night Friday and Saturday nights, and has live music Wednesday through Saturday.

Madam's Organ, 2461 18th St., N.W., 202/667-5370; www.madamsorgan.com. The popular Madam's Organ has a full schedule of bluegrass, R&B, and blues. Try to arrive before 10 Thursday through Saturday—after 11, you'll probably wait in line.

Modern, 3287 M St., N.W., 202/338-7027; www.modern-dc.com. Metro: Foggy Bottom, then walk or bus. You may not be sure if it's a bar or a retro furniture store, but this handsome, friendly bar with couches, coffee tables, a hardwood dance floor, and a dress code is a delightful exception to the rule that Georgetown bars are only for students.

9:30 Club, 815 V St., N.W., 202/265-0930; www.930.com. Metro: U Street–Cardozo. A great sound system makes this crowded club the best place in Washington to hear top-tier rock, punk, hip-hop, and country shows.

U-topia, 1418 U St., N.W.; 202/483-7669. Metro: U Street-Cardoza. This crowded bistro and club offers live jazz and Latin music nightly to a hip and eclectic crowd of all ages. Vibrant artwork adds spice, but the food and service don't always match the flair.

THEATER

Arena Stage, 1101 Sixth St., S.E., 202/488-3300; www.arenastage.com. This respected resident theater company presents a busy season on its three stages.

Ford's Theatre See p. 132.

Howard Theatre See p. 174.

Lincoln Theater See p. 174.

National Theatre See p. 143.

Shakespeare Theatre, 450 7th St., N.W., 202/547-1122. Metro: Gallery Place/Chinatown Widely acknowledged as one of the best Shakespeare companies in America, the Shakespeare Theatre stages several plays a year in a custom-built, state-of-the-art theater. Many of its reinterpretations of Shakespeare's plays are based in modern settings. See p. 134.

Signature Theatre, 2800 S. Stafford St., Arlington, 703/820-9771; http://www.sig-online.org. Especially known for its productions of modern musical theater.

Studio Theatre, 1501 14th St., N.W., 202/332-3300; www.studiotheatre.org. Metro: Dupont Circle. The third largest producing theater in Washington, Studio Theatre presents the best of contemporary theater. It is the home of Studio Theatre Acting Conservatory, which runs a widely-respected school for the theater.

Warner Theatre See p. 144.

Woolly Mammoth, 641 D St., N.W., 202/393-3939; www.woollymammoth.net. Metro: Gallery Place/Chinatown. *Variety* comments on Woolly Mammoth's "fierce dedication to the offbeat," a dedication that is pursued with genuine devotion and solid production values. After 25 years as a leader in developing new plays, this company recently moved into its first permanent home—a courtyard-style theater in the heart of downtown D.C.

ACTIVITIES

From boating to golfing to ice skating, Washington offers an amazingly diverse selection of options for outdoor enthusiasts. If you're in the mood to watch others do the work instead, you have a number of big-name sports teams from which to choose, including Michael Jordan's Wizards. For something a little different, join one of the many specialty tours—a chance to see the city from a different point of view, by walking, boating, or even by bike.

OUTDOOR ACTIVITIES

BOATING

Jack's Boathouse, 3500 K St., N.W., 202/337-9642; jacksboathouse.com. Open April–Oct. Located under Key Bridge in Georgetown, Jack's rents canoes and kayaks.

Thompson Boat Center, 2900 Virginia Ave., N.W., 202/333-9543; thompsonboatcenter.com. Open April–Oct. Canoes, rowing shells, and kayaks for rent. Lessons available. Also, all-terrain and cruiser bike rentals.

GOLF

East Potomac Park Golf Course, 972 Ohio Dr., S.W., 202/554-7660; www.golfdc.com. This public course near the Mall consists of one 18-hole, par-72 course and two 9-hole courses. Open daily from dawn until dusk. Daily cart fees.

Langston Golf Course, 268 Benning Rd., N.E., 202/397-8638. The Langston Golf Course is an 18-hole, par-72 public course that also offers a golf school, golf shop, driving range, putting green, and snack bar.

Rock Creek Park Golf Course, 16th and Rittenhouse Sts., N.W., 202/882-7332. This 4,798-yard, par-65 public course has a hilly and challenging terrain. Amenities include a golf school, golf shop, a putting green, and a snack bar. The course is open every day from dawn to dusk.

ICE SKATING

National Gallery of Art Sculpture Garden Ice Skating Rink, 7th St. and Constitution Ave., N.W., 202/737-4215. Open mid-Nov.-mid-March. This rink on the Mall affords skaters views of modern sculpture in the museum garden. The state-of-the-art sound system provides uniform sound to the skaters without distracting other visitors to the garden.

TENNIS

East Potomac Tennis Center, 1090 Ohio Dr., S.W., 202/554-5962; www.eastpotomactennis.com. Indoor and outdoor courts, seasonal membership or walk-in court rental, tennis lessons, and racquet stringing.

Rock Creek Park Tennis Center, 16th and Kennedy St., N.W., 202/722-5949; www.rockcreektennis.com. The facility has a total of 25 outdoor tennis courts: 10 hard courts and 15 clay courts. Five indoor courts are heated and available in winter.

SPECTATOR SPORTS

Baltimore Orioles, tickets through TicketMaster, 888-848-2473; www.baltimore.orioles.mlb.com. Baseball at Oriole Park at Camden Yards, Baltimore.

Baltimore Ravens, 410/261-7283; www.baltimoreravens.com. NFL football in Baltimore.

DC United, 202/587-5000; dcunited.mlsnet.com. Professional soccer at RFK Stadium.

Washington Capitals, 202/266-2277; www.washingtoncaps.com. Professional hockey at the Verizon Center.

Washington Mystics, 202/661-5050; www.wnba.com/mystics. Professional women's basketball at the Verizon Center.

Washington Nationals, 202/675-6287; www.washingtonnationals.com The Nationals' new stadium, opening for the 2008 baseball season, is located near the Washington Navy Yard in Southeast.

Washington Redskins, 301-276-6050; www.redskins.com. NFL football at FedEx Field.

Washington Wizards, 202/661-5050; www.nba.com/wizards. Professional men's basketball at the Verizon Center.

SPECIALTY TOURS

WALKING TOURS

Anecdotal History Tours, 301/294-9514; www.dcsightseeing.com. Author Anthony Pitch leads tours of monuments and memorials with a special focus on anecdotal history of events such as the Lincoln assassination and the burning of Washington in 1814. Private tours any day by appointment.

Georgetown & Dupont Circle Walking Tours 301/588-8999; www.tourdc.com. In her popular walking tours of Georgetown and Dupont Circle/Embassy Row, writer and tour guide Mary Kay Ricks serves up a lot of scandal and history. Group tours only available by advance booking.

Washington Walks, 202/484-1565; www.washington walks.com Offered April–Oct. Among the walks offered are Capital Hauntings, which seeks out the ghosts that frequent the area around Lafayette Square and the White House; Embassy Row, Washington's grandest boulevard; U St. Before Harlem; and Goodnight, Mr. Lincoln, in which families learn about the 16th President at the base of the Lincoln Memorial.

Bike the Sites, 1101 Pennsylvania Ave., N.W., 202/842-2453; www.bikethesites.com This venture offers family-oriented tours that combine biking and walking. Bike and stroller rentals also available. Located in downtown Washington, at rear of Old Post Office Pavilion (across from the Federal Triangle Metro).

BOAT TOURS & CRUISES

Dandy Restaurant Cruise Ship, Zero Prince St., Alexandria, VA, 703/683-6076; www.dandydinnerboat.com. The *Dandy* cruises from Old Town Alexandria to Georgetown, under the Potomac River bridges and past the monuments and memorials. Dinner is served aboard, and there's a marble dance floor.

***Odyssey* Cruises, Gangplank Marina,** 600 Water St. , S.W., 866/306-2469; www.odyssey cruises.com/dc. The 2- to 3-hour *Odyssey* cruises feature innovative meals, a top wine list, and live music, while taking in the sites of the nation's capital.

***Spirit of Washington*,** Pier 4, 6th & Water Sts., S.W., 202/554-8000 or 866/302-2469; www.spiritofwashington.com. With three interior decks and roomy outdoor observation decks, the *Spirit of Washington* can accommodate up to 450 people for leisurely afternoon or evening cruises. Food, entertainment, and dancing are available.

OTHER

Scandal Tours, 202/783-7212; www.gnpcomedy.com. This irreverent tour of Washington's infamous scandal sites is hosted by the critically acclaimed comedy group, Gross National Product, who give you an impudent commentary on Washington's embarrassing moments. Reservations required.Offered from April Fool's Day through Labor Day weekend on Saturdays at 1 p.m., pick-up at the Warehouse Theater at 1017 Seventh St., N.W. (one block from Mt. Vernon Square Metro stop). Reservations are required.

SpyDrive, 866/SPY-TREK or 703/642-7450; http://spytrek.com/spydrive. Former intelligence officers (U.S. and foreign) host this two-plus-hour bus tour of sites where spies operated. Available to large groups only by reservation.

Washington Photo Safari, 202/537-0937 and 877/512-5969; www.washingtonphoto safari.com. Professional photographer David Luria offers half-and full-day photography workshops in English, French, and Spanish.

HEALTH CLUBS

Some fitness clubs in Washington offer guest passes to anyone accompanying a member, or limited-time guest passes. Call the individual locations for information.

Bally Total Fitness
Call 800/515-2582 for information on all locations, or visit www.ballyfitness.com. No daily guest rate; must be a Bally Total Fitness member. The dozen clubs in the Washington area include, in the city: 2000 L St., N.W., #1B (202/331-7788).

11th Street Fitness Center
555 12th St., N.W., 202/628-5650; www.thefitnesscompany.com Members and guests enjoy reciprocity with 40 Fitness Company locations on the East Coast.

Gold's Gym
www.goldsgym.com The Gold's Gyms in the Washington area include the following; on Capitol Hill, 409 3rd St., S.W. (202/554-4653); and downtown, at 1120 20th St., N.W. (202/293-4200).

Sport and Health Clubs
www.sportandhealth.com. There are two dozen Sport and Health Clubs in the Washington area, including near Dupont Circle in the Hilton Hotel: 1919 Connecticut Ave., N.W. (202/483-4100); and in upper Northwest Washington, 4000 Wisconsin Ave, (202/362-8000).

Washington Sports Club
www.mysportsclubs.com The 19 clubs in the Washington area include the following: downtown, at 1211 Connecticut Ave., N.W. (202/296-7733); also on Capitol Hill, at 214 D St., S.E. (202/547-2255); or in Georgetown at 3222 M St., N.W., Suite 140 (202/338-0911).

INDEX

Bold page numbers indicate illustrations

A

B

C

ILLUSTRATIONS CREDITS

Cover: Richard T. Nowitz, except (left), Karen Ballard.

Photographs by Richard T. Nowitz except:
1, Karen Ballard; 9, Bob Rowan; Progressive Image/CORBIS; 14-15, Karen Ballard; 19, Bettmann/CORBIS; 20-1, WHHA; 22, WHHA; 23, CORBIS; 24, Thomas Cowperthwait & Co.; 24-25, Sisse Brimberg/Image Collection; 27, Bettmann/CORBIS; 28-29, Hulton Archive/Getty Images; 31, Martin H. Simon/CORBIS; 32, Karen Ballard; 35, Karen Ballard; 41, Ginevra de Benci, Leonardo da Vinci, Ailsa Mellon Bruce Fund, National Gallery of Art, Washington; 43, Franco Origlia/Getty Images; 56-57, Maltings Partnership; 58-59, Christie's Images/CORBIS; 66, The Historical Society of Washington, D.C.; 71 (UP), Gift of the Japan Foundation, Arthur M. Sackler Gallery, S1993.21; 71 (LO), Freer-Sackler Gallery/Smithsonian Institution; 74, National Museum of African Art/Smithsonian Institution; 77, National Air and Space Museum/Smithsonian Institution; 78, CORBIS; 80-81, Lawrence M. Porges/NGS; 82, Kay Hankins; 83, National Museum of the American Indian/Smithsonian Institution; 86-87, Maltings Partnership; 87, Self-Portrait, Vincent Van Gogh, Collection of Mr. and Mrs. John Hay Whitney, National Gallery of Art, Washington; 88, The Annunciation, Jan van Eyck, Andrew W. Mellon Collection, National Gallery of Art, Washington; 93, Courtesy of Smithsonian Institution; 94, Karen Ballard; 99, Everett C. Johnson/Folio; 100, Jamie Rose; 104, Karen Ballard; 110-111, Maltings Partnership; 112-113, WHHA; 113, White House photo by Joyce N. Boghosian; 114, Lawrence M. Porges/NGS; 117, Renwick Gallery/Smithsonian Institution; 118, Kay Hankins; 119 (LO), Albert Bierstadt, The Last of the Buffalo, 1888, Gift of Mary (Mrs. Albert) Bierstadt, Corcoran Gallery of Art, Washington, D.C.; 120, Bettmann/CORBIS; 125, Karen Ballard; 126, Taylor Kennedy; 131, Karen Ballard; 133, Info + National Museum of Women in the Arts; 134, John Skowronski; 135 (UP), John Skowronski; 135 (LO), John Skowronski; 136, National Museum of American Art/Smithsonian Institution; 137, National Portrait Gallery/Smithsonian Institution; 138, Richard T. Nowitz/CORBIS; 140, Kay Hankins; 142, Artist's Rendering courtesy of Polshek Partnership Architects; 146, Jamie Rose; 148, Karen Ballard; 149, Karen Ballard; 150-151, Karen Ballard; 159 (LO LE), Bettmann/CORBIS; 159 (UP), Karen Ballard; 159 (LO RT), Karen Ballard; 164-165 Auguste Renoir/The Phillips Collection; 166, Henri Matisse/The Phillips Collection; 167, Robert C. Lautman/The Phillips Collection; 168, Jamie Rose; 171 Karen Ballard; 174-175 Karen Ballard; 174, Bettmann/CORBIS; 175, Bettmann/CORBIS; 185, Courtesy Hillwood Museum & Gardens; 186 (UP), Courtesy Hillwood Museum & Gardens; 186 (LO), Courtesy Hillwood Museum & Gardens; 190, Jamie Rose; 192, Karen Ballard; 194, (UP), Hulton Archive/Getty Images; 194, (LO), Jamie Rose; 207, Kaseman Beckman Amsterdam Studio (KBAS), New York, NY; 208, Jamie Rose; 214, Richard T. Nowitz/CORBIS; 220-1, National Air and Space Museum, Udvar-Hazy Center/Smithsonian Institution; 222-223, Maltings Partnership; 224-225, Mount Vernon Ladies' Association; 230, Kevin Fleming/CORBIS.

Founded in 1888, the National Geographic Society is one of the largest nonprofit scientific and educational organizations in the world. It reaches more than 285 million people worldwide each month through its official journal, NATIONAL GEOGRAPHIC, and its four other magazines; the National Geographic Channel; television documentaries; radio programs; films; books; videos and DVDs; maps; and interactive media. National Geographic has funded more than 8,000 scientific research projects and supports an education program combating geographic illiteracy.

For more information, please call 1-800-NGS LINE (647-5463) or write to the following address: National Geographic Society, 1145 17th Street N.W., Washington, D.C. 20036-4688 U.S.A.

Visit us online at: www.nationalgeographic.com/books

For information about special discounts for bulk purchases, please contact National Geographic Books Special Sales: ngspecsales@ngs.org

For rights or permissions inquiries, please contact National Geographic Books Subsidiary Rights: ngbookrights@ngs.org

Published by the National Geographic Society
John M. Fahey, Jr., *President and Chief Executive Officer*
Gilbert M. Grosvenor, *Chairman of the Board*
Nina D. Hoffman, *Executive Vice President; President, Book Publishing Group*
Kevin Mulroy, *Senior Vice President and Publisher*
Elizabeth L. Newhouse, *Director of Travel Publishing*
Barbara Brownell Grogan, *Executive Editor*
Marianne R. Koszorus, *Director of Design*
Cinda Rose, *Art Director*
Carl Mehler, *Director of Maps*
R. Gary Colbert, *Production Director*
Jennifer Thornton, *Managing Editor*

Staff for this book:
Barbara A. Noe, *Senior Editor and Project Manager*
Melissa G. Ryan, *Illustrations Editor*
Kay Hankins, *Designer*
Allan Fallow, *Senior Editor*
Jane Sunderland, Carolina E. Averitt, Jarelle Stein, *Text Editors*
Caroline Hickey, *Senior Researcher*
Victoria Garrett Jones, *Editorial Researcher*
Matt Chwastyk, Joseph F. Ochlak, Nicholas P. Rosenbach, Gregory Ugiansky, XNR Productions, *Map Edit, Research, and Production*
Richard S. Wain, *Production Project Manager*
Janet Dustin, *Illustrations Assistant*
Connie D. Binder, *Indexer*
Lise Sajewski, *Editorial Consultant*

Staff for 2008 edition
Lawrence M. Porges, *Project Manager*
Diana Parsell, *Editorial Consultant*
Ruth Thompson, *Designer*
Lynsey Jacob, *Editorial Assistant*
Olivia Garnett, Marshall Kiker, Michael McNey, Carol Stroud, Jane Sunderland, Maura Walsh, Meredith Wilcox, *Contributors*
Map art drawn by Chris Orr & Associates, Southampton, England
Artwork by Maltings Partnership, Derby, England

Third edition 2008.

ISSN 1538-5515

ISBN: 978-1-4262-0225-4 (3rd edition)

Printed and Bound by Mondadori Printing, Toledo, Spain. Color separations by Quad Graphics, Alexandria, VA.

Visit the society's Web site at http://www.nationalgeographic.com.

	path. Its lack of infrastructure—only a few of the lodgings have more than a dozen rooms—means it never gets too crowded, which keeps beaches like beautiful Playa Flamenco pristine.
PONCE & THE SOUTHERN COAST 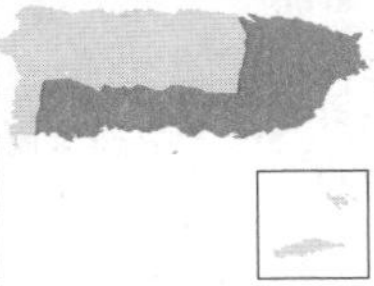	Puerto Rico's southern coast is drier than other parts of the island, and cacti are abundant. Here you'll find tropical dry forests such as the Bosque Estatal de Guánica, one of the island's most popular destinations for hikers. It's also one of the best places for bird-watching, as there are more than 100 species, including the pearly eyed thrasher, the lizard cockoo, and the nightjar. Beaches are always close at hand too, but they can be crowded, especially on holiday weekends, since this is a favored destination for Puerto Rican families. The south also has some of the island's most historic towns, including bustling Ponce, with its fascinating blend of neo-classical and Art Deco buildings.
RINCÓN & THE PORTA DEL SOL 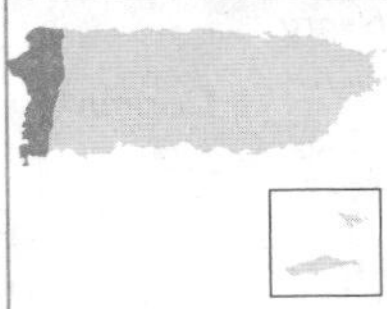	The jagged coastline of the Porta del Sol is known for its world-class surfing. There are awe-inspiring waves around Aguadilla and Isabella, but travelers have only recently begun to discover these towns. Most surfers still head to Rincón, where dozens of beaches beckon those who hanker to hang ten. The place is a magnet for expats, so expect to run into a lot of gringos. The region known as Cabo Rojo, on the south-western coast, attracts locals who pack the open-air terraces at seafood shacks along the beach at Joyuda. Flights to the airports at Aguadilla and Mayagüez make this region a quick and easy trip from the northeastern United States.
THE CORDILLERA CENTRAL 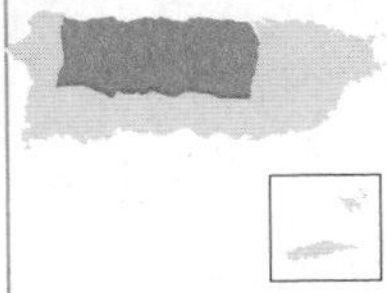	Travelers seldom explore the ridge running across the center of the island, called the Cordillera Central. That's a shame, because the scenery here is incomparable. Driving along the Ruta Panorámica, the "Panoramic Route" that traverses the heavily forested mountains, you catch glimpses of the island's northern and southern coasts. Some of the most remote nature reserves are found in the Cordillera Central. The cloud-covered Bosque Estatal de Toro Negro has waterfalls, natural pools, and the island's tallest mountain peak, Cerro de Punta. The drier Bosque Estatal de Maricao is known for its numerous species of birds. A casual, laid-back atmosphere is the norm in this region.

Puerto Rico

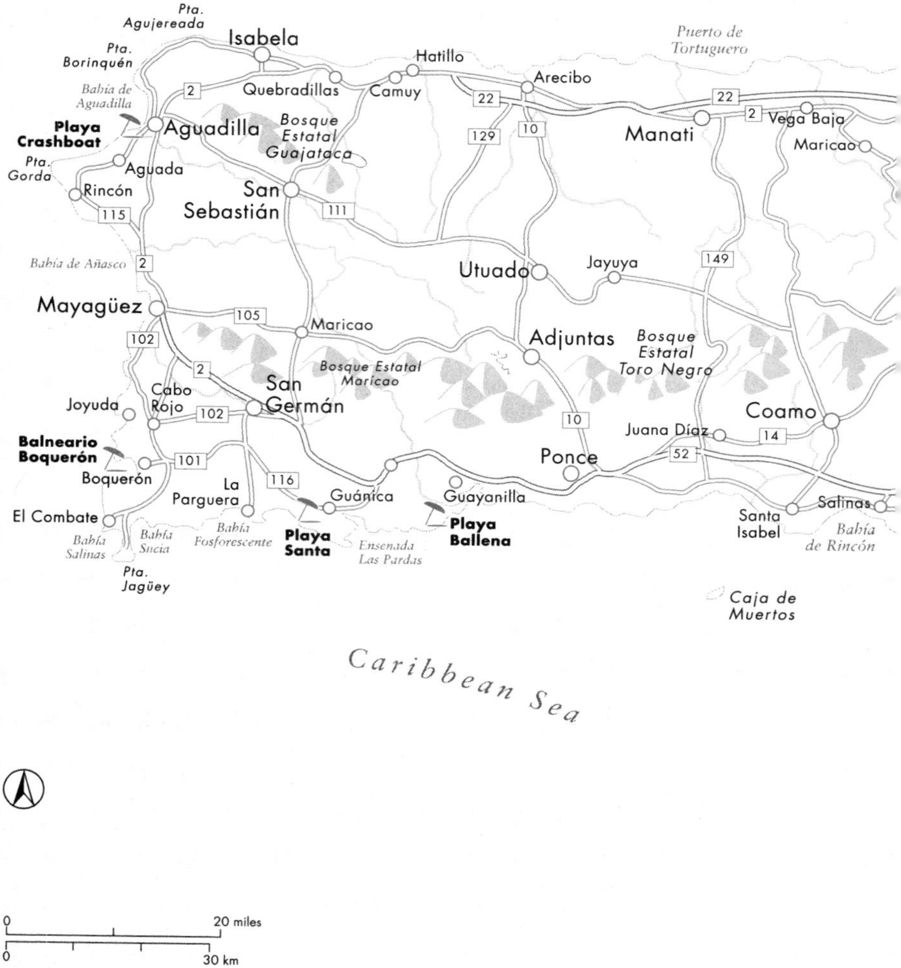

Pta. Agujereada
Pta. Borinquén
Isabela
Hatillo
Puerto de Tortuguero
Bahía de Aguadilla
Quebradillas
Camuy
Arecibo
22
2
Playa Crashboat
Aguadilla
Bosque Estatal Guajataca
129
10
Manati
Vega Baja
Maricao
Pta. Gorda
Aguada
San Sebastián
Rincón
115
111
Bahía de Añasco
Utuado
Jayuya
149
Mayagüez
105
Maricao
Adjuntas
Bosque Estatal Toro Negro
102
Bosque Estatal Maricao
Cabo Rojo
San Germán
Joyuda
Coamo
Juana Díaz
14
Balneario Boquerón
101
52
Ponce
Boquerón
116
La Parguera
Guánica
Guayanilla
Salinas
El Combate
Santa Isabel
Bahía Salinas
Bahía Sucia
Bahía Fosforescente
Playa Santa
Ensenada Las Pardas
Playa Ballena
Bahía de Rincón
Pta. Jagüey
Caja de Muertos
Caribbean Sea
0
20 miles
30 km

CONTENTS

MAPS

Be a Fodor's Correspondent

Your opinion matters. It matters to us. It matters to your fellow Fodor's travelers, too. And we'd like to hear it. In fact, we need to hear it.

When you share your experiences and opinions, you become an active member of the Fodor's community. That means we'll not only use your feedback to make our books better, but we'll publish your names and comments whenever possible. Throughout our guides, look for "Word of Mouth," excerpts of your unvarnished feedback.

Here's how you can help improve Fodor's for all of us.

Tell us when we're right. We rely on local writers to give you an insider's perspective. But our writers and staff editors—who are the best in the business—depend on you. Your positive feedback is a vote to renew our recommendations for the next edition.

Tell us when we're wrong. We're proud that we update most of our guides every year. But we're not perfect. Things change. Hotels cut services. Museums change hours. Charming cafés lose charm. If our writer didn't quite capture the essence of a place, tell us how you'd do it differently. If any of our descriptions are inaccurate or inadequate, we'll incorporate your changes in the next edition and will correct factual errors at fodors.com immediately.

Tell us what to include. You probably have had fantastic travel experiences that aren't yet in Fodor's. Why not share them with a community of like-minded travelers? Maybe you chanced upon a beach or bistro or B&B that you don't want to keep to yourself. Tell us why we should include it. And share your discoveries and experiences with everyone directly at fodors.com. Your input may lead us to add a new listing or highlight a place we cover with a "Highly Recommended" star or with our highest rating, "Fodor's Choice."

Give us your opinion instantly at our feedback center at www.fodors.com/feedback. You may also e-mail editors@fodors.com with the subject line "Puerto Rico Editor." Or send your nominations, comments, and complaints by mail to Puerto Rico Editor, Fodor's, 1745 Broadway, New York, NY 10019.

You and travelers like you are the heart of the Fodor's community. Make our community richer by sharing your experiences. Be a Fodor's correspondent.

Happy traveling!

Tim Jarrell, Publisher

FODOR'S PUERTO RICO
Editor: Brooke Barrier

Editorial Contributor: Mark Sullivan

Editorial Production: Evangelos Vasilakis
Maps & Illustrations: David Lindroth, *cartographer*; Bob Blake, Rebecca Baer, *map editors;* William Wu, *information graphics*
Design: Fabrizio LaRocca, *creative director*; Guido Caroti, Siobhan O'Hare, *art directors*; Tina Malaney, Chie Ushio, Ann McBride, *designers*; Melanie Marin, *senior picture editor;* Moon Sun Kim, *cover designer*
Cover Photo: John Stuart
Production/Manufacturing: Angela L. McLean

Fifth Edition

ISBN 978-1-4000-0731-8

ISSN 1531–0396

SPECIAL SALES
This book is available at special discounts for bulk purchases for sales promotions or premiums. Special editions, including personalized covers, excerpts of existing books, and corporate imprints, can be created in large quantities for special needs. For more information, write to Special Markets/Premium Sales, 1745 Broadway, MD 6-2, New York, New York 10019, or e-mail specialmarkets@randomhouse.com.

AN IMPORTANT TIP & AN INVITATION
Although all prices, opening times, and other details in this book are based on information supplied to us at press time, changes occur all the time in the travel world, and Fodor's cannot accept responsibility for facts that become outdated or for inadvertent errors or omissions. So **always confirm information when it matters,** especially if you're making a detour to visit a specific place. Your experiences—positive and negative—matter to us. If we have missed or misstated something, **please write to us.** We follow up on all suggestions. Contact the Puerto Rico editor at editors@fodors.com or c/o Fodor's at 1745 Broadway, New York, NY 10019.

PRINTED IN THE UNITED STATES OF AMERICA

10 9 8 7 6 5 4 3 2 1

Fodors

PUERTO RICO

5th Edition

Where to Stay and Eat for All Budgets

Must-See Sights and Local Secrets

Ratings You Can Trust

Fodor's Travel Publications New York, Toronto, London, Sydney, Auckland
www.fodors.com

ABOUT THIS BOOK

Our Ratings

Sometimes you find terrific travel experiences and sometimes they just find you. But usually the burden is on you to select the right combination of experiences. That's where our ratings come in.

As travelers we've all discovered a place so wonderful that its worthiness is obvious. And sometimes that place is so unique that superlatives don't do it justice: you just have to be there to know. These sights, properties, and experiences get our highest rating, **Fodor's Choice**, indicated by orange stars throughout this book.

Black stars highlight sights and properties we deem **Highly Recommended**, places that our writers, editors, and readers praise again and again for consistency and excellence.

By default, there's another category: any place we include in this book is by definition worth your time, unless we say otherwise. And we will.

Disagree with any of our choices? Care to nominate a place or suggest that we rate one more highly? Visit our feedback center at www.fodors.com/feedback.

Budget Well

Hotel and restaurant price categories from ¢ to $$$$ are defined in the opening pages of each chapter. For attractions, we always give standard adult admission fees; reductions are usually available for children, students, and senior citizens. Want to pay with plastic? **AE, D, DC, MC, V** following restaurant and hotel listings indicate whether American Express, Discover, Diner's Club, MasterCard, and Visa are accepted.

Restaurants

Unless we state otherwise, restaurants are open for lunch and dinner daily. We mention dress only when there's a specific requirement and reservations only when they're essential or not accepted—it's always best to book ahead.

Hotels

Hotels have private bath, phone, TV, and air-conditioning and operate on the European Plan (aka EP, meaning without meals), unless we specify that they use the Continental Plan (CP, with a Continental breakfast), Breakfast Plan (BP, with a full breakfast), or Modified American Plan (MAP, with breakfast and dinner) or are all-inclusive (AI, including all meals and most activities). We always list facilities but not whether you'll be charged an extra fee to use them, so when pricing accommodations, find out what's included.

Many Listings

- ★ Fodor's Choice
- ★ Highly recommended
- ✉ Physical address
- ✥ Directions
- 📫 Mailing address
- ☎ Telephone
- 📠 Fax
- 🌐 On the Web
- ✉ E-mail
- 🎟 Admission fee
- ⏲ Open/closed times
- Ⓜ Metro stations
- 💳 Credit cards

Hotels & Restaurants

- 🏨 Hotel
- 🛏 Number of rooms
- 👍 Facilities
- 🍽 Meal plans
- ✕ Restaurant
- ✍ Reservations
- 🚬 Smoking
- 🍷 BYOB
- ✕🏨 Hotel with restaurant that warrants a visit

Outdoors

- 🏌 Golf
- ⛺ Camping

Other

- 👶 Family-friendly
- ⇨ See also
- ✉ Branch address
- ☞ Take note

WHAT'S WHERE

SAN JUAN

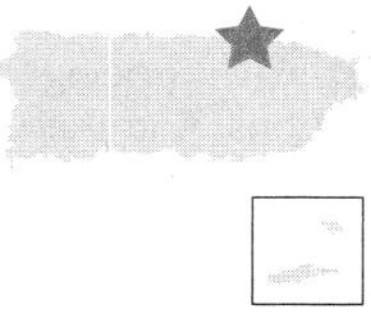

Few places remain in the Caribbean where you still can see what captivated the conquistadors. Strolling through Old San Juan's crimson-colored Puerta de San Juan, the last of the five original gateways into the city, you will find yourself on the same cobblestone streets walked by Juan Ponce de León. This is the magical part of San Juan. The rest of the city is less captivating, but with the renovation of La Concha and other resorts, areas like Condado are beginning to shake off a slightly down-at the-heels feel they've had since the late 1980s. Come to San Juan if you want to sample excellent restaurants or shop in myriad designer boutiques, especially for clothing by the island's more daring designers. And, naturally, choose San Juan if you want to party; there are few places in the Caribbean that have as varied and dynamic a nightlife scene. The city's beaches are nice, but you'll have to look further afield to find the island's finest. Don't choose San Juan if you want a quiet, get-away-from-it-all experience; the city's resorts, for all their good points, aren't really the best places to while away your hours in solitude.

EL YUNQUE & THE NORTHEAST

The most popular day trip from San Juan, El Yunque doesn't disappoint. There are more than a dozen hiking trails through this tropical forest, leading down to hidden pools and up to mountaintop observatories. If you're pressed for time, you can even experience it from your car; the waterfall called Cascada La Cola is right along the road. Don't miss oceanfront Luquillo, which has one of the island's best-known beaches and a string of *kioskos* (food stands) selling all types of seafood. West of Luquillo, the coastline gets wilder. The Reserva Natural Las Cabezas de San Juan, with its miles of mangrove forest, is one of the island's most remote nature reserves. The only real city, Fajardo, won't win any beauty contests, but it does make a good base for exploring the region.

VIEQUES & CULEBRA

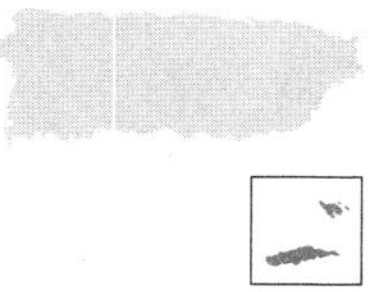

Although the rest of Puerto Rico rings with the adrenaline rush of Latin America, this pair of palm-ringed islands has the laid-back vibe of the Caribbean. It's understandable when you realize that Vieques and Culebra, off the main island's northeastern coast, are also a stone's throw from St. Thomas and St. Croix. Most famous is Vieques, in the headlines for years when protests led to the shutdown of a much-derided U.S. military base. Development is coming in fits and starts, with boutique hotels and trendy eateries that wouldn't be out of place in Miami Beach. Culebra is even more off the beaten

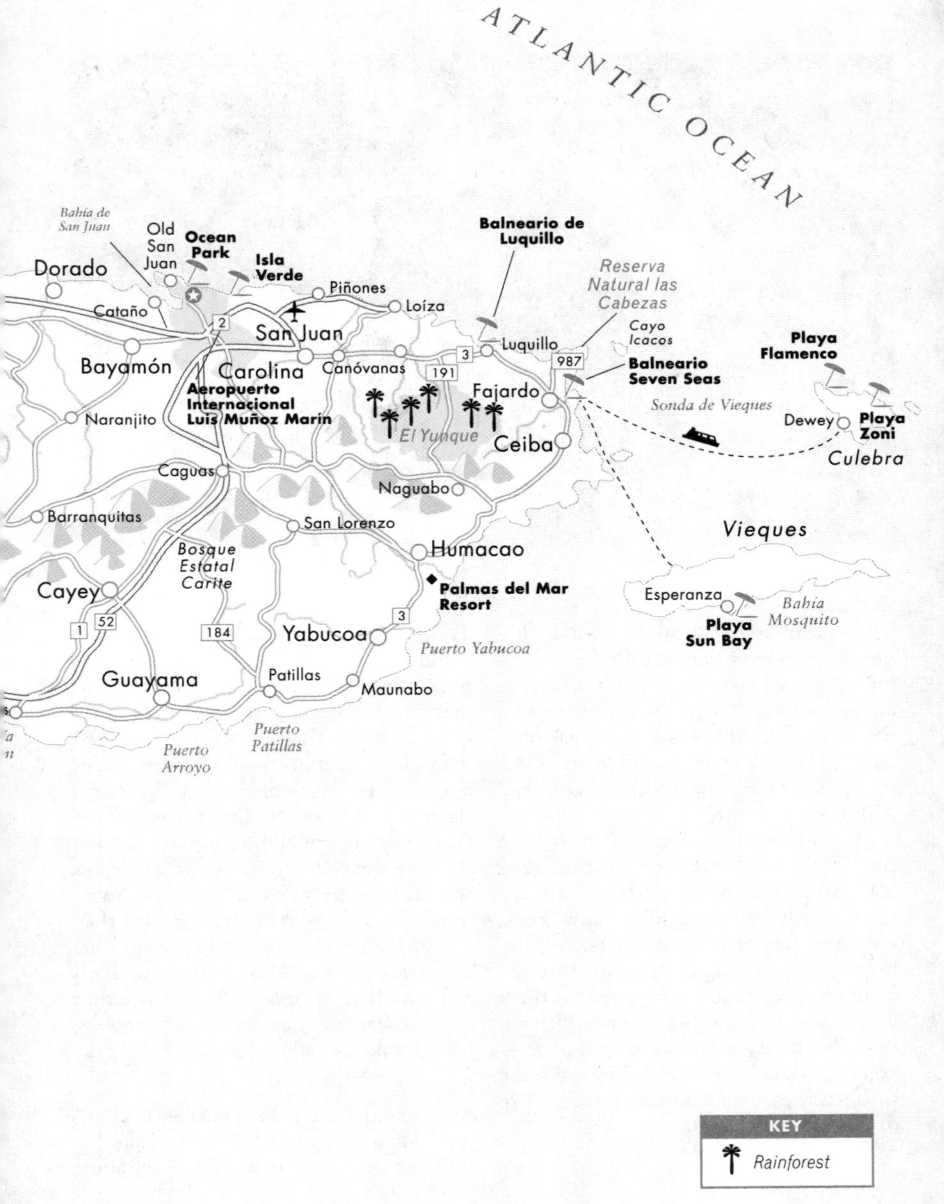
ATLANTIC OCEAN
Bahía de San Juan
Old San Juan
Ocean Park
Isla Verde
Balneario de Luquillo
Reserva Natural las Cabezas
Dorado
Cataño
Piñones
Loíza
San Juan
Luquillo
Cayo Icacos
Playa Flamenco
Bayamón
Carolina
Canóvanas
Balneario Seven Seas
Aeropuerto Internacional Luis Muñoz Marín
Fajardo
Sonda de Vieques
Naranjito
El Yunque
Ceiba
Dewey
Playa Zoni
Culebra
Caguas
Naguabo
Barranquitas
San Lorenzo
Vieques
Humacao
Bosque Estatal Carite
Palmas del Mar Resort
Cayey
Esperanza
Bahía Mosquito
Playa Sun Bay
Yabucoa
Puerto Yabucoa
Guayama
Patillas
Maunabo
Puerto Patillas
Puerto Arroyo
2
3
191
987
52
1
184
KEY
Rainforest

QUINTESSENTIAL PUERTO RICO

Coquis

The first time you hear the sound—*ko-kee, ko-kee*—you might mistake it for a bird. But then you realize that the sun has already set. This is the call of the coqui, the "little frog" that sings from dusk until dawn. They are indeed small, rarely measuring more than an inch and a half long. Although they are all called "coqui," the 16 species that live in Puerto Rico couldn't be more different. They range in color from muddy brown to olive green to mustardy yellow. Unlike many frogs, they are not strong swimmers. In fact, because their young do not pass through a tadpole stage, there is no need for them to live near large bodies of water. Bring a flashlight if you're out walking at night—you might catch a glimpse of one of these shy creatures, which are the island's more or less official animal.

Mofongo

This dish, a favorite all over the island, couldn't be simpler: mashed green plantains mixed with garlic and other flavorings and fried in a pan. Served plain, it's often a side dish. But when it's stuffed with chicken, beef, or some other meat, *mofongo* becomes one of Puerto Rico's signature entrées. In the center of the island it's often made with pork. On the coast, however, mofongo is almost always stuffed with fresh fish or shellfish. Some restaurants are even known for what they put in their plantains. A neon sign outside Tino's, one of a long line of seafood restaurants in Joyuda, touts its signature dish: an earthenware goblet overflowing with plantains and seafood.

Rum

As you enjoy your piña colada—a cocktail served in nearly every bar on the island—lift your glass to Christopher Columbus.

If you want to get a sense of contemporary Puerto Rican culture, and indulge in some of its pleasure, start by familiarizing yourself with the rituals of daily life. These are a few highlights—things in which you can take part with relative ease.

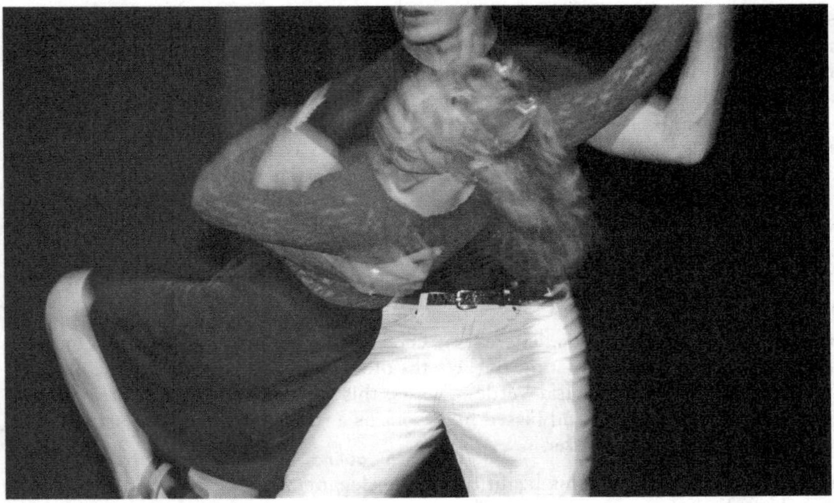

Although the explorer didn't invent the fruity cocktail, he did bring sugarcane to the Caribbean on his second voyage in 1493. Sugarcane is native to Southeast Asia, but it was cultivated in Spain at the time, and Columbus thought it would do well in the tropical "New World." Juan Ponce de Léon, the island's first governor, planted vast fields of the stuff. The first sugar mill was opened in 1524, leading to the distillation of what was then called *brebaje*. Although rum was first exported in 1897, it took a bit longer for it to become the massive industry it is today. The Bacardí family, after fleeing Cuba, set up shop near San Juan in 1959. Their company's product, lighter-bodied than those produced by most other distilleries, gained favor around the world. Today Puerto Rico produces more than 35 million gallons of rum a year. You might say it's the national drink.

Salsa

Although it's the music most identified with Puerto Rico, salsa did not originate on the island. It was born in New York City, where a sizable Puerto Rican community lived after World War II. (Puerto Rican–born Tito Puente, who helped popularize salsa, studied percussion at the Juilliard School in New York.) Salsa blends the swing music that was popular at the time with the Afro-Caribbean rhythms of rumba, mambo, and merengue. The ensemble needed to perform salsa includes a huge array of percussion instruments, including maracas, bongos, and *güiros*, the gourds that the island's indigenous Taíno people once used to mark the beat. Today, more than 50 years after it was first created, salsa remains immensely popular in Puerto Rico and is one of the iconic musical styles of the Caribbean.

IF YOU LIKE

Beaches

Sanjuaneros often pack the city's sandy stretches as well as such east-coast beaches as Luquillo. Those seeking solitude will find it on the outer islands, where the beaches are wide, spectacular, and often deserted. To the south, several stretches are broad and inviting, with plenty of seaside bars and restaurants where you can while away the hours. The west coast near the town of Rincón is popular with surfers.

Balneario de Carolina, San Juan. There's a reason this spot is the site for some of the toniest resorts in San Juan's Isla Verde—the beach, wide and warm and kissed by the surf, seems to go on forever.

Balneario Luquillo, Luquillo. This beautiful beach has all the trimmings—including lifeguards, changing rooms, and nearby kiosks where you can find tasty local cuisine and piña coladas.

Playa Crashboat, Aguadilla. The picturesque boats lining the shores here are just part of the appeal. The water has a shimmering, glassy look and is great for swimming and snorkeling.

Playa Flamenco, Culebra. Imagine a long curve of white sand and azure-tinted water. Palm trees wave in the wind. No one is there to claim the spot as theirs. It's the quintessential Caribbean beach.

Sun Bay, Vieques This crescent-shaped bay has one of the region's prettiest beaches. On weekdays, when the crowds are thin, you might also find wild horses grazing among the palm trees.

History

Puerto Rico has preserved much of its history, especially in Old San Juan, a UNESCO World Heritage Site. Walk down any cobblestone street and you'll get a sense of what it was like to be here during the Spanish Empire. Nearly as fascinating is Ponce, whose boom in the 1930s brought wonderful Art Deco buildings around the main square. For colonial splendor, there's San Germán and Guayama on the southern coast.

Capilla de Porta Coeli, San Germán. One of the oldest religious buildings in the Americas, this mission-style chapel now functions as a museum of religious art.

Casa Cautiño, Guyama. Dating from 1887, this elegant neoclassical home has a painstakingly restored exterior. You'll be swept back in time walking through the Victorian-era rooms.

Fuerte San Felipe del Morro, Old San Juan. El Morro is solid as a rock and even today seems impenetrable. Take a guided tour and see why San Juan was able to fend off invaders for 400 years.

Hacienda Buena Vista, Ponce. The grounds of this former coffee plantation are meticulously maintained. Take a guided tour to find out what it was like to be a settler taming the wilderness.

Museo de Arte de Puerto Rico, San Juan. The island's premier art museum scours the island for interesting pieces, displaying works by contemporary local artists as well as island masters like Rafael Tufiño.

Parque de Bombas, Ponce. This red-and-black striped structure has served as a firehouse since 1883. It's among the most photographed buildings in Puerto Rico.

Luxury Resorts

Most of Puerto Rico's luxury resorts are right on the beach, and those that aren't usually have a stunning view over the water. Although high-end hotels are scattered all over the island, most are along the northern and eastern coasts, which is not surprising, as these were the first places to see large-scale tourism.

La Concha, San Juan. One of the Caribbean's finest examples of tropical modernism, this showplace reopened to much fanfare in 2007. The sleek hotel—with a restaurant inside a clamshell—makes mid-century style hip again.

El Conquistador Resort & Golden Door Spa, Fajardo. This resort is big—so big, in fact, that you can easily spot it from nearby islands. Relax by the pool, play in the water park, or take an eight-minute boat ride to a private island beach.

El Convento Hotel, Old San Juan. You wouldn't recognize this as the Carmelite convent it was 350 years ago; today it's luxurious and contemporary, a fine example of sensitive planning and good decoration.

Horned Dorset Primavera, Rincón. This west-coast inn is the place to go to get away from it all in luxury. The two-story suites are impeccable.

Hacienda Tamarindo, Vieques. A tamarind tree rises up through three stories in the lobby, and the outdoor pool is touted as one of Puerto Rico's most beautiful. It's a formula for whimsical bliss.

Outdoor Activities

Does it take more than a piña colada to get you going? Does the thought of lying on the beach for a week bore you to tears? Luckily, Puerto Rico has more than enough outdoor activities to keep you occupied. Whether you prefer your adventures in the forest, on the sea, or underground, the island has something for everyone.

Kayaking in Bahía Mosquito, Vieques. The magnificence of gliding through the sparkling sea creatures at this bioluminescent bay is almost beyond description. Here nature beats special effects hands down.

Hiking in Bosque Estatal de Guánica, Guánica. This dry forest is an amazing site with its various forms of cacti and abundant bird life. Hiking here may not be for everyone—it's hot and arid—but you'll love it if you're interested in exotic flora and birds.

Soft-adventure Spelunking at Parque de las Cavernas de Río Camuy, Arecibo. The tram ride down to the caves in the limestone karst just south of Arecibo—through wild bamboo and banana plants—is worth the price of admission alone. You'll soon see that Clara Cave de Empalme is a natural wonder.

Exploring El Yunque. With 100 billion gallons of precipitation annually, this protected area truly is a rain forest. Among its sights are 240 tree species and 68 types of birds, including the endangered Puerto Rican green parrot.

GREAT ITINERARIES

LIFE'S A BEACH

This itinerary takes you west to the best beaches of the Porta del Sol, along the island's west coast, and it will get you home in a week. You can easily combine this with one of the other itineraries if you want to see more of the island.

Day 1: Dorado

Head immediately to Dorado, one of the north coast's most stunning stretches of sand. This is a favorite weekend destination for sanjuaneros, so you won't have a problem finding a place to stay. One good choice is the Embassy Suites Dorado del Mar Beach & Golf Resort. There's a string of restaurants along the town's main drag, including El Ladrillo, a longtime favorite serving *zarzuela* (seafood stew) and other traditional Spanish dishes.

Logistics: After arriving at San Juan's Aeropuerto Internacional Luis Muñoz Marín, pick up the rental car that you have arranged in advance. Take Route 165 west of San Juan, then head west on Route 693.

Day 2: Isabela & Rincón

Your destination for your second day is Rincón, on the western coast. There's no need to hurry, however. If it's a weekend, take a detour to Lago Dos Bocas, where you can have lunch at one of the waterfront restaurants. You'll have to take a boat across the lake, but we think that adds to the appeal. If it isn't a weekend, stop for a bite in Isabela, a small town that overlooks the rocky shoreline. Happy Belly's, on a stretch of shoreline called Playa Jobos, has great hamburgers. You'll probably arrive in Rincón in early afternoon, giving you plenty of time to hit the beach. If you've just received a large inheritance, you'll want to stay at the Horned Dorset Primavera. Otherwise, there are any number of inexpensive lodgings on or near the beach.

Logistics: From Dorado, drive south on 165, then west on Route 2. If you're in a hurry, save a bit of time by taking Route 22, a toll road that runs parallel to Route 2 until they meet near Arecibo. From Route 2, Route 115 takes you to Rincón.

Day 3: Cabo Rojo

The term Cabo Rojo is confusing, as "Red Cape" refers to a region, a town, and the tiny peninsula that juts off the southwestern tip of the island. The latter is where you are headed on your third day. Stop en route at Joyuda, known as the "Golden Mile" because of its string of seafood shacks. Make sure to stop at one for lunch. We like the food best at Tino's, even though it is one of the few places that doesn't have a view. Joyuda has no beachfront, so if you want to walk on the sand you'll have to head south to Boquerón. An even better idea is to continue on to El Combate. Here you'll find a less crowded beach near the neoclassical Cabo Rojo Lighthouse. (Be aware, though, that the rough road to the lighthouse is rocky.) Stay overnight in El Combate, perhaps at the recently expanded Bahía Salinas Beach Hotel.

Logistics: From Rincón, Route 115 takes you back to Route 2. Head south on Route 2 until you reach the turnoff for Route 100, which leads to all the coastal communities in Cabo Rojo.

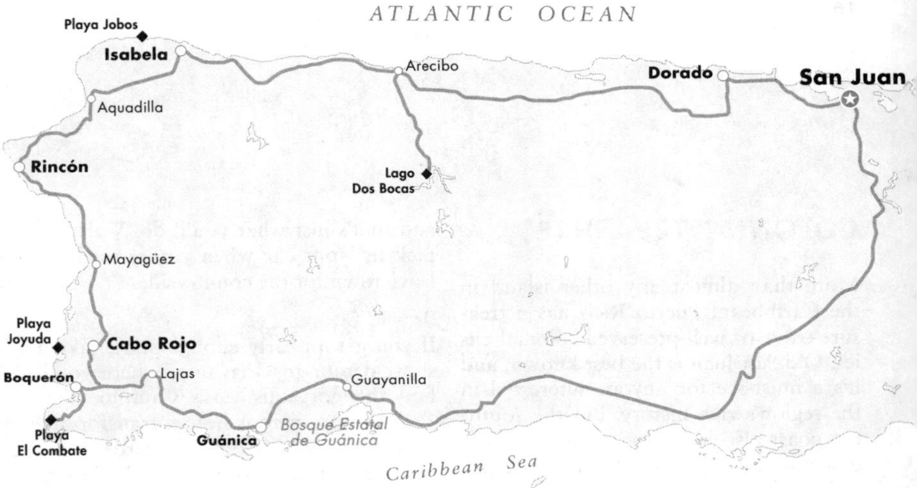

Day 4: Bosque Estatal de Guánica

From Cabo Rojo it's an easy drive to the coastal town of Guánica. Drop your stuff off at your hotel—either the expansive Copamarina Beach Resort or the intimate Mary Lee's by the Sea—and head to the Bosque Estatal de Guánica. There are several entrances to the state park, but take Route 334, because this route takes you past the park's ranger station, where you can pick up trail maps. This is a dry forest, so the scenery is unlike that of any other part of the island. You'll see more than 700 species of plants, ranging from the prickly pear cactus to the gumbo limbo tree. In the afternoon, head back to the hotel for some much-needed rest and relaxation. The beaches along the coast are beautiful, but you can also take a ferry to the offshore Gilligan's Island. The name may be a bit hokey, but the scenery is gorgeous. There's no better choice for dinner than the elegant dining room at Alexandra.

Logistics: From El Combate, head north on Route 100 until you reach the turnoff for Route 2. Follow it east until you reach Route 116, which leads south to Guánica. You can take a more direct route to Guánica, but the narrow roads won't save you any time.

TIPS

Book your hotels in advance. There are long stretches along the island's northern and western coasts that don't have any lodgings.

This drive is especially nice with a convertible. Ask your rental company about rates—you may be surprised to find they cost only $20 or $30 more a day than a compact.

The only traffic you're likely to encounter is in San Juan. If you're going to be driving through the city on a weekday morning or afternoon, add a half-hour or more to your estimated time of arrival.

Day 5: San Juan

If you have a flight home today, don't despair. The drive back to San Juan should take you less than two hours, so you can probably spend the entire morning by the beach or beside the pool.

Logistics: Route 2 takes you directly back to San Juan.

COLONIAL TREASURES

More than almost any other island in the Caribbean, Puerto Rico has a treasure trove of well-preserved colonial cities. Old San Juan is the best known, and it's a must-see for anyone interested in the region's rich history. But the southern coast also has some gems, from the graceful square in Coamo to the churches of San Germán to the heady mix of neoclassical and Art Deco masterpieces in Ponce.

Day 1: Old San Juan

If you truly want to experience Old San Juan, make sure you stay within the city walls. El Convento, once a carmelite convent, is Old San Juan's most luxurious lodging. Gallery Inn, whose mascot is a cockatoo named Campeche, has the most personality; while Da House is cheap and funky. After you drop off your suitcases, hit the cobblestone streets. Make sure to stroll along the city walls and visit one of the forts—most people pick Fuerte San Felipe del Morro, but the nearby Fuerte San Cristóbal is equally impressive. But Old San Juan isn't just for historical sightseeing. When the sun goes down, the streets of the historic district light up, becoming one of the city's nightlife centers. For dinner, head to Calle Fortaleza, where you'll find some of the city's best restaurants. Then you can while the night away at one of the happening bars or clubs.

Logistics: Believe us when we tell you that you don't want to worry about parking in Old San Juan. At San Juan's Aeropuerto Internacional Luis Muñoz Marín, take a *taxi turístico* (tourist taxi) to your hotel. The streets here were made for walking, and that's just what you'll do. Wait and pick up your car when you're ready to leave town for the countryside.

Day 2: Coamo

If you get an early enough start, take a short detour to Guayama, where you'll find the gorgeous Casa Cautiño. This 19th-century manor house, transformed into a museum, is one of Puerto Rico's most beautifully restored colonial-era structures. Continue west to Coamo, best known for its thermal springs. The best place to stay is the Parador Baños de Coamo, a rustic retreat with hot and cold pools. On Coamo's lovely main square is the gleaming white Iglesia Católica San Blás, one of the island's oldest churches. In terms of distance, Coamo isn't so far from San Juan—only about 96 km (60 mi)—so you don't have to leave at the crack of dawn to have most of a day to explore the town.

Logistics: Ponce is reached by Route 52, a modern highway that heads south of San Juan. This is a toll road, so keep your change handy.

Day 3: Ponce

Your destination on your third day is Ponce, the "Pearl of the South." You'll know you have arrived when you drive through the massive letters spelling the name of the city. The main square, the Plaza de las Delicias, is a delight. Here you'll find the Catedral de Nuestra Señora de Guadalupe, a church dating from 1835, and the Parque de Bombas, a firehouse from 1882 that is painted in bold red-and-black stripes. There are several museums around the city, but the most interesting is the small Casa Wiechers-Villaronga, a house built in 1911. In a city filled with neoclassical confections, this is

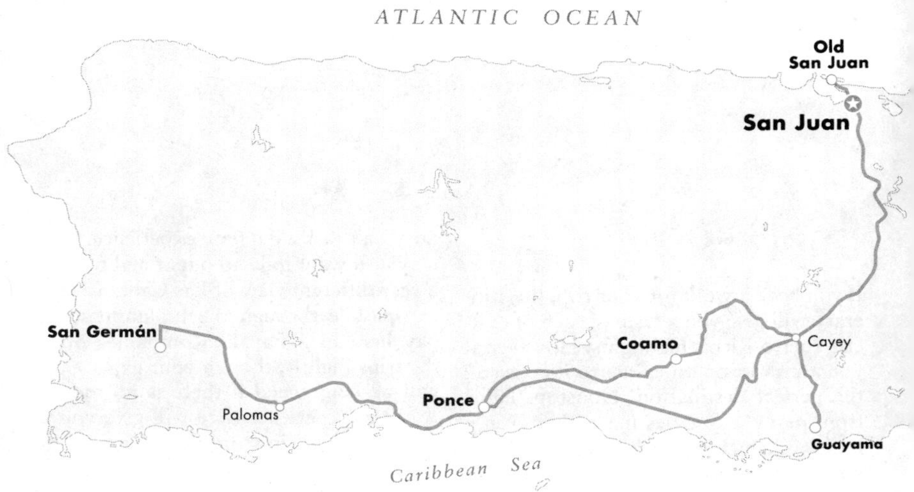

one of the most elaborate. Don't forget to stroll around the downtown streets, as the combination of neoclassical and Art Deco architecture is fascinating. One of the great pleasures of visiting Ponce is dining at Mark's at the Meliá, the city's best restaurant; conveniently, the restaurant is in Ponce's best hotel, making your choice of lodging an easy decision.

Logistics: Ponce is reached by Route 52. To get downtown, take Route 1.

Day 4: San Germán

Less than an hour west of Ponce is San Germán, a must-see for anyone interested in the colonial era. The best place to start a tour of San Germán is Plazuela Santo Domingo, the small park in the center of the historic district. At the eastern edge of the park is the Capilla de Porta Coeli. This chapel, at the top of some steep stone steps, is now a museum of religious art. Stroll west past the delightful assemblage of buildings of every architectural style from mission to Victorian. Make sure to see the other gorgeous church, called the Iglesia de San Germán de Auxerre. The best lodging in the area is the simple Villa del Rey, a few miles outside of town.

Logistics: San Germán is easy to reach—simply take Route 2 west of Ponce. When you reach Route 122, head south.

> **TIPS**
>
> If you're staying in Old San Juan, pick up your rental car at one of the hotel desks. You'll avoid an expensive taxi ride to the airport.
>
> Bring comfortable shoes for exploring these colonial-era cities. You'll be glad you brought sneakers after a few hours traipsing around on the cobblestone streets.
>
> Old San Juan and Ponce are hillier than they first appear. Take advantage of the free public transportation to the most popular tourist sites.

Day 5: San Juan

If you have time on your way back to San Juan, stop for lunch at one of the open-air eateries near Guavate, off Route 52. You can try *lechón,* whole suckling pig roasted on a spit.

Logistics: From San Germán, take Route 2 until you reach Ponce. Exit onto Route 52; a toll road takes you all the way to San Juan.

ISLAND HOPPING

If you have a week for your trip, this itinerary will give you a taste of each of eastern Puerto Rico's highlights. However, if you are short on time, Puerto Rico is still the perfect destination. Nonstop flights from many U.S. cities mean that even a long weekend is a possibility, though after you see the beaches, you may not want to limit yourself to just a night or two on Vieques or Culebra.

Day 1: El Yunque

East of San Juan is El Yunque, the undulating rain forest that covers much of the eastern edge of the island. It's a highlight of any trip to Puerto Rico, and you can still have a memorable trip if you have only one day to spend there. Several of the trails can be done in an hour or less, including one leading to the spectacular waterfalls called the Cascada La Mina. Spend the night in Río Grande; our favorite hotel along this stretch of shoreline is Wyndham's upscale Rio Mar Beach Resort & Spa, known for its seaside golf courses, lovely beach, and first-class restaurants.

Logistics: Take Route 3 east of San Juan, then head south on Route 191, which leads through El Yunque.

Day 2: Reserva Natural Las Cabezas de San Juan

Get an early start on your second day, because you've got to cover a lot of ground. Head to Fajardo, on the northeastern tip of the island. Drop your stuff off at your hotel—we prefer the smaller ones like the Fajardo Inn—then head out for a prearranged tour of the mangrove forests of the Reserva Natural Las Cabezas de San Juan. However, exploring this area isn't just a daytime experience. You may also want to head out at night to get a very different view of Las Cabezas; you can paddle through the bioluminescent bay here in a kayak. Companies offer the trips nightly, though your experience will be heightened if there is no moon. And the experience here will give you a taste of what's in store when you get to Vieques, which has a much more dramatically beautiful bio-bay.

Logistics: Take Route 3, which leads all the way to Fajardo.

Days 3 and 4: Culebra

Culebra has some of the most beautiful, powdery soft beaches that you'll find in all of Puerto Rico. It's a small, quiet island, so you won't find much to do except relax. But then, that's the draw. There are no big hotels or fancy restaurants, only small guesthouses and some villas. If this sounds like too much of a get-away-from-it-all experience for your tastes, then skip Culebra and spend more time on Vieques, which has more resorts and better restaurants. If you visit both islands, it's usually to your advantage to visit Culebra before Vieques because the latter has more flights and better connections to and from San Juan.

Logistics: Drop off your rental car in Fajardo—you'll want to rent a sturdier four-wheel-drive vehicle once you get to Culebra. Take a 90-minute ferry trip or 10-minute puddle-jumper flight to the island. We recommend taking the plane, as the views are spectacular.

Days 5 and 6: Vieques

Close—both in terms of atmosphere and geography—to the U.S. Virgin Islands, Vieques has an entirely different feel from the rest of Puerto Rico. If you've never

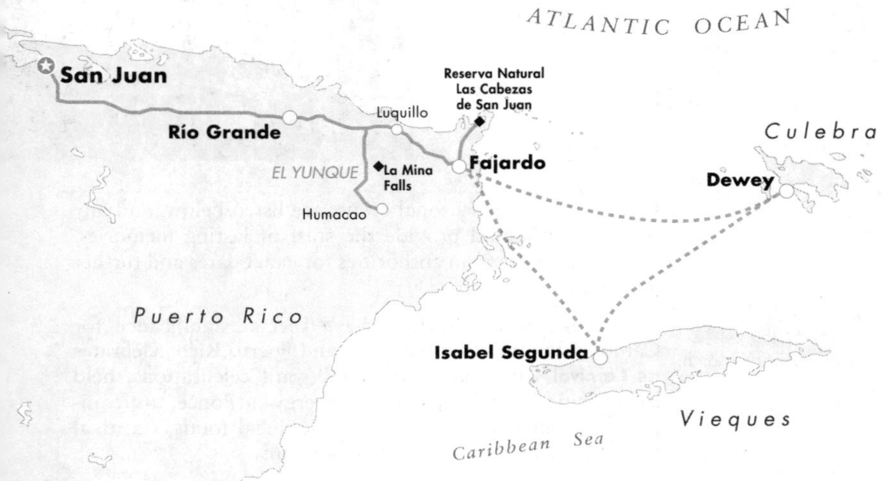

been to Vieques, we strongly recommend you spend at least one night there. The beaches are endless, the snorkeling is remarkably varied, and the bioluminescent bay is one of nature's best shows. If you've already seen Vieques—or if you aren't compelled to return again and again, as so many visitors are—you might try Culebra alone.

Logistics: You'll want to fly between Culebra and Vieques—there are often unscheduled direct flights between the islands. Otherwise you'll take a short hop to Fajardo, then continue to your destination.

Day 7: San Juan

From Vieques, take a puddle-jumper flight back to San Juan. If you want to spend a day in Old San Juan, then take a flight into Aeropuerto Fernando L. Rivas Dominici, which is a short taxi ride from San Juan's colonial heart. If you are connecting to a flight back home, then all you have to do is switch planes and you'll be on your way.

Logistics: If you are connecting to a flight back home, make sure your flight to San Juan is headed to Aeropuerto Internacional Luis Muñoz Marín. If it is going to San Juan's regional airport, Aeropuerto Fernando L. Rivas Dominici, you'll have to shuttle between the airports.

TIPS

Don't even think about taking your rental car to Vieques or Culebra. The cargo ferry runs at an erratic schedule, and may bump your vehicle at the last minute if there is no room. Besides, you need a 4x4 to navigate the island roads.

Check to see if you have to reserve in advance for certain tours, such as the daily trip to Fajardo's Reserva Natural Las Cabezas de San Juan.

Vieques and Culebra are both popular weekend destinations for Puerto Ricans, so the ferries become very crowded on weekends, and it's sometimes difficult to get on. If possible, plan your travel to the smaller islands for a weekday.

Always reserve your car in advance if you are headed to Vieques or Culebra. There are limited rentals available.

Plan your trip carefully. It's almost impossible to travel between Vieques and Culebra on a weekend.

ON THE CALENDAR

	Puerto Rico's top seasonal events are listed below, and any one of them could provide the stuff of lasting memories. Contact local tourism authorities for exact dates and further information.
ONGOING February–early March	The weeks preceding Lent have special significance for Catholicism and other religions, and Puerto Rico celebrates its **Carnival** with vigor. The flamboyant celebrations, held island-wide but with particular energy in Ponce, are complete with float parades, folk music, local foods, Carnival Queen pageants, and music competitions.
Late August–early September	Anglers of all stripes try their hand at snagging blue marlin and other game fish in the largest fishing competition in Puerto Rico, the **International Billfish Tournament,** which is hosted by the Club Náutico de San Juan. The strongest tackle might prevail—marlins can weigh as much as 900 pounds.
WINTER December	The Puerto Rico National Folkloric Ballet performs its highly anticipated **Annual Criollísimo Show** regularly during the month. The dance blends modern ballet with Puerto Rican and Caribbean music and themes. Look to the Teatro Tapia in Old San Juan or the Centro de Bellas Artes Luis A. Ferré in Santurce for schedules.
Early December	For 10 days in early December, **Humacao's Fiesta Patronale** celebrates the Virgin of the Immaculate Conception; the festival coincides with the city's sprucing up for Christmas. If you've got a hankering for loud engines and sea spray, visit the exciting **Puerto Rico International Offshore Cup** speed-boat races held every year in Fajardo, where local and international teams compete for prize money and prestige.
Mid-December	Cataño's Casa Bacardí Visitor Center hosts the **Bacardí Artisan's Fair.** With local crafts, children's activities, folk bands, and food and drink kiosks, it's arguably the largest event of its kind in the Caribbean.
Late December	The annual **Festival de los Máscaras** honors the mask-making traditions of the northwestern town of Hatillo, where colorful masks used in religious processions have been crafted for centuries. **Navidades,** or Christmas, features costumed nativity processions, concerts, and other festivities island-wide during the week leading to one of the busiest holidays of the year.

January	The annual season of the **Puerto Rico Symphony Orchestra** begins with classical and pop performances by the island's finest orchestra. Concerts are held in San Juan.
January 5–6	In Isabela the **Fiesta de Reyes Isabelinos** *(Three Kings Day)* is a two-day extravaganza that includes dramatizations of the pilgrimage to find the baby Jesus. The holiday is also celebrated in many other towns around the island.
Late January	The annual **Fiestas de la Calle San Sebastián** *(San Sebastián Street Festival)*, named after the street in Old San Juan where the festival originated, features several nights of live music in the plazas as well as food festivals and *cabezudos* parades, where folk legends are caricatured in oversize masks.
Late January–early February	Each year the Puerto Rico film industry picks talent to honor in the **Puerto Rico International Film Festival.** International stars such as Benicio Del Toro and Chita Rivera attest to the power of Puerto Rican influence in the arts, and the San Juan film festival showcases island-made films and works from around the world.
Early February	Coamo's **San Blas de Illescas Half Marathon** has been running, literally, since 1957. The race, in honor of the town's patron saint and part of its fiesta patronale, covers 21 km (13 mi) in the hills of the central town; it's so popular that competitors come from the world over, and the streets are lined with some 200,000 spectators.
Mid-February	Ponce's **Danza Week** of cultural activities celebrates the *danza,* a colonial-era dance similar to the waltz.
Late February	The mountain towns of Maricao and Yauco, centers of the island's coffee-growing region, host the annual **Festival de Café** *(Coffee Harvest Festival)*, honoring both crops and farmers. There's folk music, crafts displays, and booths selling typical foods of the region.
SPRING March	The two-day **Dulce Sueño Paso Fino Fair,** showcasing the island's famous Paso Fino horses, is held in the town of Guayama. Paso Finos are bred and trained to walk with a distinctive, smooth gait, and the horses and their trainers are held in high regard.

	Luquillo celebrates its patron saint at the **Fiestas Patronales de San José,** held each year on March 19. The festivities include traditional dances, colorful parades, and religious processions.
April	Fajardo's **Festival de Chiringas** *(Kite Festival)* features demonstrations and flying competitions, as well as food and drink booths. The annual **Regata de Veleros Copa Kelly** *(Kelly Cup Sailboat Regatta)* takes place off the coast of Fajardo.
Late April–May	Bayamón's **Chicharrón Festival** celebrates the island's famous puffy, pork-rind fritter. The city has become known for this treat thanks to the many *chicharronero* carts that line Route 2 on the way into town. The Fajardo **Festival de Bomba y Plena** turns the spotlight on Puerto Rico's lively Afro-influenced music and dance.
SUMMER June	Fortaleza Street in Old San Juan is closed to traffic for the annual "South of Fortaleza" **SoFo Culinary Week,** when more than two dozen restaurants set their chairs, tables, and bars outside on the street. In San Juan, the **Fiesta de San Juan Bautista** *(St. John the Baptist Festival)* honors the city's patron saint with a week of parades, music, dance, and, ultimately, a traditional backward walk into the ocean to bring good luck in the ensuing year. The annual **Heineken JazzFest** attracts some 15,000 aficionados to San Juan for four days of outdoor concerts by the likes of David Sánchez, George Benson, Nestor Torres, and Spyro Gyra.
Early June	The annual **Casals Festival** in San Juan honors the late, great cellist Pablo Casals, who lived in Old San Juan. The 10 days of classical-music performances feature the Puerto Rico Symphony Orchestra, as well as soloists from the island and around the world.
Late June–July	Gardenias, lilies, begonias, and thousands of tropical plants are showcased at Aibonito's annual **Fiesta de Flores** *(Flower Festival).*
July	Loíza's **Fiesta de Santiago Apóstol** *(St. James Festival)*, held in July, honors Puerto Rico's African traditions and the apostle St. James with a carnival of street parades, music, and dancing.

Early July	Río Grande celebrates its **Carnival** between the first and second week of July with music competitions, parades, and feasts.
Mid-July	The **Barranquitas Fería de Artesanía** *(Barranquitas Artisans' Fair)* offers spots to more than 200 local artisans to display their pottery, wood carvings, leather bags and belts, basketry, and other handiwork. Around July 16 such coastal towns as Naguabo, Ceiba, and Humacao conduct religious processions honoring the **Virgen del Carmen.** Offerings of flowers from the *flamboyán* tree are made to this virgin, the patron saint of fishermen, and festivities continue into the evening.
FALL October	Arecibo, on the north coast, holds the **Cetí Festival,** named after a tiny, sardinelike fish found in the area and considered a culinary delicacy.
Early October	Naguabo's **Fiestas Patronales de Nuestra Virgen del Rosario** honors Our Lady of the Rosary the first 10 days of October.
Late October	The northern town of Corozal hosts the **Festival del Plátano** *(Plantain Festival)*, which highlights this versatile staple of Puerto Rican cuisine.
Mid-November	The **Festival of Puerto Rican Music,** held in San Juan and other locations, celebrates the vibrancy of the island's folk music, highlighted by a contest featuring the *cuatro,* a traditional guitar with five double strings.
Late November	Moca's **Festival de Mundillo** *(Bobbin Lace Festival)* showcases delicate, woven lace with demonstrations and exhibits. Luquillo hosts the three-day **Festival de Platos Típicos** *(Festival of Typical Dishes)*, highlighting food and drink prepared with coconut.

WHEN TO GO

High season runs from mid-December through mid-April. Winter hotel rates are as much as 25% higher than off-season rates, and hotels tend to be packed. San Juan is also a commercial town, and hotels, except for the short season around Christmas and New Year's, are busy year-round with international business travelers. This doesn't mean the island won't have rooms in winter—rarely is space completely unavailable—but if you plan to beat that winter sleet in Duluth, make arrangements for flights and hotel space at least a few weeks ahead of time. A fun and often less expensive time to visit is during the "shoulder" seasons of fall and spring. The weather is—still—perfect, and the tourist crush is less intense.

You can always visit Puerto Rico during the less busy summer season, when temperatures are hot and hurricanes more likely. And you might even find some added bargains at this time of the year. Given its proximity to the East Coast of the United States and large number of flights, Puerto Rico can be an excellent hurricane-season option for the Caribbean. This kind of trip works best when you can visit at the last minute, when you'll be able to watch the weather report and know a storm isn't about to strike; it's also nice if you can get a bargain airfare, which might very well happen on a summer weekend. Know that business travel—not to mention the fact that San Juan serves as a major hub for American Airlines flights to the rest of the Caribbean—keeps the flights to Puerto Rico fairly full on weekdays all year long.

Climate

Puerto Rico's weather is moderate and tropical year-round, with an average temperature of about 82°F (26°C). Essentially, there are no big seasonal changes, although winter sees cooling (not cold) breezes from the north, and temperatures in higher elevations drop by as much as 20 degrees. Hurricane season in the Caribbean runs July through November.

The following are average daily maximum and minimum temperatures.

Forecasts **Puerto Rico Weather** (☎787/253–4586). **The Weather Channel** (🌐www.weather.com).

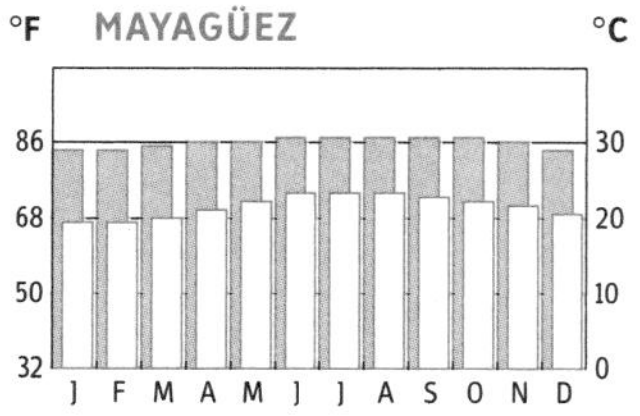

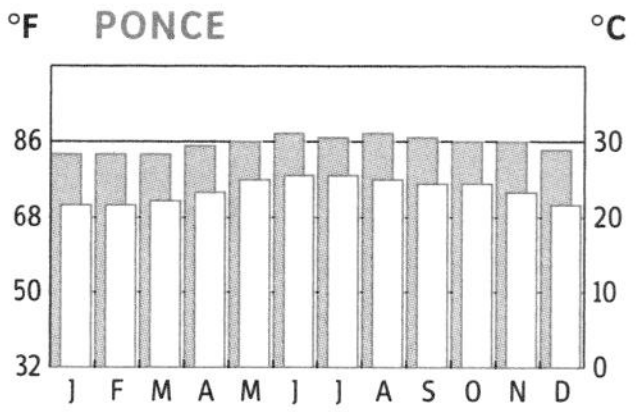

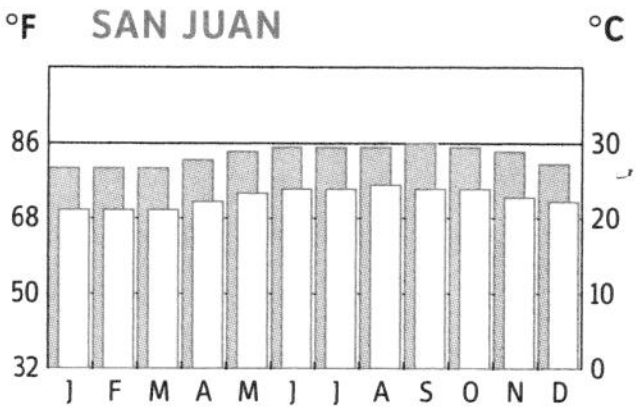

San Juan

WORD OF MOUTH

"Old San Juan is clean and beautiful with blue cobblestone streets and an abundance of restaurants, art galleries, and shops. We bought some art and even some handmade teak dominoes. We will definitely stop back here again in our travels."

—C and V

"The area surrounding [Santurce's Plaza del Mercado] has some cheap and good restaurants, and it's also a great spot for 'happy hour' nightlife from about 6 to midnight on Thursday and Friday nights. It's a very casual atmosphere and, because it starts early, locals often even take their kids."

—PR native

www.fodors.com/forums

Revised and Updated by Mark Sullivan

IF YOU ASSOCIATE PUERTO RICO'S capital with the sleepy streets of Old San Juan, then you know only part of the picture. First of all, San Juan is a major metropolis, radiating out from the spot on the Atlantic Ocean that was discovered by Juan Ponce de León. More than a third of the island's 4 million citizens proudly call themselves *sanjuaneros.* Second, this city may be rooted in the past, but it has its eye on the future. Locals go about their business surrounded by the antique and the modern, the commercial and the residential, the man-made and the natural.

By 1508 the explorer Juan Ponce de León had established a colony in an area now known as Caparra, southeast of present-day San Juan. He later moved the settlement north to a more hospitable peninsular location. In 1521, after he became the first colonial governor, Ponce de León switched the name of the island—which was then called San Juan Bautista in honor of St. John the Baptist—with that of the settlement of Puerto Rico (Rich Port). The capital of paradise was born.

Defended by the imposing Fuerte San Felipe del Morro (El Morro), Puerto Rico's administrative and population center helped to keep the island firmly in Spain's hands until 1898, when it came under U.S. control after the Spanish-American War. Centuries of Spanish rule left an indelible imprint on the city, particularly in the walled area now known as Old San Juan. The area, with its cobblestone streets lined with brightly painted, colonial-era structures, has been designated a UNESCO World Heritage Site.

Old San Juan is a monument to the past, but the rest of the city is planted firmly in the here and now. It draws migrants from elsewhere on the island to jobs in its businesses and industries. It captivates both residents and visitors with its vibrant lifestyle, as well as its balmy beaches, pulsing nightclubs, and mesmerizing museums. Once you set foot in this city, you may never want to leave.

EXPLORING SAN JUAN

San Juan's metro area stretches for 12 mi along Puerto Rico's north coast, and defining the city is rather like assembling a puzzle. Neighborhoods are irregular and sometimes overlap—locals disagree, for example, where Condado ends and Ocean Park begins. The areas most visited by tourists run along the coast.

Farthest west is Old San Juan, the showplace of the island's rich history. On this peninsula you will find the city's finest museums and shops, as well as excellent dining and lodging options. To the east is Puerta de Tierra, a narrow strip of land sandwiched between the ocean and the bay. The area is home to a couple of famous hotels and two noteworthy parks, the Parque de Tercer Milenio and the Parque Muñoz Rivera. Beyond Puerta de Tierra is Condado, a strip of shoreline crowded by resort hotels and apartment buildings. Here you'll find designer fashions in the boutiques and on the people strolling down the main drag of Avenida Ashford. Ocean Park, to the east of

SAN JUAN TOP 5

- Getting lost among the cobblestone streets of Old San Juan, a UNESCO World Heritage Site.
- Climbing the battlements of Fuerte San Felipe del Morro, the 16th-century fort that dominates the waterfront; the fort is a national historic sight.
- Window shopping along Condado's Avenida Ashford, where you'll find most of the city's designer boutiques, including the boutique of Nono Maldonado, one of the island's home-grown design talents.
- Catching a few rays at Balneario de Carolina, the award-winning beach at the eastern tip of Isla Verde and San Juan's best beach.
- Dining at Aguaviva or one one of the other stellar restaurants along the southern end of Calle Fortaleza, a strip so trendy that locals call it "SoFo."

Condado, is mostly residential, but the handful of inns and restaurants here are among the city's best. Beyond Ocean Park is Isla Verde, which looks a lot like Condado.

You may want to explore a few other neighborhoods. South of Condado and Ocean Park lies Santurce, a business district with a growing artistic community, thanks to the Museo de Arte de Puerto Rico and the Museo de Arte Contemporáneo. Hato Rey is a busy financial district, where you'll find the large Plaza las Américas Mall. The mostly residential Río Piedras area is home of the Universidad de Puerto Rico.

WHEN TO TOUR SAN JUAN

During the high season, roughly mid-December through mid-April, hotels tend to be packed, though rarely entirely full, and rates are a bit higher than in the off-season. However, a winter visit may allow you to participate in several colorful annual events on the San Juan social calendar. The January San Sebastián Street Festival, held in Old San Juan, consists of several nights of live music in the plazas, food festivals, and *cabezudos* (parades) in which folk legends are caricatured using oversize masks. A near-winter festival, the mid-November Festival of Puerto Rican Music, takes place in both San Juan venues and elsewhere on the island. The festival celebrates Puerto Rico's traditional *plena* and *bomba* folk music with competitions and concerts.

A less expensive time to visit San Juan is during the "shoulder" seasons of fall and spring, when the weather is still fantastic and the tourist crush is less intense. San Juan's weather is moderate and tropical year-round, with an average temperature of about 82°F (26°C). And although it's true that hurricane season accounts for much of the summer, San Juan is still an attractive destination during those months—many hotels charge the lowest rates of the year, restaurant reservations are easier to come by, and the streets are free of tourists.

OLD SAN JUAN

Old San Juan is compelling. Its 16th-century cobblestone streets, ornate Spanish town houses with wrought-iron balconies, busy plazas, and museums are all repositories of the island's history. Founded in 1521 by the Spanish explorer Juan Ponce de León, Old San Juan sits on a peninsula separated from the "new" parts of the city by a couple of miles and a couple of centuries. Ironically, its culture is youthful and vibrant, reflecting the sensibilities of stylish professionals, a bohemian art crowd, and skateboarding teenagers who populate the streets. You'll find more streetfront cafés and restaurants, more contemporary art galleries, more musicians playing in plazas, than anywhere else in San Juan.

At the northwest end of Old San Juan, Calle Norzagaray leads to El Morro, the old city's defense bastion. On the north side of Calle Norzagaray you'll find a small neighborhood at the foot of an embankment, bordering the ocean—this is La Perla, a rough area that you would do best to avoid. The west end of the old city faces San Juan Bay, and it's here that the sandstone walls of the original city are most evident. On Old San Juan's south side you'll find the commercial and cruise-ship piers that jut into San Juan Harbor.

Numbers in the text correspond to numbers in the margin and on the Old San Juan map.

TIMING & PRECAUTIONS

Old San Juan is a small neighborhood, approximately seven city blocks square. In strictly geographical terms, it's easily traversed in a day. But to truly appreciate the numerous museums, galleries, and cafés, it requires two or three days—and the walk described above is designed with that in mind. If you're limited to one day, you'll need to pick and choose sights according to your interests. It can be done—it's just not quite so rewarding.

Don't consider driving in Old San Juan unless you enjoy sitting in traffic jams for much of the day. Old San Juan is a walking city, with narrow, one-way streets, narrower alleys, little parking, and sights and shops packed together in an area hardly larger than ½ square mi. Some of the streets are steep and many are paved with cobblestones, so wear comfortable shoes as well as a hat and sunscreen—and drink plenty of water. Old San Juan is generally safe, but keep in mind that pickpockets visit the same places as tourists. Keep money and credit cards out of back pockets and avoid carrying open handbags. Street hustlers are few and far between, but you will meet the occasional, mostly harmless, indigent asking for money.

Free trolleys swing through Old San Juan all day, every day—departing from the main bus terminal area across from Pier 4 and taking two routes through the Old City. One route heads north to Calle Norzagaray then west to El Morro (the trolley doesn't go into El Morro, but drops you off at the long footpath leading to the fort), then south along Calle Cristo, east on Fortaleza, south on San Justo, and then back along Calle Gilberto Concepción de Gracia (also called Calle la Marina) to the piers. The other route takes you to the Plaza de Armas, south on Calle San José, then back to the piers. Both make regular stops (at signs marked PARADA) on their routes. When you're finished touring, taxis can be found in several spots: in front of Pier 2, on the Plaza de Armas, or on Calle O'Donnell near the Plaza de Colón.

WHAT TO SEE

14 **Alcaldía.** San Juan's city hall was built between 1604 and 1789. In 1841, extensive alterations were made so that it would resemble the city hall in Madrid, with arcades, towers, balconies, and an inner courtyard. Renovations have refreshed the facade of the building and some interior rooms, but the architecture remains true to its colonial style. A municipal tourist information center and an art gallery with rotating exhibits are on the first floor. ✉ *153 Calle San Francisco, Plaza de Armas, Old San Juan* ☎ *787/724–7171* 🎫 *Free* ⏲ *Weekdays 8–4.*

10 **Capilla del Cristo.** According to legend, in 1753 a young horseman named Baltazar Montañez carried away during festivities in honor of San Juan Bautista (St. John the Baptist), raced down Calle Cristo and plunged over its steep precipice. A witness to the tragedy promised to build a chapel if the young man's life could be saved. Historical records maintain the man died, but legend contends that he lived. (Another version of the story has it that the horse miraculously stopped before plunging over the cliff.) Regardless, this chapel was built, and inside is a small silver altar dedicated to the Christ of Miracles. You can visit any time, even if the gates are closed. ✉ *End of Calle Cristo, Old San Juan* ☎ *No phone* 🎫 *Free.*

20 **Casa Blanca.** The original structure on this site was a wooden house built in 1521 as a home for Ponce de León; he died in Cuba without ever having lived here. His descendants occupied the house's sturdier replacement, a lovely colonial mansion with tile floors and beamed ceilings, for the next 250 years. It was the home of the U.S. Army commander in Puerto Rico from the end of the Spanish-American War in 1898 to 1966. Several rooms decorated with colonial-era furnishings are open to the public. A guide will show you around, and then you can explore on your own. Don't miss the stairway descending from one of the bedrooms—which, despite local lore, leads to a small room and not to a tunnel to nearby El Morro. The lush garden is a quiet place to unwind. ✉ *1 Calle San Sebastián, Old San Juan* ☎ *787/725–1454* 🌐 *www.icp.gobierno.pr* 🎫 *$3* ⏲ *Tues.–Sat. 9–noon and 1–4.*

9 **Casa del Libro.** On a pleasant side street, this 18th-century house contains a museum dedicated to the artistry of the printed word. The 6,000-piece collection includes some 200 rare volumes dating back more than 500 years, as well as what appears to be legal writing on a fragment of clay from 2,000 years ago. Also on hand are several antique printing presses, one constructed in 1812 in France and later brought to Puerto Rico. There are interesting temporary exhibits as well. At this writing, repairs to the building have relocated the museum temporarily to the ground-floor courtyard of the Museo de las Americas. Construction is expected to continue through the end of 2008, so call ahead. ✉ *255*

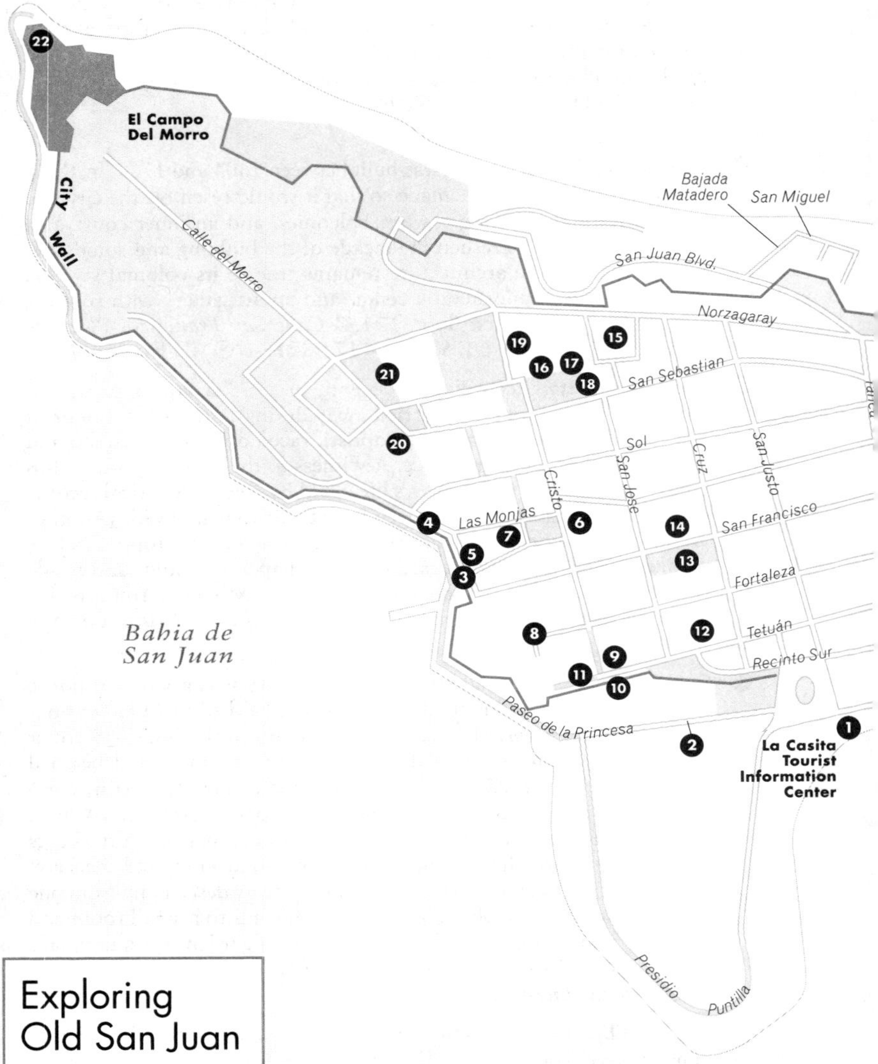

Exploring Old San Juan

- Alcaldía **14**
- Capilla del Cristo **10**
- Case Blanca **20**
- Casa del Libro **9**
- Casa de Ramón Power y Giralt **12**
- La Casita **1**
- Catedral de San Juan Bautista **6**
- Convento de los Dominicos **19**
- Fortaleza **8**
- Fuerto San Cristóbal **23**
- Fuerto San Felipe del Morro (El Morro) **22**
- Iglesia de San José **16**
- Museo de Arte y Historia de San Juan **15**
- Museo de las Américas ... **21**
- Museo del Niño **7**
- Museo de Nuestra Raíz Africana **18**
- Museo Felisa Rincón de Gautier **5**
- Museo Pablo Casals **17**
- Parque de las Palomas ... **11**
- Paseo de la Princesa **2**
- Plaza de Armas **13**
- Plaza de Colón **24**

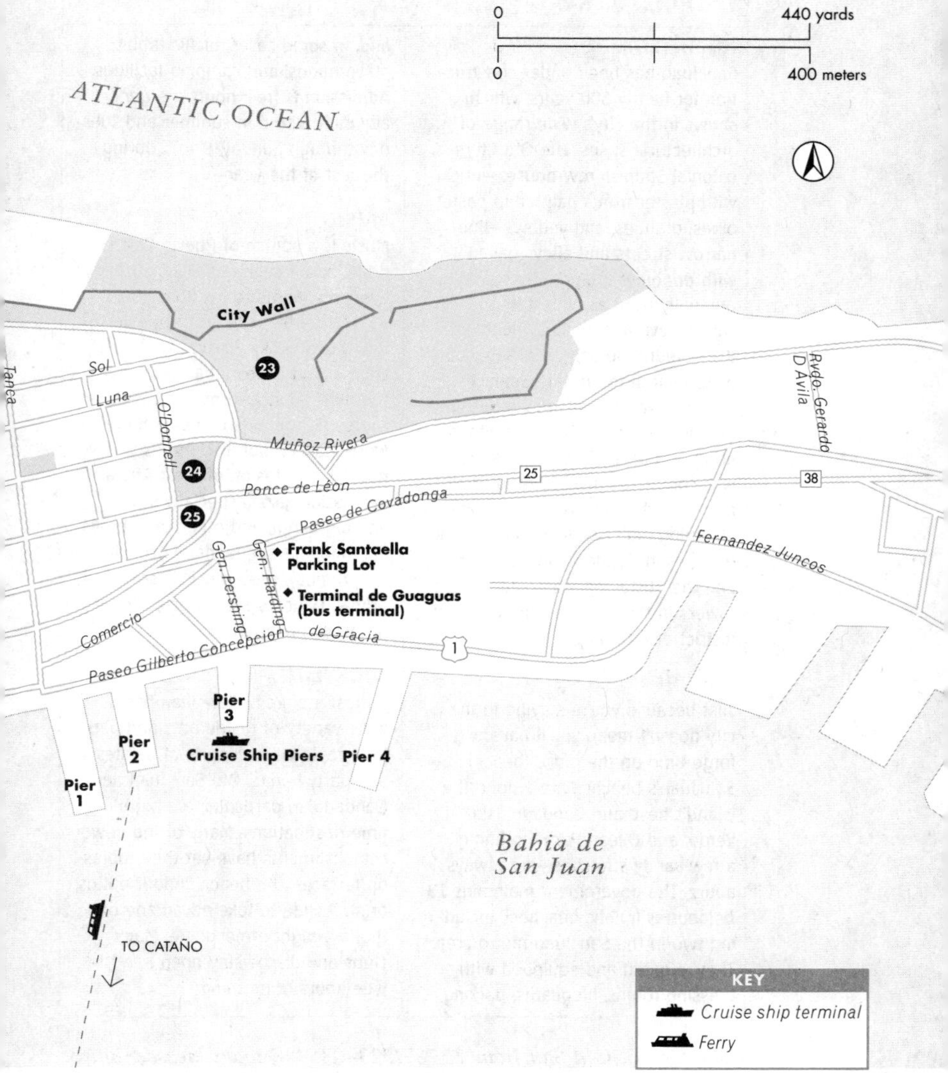

0
440 yards
0
400 meters
ATLANTIC OCEAN
City Wall
23
Sol
Luna
Tanca
O'Donnell
Muñoz Rivera
Rvdo. Gerardo D Avila
24
Ponce de Léon
25
38
25
Paseo de Covadonga
Fernandez Juncos
Gen. Pershing
Gen. Harding
Frank Santaella Parking Lot
Terminal de Guaguas (bus terminal)
Comercio
Paseo Gilberto Concepcion de Gracia
1
Pier 3
Pier 2
Pier 1
Cruise Ship Piers
Pier 4
Bahia de San Juan
TO CATAÑO
KEY
Cruise ship terminal
Ferry

IF YOU LIKE

ARCHITECTURE

San Juan has been under construction for nearly 500 years, which shows in the city's wide range of architectural styles. The Old City's colonial Spanish row houses—brick with plaster fronts painted in pastel blues, oranges, and yellows—line narrow streets and alleys paved with *adoquines* (blue-gray stones originally used as ballast in Spanish ships). Several churches, including the Catedral de San Juan Bautista, were built in the ornate Spanish Gothic style of the 16th century. The massive, white marble El Capitolio, home of Puerto Rico's legislature, was completed in 1929. And firmly rooted in the 20th century are the gleaming high-rise resorts along the beaches in Condado and Isla Verde, and the glistening steel-and-glass towers in the business and financial district of Hato Rey.

BEACHES

Just because you're staying in the city doesn't mean you'll have to forgo time on the *playa* (beach). San Juan's beaches are among the island's best, and Condado, Isla Verde, and Ocean Park—to name a few sandy stretches—are always abuzz. The government maintains 13 *balnearios* (public beaches), including two in the San Juan metro area. They're gated and equipped with dressing rooms, lifeguards, parking, and, in some cases, picnic tables, playgrounds, and camping facilities. Admission is free; hours are generally daily 9 to 5 in summer and Tuesday through Sunday, 9 to 5 during the rest of the year.

MUSIC

Music is a source of Puerto Rican pride, and it seems that increasingly everyone wants to live that *vida loca* (crazy life) espoused by Puerto Rico's own Ricky Martin. The brash Latin sound is best characterized by the music-dance form salsa, which shares not only its name with the word "sauce," but also its zesty, hot flavor. A fusion of West African percussion, jazz (especially swing and big band), and other Latin beats (mambo, merengue, flamenco, cha-cha, rumba), salsa music is sexy and primal. Dancers are expected to let go of all inhibitions.

NIGHTLIFE

Almost a big city, San Juan has a wide variety of restaurants and bars for people with all sorts of palates and party habits. Old San Juan and Condado, in particular, are big nighttime destinations. Many of the newer establishments have set their tables on terraces, the beach, indoor patios, or streetside to take advantage of the late-night atmosphere. Many clubs and discos stay open into the wee hours of morning.

Calle Cristo, Old San Juan ☎787/723–0354 ⊕www.lacasadellibro.org $2 donation suggested ⊗Tues.–Sat. 11–4:30.

12 **Casa de Ramón Power y Giralt.** The restored home of 18th-century naval hero Don Ramón Power y Giralt is now the headquarters of the Conservation Trust of Puerto Rico. On-site are several displays highlighting the physical, cultural, and historical importance of land and properties on the island under the trust's aegis. You'll find a display of musical instruments that you can play, a bird diorama with recorded bird songs, an active beehive, and a seven-minute movie discussing the trust's

efforts. Displays are in Spanish; the movie is in English or Spanish. A gift shop sells toys and Puerto Rican candies. ✉ *155 Calle Tetuán, Old San Juan* ☎ *787/722-5834* *Free* *Tues.–Sat. 9–5.*

1 **La Casita.** With a name that means "Little House," La Casita was built in the 1930s to handle traffic at the nearby port. Today the beautiful building, with yellow stucco walls and a barrel-tile roof, serves as an information center run by the Puerto Rico Tourism Company. The friendly staff will give you all the maps and brochures you can carry. ✉ *Plaza de la Dársena, Old San Juan* ☎ *787/722–1709* *www.gotopuertorico.com* *Mon.–Wed. 8:30–8, Thurs.–Fri. 8:30–5:30, weekends 9–8.*

6 **Catedral de San Juan Bautista.** The Catholic shrine of Puerto Rico had humble beginnings in the early 1520s as a thatch-roof, wooden structure. Hurricane winds tore off the thatch and destroyed the church. It was reconstructed in 1540, when it was given a graceful circular staircase and vaulted Gothic ceilings. Most of the work on the present cathedral, however, was done in the 19th century. The remains of Ponce de León are in a marble tomb near the transept. The trompe l'oeil work on the inside of the dome is breathtaking. Unfortunately, many of the other frescoes suffer from water damage. ✉ *151 Calle Cristo, Old San Juan* ☎ *787/722–0861* *www.catedralsanjuan.com* *$1 donation suggested* *Mon.–Sat. 8–5, Sun. 8–2:30.*

19 **Convento de los Dominicos.** Built by Dominican friars in 1523, this convent often served as a shelter during Carib Indian attacks and, more recently, as headquarters for the Antilles command of the U.S. Army. Now home to some offices of the Institute of Puerto Rican Culture, the beautifully restored building contains religious manuscripts, artifacts, and art. The institute also maintains a book and music shop on the premises. Classical concerts are held here occasionally. ✉ *98 Calle Norzagaray, Old San Juan* ☎ *787/721–6866* *Free* *Mon.–Sat. 9–5.*

8 **Fortaleza.** Sitting on a hill overlooking the harbor, the Fortaleza was built in 1533 as a fortress—and not a very good one. It was attacked numerous times and was occupied twice, by the British in 1598 and the Dutch in 1625. When El Morro and the city's other fortifications were finished, the Fortaleza was transformed into a palace. Numerous changes have been made to the original primitive structure over the past four centuries, resulting in the current collection of marble and mahogany, medieval towers, and stained-glass galleries. It is still the official residence of the island's governor and is the Western hemisphere's oldest executive mansion in continual use. Guided tours are conducted several times a day in English and Spanish; both include a short video presentation. Call ahead, as tours are often canceled because of official functions. The tours begin near the main gate in a yellow building called the Real Audiencia. ✉ *Western end of Calle Recinto Oeste, Old San Juan* ☎ *787/721–7000* *www.fortaleza.gobierno.pr* *Free* *Weekdays 9–5.*

NEED A BREAK?

On your hike up hilly Calle Cristo, stop at Ben & Jerry's (✉ *61 Calle Cristo, Old San Juan* ☎ *787/977-6882*) at the corner of Calle Sol. Savor Vermont ice cream under a palm tree or enjoy fresh-fruit smoothies next to a Green Mountain cow.

23 **Fuerte San Cristóbal.** This stone fortress, built between 1634 and 1785, guarded the city from land attacks. Even larger than El Morro, San Cristóbal was known in the 17th and 18th centuries as the Gibraltar of the West Indies. Five free-standing structures are connected by tunnels, and restored units include an 18th-century barracks. You're free to explore the gun turrets, officers' quarters, and passageways. Along with El Morro, San Cristóbal is a National Historic Site administered by the U.S. Park Service; it's a UN World Heritage Site as well. Rangers conduct tours in Spanish and English. ✉ *Calle Norzagaray at Calle Muñoz Rivera, Old San Juan* ☎ *787/729–6960* 🌐 *www.nps.gov/saju* *$3; $5 includes admission to El Morro* ⏲ *June–Nov., daily 9–5; Dec.–May, daily 9–6.*

22 **Fuerte San Felipe del Morro.** On a rocky promontory at the northwestern tip of the Old City is El Morro (which translates as "promontory"), a fortress built by the Spaniards between 1540 and 1783. Rising 140 feet above the sea, the massive six-level fortress covers enough territory to accommodate a 9-hole golf course. It is a labyrinth of dungeons, ramps, barracks, turrets, towers, and tunnels. Built to protect the port, El Morro has a commanding view of the harbor. You're free to wander throughout. The cannon emplacement walls are thick as a child's arm is long, and the dank secret passageways are a wonder of engineering. The fort's small but enlightening museum displays ancient Spanish guns and other armaments, military uniforms, and blueprints for Spanish forts in the Americas. There's also a gift shop. The fort is a National Historic Site administered by the U.S. Park Service; it's a UN World Heritage Site as well. Tours and a video are available in English. ✉ *Calle del Morro, Old San Juan* ☎ *787/729–6960* 🌐 *www.nps.gov/saju* *$3; $5 includes admission to Fuerte San Cristóbal* ⏲ *June–Nov., daily 9–5; Dec.–May, daily 9–6.*

Fodor's Choice ★

16 **Iglesia de San José.** With its vaulted ceilings, this church is a splendid example of 16th-century Spanish Gothic architecture. It was built under the supervision of Dominican friars in 1532, making it one of the oldest churches in the Western Hemisphere. The body of Ponce de León, the Spanish explorer who came to the New World seeking the Fountain of Youth, was buried here for almost three centuries before being moved to the Catedral de San Juan Bautista in 1913. At this writing, much-needed renovations were underway. Until it is reopened in late 2008, you can peek inside while work is in progress. ✉ *Calle San Sebastián, Plaza de San José, Old San Juan* ☎ *787/725–7501.*

15 **Museo de Arte y Historia de San Juan.** A bustling marketplace in 1855, this handsome building is now the modern San Juan Museum of Art and History. You'll find exhibits of Puerto Rican art and audiovisual shows that present the island's history. Concerts and other cultural events take place in the huge interior courtyard. ✉ *150 Calle Norza-*

garay, at Calle MacArthur, Old San Juan ☎787/724–1875 Free ⏲Tues.–Sun. 10–4.

21 **Museo de las Américas.** On the second floor of the imposing former military barracks, Cuartel de Ballajá, the museum's permanent exhibit, "Las Artes Populares en las Américas," focuses on the popular art and folk art of Latin America, including religious figures, musical instruments, basketwork, costumes, and farming and other implements. It's a small exhibit, worth a look if you're visiting other nearby attractions. ✉*Calle Norzagaray and Calle del Morro, Old San Juan* ☎*787/724–5052* 🌐*www.museolasamericas.org Free* ⏲*Tues.–Sun. 10–4.*

5 **Museo Felisa Rincón de Gautier.** This tiny museum honors Felisa Rincón de Gautier, who served as San Juan's mayor from 1946 to 1968. Throughout her life, "Doña Felisa" worked tirelessly on various public causes, from women's voting rights to health care for the poor. A fascinating figure who rose to power at a time when women and politics were not mentioned in the same breath. Even if you have no interest in her story, you can peek inside one of the historic homes of Old San Juan. ✉*51 Caleta de San Juan, Old San Juan* ☎*787/723–1897* 🌐*www.preb.com/biog/felisare.htm Free* ⏲*Mon.–Fri. 9–4.*

7 **Museo del Niño.** This three-floor, hands-on "museum" is pure fun for kids. There are games to play, clothes for dress-up, a mock plaza with market, and even a barbershop where children can play (no real scissors here). One of the newer exhibits is an immense food-groups pyramid, where children can climb to place magnets representing different foods. Older children will appreciate the top-floor garden where bugs and plants are on display, and the little ones can pretend to go shopping or to work at a construction site. For toddlers, there's a playground. Note that when it reaches capacity, the museum stops selling tickets. ✉*150 Calle Cristo Old San Juan* ☎*787/722–3791* 🌐*www.museodelninopr.org $5, $7 for children* ⏲*Tues.–Thurs. 9–3:30, Fri. 9–5, weekends noon–5:30.*

18 **Museo de Nuestra Raíz Africana.** The Institute of Puerto Rican Culture created this museum to help Puerto Ricans understand African influences in island culture. On display over two floors are African musical instruments, documents relating to the slave trade, and a list of African words that have made it into popular Puerto Rican culture. ✉*101 Calle San Sebastián, Plaza de San José, Old San Juan* ☎*787/724–4294* 🌐*www.icp.gobierno.pr $2* ⏲*Tues.–Sat. 8:30–4:30.*

17 **Museo Pablo Casals.** The small, two-story museum contains memorabilia of the famed cellist, who made his home in Puerto Rico from 1956 until his death in 1973. Manuscripts, photographs, and his favorite cellos are on display, in addition to recordings and videotapes (shown on request) of Casals Festival concerts, which he instituted in 1957. The festival is held annually in June. ✉*101 Calle San Sebastián, Plaza de San José, Old San Juan* ☎*787/723–9185 $1* ⏲*Tues.–Sat. 9:30–4:30.*

11 **Parque de las Palomas.** Never have birds had it so good. The small, shaded park bordering Old San Juan's Capilla del Cristo has a large

CLOSE UP

Peaceful Music

Cellist Pablo Casals was one of the 20th century's most influential musicians. Born in Catalonia in 1876, he studied in Spain and Belgium, settled for a time in Paris, then returned to Barcelona. Tours in Europe, the United States, and South America brought him artistic and financial success and opportunities to collaborate with other prominent musicians.

By the advent of the Spanish Civil War, he was an internationally famous musician, teacher, and conductor. He was also an outspoken supporter of a democratic Spain. Forced into exile by Franco's regime, Casals arrived in Puerto Rico, his mother's birthplace, in 1956. Here the 81-year-old maestro continued to work and teach. He established the Casals Festival of Classical Music, making the island a home for sublime orchestral and chamber works. During two weeks each June, the Puerto Rico Symphony Orchestra is joined by musicians from all over the world.

In Catalan, Casal's first name is "Pau," which appropriately means "peace." He and his friend Albert Schweitzer appealed to the world powers to stop the arms race, and he made what many experts say is his greatest work—an oratorio titled *The Manger*—his personal message of peace. Casals died in Puerto Rico in 1973, but his many legacies live on. His favorite instruments, his recordings, and some of his numerous awards are preserved at the Museo Pablo Casals.

–Karen English

stone wall with pigeonholes cut into it. Hundreds of *palomas* (pigeons) roost here, and the park is full of cooing local children chasing the well-fed birds. There's a small kiosk where you can buy refreshments and bags of seed to feed the birds. Stop to enjoy the wide views over the bay.

2 **Paseo de la Princesa.** This street down at the port is spruced up with flowers, trees, benches, street lamps, and a striking fountain depicting the various ethnic groups of Puerto Rico. Take a seat and watch the boats zip across the water. At the west end of the paseo, beyond the fountain, is the beginning of a shoreline path that hugs Old San Juan's walls and leads to the city gate at Calle San Juan.

13 **Plaza de Armas.** The old city's original main square was once used as military drilling grounds. Bordered by calles San Francisco, Rafael Codero, San José, and Cruz, it has a fountain with 19th-century statues representing the four seasons, as well as a bandstand and a small café. This is one of the most popular meeting places in Old San Juan, so you're likely to encounter everything from local bands to artists sketching caricatures to street preachers imploring the wicked to repent.

NEED A BREAK?

At Café 4 Estaciones, on the Plaza de Armas in Old San Juan, tables and chairs sit under a canvas canopy surrounded by potted plants. It's the perfect spot to put down your shopping bags and rest your tired feet. Grab a *café con leche* (coffee with hot milk), an espresso, or cold drink, and watch the children chase the pigeons.

24 **Plaza de Colón.** A statue of Christopher Columbus stands atop a high pedestal in this bustling Old San Juan square. Originally called St. James Square, it was renamed in honor of Columbus on the 400th anniversary of his arrival in Puerto Rico. Bronze plaques on the statue's base relate various episodes in the life of the great explorer. On the north side of the plaza is a terminal for buses to and from San Juan.

4 **Plazuela de la Rogativa.** According to legend, the British, while laying siege to the city in 1797, mistook the flaming torches of a *rogativa*—religious procession—for Spanish reinforcements and beat a hasty retreat. In this little plaza statues of a bishop and three women commemorate the legend. The monument was created in 1971 by the artist Lindsay Daen to mark the Old City's 450th anniversary. ✉*Caleta de las Monjas, Old San Juan.*

3 **Puerta de San Juan.** Dating back to 1520, this was one of the five original entrances to the city. The massive gate, painted a brilliant shade of red, gave access from the port. It resembles a tunnel because it passes through La Muralla, the 20-foot-thick city walls. ✉*Paseo de la Princesa, Old San Juan.*

25 **Teatro Tapia.** Named after the Puerto Rican playwright Alejandro Tapia y Rivera, this municipal theater was built in 1832 and remodeled in 1949 and again in 1987. It showcases ballets, plays, and operettas. Stop by the box office to find out what's showing. ✉*Plaza de Colón, Old San Juan* ☎*787/721–0169.*

GREATER SAN JUAN

Modern San Juan is a study in congested highways and cement-block housing complexes, as well as the resorts of Condado and Isla Verde. Sightseeing in the modern city requires more effort than it does in Old San Juan—the sights are scattered in the suburbs, accessible by taxi, bus, or a rental car, but not on foot.

Avenidas Muñoz Rivera, Ponce de León, and Fernández Juncos are the main thoroughfares that cross Puerta de Tierra, just east of Old San Juan, to the neighborhoods of Condado, Ocean Park, and Isla Verde. Puente Dos Hermanos, the "Bridge of the Two Brothers," connects Puerta de Tierra with Condado. Avenida Ashford, which splits off into Avenida Magdalena for a few blocks, travels through Condado to Ocean Park. Calle Loíza connects Ocean Park with Isla Verde. These streets can be choked with traffic, so if you are traveling more than a few blocks, consider taking the speedier Route 26.

South of the Laguna del Condado is Miramar, home to a few notable hotels and restaurants. Although it seems slightly seedy, it is clearly on its way up. South of Condado and Ocean Park is Santurce, a mostly commercial district where you'll find the Museo de Arte de Puerto Rico and the Museo de Arte Contemporáneo. Hato Rey, south of Santurce, is a busy financial district, where you'll find the large Plaza las Américas Mall. Even farther south is residential Río Piedras, home of the Universidad de Puerto Rico.

GREAT ITINERARIES

IF YOU HAVE 1 DAY

Many people find themselves with a single day—or even less—to explore San Juan. There should be no question about your destination—head to Old San Juan. Ramble through the cobblestone streets and duck into the many shops, but save plenty of time for exploring the turrets, towers, and dungeons of **Fuerte San Felipe del Morro**, the original fortress on a rocky promontory at the old city's northwestern tip.

IF YOU HAVE 3 DAYS

It's only fitting that you spend the first day on a *playa* (beach). Choose from the city's finest at Condado, Ocean Park, or Isla Verde, and park yourself in a rented chair with a good book, a cold drink, and plenty of sunscreen. In the evening, make sure you enjoy the warm weather by dining alfresco. On the second day take a walking tour of Old San Juan. What to see? **Fuerte San Felipe del Morro** is at the top of the list, but it can often be crowded. You might want to explore the equally enthralling **Fuerte San Cristóbal,** which has underground tunnels and hidden passages. The city's original fortress, the **Fortaleza,** wasn't much protection from marauding pirates, but it does a great job at sheltering the governor. And **Casa Blanca,** a home built for Juan Ponce de León, is a wonderful place to explore how the Spanish lived in the colonial days. On your third day, hop the ferry across the bay to Cataño for a tour of the **Casa Bacardí Visitor Center.** Return in time for some shopping in the high-end shops along Calle Cristo, then dinner in one of the trendy eateries on Calle Fortaleza.

IF YOU HAVE 5 DAYS

Follow the itinerary above for your first three days in San Juan. On Day 4 head for the Santurce district. You can immerse yourself in island art at the **Museo de Arte Contemporáneo de Puerto Rico** and the **Museo de Arte de Puerto Rico.** Afterward, wander through the produce stalls at the Plaza del Mercado in Santurce, with a fresh papaya or soursop shake in hand, and have your palm read. Be sure to note the giant bronze sculptures of avocados by artist Annex Burgos. On the morning of Day 5, hit the beach once more, then head to Avenida Ashford in Condado for an afternoon of shopping in its ritzy boutiques.

Numbers in the text correspond to numbers in the margin and on the Greater San Juan map.

A GOOD TOUR

East of Old San Juan on Avenida Ponce de León you'll find **El Capitolio,** Puerto Rico's magnificent capitol building. At the east end of Puerta de Tierra is the Caribe Hilton, where you'll find the small bastion **Fuerte San Gerónimo.** (It's not worth seeking out if you've seen any of the island's other fortifications.) Take Avenida Ashford east, branching off onto Avenida Magdalena and then Calle Luiza. At the corner of Avenida Ponce de León is the **Museo de Arte Contemporáneo de Puerto Rico,** with a fine collection of contemporary Puerto Rican art. If you're hungry, stop for lunch at the nearby **Plaza del Mercado.** Afterward, head east on Avenida Ponce de León, then north on Avenida José de Diego to reach the **Museo de Arte de Puerto Rico,** a former hospital that has been transformed into the island's most ambitious art museum.

From the museum, it's a straight ride south on Avenida Ponce de León (Route 25) to the Río Piedras district, where you'll find the Universidad de Puerto Rico and its **Museo de Historia, Antropología y Arte.** Less than 1 mi to the west, at the junction of routes 1 and 847, is the 75-acre **Jardín Botánico.**

TIMING Depending on what mode of transportation you choose, you can see these sights in a day; if you linger in the museums, exploring the Greater San Juan area might require two days. Buses are the least expensive but most time-consuming way to travel. Taxis are more convenient and you won't get lost—consider hiring a taxi by the hour and covering your selected sights in a couple of hours. Taxis charge $30 per hour for city tours, but the rate can be negotiable for long stretches of time. If you choose to rent a car, get a good map. San Juan's roads are well marked, but one-way streets pop up out of nowhere, and traffic jams at rush hour are frequent.

WHAT TO SEE

26 **El Capitolio.** The white-marble Capitol, a fine example of Italian Renaissance style, dates from 1929. The grand rotunda, which can be seen from all over San Juan, was completed in the late 1990s. Fronted by eight Corinthian columns, it's a very dignified home for the commonwealth's constitution. Although the Senate and the House of Representatives have offices in the more modern buildings on either side, the Capitol is where the legislators meet. You can also watch the legislature in action—note that the action is in Spanish—when it is in session, most often Monday and Tuesday. Guided tours, which take 45 minutes and include visits to the rotunda and other parts of the building, are by appointment only. ✉ *Av. Ponce de León, Puerta de Tierra* ☎ *787/977–4929* 🌐 *www.gotopuertorico.com* 🎟 *Free* 🕑 *Weekdays 9–5, weekends 9–2.*

27 **Fuerte San Gerónimo.** At the eastern tip of Puerta de Tierra, this tiny fort is perched on a hilltop like an afterthought. Added to San Juan's fortifications in the 18th century, it barely survived the British attack of 1797. Restored in 1983 by the Institute of Puerto Rican Culture, it's now open to the public. It's hard to find, but if you're intent on seeing it, go to the entrance of the Caribe Hilton. ✉ *Calle Rosales, Puerta de Tierra* ☎ *787/724–5477.*

32 The Universidad de Puerto Rico's main attraction is the **Jardín Botánico** *(Botanical Garden)*, a 75-acre forest of more than 200 species of tropical and subtropical vegetation. Gravel footpaths lead to a graceful lotus lagoon, a bamboo promenade, an orchid garden with some 30,000 plants, and a palm garden. Signs are in Spanish and English. Trail maps are available at the entrance gate, and groups of 10 or more can arrange guided tours ($25). ✉ *Intersection of Rtes. 1 and 847 at entrance to Barrio Venezuela, Río Piedras* ☎ *787/767–1710* 🌐 *www.upr.clu.edu* 🎟 *Free* 🕑 *Daily 9–4:30.*

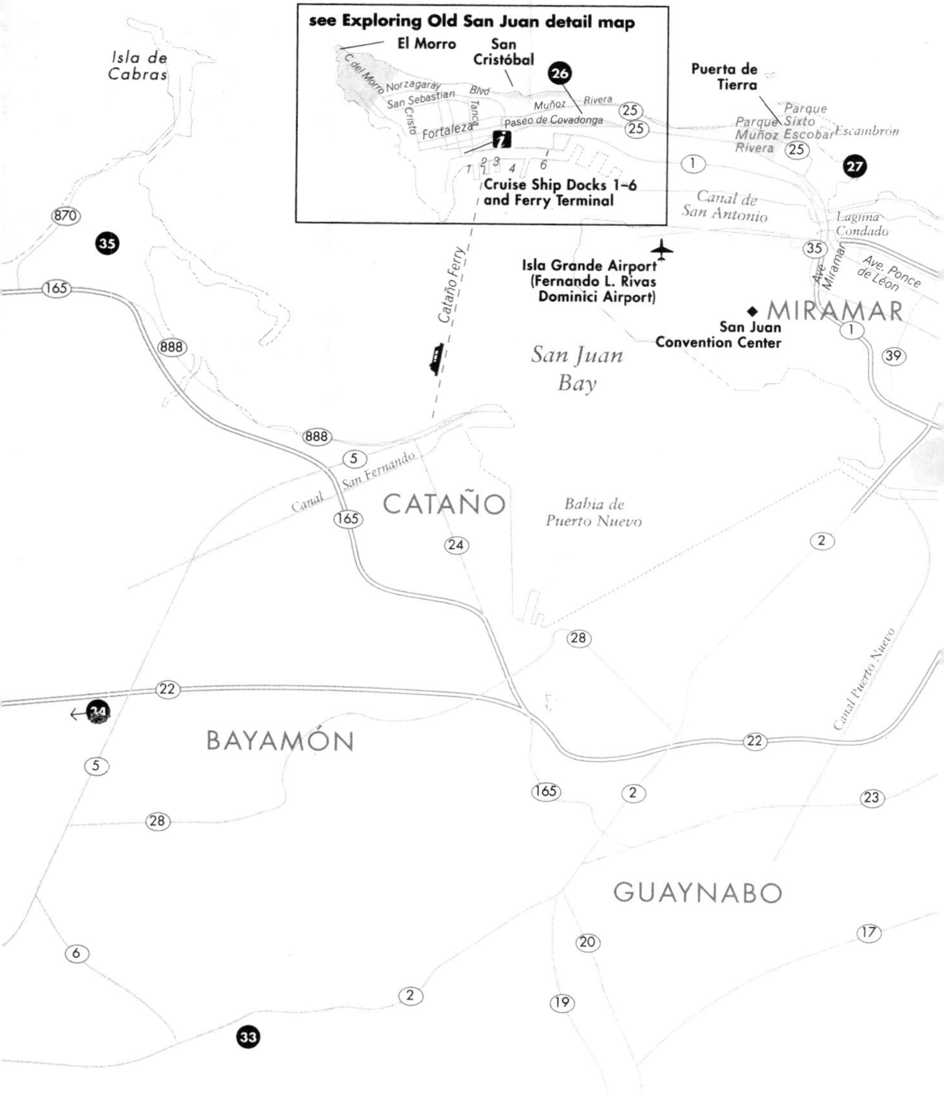

see Exploring Old San Juan detail map
El Morro
San Cristóbal
26
C del Morro
Norzagaray Blvd
San Sebastian
Cristo
Tanca
Muñoz Rivera
Paseo de Covadonga
Fortaleza
25
1 2 3 4 6
Cruise Ship Docks 1–6 and Ferry Terminal
Isla de Cabras
Puerta de Tierra
Parque Sixto Escobar
Parque Muñoz Rivera
Escambrón
27
Canal de San Antonio
Laguna Condado
Isla Grande Airport (Fernando L. Rivas Dominici Airport)
Ave. Miramar
Ave. Ponce de Léon
MIRAMAR
San Juan Convention Center
Cataño Ferry
San Juan Bay
870
35
165
888
5
Canal San Fernando
CATAÑO
Bahía de Puerto Nuevo
24
2
39
28
22
34
BAYAMÓN
Canal Puerto Nuevo
GUAYNABO
23
20
17
6
19
33

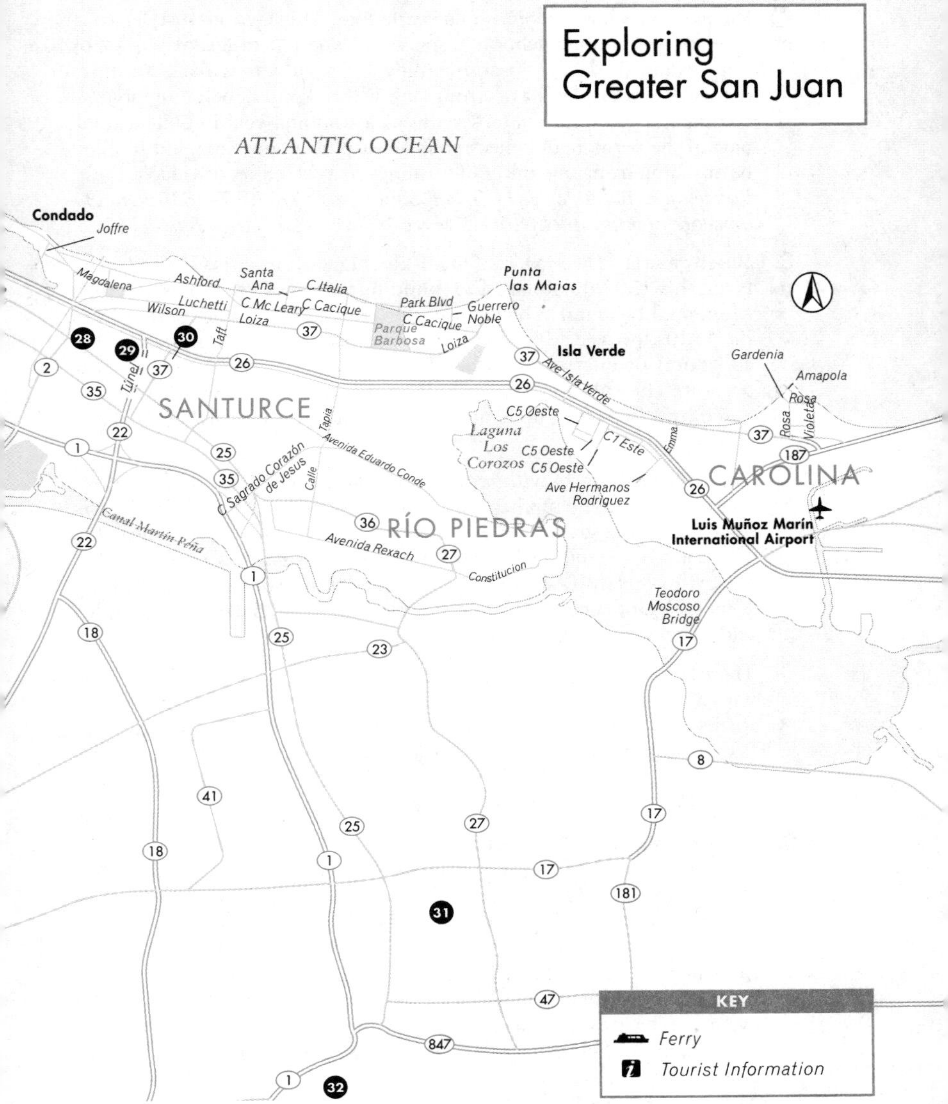
Exploring
Greater San Juan
ATLANTIC OCEAN
Condado
Joffre
Magdalena
Ashford
Santa Ana
C Italia
Punta las Maias
Wilson
Luchetti
C Mc Leary
C Cacique
Park Blvd
Guerrero Noble
Loiza
Parque Barbosa
Taft
Túnel
Isla Verde
Ave Isla Verde
Gardenia
Amapola
Rosa
Violeta
SANTURCE
Tapia
Avenida Eduardo Conde
C Sagrado Corazón de Jesus
Calle
Laguna Los Corozos
C5 Oeste
C1 Este
Emma
Ave Hermanos Rodriguez
CAROLINA
Luis Muñoz Marín International Airport
Canal Martín Peña
RÍO PIEDRAS
Avenida Rexach
Constitucion
Teodoro Moscoso Bridge
KEY
Ferry
Tourist Information

28 ★ **Museo de Arte Contemporáneo de Puerto Rico.** This Georgian-style structure, once a public school, displays a dynamic range of works by both established and up-and-coming Puerto Rican artists. Many of the works on display have strong political messages, including pointed commentaries on the island's status as a commonwealth. Only a small part of the permanent collection is on display at any time, but it might be anything from an exhibit of ceramics to a screening of videos. ✉ *Av. Ponce de León at Av. R.H. Todd, Santurce* ☎ *787/977–4030* 🌐 *www.museocontemporáneopr.org* 🎫 *Free* ⏲ *Tues.–Sat. 10–4, Sun. 1–4.*

30 Fodor's Choice ★ **Museo de Arte de Puerto Rico.** One of the biggest museums in the Caribbean, this 130,000-square-foot building was once known as San Juan Municipal Hospital. The beautiful neoclassical building, dating from the 1920s, proved to be too small to house the museum's permanent collection of Puerto Rican art dating from the 17th century to the present. The solution was to build a new east wing, which is dominated by a five-story-tall stained-glass window, the work of local artist Eric Tabales.

The collection starts with works from the colonial era, most of them commissioned for churches. Here you'll find works by José Campeche, the island's first great painter. His *Immaculate Conception,* finished in 1794, is a masterpiece. Also well represented is Francisco Oller y Cestero, who was the first to move beyond religious subjects to paint local scenes. His influence is still felt today. A gallery on the top floor is filled with works by artists inspired by Oller.

There's much more to the museum, including a beautiful garden filled with a variety of native flora and a 400-seat theater that's worth seeing for its remarkable lace curtain. And one of the city's best restaurants, Pikayo, is tucked away in the corner of the museum's massive atrium. ✉ *299 Av. José De Diego, Santurce* ☎ *787/977–6277* 🌐 *www.mapr.org* 🎫 *$6* ⏲ *Tues–Sat. 10–4, Sun. noon–4.*

29 **Plaza del Mercado.** Completely overlooked by tourists, the Plaza del Mercado is one of the most charming corners of San Juan. At its center is a massive market hall dating from 1910. Inside you'll find bushels of fruits and vegetables, many of which you probably haven't seen before. If all this food makes you hungry, dozens of storefront restaurants face the central square. These places, mostly serving seafood, are quiet during the week but bustling on the weekends, especially in the evening. The area also has many *botánicas,* small shops that sell herbs, candles, and religious items. There may even be an in-house card- or palm-reader ready to show you your future. The square is between the Museo de Arte de Puerto Rico and the Museo de Arte Contemporáneo de Puerto Rico, making it a good place to stop for lunch if you are museum hopping. ✉ *Calle Dos Hermanos at Calle Capital, Santurce.*

31 The Universidad de Puerto Rico's **Museo de Historia, Antropología y Arte** *(Museum of History, Anthropology and Art)* has archaeological and historical exhibits that deal with the Native American influence on the island and the Caribbean, the colonial era, and the history of slavery.

CLOSE UP

Art Invasion

Public art is transforming the Puerto Rican capital: here a monolithic metal dove; there avocados so big you can stretch out on them. The stained-glass blades of a windmill spin above an oceanfront drive. A bright red jack towers over children at play in a park. These are only some of the 25 works by local artists that the city commissioned from 1996 to 2000, when Governor Sila Marí Calderón was its mayor. The pieces range from realistic to abstract, and many were installed as part of larger renovations of parks, plazas, and markets.

Often the works seem perfectly at home in their environments. *Platanal,* by Imel Sierra Cabreras, has translucent panels that run across the ceiling of the restored Plaza del Mercado in Santurce. The avocados in *My Favorite Fruit* by Annex Burgos seem to spill from the entrance of this marketplace and across its front plaza. Although the large jack by María Elena Perales is a bit surreal, it's an appropriate addition to a playground in Parque Central Municipio de San Juan.

Some pieces attempt to soften or enliven their surroundings. Carmen Inés Blondet, whose *Fire Dance* is a collection of 28- to 35-foot spirals, created what seems an abstract forest in the midst of the concrete jungle. Crabs were once a common sight in Santurce (hence the name of the baseball team, the Santurce Crabbers), so Adelino González's benches for the area are bronze crabs. *Windmills of San Juan,* by Eric Tabales, is a whimsical tribute to the coast and its ocean breezes. The steel tower, with its rotating wheel of color, is on a restored oceanside drive in Ocean Park.

The works haven't been without controversy. Many residents found *Paloma,* the metallic dove that towers over a busy Condado intersection, ugly; others went so far as to assert that it was the cause of traffic jams. Mayor Jorge Santini even threatened to remove it during his campaign. But it appears to be here to stay. To soften the piece, a fountain was added to its base and it's now especially beautiful at night when the water is illuminated.

As a whole, however, the statues have made San Juan more interesting. And public art has spread around the island. In January 2002 Governor Calderón unveiled plans for the Puerto Rico Public Art Project. Its budget of $15 million has funded about 100 new works. In San Juan these include stations of the urban train, the Luis Muñoz Marín International Airport, and several government buildings and city parks. The committee also envisions installing works at nature reserves, along highways, and in school playgrounds across the island. Soon, perhaps, that new bus stop, lifeguard station, or street-vendor stand you see will truly be a work of art.

–John Marino

Art displays are occasionally mounted; the museum's prize exhibit is the painting *El Velorio* (*The Wake*), by the 19th-century artist Francisco Oller. ✉*Av. Ponce de León, Río Piedras* ☎*787/764–0000 Ext. 5852* 🌐*www.uprrp.edu* 🎫*Free* 🕑*Mon.–Wed. and Fri. 9–4:30, Thurs. 9–9, weekends 9–3.*

SAN JUAN ENVIRONS

The suburbs of Cataño, Bayamón, and Guaynabo, west and south of San Juan, are separate municipalities but in many ways are indistinguishable from the city itself. Cataño, bordered by the Bahía de San Juan in the north, is an industrial suburb, perhaps most noted for its distillery belonging to Bacardí. Bayamón can be reached within 15 to 30 minutes from central San Juan; if you come by car, stop by the attractive central park bordered by historic buildings. Guaynabo is a mix of residential and industrial areas and is worth visiting for its historical importance—Juan Ponce de León established the island's first settlement here in Caparra, and you can visit the ruins of the original fortification.

The Casa Bacardí Visitor Center is an easy trip from Old San Juan—you simply take a ferry across the harbor. The other sites are a challenge to reach, as you must navigate some of the region's most traffic-clogged streets. Do yourself a favor and take a taxi or book a tour.

WHAT TO SEE

35 **Casa Bacardí Visitor Center.** Exiled from Cuba, the Bacardí family built a small distillery here in the 1950s. Today it's one of the world's largest, with the capacity to produce 100,000 gallons of spirits a day and 221 million cases a year. You can hop on a little tram to take a 45-minute tour of the bottling plant, distillery, and museum. Yes, you'll be offered a sample. If you don't want to drive, you can reach the factory by taking the ferry from Pier 2 for 50¢ each way and then a *publico* (public van service) from the ferry pier to the factory for about $2 or $3 per person. ✉*Rte. 888, Km 2.6, Cataño* ☎*787/788–1500 or 787/788–8400* 🌐*www.casabacardi.org* 🎫*Free* ⏲*Mon.–Sat. 8:30–5:30, Sun. 10–5; last tour 1½ hrs before closing.*

33 **Ruinas de Caparra.** In 1508, Ponce de León established the island's first settlement here. The Caparra Ruins—a few crumbling walls—are what remains of an ancient fort. The small **Museo de la Conquista y Colonización de Puerto Rico** (Museum of the Conquest and Colonization of Puerto Rico) contains historical documents, exhibits, and excavated artifacts, though you can see the museum's contents in less time than it takes to say the name. Both the ruins and the museum are maintained by the Puerto Rican government's museums and parks division. ✉*Rte. 2, Km 6.6, Guaynabo* ☎*787/781–4795* 🌐*www.icp.gobierno.pr* 🎫*Free* ⏲*Tues.–Sat. 8:30–4:20.*

34 **Parque de las Ciencias Luis A. Ferré.** The 42-acre Luis A. Ferré Science Park contains a collection of intriguing activities and displays. The Transportation Museum has antique cars and the island's oldest bicycle. In the Rocket Plaza, children can experience a flight simulator, and in the planetarium the solar system is projected on the ceiling. Also on-site are a small zoo and a natural-science exhibit. It's a long drive from central San Juan, though. ✉*Rte. 167, Bayamón* ☎*787/740–6878* 🎫*$5* ⏲*Wed.–Fri. 9–4, weekends 10–6.*

WHERE TO EAT

In cosmopolitan San Juan, European, Asian, and Middle Eastern eateries vie for your attention with family-owned restaurants specializing in seafood or *comida criolla* (creole cooking). U.S. chains such as McDonald's and Subway compete with chains like Pollo Tropical, which specialize in local cuisine. Although each of the city's large hotels has two or more fine restaurants, the best dining is often in stand-alone establishments—don't be shy about venturing to such places.

Dress codes vary greatly, though a restaurant's price category is a good indicator of its formality. For less expensive places, anything but beachwear is fine. Ritzier spots will expect collared shirts for men (jacket and tie requirements are rare) and chic attire for women. When in doubt, do as the Puerto Ricans often do and dress up.

For breakfast outside of your hotel, cafés are your best bet. 'It's rare for such establishments to close between breakfast and lunch; it's slightly more common for restaurants to close between lunch and dinner. Although some places don't accept reservations, it's always a good idea to make them for dinner whenever possible. This is especially true during the busy season from November through April and on weekends at any time of the year.

SAINTS ON PARADE

Each of Puerto Rico's 78 municipalities has a patron saint, and each one celebrates an annual festival near the saint's birthday, sometimes lasting a week or more. These festivals are a great opportunity to hear live music and buy local arts and crafts. San Juan celebrates its patron-saint feast in the *noche de San Juan* on June 23, when locals take to the beach. The event culminates at midnight, when crowds plunge into the Atlantic to flip over backwards three times, a cleansing ritual expected to bring good fortune.

WHAT IT COSTS IN U.S. DOLLARS

	$$$$	$$$	$$	$	¢
AT DINNER	over $30	$20–$30	$12–$20	$8–$12	under $8

Prices are per person for a main course at dinner.

OLD SAN JUAN

CAFÉS

$$–$$$ ✕ **Café Berlin.** A handful of tables spill out onto the sidewalk at this unpretentious place overlooking Plaza Colón. There's something on the menu for everyone, from turkey breast in a mustard-curry sauce to salmon in a citrus sauce. There are even several good vegetarian dishes, including tofu in a mushroom sauce. Inside is a small bar, one of the few places in Puerto Rico that serves draft beer. Not the bargain it used to be but still very popular. ✉*407 Calle San Francisco, Old San Juan* ☎*787/722–5205* ▭*AE, MC, V.*

Where to Stay & Eat in Old San Juan

Restaurants ▼

Aguaviva **17**
Amadeus **6**
Barú **7**
La Bombonera **10**
Café Berlin **19**
Cafeteria Mallorca **11**
Cali Café Concierto **13**
La Cocina di Ivo **4**
Dragonfly **16**
La Fonda del Jibarito **8**
Lupi's **21**
La Mallorquina **12**
La Ostra Cosa **1**
Panza **22**
Parrot Club **14**
El Patio de Sam **5**
Il Perugino **3**
El Picoteo **2**
Sofia **18**
Spanglish **9**
Tantra **15**
El Toro Salao **20**

Hotels ▼

Caleta Guesthouse **2**
Chateau Cervantes **8**
Da House **6**
Gallery Inn **3**
Hotel El Converto **1**
Hotel Milano **4**
Howard Johnson Plaza de Armas **5**
Sheraton Old San Juan Hotel **7**

$–$$ ✕ **La Bombonera.** You can't miss the gorgeous stained glass on the facade of this local landmark, which was established in 1903. In the window you'll see piles of freshly baked pastries. Inside there's a long counter with salmon-colored stools and a wall lined with booths of the same interesting shade. It's extremely popular in the morning—particularly on Sunday—but it's open until 8:30 for lunch and dinner. All this even though the food is only average and the grumpy waiters give the appearance of having worked here since the day it opened. ✉ *259 Calle San Francisco, Old San Juan* ☎ *787/722–0658* ▭ *AE, MC, V.*

$–$$ ✕ **Cafetería Mallorca.** The specialty at this old-fashioned eatery is the *mallorca,* a sweet pastry that's buttered, grilled, and then sprinkled with powdered sugar. Wash one down with a terrific cup of café con leche. For something more substantial, try the breakfast mallorca, which has ham and cheese. The waitstaff—all dressed in crisp green uniforms and caps—are friendly and efficient. ✉ *300 Calle San Francisco, Old San Juan* ☎ *787/724–4607* ▭ *MC, V* ⏲ *Closed Sun.*

CARIBBEAN

$$$–$$$$ ✕ **Parrot Club.** Loud and lively, this place is intent on making sure everyone is having a good time. You're likely to strike up a conversation with the bartender as you enjoy a passion-fruit cocktail or with the couple at the next table in the covered courtyard. Something about the atmosphere—ear-splitting salsa music and murals of swaying palm trees—makes connecting easy. The menu has contemporary variations of Caribbean classics. You might start with mouthwatering crab cakes or tamarind-barbecued ribs, followed by blackened tuna in a dark rum sauce or seared sea bass with lobster, leek, and scallop confit. ✉ *363 Calle Fortaleza, Old San Juan* ☎ *787/725–7370* ✍ *Reservations not accepted* ▭ *AE, DC, MC, V.*

$$–$$$ ✕ **Amadeus.** Facing Plaza San José, this bright and airy restaurant often throws open the doors and lets its tables spill into the square. If you want a little more privacy, there's also an interior courtyard and an intimate dining room with whitewashed walls, linen tablecloths, and lazily turning ceiling fans. Expect nouvelle Caribbean appetizers such as dumplings with guava-rum sauce or plantain mousse with shrimp, and entrées such as ravioli with a goat-cheese sauce and pork with mango and sugarcane. ✉ *106 Calle San Sebastián, Old San Juan* ☎ *787/722–8635* ▭ *AE, MC, V* ⏲ *No lunch Mon.*

$–$$ ✕ **La Fonda del Jibarito.** Sanjuaneros have favored this casual, family-run restaurant for years. The conch ceviche and chicken fricassee are among the specialties on the menu of comida criollo dishes. The back porch is filled with plants, and the dining room is filled with fanciful depictions of life on the street outside. The ever-present owner, Pedro J. Ruiz, is filled with the desire to ensure that everyone is happy. ✉ *280 Calle Sol, Old San Juan* ☎ *787/725–8375* ✍ *Reservations not accepted* ▭ *AE, MC, V.*

MORNING COFFEE

If you want a good cup of morning coffee, check out one of the ubiquitous Subway sandwich shops; outlets in Puerto Rico make excellent café con leche.

CLOSE UP

On the Menu

Adobo: a seasoning made of salt, onion powder, garlic powder, and ground black pepper, usually rubbed on meats before they are roasted.

Aji-li-mojili: a dressing combining garlic and sweet, seeded chili peppers, flavored further with vinegar, lime juice, salt, and olive oil; it is traditionally served with lechón asado.

Alcapurrias: banana croquettes stuffed with beef or pork, which are very popular as a fast food.

Amarillos: fried ripe, yellow plantain slices, a common side dish.

Arepas: fried corn or bread cakes.

Asopao: a gumbo made with fish or chicken, flavored with spices such as garlic, paprika, and oregano as well as salt pork, cured ham, green peppers, chili peppers, onions, tomatoes, chorizo, and pimentos.

Batido: a tropical fruit-and-milk shake; basically, a smoothie.

Bacalaítos: deep-fried codfish fritters, which are often served as an appetizer for lunch or dinner.

Chimichurri: an herb sauce of finely chopped cilantro or parsley with garlic, lemon, and oil that is usually served with grilled meats.

Chinas: in Puerto Rico *naranjas* (oranges) are called chinas, so you'll see "jugo de china" on many breakfast menus.

Empanadillas: turnovers, bigger than *pastelillos,* filled with beef, crabmeat, conch, or even lobster.

Jueyes: land crab, which is often boiled or served in a stew.

Lechón Asado: a slow-roasted, garlic-studded whole pig, marinated in sour orange juice and coloring made from achiote, the inedible fruit of a small Caribbean shrub whose seeds are sometimes ground as a spice; it's traditionally served with *aji-li-mojili.*

Mofongo: a mix of plantains mashed with garlic, olive oil, and salt in a *pilón,* the traditional mortar and pestle used in the Puerto Rican kitchen.

Mojo or Mojito Isleño: a sauce made of olives and olive oil, onions, pimientos, capers, tomato sauce, vinegar, and a flavoring of garlic and bay leaves that is usually served with fried fish (not to be confused with Cuban rum drink, *mojito*).

Pasteles: corn or yucca stuffed with various fillings and wrapped in a plantain leaf.

Pastelillos: deep-fried cheese and meat turnovers, which are a popular fast-food snack.

Picadillo: spicy ground meat, which is used for stuffing or eaten with rice.

Pique: a condiment consisting of hot peppers soaked in vinegar, sometimes with garlic or other spices added.

Pionono: a slice of ripe plantain peel filled with picadillo, breaded and fried.

Sofrito: a seasoned base made with pureed tomatoes, sautéed onions, bell peppers, tomatoes, sweet red chili peppers, herbs and spices, cilantro (coriander), *recao,* and garlic, and colored with achiote (annato seeds); it's used in rice, soups, and stews, giving them a bright yellow coloring.

Tembleque: a coconut custard, a popular dessert; when served, it's usually sprinkled with cinnamon or nutmeg.

Tostones: crushed fried green plantains, usually served as an appetizer.

ECLECTIC

> **WORD OF MOUTH**
>
> "One of the most romantic restaurants I've been to is [La] Ostra Cosa in Old San Juan on Calle Cristo. It is wonderful seafood in a lush, outdoor courtyard. The menu lists the 'aphrodisiac value' of each item." -mom929.

$$$–$$$$ **Panza.** Tucked discreetly behind gauzy curtains, this restaurant doesn't have to shout to be heard—chef Roberto Pagan's creative cooking speaks loud and clear. Although it's rather too quaintly divided into sections called Preface, Essays, and Contents, the menu is a wonderful mix of different-size dishes, so you can have your own or share a few with friends. Our favorites include bacon-wrapped dates with blue cheese aioli and tiny tacos stuffed with slow-cooked duck. The half-moon banquettes in the front window are the perfect place to sample any of the 550 wines from the eatery's extensive cellars. ✉ *Chateau Cervantes, 329 Calle Recinto Sur, Old San Juan* ☎ *787/724–7722* *Reservations essential* *AE, D, DC, MC, V* *Closed Sun.*

$$–$$$ **Barú.** A global menu has earned Barú a solid reputation among sanjuaneros, so it's often crowded. The dishes, all served in medium-sized portions so you can order several and share, range from Middle Eastern to Asian to Caribbean. Favorites include oysters in a soy-citrus sauce, risotto with green asparagus, and carpaccio made from beef, tuna, or salmon. More substantial fare includes filet mignon with horseradish mashed potatoes and pork ribs with a ginger-tamarind glaze. The dining room, in a beautifully renovated colonial house, is dark and mysterious. ✉ *150 Calle San Sebastián, Old San Juan* ☎ *787/977–7107* *AE, MC, V* *Closed Mon. No lunch.*

$$–$$$ ★ **La Ostra Cosa.** This restaurant's succulent prawns, grilled and served with garlic butter, are supposed to be aphrodisiacs. In fact, everything on the menu is rated for its love-inducing qualities. (Look out for those labeled "Ay, ay, ay!") There are some seats indoors, but opt for a seat in the walled courtyard. With brilliant purple bougainvillea tumbling down and moonlight streaming through the trees, it's one of the city's prettiest alfresco dining spots. The gregarious owner, Alberto Nazario, brother of pop star Ednita Nazario, genuinely enjoys seeing his guests satisfied. He'll sometimes take out a guitar and sing old folk songs. Don't be surprised if the locals sing along. ✉ *154 Calle Cristo, Old San Juan* ☎ *787/722–2672* *AE, MC, V.*

$–$$$ **El Patio de Sam.** A great selection of beers—26, to be exact, including the locally brewed Medalla—make this a popular late-night spot. Just as appealing is the dimly lighted courtyard that gives the place its name. The menu consists mostly of steaks and seafood, but there are plenty of opportunities to sample Puerto Rican fare. Save room for the flan, which melts in your mouth. There's entertainment (usually a guitarist singing old standards) every night but Sunday. ✉ *102 Calle San Sebastián, Old San Juan* ☎ *787/723–1149* *AE, D, DC, MC, V.*

INDIAN

$–$$ **Tantra.** This little gem sits square in the middle of Old San Juan's restaurant row, rather ironically called SoFo (South Fortaleza Street). The menu, which combines Indian and Caribbean flavors, has traditional dishes such as tandoori chicken and inventive surprises like beef tenderloin in a casava purée. The jewel-tone interior invites you to linger, and many patrons do so for an after-dinner puff on an Asian water pipe. ✉*356 Calle Fortaleza, Old San Juan* ☎*787/977–8141* ▭*AE, MC, V.*

ITALIAN

$$$–$$$$ ★ ✕**Il Perugino.** This colonial-era house has been transformed into something out of ancient Rome. But did Romans ever feast on such appetizers as foie gras on a bed of white onions or marinated salmon with chives? As good as these are, the main courses are even better. The ravioli stuffed with chicken liver, spinach, and black truffles are a wonder, as is the pork fillet with thyme and blueberries. The extensive wine cellar, housed in the former cistern, is sure to contain the perfect complement to your meal. Everything here is discreet, from the entrance (just an awning over a doorway) to the service. ✉*105 Calle Cristo, Old San Juan* ☎*787/722–5481* ▭*MC, V.*

$$–$$$ ✕**La Cocina di Ivo.** Old San Juan's prettiest courtyard has been transformed into this traditional trattoria. The staff enters and leaves through leaded-glass doors on either side of the central courtyard that lead to the bar, the wine cellar, and intimate dining rooms. You'll want to dine alfresco, as ceiling fans keep everything cool. A fountain bubbles on one side of the courtyard, and rows of potted fig trees surround the wrought-iron café tables. The place is named for chef Ivo Bignami, and the kitchen turns out specialties of his native Milan. For a lighter meal, or a first course big enough to share with your date, order the light, fluffy gnocchi. Entrées include filet mignon in truffle sauce and veal with porcini mushrooms. For desert, try the classic and tasty tiramisu. ✉*202 Calle Cristo, Old San Juan* ☎*787/729–7070* ▭*AE, MC, V.*

$$–$$$ ✕**Sofia.** Ignore the tongue-in-cheek recordings of "That's Amore." Everything else in this red-walled trattoria is the real deal, from the gleaming vegetables on the antipasto table to the vintages on the small but well-chosen wine list. Start with the squid stuffed with sweet sausage, then move onto the linguine with clams and pancetta or the cannelloni filled with roasted duck and topped with mascarpone cheese. The plates of pasta are huge, so you might want to consider a half-order (which is more the size of a three-quarter order). Save room for—what else?—a tasty tiramisu. ✉*355 Calle San Francisco, Old San Juan* ☎*787/721–0396* ▭*AE, MC, V.*

LATIN

$$–$$$ ✕**La Mallorquina.** Dating from 1848, La Mallorquina is thought to be the island's oldest restaurant. The menu is heavy on such basic Puerto Rican and Spanish fare as *asopao* (a stew with rice and seafood) and paella, but the old-fashioned atmosphere is what really recommends the place. Nattily attired staffers zip between tables set against peach-colored walls and beneath the whir of ceiling fans. They can be a bit short with tourists, however. ✉*207 Calle San Justo, Old San Juan* ☎*787/722–3261* ▭*AE, MC, V* ⊙*Closed Sun.*

$ ✕**Spanglish.** On a quiet side street, this café has a laid-back vibe that has people coming back again and again. The food, from old family recipes, includes Puerto Rican favorites like garbanzo-bean stew flavored with ham, and sausage and veal tips simmered in wine. The creamy flan has also developed quite a following. There's a small bar in back where you can sample the trademark drink, a fruity rum punch. ⊠*105 Calle Cruz, Old San Juan* ☎*787/722–2424* ▭*MC, V.*

MEDITERRANEAN

$$–$$$$ ★ ✕ **Carli Café Concierto.** As you might guess from the name, the music is as much of a draw as the food at Carli Café Concierto. The genial owner and host, Carli Muñoz, once toured with the Beach Boys (note the gold album on the wall). Many evenings he plays the gorgeous grand piano, often accompanied by singers and musicians who happen to drop in. In the Banco Popular building that dominates the skyline, this intimate bistro has black-marble tables scattered around the room. Have a seat indoors or on the outdoor patio, and dine on such Mediterranean-Caribbean specialties as seared loin of lamb or ravioli in a light pesto sauce. ⊠*Plazoleta Rafael Carrión, Calle Recinto Sur and Calle San Justo, Old San Juan* ☎*787/725–4927* ▭*AE, MC, V* ⊙*Closed Sun.*

MEXICAN

$–$$ ✕ **Lupi's.** Dining in Old San Juan doesn't have to mean fighting for a table. This Mexican restaurant is the best of the string of laid-back eateries along Calle Recinto Sur. Plates of steaming hot tacos, burritos, and other reasonably authentic fare arrive at your table within minutes of ordering. And if you want to watch the big game—whatever it might be—it will doubtless be playing on the television over the bar. It stays open late, so this is a good place to try when other kitchens are closing ⊠*313 Calle Recinto Sur, Old San Juan* ☎*787/722–1874* ▭*AE, MC, V.*

PAN-ASIAN

$$–$$$ ✕ **Dragonfly.** It's not hard to find this little restaurant—it's the one with crowds milling about on the sidewalk. If you can stand the wait—as you undoubtedly will have to because reservations aren't accepted—you'll get to sample chef Roberto Trevino's Latin-Asian cuisine. (The best way to avoid a frustrating wait is to come when it opens at 6 PM.) The *platos* (plates) are meant to be shared, so order several for your table. Favorites include pork-and-plantain dumplings with an orange dipping sauce, smoked-salmon pizza with wasabi salsa, and lamb spareribs with a tamarind glaze. The dining room, all done up in Chinese red, resembles an opium den. ⊠*364 Calle Fortaleza, Old San Juan* ☎*787/977–3886* ✍*Reservations not accepted* ▭*AE, MC, V* ⊙*No lunch.*

SEAFOOD

$$$–$$$$ ★ ✕ **Aguaviva.** The name means "jellyfish," which explains why this ultracool, ultramodern place has lighting fixtures shaped like that sea creature. Elegantly groomed oysters and clams float on cracked ice along the raw bar. The extensive menu is alive with inventive ceviches, some with tomato or roasted red peppers and olives, and fresh takes on such classics as paella. For something more filling, try dorado served with a shrimp salsa, or tuna accompanied by seafood enchila-

das. You could also empty out your wallet for one of the *torres del mar*, or towers of the sea. This gravity-defying dish comes hot or cold and includes oysters, mussels, shrimp—you name it. Oh, and don't pass up the lobster mashed potatoes. Those alone are worth the trip—and the wait. ✉ *364 Calle Fortaleza, Old San Juan* ☎ *787/722–0665* ✍ *Reservations not accepted* 💳 *AE, D, MC, V.*

CAUTION

Sanjuaneros generally eat dinner late; if you arrive at a restaurant before 7 PM, you may be the only diners.

SPANISH

$$$ ✕ **El Picoteo.** You could make a meal of the small dishes that dominate the menu at this tapas restaurant. You won't go wrong ordering the sweet sausage in brandy or the turnovers stuffed with lobster and passing them around the table. If you're not into sharing, there are five different kinds of paella that arrive on huge plates. There's a long, lively bar inside; one dining area overlooks a pleasant courtyard, whereas the other takes in the action along Calle Cristo. Even if you have dinner plans elsewhere, consider stopping here for a nightcap. ✉ *Hotel El Convento, 100 Calle Cristo, Old San Juan* ☎ *787/723–9621* 💳 *AE, D, DC, MC, V.*

$$–$$$ ✕ **El Toro Salao.** The name means "The Salty Bull," and there's something about this place that makes its moniker entirely appropriate. (And it's not just the bullfighting posters that decorate one of the two-story-high walls.) This tapas restaurant was opened by Emilio Figueroa, who helped turn the sourthern end of Calle Fortaleza into the city's top dining destination. El Toro Salao is not on South Fortaleza, but its brash attitude clearly marks it as part of the SoFo bunch. There are plenty of small dishes to share, as well as heartier fare such as blackened tuna in sweet paprika sauce and grilled octopus with a sundried-tomato vinaigrette. The dining room, with a bar illuminated in lusty red, is pleasant enough; but the tables that spill onto the adjacent cobblestone square are even better. ✉ *367 Calle Tetuán, Old San Juan* ☎ *787/722–3330* 💳 *AE, MC, V* ⏲ *Closed Sun. No lunch.*

PUERTA DE TIERRA

SEAFOOD

$$–$$$$ ✕ **Atlántica.** This popular restaurant is across from its namesake, so it's no surprise that the seafood is the freshest around. Start with a plate of fried calamari, served lightly breaded and accompanied by a spicy sauce, then move on to the broiled lobster tail or grilled red snapper in a garlic sauce. Locals swear by the paella, which is loaded with scallops, clams, shrimp, and squid. The restaurant is just west of Playa Escambrón. ✉ *7 Calle Lugo Viñas, Puerta de Tierra* ☎ *787/722–0890* 💳 *AE, MC, V* ⏲ *Closed Mon.*

$–$$$ ✕ **Escambrón.** You can see two of the forts of Old San Juan—Fuerte San Filipe del Morro and Fuerte San Cristóbal—from the covered terrace of this seafood restaurant. The beach itself is only a few feet away. The food here is more creative than you'd expect, with dishes ranging from shrimp with cilantro and roasted-garlic butter to lobster grilled with a rum-and-butter sauce. Not in the mood for seafood? There are plenty of meat dishes, including skirt steak and pork chops. The restaurant is walking distance from the Caribe Hilton and the Normandie. ✉ *Playa Escambrón, Puerta de Tierra* ☎ *787/724–3344* ▭ *AE, MC, V.*

CONDADO

ASIAN

$$–$$$$ ✕ **Budatai.** A trio of lighting fixtures—think Chinese lanterns designed by Salvador Dalí—distinguish this place from those serving *moo goo gai pan.* This Pan-Asian eatery was designed with the same clean lines and airy spaces as the string of designer stores that are its downstairs neighbors. And judging from their bags, its hip, young customers are fortifying themselves after an exhausting day of shopping in Chanel, Gucci, and Ferragamo. This is designer food, and it fits the neighborhood beautifully. Start with the pork dumplings, made with shaved truffles and topped with flying-fish roe that adds the perfect touch of saltiness. The entrées include soy-glazed salmon with coconut hash and veal steak with lobster mashed potatoes. Sunday brunch adds some interesting items to the lunch menu, such as pistachio French toast with seared foie gras (with a $35 price tag that tops almost everything on the dinner menu). ✉ *1056 Av. Ashford, Condado* ☎ *787/725-6919* ✍ *Reservations essential* ▭ *AE, MC, V.*

$$–$$$$ ✕ **Cherry Blossom.** It's clear when you walk through the delicately etched glass doors that this place has a split personality. To the left is a sedate little sushi bar where you place your order by checking off items on the menu. (We liked the spicy crab and avocado roll, but people at the next table seemed happy with their salmon skin roll.) To the right is a more boisterous dining room where the tables are arranged around teppanyaki tables. Chefs wearing tall red hats add drama to your meal, tossing knives and dodging flames as they prepare such dishes as sautéed scallops in garlic-sake sauce, beef stir-fried with scallions, and roast duck in savory spices. Wash everything down with a Sapporo beer or a fruity specialty cocktail. ✉ *Av. Ashford at Av. Condado* ☎ *787/723–7300* ▭ *AE, D, DC, MC, V.*

$–$$$ ✕ **Great Taste.** It's no surprise that this simple Chinese and Japanese restaurant revamped its dining room with Chanel and Gucci moving in down the street. But most of its creativity is still in the kitchen. As you might guess, the menu is heavy on seafood, offering such dishes as fish with ginger and scallion and fried shrimp with crispy, minced garlic. There are plenty of meat dishes as well, including shredded duck with spicy bean sauce. (If you can't find it on the menu, look under the heading for chicken.) The dim sum menu has about 40 different choices, and the sushi bar's extensive selections put other places to shame. Be sure to check out the beautiful view over the Laguna del Condado. ✉ *1018 Av. Ashford, Condado* ☎ *787/721–8111* ▭ *AE, D, DC, MC, V.*

CAFÉS

$–$$ **La Patisserie.** Everything—from pastries to pastas—is delicious at this café, which sits on a quiet block in Condado. For breakfast, wonderful omelets are stuffed with fresh vegetables and imported cheeses. Sandwiches—from pastrami to king crab—are served during lunch on croissants, baguettes, and other types of bread. For dinner, try grilled salmon or chicken in white wine. Like most eateries in Condado, it has valet parking. ✉ *1504 Av. Ashford, Condado* ☎ *787/728–5508* ▭ *AE, MC, V.*

CARIBBEAN

$$–$$$$ Fodor's Choice ★ **Ajili-Mójili.** Set in a plantation-style house, this elegant dining room sits on the edge of Condado Bay. Traditional Puerto Rican food is prepared with a flourish. Sample the fried cheese and *bolitas de yautia y queso* (cheese and yam dumplings), then move on to the *gallinita rellena* (stuffed cornish game hen). The plantain-crusted shrimp in a white-wine herb sauce is delicious, as is the paella overflowing with shrimp, octopus, mussels, chicken, and spicy sausage. Prices, however, are pretty high—even for this level of quality. ✉ *1006 Av. Ashford, Condado* ☎ *787/725–9195* ▭ *AE, DC, MC, V.*

$$–$$$ **Yerba Buena.** Tables on the terrace are hard to come by at this restaurant, one of the most popular in Condado. That's fine, because the glassed-in dining room is even more comfortable and has exactly the same view. Cuban classics such as *ropa vieja* (meat cooked so slowly that it becomes tender shreds) seamlessly blend local dishes with imaginative presentation. The shrimp has a coconut-and-ginger sauce; the halibut fillet one of mango and orange liqueur. The restaurant claims to use the "original" recipe for its *mojito,* Cuba's tasty rum, lime, and mint drink. Live Latin jazz is played live many nights. ✉ *1350 Av. Ashford, Condado* ☎ *787/721–5700* ▭ *AE, MC, V* ⊙ *Closed Mon.*

$–$$$ **Casa Dante.** If you're curious about mofongo—sweet plantains mashed into a paste and filled with just about anything imaginable—this is where locals will send you. This self-proclaimed "casa del mofongo" adds chicken or any combination of seafood to an excellent version of the dish. You can even order it as a side alongside grilled *churrasco* or sautéed red snapper. The restaurant, which sits on the border of Isla Verde and Ocean Park, offers delivery as well. ✉ *39 Av. Isla Verde, Punta Las Marías* ☎ *787/726–7310* ▭ *MC, V* ⊙ *Closed Mon.*

CONTINENTAL

$$$–$$$$ **Augusto's.** Austrian-born chef Augusto Schreiner, a graduate of the Salzburg Culinary School, regularly wins awards for his classic European cuisine. The menu changes seasonally; some of the dishes commonly served are veal chops with roasted root vegetables and duck breast with bok choy. Particularly good is the lobster with saffron risotto. Large bouquets of flowers soften the angular lines of the formal dining room ✉ *Courtyard by Marriott Miramar, 801 Av. Ponce de León, Miramar* ☎ *787/725–7700* ▭ *AE, MC, V* ⊙ *Closed Sun. and Mon. No lunch Sat.*

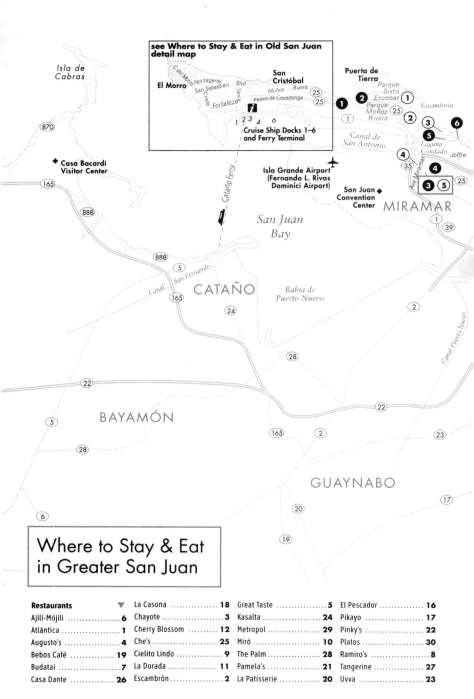

Where to Stay & Eat in Greater San Juan

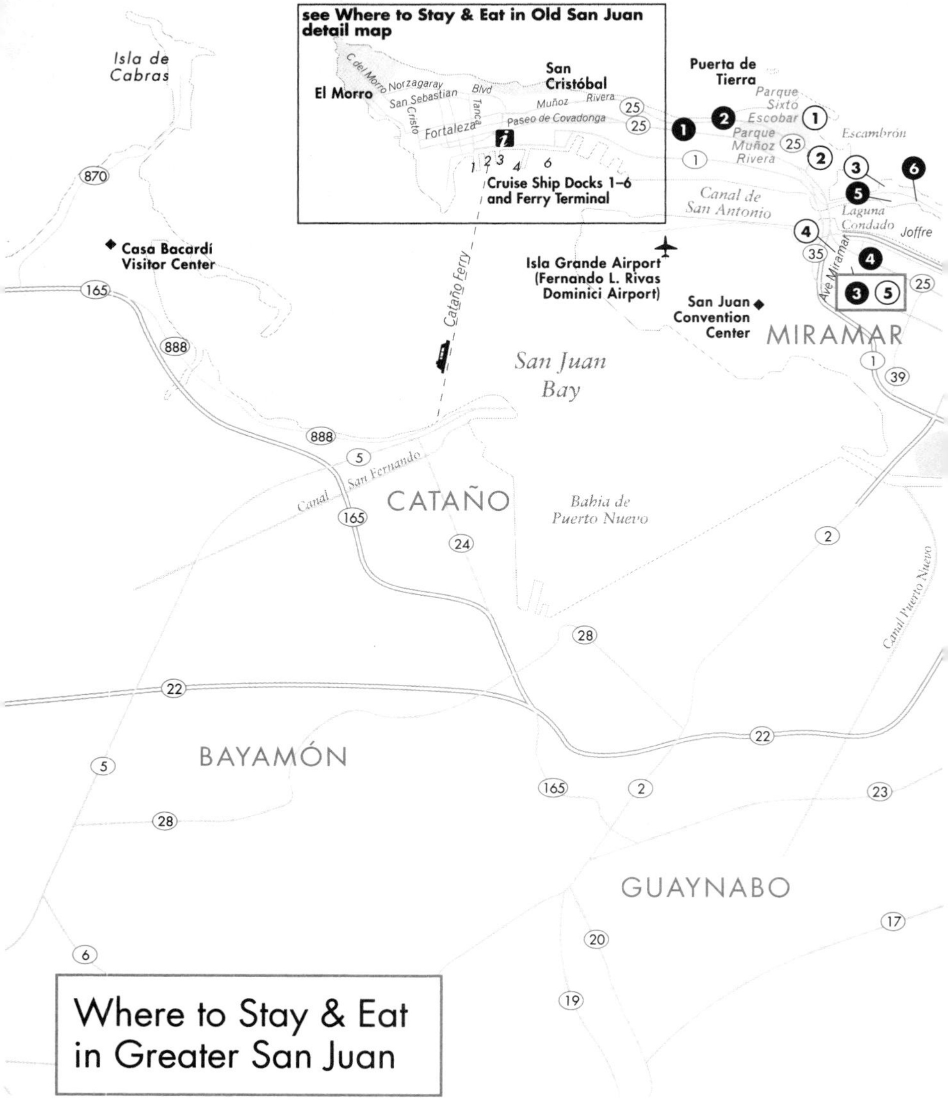

Restaurants ▼

- Ajili-Mójili **6**
- Atlántica **1**
- Augusto's **4**
- Bebos Café **19**
- Budatai **7**
- Casa Dante **26**
- La Casona **18**
- Chayote **3**
- Cherry Blossom **12**
- Che's **25**
- Cielito Lindo **9**
- La Dorada **11**
- Escambrón **2**
- Great Taste **5**
- Kasalta **24**
- Metropol **29**
- Miró **10**
- The Palm **28**
- Pamela's **21**
- La Patisserie **20**
- El Pescador **16**
- Pikayo **17**
- Pinky's **22**
- Platos **30**
- Ramiro's **8**
- Tangerine **27**
- Uvva **23**

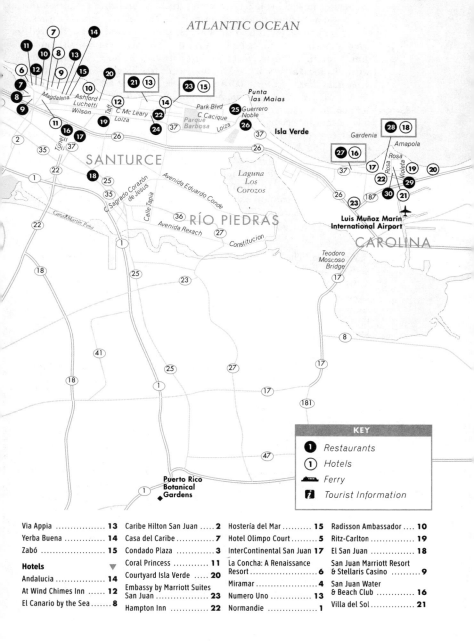

Via Appia **13**
Yerba Buena **14**
Zabó **15**

Hotels

Andalucia **14**
At Wind Chimes Inn **12**
El Canario by the Sea **8**
Caribe Hilton San Juan ... **2**
Casa del Caribe **7**
Condado Plaza **3**
Coral Princess **11**
Courtyard Isla Verde **20**
Embassy by Marriott Suites San Juan ... **23**
Hampton Inn **22**
Hostería del Mar **15**
Hotel Olimpo Court **5**
InterContinental San Juan **17**
La Concha: A Renaissance Resort ... **6**
Miramar **4**
Numero Uno **13**
Normandie **1**
Radisson Ambassador **10**
Ritz-Carlton **19**
El San Juan **18**
San Juan Marriott Resort & Stellaris Casino ... **9**
San Juan Water & Beach Club ... **16**
Villa del Sol **21**

ECLECTIC

$$$–$$$$ ★ ✕ **Chayote.** Slightly off the beaten path, this chic eatery is definitely an "in" spot. The chef gives haute international dishes tropical panache. Starters include chayote stuffed with prosciutto and corn tamales with shrimp in a coconut sauce. About half the entrées are seafood dishes, including pan-seared tuna with a ginger sauce and red snapper served over spinach. The ginger flan is a must for dessert. The sophisticated dining room, in the basement level of a newly chic hotel, is hung with works by local artists. It's in Miramar, just a few blocks from Condado. ✉ *Hotel Olimpo Court, 603 Av. Miramar, Miramar* ☎ *787/722–9385* ▭ *AE, MC, V* ⊙ *Closed Sun. and Mon. No lunch Sat.*

$$–$$$ ✕ **Zabó.** In a restored plantation house surrounded by a quiet garden, this restaurant seems as if it's out on the island somewhere. If you'd rather remember that you're in Condado, several outdoor tables sit near bustling Avenida Ashford. Make sure to order several of the tasty appetizers—such as breaded calamari in a tomato-basil sauce—so you can share them with your dinner companions. Of the notable main courses, try the veal chops stuffed with provolone and pancetta, or the miso-marinated salmon served over lemony basmati rice. ✉ *14 Calle Candida, Condado* ☎ *787/725–9494* ▭ *AE, D, DC, MC, V* ⊙ *Closed Sun. and Mon. No lunch Tues.–Thurs.*

ITALIAN

$$–$$$ ✕ **Via Appia.** The food at this no-frills café is just as authentic and tasty—from the pizza to the veal and peppers to the house red wine—as its higher-priced *paisanos*. The outdoor-seating area looks out on Condado's busy Ashford Avenue, which is usually filled with people coming from and going to the beach. The wine bar next door has a bit more ambience. ✉ *1350 Av. Ashford, Condado* ☎ *787/725–8711* ▭ *AE, MC, V.*

LATIN

$$ ✕ **Cielito Lindo.** The moment you walk in the door you know that this is the real deal. The first clue is the smell of grilled meat coming from the kitchen. The juicy flank steaks are indeed standouts, but so are the burritos and fajitas that cater to the Tex-Mex crowd. There's also a wide selection of margaritas, each one iced to perfection and served with a lime wedge. The decor—paper streamers hanging from the ceiling—will remind you of eateries in small towns all over Mexico. ✉ *1108 Av. Magdalena, Condado* ☎ *787/723–5597* ▭ *AE, MC, V.*

$–$$ ✕ **Bebos Café.** At this longtime favorite, huge platters of delicious comida criolla are constantly streaming out of the kitchen. Friendly service and low prices ensure that the place is always packed. The menu includes everything from grilled flank steak to seafood-stuffed mofongo to barbecued ribs, as well as a selection of good local desserts, such as flan and dense, moist *tres leches* cake. Breakfast is also popular. ✉ *1600 Calle Loíza, Condado* ☎ *787/268–5087* ▭ *AE, MC, V.*

SEAFOOD

$–$$$ ✕ **La Dorada.** This seafood establishment in the middle of Condado's restaurant row is surprisingly affordable. The dining room isn't much to look at—it's more along the lines of a diner. The focus here is the food. The grilled seafood platter is the specialty, but there are plenty of other excellent dishes, including mahimahi in caper sauce and codfish in green sauce. The friendly staff is genuinely welcoming. ✉ *1105 Av. Magdalena, Condado* ☎ *787/722–9583* ▭ *AE, D, MC, V.*

SPANISH

$$$–$$$$ ✕ **Ramiro's.** The smell of chef Jesús Ramiro's imaginative Castilian cooking fills this sea-green dining room. He is also known for his artistic presentation: flower-shaped peppers filled with fish mousse, a mix of seafood caught under a vegetable net, roast duckling with sugarcane honey, and, if you have room for more, a kiwi dessert sculpted to resemble twin palms. The dining room is filled with business people intent on impressing their clients—and by the looks of things, they do. ✉ *1106 Av. Magdalena, Condado* ☎ *787/721–9049* ▭ *AE, DC, MC, V.*

$$–$$$ ✕ **Miró.** Like its namesake, the painter Joan Miró, this small restaurant draws its inspiration from the Catalan region of Spain, where the cuisine is heavy on seafood and hearty tapas. Start with steamed clams with garlic or braised chorizo and peppers. Main courses include sizzling lamb chops, as well as grilled tuna with anchovy and caper butter or codfish in a red-pepper and eggplant sauce. Prints by the artist hang on the walls, adding an authentic touch to the maze of tiny dining rooms. Its new location, on busy Avenida Ashford across from the San Juan Marriott Resort, means that the place is always packed. ✉ *1214 Av. Ashford, Condado* ☎ *787/723–9593* ▭ *AE, MC, V.*

SANTURCE

ECLECTIC

$$$$ ✕ **Pikayo.** Chef Wilo Benet is clearly the star here—a plasma television in the dining room broadcasts everything that's going on in his kitchen. The Puerto Rico native artfully fuses Caribbean cuisine with influences from around the world. Veal is served in a swirl of sweet-pea couscous, for example, and beef medallions are covered with crumbled blue cheese and a red-wine reduction. The regularly changing menu is a feast for the eye as well as the palate, and might include perfectly shaped tostones (fried green plantains) stuffed with oven-dried tomatoes or mofongo topped with saffron shrimp. A changing selection of artwork is exhibited in the minimalist dining room—the restaurant is, after all, inside a museum. It's in Santurce, just south of Condado. ✉ *Museo de Arte de Puerto Rico, 299 Av. José de Diego, Santurce* ☎ *787/721–6194* ▭ *AE, MC, V* ⏲ *Closed Sun. No lunch Mon. & Sat..*

SPANISH

$$$–$$$$ ✕ **La Casona.** Business executives come here for power lunches, but La Casona is also a nice spot for a romantic dinner. The restored Spanish colonial residence in Santurce has well-appointed rooms and blooming gardens. The menu is based solidly in Spain but has many creative flourishes—start with the smoked salmon and move on to the duck breast in raspberry sauce or the rack of lamb, which is first baked and

then sautéed with brandy and fruit. ✉ *609 Calle San Jorge, Santurce* ☎ *787/727–2717* ▭ *AE, D, DC, MC, V* ⏲ *Closed Sun.*

SEAFOOD

$$ ✕ **El Pescador.** If you want food that's unmistakably Puerto Rican, head to Plaza del Mercado. Surrounding a fruit and vegetable market dating from 1910 you'll find a few dozen restaurants that are the real deal. Our favorite is El Pescador, a narrow storefront selling the freshest of seafood. If you come in the evening it might be cool enough to eat at one of the handful of tables on the square. If not, settle for the bright green dining room. The *chillo entero frito* (fried whole red snapper) and *camarones al ajillo* (shrimp with garlic) are tasty, but the standout is the *arroz con calamari* (rice with squid). This dramatic inky black dish draws oohs and aahs from surrounding customers when it arrives at your table. Parking is tough here, especially on weekends, so take a taxi. ✉ *178 Calle Dos Hermanos, Santurce* ☎ *787/721–0995* ▭ *AE, MC, V* ⏲ *Closed Mon.*

OCEAN PARK

CAFÉS

$$–$$$ ★ ✕ **Kasalta.** Those who think coffee can never be too strong should make a beeline to Kasalta, which has an amazing pitch-black brew that will knock your socks off. Make your selection from the display cases full of luscious pastries and other tempting treats. Walk up to the counter and order a sandwich, such as the savory Cubano, or such items as the meltingly tender octopus salad. For dinner there are fish dishes and other more substantial fare. ✉ *1966 Calle McLeary, Ocean Park* ☎ *787/727–7340* ▭ *AE, MC, V.*

¢–$ ✕ **Pinky's.** This tiny café near the beach is known for its gourmet wraps and sandwiches, as well as its freshly squeezed juices and fruity frappés. The pink sub is a blend of turkey, salami, and mozzarella, topped with black olives, chopped tomatoes, and basil. The surfer wrap is a mix of grilled turkey and mozzarella with pesto mayonnaise. Don't see what you want? Create your own. Seating is limited, but takeout is available. Or place your order from the beach, where speedy delivery people tend to your hunger pangs. ✉ *51 Calle María Moczo, Ocean Park* ☎ *787/727–3347* ▭ *MC, V* ⏲ *Closed Mon. No dinner.*

CARIBBEAN

$$$–$$$$ ★ ✕ **Pamela's.** If you've always dreamed of a table for two on the beach, only steps from where crashing waves meet the shore, head to this restaurant in Ocean Park. A dozen or so umbrella-covered tables are set up outside the white walls of the Numero Uno Guesthouse, the perfect place to take advantage of the cool seaside breezes. (You can choose a table in the garden if you want more privacy, or the glassed-in solarium if you prefer air conditioning.) The contemporary menu is as memorable as the setting; look for spicy shrimp sautéed with ginger and jalapeños or dorado cooked in a banana leaf. ✉ *Numero Uno Guesthouse, 1 Calle Santa Ana, Ocean Park* ☎ *787/726–5010* ▭ *AE, D, MC, V.*

LATIN

$$–$$$ ✕**Che's.** This Argentine-style steak house on the eastern edge of Ocean Beach is worth the trip. If you haven't tried churrasco, the marinated skirt steak locals love, this is the place to do it. Another specialty is the grilled sweetbreads. The hamburgers are huge, and the french fries are fresh. The wine list, which tends toward Chilean and Argentine vintages, is also a winner. It's in Ocean Park, before you get to Isla Verde. ✉*35 Calle Caoba, Punta Las Marías* ☎*787/726–7202* ▭*AE, D, DC, MC, V.*

MEDITERRANEAN

$$–$$$$ ✕**Uvva.** You might think you're in the South Pacific or Bali when you sit down at one of the bamboo tables in this romantic restaurant, complete with oiled teak ceiling beams and shutters that swing up to catch the breeze. The menu has a bit of a split personality—appetizers lean toward Caribbean favorites, whereas most entrées are Mediterranean staples. However, it all comes together in such dishes as seared tuna with a ginger-and-cilantro vinaigrette or sesame-crusted salmon served over a bed of Asian vegetables. Vegetarian options are available as well. ✉*Hostería del Mar, 1 Calle Tapia, Ocean Park* ☎*787/727–0631* ▭*AE, D, DC, MC, V.*

ISLA VERDE

CARIBBEAN

$$–$$$ ✕**Platos.** In the heart of Isla Verde, this restaurant attracts a young, hip crowd. The menu is a combination of something old, something new. Puerto Rican favorites are jazzed up, serving skirt steak with pumpkin risotto and covering grilled pork with a guava glaze. The bar is a great place for a beer in the afternoon or for cocktails before heading to the clubs. ✉*2 Calle Rosa, Isla Verde* ☎*787/791–7474* ▭*AE, MC, V.*

$–$$ ✕**Metropol.** Even though this restaurant is across from a string of hotels, it draws a largely local crowd. The reason may be the traditional dishes, drawn from Cuban and Puerto Rican recipes. You may never have encountered some of them, such as *lacón con papas a la gallega* (smoked pork hocks with boiled potatoes) and *masitas de cerdo fritas a la cubana* (chunks of fried pork). Many prefer a table in the clubby bar to the cavernous dining room. ✉*Av. Isla Verde, Isla Verde* ☎*787/791–5585* ▭*AE, D, DC, MC, V* ⌚*No dinner Sun.*

CONTINENTAL

$$–$$$$ ✕**The Palm.** The same great steaks and seafood are served here as at this popular chain's other locations, including the original in New York City. When you leave, you half expect to look up at the Brooklyn Bridge. Caricatures of local and international celebrities stare down at you from the walls. The dark wood of the bar and other furnishings lets you know you're in for some serious dining. The 10-ounce filet mignon is relatively petite, at least when compared to the rib eye that weighs in at 24 ounces. Then there's the lobster, which starts at 3 pounds and goes higher. ✉*El San Juan Hotel & Casino, 6063 Av. Isla Verde, Isla Verde* ☎*787/791–1000* ▭*AE, D, DC, MC, V.*

ECLECTIC

$$–$$$$ ✕ **Tangerine.** The dining room opens onto an oceanfront terrace, where constant breezes are as much a part of the dreamy scene as the muted-orange lighting and cream walls. This place is all about sensual pleasures, so it's no surprise that many of the menu descriptions are a bit risqué. (A plate with three types of marinated fish is named, quite simply, "Threesome.") Appetizers such as roasted pumpkin soup with lemongrass foam and crispy wild mushroom dumplings are seductive but overpriced. Artful entrées include chicken breast stuffed with eggplant puree or pan-seared sea bass with sea-urchin butter sauce. ✉ *San Juan Water & Beach Club, 2 Calle Tartak, Isla Verde* ☎ *787/728–3666* ▭ *AE, MC, V.*

WHERE TO STAY

San Juan prides itself on its plentiful clean, comfortable accommodations, and hoteliers, by and large, aim to please. Big hotels and resorts, several with casinos, and a few smaller establishments line the sandy strands along Condado and Isla Verde. Between these two neighborhoods, the Ocean Park area has homey inns, as do the districts of Miramar and Santurce, although the latter two areas aren't directly on the beach. Old San Juan has only a few noteworthy hotels, one of which has a casino.

> **CAUTION**
>
> The small, government-sponsored inns called *paradores* are primarily *en la isla* (out on the island) rather than in San Juan.

Staying in a self-catering apartment or condo has advantages over a resort, especially for families. You can cook when and what you want, and you can enjoy considerable autonomy. Several companies represent such properties in San Juan. When booking, be sure to ask about maid service, swimming pools, and any other amenities that are important to you.

PRICES

The city's rooms aren't inexpensive: for a high-end beach-resort room, expect to pay at least $200 to $300 for a double in high season—roughly mid-November through mid-April. For smaller inns and hotels, doubles start at $100 to $150. As a rule, if your room is less than $50 in high season, then the quality of the hotel might be questionable. Although most hotels operate on the European plan (EP, no meals included), a few larger establishments offer other meal plans and/or all-inclusive packages; there's only one true all-inclusive hotel in Puerto Rico, and it's not in San Juan.

WHAT IT COSTS IN U.S. DOLLARS

	$$$$	$$$	$$	$	¢
FOR 2 PEOPLE	over $350	$250–$350	$150–$250	$80–$150	under $80

Prices are for a double room in high season, excluding 9% tax (11% for hotels with casinos, 7% for paradores) and typical 5%–12% service charge.

APARTMENT RENTALS

Puerto Rico Vacation Apartments (✉ *Calle Marbella del Caribe Oeste S-5, Isla Verde,* ☎ *787/727–1591 or 800/266–3639* 🌐 *www.sanjuanvacations.com*) represents some 200 properties in Condado and Isla Verde.

OLD SAN JUAN

$$$$ Fodor'sChoice ★ **Hotel El Convento.** Carmelite nuns once inhabited this 350-year-old convent, but they never had high-tech gadgets such as in-room broadband connections or plasma TVs. The accommodations here beautifully combine the old and the new. All the guest rooms have hand-hewn wood furniture, shuttered windows, and mahogany-beamed ceilings, but some have extra appeal. Room 508 has two views of the bay, while Rooms 216, 217, and 218 have private walled patios. Guests gather on the second floor for the complimentary wine and hors d'oeuvres that are served before dinner. The second-floor El Picoteo and the courtyard Café del Níspero are good dining choices. **Pros:** Lovely building, atmosphere to spare, near plenty of dining options. **Cons:** A bit of a chain-hotel feel, near some noisy bars. ✉ *100 Calle Cristo, Old San Juan* *Box 1048, 00902* ☎ *787/723–9020 or 800/468–2779* 🌐 *www.elconvento.com* *63 rooms, 5 suites* *In-room: safe, DVD, Ethernet, Wi-Fi. In-hotel: 3 restaurants, bars, pool, gym, concierge, laundry service, public Internet, public Wi-Fi, parking (fee), no-smoking rooms* *AE, D, DC, MC, V* *EP.*

> **WORD OF MOUTH**
>
> "We love El Convento. Have stayed many times, going back in a few weeks. The rooftop pool is really nice considering you are in the middle of a city. " –jencal.

$$$$ **Sheraton Old San Juan Hotel.** This hotel's triangular shape subtly echoes the cruise ships docked nearby. Rooms facing the water have dazzling views of these behemoths as they sail in and out of the harbor. (Interior rooms, however, face black concrete walls.) The rooms have been plushly renovated and have nice touches like custom-designed beds. On the top floor you'll find a sunny patio with a pool and whirlpool bath, as well as a spacious gym with the latest equipment. Renovations in 2007 brought two new restaurants—a steak house and a burger joint—and an expansion to the once small casino. **Pros:** Harbor views, near many dining options, good array of room types. **Cons:** Noise from casino overwhelms lobby and restaurants, extra charges for everything from bottled water to Internet access. ✉ *100 Calle Brumbaugh, Old San Juan* ☎ *787/721–5100 or 866/376–7577* 🌐 *www.sheratonoldsanjuan.com* *200 rooms, 40 suites* *In-room: safe, refrigerator, Ethernet. In-hotel: restaurant, room service, bar, pool, gym, laundry service, executive floor, public Internet, parking (fee), no-smoking rooms* *AE, D, DC, MC, V* *EP.*

$$$ ★ **Chateau Cervantes.** Nothing like this hotel exists anywhere else in San Juan—or Puerto Rico, for that matter. The brainchild of local fashion icon Nono Maldonado, this luxury lodging has a look that's completely

au courant. Bursts of color from red pillows or gold upholstery on the banquettes add considerable warmth. And the amenities are above and beyond other hotels. Splurge for one of the larger suites and you'll get a butler who will mix cocktails; the two-level presidential suite comes with a car and driver. The rooftop terrace has a bar, a hot tub, and an area for massages. **Pros:** Gorgeous rooms, great restaurant, quiet side street location. **Cons:** No views, very pricey. ✉*329 Calle Recinto Sur, Old San Juan* ☎*787/724–7722* 🌐*www.cervantespr.com* *6 rooms, 6 suites* *In-room: safe, Wi-Fi. In-hotel: restaurant, bar, concierge, laundry service* *AE, D, DC, MC, V* *EP.*

$$–$$$ ★ **Gallery Inn.** You can shop from your bed at this 200-year-old mansion, as owner Jan D'Esopo has filled the rooms with her own artworks. But it's not only the rooms; the hallways, the staircases, and the roof are lined with her fascinating bronze sculptures. Even if you aren't a guest, D'Esopo will be pleased to show you around and may offer you a glass of wine too. (Just make sure that Campeche, one of her many birds, doesn't try to sneak a sip.) No two rooms are alike here, but all have four-poster beds, hand-woven tapestries, and quirky antiques in every nook and cranny. You can view the coastline from several rooms and from the spectacular rooftop terrace. The first-floor Galería San Juan displays artwork by D'Esopo and others. **Pros:** One-of-a-kind lodging, ocean views, wonderful classical music concerts. **Cons:** No restaurant, an uphill walk from rest of Old San Juan. ✉*204–206 Calle Norzagaray, Old San Juan* ☎*787/722–1808* 🌐*www.thegalleryinn.com* *13 rooms, 10 suites* *In-room: no a/c (some), refrigerator (some), no TV. In-hotel: restaurant, no elevator, no-smoking rooms* *AE, DC, MC, V* *CP.*

$–$$ **Hotel Milano.** This affordable hotel is near the best and worst of Old San Juan. On the plus side, it's on a lively street lined with interesting shops. On the other hand, the street can be noisy. For less clamor, opt for a room at the back of the five-story building. Rooms here won't win any prizes, but they are clean and comfortable. The open-air restaurant on the top floor has expansive views of the barrel-tile rooftops. The friendly staff goes above and beyond the call of duty, arranging for your laundry to be washed or confirming that your flight is departing on time. **Pros:** Budget-friendly rates, walk to shops and restaurants. **Cons:** On a busy street, noise from nearby bars. ✉*307 Calle Fortaleza, Old San Juan* ☎*877/729–9050* 🌐*www.hotelmilanopr.com* *30 rooms* *In-hotel: restaurant, bar, laundry service, no-smoking rooms* *AE, MC, V* *CP.*

$–$$ **Howard Johnson Plaza de Armas.** Located on Old San Juan's main square, this hotel couldn't be more convenient. All of the most popular sites are within easy walking distance. Some of the building's best architectural details, such as the tile floors, have been preserved. The best rooms are in the front, where shuttered doorways lead to balconies overlooking the Plaza de Armas. Some of the inner rooms are a bit cramped. The interior courtyard has a hip little bar area. **Pros:** Great location, quiet courtyard, good value. **Cons:** Some rooms have very small windows, some street noise. ✉*202 Calle San José, Old San Juan*

☎787/722–9191 🌐*www.hojo.com* 51 rooms *In-room: refrigerator (some). In-hotel: bar* AE, D, DC, MC, V CP.

$ ★ **Da House.** This hotel occupies the same building as the fabled Nuyorican Café, a concert hall that many patrons simply refer to as Da House. But if you're expecting this hangout for musicians, artists, and writers to be dark and smoky, think again. Sunlight pours in through the front windows of the bright and airy hotel. Rooms are bigger than you'd expect in a former convent, especially those with small sitting areas at the front of the building. The original tile floors have been preserved, and many of the furnishings are antiques. During the 1970s the building housed an artist collective, the Centro Nacional de las Artes, and continues in this vein by naming each of the 27 rooms for a different local artist. If you like the paintings hanging in your room, remember that they are all for sale. But it's the music that draws people here. If you're an early-to-bed person, you'll probably want a room on the top floor. (We found 402 and 403 to be the quietest.) If you plan on staying downstairs until the last encore, it won't matter which room you take. **Pros:** Hip vibe, mingle with artsy types, great rooftop bar. **Cons:** Noise from nearby bars, on a steep alley, simple accommodations. ✉*312 Calle San Fransico (entrance on Callejón de la Capellia), Old San Juan* ☎*787/977–1180* 🌐*www.dahousehotelpr.com* *27 rooms* *In-room: no TV, Ethernet. In-hotel: bar, no elevator, public Wi-Fi* *AE, MC, V* *EP.*

¢–$ **The Caleta Guesthouse.** This little lodging is in an area overlooking the Bahía de San Juan. Narrow stairs and hallways lead to rooms with unique character that can all accommodate up to four people. Some have balconies overlooking the street. Returning guests often request the Sunshine Suite, with its warm light and outstanding views. Although the hotel usually requires a minimum stay, you can sometimes arrange daily rates. **Pros:** Good value, homey feel. **Cons:** Few amenities, mismatched furnishings. ✉*151 Clara Lair St., Old San Juan* ☎*787/725–5347* 🌐*www.thecaleta.com* *8 rooms* *In-room: no a/c (some), kitchen. In-hotel: laundry facilities, no-smoking rooms* *AE, MC, V* *EP.*

PUERTA DE TIERRA

$$$–$$$$ **Caribe Hilton San Juan.** Not many hotels can lay claim to their own fort, but Fuerte San Gerónimo, which once guarded the entrance to San Juan Bay, is on the grounds of this sprawling resort. It has a private beach, a luxurious spa, and one of the best-developed kids' programs on the island. (You can take advantage of the free hour of babysitting to have a grown-up meal at Morton's or one of the other on-site restaurants.) Unfortunately, the guest rooms are a little past their prime, and the open-air lobby is crowded, noisy, and free of any charm whatsoever. **Pros:** Family-friendly atmosphere, private beach, lots of dining options. **Cons:** Some views obscured by new construction, disorganized staff, parts of hotel need refreshing. ✉*Calle Los Rosales, Puerta de Tierra* ☎*787/721–0303 or 877/464–4586* 🌐*www.hiltoncaribbean.com* *602 rooms, 44 suites* *In-room: safe, refrigerator, Ethernet.*

In-hotel: 9 restaurants, room service, bar, tennis courts, pool, gym, spa, beachfront, concierge, children's programs (ages 4–12), laundry service, public Wi-Fi, parking (fee), no-smoking rooms ▭*AE, D, DC, MC, V* 🍴*EP.*

$–$$ Fodor'sChoice ★ **Normandie Hotel.** One of the Caribbean's finest examples of Art Deco architecture, this ship-shaped hotel hosted high-society types back in the 1930s. After a stem-to-stern renovation, it's ready to sail again. Egyptian motifs in the grand ballroom and other period details have been meticulously restored. Guest rooms, many of which are as big as suites, are decorated in shades of cream and oatmeal. Business travelers will appreciate the huge desks with ergonomic chairs. Those in search of relaxation need look no further than the sparkling pool or the compact spa with its massage area overlooking the ocean. N Bar, on the second floor, has quickly become a see-and-be-seen place for the city's trendy crowd. As this writing, the Normandie was expected to be rebranded as a W Hotel, but no date had been set for the transition. **Pros:** Gorgeous property, professional staff, chic clientele. **Cons:** Need to walk to beach, not within walking distance to anything else. ✉*499 Av. Muñoz Rivera, Puerta de Tierra* ☎*787/729–2929* 🌐*www.normandiepr.com* *58 rooms, 117 suites* *In-room: safe, refrigerator, Ethernet, Wi-Fi. In-hotel: 2 restaurants, bars, pool, gym, spa, beachfront, laundry service, public Internet, public Wi-Fi, parking (fee), no-smoking rooms* ▭*AE, MC, V* 🍴*EP.*

CONDADO

$$$$ **La Concha—a Renaissance Resort.** A gem of the Tropical Modernism architectural movement, La Concha nevertheless stood empty for more than a decade as travelers headed to newer names. But the resort has been treated to a $181 million renovation and looks even better than it did when it first opened in 1958. The design team consulted with original architect Toro Ferrer to restore many of the original elements, including the round-roofed pool cabanas that give the front facade a distinctive look. The team also incorporated modern features, such as the glassed-in lobby (surrounding a bar serving dozens of kinds of rum) that opens onto a spacious patio with a multilevel swimming pool. The hotel has always been known for its beachfront restaurant set inside a giant clamshell. La Perla, clearly visible as you fly into San Juan, again sits in a shimmering reflecting pool. The sizable, geometric rooms are marvels of intelligent design—for example, a sleek leather sofa pulls out into a full-size bed. **Pros:** Amazing architecture, near the city's best shopping, all rooms face the ocean. **Cons:** Ongoing construction at two nearby properties, casino and some restaurants won't open until 2008. ✉*1077 Av. Ashford, Condado* ☎*787/721–8500* 🌐*www.laconcharesort.com* *232 rooms, 16 suites* *In-room: safe, refrigerator, Ethernet, Wi-Fi. In-hotel: 4 restaurants, room service, bars, pool, beachfront, laundry service, public Wi-Fi, no smoking rooms* ▭*AE, D, DC, MC, V* 🍴*EP.*

$$$–$$$$ **San Juan Marriott Resort & Stellaris Casino.** The shape and color of a cardboard box, this hotel doesn't add much to the skyline of Condado.

Nothing about the hotel hints that it's in the Caribbean. The nondistinctive hanger-like lobby reverberates with the exceptionally loud music of the lounge and the ringing of slot machines in the adjoining casino. It's only in the rooms that there's a bit of flair—tropical fabrics and bright colors lighten the mood considerably—and there's a view of the ocean from most of the balconies. The high points are undoubtedly the pair of pools, which add a bit of whimsy with their gushing fountains and swirling mural. **Pros:** On one of the area's best beaches, near dozens of dining options. **Cons:** Uninspired architecture, lots of conventions, overworked staff. ✉ *1309 Av. Ashford, Condado* ☎ *787/722–7000 or 800/465–5005* 🌐 *www.marriott.com* *512 rooms, 17 suites* *In-room: safe, Ethernet, Wi-Fi. In-hotel: 4 restaurants, room service, bar, tennis courts, pool, gym, beachfront, children's programs (ages 4–12), laundry service, executive floor, public Wi-Fi, parking (fee), no-smoking rooms* *AE, D, DC, MC, V* *EP.*

$$–$$$ **Condado Plaza Hotel & Casino.** This hotel looks ravishing, but its beauty is sometimes only skin deep. Because of a top-to-bottom renovation, it has the look and feel of a boutique hotel. The common areas are crisp and clean, and feature the wave pattern from the hotel's logo on everything from the ultramodern lighting fixtures to the art on the walls. Rooms are eye-popping—the ocean wing is cherry red, the bay wing glimmers in gold—and have such sleek furnishings as low-slung leather sofas near the massive windows. The latest high-tech toys, such as flast-screen TVs, are here, but we had trouble with the temperamental cordless phone and an unreliable Internet connection. Noise was also a problem. At night we could hear doors opening and closing, as well as conversations in adjoining rooms. The casino is a box-like room with gaming tables and slot machines. We're willing to give this place the benefit of the doubt, as renovations weren't quite finished when we visited in late 2007. **Pros:** Lovely interiors, great ocean views from some rooms. **Cons:** Noisy rooms, on a disappointingly small public beach, long walk to center of Condado. ✉ *999 Av. Ashford, Condado* ☎ *787/721–1000* 🌐 *www.condadoplaza.com* *570 rooms, 62 suites* *In-room: safe, refrigerator, VCR, Ethernet, Wi-Fi. In-hotel: 7 restaurants, room service, bars, tennis courts, pools, gym, beachfront, concierge, children's programs (ages 4–12), laundry service, executive floor, airport shuttle, parking (fee), no-smoking rooms* *AE, D, DC, MC, V* *EP.*

$$–$$$ **Radisson Ambassador Plaza Hotel & Casino.** It's not on the ocean, but this resort hotel is only half a block away, which means you could be strolling along the sandy beach in less than five minutes. Even closer is the rooftop pool, with a view over the rooftops of Condado. The casino's energy spills into—if not overwhelms—the narrow lobby. The rest of the hotel has the same frenetic feel. The rooms are a bit old-fashioned, with heavy draperies and fussy furnishings. The second-floor restaurant, La Scala, serves northern Italian cuisine. **Pros:** Dozens of restaurants outside the front door, nice view from many rooms. **Cons:**Chain-hotel feel, old-fashioned room decor, harried staff. ✉ *1369 Av. Ashford, Condado* ☎ *787/721–7300 or 800/333–3333* 🌐 *www.radisson.com* *146 rooms, 87 suites* *In-room: safe, refrigerator, VCR, Ethernet. In-hotel:*

2 restaurants, room service, bars, pool, gym, concierge, laundry facilities, laundry service, parking (fee), no-smoking rooms ▭*AE, D, DC, MC, V* 🍽*EP.*

$–$$ **Coral Princess.** This Art Deco building—one of the few left in Condado—has personality to spare. The ample guest rooms subtly reflect the hotel's heritage with crisp lines and simple furnishings. The hotel is a block from the neighborhood's main drag, so you don't have to fight the crowds every time you walk out the front door. The beach is five minutes away, but you can always take advantage of the swimming pool on the palm-shaded terrace or the hot tub on the rooftop. ✉*1159 Av. Magdalena, Condado* ☎*787/977–7700* 🌐*www.coralpr.com* *25 rooms, 1 apartment* *In-room: kitchen (some), Ethernet. In-hotel: bar, pool, public Wi-Fi* ▭*AE, D, DC, MC, V* 🍽*CP.*

$ **At Wind Chimes Inn.** Hidden behind a whitewashed wall covered with bougainvillea, this Spanish-style villa gives the impression of an exclusive retreat. Much about the place invites you to relax: the patios shaded by royal palms, the terra-cotta-tiled terraces, and the small pool with a built-in whirlpool spa. And the soft, ever-present jingling of wind chimes, reminds you that the beach is a block away. The inn has spacious, tropical guest rooms, and the Boat Bar, open only to guests, serves a light menu from 7 AM to 11 PM. **Pros:** Charming architecture, on the edge of Condado, near shops and restaurants. **Cons:** On a busy street, old-fashioned rooms, distracted staff. ✉*1750 Av. McLeary, Condado* ☎*787/727–4153 or 800/946–3244* 🌐*www.atwindchimesinn.com* *17 rooms, 5 suites* *In-room: kitchen (some), Wi-Fi. In-hotel: bar, pool, no elevator, public Wi-Fi, parking (fee), no-smoking rooms* ▭*AE, D, MC, V* 🍽*EP.*

$ **El Canario by the Sea.** You can't see the ocean from this three-story hotel wedged between blocky condo complexes. Walk out the front door, however, and you can be on the beach in less than a minute. Rooms are comfortable, but they won't win any prizes for decor. Continental breakfast is served on a pretty brick patio. If this location is booked, the company has two more properties in Condado. **Pros:** Near beach, shops, and restaurants, complimentary newspaper with your breakfast. **Cons:** No pool, staff seems disorganized. ✉*4 Av. Condado, Condado* ☎*787/722–8640 or 800/533–2649* 🌐*www.canariohotels.com* *25 rooms* *In-room: safe. In-hotel: no elevator, no-smoking rooms* ▭*AE, DC, MC, V* 🍽*CP.*

$ **Miramar.** This high-rise sits in the middle of Miramar, an up-and-coming neighborhood located halfway between Condado and Old San Juan. It's a good area if you want to be close to the historic district but don't want the hassle of driving through the narrow streets. There's no beach, but some of the city's best are nearby. The generously sized rooms have kitchenettes and many of those on the upper floors have nice views of Condado Bay. **Pros:** Short drive to Old San Juan and Condado, walk to excellent restaurants. **Cons:** Drab decor, not the most interesting neighborhood. ✉*606 Av. Ponce de León, Miramar* ☎*787/977–1000* 🌐*www.miramarhotelpr.com* *50 rooms* *In-room: safe, kitchen, refrigerator, Wi-Fi. In-hotel: restaurant, bar, gym, public Wi-Fi, parking (free)* ▭*AE, MC, V* 🍽*CP.*

¢–$ **Casa del Caribe.** Tucked discreetly off Ashford Avenue, this guesthouse is one of the most affordable hotels in Condado. It's surrounded by a wall, which blocks most of the traffic noise from nearby Avenida Ashford. Rooms decorated with works by local artists are simple, but comfortable. The wraparound verandah, surrounded by an overgrown garden, is the perfect place for a siesta. Monthly rates are available. **Pros:** Near plenty of restaurants, on quiet side street. **Cons:** Staff sometimes surly, common areas are unkempt. ✉ *57 Calle Caribe, Condado* ☎ *787/722–7139* 🌐 *www.casadelcaribe.net* *12 rooms, 1 suite* *In-room: kitchen (some). In-hotel: parking (fee), no-smoking rooms, some pets allowed (fee)* *AE, D, MC, V* *CP.*

¢ **Hotel Olimpo Court.** This hotel has always been a favorite of ours because of the friendly service, reasonable rates, and clean rooms. Imagine our surprise when we found the front door, which had always been a bit hard to open, transformed into two panes of glass that parted automatically. Everything else has been updated, too, from the lobby (now marble) to the rooms (now sleek). But the rates—amazingly enough—are unchanged. The on-site restaurant, Chayote, is one of the city's best and most creative. The hotel is in Miramar, very close to Condado. **Pros:** Comfortable rooms, restaurant is one of the city's best, near convention center. **Cons:** Not much happening in Miramar, unattractive block. ✉ *603 Miramar Av., Miramar* ☎ *787/724–0600* *787/977–0655* *45 rooms* *In-room: kitchen. In-hotel: restaurant, parking (no fee), no-smoking rooms* *AE, MC, V* *EP.*

OCEAN PARK

$–$$ **Hostería del Mar.** This small hotel charms you before you even walk through the door. You'll probably pause, as most people do, to admire the pond filled with iridescent goldfish before continuing into the wood-paneled lobby. The decor might be best described as South Seas meets South Beach, with spacious guest rooms decked out in colorful fabrics and rattan furnishings. Many rooms have views of the beach, which is only a few feet away. Be sure to enjoy the kitchen's creative cuisine, either in the dining room or at a table on the sand. Most of the staff is courteous and helpful. **Pros:** Lovely building, great on-site dining, good value. **Cons:** A long walk to other restaurants, no pool. ✉ *1 Calle Tapia, Ocean Park* ☎ *787/727–3302 or 877/727–3302* 🌐 *www.hosteriadelmarpr.com* *8 rooms, 5 suites* *In-room: kitchen (some). In-hotel: restaurant, bar, beachfront, parking (no fee), no elevator, no-smoking rooms* *AE, D, DC, MC, V* *EP.*

$–$$ ★ **Numero Uno.** Although the name refers to the hotel's address, Numero Uno is how guests rate this small hotel. It's common to hear people trading stories about how often they've returned to this relaxing retreat. Behind a whitewashed wall is a patio where you can catch some rays beside the small pool, enjoy a cocktail at the bar, or dine in the restaurant. (It's so good that it draws locals.) A few steps away, a sandy beach beckons, where you can relax on beach chairs and under umbrellas. Instead of the usual tropical colors, the rooms are decorated in shades of cream and gray, with custom-made furnishings, including sleek writing desks. **Pros:** Friendly atmosphere, great restaurant, good value. **Cons:** A long walk to other restaurants, small pool. ✉ *1 Calle Santa Ana, Ocean Park* ☎ *787/726–5010* 🌐 *www.numero1guesthouse.com* *11 rooms, 2 apartments* *In-room: kitchen (some), refrigerator, Ethernet. In-hotel: restaurant, bar, pool, beachfront, no elevator* ▭ *AE, MC, V* *CP.*

$ ★ **Andalucia.** In a Spanish-style house, this little inn lives up to its name with such details as hand-painted tiles and ceramic pots filled with greenery. A kidney-shaped hot tub in the central courtyard is big enough for you and four or five of your closest friends. The rooms are decorated with bamboo headboards and other tropical touches. Hosts Estaban Haigler and Emeo Cheung give you the warmest welcome imaginable, making you feel that their home is yours. When we last visited, they had added three more rooms, a couple of which are great for single travelers. One of the prettiest beaches in the city is a five-minute walk away. **Pros:** Affordable rates, helpful hosts, gorgeous courtyard. **Cons:** Not right on the beach, some rooms are smaller than others. ✉ *2011 Calle McLeary, Ocean Park* ☎ *787/309–3373* 🌐 *www.andalucia-puertorico.com* *11 rooms* *In-room: kitchen (some), refrigerator, Wi-Fi* ▭ *MC, V. In-hotel: no elevator, public Internet, public Wi-Fi* *EP.*

ISLA VERDE

$$$$ Fodor'sChoice ★ **Ritz-Carlton San Juan Hotel, Spa & Casino.** Elegant marble floors and fountains won't undermine the feeling that this is a true beach getaway. The hotel's sandy stretch is lovely, as is the cruciform pool, which is lined by statues of the chain's signature lion. Works by Latin American artists adorn the lobby lounge and the hallways leading to the well-equipped business center. Rooms have a mix of traditional wooden furnishings and wicker pieces upholstered in soft fabrics. Though most room windows are sealed shut to muffle airport noise, many suites open onto terraces and numerous rooms have balconies. You can pamper yourself at the full-service spa with aloe body wraps and *parcha* (passion-fruit juice) massages. Tastefully so, the lavish casino has a separate entrance from the lobby. **Pros:** Top-notch service, excellent restaurant options, pretty pool area. **Cons:** Bland facade, very expensive for San Juan lodging. ✉ *6961 Av. Los Gobernadores, Isla Verde* ☎ *787/253–1700 or 800/241–3333* 🌐 *www.ritzcarlton.com* *403 rooms, 11 suites* *In-room: refrigerator, Ethernet. In-hotel: 3 restaurants, room service, bars, tennis courts, pool, gym, spa, concierge, children's programs (ages 4–12), laundry service, executive floor, public Wi-Fi, parking (fee), no-smoking rooms* ▭ *AE, D, DC, MC, V* *EP.*

$$–$$$ Fodor'sChoice ★ **El San Juan Hotel & Casino.** For decades this hotel was the don't-miss destination in Isla Verde, and now it's on everyone's list again after a complete renovation in 2007. First, what hasn't changed: the intricately carved mahogany walls and ceiling in the lobby. There are three new bars beneath the coffered ceiling. The Blue Bar is in the center, down a few steps from the lobby, and set below a massive oval-shaped chandelier. You'll find the burnished warmth of Gold Bar on the right and

the shimmering Silver Bar on the left. Just outside is the pool area, furnished with a trio of poolside cabañas with such unbelievable amenities as television and air-conditioning and four-poster beds hung with gauzy curtains—all of which can be reserved in advance. (Some people even opt for breakfast in these beds.) Brava, a two-level nightclub, draws a hip crowd. Rooms are larger than most on the island, and have modern white furnishings with a few colorful accents. All have high-tech conveniences such as CD players and iPod docks. **Pros:** Beautiful pool, great dining options in and near hotel, on a fantastic beach. **Cons:** Casino noise in the lobby, self-parking lot is a long walk from the hotel entrance. ✉*6063 Av. Isla Verde, Isla Verde* ☎*787/791–1000* 🌐*www.elsanjuanhotel.com* *332 rooms, 57 suites* *In-room: safe, refrigerator, VCR, Ethernet, Wi-Fi. In-hotel: 8 restaurants, room service, bars, tennis courts, pools, gym, beachfront, concierge, children's programs (ages 5–17), laundry service, public Wi-Fi, parking (fee), no-smoking rooms* *AE, DC, MC, V* *EP.*

$$$ **Courtyard by Marriott Isla Verde Beach Resort.** This 12-story hotel tries to be all things to all people—and succeeds to a great degree. Harried business executives appreciate its location near the airport and high-tech offerings such as high-speed Internet connections. Families prefer the many dining options and the fact that the city's best beach is just outside. The place is buzzing during the day, especially around the three swimming pools. At night the action centers on the lobby bar, where people often dance to the live salsa music. (If you don't know how, you can take lessons.) **Pros:** On a great beach, family-friendly environment. **Cons:** Noise from lobby, long walk to Condado. ✉*7012 Boca de Cangrejos, Isla Verde* ☎*787/791–0404 or 800/791–2553* 🌐*www.sjcourtyard.com* *260 rooms, 33 suites* *In-room: safe, refrigerator, VCR, Ethernet, Wi-Fi. In-hotel: 3 restaurants, room service, bar, pools, gym, beachfront, laundry facilities, laundry service, public Internet, public Wi-Fi, parking (fee)* *AE, D, DC, MC, V* *BP.*

$$$ **Embassy Suites San Juan Hotel & Casino.** Overshadowing neighbors with more prestigious names, the coral-colored Embassy Suites is one of the prettiest hotels in Isla Verde. The glass elevators that whisk you up to your room overlook the plant-filled atrium that includes a pond and waterfall. Outside is a lagoon-style pool and an adjacent bar. The suites are not luxurious, but they are spacious enough for a family. The location—1 mi from the airport—makes the hotel popular with business travelers. The one drawback is that while the beach is nearby, you have to cross some busy streets to get to it. **Pros:** Family-friendly environment, pretty pool. **Cons:** Not on beach, chain-hotel feel. ✉*8000 Calle Tartak, Isla Verde* ☎*787/791–0505 or 888/791–0505* 🌐*www.embassysuitessanjuan.com* *299 suites* *In-room: safe, refrigerator, dial-up, Wi-Fi. In-hotel: 2 restaurants, room service, bar, pool, gym, laundry facilities, laundry service, public Wi-Fi, parking (fee), no-smoking rooms* *AE, D, DC, MC, V* *BP.*

$$–$$$ **Inter-Continental San Juan Resort & Casino.** Despite its name, this 16-story hotel in the heart of Isla Verde is downright dowdy. The curvy balconies on the facade are old-fashioned, and the low-ceilinged lobby does not invite you to linger. But the spacious rooms have pleasant views of the

ocean or the city; suites overlook the palm-shaded pool area. The jangling casino is just off the lobby, and on-site restaurants include the poolside Restaurant Ciao Mediterráneo, Ruth's Chris Steak House, and the Grand Market Café. **Pros:** Lovely pool, on one of the city's best beaches. **Cons:** Chain-hotel feel, unattractive facade, cramped lobby. ✉*5961 Av. Isla Verde, Isla Verde* ☎*787/791–6100 or 800/443–2009* 🌐*www.ichotelsgroup.com* *380 rooms, 22 suites* *In-room: safe, refrigerator, dial-up. In-hotel: 6 restaurants, room service, bars, pool, gym, spa, beachfront, concierge, laundry facilities, laundry service, no-smoking rooms* *AE, D, MC, V* *EP.*

$$–$$$ ★ **San Juan Water & Beach Club.** Water is everywhere at this boutique hotel, from the droplets that decorate the reception desk to the deluge that runs down the glass walls of the elevators. The soft, blue neon glow in the guest rooms, all of which are decorated in a minimalist style, adds to your under-the-sea experience. Four rooms are equipped with telescopes for stargazing or people-watching along the beach. No matter which room you choose, you'll have a view of the ocean. The lobby's Liquid lounge is a popular stop along the party trail for hipsters. Wet, the rooftop bar, lets you recline on white leather sofas as you take in the view of the skyline. **Pros:** Fun atmosphere, interesting design, great dining and nightlife options. **Cons:** Lack of closet space in rooms, long walk around block to Condado restaurants. ✉*2 Calle Tartak, Isla Verde* ☎*787/728–3666 or 888/265–6699* 🌐*www.waterandbeachclubhotel.com* *84 rooms* *In-room: safe, VCR, Ethernet. In-hotel: restaurant, room service, bars, pool, gym, beachfront, concierge, laundry service, public Wi-Fi, parking (fee), no-smoking rooms* *AE, D, DC, MC, V* *EP.*

$$ **Hampton Inn & San Juan Resort.** If you can live without being directly on the beach, you can get a room here for much less than at many of the resort's competitors across the road. The palm-shaded pool is so pleasant that you might not even make it to the beach. The guest rooms are standard issue, decorated in tropical colors, and count coffeemakers and irons among their amenities. Free coffee and tea are available around the clock in the lobby. The Guacamayo Pool Bar & Grill has a basic menu of hamburgers, fries, and the like. **Pros:** Good value, helpful staff. **Cons:** Long walk to beach, chain-hotel feel. ✉*6530 Av. Isla Verde, Isla Verde* ☎*787/791–8777 or 800/426–7866* 🌐*www.hamptoninn.com* *147 rooms, 54 suites* *In-room: safe, refrigerator, Ethernet. In-hotel: restaurant, bar, pool, gym, laundry facilities, public Wi-Fi, parking (fee), no-smoking rooms* *AE, MC, V* *CP.*

$ **Villa del Sol.** With stucco walls and a barrel-tile roof, this little hotel resembles the manor house of a hacienda. Swaying palm trees line the entrance, which takes you to an interior courtyard. Enjoy the sun from one of the chaise longues surrounding the pool or on the second-story terrace. The cheerful rooms are more spacious than you'd expect in a budget hotel. The only thing you're giving up by staying here is the beachfront, but the ocean is only a block away. **Pros:** Best value in Isla Verde, pretty building, near good dining options. **Cons:** No beach, uninteresting street. ✉*4 Calle Rosa, Isla Verde* ☎*787/791–2600* 🌐*www.villadelsolpr.com* *24 rooms* *In-room: refrigerator, Wi-Fi.*

In-hotel: restaurant, bar, pool, no elevator, public Wi-Fi, parking (no fee) ▭*AE, D, MC, V* 🍽*EP.*

NIGHTLIFE & THE ARTS

Several publications will tell you what's happening in San Juan. *Qué Pasa,* the official visitors' guide, has current listings of events in the city and out on the island. For more up-to-the-minute information, pick up a copy of the English-language *San Juan Star,* the island's oldest daily; the weekend section, which appears each Thursday, is especially useful. *Bienvenidos,* published by the Puerto Rico Hotel & Tourism Association, is also helpful. The English-language *San Juan City Magazine* has extensive calendars, as well as restaurant reviews and cultural articles.

There are also publications for Spanish-speaking visitors, including the "Wikén" section of the Spanish-language newspaper *El Nuevo Dia*; the paper also gives a weekly rundown of events on its Web site: 🌐*www.elnuevodia.com*. *Noctámbulo* is a Spanish-language pocket-size music and nightlife guide aimed at island youth that has extensive listings and is distributed in area clubs, bars, and restaurants.

NIGHTLIFE

From Thursday through Sunday, it's as if there's a celebration going on nearly everywhere in San Juan. Be sure you dress to party, particularly on Friday and Saturday nights; Puerto Ricans have flair, and both men and women love getting dressed up to go out. Bars are usually casual, but if you have on jeans, sneakers, and a T-shirt, you may be refused entry at nightclubs and discos.

Well-dressed visitors and locals alike often mingle in the lobby bars of large hotels, many of which have bands in the evening. Some hotels also have clubs with shows and/or dancing; admission starts at $10. Casino rules have been relaxed, injecting life into what was once a conservative hotel gaming scene, but you still won't be allowed in if you're wearing a tank top or shorts. There are more games as well as such gambling perks as free drinks and live music.

In Old San Juan, Calle San Sebastián is lined with bars and restaurants. Salsa music blaring from jukeboxes in cut-rate pool halls competes with mellow Latin jazz in top-flight night spots. The young and the beautiful often socialize in Plaza San José. Late January sees the Fiestas de la Calle San Sebastián, one of the Caribbean's best street parties.

Young professionals as well as a slightly older bohemian crowd fill Santurce, San Juan's historical downtown area, until the wee hours. The revitalized Plaza del Mercado (Calle Dos Hermanos at Calle Capital) has structures—many painted in bright colors—dating from the 1930s or earlier. On weekend nights the area's streets are closed to vehicular traffic. You can wander around with drinks, which are served in plastic

CLOSE UP

The Piña Colada Wars

This mixture of pineapple juice, coconut cream, and liberal amounts of rum, always garnished with a wedge of pineapple and a maraschino cherry, was invented by Ramón Marrero at the Caribe Hilton in 1954 or by Ramón Portas Mingot at the Barranchina Bar in 1963, depending on whom you believe. Was it Marrero, a young bartender who is said to have spent three months on a concoction that would appeal to patrons at the Beachcomber's Bar? (His secret? Using only fresh pineapple juice.) Or was it Mingot, an elderly bartender who was satisfying the whims of patrons at the bar in Old San Juan? (He said his were so frothy because he froze the pineapple juice and coconut cream mixture instead of simply adding crushed ice.)

The two venues have fought over bragging rights for decades. The Caribe Hilton issues press release after press release reminding people that the drink was born in its seaside bar. (If what its public relations department says is true, the drink celebrated its 50th anniversary in 2004.) The Barranchina Bar put up a plaque that tells passersby that it is the true birthplace of the beverage. The Caribe Hilton seems to have the edge. Coco López, the company that makes the coconut cream most often used in the drink, honored Marrero in 1978. In gratitude for his contributions to the "bartending arts," they presented him with a color television set. But the origins of the piña colada—which means "strained pineapple"—remains as unclear as the cocktail itself. You may have to sample several before you make up your own mind.

–Mark Sullivan

cups, and sway to music that pours from countless open-air establishments and the marketplace's front plaza.

BARS

El Batey. This wildly popular hole-in-the-wall bar won't win any prizes for its decor. Grab a marker to add your own message to the graffiti-covered walls, or add your business card to the hundreds that cover the lighting fixtures. The ceiling may leak, but the jukebox has the best selection of oldies in town. Join locals in a game of pool. ✉ *101 Calle Cristo, Old San Juan* ☎ *787/725–1787.*

Borinquen Brewing Company. Behind glass at the back, sleek metal vats hold this microbrewery's lagers and stouts. The taps sprouting from the wooden bar are a rarity in Puerto Rico, where draft beer is virtually nonexistent. The music is good, and there's often sports on TV. The island art on the walls reaffirms that you're in the Caribbean and not a mainland suburb. ✉ *4800 Av. Isla Verde, Isla Verde* ☎ *787/268–1900* ⏲ *Closed Mon.*

Coaches. This typical sports pub is well outfitted with televisions if your travel plans coincide with that game you just can't miss. Local Ivy League graduates often congregate here to watch big sporting events showcasing their alma maters. The annual Harvard–Yale football game can get ugly. The restaurant-bar also becomes a venue for live rock, Latin pop, and reggae bands at night, especially on weekends. Food offerings include U.S.-style burgers, chicken, steaks, and salads, as well as some Mexican food and local goodies. ✉*137 Av. Roosevelt, Hato Rey* ☎*787/758–3598.*

Karma. Music of all kinds, from *rock en español* to hip-hop to Latin rhythms, is played in this popular, spacious bar-lounge in the heart of Santurce, and there's often a lively crowd. A menu of Spanish and Puerto Rican tapas is available when hunger strikes. ✉*1402 Av. Ponce de León, Santurce* ☎*787/721–5925.*

CAUTION

Dress for the larger casinos in San Juan tends to be on the formal side, and the atmosphere is refined. Tank tops or shorts are usually not acceptable attire.

Liquid. In the lobby of the San Juan Water & Beach Club Hotel, glass walls filled with undulating water surround fashionable patrons seated on stools that seem carved from gigantic, pale seashells. If the wild drinks and pounding music are too much, head upstairs to Wet, a less frenetic and more welcoming space on the penthouse floor, where you can relax at the bar or on a leather banquette. ✉*San Juan Water & Beach Club, 2 Calle Tartak, Isla Verde* ☎*787/725–4664.*

CASINOS

By law, all casinos are in hotels, and the government keeps a close eye on them. They're allowed to operate from noon to 4 AM, but within those parameters individual casinos set their own hours. In addition to slot machines, typical games include blackjack, roulette, craps, Caribbean stud poker (a five-card stud game), and *pai gow* poker (a combination of American poker and the ancient Chinese game of pai gow, which employs cards and dice). That said, an easing of gaming regulations has set a more relaxed tone and made such perks as free drinks and live music more common. The range of available games has also greatly expanded. The minimum age is 18.

Condado Plaza Hotel & Casino. Popular with locals, the casino at the Condado Plaza received a top-to-bottom makeover in 2007. But, it's still one of the least interesting of the city's gaming rooms, worth a visit only if you're staying in the hotel. ✉*999 Av. Ashford, Condado* ☎*787/721–1000.*

Inter-Continental San Juan Resort & Casino. You may feel as if you're in Las Vegas here, perhaps because this property was once a Sands. A torch singer warms up the crowd at a lounge-bar outside the gaming room. Inside, a garish chandelier dripping with strands of orange lights runs the length of a mirrored ceiling. ✉*5961 Av. Isla Verde, Isla Verde* ☎*787/791–6100.*

Ritz-Carlton San Juan Hotel, Spa & Casino. With its golden columns, turquoise and bronze walls, and muted lighting, the Ritz casino is refined by day or night. There's lots of activity, yet everything is hushed. ✉*Av. Las Gobernadores, Isla Verde* ☎*787/253–1700.*

El San Juan Hotel & Casino. Slow-turning ceiling fans hang from a carved-wood ceiling, and neither the clangs of the slots nor the sounds of the salsa band disrupt the semblance of old world. The polish continues in the adjacent lobby, with its huge chandeliers and mahogany paneling.

✉6063 Av. Isla Verde, Isla Verde ☎787/791–1000.

San Juan Marriott Resort & Stellaris Casino. The crowd is casual, and the decor is tropical and bubbly at this spacious gaming room. A huge bar, where Latin musicians usually perform, and an adjacent café are right outside. *✉1309 Av. Ashford, Condado ☎787/722–7000.*

Sheraton Old San Juan Hotel & Casino. It's impossible to ignore this ground-floor casino, the only place to gamble in Old San Juan. You can see the gaming room—expanded in 2007—from the hotel's main stairway, the balcony above, and the lobby. Light bounces off the Bahía de San Juan and pours through its many windows; passengers bound off their cruise ships and pour through its many glass doors. *✉101 Calle Brumbaugh, Old San Juan ☎787/721–5100.*

RAGGAETÓN

If you go out to San Juan's popular dance clubs, you're likely to hear this hip-hop–influenced mix of Jamaican reggae and dancehall styles along with some Latin rhythms. The music has a strong electronic drum-machine beat, and the lyrics are in Spanish. Many believe the music got its start in Puerto Rico, but its popularity has spread much further.

DANCE CLUBS

Brava. A long line of young people can be spotted at the door of this chic club at the El San Juan Hotel & Casino. The two-level club, each with its own DJ and dance floor, is one of the best places for dancing. There's a different theme party Thursday to Saturday. *✉6063 Av. Isla Verde, Isla Verde ☎787/641–3500.*

Candela. This lounge–art gallery housed in an historic building hosts some of the most innovative local DJs on the island and often invites star spinners from New York or London. This is the island's top showcase for experimental dance music. The festive, late-night haunt is open Tuesday through Saturday from 8 PM onward, and the conversation can be as stimulating as the dance floor. *✉110 San Sebastián, Old San Juan ☎787/977–4305.*

Club Lazer. This multilevel club has spots for quiet conversation, spaces for dancing to loud music, and a landscaped roof deck overlooking San Juan. The crowd changes every night; Saturday is ladies' night. *✉251 Calle Cruz, Old San Juan ☎787/725–7581.*

The Noise. A young crowd frequents this Old San Juan dance club to listen to hip-hop, reggae, and underground music. Long lines often spill out the door Thursday through Saturday nights. *✉203 Calle Tacna, Old San Juan ☎787/724–3426.*

Teatro Puerto Rico. This cavernous club with an upstairs lounge hosts DJs spinning trance-like rhythms. Live music and other performances also often take place. A popular local drag queen performs Sunday nights. It's closed on Monday and Tuesday. *✉1420 Av. Ponce de León, Santurce ☎787/723–3416.*

GAY & LESBIAN BARS & CLUBS

With its sophisticated nightlife, San Juan has become a popular destination for gay and lesbian tourists. The Condado, perhaps the heart of gay San Juan, is a favorite destination for happy hour. It hosts an annual gay-pride march each June, full of music and dancing, that rivals those in similar cities around the world. Santurce, just south of Condado, is packed with bars and clubs that cater to men and women of all ages. Most are located on or near Avenida Ponce de León.

Puerto Rico Breeze (🌐*www.puertoricobreeze.com*) is a monthly newspaper covering Puerto Rico's gay and lesbian community. It's chock full of listings, articles, and advertisements on dining options, entertainment, and lodging alternatives.

Atlantic Beach. The oceanfront-deck bar of this hotel is famed in the gay community for its early-evening happy hours. But the pulsating tropical music, exotic drinks, and ever-pleasant ocean breeze make it a hit regardless of sexual orientation. Good food is also served on deck. ✉*1 Calle Vendig, Condado* ☎*787/721–6100.*

Cups. This women-oriented bar in the middle of Santurce has been a mainstay of San Juan's nightlife since 1980. Karaoke on Thursday night is especially popular. It's open Wednesday to Saturday. ✉*1708 Calle San Mateo, Santurce* ☎*787/268–3570.*

Eros. A balcony bar overlooks all the drama on the dance floor at this popular club. Most of the time DJs spin music ranging from house and hip-hop to salsa and reggaetón, but occasionally disco nights send you back to the music of the 1970s and '80s. It's open Wednesday to Sunday. ✉*1257 Av. Ponce de León, Santurce* ☎*787/722–1131.*

Junior's. Open every evening, this neighborhood bar attracts nearly equal numbers of men and women. The jukebox plays a constant stream of salsa, which often draws crowds to the dance floor. It has some of the cheapest drinks in town. ✉*613 Calle Condado, Santurce* ☎*787/723–9477.*

Starz. Dancing at this cavernous club starts at 10 PM on Friday and Saturday nights, but most people don't arrive until after midnight. There's also a popular after-the-beach party on Sunday evening. ✉*365 Av. de Diego, at Av. Ponce de León, Santurce* ☎*787/721–8645.*

LATIN MUSIC

Hijos de Borinquen. Famed artist Rafael Tufiño, who stops in once in a while and has a stool with his name on it, immortalized this beloved bar in one of his paintings. The audience often sings along with the Puerto Rican ballads; some even play maracas, cowbells, or bongos. The pitch is fevered during Andrés Jiménez's revolutionary anthem "Despierta Borinquen." It's closed Monday. ✉*151 Calle San José, at Calle San Sebastián, Old San Juan* ☎*787/723–8126.*

★ **Nuyorican Café.** There's something interesting happening at this hipper-than-hip performance space nearly every night, be it an early evening play, poetry reading, or talent show or later on a band playing Latin jazz, Cuban son, or Puerto Rican salsa. During breaks between performances the youthful, creative set converses in an alley outside the front door. It's usually closed on Monday. ✉ *312 Calle San Fransico (entrance on Callejón de la Capellia), Old San Juan* ☎ *787/977–1276.*

Rumba. The air-conditioning blasts, the music thumps, and the crowd pretends not to notice how hip the place has become. With a large dance and stage area and smokin' Afro-Cuban bands, it's one of the best parties in town. ✉ *152 Calle San Sebastián, Old San Juan* ☎ *787/725–4407.*

NIGHT BITES

San Juan is a cosmopolitan city by Caribbean standards, welcoming to all kinds of visitors, with plenty of late-night places. The establishments listed here are generally open until at least midnight during the week and 2 AM on weekends. But many are open much later. Old San Juan's Brick House, for example, proudly proclaims that its kitchen doesn't close until 3 AM.

Brick House Bar & Grill. This friendly bar and sidewalk café on Old San Juan's bustling Plaza Somohano is adjacent to the Teatro Tapia. You can get tasty burgers until 3 AM, as well as plenty of good conversation. If you eat elsewhere, you might run into your server here, after his or her shift ends. ✉ *359 Calle Tetuán, Old San Juan* ☎ *787/724–3359.*

Buren. Across the street from Hotel El Convento, this funky, tropical-color bistro with a charming interior patio serves good pizza and pasta, as well as Caribbean- and Mediterranean-inspired dishes. The house wines by the glass are all good, and there's often live jazz or flamenco music. ✉ *103 Calle Cristo, Old San Juan* ☎ *787/977–5023.*

Hard Rock Café. Are you really surprised to find that there's a Hard Rock in Old San Juan? These days, they're almost as common as McDonald's. This one, however, attracts a surprising number of locals. ✉ *253 Recinto Sur, Old San Juan* ☎ *787/724–7625.*

Makarios. Italy meets the Middle East, brick-oven pizza meets hummus, and crostinis meet falafel on a big outdoor-seating area that spills onto a plaza. The first indoor level is a sleek, modern bar with Western music and a small dining area that serves pizza and snacks. Upstairs is more serious Middle Eastern cuisine, hypnotic rhythms, and a skillful belly dancer. ✉ *356 Calle Tetuán, Old San Juan* ☎ *787/723–8653.*

El Patio de Sam. The clientele swears that this Old San Juan institution serves the island's best burgers. Potted plants and strategically placed canopies make the outdoor patio a fine place to eat in any weather. ✉ *102 Calle San Sebastián, Old San Juan* ☎ *787/723–1149.*

Señor Frog's. Latin America's answer to the Hard Rock Café, Señor Frog's attracts the cruise-ship crowd. The menu is a nod to Mexico, with south-of-the-border favorites like nachos and quesadillas. ✉ *Paseo Portuario, Old San Juan* ☎ *787/977–4142.*

THE ARTS

San Juan is the epicenter of Puerto Rico's lively arts scene, and on most nights there's usually a ballet, a play, or an art opening somewhere in town. If you're in town on the first Tuesday of the month, take advantage of Old San Juan's **Noches de Galerias** (☎ *787/723–6286*). Galleries and select museums open their doors after hours for viewings that are accompanied by refreshments and music. Afterward, people head to bars and music clubs, and the area remains festive until well past midnight. The event is so popular that finding a parking space is difficult; it's best to take a cab.

ISLAND CULTURE

The year-round festival called **LeLoLai** (☎*787/721–2400)* celebrates Puerto Rico's Indian, Spanish, and African heritage. Performances showcasing island music and folklore take place each week in different hotels around the island. It's sponsored by the Puerto Rico Tourism Company.

PERFORMING ARTS

San Juan is arguably one of the most important cultural centers of the Caribbean, both for its home-grown culture and the healthy influx of visiting artists that the local population supports. The city hosts the Puerto Rico Symphony Orchestra, the world-renowned Pablo Casals classical-music festival in winter, and an annual series of opera concerts. Many hit plays in New York and other large markets get produced locally, and there are often three or four other local theatrical productions taking place on any given weekend, many of them downright adventurous.

MAJOR EVENTS

The Casals Festival (☎*787/723–9185* 🌐*www.festcasalspr.gobierno.pr*) has been bringing some of the most important figures in classical music to San Juan ever since Pablo Casals, the famous cellist, conductor, and composer, started the festival in 1957. Casals went on to direct it until his death in 1973. It has continued to serve as a vibrant stage for top-notch classical performers since then. Most of the shows take place at the Centro de Bellas Artes Luis A. Ferré, but performances are also at the University of Puerto Rico and other venues. The festival takes place from mid-February through mid-March. Tickets are available at the box office of the Centro de Bellas Artes Luis A Ferré.

San Juan is a great place to hear jazz, particularly Latin jazz, and the annual **Puerto Rico Heineken Jazzfest** (☎*866/994–0001* 🌐*www.prheinekenjazz.com*), which takes place in June, is one of the best opportunities for it. Each year's festival is dedicated to a particular musician. Honorees have included Chick Corea, Mongo Santamaria, and Tito Puente. Although the festival was born at the Tito Puente Amphiteatro, it has since moved to the Puerta de Tierra oceanside park and sports facility right outside Old San Juan. With the Atlantic surf crashing outside the park and the stars overhead, it's a stimulating atmosphere in which to soak up fine jazz music.

TICKETS

Two major outlets sell tickets for events throughout Puerto Rico. **Ticket Center** (✉*Plaza Las Américas, 525 Av. Franklin Delano Roosevelt, Hato Rey* ☎*787/792–5000* 🌐*www.ticketcenterpr.com*) can get you seats to most large-scale events. **Ticketpop** (✉*Banco Popular, 1500 Av. Ponce de León, Santurce* ☎*787/294–0001* 🌐*www.ticketpop.com*) also sells tickets to popular events.

Anfiteatro Tito Puente *(Tito Puente Amphitheater)*. Surrounded by lagoons and trees, the open-air theater is a great spot to hear hot Latin jazz, reggae, and Spanish pop music. It's named after the late, great musician who is widely credited with bringing salsa to the rest of the world. Shows usually take place Thursday through Sunday nights. ✉*Parque Luis Muñoz Marín, Hato Rey* ☎*787/751–3353*.

Centro de Bellas Artes Luis A. Ferré *(Luis A. Ferré Center for the Performing Arts)*. With three different theaters holding up to 1,800 people, this is the largest venue of its kind in the Caribbean. There's something going on nearly every night, from pop or jazz concerts to plays, operas, and ballets. It's also the home of the San Juan Symphony Orchestra. ✉*Av. José de Diego and Av. Ponce de León, Santurce* ☎*787/725–7334*.

UNCONVENTIONAL DESIGN

Undulating waves of glass and steel form the facade of the Puerto Rico Convention Center, a futuristic meeting place that opened in San Juan in 2006. Locals tout the statistics, such as the fact that the facility's 580,000 square feet make it the largest meeting space in the Caribbean. But it's the eye-catching design—the architects call it "techno-tropic"—that has drawn raves. Located on what was once a naval base in the aptly christened "Convention District," it is convenient to Miramar, Condado, and Old San Juan.

Coliseo Roberto Clemente. The arena has become an important island venue for concerts in addition to its status as a sports facility. Rap, reggae, salsa, jazz, and pop musicians all play this venue, which holds 10,000 people. Recent concerts have included Ricky Martin and the Rolling Stones. ✉*Av. Roosevelt at Plaza las Américas, Hato Rey* ☎*787/754–7422*.

Estadio Hiram Bithorn *(Hiram Bithorn Stadium)*. Particularly big acts often use this outdoor stadium adjacent to the Roberto Clemente Coliseum, which hosts baseball games and large concerts. There's seating capacity for at least 18,000, more when the infield is used for fans. ✉*Av. Roosevelt at Plaza las Américas, Hato Rey* ☎*787/765–5000*.

Teatro Tapia. Named for Puerto Rican playwright Alejandro Tapia, the theater hosts traveling and locally produced theatrical and musical productions. Matinee performances with family entertainment are also held here, especially around the holidays. ✉*Plaza Colón, Old San Juan* ☎*787/721–0169*.

GROUPS **Orquesta Sinfónica de Puerto Rico** *(Puerto Rico Symphony Orchestra)*. The island's orchestra is one of the most prominent in the Americas. Its 76 members perform a full 48-week season that includes classical-music concerts, operas, ballets, and popular-music performances. The orchestra plays most shows at Centro de Bellas Artes Luis A. Ferré, but it also gives outdoor concerts at museums and university campuses around the island, and has an educational outreach program in island schools. Pablo Casals, the impetus for this group, helped create it in 1956. ☎*787/721–7727* 🌐*www.sinfonicapr.gobierno.pr.*

SPORTS & THE OUTDOORS

Many of San Juan's most enjoyable outdoor activities take place in and around the water. With miles of beach stretching across Isla Verde, Ocean Park, and Condado, there's a full range of water sports, including sailing, kayaking, windsurfing, kiteboarding, Jet Skiing, deep-sea fishing, scuba diving, and snorkeling.

Land-based activities include tennis and walking or jogging at local parks. With a bit of effort—meaning a short drive out of the city—you'll discover a world of championship golf courses and rain-forest trails. Baseball is big in Puerto Rico, and the players are world-class; many are recruited from local teams to play in the U.S. major leagues. The season runs from October through February. Games are played in San Juan venues, as well as others around the island.

BEACHES

The city's beaches can get crowded, especially on weekends. There's free access to all of them, but parking can be an issue in the peak sun hours—arriving early or in the late afternoon is a safer bet.

★ **Balneario de Carolina.** When people talk of a "beautiful Isla Verde beach," this is the one they're talking about. A government-maintained beach, this balneario east of Isla Verde is so close to the airport that the leaves rustle when planes take off. The long stretch of sand, which runs parallel to Avenida Los Gobernadores, is shaded by palms and almond trees. There's plenty of room to spread out and lots of amenities: lifeguards, restrooms, changing facilities, picnic tables, and barbecue grills. ✉*Carolina* 🎫*Parking $2* ⏲*Daily 8–6.*

★ **Balneario de Escambrón.** In Puerta de Tierra, this government-run beach is just off Avenida Muñoz Rivera. The patch of honey-colored sand is shaded by coconut palms and has surf that's generally gentle. Favored by families, it has lifeguards, bathhouses, bathrooms, and restaurants. ✉*Puerta de Tierra* 🎫*Parking $3* ⏲*Daily 7–7.*

Playa de Ocean Park. The residential neighborhood east of Condado and west of Isla Verde is home to this 1-mi-long (1½-km-long) stretch of golden sand. The waters are often choppy but still swimmable—take care, however, as there are no lifeguards on duty. Windsurfers say the conditions here are nearly perfect. The beach is popular with young people, particularly on weekends, as well as gay men. Parking is a bit difficult, as many of the streets are gated and restricted to residents. ✉*Ocean Park* ⏲*Daily dawn to dusk.*

Playa del Condado. East of Old San Juan and west of Ocean Park, this long, wide beach is overshadowed by an unbroken string of hotels and apartment buildings. Beach bars, water-sports outfitters, and chair-rental places abound. You can access the beach from several roads off Avenida Ashford, including Calle Cervantes and Calle Candina. The

CLOSE UP

Waving a Blue Flag

With 365 different beaches in Puerto Rico, choosing where to spread out your towel might seem like a daunting task. The decision is easier now that four have been designated with a Blue Flag. Chosen by the Foundation for Environmental Education, a non-profit agency, Blue Flag beaches have to meet 27 criteria, focusing on water quality, the presence of a trained staff, and the availability of facilities such as water fountains and restrooms.

It's no wonder that Playa Flamenco, on the island of Culebra, made the cut. After all, it's rated one of the world's best beaches. More surprisingly, two of the beaches are in San Juan: Balneario Escambrón, in Puerta de Tierra, and Balneario Carolina, in Isla Verde. The fourth is Luquillo's Balneario Monserrate. This means that three of Puerto Rico's finest beaches are within an hour's drive of the capital.

–Mark Sullivan

protected water at the small stretch of beach west of the Condado Plaza hotel is particularly calm and popular with families; surf elsewhere in Condado can be a bit strong. The stretch of sand near Calle Vendig (behind the Atlantic Beach Hotel) is especially popular with the gay community. If you're driving, on-street parking is your only option. ✉*Condado* ⏲*Daily dawn to dusk*.

BASEBALL

Does the name Roberto Clemente ring a bell? The late, great star of the Pittsburgh Pirates, who died in a 1972 plane crash delivering supplies to Nicaraguan earthquake victims, was born near San Juan and got his start in the Puerto Rican pro leagues. Many other Puerto Rican stars have played in the U.S. major leagues, including the brothers Roberto Alomar and Sandy Alomar Jr.; their father, Sandy Alomar; and Hall of Fame inductees Tony Perez and Orlando Cepeda. Baseball games in the San Juan area are played at **Estadio Hiram Bithorn** (✉*Hato Rey* ☎*787/725–2110*), named for the first Puerto Rican to play in the major leagues. It's home to the Cangrejeros de Santurce, which means the Santurce Crabbers. (No, that last part was not a joke.)

BIKING

Most streets don't have bike lanes, and auto traffic makes bike travel somewhat risky; further, all the fumes can be hard to take. That said, recreational bikers are increasingly donning their safety gear and wheeling through the streets, albeit with great care.

As a visitor, your best bet is to look into a bike tour offered by an outfitter. One popular 45-minute trip travels from Old San Juan's cobblestone streets to Condado. It passes El Capitolio and runs through either Parque del Tercer Milenio (ocean side) or Parque Luis Muñoz Rivera, taking you past the Caribe Hilton Hotel and over Puente Dos Hermanos (Dos Hermanos Bridge) onto Avenida Ashford. The truly ambitious can continue east to Ocean Park, Isla Verde, and right on out of town to the eastern community of Piñones and its beachside bike path.

At **Hot Dog Cycling** (✉*5916 Av. Isla Verde, Isla Verde* ☎*787/791–0776* 🌐*www.hotdogcycling.com*), Raul del Río and his son Omar rent mountain bikes for $30 a day. They also organize group excursions to El Yunque and other places out on the island.

DIVING & SNORKELING

The waters off San Juan aren't the best places to scuba dive, but several outfitters conduct short excursions to where tropical fish, coral, and sea horses are visible at depths of 30 to 60 feet. Escorted half-day dives range from $45 to $95 for one or two tanks, including all equipment; in general, double those prices for night dives. Packages that include lunch and other extras start at $100; those that include accommodations are also available.

Snorkeling excursions, which include transportation, equipment rental, and sometimes lunch, start at $50. Equipment rents at beaches for about $10. Avoid unsupervised areas, as rough waters and strong undertows make some places dangerous.

Eco Action Tours (☎*787/791–7509* 🌐*www.ecoactiontours.com*) offers diving trips for all skill levels. **Ocean Sports** (✉*1035 Av. Ashford, Condado* ☎*787/723–8513* ✉*77 Av. Isla Verde, Condado* ☎*787/268–2329* 🌐*www.osdivers.com*) offers certified scuba dives; airtank fill-ups; and equipment repairs, sales, and rentals. It also rents surfboards by the day.

FISHING

Puerto Rico's waters are home to large game fish such as snook, wahoo, dorado, tuna, and barracuda; as many as 30 world records for catches have been set off the island's shores. Prices for fishing expeditions vary, but they tend to include all your bait and tackle, as well as refreshments, and start at $500 (for a boat with as many as six people) for a half-day trip to $1,000 for a full day. Other boats charge by the person, starting at $150 for a full day.

Half-day and full-day excursions can be arranged through **Mike Benítez Sport Fishing** (✉*Club Náutico de San Juan, Miramar* ☎*787/723–2292* 🌐*www.mikebenitezfishingpr.com*). From the 45-foot *Sea Born* you can fish for sailfish, white marlin, and blue marlin.

GOLF

Puerto Rico is the birthplace of golf legend and raconteur Chi Chi Rodriguez—and he had to hone his craft somewhere. The island has more than a dozen courses, including some of championship caliber. Several make good day trips from San Juan. Be sure to call ahead for details on reserving tee times; hours vary and several hotel courses allow only guests to play or give preference to them. Greens fees start at $25 and go as high as $190.

Three golf clubs are within fairly easy striking distance of San Juan. The four 18-hole golf courses at the **Hyatt Hacienda del Mar** are just west of San Juan. *For more information, see Golf under Dorado in Chapter 5, Rincón & the Porta del Sol.*

> **A GOLF GREAT**
>
> Juan "Chi Chi" Rodriguez, who was born in Río Piedras, was the first Puerto Rican golfer to be inducted into the World Golf Hall of Fame.

There are more options to the east of the city. **Palmas del Mar Country Club** has two good golf courses. *For more information see Golf under Humacao in Chapter 2, El Yunque & the Northeast.* The spectacular **Rio Mar Beach Resort & Spa** has a clubhouse with a pro shop and two restaurants set between two 18-hole courses. *For more information see Golf under Río Grande in Chapter 2, El Yunque & the Northeast.*

HIKING

El Yunque, the Caribbean National Forest, is within easy striking distance of San Juan, about an hour's drive east. The park, which is officially known as the Bosque Nacional del Caribe, has more than a dozen hiking trails.

Eco Action Tours (☎*787/791–7509* 🌐*www.ecoactiontours.com*) organizes a variety of hikes and excursions throughout the island, including in El Yunque.

HORSE RACING

Try your luck with the exactas and quinielas at **Hípodromo El Comandante** (✉*Rte. 3, Km 15.3, Canóvanas* ☎*787/641–6060* 🌐*www. elcomandantepr.net*), a large thoroughbred racetrack about 20 minutes east of San Juan. On race days the dining rooms open at 12:30 PM. Post time is at 2:30 on Wednesday and Friday through Monday. There's an air-conditioned clubhouse and restaurant, as well as a bar where people dance to live rumba music on Friday after the last race. Parking and admission to the grandstand are free; clubhouse admission is $3.

KAYAKING

The Laguna del Condado is popular for kayaking, especially on weekends. You can simply paddle around it or head out under the Puente Dos Hermanos to the San Gerónimo fort right behind the Caribe Hilton and across from the Wyndham Condado Plaza. Kayaks rent for $25 to $35 an hour.

Las Tortugas Adventures (✉*Cond. La Puntilla, 4 Calle La Puntilla, Old San Juan* ☎*787/725–5169* 🌐*www.kayak-pr.com*) organizes group-kayaking trips to the Reserva Natural Las Cabezas de San Juan and the Bahía Mosquito in eastern Puerto Rico.

SPAS

Eden Spa. The treatments at this small spa sound good enough to eat—fresh fruit and sugar body wraps, for example, or the lemongrass and mint pedicure. Many of the therapies use botanicals found on the island, which explains why the scents of passion fruit and pineapple mingle in the air. The seven-room facility is across from the cruise-ship port, so cruise-ship passengers drop by for pampering. The spa is closed Sunday. ☒*331 Calle Recinto Sur, Old San Juan* ☎*787/721–6400*.

SURFING

★ Although the west-coast beaches around Isabela and Rincón are considered *the* places to surf in Puerto Rico, San Juan was actually the place where the sport got its start on the island. In 1958 legendary surfers Gary Hoyt and José Rodríguez Reyes began surfing at the beach in front of Bus Stop 2½, facing El Capitolio. Although this spot is known for its big waves, the conditions must be nearly perfect to surf here. Today many surfers head to Puerta de Tierra and a spot known as La Ocho (in front of Bus Stop 8 behind the Dumas Restaurant). Another, called the Pressure Point, is behind the Caribe Hilton Hotel.

In Condado you can surf La Punta, a reef break behind the Presbyterian Hospital, with either surfboards or boogie boards. In Isla Verde, white water on the horizon means that the waves are good at Pine Grove, the beach break near the Ritz-Carlton. East of the city, in Piñones, the Caballo has deep-to-shallow-water shelf waves that require a big-wave board known as a "gun." The surf culture frowns upon aficionados who divulge the best spots to outsiders. If you're lucky, though, maybe you'll make a few friends who'll let you in on where to find the best waves.

At Ocean Park beach, famous surfer Carlos Cabrero, proprietor of **Tres Palmas Surf Shop** (☒*1911 Av. McLeary, Ocean Park* ☎*787/728–3377*), rents boards (daily rates are $25 for boogie, $30 short boards, $35 for foam boards, and $40 for long boards), repairs equipment, and sells all sorts of hip beach and surfing gear.

TENNIS

If you'd like to use the tennis courts at a property where you aren't a guest, call in advance for information about reservations and fees. The four lighted courts of the **Club Tennis de Isla Verde** (☒*Calles Ema and Delta Rodriguez, Isla Verde* ☎*787/727–6490*) are open for nonmember use at $4 per hour, daily from 8 AM to 10 PM. The **Parque Central Municipio de San Juan** (☒*Calle Cerra, exit on Rte. 2, Santurce* ☎*787/722–1646*) has 17 lighted courts. Fees are $3 per hour from 8 AM to 6 PM and $4 per hour from 6 PM to 10 PM.

WINDSURFING & KITESURFING

★ The waves can be strong and the surf choppy, but the constant wind makes for good sailing, windsurfing, or kiteboarding (maneuvering a surfboard using a parachutelike kite), particularly in Ocean Park and Punta Las Marías (between Ocean Park and Isla Verde). In general, you can rent a Windsurfer for about $25 an hour (including a lesson).

You'll get the best windsurfing advice and equipment from Jaime Torres at **Velauno** (✉*2430 Calle Loíza, Punta Las Marías* ☎*787/728–8716* 🌐*www.velauno.com*), the second-largest full-service windsurfing center in any U.S. territory. It has rentals, repair services, and classes. It also sells new and used gear and serves as a clearinghouse for information on windsurfing events throughout the island.

SHOPPING

In Old San Juan, Calle Fortaleza and Calle San Francisco have everything from T-shirt emporiums to jewelry stores to shops that specialize in made-to-order Panama hats. Running perpendicular to those streets is Calle Cristo, lined with factory-outlet stores, including Coach, Gant, Guess, and Ralph Lauren. On weekends, artisans sell their wares at stalls around the Paseo de la Princesa.

With many stores selling luxury items and designer fashions, the shopping spirit in Condado is reminiscent of that in Miami. Avenida Ashford is considered the heart of San Juan's fashion district. High-end chain stores such as Chanel, Ferragamo, and Gucci are huddled together in what was formerly a derelict shopping strip. They are betting that the newly opened, luxury hotel La Concha will attract people ready to plunk down their platinum credit cards. A little farther west along Avenida Ashford are the one-of-a-kind clothing retailers that make this a not-to-be-missed neighborhood.

Thanks to Puerto Rico's vibrant art scene, numerous galleries and studios are opening, and many are doing so in Santurce and other neighborhoods outside the old city walls. If you prefer shopping in air-conditioned comfort, there are plenty of malls in and just outside San Juan.

MARKETS & MALLS

Look for vendors selling crafts from around the island at the **Artesanía Puertorriqueña** (✉*Plaza de la Dársena, Old San Juan* ☎*787/722–1709*). It's convenient for cruise-ship passengers, as it's across from Pier 1. Several vendors also sell handbags, hats, and other items along nearby Calle San Justo.

About 10 minutes east of San Juan you'll find **Plaza Carolina** (✉*Av. Fragosa, Carolina* ☎*787/768–0514*). Get there via Route 26. **Plaza del Sol** (✉*725 West Main Av., Bayamón* ☎*787/778–8724*) includes Old Navy and Banana Republic. It's about 30 minutes west of San

Juan. For a complete shopping experience, head to **Plaza Las Américas** (⊠*525 Av. Franklin Delano Roosevelt, Hato Rey* ☎*787/767–5202*), which has 200 shops, including the world's largest JCPenney store, the Gap, Sears Roebuck, Macy's, Godiva, and Armani Exchange, as well as restaurants and movie theaters. Off Avenida John F. Kennedy, about 15 minutes south of San Juan, **Plaza San Patricio** (⊠*Av. San Patricio at Av. Franklin Delano Roosevelt, Guaynabo* ☎*787/792–1255*) has a Boston Shoe and a Footaction USA, as well as restaurants and movie theaters.

FACTORY OUTLETS

With no sales tax, Old San Juan has turned into an open-air duty-free shop for people pouring off the cruise ships. Because they have only a few hours in port, they often pass by more interesting shops and head directly for the factory outlets on and around Calle Cristo. The prices aren't particularly good, but nobody seems to mind. Designer bags can be had at **Coach** (⊠*158 Calle Cristo* ☎*787/722–6830*). Taking up ★ several storefronts, **Ralph Lauren** (⊠*Calle Cristo and Calle Fortaleza* ☎*787/722–2136*) has perhaps the best deals around. Stop here toward the end of your trip, as there are plenty of items such as pea coats and scarves that you won't be wearing until you get home.

There's clothing for men and women at **Tommy Hilfiger** (⊠*206 Calle Cristo* ☎*787/729–2230*). The staff is eager to please.

It's not in Old San Juan, but **Belz Factory Outlet World** (⊠*Rte. 3, Km 18.4* ☎*787/256–7040*) has more than 75 factory outlet stores, including Nike, Guess, Mikasa, Gap, Levi's, and Liz Claiborne. It's in Canóvanas, about 20 minutes east of San Juan.

SPECIALTY SHOPS

ART

★ The very influencial **Galería Botello** (⊠*208 Calle Cristo, Old San Juan* ☎*787/723–9987*) displays the works of the late Angel Botelli, who was hailed as the "Caribbean Gauguin" as far back as 1943. His work, which often uses the bright colors of the tropics, usually depicts island scenes. His paintings hang in the Museo de Arte de Puerto Rico. There are works on display here by other prominent local artists as well.

★ Among those who have displayed their works at **Galería Petrus** (⊠*726 Calle Hoare, Miramar* ☎*787/289–0505* 🌐*www.petrusgallery.com*) are Dafne Elvira, whose surreal oils and acrylics tease and seduce (witness a woman emerging from a banana peel); Marta Pérez, another surrealist, whose bewitching paintings examine such themes as how life on a coffee plantation might have been; and Elizam Escobar, a former political prisoner whose oil paintings convey the horrors human beings must endure. Petrus also sells the architectonic designs of Imel Sierra (who created the sculpture *Paloma* in Condado), which combine wood and metal elements.

★ Half a block from the Museo de Arte de Puerto Rico, **Galería Raíces** (✉ *314 Av. José de Diego, Santurce* ☎ *787/723–8909*) is dedicated to showing work by such emerging Puerto Rican artists as Nayda Collazo Llorens, whose cerebral and sensitive multimedia installations examine connections and patterns in games, codes, and human memory. Raíces also displays the work of sculptors Annex Burgos and Julio Suárez. **Galería San Juan** (✉ *204–206 Calle Norzagaray, Old San Juan* ☎ *787/722–1808*) shows sensuous sculptures of faces and bodies by artist Jan D'Esopo. The gallery—a part of the guesthouse she runs—is a work of art in itself. It is a bit hard to find, so look for the busts over the front door.

ART FOR ART'S SAKE

Many galleries stay open during Old San Juan's Noches de Galerías, held from 6 to 9 on the first Tuesday of the month, September to December and February to May.

Galería Tamara (✉ *210 Av. Chardón, Suite 104-A, Hato Rey* ☎ *787/764–6465*) has abstract oil studies by Wilfredo Chiesa and oil paintings of placid home scenes by Carmelo Sobrino. **Galería Viota** (✉ *739 Av. San Patricio, Las Lomas* ☎ *787/782–1752*) features paintings and silkscreens by master Augusto Marín and large-format abstract expressionist works by Paris-based Ricardo Ramírez.

CIGARS

The **Cigar House** (✉ *255 Calle Fortaleza, Old San Juan* ☎ *787/723–5223*) has a small, eclectic selection of local and imported cigars.

CLOTHING

MEN'S CLOTHING

Aficionados of the famous Panama hat, made from delicately handwoven straw, should stop at **Olé** (✉ *105 Calle Fortaleza, Old San Juan* ☎ *787/724–2445*). The shop sells top-of-the-line hats for as much as $1,000. **Lord Jim** (✉ *250 Calle San Francisco, Old San Juan* ☎ *787/722–3589*) has a fantastic selection of leather goods, including shoes you won't find anywhere else.

After many years of catering to a primarily local clientele, **Clubman** (✉ *1351 Av. Ashford, Condado* ☎ *787/722–1867*) is still the classic choice for gentlemen's clothing. **Monsieur** (✉ *1126 Av. Ashford, Condado* ☎ *787/722–0918*) has stylish casual clothing for men. In his shop called **Otto** (✉ *69 Av. Condado, Condado* ☎ *787/722–4609*), local designer Otto Bauzá stocks his own line of casual wear for younger men.

MEN'S & WOMEN'S CLOTHING

With a hipper style than most Condado boutiques, **Abitto** (✉ *1124 Av. Ashford, Condado* ☎ *787/724–0303*) is always filled with young people waving around their credit cards. Prolific designer **David Antonio** ★ (✉ *69 Av. Condado, Condado* ☎ *787/725–0600*) runs a shop that's small but full of surprises. His joyful creations range from updated versions of the men's classic *guayabera* shirt to fluid chiffon and silk tunics ★ and dresses for women. **Nono Maldonado** (✉ *1112 Av. Ashford, Condado* ☎ *787/721–0456*) is well known for his high-end, elegant linen designs for men and women. He should know a thing or two about style—he worked for many years as the fashion editor of *Esquire*.

WOMEN'S CLOTHING

E'Leonor (✉ *1310 Av. Ashford, Condado* ☎ *787/725–3208*) is a well-established store for bridal apparel, evening gowns, and cocktail dresses as well as more casual attire. Look for designs by Vera Wang and St. John. **Lisa Cappalli** (✉ *151 Av. José de Diego, Condado* ☎ *787/724–6575*) sells her lacy, sensuous designs in this boutique. **Mademoiselle** (✉ *1504 Av. Ashford, Condado* ☎ *787/728–7440*) sells only European apparel, including NewMan, Gerard Darel, and Ungaro Fever.

Mia (✉ *1104 Av. Ashford, Condado* ☎ *787/724–2147*) is the place for sophisticated outfits that look like they belong in an art gallery—either on display or on one of the artists.

The window displays at **Nativa** (✉ *55 Calle Cervantes, Condado* ☎ *787/724–1396*) are almost as daring as the clothes it sells. **Pasarela** (✉ *1302 Av. Ashford, Condado* ☎ *787/724–5444*), which means "catwalk" in Spanish, seems a fitting name for a boutique offering designs by the likes of Nicole Miller, Luca Luca, La Perla, and Renato Nucci. **Verovero** (✉ *1302 Av. Ashford, Condado* ☎ *787/725–2332*) stocks women's shoes that look as if they were dreamed up by engineers. These gravity-defying styles are mostly from Italian designers.

Crysta (✉ *51 Calle Maria Moczo, Ocean Park* ☎ *787/727–9782*) stocks handpicked fashions from Brazil. The bikinis are fun and flirty, as are the party dresses. **Harry Robles** (✉ *1752 Calle Loíza, Ocean Park* ☎ *787/727–3885*) sells his elegant gowns in this shop.

FURNITURE & ANTIQUES

★ For nearly two decades, Robert and Sharon Bartos of **El Alcázar** (✉ *103 Calle San José, Old San Juan* ☎ *787/723–1229*) have been selling antiques and objets d'art from all over the world.

Casa Galesa (✉ *108 Calle Cruz, Old San Juan* ☎ *787/977–0400*) has gorgeous older pieces mixed in with some lovely reproductions. **Casas y Cosas** (✉ *Calle Cruz at Calle Luna, Old San Juan* ☎ *787/721–6290*) carries lovely furnishings dating back to the late 19th century. Near the Museo de Arte de Puerto Rico, **Trapiche** (✉ *316 Av. José de Diego, Condado* ☎ *787/724–1469*) stocks a fine selection of furniture and home accessories from Puerto Rico and the Dominican Republic.

GIFTS

Exotic *mariposas* cover the walls of **Butterfly People** (✉ *257 Calle de la Cruz, Old San Juan* ☎ *787/732–2432*). Clear plastic cases hold everything from a pair of common butterflies to dozens of rarer specimens in this lovely shop. Only the YOU BREAK IT, YOU BOUGHT IT signs detract from the colorful display. You can find many unique spices and sauces from around the Caribbean, kitchen items, and cookbooks at **Spicy Caribbee** (✉ *154 Calle Cristo, Old San Juan* ☎ *787/625–4690*).

CLOSE UP

Design Lions

Puerto Rico's young fashion designers have opened many a boutique and atelier in metropolitan San Juan during the last few years. Their styles may differ, but these young lions all share an island heritage—complete with a tradition of true craftsmanship—and a level of sophistication acquired after studying and traveling abroad. The result is a fascinating assortment of original, exclusive, high-quality designs.

With all the warmth and sun, it goes without saying that Puerto Rico's designers are most inspired when it comes to creations for the spring and summer seasons. Lacy, flowing creations and lightweight, if not sheer, fabrics dominate designs for women. For men the trend is toward updated linen classics in tropical whites and creams. Whatever you find will be one of a kind, with stylish—if not playful or downright sexy—lines. Some of these designers have their own shops in San Juan.

Which designers should you check out? Lisa Cappalli, a graduate of New York City's Parsons School of Design, favors lace, as lace-making is a tradition in her family. David Antonio uses upbeat colors—bold reds and vibrant oranges—in his updated classics. Harry Robles is a bit more established than his peers; he specializes in gowns for women, and his draping designs are often dramatic and always elegant. Each of these young designers has a shop in San Juan.

To see their collections, consider visiting during San Juan Fashion Week, which takes place each year in March and September. The events are full of shows and cocktail parties, all organized by the Puerto Rico Fashion Designers Group under the leadership of island-fashion icons Nono Maldonado and Mirtha Rubio.

–Isabel Abislaimán

HANDICRAFTS

Arte & Máscaras (✉ *222 Calle San José, Old San Juan* ☎ *787/724–9020*) has walls covered with festival masks made all over Puerto Rico. At the **Convento de los Dominicos** (✉ *98 Calle Norzagaray, Old San Juan* ☎ *787/721–6866*)—the convent on the north side of the old city that houses the offices of the Instituto de Cultura Puertorriqueña—you'll find baskets, masks, the famous ten-string *cuatro* guitars, *santos* (carved statues of the saints), books and tapes, and reproductions of Taíno artifacts. The **Haitian Gallery** (✉ *Calle Fortaleza and Calle O'Donnell, Old San Juan* ☎ *787/725–0986*) carries Puerto Rican crafts as well as folksy, often inexpensive, paintings from around the Caribbean. ★ **Magia** (✉ *99 Calle Cristo, Old San Juan* ☎ *787/386–6164*) is the most clever shop in San Juan. At first the items on display look like traditional crafts, but look closer and you'll notice that everything is a bit offbeat. A little wooden shrine, for example, might be sheltering an image of Marilyn Monroe.

Near Old San Juan's main square, **Mundo Tanio** (✉*151 San José, Old San Juan* ☎*787/724–2005*) sells high-quality folk art from around ★ the island. **Mi Pequeño San Juan** (✉*107 Calle Cristo, Old San Juan* ☎*787/977–1636*) specializes in tiny versions of San Juan doorways. These ceramics, all created by hand right in the shop, are a wonderful souvenir to remember your stay. You might even find the hotel where you stayed reproduced in plaster. For one-of-a-kind santos, art, and festival masks, head for **Puerto Rican Arts & Crafts** (✉*204 Calle Fortaleza, Old San Juan* ☎*787/725–5596*).

JEWELRY

In the Banco Popular building, the family-run **Abislaimán Joyeros** (✉*Plaza Don Rafael, 206 Calle Tetuán, Old San Juan* ☎*787/724–3890*) sells fine jewelry designs by Sal Prashnik and Jose Hess, as well as watches by Baume & Mercier. **Aetna Gold** (✉*111 Calle Gilberto Concepción de Gracia, Old San Juan* ☎*787/721–4756*), adjacent to the Sheraton Old San Juan Hotel, sells exquisite gold jewelry designed in Greece. For an array of watches and jewelry, visit the two floors of **Bared** (✉*154 Calle Fortaleza, Old San Juan* ☎*787/722–2172*), with a charmingly old-fashioned ambience. Look for the massive clock face on the corner.

Club Jibarito (✉*202 Calle Cristo, Old San Juan* ☎*787/724–7797*) has a fantastic collection of high-end watches by Jaeger-LeCoultre and other designers.

Diamonds and gold galore are found at **Joseph Manchini** (✉*101 Calle Fortaleza, Old San Juan* ☎*787/722–7698*). **Joyería Cátala** (✉*Plaza de Armas, Old San Juan* ☎*787/722–3231*) is known for its large selection of pearls. **Joyería Riviera** (✉*257 Fortaleza St., Old San Juan* ☎*787/725–4000*) sells fine jewelry by David Yurman and Rolex watches.

N. Barquet Joyeros (✉*201 Calle Fortaleza, Old San Juan* ☎*787/721–3366*), one of the bigger stores in Old San Juan, carries Fabergé jewelry, pearls, and gold as well as crystal and watches. **Portofino** (✉*250 Calle San Francisco, Old San Juan* ☎*787/723–5113*) has an especially good selection of watches. **Rheinhold Jewelers** (✉*Plaza Las Américas, 525 Av. Franklin Delano Roosevelt, Hato Rey* ☎*787/767–7837* ✉*Wyndham El San Juan Hotel, 6063 Av. Isla Verde, Isla Verde* ☎*787/791–2521*) sells exclusive designs by Stephen Dueck and Tiffany's.

Cristobal (✉*Plaza Ventana al Mar, 1049 Av. Ashford, Condado* ☎*787/721–8385*) sells glittery pieces in gold and silver that appeal to more modern tastes. With the huge panes of glass on the street, it's a great place to window-shop.

SAN JUAN ESSENTIALS

To research prices, get advice from other travelers, and book travel arrangements, visit www.fodors.com.

TRANSPORTATION

BY AIR

San Juan's busy Aeropuerto Internacional Luis Muñoz Marín is the Caribbean hub of American Airlines, which flies nonstop from Baltimore, Boston, Chicago, Dallas, Fort Lauderdale, Miami, Newark, New York–JFK, Orlando, Philadelphia, Tampa, and Washington, D.C.–Dulles. Continental Airlines flies nonstop from Houston and Newark. Delta flies nonstop from Atlanta, Orlando, New York–LGA, and New York–JFK. JetBlue flies nonstop from Boston, Orlando, and New York–JFK. Spirit Air flies nonstop from Fort Lauderdale and Orlando. United flies nonstop from Chicago, New York–JFK, Philadelphia, and Washington, D.C.–Dulles. US Airways flies nonstop from Baltimore, Boston, Charlotte, Pittsburgh, Philadelphia, and Washington, D.C.–Dulles. International carriers serving San Juan include Air Canada from Toronto, Air France from Paris, Iberia from Madrid, and British Airways from London.

It used to be that travelers arriving at San Juan's international airport had to transfer to nearby Aeropuerto Fernando L. Rivas Dominici (close to Old San Juan and Condado) to take a flight to Vieques or Culebra. This is no longer the case, as all the carriers servicing the islands also have flights from the international airport. Air Flamenco, Isla Nena Air Service, and Vieques Air Link offer daily flights from both airports in San Juan to Vieques and Culebra. Cape Air flies between the international airport and Vieques.

Puerto Rico is also a good spot from which to hop to other Caribbean islands. American Eagle serves many islands in the Caribbean from San Juan; Cape Air connects San Juan to St. Thomas and St. Croix. Seaborne Airlines has seaplanes departing from San Juan Piers 6 and 7 to St. Thomas and St. Croix.

International Airlines **Air Canada** (☎ *888/247–2262* ⊕ *www.aircanada.com*). **Air France** (☎ *800/237–2747* ⊕ *www.airfrance.com*). **American Airlines/American Eagle** (☎ *800/433–7300* ⊕ *www.aa.com*). **British Airways** (☎ *800/247–9297* ⊕ *www.britishairways.com*). **Continental** (☎ *800/231–0856* ⊕ *www.continental.com*). **Delta** (☎ *800/221–1212* ⊕ *www.delta.com*). **Iberia** (☎ *787/725–7000* ⊕ *www.iberia.com*). **JetBlue** (☎ *800/538–2583* ⊕ *www.jetblue.com*). **Spirit Air** (☎ *800/772–7117* ⊕ *www.spiritair.com*). **United Airlines** (☎ *800/864–8331* ⊕ *www.united.com*). **US Airways** (☎ *800/428–4322* ⊕ *www.usairways.com*).

Regional Airlines **Air Flamenco** (☎ *787/724–1818* ⊕ *www.airflamenco.net*). **Cape Air** (☎ *800/525–0714* ⊕ *www.flycapeair.com*). **Isla Nena Air Service** (☎ *787/741–6362 or 877/812–5144* ⊕ *www.islanena.8m.com*). **Seaborne Airlines** (☎ *888/359–8687* ⊕ *www.seaborneairlines.com*). **Vieques Air Link** (☎ *787/741–8331 or 888/901–9247* ⊕ *www.vieques-island.com/val*).

AIRPORTS & TRANSFERS The Aeropuerto Internacional Luis Muñoz Marín is in Isla Verde, 18 km (11 mi) east of downtown. San Juan's other airport, the small Aeropuerto Fernando L. Rivas Dominici (also known as the Isla Grande Airport) near the city's Miramar neighborhood, serves flights to and from destinations in Puerto Rico and throughout the Caribbean. (Although it was still operating at this writing, the airport's future was uncertain.)

Before you leave for Puerto Rico, check with your hotel about transfers: many area establishments provide transport from the airport, free or for a fee, to their guests. Otherwise, your best bets are *taxis turísticos* (tourist taxis). Uniformed officials at the airport can help you make arrangements. They will give you a slip with your exact fare written on it to hand to the driver. Rates are based on your destination. A taxi turístico to Isla Verde costs $10. It's $15 to Condado and $19 to Old San Juan. There's a 50-cent charge for each bag handled by the driver.

The Baldorioty de Castro Expressway (Route 26) runs from the airport into the city. Exits are clearly marked along the way, though you should check with your hotel to determine which one is best for you to take. With regular traffic, the drive from the airport all the way west to Old San Juan takes about 20 minutes, but you should plan on 40 minutes.

Information **Aeropuerto Fernando L. Rivas Dominici** (☎ *787/729–8711*). **Aeropuerto Internacional Luis Muñoz Marín** (☎ *787/791–4670*).

BY BOAT & FERRY

Cruise ships pull into the city piers on Calle Gilberto Concepción de Gracia. There are often hundreds of people fighting over the handful of taxis lined up along the street. Save yourself the hassle and walk the few blocks to Old San Juan. If you are headed to other neighborhoods, take a taxi from nearby Plaza Colón.

The ferry between Old San Juan and Cataño is operated by the Autoridad de los Puertos. It costs a mere 50 cents one-way and runs daily every 15 or 30 minutes from 5:45 AM until 10 PM. The ferry, which departs from Pier 2, is the one to take if you wish to visit the Bacardí Rum Factory.

Information **The Autoridad de los Puertos** (☎ *787/788–1155*).

BY BUS

The Autoridad Metropolitana de Autobuses (AMA) operates buses that thread through San Juan, running in exclusive lanes on major thoroughfares and stopping at signs marked PARADA. Destinations are indicated above the windshield. Bus B-21 runs through Condado all the way to Plaza Las Américas in Hato Rey. Bus A-5 runs from San Juan through Santurce and the beach area of Isla Verde. Fares are 75[cen] and are paid in exact change upon entering the bus. Most buses are air-conditioned and have wheelchair lifts and lock-downs.

Information **AMA** (☎ *787/767–7979*).

BY CAR

Although car rentals in Puerto Rico are inexpensive (rates can start at about $39 a day), we don't recommend that you rent a car if you are staying only in San Juan (at most, you might want to rent a car for a day to explore more of the island). Parking is difficult in San Juan—particularly in Old San Juan—and many hotels charge hefty daily rates; also, traffic can be very heavy at times. With relatively reasonable taxi rates, it simply doesn't pay to rent a car unless you are going out of the city.

The main highways into San Juan are Route 26 from the east (it becomes the Baldorioty de Castro Expressway after passing the airport), Route 22 (José de Diego Expressway) from the west, and Route 52 (Luis A. Ferré Expressway) from the south.

Avenidas Ashford and McLeary run along the coastal neighborhoods of Condado and Ocean Park. The main inland thoroughfares are avenidas Fernández Juncos, Ponce de León, and Luis Muñoz Rivera, which travel from Old San Juan, through Puerta de Tierra and Santurce, and on to Hato Rey. Running north–south are avenidas Franklin Delano Roosevelt and Central (also known as Piñeiro), which intersect Muñoz Rivera and Ponce de León. Avenida Kennedy runs mostly north–south and leads to the suburbs of Bayamón and Guaynabo.

GASOLINE There aren't many gas stations in Old San Juan, but they're abundant elsewhere in the city. Some close at 11 PM or so; others are open 24 hours.

PARKING There's some on-street parking, but meters are often broken. No-parking zones are indicated with yellow paint or signs, though rarely both. Just because a spot on the street is painted white (or not at all), doesn't mean it's a parking space. Always look for signs limiting the number of hours you can leave your car. Fines for parking illegally range from $15 to $250.

In Old San Juan, park at La Puntilla, at the head of Paseo de la Princesa. It's an outdoor lot with the Old City's cheapest rates (they start at 50¢ an hour). You could also try the Felisa Rincón de Gautier lot on Calle Gilberto Concepción de Gracia or the Frank Santaella lot between Paseo de Covadonga and Calle Gilberto Concepción de Gracia. Parking starts at $1.25 for the first hour. The lots open at 7 AM and close at 10 PM weekdays and as late as 2 AM on weekends.

ROAD CONDITIONS City streets (the occasional pothole aside) and some highways are in good condition, but several of the older, heavily trafficked routes aren't well maintained. People tend to ignore the law prohibiting jaywalking; watch out for pedestrians when driving in town.

RULES OF THE ROAD Speed limits are posted in miles, distances in kilometers. In general, city speed limits are 35 mph; on the highways they're 55 to 65 mph. Right turns on red lights are permitted. Seat belts are required; the fine for not using them is $50.

TRAFFIC Traffic jams are common—particularly at rush hours (7 AM to 9 AM and 3 PM to 6 PM)—throughout the metropolitan area. Several areas along main highways are undergoing repairs; be prepared for sudden slowdowns.

Major Agencies **Avis** (☎ *787/774-3556*). **Hertz** (☎ *787/654-3131*). **National** (☎ *787/791-1805*). **Thrifty** (☎ *787/367-2277*).

Local Agencies **Charlie Car Rental** (☎ *787/791-1101* ⊕ *www.charliecars.com*). **L&M Car Rental** (☎ *787/725-8307*). **Vias** (☎ *787/791-4120*).

BY TAXI

The Puerto Rico Tourism Company oversees a well-organized taxi program. Taxis turísticos, which are painted white and have the *garita* (sentry box) logo, charge set rates based on zones; they run from the airport and the cruise-ship piers to Isla Verde, Condado, Ocean Park, and Old San Juan, with rates ranging $10 to $19. Make sure to agree on a price before you get inside. City tours start at $30 per hour.

Although you can hail cabs on the street, virtually every San Juan hotel has taxis waiting outside to transport guests; if none are available, you or a hotel staffer can call one. Major Taxi and Metro Taxi are reliable companies. Note that these radio taxis might charge an extra $1 for the pickup.

Information **Major Taxi** (☎ *787/723-2460*). **Metro Taxi** (☎ *787/725-2870*).

BY TRAIN

The Tren Urbano, an elevated light-rail system, travels throughout the metropolitan area, with stops at the University of Puerto Rico and Bayamón, but does not stop near the main tourist areas or at the airport, so you're unlikely to ride it if you're in town for tourism. The fare is $1.50, which includes transfers to city buses. The system runs from 5:30 AM to 11 PM and is operated by the Alternativa de Transporte Integrado, better known as the ATI.

Information **Alternativa de Transporte Integrado** (☎ *787/723-3760* ⊕ *www.ati.gobierno.pr*).

CONTACTS & RESOURCES

BANKS & EXCHANGE SERVICES

Banks are generally open weekdays from 9 to 5. The island's largest bank is Banco Popular de Puerto Rico, which has currency-exchange services, and branches and ATMs all over the island. Other banks include Citibank, with a branch across the street from the Radisson Ambassador Plaza in Condado and another convenient branch near the cruise-ship pier in Old San Juan.

Information **Banco Popular de Puerto Rico** (✉ *1060 Av. Ashford, Condado* ☎ *787/725-4197* ✉ *Plaza Las Américas, 525 Av. Franklin Delano Roosevelt, Hato Rey* ☎ *787/753-4590* ✉ *1818 Av. Loíza, Ocean Park* ☎ *787/721-5557*). **Citibank** (✉ *206 Calle Tanca, Old San Juan* ☎ *787/721-0108* ✉ *1358 Av. Ashford, Condado* ☎ *787/721-5656*).

EMERGENCIES

General Emergencies **Ambulance, police, and fire** (☎ *911*).

Hospitals **Ashford Presbyterian Memorial Community Hospital** (✉ *1451 Av. Ashford, Condado* ☎ *787/721–2160*). **Clínica Las Américas** (✉ *400 Av. Franklin Delano Roosevelt, Hato Rey* ☎ *787/765–1919*).

Pharmacies **Puerto Rico Drug Company** (✉ *157 Calle San Francisco, Old San Juan* ☎ *787/725–2202*). **Walgreens** (✉ *1130 Av. Ashford, Condado* ☎ *787/725–1510* ✉ *1963 Av. Loíza, Ocean Park* ☎ *787/728–0083*).

INTERNET, MAIL & SHIPPING

In San Juan, Internet cafés are few and far between. If that weren't bad enough, many hotels have yet to install high-speed Internet access in their rooms. Your best bet is to use your hotel business center.

In Condado and Isla Verde, branches of Cyber Net are open weekdays until 10 and weekends until midnight.

San Juan post offices offer Express Mail next-day service to the U.S. mainland and to Puerto Rican destinations. Post offices are open weekdays from 7:30 to 4:30 and Saturday from 8 to noon.

Letters addressed to San Juan should carry the recipient's name, the street number and name or post-office box, and "San Juan, PR," plus the five-digit U.S. Postal Service Zip Code. San Juan consists of various neighborhoods, which you don't need to include on an envelope, but knowing them may help you get around. From east to west, roughly, these include Old San Juan, Puerto de Tierra, Condado, Miramar, Ocean Park, Isla Verde, Santurce, and Hato Rey. The metropolitan area includes such suburbs as Cataño, Carolina, Guaynabo, and Bayamón.

Internet Cafés **Cyber Net** (✉ *1128 Av. Ashford, Condado* ☎ *787/724–4033* ✉ *5980 Av. Isla Verde, Isla Verde* ☎ *787/728–4195*).

Post Offices **Old San Juan Branch** (✉ *153 Calle Fortaleza, Old San Juan* ☎ *787/723–1277*). **Puerta de Tierra Branch** (✉ *163 Av. Fernandez Juncos, Puerta de Tierra* ☎ *787/722–4134*).

OVERNIGHT SERVICES Most major courier services—Federal Express, UPS, Airborne Express—do business in Puerto Rico. Your best bet is to let the staff at a UPS store help you with your shipping. The company has several branches in the metropolitan area, including Old San Juan and Condado.

Information **UPS Store** (✉ *400 Calle Calaf, Old San Juan* ☎ *787/250–0501* ✉ *1357 Av. Ashford, Condado* ☎ *787/724–8678* ✉ *1507 Av. Ponce de León, Santurce* ☎ *787/723–0613*).

MEDIA

The English-language daily, the *San Juan Star,* covers local and international news and local events. Radio Oso, WOSO 1030 on the AM dial, provides the local English-speaking community with up-to-the-minute news.

TOUR OPTIONS

In Old San Juan free trolleys can take you around, and the tourist board can provide you with a copy of *Qué Pasa,* which contains a self-guided walking tour. The Caribbean Carriage Company gives tours of Old San Juan in horse-drawn carriages. It's a bit hokey, but it gets you off your feet. Look for these buggies at Plaza de la Dársena near Pier 1; the cost is $35 to $75 per couple.

Wheelchair Getaway offers city sightseeing trips as well as wheelchair transport from airports and cruise-ship docks to San Juan hotels. Colonial Adventure at Old San Juan offers group tours of the city's historic buildings. Legends of Puerto Rico has tours of Old San Juan as well as the modern neighborhoods that few travelers ever visit.

Information **Caribbean Carriage Company** (☎ *787/797–8063*). **Colonial Adventure at Old San Juan** (☎ *787/793–2992 or 888/774–9919*). **Legends of Puerto Rico** (☎ *787/605–9060* ⊕ *www.legendsofpr.com*). **Wheelchair Getaway** (☎ *787/883–0131 or 800/868–8028*).

VISITOR INFORMATION

You'll find Puerto Rico Tourism Company information officers (identified by their caps and shirts with the tourism company patch) near the baggage-claim areas at Luis Muñoz Marín International Airport. It's open daily from 9 AM to 10 PM in high season and daily from 9 AM to 8 PM in low season.

In San Juan the tourism company's main office is at the old city jail, La Princesa, in Old San Juan. It operates a branch in a pretty yellow colonial building in Plaza de la Dársena called La Casita. It's open Monday to Wednesday 8:30 to 8, Thursday to Friday 8:30 to 5:30, and weekends 9 to 8. Be sure to pick up a free copy of *Qué Pasa,* the official visitor guide. Information officers are posted around Old San Juan (look for them at the cruise-ship piers and at the Catedral de San Juan Bautista) during the day.

La Oficina de Turismo del Municipio de San Juan, run by the city, has offices in Old San Juan (at the Alcaldía) and in Condado (in front of the Condado Plaza Hotel on Avenida Ashford). Both are open weekdays from 8 to 4.

Information **Oficina de Turismo del Municipio de San Juan** (✉ *Alcaldía, 153 Calle San Francisco, Old San Juan* ☎ *787/724–7171* ✉ *999 Av. Ashford, Condado* ☎ *787/740–9270*). **Puerto Rico Tourism Company** (✉ *Plaza de la Dársena, near Pier 1, Old San Juan* 📫 *Box 902-3960, Old San Juan Station, San Juan00902-3960* ☎ *787/721–2400 or 787/722–1709* ✉ *Luis Muñoz Marín International Airport* ☎ *787/791–1014 or 787/791–2551* ⊕ *www.gotopuertorico.com*).

El Yunque & the Northeast

WORD OF MOUTH

"We got an early start and were at the El Yunque Rain Forest by 7:30 AM, before the mobs of tourists arrived. We drove to the top and walked around the forest by ourselves. During this time, we only saw one other couple!"

–CandV

www.fodors.com/forums

Revised and Updated by Mark Sullivan

TREE FROGS, RARE PARROTS, AND wild horses only start the list of northeastern Puerto Rico's offerings. The backdrops for encounters with an array of flora and fauna include the 28,000-acre El Yunque, the only tropical rain forest in the U.S. National Forest system; the seven ecosystems in the Reserva Natural Las Cabezas de San Juan; and Laguna Grande, where tiny sea creatures appear to light up the waters.

The natural beauty and varied terrain continue in the area's towns as well. Río Grande—which once attracted immigrants from Austria, Spain, and Italy—sits on the island's only navigable river. Naguabo overlooks what were once immense cane fields as well as Cayo Santiago, where the only residents are monkeys.

You can golf, ride horses, hike marked trails, and plunge into water sports throughout the region. In many places along the coast, green hills cascade down to the ocean. On the edge of the Atlantic, Fajardo serves as a jumping-off point for diving, fishing, and catamaran excursions. Luquillo is the site of a family beach so well equipped that there are even facilities enabling wheelchair users to enter the sea.

If you wish to get away from it all with a neatly packaged trip, eastern Puerto Rico has some of the island's top resorts: the El Conquistador Resort and the Westin Río Mar. You'll also find the island's only all-inclusive resort, the Paradisus Puerto Rico. The extensive facilities and luxury services at these large, self-contained complexes make the list of regional offerings more than complete.

EXPLORING EL YUNQUE & THE NORTHEAST

As the ocean bends around the northeastern coast, it laps onto beaches of soft sand and palm trees, crashes against high bluffs, and almost magically creates an amazing roster of ecosystems. Beautiful beaches at Luquillo are complemented by more rugged southeastern shores. Inland, green hills roll down toward plains that once held expanses of coconut trees, such as those still surrounding the town of Piñones, or sugarcane, as evidenced by the surviving plantations near Naguabo and Humacao.

ABOUT THE RESTAURANTS

Some restaurants carry the tourist board's *meson gastronómico* designation. Such establishments specialize in typical island food. The eastern region has both formal restaurants, where reservations are very necessary, and casual beach-side eateries, where you can walk in unannounced in beach attire and have a fine meal of fresh fish. Bills generally don't include service charges, so a 15% tip is customary and expected. Most restaurants are open for dinner from late afternoon until at least 10 PM.

WHAT IT COSTS IN U.S. DOLLARS					
	$$$$	**$$$**	**$$**	**$**	**¢**
AT DINNER	over $30	$20–$30	$12–$20	$8–$12	under $8

Prices are per person for a main course at dinner.

NORTHEAST TOP 5

- Hiking past the waterfalls of El Yunque, the only rain forest within the U.S. National Forest system. But come prepared: bring binoculars, a camera with a zoom lens, bottled water, and sunscreen; wear a hat or visor, good walking shoes, and comfortable clothes.
- Taking a dip at the Balneario de Luquillo, one of the prettiest beaches in Puerto Rico. Not only is it a family favorite, but it also has a wheelchair ramp.
- Sitting elbow-to-elbow with locals at one of the dozens of outdoor seafood shacks on the highway before you get to the Balneario de Luquillo. There are at least 50 to choose from.
- Gasping at the eye-popping views from the lighthouse at Reserva Natural Las Cabezas de San Juan.
- Hitting the tree-lined fairways of the two good golf courses at Palmas del Mar.

ABOUT THE HOTELS

The east coast has a wide variety of lodgings, from government-approved paradores to small lodges in the mountains to large, lavish resorts along the coast. The Rio Mar Beach Resort & Spa is a good option, as is the El Conquistador Resort & Golden Door Spa.

WHAT IT COSTS IN U.S. DOLLARS

	$$$$	$$$	$$	$	¢
FOR 2 PEOPLE	over $350	$250–$350	$150–$250	$80–$150	under $80

Prices are for a double room in high season, excluding 9% tax (11% for hotels with casinos, 7% for paradores) and 5%–12% service charge.

TIMING

In general, the island's northeast coast—preferred by those seeking abandoned beaches and nature reserves rather than casinos and urban glitz—tends to be less in demand than San Juan. The exception is Easter and Christmas, when Luquillo and Fajardo become crowded with local sun lovers, merrymakers, and campers. Island festivals also draw crowds, but planning a trip around one of them will give you a true sense of the region's culture. Be sure to make reservations well in advance if you're visiting during high season, which runs from December 15 through April 15.

THE NORTHEASTERN COAST

Just east of San Juan, at the community of Piñones, urban chaos is replaced with the peace of winding, palm-lined roads that are interrupted at intervals by barefoot eateries and dramatic ocean views. Farther southeast and inland is Río Grande, a community that grew by virtue of its location beside the island's only navigable river. The river rises within El Yunque, the short name for El Yunque National Forest,

IF YOU LIKE

BEACHES

The Atlantic east coast is edged with sandy, palm-lined shores that are occasionally cut by rugged stretches. Some of these beaches are quiet, isolated escapes. Others—such as Luquillo and Seven Seas near Fajardo—are jammed with water-loving families, especially on weekends and during the Easter holidays.

GREAT FOOD

Puerto Ricans love sybaritic pleasures, and that includes enjoying a well-prepared meal—whether it be Continental, Nueva Latina, or authentically native cuisine. In the east you'll find fine fare of all types. On the traditional side, look for the deep-fried snacks (often stuffed with meat or fish) known as *frituras,* as well as numerous dishes laced with coconut. Plantains are the star ingredient in the hearty *mofongo,* a seafood-stuffed dish, or as *tostones* (fried plantain chips). Fresh fish is commonly prepared with tomatoes, onions, and garlic, or some combination of the three.

GOLF

There's something to be said for facing a rolling, palm-tree-lined fairway with the distant ocean at your back. And then there are the ducks, iguanas, and pelicans that congregate in the mangroves near some holes. That's what golf in eastern Puerto Rico is all about. The Arthur Hills–designed course at El Conquistador is one of the island's best. The Flamboyán course, a Rees-Jones creation at Palmas del Mar Country Club, consistently gets raves, as do the courses at the Westin Río Mar. An old-time favorite is the Bahía Beach Plantation course, which was developed on a former coconut plantation.

a sprawling blanket of green covering a mountainous region south of Río Grande. Back on the coast, Balneario de Luquillo (Luquillo Beach) has snack kiosks, dressing rooms, showers, and facilities that enable wheelchair users to play in the ocean.

Southeast of Luquillo sits the Reserva Natural Las Cabezas de San Juan, with its restored lighthouse and variety of ecosystems. Anchoring the island's east coast is Fajardo, a lively port city with a large marina, ferry service to the outer islands, and a string of offshore cays. Catamarans based here sail to and from great snorkeling spots, yachts stop by to refuel or stock up on supplies, and local fishing craft chug in and out as part of a day's work.

PIÑONES

16 km (10 mi) east of San Juan.

Funky Piñones is little more than a collection of open-air, seaside eateries. Sand floors, barefoot patrons, and tantalizing seafood—traditionally washed down with icy beer—have made it popular with locals, especially on weekend evenings. Chilled *agua de coco* is served right from the coconut. During the day you can rent a bike and follow the marked seaside trail that meanders for 11 km (7 mi). At this writing, plans were on the table to expand the bike path all the way to Isla Verde in San Juan.

The area has grown as a nightlife designation, as fancier establishments, some with live music, have opened up. And there are raucous open-air dance halls playing mostly Dominican merengue or local rap, which is influenced by salsa and reggae. But the action begins to cook before sunset. As mid-afternoon turns into evening and people begin to leave the beach for refreshments, the air is thick with smoke from grilled fish, beef and chicken kabobs, and the kettles of oil used to fry codfish and crab fritters. When the giant orange Caribbean sun starts to fall behind the San Juan skyline, salsa and merengue—not to mention reggae and Latin pop—start to blare out from the jukeboxes and sound systems of the dozens of ramshackle establishments dotting Route 187, the sector's main road. Traffic on the two-lane road into and out of the area is daunting on Friday and Saturday nights, when many of these open-air bars host merengue combos, Brazilian-jazz trios, or reggae bands.

One of the most pleasant ways to pass the time is walking along the **Paseo Piñones.** This 6½-mi boardwalk passes through sand dunes and crosses lagoons and mangrove forests. All the while, a line of coconut palms shades you from the sun. You'll share the path with bikers, joggers, and in-line skaters. Food kiosks abound. ⊠*Piñones.*

WHERE TO EAT

$$–$$$ ✕**Bamboobei.** You can't miss this funky hangout because of its eye-catching color scheme. But behind the brilliant blue building is a great deck that looks across a bike path to the beach. There's always live music on weekends—jazz on Saturday, something else on Friday. Other times you can just enjoy the rhythms floating out from the speakers. The menu is pretty much what you'd expect—heavy on the seafood—but lots of coconut and tropical fruit jazz things up. ⊠*Rte. 187, Km 5* ☎*787/253–0948* ▭*MC, V.*

$$–$$$ ✕**Soleil.** A bit more refined than some of its neighbors, this restaurant actually sits on a wooden platform positioned *above* the sand. Even nicer is the upstairs deck that lets you gaze at the ocean instead of the parking lot. The grilled steak served with chimichurri is as good as it gets, and juicy barbecued chicken with tamarind sauce is equally tasty. There are a couple of bars, and bands playing Latin music set the scene on weekend nights. Call ahead and you can arrange free transportation to and from your hotel—a very good deal. ⊠*Rte. 187, Km 4.6* ☎*787/253–1033* ▭*AE, MC, V.*

$$–$$$ ✕**The Waterfront.** Farther down the beach than its rowdier rivals, this restaurant attracts a slightly older crowd of *sanjuaneros* whose primary objective is eating rather than drinking. The menu is also more mature, offering such entrées as red snapper in garlic sauce or lobster tails in lemon butter. If you can't decide, the sampler platter has everything from fried fritters to fresh oysters. You can choose a table in the dimly lighted dining room or outside on the covered patio. ⊠*Rte. 187, Km 5* ☎*787/791–5859* ▭*AE, MC, V.*

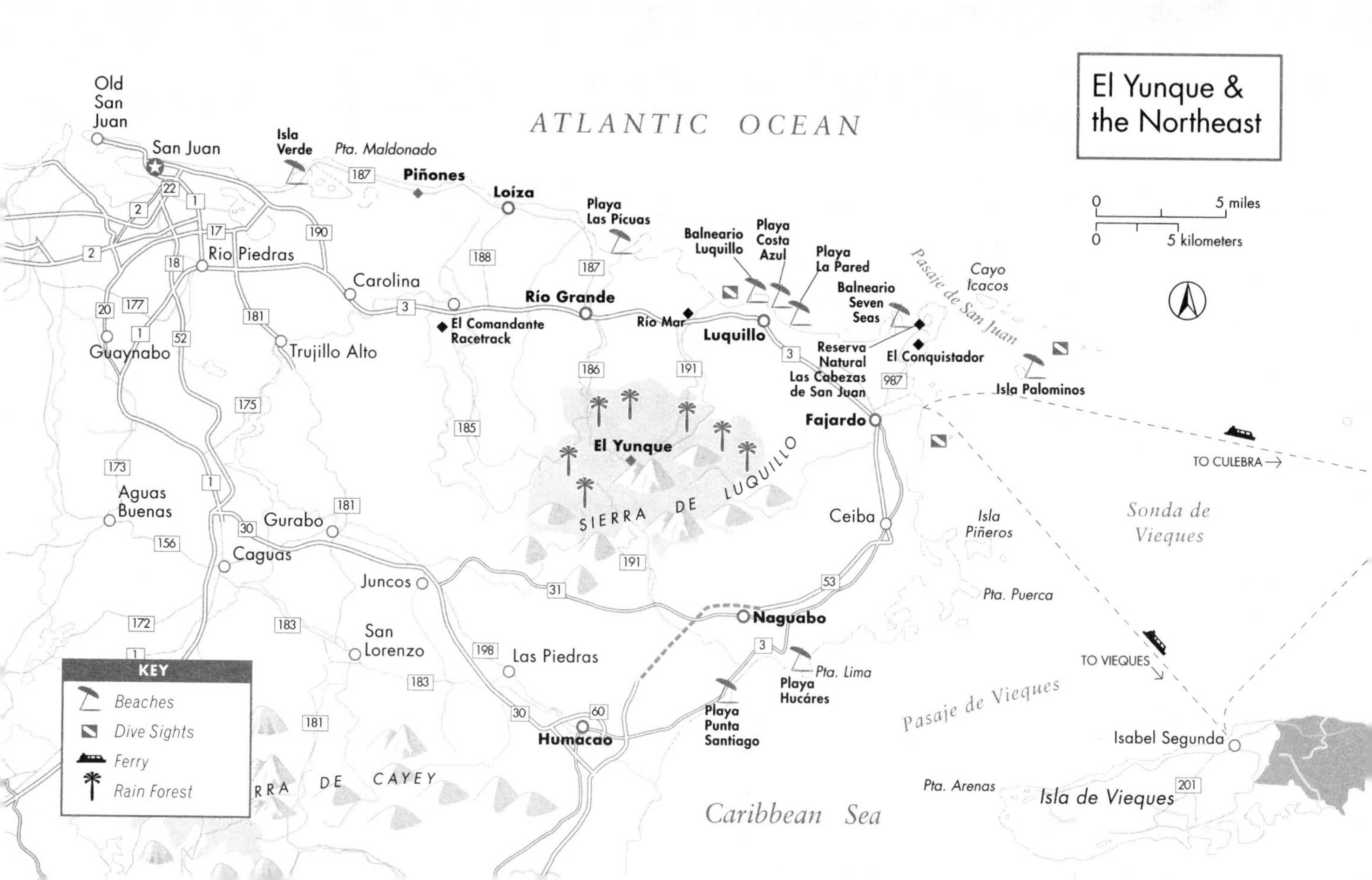
El Yunque & the Northeast
0 5 miles
0 5 kilometers
ATLANTIC OCEAN
Old San Juan
San Juan
Isla Verde
Pta. Maldonado
Piñones
Loíza
Playa Las Picuas
Balneario Luquillo
Playa Costa Azul
Playa La Pared
Balneario Seven Seas
Cayo Icacos
Pasaje de San Juan
Rio Piedras
Carolina
Río Grande
Río Mar
Luquillo
Reserva Natural Las Cabezas de San Juan
El Conquistador
Isla Palominos
El Comandante Racetrack
Guaynabo
Trujillo Alto
Fajardo
TO CULEBRA
El Yunque
SIERRA DE LUQUILLO
Ceiba
Isla Piñeros
Sonda de Vieques
Aguas Buenas
Gurabo
Caguas
Juncos
Pta. Puerca
Naguabo
San Lorenzo
Las Piedras
Pta. Lima
Playa Hucáres
TO VIEQUES
Playa Punta Santiago
Pasaje de Vieques
Humacao
Isabel Segunda
RRA DE CAYEY
Pta. Arenas
Isla de Vieques
Caribbean Sea
KEY
Beaches
Dive Sights
Ferry
Rain Forest

CAUTION

Leave yourself plenty of time for driving to El Yunque or any of the resorts in the northeast. Route 3, the main route east, is notorious for its bumper-to-bumper traffic.

$–$$ ✕ **Pulpo Loco by the Sea.** Talk about truth in packaging—the Crazy Octopus has its palm-shaded tables planted firmly in the sand just a few yards from the ocean. As you might guess, octopus, oysters, mussels, and crab lead the lineup at this colorful seafood shack, though you can always munch on local favorites such as fried codfish fritters. If your thirst is greater than your hunger, you can opt for a beer served in a plastic cup. The friendly staff seems to know all the customers on a first-name basis. ✉ *Rte. 187, Km 4.5* ☎ *787/791–8382* ▭ *AE, MC, V.*

$ ✕ **The Reef.** This place has one of the most dazzling views of San Juan, especially in the evening when the city lights are twinkling. Perched atop a coastal bluff, it's located at the first left once you cross the bridge into Piñones. Grab one of the tables on the deck and order some of the simple seafood dishes, including octopus or king-crab salads, served in *vasos* or on *platos* (glasses or plates). ✉ *Off Rte. 187, Km 1* ☎ *787/791–1973* ▭ *MC, V.*

NIGHTLIFE

Nearly all the restaurants and cafés in Piñones have bands on weekends, mostly playing roof-shaking jazz and island rhythms, and locals go as much for the drinks and live entertainment as for the food. A largely Dominican clientele frequents many of these beachfront dance halls, and you're likely to see some smoking merengue dancing. Couples also twirl to salsa, bounce to bomba, or move to the grittier beats of local rap. You'll easily find several open-air establishments drawing weekend crowds for their steamy dance floors inside and smoking barbecue pits outside.

The Reef (✉ *Off Rte. 187, Km 1* ☎ *787/791–1973*) has a jukebox for those rare evenings when there isn't live music. You can also shoot some eight ball at one of the pool tables. **Soleil** (✉ *Rte. 187, Km 4.5* ☎ *787/253–1033*) has bars upstairs as well as down, so you never have to go far to order a drink. This place can get packed on weekends.

SPORTS & THE OUTDOORS

Piñones is bordered by a 10-mi strip of beaches along the coast, which winds to a bluff called Vacia Talega, a once infamous lovers' lane with a wonderful view of an unspoiled coast lined with dense palm groves and towering sea grapes. The area has some fine surf, and several spots have become favorites of local and visiting surfers. You'll also find good fishing, snorkeling, and scuba opportunities. Away from the coast is Torrecilla Baja, one of the largest mangrove swamps on the island.

BEACHES If you want to find solitary coastline near Piñones, you can. The water is fine; however, the surf is strong, and swimming—especially in winter—can be dangerous at some beaches. You'll find a **Playa de Piñones** (✉ *Route 187, Km 8*) right in front of the cluster of food kiosks built by the government for resident cooks. A large barrier reef blocks the strong currents and serves as the foundation for the large bathing pools in front of a sandy beach.

> **CAUTION**
>
> Environmental concerns and a lack of infrastructure have so far held up large projects that are still planned for the area, but the pressure to build continues. For now, Piñones is the largest undeveloped coastal area near San Juan, and only a 10-minute drive from Isla Verde. Visit now, before it's spoiled by overdevelopment.

BICYCLING The area's big outdoor attraction is a bike path that follows the swaying coconut palms on a quiet, breezy stretch, sometimes crossing over the main roadway but mostly running parallel to it. Along most of its 7 mi, it's a wooden boardwalk for bicycles. On weekends and holidays you can rent bikes from several places along Route 187 and explore the path on your own. The going rate is $5 per hour. Many are clustered at the start of the bike trail, at the first left once you cross the bridge into Piñones. If you want to rent a bike, head to **Pulpo Loco by the Sea** (✉*Rte. 187, Km 5* ☎*787/791–8382*).

DIVING & FISHING TRIPS Locals go fishing and crabbing right off the coast, and it's likely that the crab fritters you eat in any beachfront shack are local as well. Boating, deep-sea fishing, and scuba-diving trips are run out of the marina right below the bridge from Isla Verde. **Cangrejos Yacht Club** (✉*Rte. 187, Km 1* ☎*787/791–1015* 🌐*www.cangrejosyachtclub.com*) is open Monday through Saturday from 8 to 5 and Sunday from 10 to 3. At **Puerto Rico Angling** (☎*787/724–2079* 🌐*www.puertoricofishing.com*), José Campos and his son run offshore deep-sea fishing trips for up to six people. They also offer fishing trips through the area's lagoon system.

KAYAKING You can rent kayaks and paddle through the mangrove swamp that runs along the interior of Piñones; the swamp is rich in flora and fauna—both marine and bird life. **Las Tortugas Adventures** (✉*Cond. La Puntilla, 4 Calle La Puntilla, Apt. D1–12, Old San Juan* ☎*787/725–5169 or 787/889–7734* 🌐*www.kayak-pr.com*) is a reputable outfitter based in Old San Juan that leads organized kayak trips into the mangrove waterway, a nature reserve under the jurisdiction of the commonwealth's Department of Natural & Environmental Resources. Trip lengths vary from two to four hours, and prices range from $45 to $65 per person, depending on group size and the extent of the excursion.

SHOPPING

Just west of Piñones is the town of Loíza, where you'll find **Artesanías Castor Ayala** (✉*Rte. 187, Km 6.6, Loíza* ☎*787/876–1130*). Among the offerings here are coconut-shell festival masks dubbed "Mona Lisas" because of their elongated smiles. Craftsman Raúl Ayala Carrasquillo has been making these pieces for more than 40 years, following in the footsteps of his late father. Collectors prize these wild masks, most with tentacle-like horns. ⚠ **Buyer beware: these masks have been much-copied by other artisans, so look for the signature on the back.**His one-room shop, in a shack that was painted yellow many years ago, is on the road between Loíza and Río Grande.

At **Estúdio de Arte Samuel Lind** (✉ *Rte. 187, Km 6.6, Loíza* ☎ *787/876–1494*), located on a short, dusty lane across the street from the Artesanías Castor Ayala, artist Samuel Lind sculpts, paints, and silk-screens images that are quintessentially Loízano. Lind's work is displayed in the two floors of his latticework studio. Of special note are his colorful folk-art posters.

RÍO GRANDE

35 km (21 mi) southeast of San Juan.

This urban cluster of about 50,000 residents proudly calls itself "The City of El Yunque," as it's the closest community to the rain forest and most of the reserve falls within its district borders. Two images of the rare green parrot, which makes its home in El Yunque, are found on the city's coat of arms; another parrot peeks out at you from the town's flag. The city is also near the posh Rio Mar Beach Resort & Spa, known for its seaside golf courses, lovely beach, and first-class restaurants.

CHIMICHURRI

When you get a steak in Puerto Rico, it usually is served with a little glass jar of a green herb-filled sauce with a small, plastic spoon. This is *chimichurri*, the traditional accompaniment to grilled steak. The sauce, made from finely chopped cilantro or parsley, garlic, lemon, and oil, can be sprinkled liberally or sparingly over the meat to give it a slight kick. You will rarely find steak sauce in Puerto Rico, except at an American chain, though you can frequently get ketchup if chimichurri isn't to your liking.

Río Espíritu Santo, which runs through Río Grande, begins in El Yunque's highest elevations and is the island's only navigable river. It was once used to transport lumber, sugar, and coffee from plantations, and immigrants flocked to the region to take advantage of the employment opportunities. Many of today's residents can trace their families to Spain, Austria, and Italy.

The **Museo del Cartel José Hernández** is devoted to posters and the artists who design them. The collection dates from the 1950s and includes many eye-popping posters created for island festivals and art exhibits. Call ahead, as when we visited the museum was closed for renovations until 2008. ✉ *37 Calle Pimentel, El Centro* ☎ *787/887–2370* 🎟 *Free* ⏲ *Tues.–Sun. 9–5.*

SPORTS & THE OUTDOORS

HORSEBACK RIDING

★ **Hacienda Carabalí** (✉ *Rte. 992, Km 4, north of entrance to El Yunque* ☎ *787/690–3781*), a family-run operation, is a good place to jump in the saddle and ride one of Puerto Rico's Paso Fino horses. Hour-long rides ($32) take you around the 600-acre ranch, while two-hour treks take you to a river where you and your horse can take a dip. If you prefer something more high tech, rent a four-wheeler for an excursion through the foothills of El Yunque. After your adventure, quench your thirst at the Bamboo Lounge.

GREAT ITINERARIES

IF YOU HAVE 1 DAY

If you have only a day, or even less than a day, to visit eastern Puerto Rico, you should make a beeline to **El Yunque.** Route 3 is the quickest way. This rain forest has hiking trails of various lengths leading to secluded waterfalls and mountaintop towers with spectacular views. It's wonderful to explore even if you never get out of your car. If you are staying overnight, your best bet is nearby **Río Grande.**

IF YOU HAVE 3 DAYS

If you have a bit more time, you can see much more of the region. To avoid the unrelenting string of strip malls along Route 3, take Route 187 as it winds along the coast. Stop for lunch at one of the seafood shacks that line the beach as **Pinoñes.** Spend the night in or near **Río Grande,** a town that makes a good base for exploring the region. On your second day, get up early to beat the crowds to **El Yunque.** Make sure to bring binoculars and watch for the rare Puerto Rican green parrot. On Day 3 you should head to **Luquillo,** which has one of the prettiest beaches on the island. Make sure to stop for lunch in one of the *kioskos* (food stands) on Route 3 just before you reach the town.

IF YOU HAVE 5 DAYS

If you have five days, follow the three-day itinerary above. On Day 4 head east along Route 3 to the coastal city of **Fajardo,** which has plenty of accommodations in every price range. Make sure you have called ahead to reserve a spot on a tour of Reserva Natural Las Cabezas de San Juan. If there's no moon, sign up for a late-night excursion to the reserve's bioluminescent bay. On Day 5 take a snorkeling trip to some of the nearby coral reefs. Many people who travel to Fajardo take advantage of the ferry service to the smaller islands of Vieques or Culebra.

WHERE TO EAT

$$$–$$$$ ★ ✕ **Palio.** Northern Italian dishes, such as rack of lamb with olive tapenade and fillet of beef with a sweet Muscat grape reduction, are the star attractions at this top-notch restaurant. The amiable staff serves everything with a flourish, whipping up the salads and other dishes beside your table. Specialty coffees are served in mugs engulfed in blue flames, a showstopper that people at neighboring tables applaud. The dining room, with its black-and-white checkerboard floor and dark-wood paneling, is among the island's most elegant. You can catch a glimpse of the sea through the floor-to-ceiling windows. ✉ *Rio Mar Beach Resort & Spa, 6000 Río Mar Blvd., Río Grande* ☎ *787/888–6000* ✍ *Reservations essential* ▭ *AE, D, DC, MC, V* ⏲ *No lunch.*

$$–$$$ ✕ **Shimas.** The designers of this Asian-style eatery certainly had their tongues in their cheeks. Keeping the place cool are Japanese-style fans that wave at you from the ceiling. The sushi bar is a big draw, as are the Chinese and Thai entrées on the cross-cultural menu. Start with the duck spring rolls, then move on to the lobster with a sweet-and-spicy sauce. ✉ *Rio Mar Beach Resort & Spa, 6000 Río Mar Blvd., Río Grande* ☎ *787/888–6000* ✍ *Reservations essential* ▭ *AE, D, DC, MC, V* ⏲ *No lunch.*

2

$-$$$ ✕ **Bamboo Lounge.** The foothills of El Yunque are the backdrop for this tree-shaded restaurant. On the grounds of the famous Hacienda Carabalí, the open-air eatery serves food that will satisfy those just off the trail, as well as those who spent the day lounging by the pool. The food is Caribbean, but the chef often adds a twist to the traditional recipes. You'll find local favorites like grilled halibut, but it is served here with capers. Locals swear by the broiled lobster tail in garlic sauce. ✉ *Hacienda Carabalí, Rte. 992, Km 4, north of entrance to El Yunque* ☎ *787/690–3781* ▭ *AE, MC, V* ⏲ *Closed Mon.–Thurs. No lunch Fri.*

$-$$$ ✕ **Richie's.** Perched on a mountaintop, this restaurant—a well-located option for Westin Río Mar guests who don't want to dine on-property—has a pair of open-air dining rooms overlooking the coastline. It's no surprise that seafood is the specialty here—try the fried plantains filled with shrimp, conch, octopus, or lobster for an appetizer, then move on to grouper stuffed with crab and served in a spicy sauce. Bring some insect repellent at night, as some readers have mentioned problems with mosquitoes. ✉ *Río Mar Blvd., just past entrance to the Rio Mar Beach Resort & Spa, Río Grande* ☎ *No phone* ▭ *AE, MC, V.*

> **IT'S THE BOMBA**
>
> The *bomba*—a dance for which the northeastern coast is famous—can be traced to the Kongo people of West Africa. Sometimes wearing a flouncy white dress, the woman of a dancing couple moves in a relatively fixed pattern of steps while her partner improvises to the drumbeat. A lead singer and a choir perform a call-and-response song—recounting a local story or event—while percussionists play maracas, *fuas* (wooden sticks that are smacked against a hard surface), *buleadores* (low-timbre, barrel-shape drums), and *subidores* (higher-pitch drums).

$-$$ ✕ **Antojitos Puertorriqueñes.** The menu here couldn't be simpler—dishes like fried pork with plantains or stewed crab with beans and rice are your best options. The premises are just as straightforward, a covered patio with plastic tables and chairs. But at these prices, who can complain? ✉ *160 Río Mar Blvd Río Grande.* ☎ *787/888–7378* ▭ *No credit cards.*

WHERE TO STAY

$$$$ **Grand Meliá Puerto Rico.** Located on an enviable stretch of pristine coastline is this massive resort, formerly an all-inclusive hotel called Paradisus Puerto Rico. The open-air lobby, with its elegant floral displays, resembles a Japanese garden, and the swimming pool's columns call to mind ancient Greece. Although the mishmash of styles don't quite come together in a coherent way, the resort does a decent job of being all things to all people. The 500 suites, many of which have hot tubs, are spread among two-story bungalows. Loads of them look onto the two 18-hole golf courses that, with patches of dead grass, are in need of some grooming. **Pros:** Beautiful setting, lovely pool area. **Cons:** Neighborhood is full of noisy construction projects, facade is blank and uninviting, unhelpful staff. ✉ *Rte. 968, Km 5.8, Coco Beach* ☎ *787/657–1026 or 800/336–3542* 🌐 *www.meliahotels.com* *500*

suites ☝*In-room: safe, refrigerator. In-hotel: 6 restaurants, room service, bars, golf courses, tennis courts, pool, gym, spa, beachfront, diving, water sports, children's programs (ages 4–12), concierge, laundry service, public Internet* ▭*AE, D, MC, V* 🍽*EP.*

$$$$ ★ **Rio Mar Beach Resort & Spa—a Wyndham Grand Resort.** On more than 500 acres, this sprawling resort is geared toward outdoor activities. Many people come to play the championship golf courses or hike in the nearby rain forest. But the biggest draw is the 2-mi-long stretch of sand just steps from the door. There's a kiosk near the swimming pools that rents sailboats and other equipment; a dive shop organizes excursions to nearby places of interest. Even the extensive programs for children are mostly outdoors. The seven-story hotel, which wraps around lush gardens, never feels overwhelming. Some rooms are on the small side but are cleverly designed to make use of all the available space. Wyndham took over the property in 2007 and, among other improvements, added their comfy "Be Well" beds. The Mandara Spa transports you to the South Pacific with its hand-carved wood furnishings from Bali. **Pros:** On one of the island's best beaches, great restaurants in and near the hotel, plenty of outdoor activities. **Cons:** Dark and depressing parking garage, long lines at check-in desk. ✉*6000 Río Mar Blvd., Río Grande* ☎*787/888–6000 or 877/636–0636* 🌐*www.wyndhamriomar.com* ⇨*528 rooms, 72 suites, 59 villas* ☝*In-room: safe, VCR, Ethernet. In-hotel: 7 restaurants, bars, golf courses, tennis courts, pools, gym, spa, beachfront, diving, water sports, bicycles, children's programs (ages 4–12), concierge, laundry service, public Internet, public Wi-Fi, airport shuttle, no-smoking rooms* ▭*AE, D, DC, MC, V* 🍽*EP.*

NIGHTLIFE

Pick a game—Caribbean stud poker, blackjack, slot machines—and then head to the Las Vegas–style casino at the **Rio Mar Beach Resort & Spa** (✉*6000 Río Mar Blvd., Río Grande* ☎*787/888–6000*). If all that betting makes you thirsty, step into the Players Bar, which is connected to the gaming room.

SPORTS & THE OUTDOORS

Activities in Río Grande region are mostly oriented around the two big resorts, the Rio Mar Beach Resort & Spa and the Grand Meliá Puerto Rico.

DIVING & SNORKELING The **Dive Center** (✉*Rio Mar Beach Resort & Spa, 6000 Río Mar Blvd., Río Grande* ☎*787/888–6000* 🌐*www.wyndhamriomar.com*) offers scuba and snorkeling rentals and lessons. Large catamaran snorkeling trips leave from the resort for the calm seas and deserted islands off the cost of northeastern Puerto Rico. The cost is $75 to $140 per person, including snacks. The trips offer awesome sunbathing and snorkeling opportunities.

GOLF The **Berwind Country Club** (✉*Rte. 187, Km 4.7* ☎*787/876–3056*) has an 18-hole course known for its tight fairways and demanding greens. It's open to nonmembers from Tuesday through Friday, with greens fees of $65, which includes a cart and bucket of balls. On Sunday afternoons nonmembers can play if they make arrangements in advance.

Coco Beach Golf & Country Club (✉ *Grand Melía Puerto Rico, 100 Clubhouse Dr.* ☎ *787/657–2000* 🌐 *www.cocobeachgolf.com*) has two 18-hole courses designed by Tom Kite and Bruce Besse. The courses are bordered by the coastline and offer a view of El Yunque. When we stopped by, the grass was patchy in many places. Greens fees are between $140 and $160.

★ The spectacular **Río Mar Country Club** (✉ *Rio Mar Beach Resort & Spa, 6000 Río Mar Blvd., Río Grande* ☎ *787/888–7060* 🌐 *www.wyndhamriomar.com*) has a clubhouse with a pro shop and two restaurants between two 18-hole courses. The River Course, designed by Greg Norman, has challenging fairways that skirt the Mameyes River. The Ocean Course has slightly wider fairways than its sister; iguanas can usually be spotted sunning themselves near its fourth hole. If you're not a resort guest, be sure to reserve tee times at least 24 hours in advance. Greens fees range from $165 to $190, depending on tee time.

TENNIS The facilities at the **Peter Burwash International Tennis Center** (✉ *Rio Mar Beach Resort & Spa, 6000 Río Mar Blvd., Río Grande* ☎ *787/888–6000* 🌐 *www.wyndhamriomar.com*) are the best in the area. Besides the 13 courts with spectacular views, there are lessons for everyone from novices to old pros.

WATER SPORTS You can rent sea kayaks ($25 an hour for single-person kayaks, $35 and $45 for two- and three-person models) from **Iguana Water Sports** (✉ *Rio Mar Beach Resort & Spa, 6000 Río Mar Blvd., Río Grande* ☎ *787/888–6000* 🌐 *www.wyndhamriomar.com*). The helpful staff also rents everything from rafts ($10 a day) to windsurfing equipment ($25 an hour).

SHOPPING

The picturesque **Treehouse Studio** (✉ *Unmarked road off Rte. 3* ☎ *787/888–8062*), not far from the rain forest, sells vibrant watercolors by Monica Laird, who also gives workshops. Call for an appointment and directions.

EL YUNQUE

Fodor's Choice ★ 11 km (7 mi) southeast of Río Grande; 43 km (26 mi) southeast of San Juan.

More than 28,000 acres of verdant foliage and rare wildlife make up El Yunque, the only rain forest within the U.S. National Forest system. Formally known as the El Yunque National Forest, El Yunque's odd name is believed to be derived from the Taíno word *yukiyú* (good spirit), although some people say it comes directly from *yunque,* the Spanish word for "anvil," because some of the forest's peaks have flattened tops.

Rising to more than 3,500 feet above sea level, this protected area didn't gain its "rain forest" designation for nothing: more than 100

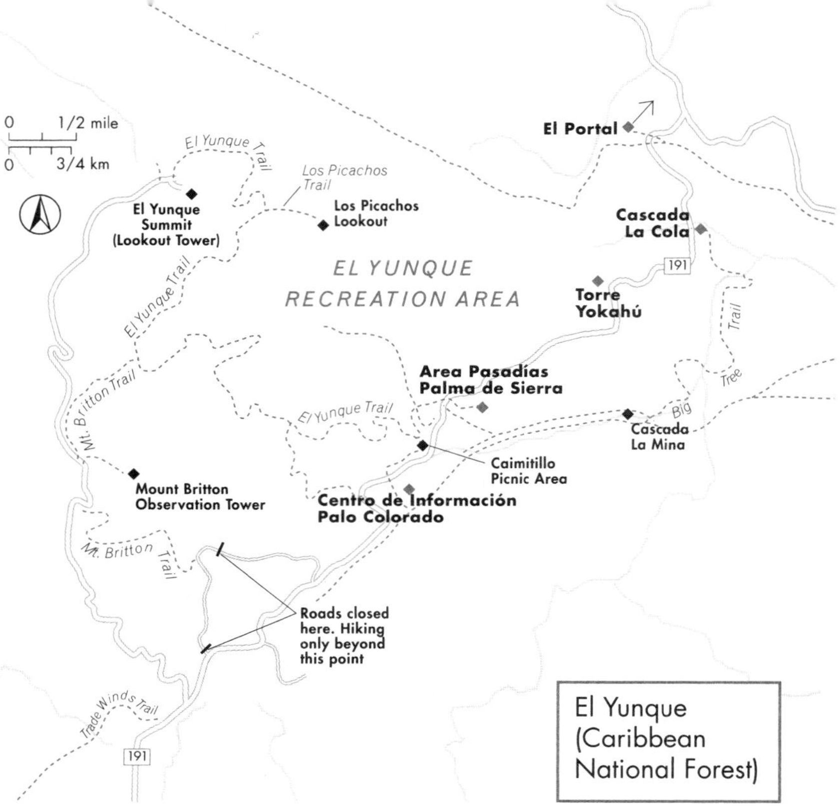

El Yunque (Caribbean National Forest)

billion gallons of precipitation fall over it annually, spawning rushing streams and cascades, 240 tree species, and oversized impatiens and ferns. In the evening millions of inch-long *coquís* (tree frogs) begin their calls. El Yunque is also home to the *cotorra,* Puerto Rico's endangered green parrot, as well as 67 other types of birds.

The forest's 13 hiking trails are extremely well maintained; many of them are easy to navigate and less than 1 mi long. If you prefer to see the sights from a car, as many people do, simply follow Route 191 as it winds into the mountains. Several observation points are located along this often narrow road, which is the park's main thoroughfare. Las Cabezas observation point is at Km 7.8; Cascada La Cola, one of two waterfalls where you can take a refreshing dip (the other, La Mina, is to the south), lies just past Km 8.1; and the Torre Yokahú observation point sits at Km 8.9. When hurricanes and mud slides haven't caused portions of the road to be closed, you can drive straight from the entrance to Km 13, the base of Pico El Yunque, the peak that forms the centerpiece of this amazing park.

Arrive early and plan to stay the entire day. The road into El Yunque opens at 7:30 AM and closes at 6 PM. You'll be charged an admission fee if you visit El Portal, the information center that has an interesting movie and interactive exhibits, but everything else is free. There are picnic areas with sheltered tables and bathrooms, as well as several basic eateries along the road through the rain forest.

A lizard's tongue darts across three movie screens, a forest erupts in flames, a tiny seedling pushes up from the ground and flourishes. Before you begin exploring El Yunque, check out the high-tech, interactive displays—explaining rain forests in general and El Yunque in particular—at **El Portal,** the information center near the northern entrance. The beautifully designed facility is a good stop for families, as many of the exhibits are geared toward youngsters. Kids especially may like a short film narrated by actor Jimmy Smits (whose mother is Puerto Rican) about efforts to save the endangered Puerto Rican parrot. New on the scene are four nature dioramas called "Understanding the Forest," which will help answer many of the questions kids might have. All exhibits are in English and Spanish. This is also a good place to pick up a map of the park and talk to rangers about which trails are open. You can stock up on water, snacks, film, and souvenirs at the small gift shop. ✉*Rte. 191, Km 4.3, off Rte. 3* ☎*787/888–1880* 🌐*www.fs.fed.us/r8/caribbean* 🎫*$3* ⏲*Daily 9–5*. The first spectacular sight you're likely to see in El Yunque is **Cascada La Cola** *(La Cola Falls)*, which plunges 85 feet down a flat sheet of solid rock. The waterfall is inches from the road, so it's visible to those who don't want to navigate the trails. (Some people even take pictures from their cars.) The gate to the park, which opens at 7:30 AM and closes at 6 PM, is just before the falls. ✉*Rte. 191, Km 8.1*. Resembling the turret of a castle, **Torre Yokahú** *(Yokahú Observation Tower)* rises unexpectedly from a little hill not far from the road. A peek through the windows of its circular stairway gives you a hint of the vistas awaiting you at the top: 1,000-year-old trees, exotic flowers in brilliant hues, and birds in flight. Postcards and books on El Yunque are sold in the small kiosk at the tower's base. The parking lot has restrooms. ✉*Rte. 191, Km 8.9*. Just beyond the halfway point along the road into El Yunque, the **Area Pasadías Palma de Sierra** is a great place to stop for trail updates. El Yunque's steep slopes, unstable wet soil, heavy rainfall, and exuberant plant life result in the need for intensive trail maintenance; some trails must be cleared and cleaned at least twice a year. Rangers at the office here have information on closures, conditions of open trails, what flora and fauna to look for, and any activities planned that day. There are restrooms and water fountains near the parking lot. ✉*Rte. 191, Km 11.6*. Palo Colorado, the red-bark tree in which the endangered cotorra nests, dominates the forest surrounding the **Centro de Información Palo Colorado.** The center—home to Forest Adventure Tours and its two-hour, ranger-led hikes (reservations are required)—is the gateway for several walks. The easy Baño del Oro Trail loops 2 km (1 mi) through an area

THE NAME GAME

El Yunque has had many names over the years. Former President Theodore Roosevelt named it the Luquillo Forest Reserve in 1903, and former President Franklin Roosevelt changed its name to the Caribbean National Forest. In 2007 the area officially became El Yunque National Forest.

dubbed the Palm Forest. The even shorter El Caimitillo Trail starts at the same place and runs for about 1 km (½ mi). Although the challenging El Yunque–Mt. Britton Trail begins as asphalt, it turns to gravel as it climbs Pico El Yunque. At a higher elevation you can follow the Mt. Britton spur to an observation tower built in the 1930s. Without detours onto any of the side trails, the El Yunque Trail takes about three hours round-trip and includes some mild ascents. Signs clearly mark each turnoff, so it's hard to get lost if you stay on the path. All the trails here are edged by giant ferns, bamboo, and oversized impatiens. There are restrooms and parking at the center and a picnic area nearby. ✉ *Rte. 191, Km 11.9* ☎ *787/888–5646* 🌐 *www.fs.fed.us/r8/caribbean* 🎫 *Free* ⏲ *Daily 8–5.*

> **SHORT ON TIME?**
>
> If you're only going to drive through El Yunque, you can probably skip the El Portal information center. There's only one road through the park, so you can't get lost.

WHERE TO EAT

$$–$$$ ✕ **Las Vegas.** The food is a cut above what you'd expect to find in such an out-of-the-way place. Look for red snapper served with fried plantains or crab turnovers with melon chutney. The roasted lamb in a wine-and-herb sauce makes a hearty dinner. In a region where eating outdoors on plastic tables and chairs is the norm, the dining room's wooden furnishings are a blessing. ✉ *Rte. 191, Km 1.3* ☎ *787/809–6586* 💳 *AE, MC, V* ⏲ *Closed Mon.–Tues.*

$ ✕ **Yuquiyu Delights.** If you've been hiking all morning in the rain forest, this open-air dining room will be a sight for sore eyes. The covered terrace is scattered with tables whose copper tops add a touch of elegance. The chalkboard out front usually lists a few specials, often local favorites such as *chuleta frita* (fried pork chop). Even if you're not looking for a full meal, there's a little shop where you can stock up on water for the trail or snacks for the ride home. ✉ *Rte. 191, Km 11.3* ☎ *No phone* 💳 *No credit cards* ⏲ *Closed Tues. No dinner.*

¢ ✕ **Muralla.** The rangers at El Yunque swear by this place, a cement-block building just past Cascada La Cola. You won't find a cheaper meal anywhere in Puerto Rico, that's for sure. The *arroz habichuela con pollo* (fried chicken with rice and beans) is a steal at less than $5. The barking dog on the roof and the unusual artwork in the open-air dining room—a huge blob of papier mâché that may or may not be a boulder—add to the atmosphere. Get here early, as the place closes at 5 PM. ✉ *Rte. 191, Km 7.4* ☎ *No phone* 💳 *No credit cards* ⏲ *Closed Thurs. No dinner.*

SHOPPING

While in El Yunque, buy a recording of the tree frog's song, a video about the endangered green parrot, or a coffee-table book about the rain forest at the large **El Yunque Gift Shop** (✉ *El Portal, Rte. 191, Km 4.3* ☎ *787/888–1880*). Tucked among the rain-forest gifts are other Puerto Rican items, including note cards, maps, soaps, jams, and coffee.

★ Not far from the entrance to El Yunque are half a dozen souvenir shops selling identical T-shirts. A cut above the rest is **Coquí International** (✉*Rte. 955, near intersection of Rte. 191* ☎*787/888–1880*). A trail of colorful coquís (tree frogs) painted on the floor takes you past artists selling original paintings, hand-woven placemats, and one-of-a-kind items of clothing. And if you have to buy a T-shirt, the designs here can be found nowhere else.

WORD OF MOUTH

"[At El Yunque] we took the La Mina trail (long walk with lots of stairs) and swam in the waters below the waterfall—very cool."
–paulav

EN ROUTE

All along Route 3, from Canóvanas to Fajardo, roadside stands and kiosks sell fruit and sugarcane beverages, fried snacks, and fresh seafood. Artisans also sell their wares, handmade hammocks, and even tropical birds. For locals driving from El Yunque or Río Grande to Luquillo, the trip would be unthinkable without a stop at the *friquitines* (seafood kiosks) that line Route 3 west of the beach turnoff. They're busy all day, serving passing truckers, area businesspeople, and sand-covered families en route to or from the beach in Luquillo. Although some kiosks have larger seating areas than others, they all offer much the same fare, including cold drinks, plates of fried fish (head and tail still attached), conch salad, and fritters (usually codfish or corn).

LUQUILLO

13 km (8 mi) northeast of Río Grande; 45 km (28 mi) east of San Juan.

Known as the "Sun Capital" of Puerto Rico, Luquillo has one of the island's best-equipped family beaches. It's also a community where fishing traditions are respected. On the east end of Balneario de Luquillo, past the guarded swimming area, fishermen launch small boats and drop nets in open stretches between coral reefs.

Like many other Puerto Rican towns, Luquillo has its signature festival, in this case the Festival de Platos Típicos (Festival of Typical Dishes), a late-November culinary event that revolves around one ingredient: coconut. During the festivities, many of the community's 18,000 residents gather at the main square to sample treats rich with coconut or coconut milk. There's also plenty of free entertainment, including folk shows, troubadour contests, and salsa bands.

BEACHES

Fodor's Choice ★ Just off Route 3, gentle, shallow waters lap the edges of palm-lined **Balneario de Luquillo,** which is a magnet for families. It's well equipped with dressing rooms and restrooms, lifeguards, guarded parking, food stands, picnic areas, and even cocktail kiosks. Its most distinctive facility, though, is the Mar Sin Barreras (Sea Without Barriers), a low-sloped ramp leading into the water that allows wheelchair users to take a dip. The beach is open every day but Monday, from 9 to 5. Admission is $2 per car. ✉*Off Rte. 3.*

CLOSE UP

210 Parrots & Counting

The Taíno Indians called it the *iguaca,* Spanish speakers refer to it as the *cotorra,* and scientists know it as *Amazona vittata.* Whatever moniker it takes, the Puerto Rican green parrot—the only one native to the island—is one of the world's rarest birds. It nests primarily in the upper levels of El Yunque and in the nearby Sierra de Luquillo. The bird is almost entirely green, though there are touches of blue on its wings, white rings around its eyes, and a red band just above its beak. It's only about 12 inches long, and its raucous squawk doesn't match its delicate appearance. The parrots mate for life. In February (the rain forest's driest season), they build nests within tree hollows and lay three to four eggs. Both parents feed the young.

When the Spanish arrived, the parrot population was an estimated 1 million on the main island, Vieques, and Culebra. But deforestation, hurricanes, and parasites have reduced the population (parrot hunting was common before being outlawed in 1940). By 1967 there were only 19 birds; a 1975 count totaled only 13.

But things are looking up, especially with work beginning on a $2.5-million, state-of-the-art breeding facility in El Yunque. At this writing, an estimated 30 green parrots were living in the wild and another 180 were in captivity. Officials are optimistic that the numbers will continue to grow. If you're very observant (and very lucky), you just might spot one.

Waving palm trees and fishing boats add charm to the small **Playa Costa Azul,** although the ugly residential buildings along the water make an unattractive backdrop. The water here is good for swimming, and the crowds are thinner than elsewhere, but there are no facilities. ⊠*Off Rte. 193, near Rte. 3.*

Playa La Pared, literally "The Wall Beach," is a surfer haunt. Numerous local competitions are held here throughout the year, and several surfing shops are close by in case you need a wet suit or a wax for your board. The waves here are medium-range. It's very close to Balneario de Luquillo, but has a separate entrance. There are no facilities. ⊠*Off Rte. 3.*

WHERE TO EAT

$–$$ ✕ **Brass Cactus.** "Gringoland" is how one local described this Tex-Mex eatery. So many English-speaking tourists frequent the place that management doesn't bother printing the menu in Spanish. But the tender ribs and burgers melt in your mouth, and the helpings of crispy fries are generous. Nearly every dish—from the jalapeño burger to the mahimahi wrap—is made to be washed down with beer. Televisions broadcast the latest sporting events, and on the weekend bands often replace the jukebox. ⊠*Off Rte. 3, near main entrance to Luquillo* ☎*787/889–5735* ▭*AE, MC, V.*

¢–$ ✕ **Lolita's.** When it comes to Mexican food, this place is the real deal. Sure, you could order one of the dozen or so burritos, but why play it safe? Order *carne tampiqueña* (marinated skirt steak), *enchiladas suizas* (enchiladas in a mild green sauce), or *mole con pollo* (chicken in a spicy sauce laced with chocolate) and you'll know where you want to go for your next trip. Everything is washed down with oversized margaritas, of course. Those who eschew tequila can try the house sangrîa or one of the many Mexican beers. There's also an unusually varied wine list. The pleasant dining room, decorated with slightly kitschy paintings of village life, is on the second floor of a building just east of Luquillo. ✉*Rte. 3, Km 41.3, Barrio Juan Martín* ☎*787/889–5770 or 787/889–0250* ▭*AE, MC, V.*

WORD OF MOUTH

["We drove to Luquillo Beach and had tapas on our beach chairs (which they carry down to the beach for you for only $5 each). The beach was large and there were a lot of people there, but a great stop nonetheless!" –CandV

¢ ✕ **La Parrilla.** There are more than 50 *kioskos,* or food stands, along the highway on the way to Luquillo Beach. They all serve basically the same thing—fried seafood. Unlike its weekends-only neighbors, this place is so popular with locals that it's open every day. True to its name, it also has a grill, so you can add some sizzle to your shrimp, salmon, or red snapper. There are even a couple of steaks on the menu that are guaranteed to slay the biggest appetite. Like all of its neighbors, this place faces the street, but there's a comfortable patio in the rear where you can escape the traffic noise. ✉*Luquillo Beach, Kiosk #2* ☎*787/889–0590* ▭*No credit cards.*

WHERE TO STAY

¢–$ **Yunque Mar.** A sign near the door says WELCOME TO PARADISE. That might be overstating its charm a bit, but this low-slung hotel is certainly pleasant. It has the barrel-tile roofs and white stucco walls that typify Spanish colonial style. The modest rooms line corridors on two floors; the ocean-view rooms upstairs cost more, but are worth it. For another $10 you get a private balcony that's a stone's throw from the water. It's just west of the Balneario de Luquillo, but the beach here is nearly as nice and almost always deserted. The on-site seafood restaurant, La Yola, is a favorite with locals. **Pros:** On a lovely beach, great restaurant, friendly owners. **Cons:** Building is on a crowded street, bland decor. ✉*6 Calle 1, Fortuna* ☎*787/889–5555* *15 rooms, 2 suites* *In-hotel: restaurant, bar, pool, no elevator* ▭*AE, MC, V* *EP.*

SPORTS & THE OUTDOORS

SURFING Not far from Playa La Pared, **La Selva Surf Shop** (✉*250 Calle Fernández Garcia Luquillo* ☎*787/889–6205* *www.rainforestsafari.com/selva.html*) has anything a surfer could need, including news about current conditions. The family-run shop sells sunglasses, sandals, bathing suits, and other beach necessities.

FAJARDO

11 km (7 mi) southeast of Luquillo; 55 km (34 mi) southeast of San Juan.

Fajardo, founded in 1772, has historical notoriety as a port where pirates stocked up on supplies. It later developed into a fishing community and an area where sugarcane flourished. (There are still cane fields on the city's fringes.) Today it's a hub for the yachts that use its marinas, the divers who head to its good offshore sites, and the day-trippers who travel by catamaran, ferry, or plane to the off-islands of Culebra and Vieques. With the most significant docking facilities on the island's eastern side, Fajardo is a bustling city of 37,000—so bustling, in fact, that its unremarkable downtown is often congested and difficult to navigate.

A few miles north of Fajardo is the fishing area known as **Las Croabas,** where seafood is sold in open-air restaurants along the ocean. In the middle of town is a small park with a lovely waterfront walk. ✉*Rte. 3, Km 51.2.*

Marina Puerto del Rey, home to 1,100 boats, is one of the Caribbean's largest marinas. This is the place to hook up with a scuba-diving group, arrange an excursion to Vieques's bioluminescent bay, or charter a fishing boat. The marina, located south of Fajardo, also has several restaurants and boating-supply stores. ✉*Rte. 9987, off Rte. 987* ☎*787/860–1000* 🌐*www.puertodelrey.com.*

The small **Marina Puerto Real** doesn't have much to recommend it, except that it's near the terminal for ferries to Vieques and Culebra. Just outside the gates is Rosa's Sea Food, one of the best restaurants on this part of the coast. ✉*Rte. 9987, off Rte. 987* ☎*787/863–2188.*

Villa Marina is the second-largest marina in Fajardo and home to charter fishing boats as well as several catamaran operators who give day tours for swimming and snorkeling to the deserted islands right off Puerto Rico's northeast coast. ✉*Rte. 987, Km 1.3* ☎*787/863–5131* 🌐*www.villamarinapr.com.*

The 316-acre **Reserva Natural Las Cabezas de San Juan,** on a headland north of Fajardo, is owned by the nonprofit Conservation Trust of Puerto Rico. You ride in open-air trolleys and wander down boardwalks through seven ecosystems, including lagoons, mangrove swamps, and dry-forest areas. Green iguanas skitter across paths, and guides identify other endangered species. A half-hour hike down a wooden walkway brings you to the mangrove-lined **Laguna Grande,** where bioluminescent microorganisms glow at night. The restored **Fajardo Lighthouse** is the final stop on the tour; its Spanish-colonial tower has been in operation since 1882, making it Puerto Rico's second-oldest lighthouse. The first floor houses ecological displays; a winding staircase leads to an observation deck. The only way to see the reserve is on a mandatory guided tour; reservations are required. ✉*Rte. 987, Km 6* ☎*787/722–5882 (weekdays) or 787/860–2560 (weekends)* 🌐*www.fideicomiso.org* 🎟*$7* ⏲*Tours Wed.–Sun. at 8:30, 9:30, 10, 10:30, and 2.*

BEACHES

A long stretch of powdery sand near the Reserva Natural Las Cabezas de San Juan, **Balneario Seven Seas** may turn out to be the best surprise of your trip. Facilities include picnic tables, changing areas, restrooms, and showers. Many restaurants are just outside the gates. On weekends the beach attracts crowds keen on its calm, clear waters—perfect for swimming and other water sports. If you haven't tried sea kayaking before, this is a good place to learn. ✉*Rte. 987, Las Croabas.*

> **WORD OF MOUTH**
>
> "There are several casual restaurants along the Seven Seas beach in Las Croabas, [and] most specialize in 'arepas rellenas'—fried dumplings/turnovers that are filled with seafood." –marigross

WHERE TO EAT

$$$–$$$$ ✕**Blossoms.** Hung with elaborate lanterns, this dining room is a fanciful version of the Far East. The first thing you'll notice is the sound of meats and vegetables sizzling on the large teppanyaki tables. The chefs here know they're on stage and perform with a flourish. Despite the abundance of fresh fish, sushi bars are a rarity in this part of Puerto Rico. But the excellent one here has a seemingly endless array of dishes. Want traditional Chinese fare? Try the fancifully named "Passion Love Boat" (lobster and shrimp) or "Full Steam Ahead" (steamed fish with scallions and black mushrooms). ✉*El Conquistador Resort & Golden Door Spa, Rte. 987, Km 3.4* ☎*787/863–1000* *Reservations essential* ▭*AE, D, DC, MC, V* ⊙*No lunch Mon.–Sat.*

$$$–$$$$ ✕**Pasión por el Fogón.** The name refers to the passion chef Myrta Pérez possesses for taking traditional dishes and making them into something special. Pérez loves to present her dishes in unexpected ways—for example, the flank steak was rolled into a cylinder and stood on one end. But what makes this dish remarkable is the slightly sweet tamarind sauce that brings out the meat's earthy flavors. If you're a seafood lover, start with the lemony ceviche, then move on to the Lobster medallions broiled in butter. Owner Norma Guadaloupe, who will no doubt greet you at the door, often wears a brilliant shade of red that matches the main dining room's walls. It seems to be a case of a food lover wearing her heart on her sleeve. ✉*Rte. 987, Km 2.3* ☎*787/863–3502* ▭*MC, V.*

$$–$$$$ ✕**Otello's.** You can dine inside, enveloped in the soft glow cast by dozens of candles, or head outside to the terrace for a meal under the stars at this northern Italian restaurant. One of many at the El Conquistador Resort, it's among the best on the island's eastern coast. It's also one of the most elegant, with pale green walls, crisp linens, and delicate crystal. Start with the minestrone soup—a guaranteed winner—and follow it with fettuccine tossed with grilled shrimp or risotto with wild mushrooms. The house specialty is fettuccine with peas and mushrooms in a cream sauce. ✉*El Conquistador Resort & Golden Door Spa, Rte. 987, Km 3.4* ☎*787/863–1000* *Reservations essential* ▭*AE, D, DC, MC, V* ⊙*No lunch.*

$$$ ✕**Calizo.** There's a string of seafood shacks on the island's northeastern coast, all serving delicious fried fish. This open-air eatery, one of the

best in the village of Las Croabas, takes things up a notch or two. Look for dishes like conch salad in a spicy vinaigrette, mahimahi in a honey-and-white wine sauce, or chunks of lobster sautéed in garlic. Wash it all down with an icy cold beer on tap. It's almost across from the Balneario Seven Seas, making it a great place to refuel after a day at the beach. ✉*Rte. 987, Las Croabas* ☎*787/706–7337* ▭*MC, V.*

> **WORD OF MOUTH**
>
> "The Conquistador has a beautiful, world-class setting. You can stay 'down' by the marina, which will facilitate going to the beach. If you stay 'up' then you will be where the action is." –marigross

$$–$$$ ✕ **Anchor's Inn.** Seafood is the specialty at this shipshape restaurant. This is a great place to sample such local favorites as *chillo entero* (fried whole red snapper), among others. When the porthole windows are flung open, a nice breeze blows through the dining room. The convenient location, down the road from El Conquistador Resort, lures travelers who have had enough hotel food. ✉*Rte. 987, Km 2.7* ☎*787/863–7200* *Reservations not accepted* ▭*AE, MC, V* *Closed Tues.*

$–$$ ✕ **Rosa's Sea Food.** Despite its name, this family-run restaurant just outside the gates of Marina Puerto Real is also a good spot for beef and chicken. But if you want to see what people from all around the island are raving about, stick with the seafood. The specialty here is pieces of lobster, simmered with onions, tomatoes, and red peppers. Grilled and sautéed selections of fresh fish, from tuna to red snapper, are also a success. You can't miss the restaurant, as it's inside a two-story house painted a vivid shade of pink. ✉*536 Calle Tablado, off Rte. 195* ☎*787/863–0213* *Reservations not accepted* ▭*AE, MC, V* *Closed Wed.*

WHERE TO STAY

$$$–$$$$ **Fodor's Choice** ★ **El Conquistador Resort & Golden Door Spa.** The name means "The Conqueror," and this sprawling complex certainly has claimed the northeastern tip of the island. Perched on a bluff overlooking the ocean, it is one of Puerto Rico's loveliest destination resorts. Arranged in five "villages," the whitewashed buildings bring to mind the colonial era. Guest rooms were completely renovated—right down to the floors—in 2007. The ultramodern furnishings are all low to the ground, making sure nothing obscures the ocean views. The resort's beach is just offshore on Palomino Island; a shuttle boat takes you there in eight minutes. At the resort there are several different pools, as well as a water park for kids (and kids at heart). For grown-ups, the Japanese-influenced Golden Door is widely considered among the Caribbean's best spas. The Strip House is the newest of the cluster of top-drawer restaurants. **Pros:** Some of the island's best rooms, unbeatable views of the nearby islands, good dining options in and near hotel. **Cons:** Must take a boat to the beach, long waits at the funicular taking guests between levels, self-parking lot is a long distance from the front door. ✉*1000 Av. El Conquistador, Box 70001, Fajardo* ☎*787/863–1000 or 800/468–0389* *www.elconresort.com* *750 rooms, 17 suites, 155 villas* *In-room: safe, refrigerator, VCR, Ethernet, Wi-Fi. In-hotel: 17* *restaurants, bars, golf course, tennis courts, pools, gym, spa, beachfront, diving, water sports, children's programs (ages 4–12), laundry service, public Wi-Fi, airport shuttle, parking (fee), no-smoking rooms* ▭*AE, D, DC, MC, V* 🍴*EP.*

2

$–$$ **Fajardo Inn.** The butterscotch-colored buildings that make up this hilltop resort offer lovely views of the islands poking out of the Atlantic Ocean. A bit closer is the pool lined with shimmering aquamarine tiles, surrounded by gardens filled with wild ginger and other colorful plants. All rooms have simple furnishings and white-tile floors; some have balconies that let you enjoy the sunrise. Two restaurants, Starfish and Blue Iguana, are so good that they attract locals. The closest beach is the public Balneario Seven Seas, about a five-minute drive away. **Pros:** Beautiful grounds, family-friendly environment, good value. **Cons:** Not on the beach, motel-like rooms. ✉*Rte. 195, 52 Parcelas, Beltran Sector, Fajardo* ☎*787/860–6000 or 888/860–6006* 🌐*www.fajardoinn.com* *54 rooms* *In-room: kitchen (some), refrigerator (some). In-hotel: 2 restaurants, bar, pool, tennis court, public Internet, laundry service, parking (no fee), no-smoking rooms* ▭*AE, MC, V* 🍴*EP.*

$ **Ceiba Country Inn.** Although it's close to the rain forest, Fajardo has few lodgings that take advantage of the area's gorgeous greenery. For that reason you might want to drive five miles south to the town of Ceiba, where amidst the rolling hills you'll find this unassuming little inn. Colorful birds—the same ones you'll see in nearby El Yunque—flutter through the tropical foliage. Don't worry, you won't miss the ocean. From the sunny patio you have a view of Culebra, one of the small islands to the east of Puerto Rico. The same seascape is available from several of the simply furnished rooms—just ask for Room 1, 2, 8, or 9. Owners Sue Newbauer and Dick Bray, along with six (at last count) dogs, will make you feel right at home. **Pros:** Gorgeous setting, friendly owners. **Cons:** Very steep driveway, not for those with pet allergies. ✉*Rte. 977, Km. 1.2, Ceiba* ☎*787/885–0471* 🌐*www.geocities.com/countryinn00735* *9 rooms* *In-room: refrigerator. In-hotel: bar, no elevator, no-smoking rooms* ▭*AE, MC, V* 🍴*CP.*

NIGHTLIFE

Most of the evening action takes place in the El Conquistador Resort's lounges, but there are a few neighborhood bars where locals drink beer. You can play slots, blackjack, roulette, and video poker at **El Conquistador Casino** (✉*El Conquistador Resort & Golden Door Spa, 1000 Av. El Conquistador* ☎*787/863–1000*), a typical hotel gambling facility within the resort's lavish grounds.

SPORTS & THE OUTDOORS

GOLF ★ The 18-hole Arthur Hills–designed course at **El Conquistador Resort & Golden Door Spa** (✉*1000 Av. El Conquistador* ☎*787/863–6784*) is famous for its 200-foot changes in elevation. From the highest spot, on the 15th hole, you have great views of the surrounding mountains. The trade winds make every shot challenging. Greens fees for resort guests range from $100 to $165 and are even steeper for nonguests.

DAY SAILS Several reputable catamaran and yacht operators in Fajardo make excursions to the reefs and sparkling blue waters surrounding a handful of small islets just off the coast. Many of the trips include transportation from San Juan and transportation to and from San Juan–area hotels. Whether or not you're staying in Fajardo, if you take a day trip on the water you'll see classic Caribbean scenes of coral reefs rife with sea life, breathtakingly clear water, and palm-fringed, deserted beaches. The day sails, with stops for snorkeling, include swimming breaks at deserted beaches and picnic lunches. Most of the craft are outfitted for comfort, with quality stereo systems and full-service bars. Many competent operators offer a nearly identical experience, so your selection will probably be based on price and which operators serve your San Juan hotel, or which operate out of the marina in Fajardo that you are visiting. Prices range from $55 to $95; price is affected by whether you join a trip in San Juan or in Fajardo and by what is included in the cost. Ask if extras, such as picnic lunches and a full-service bar, are included. They are quickly becoming standard features.

At **East Winds Excursions** (✉ *Marina Puerto del Rey, Rte. 3, Km 51.4* ☎ *787/860–3434 or 877/937–4386* 🌐 *www.eastwindcats.com*) catamarans ranging in size from 45 feet to 65 feet take you offshore for snorkeling. Two of the catamarans are powered, and this cuts down tremendously on the travel time to outlying islands. Trips include stops at isolated beaches and a lunch buffet, included in the price. All craft are outfitted with swimming decks, freshwater showers, and full-service bars. These vessels are some of the plushest for day sails in the area.

Erin Go Bragh (✉ *Marina Puerto del Rey, Rte. 3, Km 51.4* ☎ *787/860–4401 or 787/409–2511* 🌐 *www.egbc.net*) is a sailing yacht based in Fajardo that takes a tour of the glistening waters and islands offshore. It is known for its barbecue picnic lunches. Snorkel and fishing equipment are provided. Longer charters are available for groups.

The *Spread Eagle II* (✉ *Puerto del Rey Marina, Rte. 3, Km 51.4* ☎ *787/887–8821 or 888/523–4511* 🌐 *www.snorkelpr.com*) is a 51-foot catamaran that heads out to isolated beaches on the islands off Fajardo. The trip includes an all-you-can-eat buffet and unlimited piña coladas. To top it off, you get a free snorkel to bring home. Sunset and moonlight cruises are also available.

At Villa Marina, **Fajardo Tours** (✉ *Villa Marina, Rte. 987, Km 1.3* ☎ *787/863–2821* 🌐 *www.travelerpr.com*) has a 54-foot catamaran called the *Traveler* that takes you to pristine coral reefs for an afternoon of snorkeling. Of course, there's the usual lunch buffet and plenty of rum punch.

DIVING The waters off eastern Puerto Rico are probably the best suited for scuba diving and snorkeling and compare favorably to other Caribbean diving destinations. Most operators will take you on dives up to 65 feet down, where visibility averages 40 feet to 60 feet and the water is still warm. The east has bountiful coral reefs, with a good mix of hard and soft coral, as well as a large variety of marine life. Fine snorkeling and diving spots can be found immediately offshore from Fajardo, and there are many small, uninhabited islets from which to dive just off the coast. Experienced divers will find more than enough variety to satisfy themselves, and those starting out will find eastern Puerto Rico a perfect place, with easy dives offering a taste of the beauty of life underwater.

La Casa del Mar Dive Center (✉*El Conquistador Resort & Golden Door Spa, 1000 Av. El Conquistador* ☎*787/863–1000 Ext. 7919 or 787/860–3483lacasadelmar@hotmail.com*) focuses its scuba and snorkeling activity on the islets of Palominos, Lobos, and Diablo. It also offers boating charters and trips to Vieques's bioluminescent bay. A two-tank morning dive costs from $99 to $124, depending on your equipment needs; single-tank afternoon dives are $69 to $94. An afternoon of snorkeling costs $50 per person.

At **Sea Ventures Pro Dive Center** (✉*Marina Puerto del Rey, Rte. 3, Km 51.4* ☎*787/863–3483* 🌐*www.divepuertorico.com*) you can get your diving certification, arrange dive trips to 20 offshore sites, or organize boating and sailing excursions. A two-tank dive for certified divers, including equipment, is $99.

KAYAKING

Several tour operators, including some based in San Juan, offer nighttime kayaking tours in the bioluminescent bay at the Reserva Natural Las Cabezas de San Juan, just north of Fajardo.

Eco Action Tours (☎*787/791–7509 or 787/640–7385* 🌐*www.ecoactiontours.com*) provides transportation and gives kayak tours of the shimmering Fajardo bay every night, with pickup service in the Fajardo area and San Juan hotels. The outfit also offers sailing tours to Culebra, daylong snorkeling trips, and Jet Ski rentals.

Las Tortugas Adventures (☎*787/725–5169 or 787/889–7734* 🌐*www.kayak-pr.com*) provides transportation from San Juan for a one-day kayaking trip in the Reserva Natural Las Cabezas de San Juan. Rates include transportation from San Juan, but it's possible to join up with the group in Fajardo.

SHOPPING

Maria Elba Torres runs the **Galería Arrecife** (✉*El Conquistador Resort & Golden Door Spa, 1000 Av. El Conquistador* ☎*787/863–3972*), which shows only works by Caribbean artists. Look for ceramics by Rafael de Olmo and jewelry made from fish scales. Chocolate-loving Laurie Humphrey had trouble finding a supplier for her sweet tooth, so she opened the **Paradise Store** (✉*Rte. 194, Km 0.4* ☎*787/863–8182*). Lindt and other gourmet chocolates jam the shop, which also sells flowers and such gift items as Puerto Rican–made soaps.

THE EASTERN COAST

From Fajardo, a good way to explore the southeast is to travel along the old coastal road, Route 3, as it weaves on and off the shoreline and passes through small towns. The route takes a while to travel but offers terrific beach and mountain scenery.

NAGUABO

18 km (11 mi) southwest of Fajardo.

In this fast-growing municipality's downtown, pastel buildings give the main plaza the look of a child's nursery: a golden-yellow church on one side faces a butter-yellow city hall, and a pink-and-blue amphitheater anchors one corner. It's a good spot for people watching until the heat drives you to the beach.

Offshore, Cayo Santiago—also known as Monkey Island—is the site of some of the world's most important rhesus monkey research. A small colony of monkeys was introduced to the island in the late 1930s, and since then scientists have been studying their habits and health, especially as they pertain to the study of diabetes and arthritis. You can't land at Cayo Santiago, but Captain Frank Lopez sails a small tour boat—*La Paseadora Naguabeña*—around it.

BEACH

Playa Húcares is *the* place to be. Casual outdoor eateries and funky shops vie with the water for your attention. Two Victorian-style houses anchor one end of the waterfront promenade; a dock with excursion boats anchors the other. ✉*Off Rte. 3, south of Naguabo.*

WHERE TO STAY & EAT

$ ✕**Chumar.** As at the other seafood shacks along Playa Húcares, you order at the counter and then grab a seat at one of the plastic tables lining the sidewalk. It's right on the ocean, so you are almost guaranteed fresh fish. Paper plates and plastic cutlery accompany the down-home seafood. Afterward you can stroll along the waterfront walkway across the street. ✉*Rte. 3, Km 66, Playa Húcares* ☎*787/874–0107* ▭*MC, V.*

$ **Casa Cubuy Ecolodge.** El Yunque's southern edge is the setting for this hotel. If you're up for a hike, set off on your own for a short one or hire a local guide for a daylong adventure that takes you through thick rain forest to hidden waterfalls. If you'd rather relax, hammocks await you on the tiled veranda. Guest rooms are simple—no phones or TVs—but comfortable, with tile floors, rattan furniture, and windows that show off one of the island's best views. You must climb many stairs to reach the upper rooms; if this is a problem, request one on the lower level. The proprietor, who believes that healthful eating translates into healthful living, serves tasty and wholesome breakfasts. Light picnic lunches can also be ordered in the morning to take with you on hikes, and dinner is available for groups of four or more. **Pros:** Spectacular setting, close to some of the island's best hiking trails, doting staff. **Cons:** Basic rooms, up a terrible road. ✉*Rte. 191, Km 22, Barrio Río Blanco* ☎*787/874–6221* 🌐*www.casacubuy.com* *8 rooms* *In-room: no a/c, no TV. In-hotel: no elevator, no-smoking rooms* ▭*AE, MC, V* *BP.*

SPORTS & THE OUTDOORS

Captain Frank Lopez will sail you around Cayo Santiago aboard *La Paseadora* (✉ *Playa Húcares dock, Rte. 3, Km 66.6* ☎ *787/850–7881*). Lopez, a charming, well-informed guide, gears the outings to the group. In an hour or 90 minutes, you can motor around the island and watch the monkeys. You can also make arrangements in advance for snorkeling stops or for the captain to drop you off at another islet and pick you up later.

WORD OF MOUTH

"Casa Cubuy [Ecolodge] is located in the nearby rain forest. Wonderful rooms, views, hiking & breakfasts. You could see three waterfalls from our room. Just remember to take along some food or snacks. If they don't have six people request dinner, you are on your own and it is a long ride back into town." –SAnParis

HUMACAO

15 km (9 mi) southwest of Naguabo; 55 km (34 mi) southeast of San Juan.

Travelers flock to the Humacao area for one reason: the sprawling resort community called Palmas del Mar and its two world-class golf courses, the Flamboyán and the Palm. Although it's not thought of as a tourist destination, Humacao does have a handful of interesting neo-colonial buildings along its traffic-clogged downtown streets. These are worth a peek if you're stuck here on a rainy day.

The former residence of sugar baron Antonio Roig Torruellas, **Museo Casa Roig** was built in 1919. Czech architect Antonio Nechodoma designed the facade, unusual for its wide eaves, mosaic work, and stained-glass windows with geometric patterns. This building, which bears more than a passing resemblance to those of Frank Lloyd Wright—was Puerto Rico's first 20th-century building to be included on the register of National Historic Places. The Roig family lived in the home until 1956; it was then abandoned before being turned over to the University of Puerto Rico in 1977. It's currently a museum and cultural center that houses historical photos, furniture, and rotating exhibits of works by contemporary island artists. ✉ *66 Calle Antonio López* ☎ *787/852–8380* 🌐 *www.uprh.edu/~museocr* 🎫 *Free* 🕑 *Wed.–Fri. and Sun. 10–4.*

Plaza de Humacao, downtown's broad square, is anchored by the pale pink Catedral Dulce Nombre de Jesús (Sweet Name of Jesus Cathedral), which dates from 1869. It has a castlelike facade, and even when its grille door is locked, you can peek through to see the sleek altar, polished floors, and stained-glass windows dominated by blues. Across the plaza, four fountains splash under the shade of old trees. People pass through feeding the pigeons, children race down the promenade, and retirees congregate on benches to chat. Look for the little monument with the globe on top; it's a tribute to city sons who died in wars. ✉ *Av. Font Martel at Calle Ulises Martinez.*

As you travel from Naguabo to Humacao, you'll pass stretches of beach and swaths of undeveloped land, including the swamps, lagoons, and forested areas of the **Refugio de Vida Silvestre de Humacao.** This nature reserve has an information office, restrooms, and camp sites. ✉ *Rte. 3, Km 74.3* ☎ *787/852–4440* *Free* ⏲ *Weekdays 7:30–4:30.*

BEACH

Right beside the Refugio de Vida Silvestre de Humacao, **Playa Punta Santiago** is a long shore with closely planted palm trees that are perfect for stringing up hammocks. The beach, one of 12 government-operated public beaches, has changing facilities with showers and restrooms, food kiosks, and lifeguard stations. Parking is $3. ✉ *Rte. 3, northeast of Humacao.*

WHERE TO EAT

$$$–$$$$ Fodor's Choice ★ ✕ **Chez Daniel.** When the stars are out, it would be hard to find a more romantic setting than this waterfront eatery in the Anchor's Village Marina. Dozens of gleaming white boats are anchored so close that you could practically hit them with a baguette. The dining room has a chummy atmosphere, probably because many patrons seem to know each other. If you'd prefer alone time, ask for a table on one of the private terraces. Chef Daniel Vasse's French country–style dishes are some of the best on the island. The exceptional Catalan-style bouillabaisse is full of fresh fish and bursts with the flavor of a white garlic sauce. Pair it with a bottle from the extensive wine cellar. Sunday brunch, with its seemingly endless seafood bar, draws people from all over the island. ✉ *Palmas del Mar, Anchor's Village Marina, Rte. 906, Km 86.4* ☎ *787/850–3838* *Reservations essential* ▭ *AE, MC, V* ⏲ *Closed Tues. No lunch Mon.–Thurs.*

$–$$ ✕ **Bistro Rico.** You can't eat at Chez Daniel every night, which is probably why Daniel Vasse opened this bistro a stone's throw away from his original restaurant. The menu here is mostly made up of sandwiches, but don't expect anything too ordinary. The sliced duck breast with caramelized red onions is simple but satisfying, as is the codfish with slices of hard-boiled eggs or the filet mignon with bearnaise sauce. The handful of entrées includes—of course—a smashing quiche Lorraine. The staff is friendly, and the simple decor is livened up with some slightly kitschy seaside murals. ✉ *Palmas del Mar, Anchor's Village Marina, Rte. 906, Km 86.4* ☎ *787/850–3838* ▭ *AE, MC, V* ⏲ *Closed Sun.*

WHERE TO STAY

$$ **Four Points by Sheraton at Palmas del Mar Hotel & Casino.** The only hotel in Palmas del Mar, the Four Points by Sheraton, sits amid acres and acres of condo developments. It's surprisingly modest in scale, given its opulent surroundings. The rooms could be at any hotel, but those fitted with plantation-style furnishings are more luxurious. None of the rooms has a view of the ocean, but all of them have balconies overlooking the infinity pool or the lush grounds. Because you have access to the facilities at Palmas del Mar, you can stroll around the marina, play a few games of tennis, or hit the links at the two championship golf courses. **Pros:** Access to all the resort's amenities, near excellent restaurants, beautiful pool area. **Cons:** Uninspired architecture, standard-issue rooms, small casino. ✉ *170 Candelero Dr.* ☎ *787/850–6000* 🌐 *www.starwoodhotels.com* *107 rooms* *In-room: safe, Ethernet, Wi-Fi. In-hotel: restaurant, room service, bars, golf courses, tennis courts, pool, gym, beachfront, diving, water sports, public Wi-Fi, airport shuttle* *AE, D, DC, MC, V* *EP.*

2

$ **Palmas de Lucía.** Lights shaped like palm trees illuminate the pool area at this family-run hotel. Don't worry—plenty of the real thing are flourishing on the pretty stretch of beach just outside. The rooms are larger than you'd expect for the price, and have spotless kitchenettes. Kids like chatting with Coquí, the M&M-munching macaw that resides in the lobby. The hotel is in Yabucoa, several miles south of Humacao. **Pros:** An off-the-beaten-path feel, friendly staff. **Cons:** A 15-minute drive to restaurants, a bit difficult to find. ✉ *Rte. 901 at Rte. 9911, Yabucoa* ☎ *787/893–4423* 🌐 *www.palmasdelucia.com* *34 rooms* *In-room: refrigerator. In-hotel: restaurant, laundry service* *AE, MC, V* *EP.*

NIGHTLIFE

The small casino at the **Four Points by Sheraton Palmas del Mar Resort** (✉ *170 Candelero Dr.* ☎ *787/850–6000*) offers everything from blackjack to slot machines. The action is liveliest on weekends.

SPORTS & THE OUTDOORS

FISHING At **Karolette Sport Fishing** (✉ *Palmas del Mar, Anchor's Village Marina* ☎ *787/850–7442* 🌐 *www.karolette.com*), you're in the capable hands of Captain Bill Burleson, who has fished these waters since 1966. He'll take you out for excursions in his bright yellow Bertram powerboat. A half day of fishing along the continental shelf costs $680, while a full day (usually more than nine hours) of deep-water fishing costs $1,250. If nobody makes a catch, he'll cut the fee in half.

Maragata Charters (✉ *Palmas del Mar, Anchor's Village Marina* ☎ *787/637–5786* 🌐 *www.maragatacharters.com*) takes anglers out to the continental shelf on a 38-foot power catamaran. For a four-hour tour, the cost for six people is $600, while an eight-hour tour is $1,020.

GOLF ★ **Palmas del Mar Country Club** (✉ *Rte. 906* ☎ *787/285–2256* 🌐 *www.palmascountryclub.com*) has two good golf courses: the Rees Jones–designed Flamboyán course, named for the nearly six dozen flamboyant trees that pepper its fairway, winds around a lake, over a river, and to the sea before turning toward sand dunes and wetlands. It's been rated one of the top five courses in the world. The older Gary Player–designed Palm course has a challenging par 5 that scoots around wetlands. Greens fees are $70 to $100.

EL YUNQUE & THE NORTHEAST ESSENTIALS

To research prices, get advice from other travelers, and book travel arrangements, visit www.fodors.com.

TRANSPORTATION

BY AIR

Air Flamenco, Isla Nena Air Service, and Vieques Air Link offer several daily flights between Fajardo and San Juan, as well as between Fajardo and Vieques and Culebra. Trips to any of these destinations are between 10 and 15 minutes; the cost ranges from $40 to $100 round-trip.

Information **Air Flamenco** (☎ *787/724–1818* 🌐 *www.airflamenco.net*). **Isla Nena Air Service** (☎ *787/741–6362 or 877/812–5144* 🌐 *www.islanena.8m.com*). **Vieques Air Link** (☎ *787/741–8331 or 888/901–9247* 🌐 *www.viequesisland.com/val*).

AIRPORTS Fajardo is served by the one-room Aeropuerto Diego Jiménez Torres, which is just southwest of the city on Route 976. The landing field at Aeropuerto Regional de Humacao is used mostly by private planes.

Information **Aeropuerto Diego Jiménez Torres** (☎ *787/860–3110*). **Aeropuerto Regional de Humacao** (☎ *787/852–8188*).

BY BUS

Públicos travel between San Juan and Fajardo, stopping en route at the ferry terminal. The full journey can take up to two hours, depending on where you board and where you are dropped off. However, the fare is a huge bargain at $5 (pay the driver as you board). To get to Fajardo, you simply flag públicos down anywhere along Route 3.

Within cities and towns, local buses pick up and discharge at marked stops and cost 35¢ to 50¢. You enter and pay (the exact fare is required) at the front of the bus and exit at the front or the back.

BY CAR

Unless you are planning to hop directly onto a ferry to Vieques or Culebra, you should consider renting a car in eastern Puerto Rico. Even the destination resorts are fairly isolated, and you may appreciate the mobility if you want to get out and have a meal away from the resort, or explore El Yunque or some of the great beaches on your own. Rates generally start at about $35 a day, but it may be possible to rent directly from your lodging, so ask about packages that include lodging and a car rental.

From San Juan the east coast is accessible via Route 3, or Route 187 if you want to visit Loíza. At Fajardo the road intersects with Route 53, a fast toll road that continues down the coast. Route 3, however, also continues along the coast and provides a more scenic, if slower, trip.

EMERGENCY SERVICES Rental-car agencies usually give customers emergency road-service numbers to call. There's no AAA service on Puerto Rico.

GASOLINE Gas stations are found along major roads and within cities and towns. Gasoline is sold in liters, not gallons. Although few eastern stations have round-the-clock hours, many are open until midnight and most are open seven days a week. Note that gas is rarely self-service; an attendant usually pumps it for you.

PARKING Although parking can be a nightmare (a pricey one at that) in San Juan, it's no problem out on the island except during festivals. Some midsize cities have metered on-street parking as well as lots; in smaller communities, street parking is the norm and is generally free. Most of the bigger resorts charge for parking.

ROAD CONDITIONS The main roads are in good shape, but many highway-exit and other signs have been blown down by hurricanes, and may or may not have been replaced. When it rains, be alert for flash flooding, even on the major highways.

Agencies **Avis** (✉ *El Conquistador Resort & Golden Door Spa, 1000 Av. El Conquistador, Fajardo* ☎ *787/863–2735* ✉ *170 Candelero Dr., Humacao* ☎ *787/285–1376* ✉ *Rio Mar Beach Resort & Spa, 6000 Río Mar Blvd., Río Grande* ☎ *787/888–6638* 🌐 *www.avis.com*). **L & M** (✉ *Rte. 3 Marginal, Km 43.8, Fajardo* ☎ *787/860–6868* 🌐 *www.lmcarrental.net*). **Leaseway of Puerto Rico** (✉ *Rte. 3, Km 44.4, Fajardo* ☎ *787/860–5000*).

BY FERRY

The Puerto Rico Ports Authority runs passenger ferries from Fajardo to Culebra and Vieques. Service is from the ferry terminal in Fajardo, about a 90-minute drive from San Juan. A municipal parking lot next to the ferry costs $5 a day—handy if you are going to one of the islands for the day. On Culebra the ferry pulls right into a nicely renovated terminal in downtown Dewey. The Vieques ferry dock is in downtown Isabel Segunda.

The ferries have a limited number of seats, so get to the terminal well ahead of time. This means an hour or more before the departure time in Fajardo, somewhat less in Vieques and Culebra. Advance reservations are not accepted. In Fajardo, the ticket counter is in the small building across the street from the actual terminal. In Vieques and Culebra, the ticket counters are at the entrance to the terminals. The food kiosks at Fajardo and Vieques open in time for the early morning departures; Culebra doesn't have any eateries nearby.

In addition to the regular ferries, there are cargo ferries with weekday departures. These ferries are notorious for canceling departures at the last minute, leaving travelers stranded. If they are carrying hazardous cargo, such as fuel oil, they will refuse passage even to those who have already bought tickets. And don't even think about using one to transport your rental car to Vieques or Culebra. Even if you can get your car onboard, they might not be able to bring it back for a week or more. That's sure to throw a monkey wrench in your travel plans.

FARES & SCHEDULES The Fajardo–Vieques passenger ferry departs from Vieques weekdays at 9 AM, 1 PM, 3 PM, 4:30 PM, and 8 PM, returning at 6:30 AM, 11 AM, 3 PM, and 6 PM. On weekends ferries depart from Vieques at 9 AM, 3

PM, and 6 PM, returning at 6:30 AM, 1 PM, and 4:30 PM. Tickets for the 90-minute journey are $2 each way.

The Fajardo-Culebra ferry leaves Culebra daily at 9 AM, 3 PM, and 7 PM, returning at 6:30 AM, 1 PM, and 5 PM. The 90-minute trip is $2.25.

Ferry schedules change with alarming frequency. Call to confirm before you plan your trip, especially if you are planning to travel on the weekend.

Information **Puerto Rico Ports Authority** (☎ *787/863-0705*).

Ferry Terminals **Culebra Terminal** (☎ *787/742-3161*). **Fajardo Terminal** (☎ *787/863-4560*). **Vieques Terminal** (☎ *787/741-4761*).

BY TAXI

You can flag cabs down on the street, but it's faster and safer to have your hotel call one for you. Either way, make sure the driver is clear on whether he or she will charge a flat rate or use a meter to determine the fare. In most places the cabs are metered. Instead of renting a car, some people opt to take a taxi to Fajardo. The cost from the San Juan area should be about $80 for up to five people.

Information **Fajardo Taxi Service** (☎ *787/860-1112*). **Humacao Taxi** (☎ *787/852-6880*).

CONTACTS & RESOURCES

BANKS & EXCHANGE SERVICES

Banks and ATMs (or ATHs, as they're called here) are plentiful. Banks are usually open weekdays from 9 to 5; very few open on Saturday, and those that do are open only until noon.

Information **Banco Popular** (✉ *Rte. 3, Km 42.4, Fajardo* ☎ *787/860-1570*). **Banco Roig** (✉ *55 Calle Antonio Lopez, Humacao* ☎ *787/852-8601*).

EMERGENCIES

Emergency Numbers **General** (☎ *911*). **Medical Clinics** (☎ *787/876-2042 in Loíza, 787/823-2550 in Río Grande, 787/889-2620 in Luquillo, 787/863-2550 in Fajardo, 787/874-7440 in Naguabo*).

Hospitals **Hospital Dr. Dominguez** (✉ *300 Font Martelo, Humacao* ☎ *787/852-0505*). **Hospital Gubern** (✉ *110 Antonio Barcelo, Fajardo* ☎ *787/863-0669*). **Hospital San Pablo del Este** (✉ *Av. General Valero, Km 2.4, Fajardo* ☎ *787/863-0505*). **Ryder Memorial Hospital** (✉ *Salida Humacao-Las Piedras, Humacao* ☎ *787/852-0768*).

Pharmacies **Walgreens** (✉ *Fajardo Plaza, Fajardo* ☎ *787/860-1060* ✉ *Oriental Plaza, Humacao* ☎ *787/852-1868*).

INTERNET, MAIL & SHIPPING

Puerto Rico is part of the U.S. postal system, and most communities of any size have multiple post office branches. Some aren't open on Saturday, however. Big hotels and resorts also have postal drop boxes.

There are very few Internet cafés in this part of the country, but all of the larger hotels have in-room Internet access.

Post Offices **Fajardo main post office** (✉ *102 Calle Garrido Morales E, Fajardo* ☎ *787/863-0802*). **Naguabo main post office** (✉ *100 Rte. 31, Naguabo* ☎ *787/874-3115*).

OVERNIGHT SERVICES

Puerto Rico has express overnight mail delivery through the U.S. Postal Service as well as Federal Express, which usually operates through office supply stores or other commercial outlets. (Note that FedEx doesn't offer Saturday pickup on the island.)

Information **OfficeMax** (✉ *Rte. 3, Fajardo* ☎ *800/463-3339*). **Post Net** (✉ *Rte. 3, Río Grande* ☎ *800/463-3339* ✉ *118 Av. Ortiz Estela, Humacao* ☎ *800/463-3339*).

SAFETY

Although crime isn't as high in the island's eastern areas as it is in San Juan, use prudence. Avoid bringing valuables with you to the beach; if you must do so, be sure not to leave them in view in your car. It's best to keep your car locked while driving, and steer clear of out-of-the way beaches after sunset.

VISITOR INFORMATION

The island's tourism offices are hit and miss when it comes to helpful material. The cities usually offer information through offices connected to city hall, and most are open only during business hours on weekdays.

Information **Fajardo Tourism Office** (✉ *6 Av. Muñoz Rivera, Fajardo* ☎ *787/863-1400*). **Luquillo Tourism Office** (✉ *154 Calle 14 de Julio, Luquillo* ☎ *787/889-2851*). **Naguabo Tourism Office** (✉ *Rte. 3, Km 66.6, Playa Húcares, Naguabo* ☎ *787/874-0389*). **Río Grande Office of Tourism and Culture** (✉ *Calle San José, Plaza de Recreo, Río Grande* ☎ *787/887-2370*).

Vieques & Culebra

WORD OF MOUTH

"We loved Vieques and its choice of so many beautiful beaches. We had Blue Beach to ourselves several days and thought the snorkeling was pretty good as well."

—BeachGirl247

"Most of the islands have pretty shades of blue and green. But I was in Culebra, and the water there sparkled like I never saw water sparkle before. It was like looking at diamonds!!!!!"

—noonema

www.fodors.com/forums

Revised and Updated by Mark Sullivan

ALTHOUGH THE ISLANDS OF VIEQUES and Culebra are only a few miles off the coast of Puerto Rico, they feel like another world. While the rest of the mainland rings with the adrenaline rush of Latin America, this pair of palm-ringed islands has the laid-back vibe of the Caribbean. Not surprising, as St. Thomas and St. Croix are clearly visible from the eastern edges of Culebra.

Vieques and Culebra are alike in many ways. Neither has much traffic—in fact, you won't find a single traffic light on either island. High-rise hotels haven't cast a shadow on the beautiful beaches. And there are no casinos, fast-food chains, strip malls, or most other trappings of modern life. "Barefoot" is often part of the dress code at the casual restaurants, and the hum you hear in your room more likely than not comes from a ceiling fan rather than an air-conditioner.

But each island has its own personality. Vieques is the biggest of the siblings, so it gets the most attention. The island, 21 mi long and 4 mi wide, has two small communities. Isabel Segunda, the town on the northern shore where the ferry docks, is a knot of one-way streets. It's not pretty, but it has a couple of interesting sights, including a hilltop fortress. On the southern shore is the town of Esperanza, little more that a string of low-cost restaurants and hotels along a waterfront promenade. Nearby is the world-famous Bahía Mosquito, a bioluminescent bay that twinkles like the night sky. The bulk of the island is a national park, the Vieques National Wildlife Refuge. Within the park you'll find dozens of beaches with names such as Red, Green, and Blue, as well as many more that have no official name.

At 7 mi long and 4 mi wide, Culebra is much smaller. There's only one community, the tiny town of Dewey. People come to Culebra to see Playa Flamenco, consistently rated as one of the two or three best beaches in the world, as well as many lesser-known but equally beautiful beaches. The island is mostly unspoiled, a quality that brings many people back year after year.

Getting to the islands is much easier than in years past. Both are accessible from Fajardo—either on 90-minute ferry trips or 10-minute puddle-jumper flights. There are also flights from either of San Juan's airports that take between 20 and 30 minutes. The flights are scenic, skirting the main island's northern coast before heading out over the azure waters of the Caribbean.

EXPLORING VIEQUES & CULEBRA

It's nearly impossible to see either island without renting a car. Sure, you could stay at one of the small hotels along the waterfront in Vieques, eating at the handful of restaurants within walking distance, but you'd miss out on most of what the island has to offer. Scooters are another option for getting around, especially on tiny Culebra, but they aren't a good idea if you are headed to the beach. Roads are dusty, paved with loose gravel, and riddled with huge potholes.

VIEQUES & CULEBRA TOP 5

- Swimming after dark in Bahía Mosquito, the astounding bioluminescent bay on Vieques.
- Catching some rays on Culebra's Playa Flamenco, consistently ranked as one of the world's best beaches.
- Hiking to the deserted lighthouse on one of the islands that make up the Refugio Nacional de Vida Silvestre de Culebra.
- Watching the sunset from the cantilevered deck at Al's Mar Azul, the best happy hour spot on Vieques.
- Discovering Playa Media Luna, or one of the dozens of other deserted beaches that fringe Vieques.

ABOUT THE RESTAURANTS

Most of the restaurants on Vieques and Culebra are extremely casual, meaning that the dress code doesn't get much stricter than NO SHOES, NO SHIRT, NO SERVICE. Because even the most formal restaurants on the islands are on covered terraces or in open-air dining rooms, there's not a single establishment where you'll be frowned on for wearing shorts. Pack a couple of nice shirts and you'll be set.

Caribbean cuisine—meaning lots of fresh fish and local produce—is the norm here. Even if a restaurant focuses on a different type of food, you can be sure that mangos, papayas, and other tropical fruits will make an appearance. Bills often include a service charge; if it isn't included, a 15% tip is customary. Most restaurants are open for dinner from about 6 PM until at least 10 PM.

WHAT IT COSTS IN U.S. DOLLARS

	$$$$	$$$	$$	$	¢
AT DINNER	over $30	$20–$30	$12–$20	$8–$12	under $8

Prices are per person for a main course at dinner.

ABOUT THE HOTELS

Vieques has a wide variety of lodgings, from surf shacks across from the beach to boutique hotels high up on secluded hillsides. There's something here for everyone. Looking for tropical splendor? Try Hacienda Tamarindo or the Inn on the Blue Horizon. Interesting architecture? There's Hix Island House or Bravo Beach Resort. An intimate inn where you'll meet all of your fellow travelers? Head to Casa de Amistad or Trade Winds.

Culebra has fewer options. Dewey, the island's only town, has a handful of small inns that are easy on the wallet. Scattered around the island

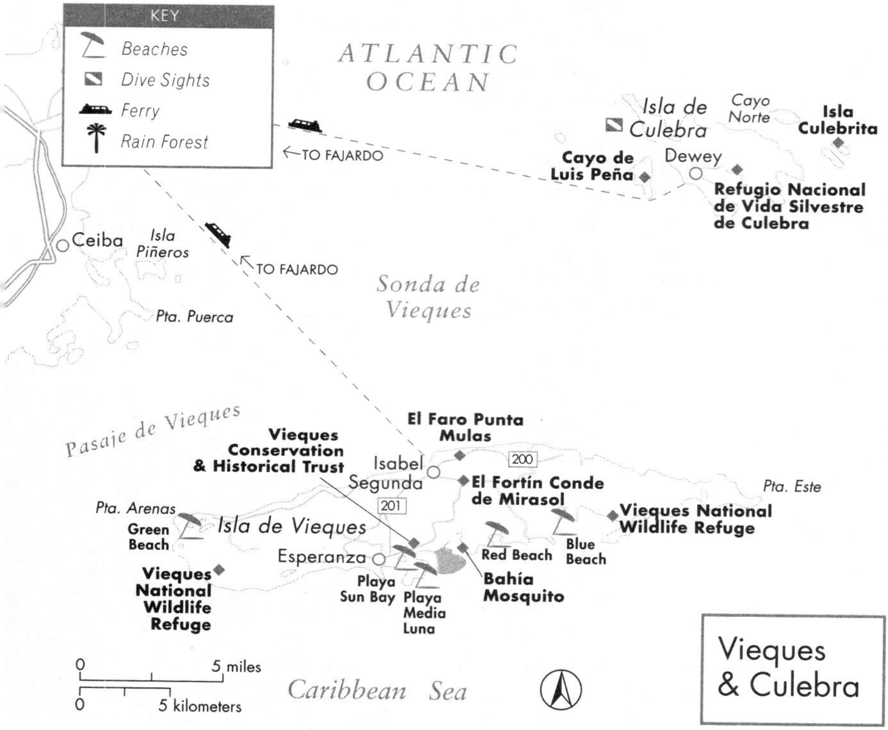

are a couple of more luxurious lodgings. Nothing here remotely resembles a chain hotel, and that's how the locals like it.

WHAT IT COSTS IN U.S. DOLLARS					
	$$$$	$$$	$$	$	¢
FOR 2 PEOPLE	over $350	$250–$350	$150–$250	$80–$150	under $80

Prices are for a double room in high season, excluding 9% tax (11% for hotels with casinos, 7% for paradores) and 5%–12% service charge.

TIMING

Roughly speaking, high season runs from December 15 through April 15. The crowds are the most unbearable at Christmas and Easter, when Vieques and Culebra are packed with families enjoying the sun and sand. Be sure to make reservations well in advance if you're visiting during the holidays. The shoulder season, when prices are a bit lower, is a good option. Remember, however, that some restaurants and hotels are only open during the high season. The only time you might want to avoid is late August through late October, when most hurricanes roll through the area.

IF YOU LIKE

BEACHES

Beautiful beaches abound on Vieques and Culebra. Many of the best stretches of sand on Vieques—Red Beach, Blue Beach, and Green Beach, to name a few—are on land that was once part of a naval base. This means that development hasn't reared its ugly head. It also means there are few, if any, amenities at most of these beaches, so bring plenty of water and a picnic lunch. The beaches on Culebra are just as unspoiled. Playa Flamenco, on the island's northern coast, is considered one of the best in the world.

SEAFOOD

Hopefully you like seafood, because that's what you'll get at almost every eatery on Vieques and Culebra. The good news is that the fish is as fresh as you'll find anywhere, since that red snapper was probably splashing around in the Caribbean that very morning. Unlike some other parts of Puerto Rico, here you can order your fish in any number of ways. Chefs are experimenting with European and Asian cooking techniques, so you may find your fish smoked or even in a sushi roll.

WATER SPORTS

Some of the best snorkeling and diving can be found in the waters surrounding Vieques and Culebra. You can sign up for a half-day or full-day excursion to nearby coral reefs, which are teeming with colorful fish. It's also possible to grab a mask and snorkel, and then simply wade out a few yards to see what you can see. Playa Esperanza, on the southern coast of Vieques, is a good place for beginners. More experienced snorkelers will prefer Blue Beach or Green Beach.

VIEQUES

13 km (8 mi) southeast of Fajardo.

Looking for a place to play Robinson Crusoe? Then head to Vieques, where you can wander along almost any stretch of sand and never see another soul. You can while away the hours underneath coconut palms, wade in the warm water, or get a mask and snorkel and explore the coral reefs that ring the island.

For many years the island was known mostly for the conflict between angry islanders and aloof federal officials. Over the course of six decades, the U.S. Navy used two-thirds of Vieques, mostly on the island's eastern and western tips, as a bombing range. Residents complained that their mighty neighbor stifled economic development and harmed the environment. After an April 1999 bombing accident took the life of one resident, waves of protests that brought the maneuvers to a standstill, and political pressure from the island's government, the military reluctantly agreed to leave on May 1, 2003.

Ironically, the military's presence helped to keep the island pristine by limiting the land available for rambling resorts. Today, most of the military's holdings have been turned into the Vieques National Wildlife Refuge. The western end of the island has the most public access. Here

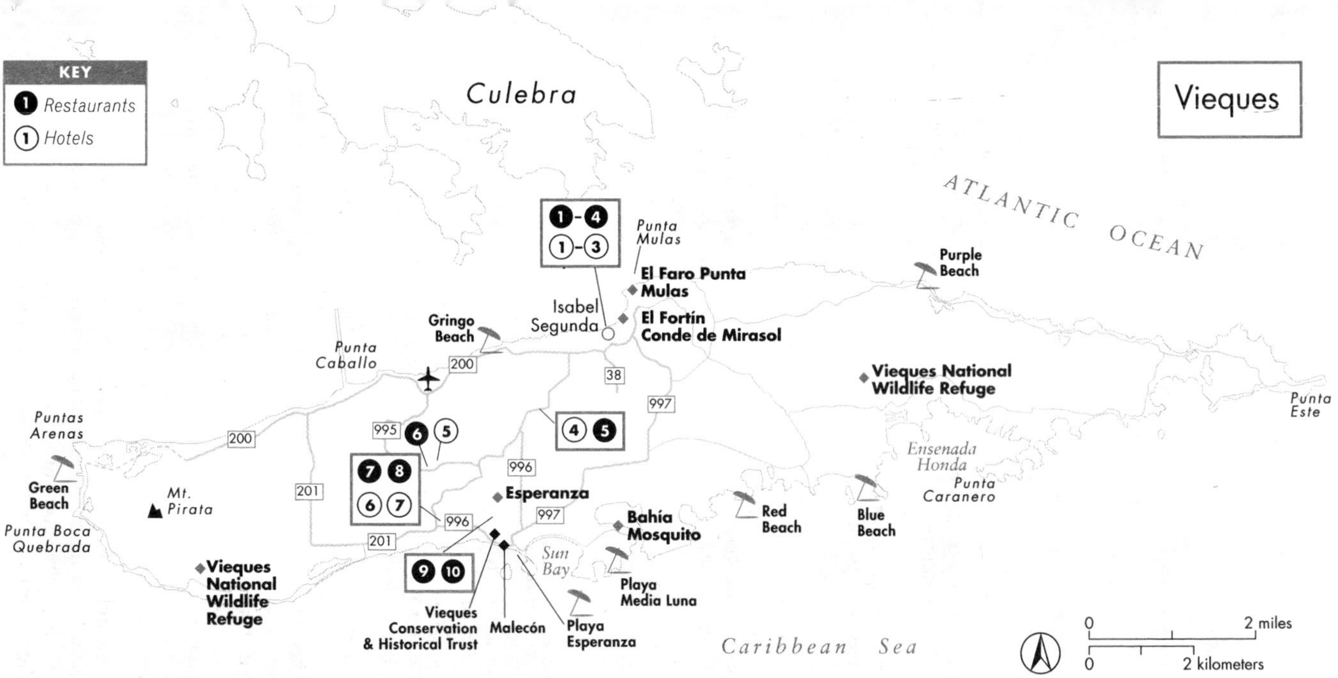

Restaurants	▼
Bananas	10
BBH	3
Bilí	9
Blue Macaw	4
Café Media Luna	2
Carambola	7
Chez Shack	6
Duffy's	8
Island Steakhouse	5
Uva	1

Hotels	▼
Bravo Beach Hotel	1
Casa de Amistad	3
Crow's Nest	4
Hacienda Tamarindo	6
Hix Island House	5
Inn on the Blue House	7
Trade Winds	2

CLOSE UP

Vieques Libre

For nearly six decades, the U.S. Navy had a stranglehold on Vieques. It controlled the island's eastern and western ends and exerted enormous influence over the destiny of the civilian area sandwiched in between. Though long protested, the bombing continued. When an off-target bomb killed a civilian on Navy land in April 1999, opposition began to transform the island's placid beaches into political hotbeds. As a result of the protests that followed, the Navy finally withdrew from its Atlantic Fleet training grounds in May 2002.

Protesters camping out on the bombing range kept it shut down from 1999 to 2000. Hundreds of Puerto Rican residents were arrested for trespassing on Navy land during war games. They were joined by celebrity protesters from the United States, including environmental lawyer Robert F. Kennedy Jr. (who gave his baby daughter the middle name "Vieques"), the wife of Reverend Jesse Jackson, and Reverend Al Sharpton, all of whom were arrested for trespassing on the bombing range. For much of 2000 and 2001, protests were so commonplace that there were semipermanent encampments of opponents. Songs with such titles as "Paz Pa' Vieques" ("Peace for Vieques") began to surface, as did bumper stickers and T-shirts with protest slogans. Latin pop celebrities such as singer–songwriter Robie Draco Rosa (who wrote such Ricky Martin hits as "Livin' la Vida Loca"), actor Edward James Olmos, singer Millie Corejter, Puerto Rican rock band Fiel a la Vega, protest-singer Zoraida Santiago, local actors, painters, doctors, and lawyers, added to the fanfare when they joined the activities.

President Bill Clinton finally agreed that residents could vote on whether to continue to host the Navy. A nonbinding referendum held in 2001 found that 68% of the island's voters wanted the military to leave immediately. Although some members of Congress argued that the Navy should stay indefinitely—their cries grew louder after September 11, 2001, when even local protesters called for a moratorium on civil disobedience—the administration agreed to withdraw the troops. In 2003, the naval base was officially closed.

The Navy's departure has undoubtedly spurred development on Vieques—one need only look at the additions to the tiny airport and plans for a modern ferry terminal. Amenities such as a golf course running along the northern coast are also in the works. But locals are working to make sure that the island retains its laid-back character. By the end of 2005, much of the former military base had already been transformed into the Vieques National Wildlife Refuge. This move should preserve most of the island in its unspoiled state.

you'll find Monte Pirata, the island's highest peak. (At 987 feet, it isn't much of a mountain, but it looks impressive.) More and more of the eastern part of the island is being opened every year. The park is your gateway to some of the island's best beaches, including Green Beach in the west and Red and Blue beaches in the east.

GREAT ITINERARIES

IF YOU HAVE 1 DAY

If you are headed to one of the islands for an overnight excursion, your best bet is **Vieques.** Get here by plane, either from San Juan or Fajardo, to maximize your time on the island. Spend the day exploring the beaches, especially the half-moon–shaped Sun Bay. In the evening you can dine at one of the oceanfront restaurants in Esperanza, then head off for an excursion to **Bahía Mosquito,** a bay filled with glow-in-the-dark dinoflagellates. Dive in and your body will be outlined in an eerie blue phosphorescence. Spend the night in Esperanza or Isabel Segunda.

IF YOU HAVE 3 DAYS

If you have a few days, you can see most of Vieques. Start your first day in Isabel Segunda, where you can take a few snapshots of **El Faro Punta Mulas,** then explore the hilltop fortress called **El Fortín Conde de Mirasol.** Head off for an afternoon by the ocean, perhaps at Green Beach or one of the delightfully deserted beaches on the northern part of the island. Enjoy the sunset from Al's Mar Azul, a favorite hangout for expats, or from the deck of a catamaran. In the cool of the evening, have dinner in one of the chic eateries in Isabel Segunda. On your second day, go for a hike in the **Vieques National Wildlife Refuge,** at either end of the island, a swath of wilderness that was once a naval base. Head for lunch at Sun Bay, a popular beach that has its own snack bar, or pack a picnic and head off to Playa Media Luna or one of the little-known gems on the southern coast. After dinner, make sure to book a tour of **Bahía Mosquito.**

IF YOU HAVE 5 DAYS

If you have a few more days, you can see both Vieques and Culebra. After following the itinerary above, head to Culebra on your fourth day. (One of the 10-minute flights between the islands is the best—and often the only—way to travel between them.) Your destination should be Playa Flamenco, a U-shaped beach bordered by an unbroken string of palm trees. The mountains beyond make a striking backdrop. Dine that evening in one of the eateries in or around the only town, the diminutive Dewey. On your last day, try snorkeling in **Refugio Nacional de Vida Silvestre de Culebra,** the island's lovely nature preserve. One of the best places is **Isla Culebrita,** an islet dominated by a deserted lighthouse.

EXPLORING VIEQUES

Just because Vieques is sleepy doesn't mean there's nothing to do besides hit the beach. There are two communities—Isabel Segunda and Esperanza—where you can dine at an open-air eatery, stock up on supplies, or book a trip to the astonishing Bahía Mosquito, perhaps the world's most luminous bioluminescent bay.

ISABEL SEGUNDA

29 km (18 mi) southeast of Fajardo by ferry.

As the transportation hub of Vieques, Isabel Segunda is unavoidable. The ferry drops off passengers at the town's dock, and propeller planes deposit passengers at the tiny airport to the west. If you want to rent a car, or gas up the one you already have, you need to make a trip to Isabel Segunda.

But Isabel Segunda (or Isabel II, as it's often labeled on maps) has some charms that are not immediately apparent. There's a lovely lighthouse on the coast just east of the ferry dock, and on the hill above town you'll find the last fort the Spanish constructed in the New World. You can also find some of the best bars and restaurants here, as well as lodgings ranging from funky to fancy.

> **CAUTION**
>
> If you plan to rent a car on Vieques or Culebra, make sure you reserve it in advance, especially when visiting during high season. The rental agencies have a limited number of vehicles, and when they are gone, you're out of luck.

El Faro Punta Mulas, a Spanish-built lighthouse beside the ferry dock in Isabel Segunda, dates from 1895. It was built to guide vessels into the harbor, which is surrounded by a chain of dangerous reefs. Its red light is rumored to be seen from as far away as St. Croix and St. Thomas. In 1992 the elegant structure was carefully restored and transformed into a maritime museum that traces much of the island's history, including the visit by South American liberation leader Simón Bolívar. Sadly, the museum had been closed for several years when this book was updated, and there were no plans to reopen it. The lighthouse itself is worth a look, however. ✉ *At end of Rte. 200* ☎ *787/741–0060.*

On a hilltop overlooking Isabel Segunda is **El Fortín Conde de Mirasol** *(Count of Mirasol Fort)*, the last military structure built by the Spanish in the New World. It was erected on Vieques's northern coast in 1840 at the order of Count Mirasol, then governor of Puerto Rico. It took more than a decade to complete, which meant Mirasol had to repeatedly ask for more money. (Queen Isabel, on being petitioned yet again, asked Mirasol whether the walls were made of gold.) The fort helped solidify Spanish control of the area, keeping British, French, Dutch, and Danish colonists away and dissuading pirates from attacking Isabel Segunda. After sitting empty for several decades, it was transformed into a museum in 1991. The museum has an impressive collection of artifacts from the Taíno Indians and other cultures that thrived on this and nearby islands before the arrival of the Spanish. It also has exhibits on the island's years as a sugar plantation and its occupation by the U.S. Navy. ✉ *471 Calle Magnolia, Isabel Segunda* ☎ *787/741–1717* 🌐 *www.enchanted-isle.com/elfortin* 🎫 *$2* ⏲ *Wed.–Sun. 10–4.*

ESPERANZA

10 km (6 mi) south of Isabel Segunda

The only time there's a traffic jam in Esperanza is when one of the wild horses frequently seen on the nearby beaches wanders into the road. This community, once a down-at-heel fishing village, is now a string of budget bars, restaurants, and hotels. All of them overlook Playa Esperanza, a shallow stretch of sand made all the more picturesque by the presence of a tiny islet called Cayo Afuera.

In the evening, there's not a better way to enjoy the sunset than a stroll along Esperanza's **Malecón,** a waterfront walkway running the length of the beach.

> **WORD OF MOUTH**
>
> "What's great about the beaches in Vieques is that there's nothing—and nobody—on most of them. Our children love exploring and checking out different beaches."
>
> –ccc.

The **Vieques Conservation & Historical Trust** was established to help save Bahía Mosquito, one of the last remaining bioluminescent bays in the world. The small museum, located on the main drag in Esperanza, has interesting information about the bay, as well as the island's flora and fauna. A little pool lets kids get acquainted with starfish, sea urchins, and other denizens of the not-so-deep. There's also a tiny gift shop where the profits are funneled back into the foundation. Call ahead if you're coming at lunch time, as the place is sometimes closed for an hour or so. ⊠ *138 Calle Flamboyán, Esperanza* ☎ *787/741–8850* 🌐 *www.vcht.com* *Free* *Tues.–Sun. 11–4.*

ELSEWHERE ON VIEQUES

Isabel Segunda and Esperanza are just a tiny portion of Vieques. Most of the island—more than two-thirds of it, in fact—was commandeered by the military until 2003. It's now a nature preserve that draws thousands of visitors each year.

Fodor's Choice ★ East of Esperanza, **Bahía Mosquito** *(Mosquito Bay)* is also known as Bioluminescent Bay or Phosphorescent Bay. It's one of the world's best spots to have a glow-in-the-dark experience with undersea dinoflagellates. Tour operators offer kayak trips or excursions on nonpolluting boats to see the bay's tiny microorganisms, which appear to light up when the water around them is agitated. Dive into the bay and you'll emerge covered in sparkling water. Look behind your boat, and you'll see a twinkling wake. Even the fish that jump from the water will bear an eerie glow. The high concentration of dinoflagellates sets the bay apart from the other spots (including others in Puerto Rico) that are home to these tiny organisms. The bay is at its best when there's little or no moonlight; rainy nights are beautiful, too, because the raindrops splashing in the water produce ricochet sparkles. Sharon Grasso of Island Adventures offers some of the best excursions to the bay. ⊠ *Reach via unpaved roads off Rte. 997.*

A portion of the west and the entire eastern end of the island is being administered as the **Vieques National Wildlife Refuge,** comprising 18,000 acres—about 14,900 acres on the eastern end and 3,100 acres on the west—which will make it the biggest protected natural reserve in Puerto Rico. Most of eastern Vieques is being administered by the U.S. Fish & Wildlife Service as a nature reserve, except for the 900-acre bombing range on the far eastern end, which will be permanently closed off, a consequence of its contamination by the ammunition shot over its 60-year existence. But most of the rest of eastern Vieques is pristine nature, astonishingly beautiful and well forested, with a hilly center region overlooking powder-white sandy beaches and a coral-ringed coastline; it served mainly as a buffer zone between the military maneuvers and civilian population. The vast majority of this acreage remains off-limits to visitors as authorities carry out a search for unexploded munitions and contaminants. Cleanup plans were still being drawn up at this writing, but the Puerto Rico government hopes they will increase public access to the island. *Box 1527, 00765* *787/741–2138* *www.fws.gov/caribbean/vieques.*

BEACHES

Many of the beaches around the island have oddly similar names: Red Beach, Blue Beach, and Green Beach. The U.S. Navy, lacking any imagination, simply assigned them random colors. Some beaches are known by one name by tourists, another by locals. Islanders know Sun Bay as Sombé.

Blue Beach. Beyond Red Beach, you'll find a handful of covered cabañas here. There can be strong surf in some spots, making swimming difficult at times. ✉ *Off Rte. 997, east of Red Beach.*

Green Beach. On the western edge of the island is this beach, which is reached via a dirt road. Miles of coral reef just off shore attract snorkelers and divers. From the shore you can catch a glimpse of El Yunque on the mainland. ✉ *At the western end of Rte. 200.*

Playa Esperanza. The most accessible beach is across from the town of the same name. People staying in any of the inexpensive accommodations in Esperanza can simply walk across the road. There are some good opportunities for snorkeling, especially around Cayo Afuera, an uninhabited islet. Manatees are occasionally spotted here, as well as barracudas and nurse sharks. If you're looking for swimming or sunbathing, there are much better beaches nearby. ✉ *Esperanza Malecón, Esperanza.*

★ **Playa Media Luna.** An unpaved road east of Playa Sun Bay leads to a pretty little beach that's ideal for families because the water is calm and shallow. This is a good spot to try your hand at snorkeling. Take note, though, that there are no facilities. ✉ *Off Rte. 997, east of Playa Sun Bay.*

Red Beach. Located on former U.S. Navy land on the eastern end of Vieques, this beautiful beach is reached via a well-maintained dirt road. It's open daily from sunrise to sunset. The water is crystal clear, and its location in Bahía Corcho means that the waves are usually not so strong. ✉ *Off Rte. 997, east of Playa Media Luna.*

★ **Sun Bay.** Of Vieques's more than three dozen beaches, this one east of Esperanza is easily the most popular. Its 1-mi-long white sands skirt a crescent-shaped bay. You'll find

WORD OF MOUTH

"Do not miss Sun Bay. I thought it was the prettiest beach there. I absolutely loved it. The Jeep was key. We are sooooo glad we rented a Jeep. It was a necessity."
–lv2trvl

CLOSE UP

Underwater Fireworks

On most moonless nights strings of kayaks float along the surface of Bahía Mosquito. The people have come to this otherwise unremarkable bay on the island of Vieques to witness one of nature's most eye-popping events. As a paddle skims the top of the water, thousands of points of light appear just below the surface. Behind each kayak is a blue-green glow that slowly fades. Those who trail their fingers in the water can see the outline of every digit.

This glow is produced by dinoflagellates, single-celled organisms that are found all over the world. But the species found in the Caribbean, called Pyrodinium bahamense, happens to glow when the surrounding water is disturbed in any way. The concentration of dinoflagellates in Bahía Mosquito is an astounding 720,000 per gallon—more than anywhere else on earth. This accounts for the nightly display of underwater fireworks.

Bahía Mosquito—which means, of course, Mosquito Bay—is not the only bioluminescent bay in Puerto Rico. There are a handful of others, including Fajardo's Laguna Grande and La Parguera's Bahía de Fosforescente. But they can't compare with the glittering waters of Bahía Mosquito. That's why travelers flock here from all around Puerto Rico.

The conditions at Bahía Mosquito are perfect for growing dinoflagellates. A mangrove forest surrounding the bay constantly drops leaves and branches into the water. As bacteria eat the decaying matter, they produce prodigious amounts of vitamin B12—an essential part of the dinoflagellate diet. The lagoon's mouth, resembling the neck of a bottle, keeps the nutrients from being swept out to sea. The narrow mouth also keeps the brackish water in and the salty water out. These tiny creatures, like the rest of us, are healthier when they don't have so much salt in their diet.

Other bioluminescent bays around the world have lost their luster, mostly because of pollution. Light pollution is one of the main causes, as the dinoflagellates can't compete with the glare of headlights or the glow of street lamps. (Even the moon makes the glow difficult to discern.) On Vieques, conservation-minded citizens constantly remind their neighbors to make sure their outdoor lights are shaded so they point downward. They have also fought development near the bay, including a new road and a sports complex that would have destroyed the bay almost overnight.

Another problem is water pollution, which includes industrial waste, sewage drainage, and agricultural runoff. Spillage from the gas- and diesel-powered boats that take tourists to see the spectacle, ironically, is often the culprit. The smoke-belching boats that depart for La Parguera's Bahía de Fosforescente every night are slowly putting themselves out of business. The display in La Parguera, once as dazzling as the one in Vieques, is dismal.

On Vieques pollution-spewing boats are banned from Bahía Mosquito. Instead, there are kayaks and electric-powered pontoon boats that barely cause a ripple on the surface. But there are plenty of waves when the passengers dive into the inky black water, leaving behind them a trail of light that reminds many people of the tail of a comet.

food kiosks, picnic tables, and changing facilities. On weekdays, when the crowds are thin, you might also find wild horses grazing among the palm trees. Parking is $3, but often no one is at the gate to take your money. ✉ *Rte. 997, east of Esperanza.*

WHERE TO EAT

$$$$ ✕**Carambola.** It's hard to imagine a more romantic setting than this dining room with unbeatable views of the ocean. Indoors is a long wooden table, surrounded by chairs upholstered in a delectable shade of chocolate brown. Through the open doors are smaller tables scattered around the open-air terrace. The service is formal, and so are the meals. You choose between a five- or seven-course set meal featuring such main courses as lamb chops with a lentil balsamic salad or tilapia served with lemon potatoes. Of course, none of this comes cheap. For about the same price for a single meal here, you can have dinner for two at any of the island's other eateries. ✉ *Inn on the Blue Horizon, Rte. 996, Km 4.2, Esperanza* ☎ *787/741–3318* ✍ *Reservations essential* 💳 *AE, MC, V.*

$$$–$$$$ ✕**Blue Macaw.** Polished wood and brushed steel give this newcomer a sleek, sexy look. It's hard to resist the curvy banquette in the front dining room, but on a cool evening it's even harder to pass up a table in the enclosed rear courtyard. The food here isn't about throwing together a lot of different ingredients. Instead, the kitchen turns out a well-traveled menu of such classic dishes as crispy duck with plum sauce, osso bucco with braised vegetables, and lamb tenderloin in a raspberry sauce. Not that hungry? Plenty of smaller dishes are perfect for sharing, including quesadillas with smoked chicken. ✉ *Calle Antonio Mellado, at Calle Luis Muñoz Rivera, Isabel Segunda* ☎ *787/741–4000* ✍ *Reservations essential* 💳 *AE, MC, V* ⏲ *Closed Sun. and Mon. No lunch.*

$$$–$$$$ Fodor'sChoice ★ ✕**Uva.** On Vieques, chef Carlos Alzogaray has single-handedly changed how people approach seafood. At this Caribbean-fusion eatery, he serves mahimahi, as does everyone else, but he offers it as ceviche with a lemon–passion fruit sauce. He marinates tuna steak in a soy-ginger sauce and serves it with baby bok choy, and even rethinks lobster, which appears as carpaccio with avocado ragout. Meat dishes include a grilled hanger steak with shrimp mashed potatoes. There's also a great wine list, as you might guess from the thousands of corks covering the pillars. The friendly staff is always ready to help with wine pairings. ✉ *359 Calle Antonio Mellado, at Calle Luis Muñoz Rivera, Isabel Segunda* ☎ *787/741–2050* ✍ *Reservations essential* 💳 *AE, MC, V* ⏲ *Closed Tues.*

$$–$$$$ ✕**Island Steakhouse.** When islanders go out to dinner, they often end up at this spot far away from the beach. But its location on a rather secluded hilltop doesn't mean fewer crowds. It's especially hard to secure at table on Fridays, when the chef throws the regular menu out the window and cooks up "novo Latino" fare. On a normal night, get one of the sizzling steaks, which range in size from petite to hearty—the rib eye, one of the most popular items, weighs in at 20 ounces. There's also seafood, of course, including an exceptional lobster basted with

spiced rum. The second-floor terrace might remind you of a tree house, as it looks directly into the branches. The restaurant is on Route 201, between Isabel Segunda and Esperanza. ✉ *Crow's Nest, Rte. 201, Km 1.6* ☎ *787/741–0011* *Reservations essential* ▭ *AE, MC, V* ⊙ *Closed Mon.–Thurs. No lunch.*

$$–$$$ ✕ **Café Media Luna.** Tucked into a beautifully restored building in Isabel Segunda, this eatery has been a favorite for many years. Its popularity might be due to the convenient downtown location or the intimate tables on the balconies that surround the second-floor dining room. More likely, however, it's the creativity of the cooks. (You can watch all the action, as the kitchen is in full view.) Try the cornish hen in a sweet-spicy coconut sauce or the seared yellowfin tuna served with vegetable tempura. If you're not too famished, share one of the tasty pizzas. Half a dozen are on offer at any given time. ✉ *351 Calle Antonio Mellado, Isabel Segunda* ☎ *787/741–2594* *Reservations essential* ▭ *AE, MC, V* ⊙ *Closed Mon.–Wed. No lunch.*

$$–$$$ ✕ **Chez Shack.** This restaurant is not a shack—but it's close. It's in a delightfully ramshackle building on a one-lane road winding through the hills. The dining room is inches from the pavement, but it's unlikely a single car will pass by while you're enjoying your meal. Chicken, beef, and seafood are grilled to tender perfection. The restaurant is justifiably famous for its weekly barbecue night with a steel band. If you can't make it that evening, good jazz or island rhythms usually flow out of the sound system. The restaurant is a bit off the beaten track on Route 995, off Route 201. ✉ *Rte. 995, Km 1.8* ☎ *787/741–2175* *Reservations essential* ▭ *AE, MC, V.*

$–$$$ ✕ **Bananas.** If you're looking for authentic island cuisine, this ain't it. This longtime favorite, across from the waterfront in Esperanza, is geared almost entirely to gringos. However, that doesn't mean the grub isn't good. Find a spot at one of the curvy concrete tables and order the red-snapper sandwich (popular at lunchtime), or go all out for baby back ribs or jerk chicken. The salads are excellent, including the *caribeño* (fresh greens with curried chicken) and the *festival* (greens with grilled chicken, blue cheese, and cranberries). When the sun goes down, Bananas is one of the hot spots on this side of the island. ✉ *142 Calle Flamboyán, Esperanza* ☎ *787/741–8700* ▭ *AE, MC, V.*

$–$$$ ✕ **Bilí.** Next door to Bananas, this place deserves better than the overflow from its more established neighbor. It has the same view, sleeker decor, and more authentic food. For lunch, order a tasty sandwich such as skirt steak with mango, peppers, blue cheese, and caramelized onions, accompanied by cassava fries. For something heartier, try fried chicken with a guava glaze or angel-hair pasta with crabmeat stewed in coconut milk and tomatoes. Stop by for a beer in the evening and you won't have to shout to be heard. ✉ *144 Calle Flamboyán, Esperanza* ☎ *787/741–1382* ▭ *AE, MC, V.*

$–$$ ✕ **BBH.** There isn't a bad seat in the house in this stylish dining room. Choose one of the comfortable couches near the door, a stool at the bar, or a banquette overlooking the swimming pool. A few choice tables are outside on the covered terrace. Just as good as the seating options are the numerous small dishes created by chef Christopher Ellis. Not content to stay in Spain, his tapas-style menu travels the globe. Some items, like the chipotle-barbecued pork, clearly come from Mexico. The mussels, in red coconut-curry broth, have an Asian flair. If there is a wait for a table, your server will suggest you enjoy a cocktail at the Palms, which is right around the corner. ✉*North Shore Rd., Isabel Segunda* ☎*787/741–1128* *Reservations essential* *AE, D, MC, V.*

$ **Duffy's.** More than half of the customers crowd around the bar here, which might make you think the food must be pub grub. And that's right, to a point. You have your standard burger and fries, but this hunk of beef is the real deal. The rest of the menu tends towards wraps and sandwiches, and is a step above your usual beach food. So why do people ignore the dozen or so tables scattered around the open-air dining room in favor of sitting elbow-to-elbow at the bar? Turns out that owner Michael Duffy, son of the owner of Chez Shack, is a real character. Locals love chewing the fat with him, and you will, too. ✉*140 Calle Flamboyán, Esperanza* ☎*787/741–7600* *AE, MC, V.*

WHERE TO STAY

$$–$$$$ **Inn on the Blue Horizon.** This inn, consisting of six Mediterranean-style villas, was the tiny island's first taste of luxury. It's still one of the most sought-after accommodations, to a large extent because of its breathtaking setting on a bluff overlooking the ocean. The entire place is often booked months in advance by wedding parties and other big groups. Everything is geared toward romance, from the intimate guest rooms to the open-air bar, where the staff will make any cocktail you can name—or create a new one and name it after you. Carambola's, located here, is the island's most formal restaurant, but many people opt for a meal at the bar. **Pros:** Eye-popping view, elegant accommodations, good dining options. **Cons:** Aloof staff, pricey for what you get. ✉*Rte. 996, Km 4.2, Esperanza, Vieques* *Box 1556, Vieques00765* ☎*787/741–3318* *www.innonthebluehorizon.com* *10 rooms* *In-room: no phone, no TV. In-hotel: restaurant, bar, pool, beachfront, bicycles, no elevator, no kids under 14* *AE, MC, V* *BP.*

$$–$$$ Fodor's Choice ★ **Hix Island House.** Constructed entirely of concrete—wait, keep reading!—this award-winning hotel on 13 secluded acres is one of the most striking in Puerto Rico. Architect John Hix set out to echo the gray granite boulders strewn around Vieques, and his success is apparent in the resulting three buildings that blend beautifully with the environment. A spare aesthetic permeates the rooms, which have sinewy lines and sexy curves unlike the blocky spaces in most concrete buildings. Sunny terraces, unglazed windows, and showers that are open to the stars (yet still very private) keep nature nearby. The resort's embrace of the environment goes beyond form into function, with the use of recycled water and solar-power systems. Even the swimming pool is ecofriendly; the staff avoids using excess chemicals when cleaning it. The hotel is on Route 995, off Route 201. **Pros:** Eye-popping architecture, secluded setting, friendly staff. **Cons:** No windows means some bugs in the rooms, pool can get a bit cloudy. ✉*Rte. 995, Km 1.5, Box 1556, Vieques* ☎*787/741–2302* *www.hixislandhouse.com*

13 rooms In-room: no a/c, no phone, kitchen, refrigerator, no TV. In-hotel: pool, no elevator AE, MC, V CP.

> **WORD OF MOUTH**
>
> "The concierge [at Bravo Beach Hotel] was very helpful with making dinner reservations and arranging a kayak trip to the bio-luminescent bay, which is not to be missed." –trekker

$$ Fodor's Choice ★ **Bravo Beach Hotel.** If this boutique hotel were plopped down into the middle of South Beach, no one would raise an eyebrow. What was once a private residence has been expanded to include four different buildings, all with views of nearby Culebra from their balconies. The guest rooms have a minimalist flair, brightened by splashes of red and yellow. High-tech offerings include a Sony PlayStation in every room. And if you're traveling with an entourage, the two-bedroom villa has plenty of entertaining space. One of the pools is the setting for the Palms, a chic lounge; the other provides a backdrop for the not-to-be-missed tapas bar. The hotel is on a pretty stretch of beach, several blocks north of the ferry dock in Isabel Segunda. **Pros:** Gorgeous building, beautiful pools, good dining options. **Cons:** Unattractive neighborhood, staff seems overtaxed. *North Shore Rd., Isabel Segunda 787/741–1128 www.bravobeachhotel.com 9 rooms, 1 villa In-room: no phone, Wi-Fi. In-hotel: restaurant, bar, pools, no kids under 14 AE, D, MC, V BP.*

$$ **Crow's Nest.** This butter-yellow guesthouse sits on a hilltop and has stunning views of the ocean in the distance. If you want to go to the beaches in or around Esperanza and Isabel Segunda, they are within a few minutes' drive. Or you can relax by the swimming pool. The large rooms have balconies that overlook lovely gardens. Island Steakhouse, housed on a second-floor terrace, is one of the most popular restaurants on Vieques. Less expensive is El Jardín, an Asian-Caribbean eatery on the patio. The hotel is on Route 201, between Isabel Segunda and Esperanza. **Pros:** Hilltop location, good dining options. **Cons:** Far from beach, not the prettiest building. *Rte. 201, Km 1.6, 787/741–0033 or 888/484–3783 www.crowsnestvieques.com 15 rooms, 2 suites In-room: kitchen (some), refrigerator, dial-up. In-hotel: 2 restaurants, pool, no elevator, no kids under 12 AE, MC, V BP.*

$$ Fodor's Choice ★ **Hacienda Tamarindo.** The century-old tamarind tree rising through the center of the main building gives this plantation-style house its name. With its barrel-tile roof and wood-shuttered windows, it's one of the most beautiful on the island. You can easily find a spot all to yourself, whether it's on a shady terrace or beside the spectacular pool. Linda Vail, who runs the place along with her husband, Burr, decorated each guest room individually. "Caribbean chic" may be the best way to describe her effortless way of combining well-chosen antiques, elegant wicker furniture, and vintage travel posters. The nicest room might be Number One, which is in a separate building and has a private terrace overlooking the ocean. If you want more privacy, there's also a nicely furnished villa. The made-to-order breakfasts served on the second-floor terrace are a great reason to get up early. **Pros:** Beautiful views, nicely designed rooms, best breakfasts on the island. **Cons:** Drive to

beaches, small parking lot. ✉*Rte. 996, Km 4.5, Esperanza* *Box 1569, Vieques00765* ☎*787/741–8525* 🌐*www.haciendatamarindo.com* *16 rooms* *In-room: no phone, no TV, Wi-Fi. In-hotel: pool, public Wi-Fi, no elevator, no kids under 15* *AE, MC, V* *BP.*

$ **Trade Winds.** The best of a string of inexpensive guesthouses along the main road in Esperanza, this place has an unbeatable location across from the waterfront promenade. A number of eateries are only a short stroll away. Rooms are basic but more than adequate if you plan on spending most of your time at the beach. They share several terraces, all of which overlook the ocean. **Pros:** Good value, many nearby dining options. **Cons:** Right on the street, not the most attractive building. ✉*142 Calle Flamboyán, Esperanza* *Box 1012, Vieques 00770* ☎*787/741–8666* 🌐*www.enchanted-isle.com/tradewinds* *11 rooms* *In-room: refrigerator. In-hotel: restaurant, bar, no elevator* *AE, MC, V* *EP.*

3

¢–$ **Casa de Amistad.** A groovy vibe permeates this small guesthouse not far from the ferry dock in Isabel Segunda. Citrus colors and wicker furnishings give it a tropical touch. It's hard not to feel at home here, especially when you use the common kitchen to pack a picnic lunch or borrow an umbrella for your trip to the beach. The rooftop terrace is a great place to chill out. An on-site gift shop sells original art by the owners. **Pros:** Gay-friendly, funky furnishings. **Cons:** On an unattractive block, drive to beaches. ✉*27 Calle Benito Castano, Isabel Segunda* ☎*787/741–3758* 🌐*www.casadeamistad.com* *7 rooms* *In-hotel: pool, no elevator, public Internet* *MC* *EP.*

PRIVATE VILLA RENTALS

One good way to visit Vieques is to rent one of the beautiful vacation homes that have been built in the hilly interior or along the coasts. These are concentrated in three major areas: Bravos de Boston, Esperanza, and Pilón. Several local real-estate agents deal in short-term rentals of at least a week. A list of properties is available from gay-friendly **Rainbow Realty** (✉*Rte. 996, Esperanza* ☎*787/741–4312* 🌐*www.enchanted-isle.com/rainbow*).

$$$$ **Paso Fino.** One of the few wooden houses on Vieques, this charming place has a steeply pitched roof that results in many interesting nooks and crannies—perfect for youngsters to explore. The owner envisioned the three separate apartments as a gathering place for extended families. The top two floors make up one apartment with three bedrooms and two baths, as well as a small bed in an alcove under the open stairs. Downstairs is a smaller space with two bedrooms and two bathrooms. Across the patio with the shimmering salt-water pool is a two-story casita with two bedrooms and two baths. (Families who don't need all the bedrooms often use it as a pool house. Each apartment has a full kitchen and private outdoor areas that are perfect for impromptu dinner parties. This house has no air-conditioning, so it's most popular during the cooler months. ✉*Bravos de Boston* ☎*787/741–4312* 🌐*www.enchanted-isle.com/rainbow* *7 bedrooms, 6 bathrooms* *In-room: no a/c. In-hotel: pool, laundry facilities.* *MC, V.*

$$$–$$$$ **Hacienda Buena Vista.** At this hilltop retreat you win the jackpot: the much-sought-after 360-degree views. From this vantage point you can gaze across to the northern and southern coasts. The main house, painted a buttery yellow, is where you'll find two of the bedrooms, as well as a sunny porch and a covered terrace where you can take your meals alfresco. (The main kitchen, one of three on the property, is just inside.) Down the hill, a lovely pool overlooks the northern coast. A nearby casita also has sleeping quarters, so families or friends can enjoy being together, but not 24 hours a day. The air-conditioning is only in the bedrooms. Note: the beginning of the driveway is rocky, so make sure you have a four-wheel-drive vehicle. ✉ *Los Chivos area* ☎ *787/741–4312* 🌐 *www.enchanted-isle.com/rainbow* *3 bedrooms, 4 bathrooms* *In-room: no a/c (some). In-hotel: pool.* *MC, V.*

$$$ **Casita Linda.** On the grounds of the Hacienda Tamarindo, this small villa gives you access to all the amenities, from the refreshing pool to the best breakfasts on the island. But it's just as easy to forget that the small inn exists, since your windows and spacious terrace face the other direction, toward the ocean. Rather than the usual wicker, this villa is filled with the plush furnishings you'd expect in a boutique hotel. There's a full kitchen, so you only need to go out to dinner when you're in the mood. The two bedrooms are across from each other, making this a good choice for two couples. A nearby suite can be booked jointly with the villa, so three couples can travel together. ✉ *Rte. 996, Km 4.5, Esperanza* ☎ *787/741–8525* 🌐 *www.haciendatamarindo.com* *2 bedrooms, 1 bathrooms* *In-room: VCR, Wi-Fi. In-hotel: pool, no kids under 15, no-smoking rooms.* *AE, MC, V.*

$$$ **Casa La Puerta.** This Spanish-style house is all about the view. As you relax beside the pool or on the expansive covered terrace you have unobstructed views of the island's southern coast. With no other houses in sight, you can easily imagine how things once looked on the island. (You can also go skinny-dipping and nobody will be the wiser.) The main house is compact but seems rambling because of many private alcoves. Dramatic archways lead from the kitchen and dining areas to the two smaller bedrooms. Across the terrace is the master bedroom, allowing for plenty of privacy. Only two of the three bedrooms have air-conditioning; the smallest of the three has windows on three sides that invite the breeze. ✉ *Destino* ☎ *787/741–4312* 🌐 *www.enchanted-isle.com/rainbow* *3 bedrooms, 2 bathrooms* *In-room: no a/c (some), VCR. In-hotel: pool.* *MC, V.*

NIGHTLIFE

Not far from the ferry terminal, **Al's Mar Azul** (✉ *Calle Plinio Peterson, Isabel Segunda* ☎ *787/741–3400*) is where everyone gathers to watch the sunset. The main virtue of this open-air bar is a deck overlooking the ocean. You'll find dart boards, pool tables, and a jukebox. **The Palms** (✉ *North Shore Rd., Isabel Segunda* ☎ *787/741–1128*) is the most stylish bar on the north side of the island. Sip creative cocktails under the eponymous trees as you admire the crystalline pool.

Bananas (✉*142 Calle Flamboyán, Esperanza* ☎*787/741–8700*) is the place for burgers and beer—not necessarily in that order. There's sometimes live music and dancing.

Duffy's. (✉*140 Calle Flamboyán, Esperanza* ☎*787/741–7600*) has quickly become one of the most popular bars on the island, thanks to the jawboning of owner Michael Duffy. **La Nasa** (✉*Calle Flamboyán, Esperanza* ☎*No phone*) is the only establishment on the waterfront side of the street in Esperanza. This simple wooden shack, decorated with strings of Christmas lights the entire year, serves up cheap and very cold beer and rum drinks. Locals congregate on plastic chairs out front or stare off into the placid Caribbean from an open-air back room.

WORD OF MOUTH

"We have done the bio bay tour with Island Adventures on the pontoon boat a number of times. I prefer it to the kayak trip because it is easier to get in and out of the bay. Also on the way in and out you get a good bit of info on the flora and fauna of the island."

—soggydollar.

3

SPORTS & THE OUTDOORS

BIKING

The friendly folks at **La Dulce Vida** (☎*787/741–0495* 🌐*www.bikevieques.com*) can set you up with mountain bikes and all the equipment you need starting at $25. They'll even bring the bikes to wherever you happen to be staying. Customized tours of the island—which range from easy rides on country roads to muddy treks into the hills—are $30 to $65 per hour. But you need to book the tours far in advance.

BOATING & KAYAKING

Any number of companies offer trips to Bahía Mosquito, the most famous of the island's bioluminescent bays. Most are trips in single-person kayaks, which can be a challenge if you don't have experience or if you aren't in the best shape. A better option for most people is a boat. Make sure it's an electric-powered model, as the gas-powered ones are bad for the environment.

Aqua Frenzy Kayaks (✉*At dock area below Calle Flamboyán, Esperanza* ☎*787/741–0913*) rents kayaks and arranges kayak tours of Bahía Mosquito and other areas. Reservations are required for the excursion to glowing Bahía Mosquito; the excursion costs $30. Make reservations at least 24 hours in advance.

Blue Caribe Kayaks (✉*149 Calle Flamboyán, Esperanza* ☎*787/741–2522* 🌐*www.enchanted-isle.com/bluecaribe*) offers kayak trips to Bahía Mosquito for about $30, as well as trips to deserted parts of the coast and nearby islets. You can also rent a kayak and set off on your own.

★ **Island Adventures** (✉*Rte. 996, Esperanza* ☎*787/741–0720* 🌐*www.biobay.com*) is run by former schoolteacher Sharon Grasso, who will take you to Bahía Mosquito aboard nonpolluting, electrically powered pontoon boats. The best part is leaping into the water, where the outline of your body will be softly illuminated. The cost is about $30 per person.

Marauder Sailing Charters (☎*787/435–4858*) operates the *Marauder*, a 34-foot sailing yacht anchored off Esperanza. It sails around the southern coast, allowing a close-up look at the pristine nature of most of the island. There's a midday stop at a secluded spot for swimming, snorkeling, and sunbathing, followed by a gourmet lunch. The yacht, run by Kris Dynneson and Barbara Berger, has a good sound system and open bar.

DIVING & SNORKELING

If you want to get your own snorkeling or diving equipment, head to **Black Beard Sports** (✉*101 Calle Muñoz Rivera, Isabel Segunda* ☎*787/741–1892* 🌐*www.blackbeardsports.com*). This funky little store in downtown Isabel Segunda also arranges diving trips and certification courses.

Blue Caribe Kayaks (✉*149 Calle Flamboyán, Esperanza* ☎*787/741–2522* 🌐*www.enchanted-isle.com/bluecaribe*) will rent you snorkels, masks, and fins for $12 a day. The efficient staff can also arrange snorkeling trips to nearby islets.

Nan-Sea Charters (☎*787/741–3224* 🌐*www.nanseacharters.com*) promises to take you snorkeling at a beach so remote that it doesn't have a name. The cost for a two-dive trip is $100 per person, not including equipment rental.

FISHING

Caribbean Flyfishing Company (☎*787/741–1337* 🌐*www.caribbeanflyfishingco.com*) and Captain Franco Gonzales will take you on any type of fishing trip that you have in mind, from short trips to the shallows to longer journeys to the open ocean.

JET SKIING

In a shack near the beach, the **Fun Brothers** (✉*Calle Flamboyán, Esperanza* ☎*787/741–1337* 🌐*www.fun-brothers.com*) rent out the latest equipment to ride the waves. Jet Skis are $40 for a half-hour, $80 for an hour.

SHOPPING

Most residents do their shopping on the mainland, so there are very few shops on Vieques. You'll find mostly clothing stores that lean toward beach attire, as well as a few art galleries.

Casa Vieja Gallery (✉*Rte. 201, Esperanza* ☎*787/741–3078*) is where several local artists show and sell their work. **Diva's Closet** (✉*134 Calle Flamboyán, Esperanza* ☎*787/741–7595*), which is next door to Kim's Cabin, carries an array of women's clothes. Here you'll find everything you need for the beach or for brunch. **Kim's Cabin** (✉*136 Calle Flamboyán, Esperanza* ☎*787/741–0520*), which has been in business on Vieques since the early 1990s, is a local institution. There's jewelry in the front room and the two other rooms have clothing for men and women.

★ **Siddhia Hutchinson Fine Art Studio & Gallery** (✉*15 Calle 3, Isabel Segunda* ☎*787/741–8780*) is north of the ferry dock. The artist has lived on Vieques since the early 1990s, creating pastel watercolor prints of Caribbean scenes, as well as limited-edition ceramic dinnerware. The gallery is open Monday through Saturday, 10 AM to 4 PM.

CULEBRA

28 km (17 mi) east of Fajardo by ferry

Culebra is known around the world for its curvaceous coastline. Playa Flamenco, the tiny island's most famous stretch of sand, is considered one of the top two or three best beaches in the world. If Playa Flamenco gets too crowded, as it often does around Easter or Christmas, many other neighboring beaches will be nearly deserted. And if you crave complete privacy, hire a motorboat to take you to one of the nearby islets such as Isla Culebrita or Cayo Luis Peña. It won't be difficult to find a little cove that you will have all to yourself.

Archaeological evidence shows that Taíno and Carib peoples lived on Culebra long before the arrival of the Spanish in the late 15th century. The Spanish didn't bother laying claim to it until 1886; its dearth of fresh water made it an unattractive location for a settlement. The U.S. Navy, however, thought it was a very valuable piece of real estate. It used this island, as well as nearby Vieques, for target practice beginning in the early 20th century. Despite their smaller numbers, the residents of Culebra were more successful in their efforts to oust the military. The troops left Culebra in 1975.

EXPLORING CULEBRA

Almost everything about Culebra is diminutive. The island's only community, named in honor of U.S. Admiral George Dewey, is set along a single street leading from the ferry dock. You can explore all the shops along Calle Pedro Márquez in a half-hour. The one-room airport is a mile or so to the north. Except for one sprawling resort, no hotels have more than a dozen rooms.

Commissioned by President Theodore Roosevelt in 1909, **Refugio Nacional de Vida Silvestre de Culebra** is one of the nation's oldest wildlife refuges. Some 1,500 acres of the island make up a protected area. It's a lure for hikers and bird-watchers: Culebra teems with seabirds, from laughing gulls and roseate terns to red-billed tropic birds and sooty terns. Maps of trails in the refuge are hard to come by, but you can stop by the U.S. Fish & Wildlife Service office east of the airport to find out about trail conditions and determine whether you're headed to an area that requires a permit. The office also can tell you whether the leatherback turtles are nesting. From mid-April to mid-July, volunteers help to monitor and tag these creatures, which nest on nearby beaches, especially Playa Resaca and Playa Brava. If you'd like to volunteer, you must agree to help out for at least three nights. ✉*Rte. 250, north of Dewey* ☎*787/742–0115* 🌐*southeast.fws.gov* 🎫*Free* ⏲*Daily dawn to dusk.*

WORD OF MOUTH

"Without question, Playa Flemenco, Culebra, is the most spectacular [beach on Puerto Rico]." –RichF.

Part of the Refugio Nacional de Vida Silvestre de Culebra, **Isla Culebrita** is clearly visible from the northeast corner of Culebra. This islet is a favorite destination for sunbathers who want to escape the crowds at Playa Flamenco. On the northern shore there are several tide pools; snuggling into one of them is like taking a warm bath. Snorkelers and divers love the fact that they can reach the reef from the shore. You can also hike around the island and visit the ruins of an old lighthouse. To get there, take a dive boat or hire a water taxi.

A kayak is a great way to reach **Cayo Luis Peña,** an islet just off the western edge of Culebra. There are a handful of protected beaches where you can soak up the sun and not run into a single soul. Cayo Luis Peña is also part of the Refugio Nacional de Vida Silvestre de Culebra.

BEACHES

Fodor'sChoice ★ **Playa Flamenco.** On the island's north coast is an amazingly lovely stretch of white sand. This beach, with its almost perfect half-moon shape, is consistently ranked as one of the two or three best in the world. Once you see it, you'll know why. Mountains rise up on all sides, making it feel miles away from civilization. It's only when the propeller planes fly low over the beach that you remember that the airport is just over the ridge. During the week Playa Flamenco is pleasantly uncrowded; on the weekend, though, it fills up fast with day-trippers. This is the only beach on Culebra with amenities such as restrooms, showers, and kiosks selling simple fare. ✉*Rte. 251, west of the airport.*

Playa Melones. Just west of Dewey, this beach is a favorite spot for snorkelers. The reef that runs around the rocky point is easy to reach from shore. Locals swear that this is the best place to watch the sunset, and we admit we haven't found a better one. To get here, head uphill on the unmarked road behind the church. ✉*Off Rte. 251, west of Dewey.*

Playa Zoni. On the island's northeastern end, this beach is long and narrow, making it great for afternoon strolls. From the shore you can catch a glimpse of Isla Culebrita, not to mention St. Thomas and St. Croix. ✉*At the end of Rte. 250, 11 km (7 mi) northeast of Dewey.*

WHERE TO EAT

$$–$$$ ★ ✕**Juanita Bananas.** Trees overflowing with bananas, papayas, and passion fruit line the walkway that leads to one of Culebra's best eateries. Chef Jennifer Daubon, whose parents once ran a restaurant on the

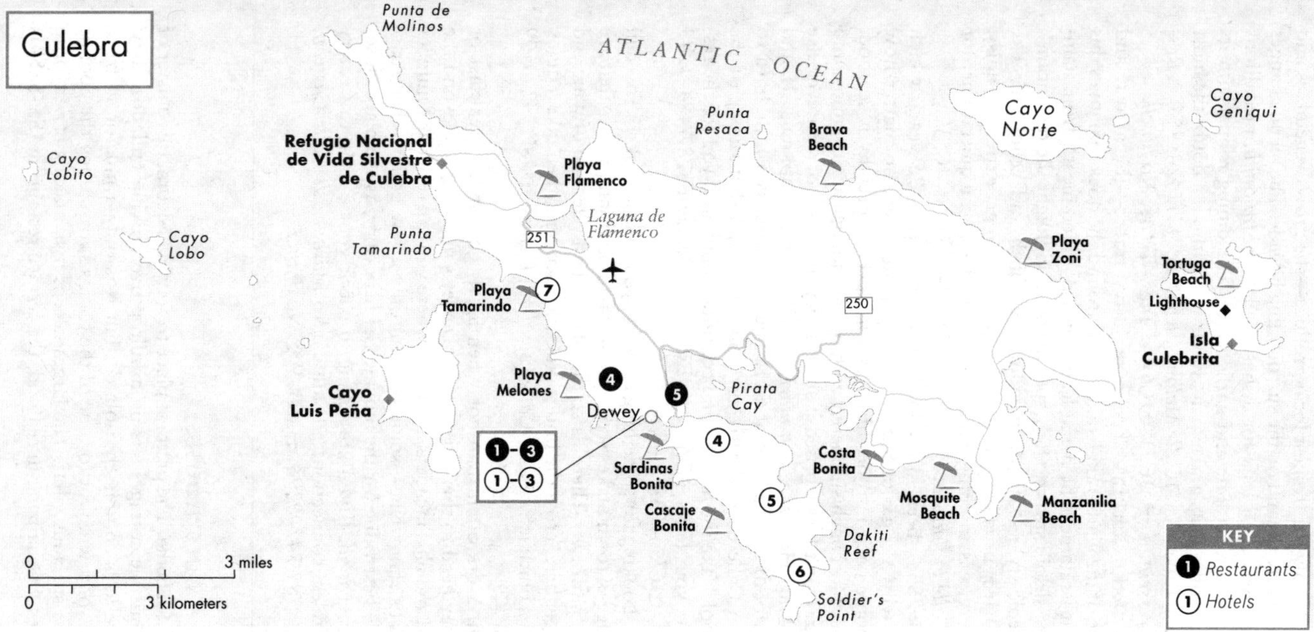

Restaurants ▼

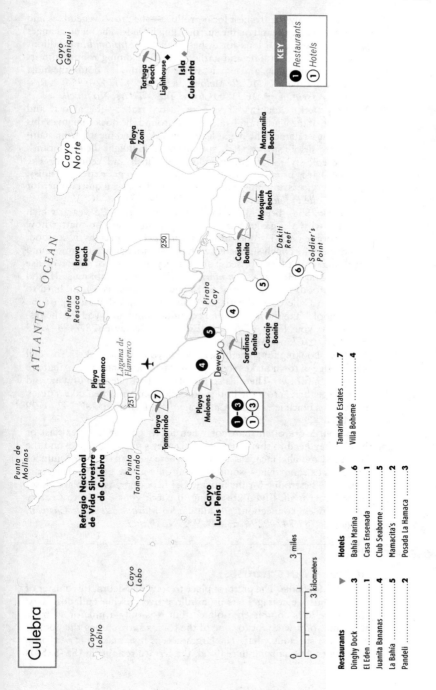

- Dinghy Dock 3
- El Eden 1
- Juanita Bananas 4
- La Bahía 5
- Pandeli 2

Hotels ▼

- Bahía Marina 6
- Casa Ensenada 1
- Club Seaborne 5
- Mamacita's 2
- Posada La Hamaca 3
- Tamarindo Estates 7
- Villa Boheme 4

island, uses only the freshest local produce—she grows vegetables and herbs on an acre of land on the surrounding hillside. The menu changes with the seasons, but look for dishes like lobster *limonjili,* medallions of lobster in a fresh lime and garlic sauce. The dining room, with its low lights, soft music, and expansive view, is without a doubt the most romantic in Culebra. ✉ *Calle Melones, Km 1* ☎ *787/742–3855* *Reservations essential* ▭ *MC, V* ⏲ *Closed Tues.–Thurs. No lunch.*

$–$$$ ✕ **Dinghy Dock.** Culebra's version of heavy traffic—the arrival and departure of the water taxi—takes place around the dock that gives this restaurant its name. The menu leans toward grilled meats, from hamburgers to sirloin steaks. Daily specials often highlight the restaurant's forte: creole-style seafood, including swordfish and yellowtail. The adjacent bar is usually packed with expats. It can get extremely noisy, and the service is anything but doting, so don't expect a quiet dinner for two. ✉ *Calle Fulladoza, Dewey* ☎ *787/742–0581* ▭ *MC, V.*

$–$$ ★ ✕ **La Bahía.** She's been in the kitchen for more than 25 years, which explains why Margarita Suárez never gets flustered, no matter how many people pack into her little restaurant. Her specialty is seafood, and dishes like conch simmered with onions and garlic are simple and satisfying. Don't be surprised if she offers you a taste of whatever else she's cooking. Her *arroz con mariscos* (rice with shrimp, mussels, and other seafood) is a bargain at $11. The restaurant is a little hard to find; from Calle de Escudero, turn onto the road that runs past the new school. Take the first left and continue uphill until you see the restaurant on your left. ✉ *Off Calle Escudero, Dewey* ☎ *787/484–1243* ▭ *MC, V* ⏲ *Closed Mon.–Wed.*

¢ ✕ **El Eden.** Looking for something to pop in your picnic basket? This deli on the edge of town makes scrumptious salads and sandwiches that are big enough for two. There's also the island's best selection of wine and beer. To get here, cross the bridge on Calle Escudero, then take a quick right and a quick left. ✉ *Off Calle Escudero, Dewey* ☎ *787/742–0509* ▭ *MC, V.*

¢ ★ ✕ **Pandeli.** More often than not when locals go out for breakfast or lunch, they head to this little café on Dewey's main street. Beyond the smart red and blue facade is a counter where you can order any number of delicious sandwiches, some of them only a few dollars. The roast beef is the best value for the money. Get here early, as the place closes in mid-afternoon. If you are aching to check your e-mail, this eatery has a wireless connection. ✉ *Calle Pedro Márquez at Calle Castelar, Dewey* ☎ *787/742–0296* ▭ *MC, V* ⏲ *No dinner.*

WHERE TO STAY

HOTELS & GUESTHOUSES

$$ ✕ **Club Seaborne.** The prettiest place to stay in Culebra, this cluster of plantation-style cottages sits on a hilltop overlooking Fulladoza Bay. The place feels completely isolated, but it is only a mile or so from the center of town. Opt for one of the rooms surrounding the pool or one of the spacious villas. The largest sleeps five, making it a favorite of families. Specializing in seafood, the terrace restaurant ($$–$$$) is

one of the best on the island. The friendly staff is happy to help you set up snorkeling and diving trips or arrange transportation to the beach. **Pros:** Lovely cottages, well-regarded restaurant, nice view. **Cons:** Staff can seem overworked, some steps to negotiate. ✉ *Calle Fulladoza, Km 1.5* *Box 357, Culebra00775* ☎ *787/742–3169* 🌐 *www.clubseabourne.com* *3 rooms, 8 villas, 1 cottage* *In-room: kitchen (some). In-hotel: restaurant, bar, pool, no elevator* *AE, MC, V* *CP.*

$–$$ **Bahía Marina.** If you're looking for space to spread out, these one-bedroom apartments are for you. Each sleeps four, thanks to a fold-out couch in the living room. Full kitchens are equipped with everything you need to make dinner for the family. Step outside onto your private deck or head out to the swimming pool, and you'll have unobstructed views of the hills surrounding Fulladoza Bay. At last check, the hotel was putting the finishing touch on 24 units, bringing the total to 39. The second-floor restaurant, Dakity ($$–$$$), takes full advantage of the island's fresh seafood. **Pros:** Beautiful setting, good restaurant. **Cons:** Feels like an apartment complex, up a steep driveway, lots of steps to negotiate. ✉ *Calle Fulladoza, Km 1.5* *Box 807, Culebra00646* ☎ *787/742–0535* 🌐 *www.bahiamarina.net* *39 apartments* *In-room: kitchen, refrigerator, Wi-Fi. In-hotel: restaurant, room service, bar, pool, no elevator, public Wi-Fi* *AE, MC, V* *CP.*

$ **Mamacita's.** PLEASE DON'T FEED THE IGUANAS, reads a sign hanging on the terrace of this longtime favorite. Set beneath lazily turning ceiling fans, the disarmingly charming restaurant ($–$$$) overlooks a canal filled with fishing boats. The menu, which is scribbled on a chalkboard, includes dishes like pork tenderloin with pineapple or salmon with a cilantro sauce. The bar gets crowded during happy hour, which starts early in these parts. If you like it so much you don't want to leave, there are guest rooms upstairs with tropical furnishings. The best have balconies overlooking the canal. **Pros:** Friendly staff, comfortable rooms, pick-up point for water taxis. **Cons:** Some noise from restaurant and bar below, on a narrow street. ✉ *66 Calle Castelar, Dewey* ☎ *787/742–0090* 🌐 *www.mamacitaspr.com* *10 rooms, 1 suite* *In-room: kitchen (some), refrigerator (some). In-hotel: restaurant, bar, no elevator* *AE, MC, V* *EP.*

$$ **Tamarindo Estates.** On a 60-acre estate on the western coast of Culebra, this string of one- and two-bedroom beach cottages is on a long, sandy beach. Most of the cottages are a bit farther inland, affording great views of the coastline from their covered verandas. Each has a full kitchen. There's a shared beach house with showers and other amenities, including a pool with an oceanfront deck. The waters of nearby Luis Peña Channel are perfect for snorkeling, and it's about a 10-minute drive to Flamenco Beach. **Pros:** Isolated location, pretty pool area. **Cons:** Short walk to the beach, far from dining options. ✉ *Off Rte. 251* *Box 313, Culebra00775* ☎ *787/742–3343* 🌐 *www.tamarindoestates.com* *16 cottages* *In-room: kitchen, VCR. In-hotel: pool, beachfront* *MC, V* *EP.*

$–$$ **Casa Ensenada.** You'll feel like you're staying in a friend's house when you arrive at this inn on the edge of town. It doesn't look like much from the street, but the palm-shaded patio in the back looks out on the sailboats cruising around Ensenada Bay. If you can't wait to join them, you can rent a boat from the dock. Otherwise, just relax with a cocktail in one of the deck chairs. There are three rooms in the main house, each with a full kitchen stocked with all the utensils you need to make dinner. **Pros:** On the water, friendly owners. **Cons:** Not a lot of privacy, on a busy street. ✉ *142 Calle Escudero, Dewey* ☎ *787/742–3559* 🌐 *www.casaensenada.com* ⇒ *3 rooms* ♁ *In-room: kitchen, Ethernet. In-hotel: public Internet.* ▭ *MC, V* 🍽 *EP.*

$ **Posada La Hamaca.** The shady terrace behind this little lodging sits on a mangrove-lined canal where owner Al Custer docks his motorboat. The guest rooms—as simple as they come—have louvered windows with the same view. The inn sits on the edge of Dewey, putting you within walking distance of restaurants, shops, and grocery stores. The staff sends you off to the beach with a little cooler filled with ice. **Pros:** Walk to shops and restaurants, laid-back atmosphere, cheap rates. **Cons:** Basic furnishings, constant clunking noises from adjacent bridge. ✉ *68 Calle Castelar, Dewey* ☎ *787/742–3516* 🌐 *www.posada.com* ⇒ *10 rooms, 1 apartment* ♁ *In-room: no phone, kitchen (some). In-hotel: no elevator* ▭ *MC, V* 🍽 *EP.*

$ **Villa Boheme.** This guesthouse's shady terrace, with several hammocks hanging between the palm trees, is a great place to hang out. You may not feel the need to do anything more strenuous than reach for your margarita, but if you do, there are some kayaks that you can rent to explore Ensenada Bay. Rooms are simple, but each one has a view of the water; all share a communal kitchen, but some have kitchens of their own. This Spanish-style lodging, painted a particularly pretty shade of apricot, is one of the most distinctive on the island. **Pros:** Expansive view of the bay, walk to restaurants and shops. **Cons:** Basic furnishings, room colors tend to be overwhelming. ✉ *Calle Fulladoza, Dewey* ☎ *787/742–3508* 🌐 *www.villaboheme.com* ⇒ *12 rooms* ♁ *In-room: kitchen (some), refrigerator (some). In-hotel: no elevator* ▭ *AE, MC, V* 🍽 *EP.*

VILLA RENTALS

Lovely vacation homes are scattered around the island. **Culebra Island Realty** (✉ *Calle Escudero, Dewey* ☎ *787/742–0052* 🌐 *www.culebraislandrealty.com*) has a few dozen properties for rent, ranging from studios to three-bedroom houses.

$$$$ **Casa Aquabella.** On a tip of the island rarely seen by travelers, four-bedroom Casa Aquabella gazes down on the long expanse of Playa Zoni. Across the ocean you can usually see St. Thomas in the distance. This is not one building but three connected by walkways. At the center are the common areas (rather blandly decorated) and a gorgeous infinity pool. The best feature might be the deck, where you can cook fresh fish on a gas grill and then enjoy an alfresco meal. One strike against it: there's only air-conditioning in the bedrooms. ✉ *Off Rte. 250, Playa Zoni area* ☎ *787/742–0052* 🌐 *www.culebraislandrealty.com* ⇒ *4 bedrooms, 4 bathrooms* ♁ *No a/c (some), pool.* ▭ *No credit cards.*

NIGHTLIFE

Dinghy Dock (✉ *Calle Fulladoza, Dewey* ☎ *787/742–0581*) is the spot where the island's expat community begins piling into the bar around sunset. It can be a raucous scene, especially when there's a band. The party continues into the wee hours, even during the week. **El Batey** (✉ *Calle Escudero, Dewey* ☎ *787/742–3828*) is popular on the weekends, when locals dance to salsa music. It's in a cement-block building halfway between the airport and the town.

SPORTS & THE OUTDOORS

BIKING

Since there's very little traffic, biking is a good way to explore the island. You can rent bikes for $20 a day at **Culebra Bike Shop** (✉ *Calle Fulladoza, Dewey* ☎ *787/742–2209*). The shop is next door to the Dinghy Dock.

> **WORD OF MOUTH**
>
> "Culebra is not for someone looking to be pampered, or someone who wants a golf vacation or shopping vacation. But if you want quiet and solitude and beauty (especially underwater!), this might be for you. I have very fond memories of this island." –cj

BOATING & KAYAKING

At **Culebra Boat Rental** (✉ *142 Calle Escudero, Dewey* ☎ *787/742–3559*) affable Butch Pendergast will rent you anything from a two-person sailboat ($100 a day) to a six-person motorboat ($215 a day). The rates go down quite a bit if you rent for more than one day.

Run by Captain Luís Grundler, **Culebra Water Taxi** (✉ *66 Calle Castelar, Dewey* ☎ *787/360–9807* 🌐 *culebraboats.com/culebra-water-taxi*) has kayak and snorkeling trips to Dakity Bay that cost $45 per person, including lunch.

The glass-bottom boat at **Tanamá** (☎ *787/501–0011*) lets you explore the undersea world without even getting wet.

DIVING & SNORKELING

Run by Monica and Walter Rieder, **Culebra Divers** (✉ *4 Calle Pedro Marquez, Dewey* ☎ *787/742–0803* 🌐 *www.culebradivers.com*) caters to people who are new to scuba diving. You travel to dive sites on one of the company's pair of 26-foot cabin cruisers. One-tank dives are $65, and two-tank dives are $95. You can also rent a mask and snorkel to explore on your own. The office is in downtown Dewey, across from the ferry terminal.

SHOPPING

Culebra is smaller than Vieques but has much better shopping. Dewey has several shops on its main drag that sell trendy jewelry, fashionable clothing, and a range of souvenirs from tacky to terrific.

Butiki (✉ *Calle Escudio, Dewey* ☎ *787/267–7284*) is the cream of the crop. You'll find everything from lovely jewelry to original paintings.

And co-owner Stephanie Blake is so helpful that the city should shut down the tourism office and send people here.

La Cava (✉ *138 Calle Escudio, Dewey* ☎ *787/742–0566*) stocks a little bit of everything. Forgot your snorkel? Left your bathing suit at home? This is a good place to find a replacement.

In a wooden shack painted vivid shades of yellow and red, **Fango** (✉ *Calle Castelar, Dewey* ☎ *787/556–9308*) is the island's best place for gifts. Jorge Acevedo paints scenes of island life, while Hannah Staiger designs sophisticated jewelry. The shop is no bigger than a walk-in closet, but you could easily spend half an hour browsing among their one-of-a-kind works.

On Island (✉ *4 Calle Pedro Marquez, Dewey* ☎ *787/742–0439*) has a selection of black and white prints of the island's flora and fauna, and a nice display of handmade jewelry.

Paradise (✉ *6 Calle Salisbury, Dewey* ☎ *787/742–3565*) is a good spot for souvenirs ranging from wrought-iron iguanas to hand-carved seagulls to plush baby turtles.

VIEQUES & CULEBRA ESSENTIALS

To research prices, get advice from other travelers, and book travel arrangements, visit www.fodors.com.

TRANSPORTATION

BY AIR

It used to be that travelers arriving at San Juan's Aeropuerto Internacional Luis Muñoz Marín had to transfer to nearby Aeropuerto Fernando L. Rivas Dominici to take a flight to Vieques or Culebra. This is no longer the case, as all carriers servicing the islands now have flights from Aeropuerto Internacional Luis Muñoz Marín.

Air Flamenco, Isla Nena Air Service, and Vieques Air Link offer daily flights from both airports in San Juan to Vieques and Culebra. Cape Air flies between the international airport and Vieques. Trips from either airport in San Juan last between 20 and 30 minutes, whereas those from Fajardo last about 10 minutes. One-way fares vary quite a bit, but are between $120 and $150 from San Juan and between $40 and $50 from Fajardo. These companies use small propeller planes that hold a maximum of nine passengers (one sits next to the pilot).

It's been delayed for years, but American Eagle still plans to begin daily flights between San Juan and Vieques. This will mean that travelers flying on American won't have to deal with their checked bags in San Juan. The 64-seat plane—seven times larger than those used by the competition—will be the only plane en route to Vieques that has a flight attendant.

Information **Air Flamenco** (☎ *787/724–1818* 🌐 *www.airflamenco.net*). **American Eagle** (☎ *800/433–7300* 🌐 *www.aa.com*). **Cape Air** (☎ *800/525–0280* 🌐 *www.*

flycapeair.com). **Isla Nena Air Service** (☎ *787/741-6362 or 877/812-5144* 🌐 *www.islanena.8m.com*). **Vieques Air Link** (☎ *787/741-8331 or 888/901-9247* 🌐 *www.vieques-island.com/val*).

AIRPORTS Most international travelers fly to Vieques and Culebra from San Juan's Aeropuerto Internacional Luis Muñoz Marín (SJU) or San Juan's Aeropuerto Fernando L. Rivas Dominici (SIG; also known as Aeropuerto Isla Grande). A smaller number fly from Fajardo's Aeropuerto Diego Jiménez Torres (FAJ), which is just southwest of the city on Route 976.

3

Aeropuerto Antonio Rivera Rodríguez (VQS), on Vieques's northwest coast, is a 10-minute cab ride from Isabel Segunda or a 15-minute taxi ride from Esperanza. The airlines have offices on the top floor of the octagonal main terminal, and the single gate is on the lower level. There are no amenities to speak of, but there's an open-air eatery across the road. At this writing, American Eagle had broken ground on an addition to the main terminal that will have a separate gate for its flights. The new addition will also have a car-rental agency.

Culebra's Aeropuerto Benjamin Rivera Noriega (CPX) is at the intersection of Route 250 and Route 251. The one-room facility has two car-rental agencies and a scooter-rental kiosk. There's a small café inside the terminal, and several others are across the road. The airport is about three minutes from downtown Dewey.

Information **Aeropuerto Antonio Rivera Rodríguez** (✉ *Vieques* ☎ *787/741-0515*). **Aeropuerto Benjamin Rivera Noriega** (✉ *Culebra* ☎ *787/742-0022*).

BY BUS

There is no public bus system around Puerto Rico. If you are planning to take a ferry to Vieques or Culebra, you can take a *público* (a privately operated, shared minivan) from San Juan to Fajardo. The two-hour journey costs about $6, depending on where you board and where you are dropped off; if you take this very inexpensive mode of transportation, expect things to be a bit crowded. There are no central terminals: you simply flag públicos down anywhere along the route.

Vieques and Culebra are served by their own inexpensive públicos, whose drivers often speak English. Just flag them down along their routes. Rates vary depending on your destination, but are usually under $5.

BY CAR

Thinking about getting around on Vieques or Culebra without a car? Think again. If you plan on staying in a town, there's no need for a car. If you want to do anything else—say, go to the beach—you need a way to get there. And don't think about taking that car you rented in San Juan to the off-islands. The main roads are in great shape, but the secondary roads are so riddled with potholes that an SUV is a must.

On Vieques and Culebra you'll find local agencies, including several that specialize in SUVs. Rates are between $40 to $80 a day, depending on the age of the car. It's sometimes possible to rent directly from your hotel or guesthouse, so ask about packages that include lodging and a car rental. If you plan to head out to remote beaches, seriously consider a four-wheel-drive vehicle.

> **WORD OF MOUTH**
>
> "Based on conversations with friendly locals, the ferry runs in streaks—there will be months without a problem, and then a couple of months where nothing runs on time." –paulav.

On Vieques, try Island Car Rental, Maritza Car Rental, or Martineau Car Rental. On Culebra, Carlos Jeep Rental has an office in the airport.

There are only a handful of major roads on Vieques and Culebra. On Vieques, Route 200 leads from the airport to Isabel Segunda, and Route 997 leads from Isabel Segunda to Esperanza. There's also a longer, more scenic route between the two towns: from Isabel Segunda, take Route 200 west to Route 201 south. After about 1 mi, take Route 996 to Esperanza.

Culebra has two major roads. Route 250 leads east and south of the airport. Route 251 leads northeast to Playa Flamenco.

EMERGENCY SERVICES Rental-car agencies usually give customers emergency road-service numbers to call. There's no AAA service in Puerto Rico.

GASOLINE Gas stations are found only in Isabel Segunda on Vieques and Dewey on Culebra. Gas shortages are common on the islands, especially during high season. Even during low season there can be long lines at gas stations.

ROAD CONDITIONS The main roads are in fairly good shape, but many highway-exit and other signs have been blown down by hurricanes and may or may not have been replaced. When it rains, be alert for flash flooding, even on the major roads.

Agencies **Carlos Jeep Rental** (✉ *Aeropuerto Benjamin Rivera Noriega, Culebra* ☎ *787/742–3514* 🌐 *www.carlosjeeprental.com*). **Island Car Rental** (✉ *Rte. 201, Vieques* ☎ *787/741–1666* 🌐 *www.enchanted-isle.com/islandcar*). **Maritza's Car Rental** (✉ *Rte. 201, Vieques* ☎ *787/741–0078*). **Martineau Car Rental** (✉ *Rte. 200, Km 3.4, Vieques* ☎ *787/741–0087* 🌐 *www.martineaucarrental.com*).

BY FERRY

The Puerto Rico Ports Authority runs passenger ferries from Fajardo to Culebra and Vieques. Service is from the ferry terminal in Fajardo, about a 90-minute drive from San Juan. A municipal parking lot next to the ferry costs $5 a day—handy if you are going to one of the islands for the day. On Culebra the ferry pulls right into a nicely renovated terminal in downtown Dewey. The Vieques ferry dock is in downtown Isabel Segunda.

There are a limited number of seats on the ferries, so get to the terminal in plenty of time. This means an hour or more ahead of the departure time in Fajardo, somewhat less in Vieques and Culebra. The Puerto Rico Ports Authority claims to take phone reservations daily from 8 to 11 and 1 to 3. In reality, it's very difficult to get anyone to answer this number.

In Fajardo, the ticket counter is in the small building across the street from the actual terminal. In Vieques and Culebra, the ticket counters are at the entrance to the terminals. There are food kiosks at Fajardo and Vieques that are open even for the early morning departures. Culebra doesn't have any eateries nearby.

Aside from the regular ferries, cargo ferries also offer weekday departures. However, they are notorious for canceling departures at the last minute, leaving travelers stranded. If they are carrying hazardous cargo, such as fuel oil, they will refuse passage even to those who have already bought tickets. And don't even think about using one to transport your rental car to Vieques or Culebra. If you are able to get your car onboard, you might find that they can't bring it back for a week or more. That's sure to throw a monkey wrench into your travel plans.

FARES & SCHEDULES The Fajardo–Vieques passenger ferry departs from Vieques weekdays at 9 AM, 1 PM, 3 PM, 4:30 PM, and 8 PM, returning at 6:30 AM, 11 AM, 3 PM, and 6 PM. On weekends ferries depart from Vieques at 9 AM, 3 PM, and 6 PM, returning at 6:30AM, 1 PM, and 4:30 PM. Tickets for the 90-minute journey are $2 each way.

The Fajardo-Culebra ferry leaves Culebra daily at 9 AM, 3 PM, and 7 PM, returning at 6:30 AM, 1 PM, and 5 PM. The 90-minute trip is $2.25.

Ferry schedules change with alarming frequency. Call to confirm before you plan your trip, especially if you are planning to travel on the weekend.

Information **Puerto Rico Ports Authority** (☎ *787/860–2005 or 800/981–2005 for reservations*).

Ferry Terminals **Culebra Terminal** (☎ *787/742–3161*). **Fajardo Terminal** (☎ *787/863–4560*). **Vieques Terminal** (☎ *787/741–4761*).

BY TAXI

You can flag down taxis on the street, but it's faster and safer to have your hotel call one for you. Either way, agree on how much the trip will cost before you get inside the taxi.

Information **Lolo Felix Tours** (✉ *Vieques* ☎ *787/485–5447*). **Willy's Taxi** (✉ *Culebra* ☎ *787/742–3537*).

CONTACTS & RESOURCES

BANKS & EXCHANGE SERVICES

There are only a handful of banks on Vieques and Culebra, but they have 24-hour ATMs (or ATHs, as they're known here). The local branches of Banco Popular are open weekdays from 9 to 5.

Information **Banco Popular** (✉ *115 Calle Muñoz Rivera, Isabel Segunda, Vieques* ☎ *787/741–2071* ✉ *15 Calle Pedro Marquez, Dewey, Culebra* ☎ *787/742–0220*).

EMERGENCIES

Vieques has a pharmacy and a hospital, but Culebra does not have either. Make sure you stock up on all supplies—such as allergy medications, contact-lens solution, or tampons—before heading to the island.

Emergency Numbers **General Emergencies** (☎ *911*).

Hospitals **Hospital Susana Centeno** (✉ *Rte. 997, Isabel Segunda, Vieques* ☎ *787/741–3283*).

Pharmacies Farmacia Isla Nena (✉ *Calle Muñoz Rivera, Isabel Segunda, Vieques* ☎ *787/741–1906*).

ENGLISH-LANGUAGE MEDIA

On Vieques, look for the monthly *Vieques Events,* which includes everything from the latest news to a calendar of cultural events.

Pick up a copy of the colorful *Culebra Guide,* available for $3 at most local shops. The map in its centerfold is especially helpful.

INTERNET, MAIL & SHIPPING

Internet cafés are a rare commodity once you leave San Juan. On Culebra there are a few terminals at Excétera, where you can get online for $15 an hour.

Vieques has a post office on the main street in Isabel Segunda, and Culebra has one on the main street in Dewey. Culebra's post office functions as a town center, and usually has a group of locals out front chewing the fat. It's in an older building with a hand-carved front door.

Internet Café Excétera (✉ *126 Calle Escudero, Dewey* ☎ *787/742–0844*).

Post Offices Culebra Post Office (✉ *Calle Pedro Marquez, Dewey, Culebra* ☎ *787/742–3288*). **Vieques Post Office** (✉ *97 Calle Muñoz Rivera, Suite 103, Isabel Segunda, Vieques* ☎ *787/741–3891*).

SAFETY

Although crime isn't as prevalent on Vieques as it is in San Juan, be on your guard. Avoid bringing valuables with you to the beach; if you must do so, be sure not to leave them in view in your car. Rental agencies advise that you leave your car unlocked when parked at a beach so thieves won't break the windows to get inside. There's very little crime on Culebra.

VISITOR INFORMATION

The island's tourism offices are hit and miss when it comes to offering helpful material. The Vieques Tourism Office, across from the main square in Isabel Segunda, has a friendly staff that has very little to give you. If you need information, ask them to print out a complete list of local businesses. It's open Monday to Saturday 8 to 4:30.

The Culebra Tourism Office, near the ferry dock, has very little information on hand. The staffers will help you as best they can, even recommending restaurants that are off the beaten path. The office is open weekdays 9 to 5.

Information Culebra Tourism Office (✉ *250 Calle Pedro Marquez, Dewey, Culebra* ☎ *787/742–3521*). **Vieques Tourism Office** (✉ *449 Calle Carlos Lebrón, Isabel Segunda, Vieques* ☎ *787/741–5000*).

WEB SITES

The Web site Enchanted Isle has plenty of information about Vieques and Culebra; the Web site Isla Vieques has information about Vieques only.

Information Enchanted Isle (🌐 *www.enchanted-isle.com*). **Isla Vieques** (🌐 *www.isla-vieques.com*).

Ponce & the Southern Coast

WORD OF MOUTH

"Ponce is the second largest city on the island and has plenty of cultural and leisure activities for visitors. I believe San German would be just a day trip, as it is a very small town, and their main tourist attraction is the Porta Coelli Church, which is very old."

–Mily

"La Parguera is a nice town with many restaurants—great seafood! There are also several nice hotels in the area, as well as condos available for rent. Many boat excursions and other water activities available. Don't miss the nightly boat trips out to the bay where you will see the wonder of phosphorescent bay."

–kenm3

www.fodors.com/forums

Revised and Updated by Mark Sullivan

FROM LUSH TROPICAL MOUNTAINS TO arid seacoast plains, Puerto Rico's southern region lets you sample the island from a local's perspective. The south is where San Juan families escape the hustle and bustle of the city for weekends on the beach. Though rich in history, the area also provides ample opportunities for golf, swimming, hiking, and cave exploration. Snaking roads between major highways reveal a glimpse of how rural Puerto Ricans enjoy life. Every mile or so you'll see a café or bar, which is the local social center. The only traffic jams you'll likely encounter will be caused by slow-moving farmers taking their goods to the local market.

At the center of everything is Ponce, a city called the "Pearl of the South." Farmers attracted to the rich soil in the area, which was perfect for growing sugarcane, founded Ponce in 1692. Evidence found at the Tibes Indian ceremonial site, just north of the city, suggests that people have been living here since 400 BC. Many residents still carry the last names of the dozens of European pioneer families who settled here during the 19th century. The region's largest city, Ponce, is home to some of the island's most interesting architecture and one of its most important art museums. Nearby San Germán, the second-oldest city in Puerto Rico, is known for its two historic main squares, well preserved in a wide variety of architectural styles.

On the coast, Guayama and Patillas show off their splendors as little-known destinations for beachgoers. But the real beach party is at La Parguera, which attracts a young but noisy crowd. If you're willing to explore beyond the casinos, high-rises, and daily traffic congestion of the island's capital, the south is a wise escape from Puerto Rico's usual tourist fare. Don't be surprised by the help many of its residents will offer whether you ask for it or not. Southern *puertorriqueños* are known for their friendliness as well as their hospitality.

EXPLORING PONCE & THE SOUTHERN COAST

The southeastern part of the island has a rugged shoreline, where cliffs drop right into the water. This is a little-explored section of the coast, which means that on one hand the beaches aren't crowded, but on the other there aren't many places to find a decent meal or bed down for the night. Covered with dry vegetation, the southwest's ragged coast has wonderful inlets and bays and jagged peninsulas that make for breathtaking views. This region is a popular destination for Puerto Rican families, so expect crowds on weekends.

ABOUT THE RESTAURANTS

Not all the culinary hot spots are in San Juan. In fact, people from the capital drive to Ponce or Guánica to see what's new on the horizon. Some of the more ambitious restaurants in this part of Puerto Rico are experimenting with fusion cuisine, which means you might find pork with tamarind glaze or guava sauce or snapper in a plantain crust. But what you'll mostly find is open-air eateries serving simple, filling fare. The southern coast is known for seafood. A 15% to 20% tip is customary; most restaurants won't include it in the bill, but it's wise to check.

SOUTHERN COAST TOP 5

- Marvel at the Parque de Bombas, a century-old firehouse whose red-and-black color scheme has inspired thousands of photographers.
- Hike through the Bosque Estatal de Guánica, where the cactus may make you think you're in the American Southwest.
- Sample a cup of the local brew at historic Hacienda Buena Vista, a beautifully restored coffee plantation outside of Ponce.
- Stroll around San Germán, whose cobblestone streets are lined with architectural treasures.
- Step back in time at Casa Cautiño, a lovingly restored colonial-era residence in the sleepy community of Guayama.

WHAT IT COSTS IN U.S. DOLLARS

	$$$$	$$$	$$	$	¢
AT DINNER	over $30	$20–$30	$12–$20	$8–$12	under $8

Prices are per person for a main course at dinner.

ABOUT THE HOTELS

Modest, family-oriented establishments near beaches or in small towns are the most typical accommodations. Southern Puerto Rico doesn't have the abundance of luxury hotels and resorts found to the north and east; however, the Hilton Ponce & Casino and the Copamarina Beach Resort are self-contained complexes with a dizzying array of services.

WHAT IT COSTS IN U.S. DOLLARS

	$$$$	$$$	$$	$	¢
FOR 2 PEOPLE	over $350	$250–$350	$150–$250	$80–$150	under $80

Prices are for a double room in high season, excluding 9% tax (11% for hotels with casinos, 7% for paradores) and 5%–12% service charge.

TIMING

The resort towns of Patillas, Guánica, and La Parguera are also popular with Puerto Ricans during Easter and Christmas and during the summer, when children are out of school. Ponce's spirited pre-Lenten carnival, held the week before Ash Wednesday, draws many visitors. Note that during busy times some *paradores*, small government-sponsored inns, and hotels require a minimum two- or three-night stay on weekends.

IF YOU LIKE

BEACHES
On Puerto Rico's southern coast you'll find surfing beaches and calm bays for swimming. Ballena Bay, near Guánica, has oft-deserted sandy stretches. Boat operators make trips to such uninhabited cays as Gilligan's Island off the coast of Guánica and Caja de Muertos off Ponce.

DIVING & SNORKELING
Southern Puerto Rico is an undiscovered dive destination, which means unspoiled reefs and lots of fish. You can arrange for dive boats at Caribe Playa Beach Resort in the southeast, Ponce's La Guancha, and the Copamarina Beach Resort in the southwest. Shore diving and snorkeling are best around islands or cays or along the southwestern coast.

HIKING
Vegetation in the region is dramatically different from that of the rest of the island. Near Guánica is the 9,900-acre Bosque Estatal de Guánica, a rare dry tropical forest. With more than 100 species of birds, it's known for its excellent bird-watching. There are good trails throughout the area, but printed guides and trail maps are hard to come by. Ask locals for directions to their favorite paths.

PONCE

34 km (21 mi) southwest of Coamo.

"Ponce is Ponce and the rest is parking space" is the adage used by the residents of Puerto Rico's second-largest city (population 194,000) to express their pride in being a *ponceño*. The rivalry with the island's capital began in the 19th century, when European immigrants from England, France, and Spain settled here. Because the city's limits extend from the Caribbean to the foothills of the Cordillera Central, it's a lot hotter in climate than San Juan. Another contrast is the neoclassical architecture of the elegant homes and public buildings that surround the main square.

Many of the 19th-century buildings in Ponce Centro, the downtown area, have been renovated, and the Museo de Arte de Ponce—endowed by its late native son and former governor Luis A. Ferré—is considered one of the Caribbean's finest art museums. Just as famous is Ponce's pre-Lenten carnival. The colorful costumes and *vejigante* (mischief maker) masks worn during the festivities are famous throughout the world. The best dining in Ponce is just west of town. Seafood restaurants line the highway in an area known as Las Cucharas, named for the spoon-shape bay you'll overlook as you dine.

EXPLORING PONCE

Las Delicias Plaza (Plaza of Delights) with its trees, benches, and famous lion fountain is a perfect people-watching square in which to spend an hour or two on a Sunday afternoon. The old red-and-black firehouse is right on the plaza and has a fire-fighting museum on its second floor. Ponce is known for its museums and has several dedicated to music, art, history, sports, and architecture. Ponceños are proud of their city, called the "Pearl of the South," and offer all visitors a warm welcome.

GETTING AROUND

Getting around Ponce couldn't be easier. You can catch a free, city-run trolley or *"chu chu"* train from Plaza las Delicias to the major attractions. On weekends there are free horse-and-carriage rides around the plaza, or if the weather is pleasant, as it often is, you could just walk. All the downtown sites are within a few blocks of the main square.

PONCE CENTRO

At the heart of Ponce Centro is the Plaza las Delicias, with trees, benches, and the famous lion fountain. Several interesting buildings are on this square or the adjacent streets, making the area perfect for a leisurely morning or afternoon stroll.

Numbers in the text correspond to numbers in the margin and on the Ponce map.

WHAT TO SEE

2 **Casa Armstrong-Poventud.** Banker and industrialist Carlos Armstrong and his wife Eulalia Pou lived in this neoclassical house designed and built for them in 1901 by Manuel V. Domenech. As this book went to press, the building was in the beginning stages of a top-to-bottom renovation. If it isn't finished when you visit, you can still admire the ornate facade, which is chock-full of columns, statues, and intricate moldings. ✉*Calle Union, across from Catedral de Nuestra Señora de Guadalupe, Ponce Centro.*

7 **Casa Wiechers-Villaronga.** In a city filled with neoclassical confections, this is one of the most elaborate. Alfredo B. Wiechers, who returned to his native Ponce after studying architecture in Paris, designed the house. Though small in scale, it makes a big impression with details like huge arched windows and a massive rooftop gazebo. No wonder that soon after it was completed in 1911 the Villaronga-Mercado family decided to make it their own. Check out the stained-glass windows and other fanciful touches. Inside you'll find original furnishings and exhibits on Wiechers and other Ponce architects of his era. ✉*Calle Reina and Calle Méndez Vigo, Ponce Centro* ☎*787/843–3363* *Free* ⏲*Wed.–Sun. 8:30–4:30.*

Fodor's Choice ★

1 **Catedral de Nuestra Señora de Guadalupe.** This pale blue cathedral has always been one of the city's jewels, but it regained much of its luster after a complete renovation in 2007. Dedicated to the Virgin of Guadalupe, it is built on the site of a 1670 chapel destroyed by earthquakes. Part of the current structure, where mass is still held, dates from 1835. After another earthquake in 1918, new steeples and a roof were put on and neoclassical embellishments were added to the facade. Inside you'll see stained-glass windows and two alabaster altars. ✉*Plaza las Delicias, Ponce Centro* ☎*787/842–0134* ⏲*Services daily 6* AM *and 11* AM.

Southern Puerto Rico
Caribbean Sea
KEY
Beaches
Dive Sights
Panoramic Route
Rain Forest
0
10 miles
0
10 kilometers
Rincón
Bahía de Añasco
San Sebastián
Añasco
Lares
Las Marías
Mayagüez
Pta. Guanajibo
Las Vegas
Marícao
Reserva Forestal Marícao
Panoramic Route
Cordillera Central
Joyuda
Playa Joyuda
Buyé
Boquerón
Balneario Boquerón
El Combate
La Playuela
Bosque Estatal de Boquerón
Refugio de Vida Silvestre
San Germán
Lajas
La Parguera
Playita Rosada
Bahía Fosforescente
Sabana Grande
Ensenada
Pta. Brea
Guánica
Playa Santa
Balneario Caña Gorda
Punta Jacinto
Gilligan's Island
Bosque Estatal de Guánica
Bahía Ballena
Yauco
Palomas
Guayanilla
Peñuelas
Bosque Estatal de Rio Abajo
Florida
Utuado
Jayuya
Collores
Adjuntas
Reserva Forestal Toro Negro
Coto Laurel
Ponce
El Tuque
La Guancha
Calzada
Ciales
Villalba
Juana Díaz
Potala Pastillo
Caja de Muertos
Orocovis
Barranquitas
El Cañon de San Cristóbal
Coamo
Baños de Coamo
Santa Isabel
Pta. Petrona
Corozal
Morovis
Naranjito
Comerío
Cidra
Aibonito
Monumento al Jibaro
Cayey
Salinas
Bahía de Rincón
Coquí
Cayos de Barcas
Cayos Caribes
Guaynabo
Aguas Buenas
Caguas
San Lorenzo
Bosque Estatal Carite
Sierra de Cayey
Guayama
Arroyo
Balneario Punta Guilarte
Patillas
El Bajo de Patillas
Inches
Channel
Maunabo
Pta. Yeguas
Faro De Manaubo
Yabucoa
Humacao
Las Piedras
Juncos
Gurabo
Trujillo Alto
El Yunque
115
2
109
111
108
120
128
102
132
10
140
141
143
146
139
14
149
150
155
157
152
156
167
173
172
1
52
175
181
185
66
3
30
31
183
179
15
184
53

GREAT ITINERARIES

IF YOU HAVE 1 DAY

Many residents of San Juan think nothing of a day trip to **Ponce**. If you head south on Route 52 you'll reach the city called the "Pearl of the South" in less than two hours. There's plenty to do here, including a tour of the Museo de Arte de Ponce. The best way to spend an hour or two is to stroll around the lovely Plaza de las Delicias. Make sure to dine in one of the outstanding restaurants, especially Mark's at the Meliá.

IF YOU HAVE 3 DAYS

From San Juan, head south on Route 52 until you reach **Ponce**, the Pearl of the South. Spend the afternoon strolling around the Plaza de las Delicias, poking into the beautiful Catedral de Nuestra Señora de Guadalupe and the striking Parque de Bombas. On the following day, visit some of the other attractions in and around the city, perhaps the Museo de Arte de Ponce, the Castillo Serrallés, or Hacienda Buena Vista. Dedicate your final day to **Guánica**, where you'll find wonderful beaches and deserted cays; spend the night here before heading back to San Juan. If you are in the mood for hiking, there's the Bosque Estatal de Guánica.

IF YOU HAVE 5 DAYS

Make a leisurely trip south from San Juan on Route 52, spending a night in **Coamo**. These hot springs were thought by some to be Ponce de León's Fountain of Youth. Continue on your second day to **Ponce** for two days of exploring. Travel west along the coast and settle at a waterfront hotel in **Guánica**. In the evening you can take a boat trip to the bioluminescent bay at **La Parguera**. On your last day explore the beautifully preserved colonial city of **San Germán**, making sure to see the lovely colonial-era chapel known as the Capilla de Porta Coeli.

4

❺ **Museo de la Historia de Ponce.** Housed in two adjoining neoclassical mansions, this museum includes 10 exhibition halls covering the city's residents, from the Taíno Indians to the Spanish settlers to the mix of the present. Hour-long guided tours in English and Spanish give an overview of the city's history. The descriptions are mostly in Spanish, but displays of clothing from different eras still are interesting to see. ✉ *51–53 Calle Isabel, Ponce Centro* ☎ *787/844–7042* 🎟 *Free* 🕙 *Tues.–Sat. 9–5.*

❻ **Museo de la Música Puertorriqueña.** At this museum you'll learn how Puerto Rican music has been influenced by African, Spanish, and Native American cultures. On display are dozens of instruments, such as the *triple* (a small string instrument resembling a banjo), as well as memorabilia of local composers and musicians. The small museum takes up several rooms in a neoclassical former residence, which alone is worth the trip. ✉ *Calle Isabel and Calle Salud, Ponce Centro* ☎ *787/848–7016* 🎟 *Free* 🕙 *Wed.–Sun. 8:30–4:30.*

❸ **Parque de Bombas.** After El Morro in Old San Juan, this distinctive red-and-black–striped building may be the second most photographed building in Puerto Rico. Built in 1882 as a pavilion for an agricultural and industrial fair, it was converted the following year into a firehouse.

Fodor's Choice ★

Casa Armstrong-Poventud 2
Case Wiechers-Villaronga 7
Catedral de Nuestra Señora de Guadalupe 1
Museo de la Historia de Ponce 5
Museo de la Música Puertorriqueña ...6
Parque de Bombas 3
Teatro La Perla 4

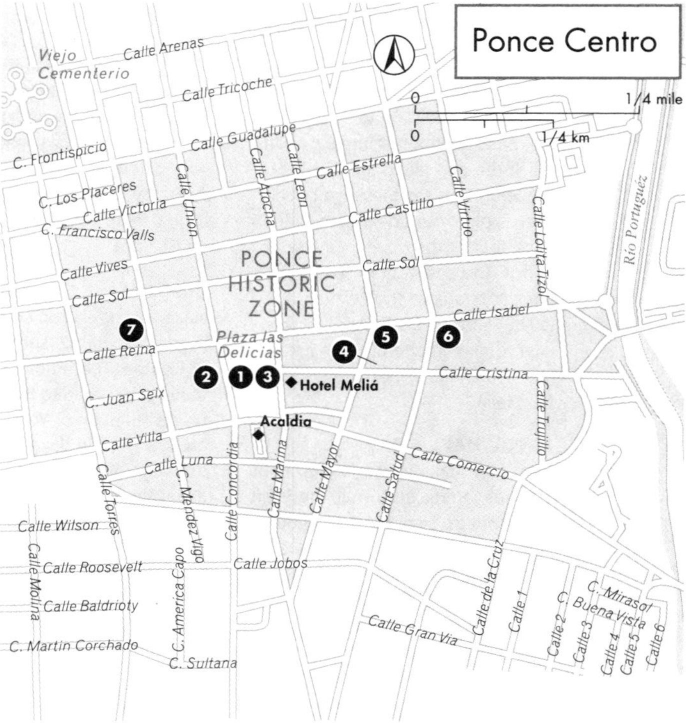

Today it's a museum tracing the history—and glorious feats—of Ponce's fire brigade. Kids love the antique fire truck on the lower level. Short tours in English and Spanish are given on the half hour. ■ **TIP→ The island's most helpful tourism officials staff a small information desk inside the door. Go ahead, ask them anything.** ✉ *Plaza las Delicias, Ponce Centro* ☎ *787/284–3338* 🎫 *Free* ⏲ *Wed.–Mon. 9–5:30.*

NEED A BREAK?

An institution for more than 40 years, King's (✉ *9223 Calle Marina* ☎ *787/843-8520*), across from Plaza las Delicias, is *the* place for ice cream in Ponce. It serves 12 varieties, from tamarind and passion fruit to classics chocolate and vanilla. A bench in the tiny storefront seats three, but most folks take their cups and cones across the street and stake out shady benches around the fountain. King's is open daily from 8 AM to midnight.

❹ **Teatro La Perla.** This theater was restored in 1941 after an earthquake and fire damaged the original 1864 structure. The striking interior contains seats for 1,047 and has excellent acoustics. It's generally open for a quick peek on weekdays. ✉ *Calle Mayor and Calle Cristina, Ponce Centro* ☎ *787/843–4322* 🎫 *Free* ⏲ *Weekdays 8–4:30.*

GREATER PONCE

The greater Ponce area has some of Puerto Rico's most notable cultural attractions, including one of the island's finest art museums and its most important archaeological site.

Numbers in the text correspond to numbers in the margin and on Greater Ponce map.

DON'T SWEAT IT

Several of the city's most popular museums—Casa Wiechers-Villaronga and the Museo de la Música Puertorriqueña—are not air-conditioned, so they close early when the weather is hot. If you want to see these sites, make sure to arrive before 11 AM.

WHAT TO SEE

4 **Castillo Serrallés.** This lovely Spanish-style villa—such a massive house that people in the town below referred to it as a castle—was built in the 1930s for Ponce's wealthiest family, the makers of Don Q rum. Guided tours give you a glimpse into the lifestyle of a sugar baron. The dining room is a highlight, with its original hand-carved furnishings. A permanent exhibit explains the area's sugarcane and rum industries. The extensive garden, with sculptured bushes and a shimmering reflection pool, is considered the best kept on the island. ✉ *17 El Vigía, El Vigía* ☎ *787/259–1774* 🌐 *home.coqui.net/castserr* 🎫 *$6, $9 includes admission to Cruceta El Vigía* ⏲ *Tues.–Thurs. 9:30–5, Fri.–Sun. 9:30–5:30.*

5 **Centro Ceremonial Indígena de Tibes.** This archeological site, discovered after flooding from a tropical storm in 1975, is the most important on the island. The ancient ceremonial center dates from AD 300 to 700 and includes nine playing fields used for a ritual ball game that some think was similar to soccer. The fields are bordered by smooth stones, some of which are engraved with petroglyphs that researchers say might have ceremonial or astronomical significance. The most eye-catching part of the site is the *Plaza de Estrella,* or Plaza of the Star, where the stones are arranged in a pattern that resembles a rising sun. Experts say it might have been used to chart the seasons. A village with several thatch huts has been reconstructed in an original setting. Be sure to visit the small museum before taking a walking tour of the site. ✉ *Tibes Indian Ceremonial Center, Rte. 503, Km 2.8, Barrio Tibes* ☎ *787/840–2255 or 787/840–5685* 🌐 *ponce.inter.edu/tibes/tibes.html* 🎫 *$3* ⏲ *Tues.–Sun. 9–noon and 1–4.*

3 **Cruceta El Vigía.** At the top of Cerro Vigía—a hill where the Spanish once watched for ships, including those of marauding pirates—is this colossal concrete cross. You can climb the stairs or take an elevator to the top of the 100-foot cross for a panoramic view across the city. Purchase tickets at nearby Castillo Serrallés. ✉ *Across from Castillo Serrallés, El Vigía* ☎ *787/259–3816* 🌐 *home.coqui.net/castserr* 🎫 *$4, $9 includes admission to Castillo Serrallés* ⏲ *Tues.–Sun. 9–5:30.*

2 **La Guancha.** Encircling the cove of a working harbor, the seaside boardwalk features kiosks where vendors sell local food and drink. The adjacent park has a large children's area filled with playground equipment and on weekends, live music. The nearby public beach has restrooms,

A GOOD WALK

Start on the tree-lined Plaza las Delicias. (You'll find parking nearby on Calle Marina, Calle Isabel, and Calle Reina.) Dominating it is the **Catedral Nuestra Señora de Guadalupe**, dating from 1835. Across the street is the **Casa Armstrong-Poventud**, home of the Institute of Culture's Ponce branch. Leaving Armstrong-Poventud, cross back to the plaza, circle south by the Alcaldía, and continue to the plaza's east side to visit the red-and-black striped fire station, **Parque de Bombas**.

From the intersection of Calles Marina and Cristina, take Calle Cristina a block east to one of the city's first restoration projects, **Teatro La Perla**, at the corner of Cristina and Mayor. One block north of the theater, at Calles Mayor and Isabel, is a former home that's now the **Museo de la Historia de Ponce**. A block east, at the corner of Calles Salud and Isabel, is the **Museo de la Música Puertorriqueña**. Four blocks west (you will go by Plaza las Delicias again, and Calle Isabel will turn into Calle Reina) is the 1911 architectural masterpiece **Casa Wiechers-Villaronga**. For more early-20th-century architecture, continue west on Calle Reina, where you'll see examples of *casas criollas,* wooden homes with the spacious front balconies that were popular in the Caribbean during the early 1900s.

TIMING

Although it's possible to see Ponce Centro in one morning or afternoon, it's best to devote a full day and evening to it. Explore the streets and museums during daylight, then head for the plaza at night when the lion fountain and street lamps are lighted and townspeople stroll the plaza.

changing areas, a medical post, and plenty of free parking. ✉ *End of Rte. 14, La Guancha* ☎ *787/844–3995.*

6 **Hacienda Buena Vista.** Built by Salvador de Vives in 1838, Buena Vista was one of the area's largest coffee plantations. It's a technological marvel—water from the nearby Río Canas was funneled into narrow brick channels that could be diverted to perform any number of tasks, including turning the waterwheel. (Seeing the two-story wheel slowly begin to turn is thrilling, especially for kids.) Nearby is the two-story manor house, filled with furniture that gives a sense of what it was like to live on a coffee plantation nearly 150 years ago. Make sure to take a look in the kitchen, dominated by a massive hearth. In 1987 the plantation was restored by the Puerto Rican Conservation Trust, which leads four tours a day (one in English). The tours are by reservation only, so make sure to call several days ahead. After seeing the plantation, you can buy coffee beans and other souvenirs at the gift shop. Allow yourself an hour to travel the winding road from Ponce. ✉ *Rte. 123, Km 16.8, Sector Corral Viejo* ☎ *787/722–5882 weekdays, 787/284–7020 weekends* *$5* *Fri.–Sun., by reservation only.*

Fodor's Choice ★

1 **Museo de Arte de Ponce.** This building—designed by Edward Durrell Stone, who also designed the original Museum of Modern Art in New York City and the Kennedy Center in Washington, DC—is easily iden-

Fodor's Choice ★

CLOSE UP

Masked Mischief

A week before Ash Wednesday, *vejigantes* (pronounced veh-hee-GAN-tays), wearing long, colorful robes and brightly painted horned masks, turn the normally placid city of Ponce into a hotbed of rowdiness. These masked mischief-makers prowl city streets for a week, scaring anyone in their path. Some historians date this tradition to a Spanish one of the 1600s that targeted lapsed Christians. Men in long robes and grotesque masks waved cow bladders, or *vejigas,* on long sticks at passersby, attempting to frighten them back into churches for Lent. Today balloons and plastic bottles have replaced cow bladders, and the playful masks present Ponce's exquisite folk art to the world.

Unlike carnival masks from other parts of the island, which are made of coconut shells *(Loíza)* or fine metallic screening *(Hatillo),* Ponce masks are made of papier-mâché. Many have African and Native American elements; it's even possible to detect influences from ancient Greece and Rome. All masks have at least two horns, but most have several protruding from the forehead, chin, and nose. Some antique masks are known to have more than 100 horns.

At the beginning of the 20th century, masks were usually painted red with yellow dots or vice versa, but today they come in every imaginable color and pattern. You'll also find them for sale at crafts stores and arts festivals. Small, simple masks start at around $20 or $30; larger ones by well-known makers can cost as much as $100. One of the best-known mask-making families today is the Caraballo family from the Playa de Ponce area.

tified by the hexagonal galleries on the second story. It has one of the best art collections in Latin America, which is why residents of San Juan frequently make the trip down to Ponce. The 3,000-piece collection includes works by famous Puerto Rican artists such as Francisco Oller, represented by a lovely landscape called *Hacienda Aurora.* There are plenty of European works on display as well, including paintings by Peter Paul Rubens and Thomas Gainsborough. The highlight of the European collection is the Pre-Raphaelite paintings, particularly the mesmerizing *Flaming June,* by Frederick Leighton, which has become the museum's unofficial symbol. Watch for special exhibits, such as a recent one examining the work of Rodin. ✉ *2325 Av. Las Américas, Sector Santa María* ☎ *787/848–0505* 🌐 *www.museoarteponce.org* 🎫 *$5* 🕓 *Daily 10–5.*

BEACHES

Caja de Muertos *(Coffin Island).* This island a few miles off the coast has the best beaches in the Ponce area and is, perhaps, the second-best spot in southern Puerto Rico for snorkeling, after La Parguera. Ask one of the many boatmen at La Guancha to take you out for about $30 round-trip. ✉ *Boats leave from La Guancha, at the end of Rte. 14, Ponce.*

La Guancha. Ponce's public beach isn't anything to write home about, but the shallow water makes it nice for children. There's some shade under thatched umbrellas, but bring sunscreen. ✉*At the end of Rte. 14, Ponce.*

El Tuque. This beach has a swimming area and picnic tables. ✉*Rte. 2, approx. 5 km (3 mi) west of Ponce.*

WHERE TO EAT

$$–$$$$ Fodor'sChoice ★ ✕**Mark's at the Meliá.** Hidden behind an etched-glass door, this discreet restaurant is one of the best on the island. Chef Mark French has won praise for his creative blend of European cooking techniques and local ingredients. His skill results in appetizers like terrine of foie gras with dried-cherry compote and smoked salmon topped with caramelized mango. The menu changes often, but you're likely to see such entrées as plantain-crusted dorado and rack of lamb with a goat-cheese crust. The chocolate truffle cake draws fans from as far away as San Juan. This is a family-run business, so Mark's wife, Melody, will likely greet you at the door. ✉*Hotel Meliá, 75 Calle Cristina, Ponce Centro, Ponce* ☎*787/284–6275* ✍*Reservations essential* ▭*AE, MC, V* ⏲*Closed Mon. and Tues.*

> **WORD OF MOUTH**
>
> "Ponce has more cultural things to see [than Isla Verde in San Juan]: Castillo Serralles, Torre del Vigía (watch tower), the firehouse, Museo de Arte de Ponce (the best art museum in PR), etc. So it just depends on what you are looking for, nightlife or culture."
>
> –majoquito

$$–$$$ ★ ✕**Cabuqui.** On sweltering hot days, it takes a lot to make *ponceños* leave their homes. Yet they come out in droves to the tree-shaded courtyard of the Cubuqui, the hottest new restaurant in Ponce. When a breeze shakes the flower-covered branches, things cool down considerably. And if nature doesn't cooperate, there are always the three air-conditioned dining rooms. The menu is extremely well traveled, stopping in Argentina (churrasco served with homemade chimichurri) and France (veal fillet in a red wine sauce) before heading back to Puerto Rico for such dishes as *masitas de cerdo* (chunks of perfectly seasoned pork). The wine list, which includes many bottles from Spain and Chile, is quite reasonable. There's always live music, whether it's a small band playing jazz or a single accordionist losing himself in a tango. ✉*32 Calle Isabel, Ponce Centro* ☎*787/984–5696* ▭*AE, MC, V.*

$$–$$$ ✕**Pito's Seafood.** Choose from the waterfront terrace or one of the enclosed dining rooms at this longtime favorite east of Ponce in Las Cucharas. No matter where you sit, you'll have a view of the ocean. The main attraction is the freshly caught seafood, ranging from lobster and crab to salmon and red snapper. To indulge yourself, try the shrimp wrapped in bacon—a specialty of the house. There's also a wide range of chicken and beef dishes. From the expansive wine cellar you can select more than 25 different wines by the glass. There's live music on Friday and Saturday nights. ✉*Rte. 2, Sector Las Cucharas* ☎*787/841–4977* ▭*AE, MC, V.*

$$–$$$ ✕**Rincón Argentina.** Housed in a beautifully restored criollo-style house, Rincón Argentina is one of the city's most popular restaurants. Com-

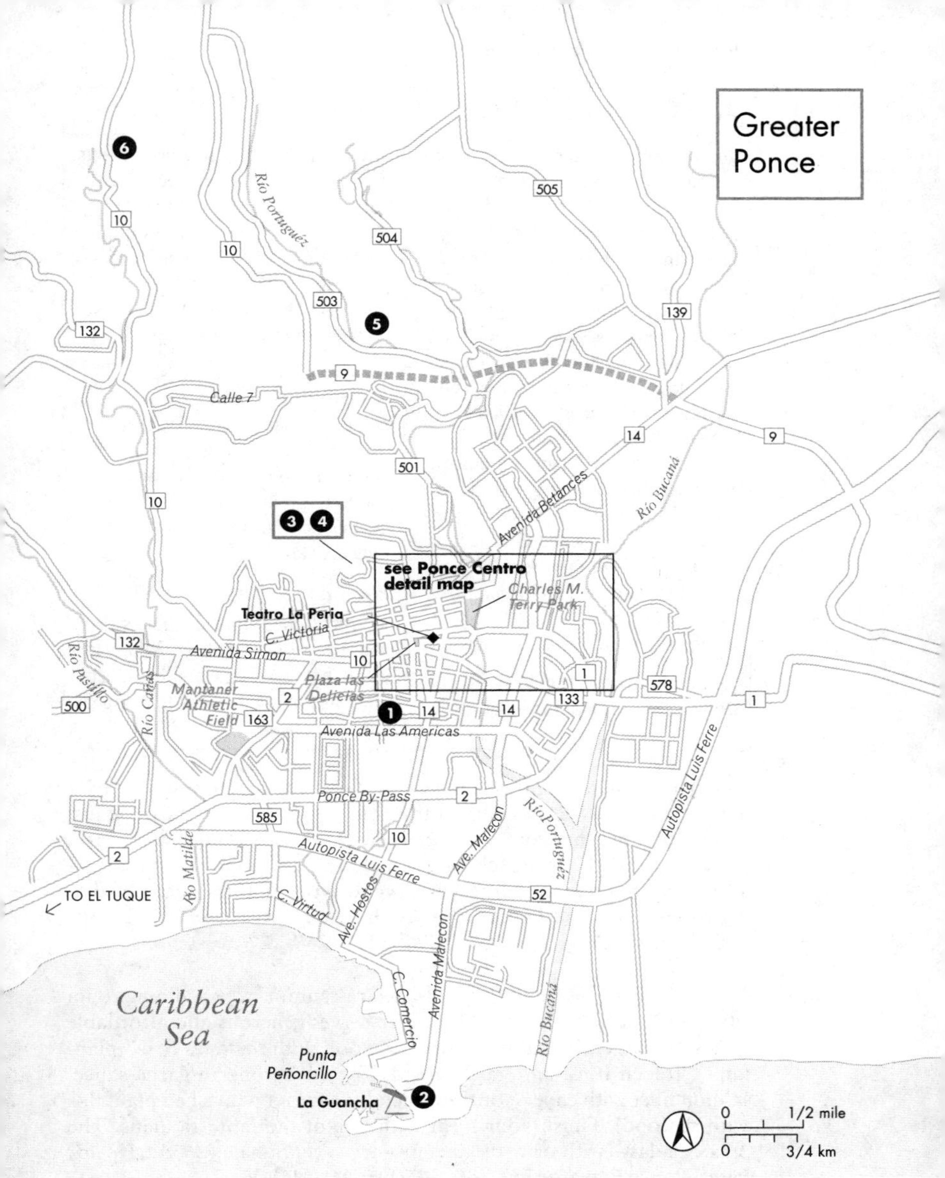

Castillo Serrallés **4**

Centro Ceremonial Indígena de Tibes **5**

Cruceta El Vigía **3**

La Guancha **2**

Hacienda Buena Vista **6**

Museo de Art de Ponce **1**

A GOOD TOUR

The **Museo de Arte de Ponce** is on Avenida Las Américas, south of Plaza las Delicias and not far from the Luis A. Ferré Expressway (Route 52). Anyone with a taste for art can happily while away many hours in its galleries. East of the museum you can pick up Route 14 south to the Caribbean and **La Guancha,** a boardwalk with food kiosks, a playground, and a child-friendly public beach. It's a good place to relax and let the younger generation work off energy. From here, if you retrace your path north past downtown you'll be heading to Calle Bertoly and El Vigía (Vigía Hill), where the **Cruceta El Vigía** towers over the city and the **Castillo Serrallés,** a former sugar baron's villa, is a popular attraction.

Farther north on Route 503 is the **Centro Ceremonial Indígena de Tibes,** which displays native artifacts dating back more than 1,500 years. You'll have to backtrack to reach Route 10, then head north to **Hacienda Buena Vista,** a former coffee plantation that's been restored by the Puerto Rican Conservation Trust. (Call ahead to arrange a tour.)

You can drive to all these sights or hop on the free trolleys or *chu chu* trains that run from Plaza las Delicias to the museum, La Guancha, and El Vigía. You'll need a car or a cab to reach the Centro Ceremonial Indígena de Tibes or Hacienda Buena Vista.

TIMING

To visit all the sights mentioned above you'll need at least 2 days. If you don't want to devote that much time, visit only the sights that appeal most to you.

pletely unpretentious, this is the kind of steak house you find all over South America. The specialty of the house is *parrilladas,* meaning just about anything that comes off the grill. Don't pass up the skirt steak, served here with lip-smacking chimichurri. On cool evenings, take a table on the terrace. Otherwise, wander through the maze of dining rooms until you find a table you like. ✉*69 Calle Salud, at Calle Isabel, Ponce Centro, Ponce* ☎*787/840–3768* ✍*Reservations essential* ▭*AE, MC, V.*

$–$$$ ✕**El Ancla.** Families favor this laid-back restaurant, whose dining room sits at the edge of the sea. The kitchen serves generous and affordable plates of fish, crab, and other fresh seafood with *tostones* (fried plantains), french fries, and garlic bread. Try the shrimp in garlic sauce, salmon fillet with capers, or the delectable *mofongo* (mashed plantains with seafood). Finish your meal with one of the fantastic flans. The piña coladas—with or without rum—are exceptional. ✉*9 Av. Hostos Final, Ponce Playa* ☎*787/840–2450* ▭*AE, MC, V.*

¢ ✕**Café Tompy.** The prices are right at this no-frills cafeteria, which draws many locals for lunch. You can sample such down-home Puerto Rican cuisine as roasted chicken marinated with local spices or slices of roast pork in a honey-sweet glaze. You can pile on the side dishes, which include toasted plantains and creamy potato salad. There's also a selection of sandwiches piled high with meats and cheeses. It's open daily for lunch and dinner, and for breakfast every day except Sunday. ✉*56 Calle Isabel, Ponce Centro* ☎*787/840–1965* ▭*MC, V.*

WHERE TO STAY

$$–$$$ **Hilton Ponce Golf & Casino Resort.** The south coast's biggest resort sits on a black-sand beach about 6 km (4 mi) south of Ponce. Everything on this 80-acre property is massive, beginning with the open-air lobby. Constructed of reinforced concrete, like the rest of the hotel, it requires huge signs to point you in the right direction. All its bright, spacious rooms are decorated in a lush, tropical motif and have balconies overlooking the sea. A large pool is surrounded by palm trees and has a spectacular view of the Caribbean. Golf lovers will appreciate the 27-hole course at the adjacent Costa Caribe Resort, which has a clubhouse with its own restaurant and lounge. **Pros:** Good golf, large casino. **Cons:** Not on beach, isolated location, bland rooms. ✉ *1150 Av. Caribe, La Guancha* *Box 7419, Ponce00732* ☎ *787/259–7676 or 800/445–8667* 🌐 *www.hiltoncaribbean.com* *253 rooms* *In-room: safe, refrigerator, Ethernet. In-hotel: 4 restaurants, room service, bars, golf courses, tennis courts, pool, gym, spa, beachfront, bicycles, children's programs (ages 8–12), parking (fee)* *AE, D, DC, MC, V* *EP.*

$ **Holiday Inn Ponce.** Perched on a hilltop, this hotel has a sweeping view of the southern coast. In exchange for that view from your private balcony, however, you give up direct access to the beach. The pair of pools, one for the kids, is a bit of a consolation. Romantic music wafting from the lobby bar and the dance beat that pulsates from the disco lend considerable Latin flair to the hotel. Adding to the energy is the sound of slot machines that echoes through the lobby. The Tanama restaurant serves Spanish, Puerto Rican, and nouvelle cuisine; several seafood restaurants are also in the nearby Las Cucharas area. **Pros:** Very friendly staff, plenty of activities. **Cons:** No beach, motel-style rooms, modest casino. ✉ *3315 Ponce Bypass, El Tuque* ☎ *787/844–1200 or 800/465–4329* 🌐 *www.holidayinn.com/ponce* *116 rooms* *In-room: safe, refrigerator, Wi-Fi. In-hotel: restaurant, room service, bars, pools, gym, laundry service, public Internet, public Wi-Fi, parking (no fee)* *AE, D, DC, MC, V* *EP.*

$ **Hotel Meliá.** In the heart of the city, this family-owned hotel has long been a local landmark. Its neoclassical facade, with flags from a dozen countries waving in the breeze, will remind you of small lodgings in Spain. The lobby, with wood-beamed ceilings and blue-and-beige tile floors, is well worn but extremely charming. The best rooms have French doors leading out to small balconies; the six suites have terrific views of the main square. Breakfast is served on the rooftop terrace, which overlooks the mountains. A waterfall drops into the beautiful tiled swimming pool. The restaurant, Mark's at the Meliá, is one of the best on the island. **Pros:** Great location on the main square, walking distance to downtown sites, good dining options in and near hotel. **Cons:** Rooms are somewhat outdated, front rooms are a bit noisy. ✉ *75 Calle Cristina, Ponce Centro* *Box 1431, Ponce00733* ☎ *787/842–0260 or 800/448–8355* 🌐 *www.hotelmeliapr.com* *72 rooms, 6 suites* *In-room: Wi-Fi. In-hotel: restaurant, bar, pool, public Internet, parking (fee)* *AE, MC, V* *CP.*

$ **Howard Johnson.** Near the airport, this hotel is a good choice if you have an early-morning flight. The rooms are pretty much what you'd expect from a chain hotel, but all have balconies overlooking a palm-shaded pool. There's not much in the way of amenities, but the smiling staff provides little extras like in-room coffeemakers with an unlimited supply of freshly ground beans. *103 Turpó Industrial Park, Airport 787/841–1000 www.hojo.com 120 rooms In-room: refrigerator (some), Ethernet, Wi-Fi. In-hotel: restaurant, room service, bar, pools, gym AE, D, DC, MC, V EP.*

¢–$ **Fox Delicias.** The facade of this hotel—an Art Deco fantasy with streamlined columns soaring heavenward and brightly colored mosaics swirling above the front door—once graced a movie palace. Don't be surprised if you stop and stare the moment you step into the cozy, brick courtyard. The interior could only pale by comparison. Once a shopping mall, this boutique hotel still feels like it should be filled with boutiques. The restaurants are behind windows where locals used to browse. The rooms are clean and comfortable, with some cool modern furnishings. **Pros:** Gorgeous facade, near all downtown sites. **Cons:** Some rooms have no windows, staff seems distracted. *6963 Calle Isabel, Ponce Centro 787/290–5050 www.hotelfoxdelicias.com 30 rooms In-hotel: 2 restaurants, bars, parking (fee) AE, MC, V EP.*

¢ **Hotel Bélgica.** Near the central square, this hotel is both comfortable and economical. A stairway off the large 1940s-era lobby leads to clean rooms with wrought-iron headboards and other furnishings. Those on the front of the building have balconies with wooden shutter–style doors. The rooms vary widely in size (Room 3 is one of the largest), and some windows open onto an air shaft, so ask to see a few before you decide. The hotel has no restaurant, but there are plenty of options in the neighborhood. **Pros:** A taste of old Ponce, friendly staff. **Cons:** Front-facing rooms are noisy, very basic rooms, lots of steps to upstairs rooms. *122 Calle Villa, Ponce Centro 787/844–3255 www.hotelbelgica.com 20 rooms In-hotel: no elevator, some pets allowed MC, V EP.*

NIGHTLIFE & THE ARTS

NIGHTLIFE

BARS & CLUBS On the main square, **Café Palermo** (*Calle Union at Calle Villa, Ponce Centro 787/448–8112*) is a hole in the wall. Still, locals crowd around the bar every night of the week. **Fusion** (*28 Calle Isabel, Ponce Centro 787/842–2544*) has a laid-back lounge area that makes you want to order a fancy cocktail. You can also belly up to the chic bar.

Wrapping around an interior courtyard, **Paseo's** (*Calle Isabel at Calle Mayor, Ponce Centro 787/843–6703*) draws a college-age crowd.

CASINOS The casinos in Ponce can't hold a candle to their counterparts in San Juan. **Hilton Ponce Golf & Casino Resort** (*Rte. 14, 1150 Av. Caribe, La Guancha 787/259–7676*) has a rather cramped casino that stays open nightly until 4 AM. **Holiday Inn Ponce** (*3315 Ponce Bypass,*

El Tuque ☎*787/844–1200*) has a small casino just off the lobby. It is open nightly until 4 AM.

THE ARTS

The **Museo de Arte de Ponce** (✉*2325 Av. Las Américas, Sector Santa María* ☎*787/848–0505*) occasionally sponsors chamber-music concerts and recitals by members of the Puerto Rico Symphony Orchestra. Check for Spanish-language theater productions and concerts at the **Teatro La Perla** (✉*Calle Mayor and Calle Cristina, Ponce Centro* ☎*787/843–4322*).

> **TAKE A WALK**
>
> In downtown Ponce, people embrace the Spanish tradition of the *paseo,* an evening stroll with family and friends around Plaza las Delicias, which is spectacular at night when its old-fashioned street lamps glow and the fountain is lit. The boardwalk at La Guancha is also a lively scene with bands playing on weekends.

SPORTS & THE OUTDOORS

DIVING & SNORKELING

You'll see many varieties of coral, parrotfish, angelfish, and grouper in the reefs around the island of Caja de Muertos. Snorkeling around La Guancha and the beach area of the Ponce Hilton is also fairly good.

Rafi Vega's **Island Venture** (☎*787/842–8546* 🌐*www.islandventurepr.com*) offers two-tank dive excursions for $65, as well as snorkeling trips for $35. The company also takes day-trippers from La Guancha to Caja de Muertos—a 45-minute boat ride—for a day of relaxing on the beach.

SHOPPING

On holidays and during festivals, artisans sell wares from booths in the Plaza las Delicias. Souvenir and gift shops are plentiful in the area around the plaza, and Paseo Atocha, a pedestrian mall with shops geared to residents, runs north of it.

Den Cayá (✉*72 Calle Isabel, Ponce Centro* ☎*787/649–7763*), a fun and funky store, has a wide variety of crafts from around the island as well as from around the world.

Mi Coquí (✉*9227 Calle Marina, Ponce Centro* ☎*787/841–0216*) has shelves filled with carnival masks, colorful hammocks, freshly ground coffee, and bottles and bottles of rum.

Plaza del Caribe Mall (✉*Rte. 2, Km 224.9* ☎*787/259–8989*), just outside town, is one of the island's largest malls and has such stores as Sears, JCPenney, and the Gap.

Ponce Mall (✉*Rte. 2, Km 225.8* ☎*787/844–6170*), with more than 25 stores, is an older shopping center with many local clothing and discount stores.

Utopia (✉78 *Calle Isabel, Ponce Centro* ☎*787/848–8742*) sells carnival masks and crafts.

THE SOUTHEASTERN COAST

> **WORD OF MOUTH**
>
> "If you decide to rent a car, just be aware that most of the road signs are solely in Spanish. While the roads were pretty well marked, if you don't know left (*izquierda*) from right (*derecho*), you'll face a few challenges!" —Callaloo

As you cross the Cordillera Central, the scenery becomes drier and more rugged. The Caribbean sparkles in the distance, and the plain between the sea and the mountains, once the heart of the sugarcane industry, is now the domain of cattle. Tucked into the foothills is Coamo, a popular hot-springs resort since the early 1900s. Closer to the coast is Guayama, with a tree-lined square surrounded by many historic buildings.

COAMO

34 km (21 mi) northeast of Ponce, 33 km (20 mi) southwest of Cayey; 20 km (13 mi) northwest of Salinas.

Founded by the Spanish in 1579, Coamo was the third city established in Puerto Rico. It dominated the south of the island until the mid-1880s, when political power shifted to Ponce. Coamo town, however, remained an important outpost; several decisive battles were fought here during the Spanish-American War in 1898.

The thermal springs outside Coamo are believed by some to be the Fountain of Youth for which Ponce de León was searching. In the mid-1800s a fashionable resort was built nearby, and people have been coming to soak in the waters ever since. Coamo is also famous for the San Blas Half-Marathon, which brings competitors and spectators from around the world. The race, held in early February, covers 18 km (13 mi) of the city's hilly streets.

On Coama's main square, the **Iglesia Católica San Blás** has a gorgeous neoclassical facade. Dating from 1563, the whitewashed building is one of the oldest churches on the island. ✉*Calle Mario Braschetti* ☎*787/825–1122* ⏲*Daily 6:30–noon.*

Off the main square, the **Museo Histórico de Coamo** is appropriately housed in the former residence of one of the city's illustrious citizens, Clotilde Santiago, a wealthy farmer and merchant born in 1826. The museum is on the second floor of this sprawling, tangerine-colored building that dates from 1863. Several rooms are decorated with colonial-style furnishings; photographs of the town and the Santiago family line the walls. ✉*29 Calle José I. Quintón* ☎*787/825–1150* 🎟*Free* ⏲*Weekdays 8–4:30.*

Outside Coamo on Route 546 you can take a dip at the famous **Baños de Coamo,** thermal springs that are said to have curative powers. Parador Baños de Coamo allows day-trippers to bathe in its own warm pool for $5 (parador guests enjoy it on the house). There's also a free public bathing area at the end of a path behind the parador. ✉ *Rte. 546, Km 1* ☎ *787/825–2186* 🎫 *$5* ⏲ *Daily 10–5:30.*

WHERE TO EAT

¢–$ ✕ **La Ceiba.** The highway leading to Coama is lined by dozens of fast-food restaurants. Luckily, there are a few family-owned eateries worth stopping for, one of the best of which is this open-air cantina. You'll find the usual tacos, burritos, quesadillas, and fajitas, as well as some interesting Puerto Rican dishes like chicken breast stuffed with shrimp. World-class margaritas are served at the bar. ✉ *Rte. 153* ☎ *787/825–2299* 💳 *MC, V.*

4

WHERE TO STAY

$ **Parador Baños de Coamo.** On weekends musicians wander around the central courtyard of this rustic country inn. Simple rooms—in four two-story buildings—have soaring ceilings and open onto latticed, wooden verandahs. Thermal water flows from natural springs into a swimming pool a few steps up from a cool-water pool, where you can still see walls built for the original resort that date back to 1847. The oldest building still intact is the 19th-century dining room, which serves huge portions of tasty *churrasco* (skirt steak) along with rice and beans. The open-air bar is popular in the afternoons. **Pros:** Relaxing atmosphere, pleasant staff. **Cons:** Uninteresting room decor, pools could be cleaner. ✉ *Rte. 546, Km 1, Box 1867, Coamo* ☎ *787/825–2186 or 787/825–2239* *48 rooms* *In-hotel: restaurant, 2 bars, 2 pools, no elevator* 💳 *AE, D, MC, V* *EP.*

SPORTS & THE OUTDOORS

GOLF The **Coamo Springs Golf Club & Resort** (✉ *Rte. 546* ☎ *787/825–1370* 🌐 *www.coamosprings.com*) is popular for its rugged beauty. It's the only 18-hole, par-72 course with Bermuda grass on the island. When it's raining in the capital, sanjuaneros may drive down here for a day of play. The 6,647-yard course, designed by Ferdinand Garbin, is open daily.

SALINAS

41 km (27 mi) east of Ponce.

Most visitors are familiar with this town only because of seeing its name on an exit sign along Route 52. Islanders, however, know that the road from the expressway exit to Salinas leads to some of Puerto Rico's best seafood restaurants. Most of them are along the seafront in the Playa de Salinas area, reached by heading south on Route 701.

WHERE TO EAT

$–$$$ ✕ **Costa Marina.** At the Marina de Salinas, this seafood restaurant has porthole windows that look out onto the dozens of sailboats anchored nearby. From the steeply sloped ceiling hang strings of semaphore flags and huge model ships. Some of the specialties include *ensalada* *de carrucho* (conch salad) and *arroz mamposteao de jueyes* (rice with crab). Make sure to try fish with the local mojo isleño. ✉ *Calle Chapin G-8* ☎ *787–824–6647* ▭ *AE, MC, V.*

SALINAS HAS THE MOJO

When you stop in Salinas—and you should—be sure to try local seafood with *mojo isleño,* a popular sauce made from tomatoes, onions, and spices, which was created here.

WHERE TO STAY

$ **Marina de Salinas.** Several different types of mangroves shade this hotel at the Marina de Salinas. Many guests arrive by private yacht, but there's no reason you can't show up in a car. The spacious rooms are cheerfully decorated with tropical colors. Your dining options include Costa Marina, a restaurant that's also in the marina, or a string of seafood restaurants along the road. It's a bit difficult to find; follow the signs leading to the PLAYA DE SALINAS. **Pros:** Off-the-beaten-path vibe, lovely mangrove trees, friendly staff. **Cons:** Far from other dining options, basic rooms. ✉ *Calle Chapin G-8* ☎ *787/824–3185 or 787/752–8484* ⊕ *www.marinadesalinas.com* *32 rooms* *In-hotel: restaurant, bar, pool, no elevator* ▭ *AE, MC, V* *EP.*

GUAYAMA

29 km (18 mi) east of Salinas, 28 km (17 mi) southeast of Cayey; 49 km (31 mi) southeast of Barranquitas.

Guayama was founded in 1736, but the city was destroyed by fire in the early 1800s. It quickly recovered when the sugarcane industry grew by leaps and bounds, and the wealth that the surrounding plantations brought to town is evident in the number of striking neoclassical homes on the streets surrounding the main square. Some have been beautifully restored, whereas others are crumbling. One of the finest 19th-century homes, Casa Cautiño, is now a museum.

The nearby countryside is home to Paso Fino horses. Each March at the Marcelino Blondet Stadium you can watch these high-stepping show horses strut their stuff during the Feria Dulce Sueño, a fair named after one of the island's most famous Thoroughbreds. Folk music and crafts are part of the festivities.

★ Built for sugar, cattle, and coffee baron Genaro Cautiño Vázquez and his wife Genoveva Insúa, **Casa Cautiño** is an elegant neoclassical home dating from 1887. The painstakingly restored exterior features a balcony with ornate grillwork. You'll be swept back in time walking through the home's rooms, which are filled with the original Victorian-era furnishings. Don't miss the modern-for-its-time bathroom, complete with a standing shower. The museum is on the main square. ✉ *1 Calle Palmer, at Calle Vicente Palé Matos* ☎ *787/864–9083* *Free* *Tues.–Sat. 9–4:30, Sun. 10–4.*

NEED A BREAK?

The fruit-flavored ice cream at Rex Cream (✉ *24 Calle Derkes* ☎ *No phone*) is hard to pass up. Flavors vary, depending on what produce is in season, but

often include lime, pineapple, tamarind, and *guanábana* (soursop). You can also get milk shakes—the mango shake is outstanding.

Just a few blocks from the main square, the **Centro de Bellas Artes** is housed in a beautifully restored neoclassical building. Paintings by local artists fill its 11 rooms. ✉ *Calle McArthur* ☎ *787/864–7765* *Free* *Tues.–Fri. 9–4:30, Sat. 10–4:30.*

One of the prettiest churches on the southern coast, **Iglesia San Antonio de Padua** was begun in 1827 but not completed until 40 years later. Don't set your watch by the time on the clock; the hand-painted face forever reads 11:30, the time the church was "baptized." The bells in the tower were cast in gold and bronze in 1835. ✉ *5 Calle Ashford* ☎ *787/864–7765.*

4

Not far from Guayama, **El Tren del Sur** *(The Train of the South)* takes passengers for one-hour trips along an old rail line beginning in Arroyo. The train carried cane from the fields to the mills from 1915 to 1958; today it's one of the island's few working trains. Call in advance; service frequently is disrupted for repairs. ✉ *Rte. 3, Km 130.9* ☎ *787/271–1574* *$3* *Trains run hourly on weekends and holidays 9:30–4:30.*

WHERE TO EAT

¢ **El Suarito.** You're surrounded by history at this restaurant in a building that dates from 1862. The site has seen life as a repair shop for horse-drawn buggies, a gas station, and—since the mid-1950s—a restaurant. The place is always hopping with townspeople who stop by at all hours for a meal or a drink. You can get eggs and toast for breakfast, sandwiches throughout the day, and roasted chicken or liver and onions for dinner. ✉ *6 Calle Derkes, at Calle Hostos* ☎ *787/864–1820* *MC, V* *Closed Sun.*

WHERE TO STAY

$ **Molino Inn.** This tidy hotel is on the outskirts of Guayama, near the ruins of a Spanish *molino* (sugar mill). Nine acres of lush, attractive grounds—including flower beds and a large pool—surround its two buildings. In stark contrast, the rooms are plain and provide only the basics. Join the local business crowd for the international and Caribbean cuisines at the restaurant. **Pros:** Convenient location, staff bends over backward to be helpful. **Cons:** Unattractive building, bland rooms. ✉ *Av. Albizu Campos at Rte. 54, Box 2393, Guayama* ☎ *787/866–1515* *molinoinn.net* *20 rooms* *In-hotel: restaurant, bar, tennis court, pool, laundry service* *AE, MC, V* *EP.*

SPORTS & THE OUTDOORS

GOLF Running through an old sugar plantation, the **Aguirre Golf Club** (✉ *Rte. 705, Km 3, Aguirre* ☎ *787/853–4052*) was built in 1925 for the executives of a local sugar mill. Open daily, the 9-hole course is short but tough. The **El Legado Golf Resort** (✉ *Rte. 153 at intersection 713* ☎ *787/866–8894* *www.ellegadogolfresort.com*), designed by golf legend and native son Chi Chi Rodríguez, is one of the island's best new courses. The 7,213-yard, 18-hole course has 12 lakes.

PATILLAS

6 km (4 mi) northeast of Arroyo.

Patillas, the so-called "Emerald of the South," is a tranquil city of about 22,000, with a small plaza and steep, narrow streets. The best sightseeing is along the coast east of town, where Route 3 skirts the Caribbean. This stretch passes rugged cliffs and beautiful beaches, many of which have not yet been discovered by visitors.

WHERE TO EAT

$$ ✕ **El Mar de la Tranquilidad.** Get a table on the terrace at the edge of the Caribbean. You'll find good Puerto Rican cuisine and lots of seafood, including lobster, red snapper, and mofongo. Be sure to sample one of the restaurant's daiquiris—there's a huge list from which to choose. ✉ *Rte. 3, Km 118.9* ☎ *787/839–6469* ▭ *AE, MC, V* ⊙ *No dinner Mon.–Wed.*

WHERE TO STAY

$ **Caribbean Paradise.** It's not right on the beach, but this family-run hotel is only a block away. Many of the second-floor rooms have views of the water, and all of them look out onto the little pool. There are many activities for kids, including a playground and a game room. **Pros:** Perfect for families, good value. **Cons:** Bland building, brusque staff. ✉ *Rte. 3, Km 114.3* *Box 1092, Patillas 00723* ☎ *787/839–5885* ⊕ *www.caribbeanparadisepr.com* *23 rooms* *In-hotel: restaurant, pool, no elevator* ▭ *AE, MC, V* *EP.*

$ ★ **Caribe Playa Beach Resort.** A good base from which to explore the southeastern coast, this small hotel sits on a crescent-shaped beach that's a little rocky but still good for a refreshing dip. Unwind by the pool, in a hammock tied between coconut trees, or in the informal library. You can arrange for boat rides, fishing trips, and scuba-diving excursions. Beachfront rooms are spacious and have small kitchenettes. The Seaview Terrace is open for breakfast, lunch, and dinner; reservations are required for dinner. **Pros:** Lovely setting, friendly staff. **Cons:** Some rooms are dark, some traffic noise. ✉ *Rte. 3, Km 112.1* *HC 764, Box 8490, Patillas 00723* ☎ *787/839–7719 or 787/839–6339* ⊕ *www.caribeplaya.com* *32 rooms* *In-room: kitchen, refrigerator. In-hotel: restaurant, pool, beachfront, diving, no elevator, some pets allowed* ▭ *AE, MC, V* *EP.*

OFF THE BEATEN PATH

Faro De Maunabo. Route 3 going eastward intersects with Route 901, the eastern portion of the cross-island Ruta Panorámica. Along the way you'll pass animals grazing in fields and cliffs that drop straight down to the ocean. If you turn off on Route 760 and take it to the end, you'll be rewarded by a dramatic view of the Faro de Maunabo (Maunabo Lighthouse, not open to the public) at Punta Tuna.

THE SOUTHWESTERN COAST

With sandy coves and palm-lined beaches tucked in the coastline's curves, southwestern Puerto Rico fulfills everyone's fantasy of a tropical paradise. The area is popular with local vacationers on weekends and holidays, but many beaches are nearly deserted on weekdays. Villages along the coast are picturesque places where oysters and fresh fish are sold at roadside stands.

WORD OF MOUTH

"While [in Guánica] we did some hiking in the Guánica tropical dry forest, and a little kayaking in the bay. We also had an unexpectedly fantastic lobster dinner at a little hole-in-the-wall restaurant just down the street from Mary Lee's called San Jacinto Seafood Restaurant." –trekker

GUÁNICA

38 km (24 mi) west of Ponce.

Juan Ponce de León first explored this area in 1508, when he was searching for the elusive Fountain of Youth. Nearly 400 years later, U.S. troops landed first at Guánica during the Spanish-American War in 1898. The event is commemorated with an engraved marker on the city's *malecón,* or jetty. Sugarcane dominated the landscape through much of the 1900s, and the ruins of the old Guánica Central sugar mill, closed in 1980, loom over the town's western area, known as Ensenada. Today most of the action takes place at the beaches and in the forests outside of Guánica.

Fodor'sChoice ★ The 9,900-acre **Bosque Estatal de Guánica** *(Guánica State Forest)*, a United Nations Biosphere Reserve, is a great place for hiking expeditions. It's an outstanding example of a tropical dry coastal forest, with some 700 species of plants ranging from the prickly pear cactus to the gumbo limbo tree. It's also one of the best places on the island for bird-watching, since you can spot more than 100 species, including the pearly eyed thrasher, the lizard cockoo, and the nightjar.

One of the most popular hikes is the **Ballena Trail,** which begins at the ranger station on Route 334. This easy 2-km (1¼-mi) walk follows a partially paved road and takes you past a mahogany plantation to a dry plain covered with stunted cactus. A sign reading GUAYACÁN CENTENARIO leads you to an extraordinary guayacán tree with a trunk that measures 6 feet across. The moderately difficult **Fuerte Trail** takes you on a 5 ½-km (3½-mi) hike to an old fort built by the Spanish Armada. It was destroyed during the Spanish-American War in 1898, but you can still see the ruins of the old observatory tower.

In addition to the main entrance on Route 334, you can enter on Route 333, which skirts the forest's southwestern quadrant. You can also try the less-explored western section, off Route 325. ✉ *Enter along Rte. 334, 333, or 325* ☎ *787/821–5706* *Free* *Daily 9–5.*

Off the southwest coast, near Guánica, is **Gilligan's Island,** a palm-ringed cay skirted by gorgeous beaches. You'll find picnic tables and restrooms but few other signs of civilization on this tiny island, officially part of the Bosque Estatal de Guánica. Wooden boats line up at the small dock in the San Jacinto section of Guánica, off Route 333 just past the Copamarina Beach Resort. Boats depart every hour from 10 to 5 (except Monday, when rangers close the island to visitors). Round-trip passage is $6. The island is often crowded on weekends and around holidays, but during the week you can find a spot to yourself. Nearby **Isla de Ballena,** reached by the same ferry, is much less crowded. ✉ *Rte. 333 or 334* ☎ *787/821–5706* *Free* *Daily 9–5.*

BEACHES

Balneario Caña Gorda. The gentle water at this beach on Route 333 washes onto a wide swath of sand fringed with palm trees. There are picnic tables, restrooms, showers, and changing facilities. ✉ *Rte. 333, west of Copamarina Beach Resort.*

Playa Jaboncillo. Rugged cliffs make a dramatic backdrop for this little cove off Route 333, but the water can be rough. The road down to the beach is extremely rocky, so think twice if you don't have a four-wheel-drive vehicle. ✉ *Rte. 333, west of Copamarina Beach Resort.*

Playa Santa. You can rent canoes, kayaks, and pedal boats at this beach at the end of Route 325 in the Ensenada district. ✉ *Rte. 325, west of Guánica.*

WHERE TO EAT

$$–$$$ ★ **Alexandra.** Puerto Ricans drive for miles to reach this restaurant in the Copamarina Beach Resort. You won't find such creative cuisine anywhere else west of Ponce. The kitchen makes traditional dishes into something special; take the free-range chicken with cumin-and-thyme butter, for example, or the grilled pork chops with pineapple chutney. A standout is the risotto, which surrounds tender mussels with rice flavored with saffron, basil, and tomatoes. The elegant dining room looks out onto well-tended gardens; if you want to get closer to the flora, ask for a table outside on the terrace. The only disappointment may be noisy children, who tend to run in and out. ✉ *Rte. 333, Km 6.5* ☎ *787/821–0505 Ext. 766* *Reservations essential* *AE, MC, V.*

$–$$ **San Jacinto.** Popular with day-trippers to Gilligan's Island, this modest restaurant sits right at the ferry terminal. This doesn't mean, however, that the dining room has views of the Caribbean. For those, grab one of the concrete picnic tables outside. The menu is almost entirely seafood, running the gamut from fried snapper to broiled lobster. When it's not high season the menu can be limited to two or three items. ✉ *Off Rte. 333* ☎ *787/821–4941* *MC, V.*

WHERE TO STAY

$$–$$$ Fodor's Choice ★ **Copamarina Beach Resort.** Without a doubt the most beautiful resort on the southern coast, the Copamarina is set on 16 palm-shaded acres facing the Caribbean Sea. The fruit trees and other plants are meticulously groomed, especially around the pair of swimming pools (one popular with kids, the other mostly left to the adults). All the guest rooms are generously proportioned, especially in the older building. Wood shutters on the windows and other touches lend a tropical feel. A

small Asian-influenced spa blends seamlessly with the rest of the hotel. Both the elegant Alexandra and the more casual alfresco Las Palmas Café serve good food. All-inclusive packages, which include all meals and activities, are available. **Pros:** Tropical decor, plenty of activities, great dining options. **Cons:** Sand at the beach has a gummy feel, noise from the many kids. ✉*Rte. 333, Km 6.5, Box 805, Guánica* ☎*787/821–0505 or 800/468–4553* 🌐*www.copamarina.com* *104 rooms, 2 villas* *In-room: safe, refrigerator, Wi-Fi. In-hotel: 2 restaurants, room service, bars, tennis courts, pools, gym, spa, beachfront, diving, water sports, laundry facilities* *AE, MC, V* *EP.*

> **WORD OF MOUTH**
>
> "Copamarina is an attractive, pleasant hotel for a low-key getaway. It's a good base for exploring that part of the island (the dry forest, Gilligan's Island, other beaches nearby) and for some water sports." –PRnative.

4

$–$$ Fodor'sChoice ★ **Mary Lee's by the Sea.** This meandering cluster of apartments sits upon quiet grounds full of brightly colored flowers. It's home to Mary Lee Alvarez, and she'll make you feel like it's your home as well. Most units have ocean views; in the others you'll catch a glimpse of the mangroves by the shore as well as the cactus growing in the nearby Bosque Estatal de Guánica. Each of the one-, two-, and three-bedroom units is decorated in bright colors. Every unit is different, but most have terraces hung with hammocks and outfitted with barbecue grills. You can rent kayaks to drift along the coast or hop a boat bound for Gilligan's Island. **Pros:** Feels like a home away from home, warm and friendly owner, near pristine beaches and forests. **Cons:** Weekly maid service unless requested daily, no nightlife options. ✉*Rte. 333, Km 6.7* *Box 394, Guánica 00653* ☎*787/821–3600* 🌐*www.maryleesbythesea.com* *10 apartments* *In-room: no phone, kitchen (some), no TV. In-hotel: laundry facilities, laundry service, some pets allowed* *MC, V* *EP.*

$ **Parador Guanica 1929.** This colonial-style building dates back to 1929, when it housed executives from the nearby sugar plantation. It's extremely pretty, with lovely arches adding more character than you usually find along the southern coast. There's a lovely view of the ocean, but no beach. The staff members are hospitality students, and they try their darnedest to make a good impression. Despite the name, the hotel is actually in Ensenada, just west of Guaníca. **Pros:** Historic setting, hard-working staff, pretty pool area. **Cons:** No beach, slightly off the beaten path. ✉*Rte. 3116, Km. 2.5, Ensenada* ☎*787/821–0099* 🌐*www.guanica1929.com* *29 rooms* *In-hotel: restaurant, bar, pool* *AE, MC, V* *EP.*

SPORTS & THE OUTDOORS

DIVING & SNORKELING Dramatic walls created by the continental shelf provide great diving off the Guánica coast. Shallow gardens around Gilligan's Island and Cayo de Caña Gorda (off Balneario Caña Gorda) also attract snorkelers and divers. **Dive Copamarina** (✉*Copamarina Beach Resort, Rte. 333, Km 6.5* ☎*787/821–0505*) offers instruction and trips.

SPORTS & THE OUTDOORS

HORSEBACK RIDING In nearby Yauco, **Gaby's World** (✉*Rte. 127, Km 5.1, Yauco* ☎*787/856–2609*) is a 204-acre horse ranch that conducts ½-hour, 1-hour, and 2-hour rides through the hills surrounding Yauco. There are also pony rides for children. The on-site steak house serves Yauco's specialty, *chuletas can-can.*

LA PARGUERA

13 km (8 mi) west of Guánica; 24 km (15 mi) southwest of Yauco.

La Parguera is best known for its bioluminescent bay. Although it is not nearly as spectacular as the one of the island of Vieques, it's still a beautiful sight on a moonless night. Glass-bottom boats lined up at the town dock depart several times each evening for 45-minute trips across the bay. During the day, you can explore the nearby mangrove forest.

The town bursts at the seams with vacationers from other parts of the island on long holiday weekends and all during the summer. The town's dock area feels a bit like Coney Island, and not in a good way. Vendors in makeshift stalls hawk cheap souvenirs, and ear-splitting salsa music pours out of the open-air bars. There are signs warning people not to drink alcoholic beverages in the street, but these are cheerfully ignored.

If you're driving through the area between February and April, keep your eyes open for roadside vendors selling the area's famous pineapples, called *piñas cadezonas.* In late June there's the colorful Fiesta de San Pedro, honoring the patron saint of fishermen.

On moonless nights, large and small boats line up along the dock to take visitors out to view the **Bahía de Fosforescente** *(Phosphorescent Bay).* Microscopic dinoflagellates glow when disturbed by movement, invading the waves with thousands of starlike points of light. The bay's glow has been diminished substantially by pollution—both light pollution from nearby communities and water pollution from toxic chemicals being dumped into the bay. (And, yes, the smoke-belching boats that take tourists to the bay are doing damage, too.) If you've seen the bioluminescent bay in Vieques, give this one a pass. If not, you may find it mildly interesting. ✉*East of La Parguera.*

The eastern section of the **Bosque Estatal de Boquerón** *(Boquerón State Forest)* is made up of miles of mangrove forests that grow at the water's edge. Boats from the dock in La Parguera can take you on cruises through this important breeding ground for seabirds. You can also organize a kayak trip. ✉*East of La Parguera.*

BEACHES

Cayo Caracoles. You can take a boat to and from this island for $5 per person. There are mangroves to explore as well as plenty of places to swim and snorkel. ✉*Boats leave from marina at La Parguera, off Rte. 304.*

Isla Mata de la Gata. For about $5 per person boats will transport you to and from this small island just off the coast for a day of swimming and snorkeling. ✉*Boats leave from marina at La Parguera, off Rte. 304.*

Playita Rosada. The small beach doesn't compare to some of the longer beaches on the southwestern coast, but it's a convenient place for a quick swim. ✉*At the end of Calle 7.*

> **WORD OF MOUTH**
>
> "The boat trip [to Bahía de Fosforescente in La Parguera] was good. I do think it is worthwhile although from what I have heard, this bioluminescent bay does not even compare to the one on the island of Vieques. We knew we weren't going to make that one so we decided to do this one . . . It was interesting nonetheless, but does not have the brilliance that Vieques has." –Juldie

WHERE TO EAT

$$–$$$ ✕**La Casita.** The so-called "Little House" isn't little at all—it's a sizable establishment that sits smack in the middle of the town's main road. Generous portions make this family-run restaurant one of the town's favorites. Try the *asopao,* which is made with shrimp, lobster, or other types of seafood. You can take a table in the rather bland ground-floor dining room or on the second-floor terrace, which has a view of the water. ✉*Rte. 304, Km 3.3* ☎*787/899–1681* ▭*MC, V.*

$$–$$$ ✕**La Pared.** Many restaurants in La Parguera sit beside the bay, but very few have an actual view. This elegant, second-floor dining room at the rear of Posada Porlamar overlooks a lovely stretch of coastline ringed by mangrove trees. The menu is the best in town, going well beyond traditional surf-and-turf offerings. There's the standard rack of lamb, for example, but here you'll find it topped with goat cheese. The lobster tail is as fresh as anywhere else on the strip, but is topped with a tasty *guanabana* (soursop) sauce. ✉*Posada Porlamar, Rte. 304, Km 3.3* ☎*787/899–4015* ▭*MC, V.*

WHERE TO STAY

$ **Posada Porlamar.** You might not realize it at first, but this small hotel is all about the water. Most of the comfortable rooms have views of the mangrove-ringed bay, as do the restaurant, café, and bar. In the rear you'll find a dock where you can rent a boat to explore the coastline, as well as a full-service dive shop where you can arrange snorkeling and diving excursions. And when you're finished exploring, you can relax by the pretty pool. The hotel is on La Parguera's main drag, but far enough from the action that it's quiet at night. **Pros:** Water views everywhere, excellent dining on the premises and nearby. **Cons:** Bland room decor, a lot of steps to negotiate. ✉*Rte. 304, Km 3.3* *Box 3113, Lajas00667* ☎*787/899–4343* *www.parguerapuertorico.com* *38 rooms* *In-hotel: restaurant, bar, pool, no elevator* ▭*MC, V* *EP.*

$ ★ **Villa del Mar.** What sets this family-run inn apart is the warmth of the staff, all of whom promise to take care of anything you need. The hotel, painted refreshing shades of lemon and lime, sits on a hill overlooking the boats in the bay. The last time we checked this place out, the staff was putting the final touches on a new restaurant with a knockout view. Not all of the squeaky clean rooms have views, so make sure to specify when you call for reservations. Downstairs you'll find an open-air lounge area near the reception desk and a shimmering pool in the courtyard. To find this hotel, take the first left as you drive into La Parguera. **Pros:** Unbeatable vistas, peace and quiet. **Cons:** Bland room decor, a good number of steps to climb. ✉ *3 Av. Albizu Campos* ⓓ *Box 1297, San Germán* ☎ *787/899–4265* 🌐 *www.pinacolada.net/villadelmar* *25 rooms* *In-room: no phone. In-hotel: restaurant, bar, pool, no elevator* *AE, MC, V* *EP.*

$ **Villa Parguera.** The rooms in this gingerbread-trimmed hotel are clustered around small courtyards filled with bright tropical flowers. Many have balconies overlooking the bay, so make sure to look at a few rooms before you decide. A spacious dining room overlooking the pool serves excellent Puerto Rican and international dishes. On Saturday night there's live music and a floor show in the dance club. The staff can be a little brusque at times. **Pros:** Family atmosphere, plenty of entertainment options, walking distance to the marina. **Cons:** Bland rooms, pool area gets crowded, noise from nearby bars. ✉ *Rte. 304, Km 3.3* ⓓ *Box 273, Lajas00667* ☎ *787/899–7777* 🌐 *www.villaparguera.net* *70 rooms* *In-hotel: restaurant, bar, pool, no elevator* *AE, D, DC, MC, V* *EP.*

NIGHTLIFE & THE ARTS

La Parguera's dock area heats up after sunset, when crowds come to take excursions to the Bahía de Fosforescente. On weekends **Mar y Tierra** (✉ *Rte. 304, Km 3.3* ☎ *787/899–4627*) is the most popular place in the strip. The open-air establishment has a couple of pool tables that are always in use. Pay attention to the sign that tells you not to put your feet on the wall.

The live floor show at **Villa Parguera** (✉ *Rte. 304, Km 2.3* ☎ *787/899–7777 or 787/899–3975*) includes a buffet. The show changes frequently, but includes live music, dancing, and comedy of the seltzer-in-your-pants variety.

SPORTS & THE OUTDOORS

DIVING & SNORKELING

Endangered leatherback turtles, eels, and an occasional manatee can be seen from many of the sites that attract divers and snorkelers from all parts. There are more than 50 shore-dive sites off La Parguera. **Paradise Scuba** (✉ *Hostal Casa Blanca, Rte. 304, Km 3.5* ☎ *787/899–7611*) has classes and trips, including night-snorkeling excursions in phosphorescent waters.

FISHING

You can spend a day or half-day fishing for blue marlin, tuna, or reef fish with Captain Mickey Amador at **Parguera Fishing Charters** (✉ *Rte. 304, Km 3.8* ☎ *787/382–4698 or 787/899–4698*). Lunch is included in the price.

SHOPPING

Outdoor stands near Bahía Fosforescente sell all kinds of souvenirs, from T-shirts to beaded necklaces. In La Parguera's center, there are several small souvenir shops, including **Nautilus** (✉ *Rte. 304* ☎ *787/899–4565*), that sell posters, mugs, and trinkets made from shells.

SAN GERMÁN

10 km (6 mi) north of La Parguera, 166 km (104 mi) southwest of San Juan.

During its early years, San Germán was a city on the move. Although debate rages about the first settlement's exact founding date and location, the town is believed to have been established in 1510 near Guánica. Plagued by mosquitoes, the settlers moved north along the west coast, where they encountered French pirates and smugglers. In the 1570s they fled inland to the current location, but they were still harassed. Determined and creative, they dug tunnels and moved beneath the city (the tunnels are now part of the water system). Today San Germán has a population of 39,000, and its intellectual and political activity is anything but underground. It's very much a college town, and students and professors from the Inter-American University often fill the bars and cafés.

Around San Germán's two main squares—Plazuela Santo Domingo and Plaza Francisco Mariano Quiñones (named for an abolitionist)—are buildings done in every conceivable style of architecture found on the island including mission, Victorian, Creole, and Spanish colonial. The city's tourist office offers a free, guided trolley tour. Most of the buildings are private homes; two of them—the Capilla de Porta Coeli and the Museo de Arte y Casa de Estudio—are museums. Strip malls surround the historical center, and the town is hemmed to the south and west by busy seaside resorts.

WHAT TO SEE

Numbers in the text correspond to numbers in the margin and on the San Germán map.

6 **Alcaldía Antigua** *(Old Municipal Building).* At the eastern end of Plaza Francisco Mariano Quiñones, this Spanish colonial–style building served as the town's city hall from 1844 to 1950. Once used as a prison, the building is now the headquarters for the police department. ✉ *East end of Plaza Francisco Mariano Quiñones.*

1 ★ **Capilla de Porta Coeli** *(Heaven's Gate Chapel).* One of the oldest religious buildings in the Americas, this mission-style chapel overlooks the long, rectangular Plazuela de Santo Domingo. It's not a grand building, but its position at the top of a stone stairway gives it a noble air. Queen Isabel Segunda decreed that the Dominicans should build a church and monastery in San Germán, so a rudimentary building was built in 1609, replaced in 1692 by the structure that can still be seen today. (Sadly, most of the monastery was demolished in 1866, leaving only a vestige of its facade.) The chapel now functions as a museum of religious art, displaying painted wooden statuary by Latin American and Spanish artists. ✉ *East end of Plazuela Santo Domingo* ☎ *787/892–5845* 🌐 *www.icp.gobierno.pr* *Free* ⏲ *Wed.–Sun. 8:30–noon and 1 to 4:15.*

3 **Casa Acosta y Forés.** A few doors down from Casa de los Kindy is this beautiful yellow-and-white wooden house dating from 1918. Although

the front of the house is typical criollo architecture, the side entrance is covered with an ornate Victorian-style porch. The house isn't open to the public. ✉ *70 Calle Dr. Santiago Veve.*

9 **Casa de Lola Rodríguez de Tió** On the National Registry of Historic Places, this house bears the name of poet and activist Lola Rodríguez de Tió. A plaque claims she lived in this creole-style house, though town officials believe it actually belonged to her sister. Rodríguez, whose mother was a descendent of Ponce de León, was deported several times by Spanish authorities for her revolutionary ideas. She lived in Venezuela and then in Cuba, where she died in 1924. The museum, which houses Rodríguez's desk and papers, isn't open regular hours; call ahead to schedule a tour. ✉ *13 Calle Dr. Santiago Veve* ☎ *787/892–3500* *Free* *By appointment only.*

4 **Casa Kindy.** East of the Plazuela de Santo Domingo, this 19th-century home is known for its eclectic architecture, which mixes neoclassical and criollo elements. Note the elegant stained-glass windows over the front windows. It's now a private residence. ✉ *64 Calle Dr. Santiago Veve.*

2 **Casa Morales.** Facing Plazuela de Santo Domingo, this Victorian-style house was designed in 1913 by architect Pedro Vivoni for his brother,

A GOOD TOUR

The best place to start is Plazuela Santo Domingo, the sun-baked park in the center of the historic district. At the eastern edge of the park is the **Capilla de Porta Coeli**, perched at the top of an imposing set of stairs. From the top you get a good view of the rest of the city. Several historic homes, none of them open to the public, are within a block of the Capilla de Porta Coeli. Across the street is the **Casa Morales**, striking for its Victorian-style gables. It would not look out of place in any New England hamlet. Half a block east on Calle Dr. Santiago Veve are two criollo-style houses, **Casa Kindy** and **Casa Acosta y Forés**. A block south of the Capilla de Porta Coeli is one of the most beautiful homes in San Germán, **Casa Perichi**.

Head west through Plazuela Santo Domingo. The hulking yellow building you see at the northwest corner of the park is the rear of the **Alcaldía Antigua**. It faces the town's other park, the Plaza Francisco Mariano Quiñones. This park is more popular with locals, as the tree-shaded benches are a pleasant place to watch the world go by. On the park's northern edge is **La Casona**, one of the town's best-preserved criollo-style buildings. The most imposing structure on the park, however, is the **Iglesia de San Germán de Auxerre**.

A block and a half west of the church is the **Casa de Lola Rodríguez de Tió**, on Calle Dr. Santiago Veve. It's one of the best examples of criollo-style architecture in the city. Backtrack to Calle Esperanza and head two blocks south to where you'll find the **Museo de Arte y Casa de Estudio**.

TIMING

San Germán's historic district is compact, so you can cover all the sights in about an hour. You'll want to budget a bit more time to stroll around the nearby streets. Be sure to wear comfortable shoes, as there will be a lot of walking uphill and downhill on cobbled streets.

4

Tomás Vivoni. The gleaming white structure has numerous towers and gables. The current owners have kept it in mint condition. It is not open to the public. ✉*38 Calle Ramos.*

5 **Casa Perichi.** You'll find an excellent example of Puerto Rican ornamental architecture in this elegant mansion, which sits a block south of Plazuela Santo Domingo. This gigantic white home, on the National Register of Historic Places, was built in 1920. Note the sensuous curves of the wraparound balcony and wood trim around the doors. It's not open to the public. ✉*94 Calle Luna.*

7 **La Casona.** On the north side of Plaza Francisco Mariano Quiñones, this two-story home was built in 1871 for Tomás Agrait. (If you look closely, you can still see his initials in the wrought-iron decorations.) For many years it served as a center of cultural activities in San Germán. Today it holds several shops. ✉*Calle José Julien Acosta and Calle Cruz.*

8 **Iglesia de San Germán de Auxerre.** Dating from 1739, this neoclassical church has seen many additions over the years. For example, the

CLOSE UP

Lives of the Santos

When they arrived on Puerto Rico, Spanish missionaries spread the word of God and fostered spirited folk art. Since few people were literate, the missionaries often commissioned local artisans to create pictures and statues depicting Bible stories and saints or *santos*. These figures—fashioned of wood, clay, stone, or even gold—are still given a place of honor in homes throughout the island.

Early *santeros* (carvers) were influenced by the Spanish baroque style. Later figures are simple and small, averaging about 8 inches in height. The carving of santos is usually a family tradition, and most of today's santeros have no formal art training. San Germán has been associated with santos-making since the origins of the art form, and the Rivera family has been known for its carvings for more than 150 years.

Each santo has a traditional characteristic. You can spot the Virgin by her blue robes, St. Francis by the accompanying birds and animals, St. Barbara by her tower, and the Holy Spirit by its hovering dove. St. John, the island's patron saint, is an ever-popular subject, as is the Nativity, which might depict only the Holy Family, or the family with an entire cast of herald angels, shepherds, and barnyard animals.

Carvings of Los Santos Reyes (The Three Kings) are also popular. Their feast day, January 6, is important on Puerto Rico. Celebrations often continue for days before or after the actual holiday, when it's difficult to find a home without an image of these regal characters on display. In Puerto Rico one king is often depicted strumming the *cuatro*, an island guitar.

–Karen English

impressive crystal chandelier was added in 1860. Be sure to take a look at the carved-wood ceiling in the nave. This church is still in use, so the only time you can get a look inside is during services. ✉ *West side of Plaza Francisco Mariano Quiñones* ☎ *787/892–1027* ⏲ *Mass Mon.–Sat. at 7* AM *and 7:30* PM *and Sun. at 7, 8:30, 10* AM, *and 7:30* PM.

⑩ **Museo de Arte y Casa de Estudio.** This early-20th-century home—built in the criollo style with some obvious neoclassical influences—has been turned into a museum. Displays include colonial furnishings, religious art, and artifacts of the indigenous peoples; there are also changing exhibits by local artists. ✉ *7 Calle Esperanza* ☎ *787/892–8870* 🎫 *Free* ⏲ *Wed.–Sun. 10–noon and 1–3.*

WHERE TO EAT

$–$$ ✕ **Chaparritas.** On San Germán's main drag, this place certainly feels like a traditional cantina. The Mexican food here is the real deal. Although you'll find some dishes that are more Tex than Mex, such as the cheesy nachos, the kitchen does best with more authentic tacos, burritos, and enchiladas. For something a bit more off the wall, try the shrimp fried in tequila. ✉ *Calle Luna 171* ☎ *787/892–1078* ⏲ *Closed Sun.–Wed.*

¢–$ ★ ✕ **Tapas Café.** One of the biggest surprises in San Germán is this wonderful little restaurant facing Plaza Santo Domingo. The dining room looks like a Spanish courtyard, complete with blue stars swirling around the ceiling. Don't expect tiny portions just because the eatery serves tapas—several of the dishes, including the medallions of beef topped with a dab of blue cheese, could pass as full entrées anywhere. You'll find old favorites on the menu, including spicy sausage in red wine, but some new creations as well, such as the yam-and-codfish fritters. ✉*50 Calle Dr. Santiago Veve* ☎*787/264–0610* ▭*MC, V* ⊙*Closed Mon. and Tues. No lunch Wed. and Thurs.*

WHERE TO STAY

$ **Villa del Rey.** On a quiet country road, Villa del Rey is set among banana and papaya trees. This family-run inn couldn't be simpler, but it's clean and comfortable. The rooms are larger than you'll find in most of the region's lodgings. The patio around the pool is a bit run-down, but the pool itself is refreshing on a hot afternoon. A restaurant and bar are planned for the future. ✉*Rte. 361, Km 0.8, off Rte. 2* *Box 3033, San Germán 00667* ☎*787/264–2542 or 787/642–2627* ⊕*www.villadelrey.net* *19 rooms* *In-room: kitchen (some). In-hotel: pool, no elevator* ▭*MC, V* *EP.*

4

PONCE & THE SOUTHERN COAST ESSENTIALS

To research prices, get advice from other travelers, and book travel arrangements, visit www.fodors.com.

TRANSPORTATION

BY AIR

Aeropuerto Mercedita (PSE) is about 8 km (5 mi) east of Ponce's downtown. The airport is so tiny that between flights there may be nobody in the terminal besides you and a bored-looking security guard. Needless to say, there are almost no amenities. The only international flights are on Continental, which shuttles between Ponce and Newark, and JetBlue, which flies between Ponce and Fort Lauderdale and New York–JFK. Cape Air flies several times a day from San Juan.

Taxis at the airport operate under a meter system, so expect to pay about $6 to get to downtown Ponce. Some hotels have shuttles from the airport, but you must make arrangements in advance.

Airlines **Cape Air** (☎*800/525–0280* ⊕*www.flycapeair.com*). **Continental** (☎*800/231–0856* ⊕*www.continental.com*). **JetBlue** (☎*800/538–2583* ⊕*www.jetblue.com*).

Airport **Aeropuerto Mercedita** (*PSE* ✉*Rte. 506 off Rte. 52, Ponce* ☎*787/842–6292*).

BY BUS

There's no easy network of buses linking the towns in southern Puerto Rico with the capital of San Juan or with each other. Some municipalities and private companies operate buses or *públicos* (usually large vans) that make many stops. Call ahead; although reservations aren't usually required, you'll need to check on schedules, which change frequently. The cost of a público from Ponce to San Juan is about $15 to $20; agree on a price before starting your journey.

Information **Choferes Unidos de Ponce** (*Terminal de Carros Públicos, Calle Vives and Calle Mendéz Vigo, Ponce Centro, Ponce 787/842-1222*). **Línea Sangermeña** (*Terminal de Carros Públicos, Calle Luna at entrance to town, San Germán 787/722-3392*).

BY CAR

A car is pretty much a necessity if you are exploring Puerto Rico's southern coast. Without one you'd find getting anywhere—even to the beach or to a restaurant—frustrating. You can rent cars at the Luis Muñoz Marín International Airport and other San Juan locations. There are also car-rental agencies in some of the larger cities along the south coast. Rates run about $35 to $45 a day, depending on the car. You may get a better deal if you rent a car for a week or more. Test your vehicle before heading out to be sure it runs properly.

A road map is essential in southern Puerto Rico. So is patience: allow extra time for twisting mountain roads and wrong turns. Some roads, especially in rural areas, aren't plainly marked. The fastest route through the region is the Luis A. Ferré Expressway (Route 52), a toll road that runs from San Juan to Ponce, crossing the island's central mountain range. The trip takes about 1½ hours.

Information **Avis** (*Mercedita Airport, Ponce 787/842-6154*). **Budget** (*Mercedita Airport, Ponce 787/848-0907*). **Dollar** (*Av. Los Caobos and Calle Acacia, Ponce 787/843-6940*). **Leaseway of Puerto Rico** (*Rte. 3, Km 140.1, Guayama 787/864-8149 www.leasewaypr.com Ponce 787/843-4330*).

EMERGENCY SERVICES There's no AAA service in Puerto Rico, but independent tow trucks regularly scout the Luis A. Ferré Expressway (Route 52) looking for disabled vehicles. Police also patrol the expressway. A number of towing companies will send trucks on request.

Information **Alfredo Towing Service** (*787/251-6750*). **Dennis Towing** (*787/504-5724*).

GASOLINE Gas stations are plentiful, particularly near expressway exits and at town entrances on secondary roads. Some stations are open 24 hours, but many close at around midnight or 1 AM. Prices in Puerto Rico are given in liters.

PARKING You can find free on-street parking in most southern cities; metered parking is rare. Larger communities have lots in their downtown areas. Prices are usually less than $1 an hour.

ROAD CONDITIONS Major highways in southern Puerto Rico are well maintained. You may encounter some construction on Highway 2 between Ponce and Guánica. Watch out for potholes on secondary roads, especially after heavy rains.

BY PUBLIC TRANSPORTATION

Ponce offers free transportation to its major attractions on its *"chu chu"* train. (It's actually a tram.) They run daily from 8:30 AM to about 7:30 PM, and leave from Plaza las Delicias. On Sunday, Guayama has a free trolley that runs to many sights. A trolley tour of San Germán is available by appointment.

Information **Guayama Trolley** (✉ *Acaldía de Guayama, Calle Vicente Pales, Guayama* ☎ *787/864–7765*). **Ponce Trolley & Chu Chu** (✉ *Plaza las Delicias, Ponce Centro, Ponce* ☎ *787/841–8160*). **San Germán Trolley** (✉ *Acaldía de San Germán, 136 Calle Luna, San Germán* ☎ *787/892–3500*).

BY TAXI

In Ponce you can hail taxis in tourist areas and outside hotels. In smaller towns it's best to call a taxi. You can also hire a car service (make arrangements through your hotel); often you can negotiate a rate that's lower than what you would pay for a taxi.

Information **Borinquen Taxi** (☎ *787/843-6000 in Ponce*). **Ojeda Taxi** (☎ *787/259–7676 in San Germán*).

4

CONTACTS & RESOURCES

BANKS & EXCHANGE SERVICES

You'll find plenty of banks in the region, and many supermarkets, drug stores, and gas stations have ATMs. Banks are normally open weekdays from 9 AM to 3 PM or 4 PM. Some banks—such as the Scotiabank branch in Ponce—are also open until noon on Saturday. You can exchange foreign currency in Banco Popular branches; Scotiabank exchanges Canadian currency. Western Union service is available at Pueblo Supermarkets.

Information **Banco Popular** (✉ *Plaza Guayama, Rte. 3, Km 134.9, Guayama* ☎ *787/866–0180* ✉ *Plaza las Delicias, Ponce Centro, Ponce* ☎ *787/843–8000*). **Scotiabank** (✉ *Plaza las Delicias, Ponce Centro, Ponce* ☎ *787/259–8535*).

EMERGENCIES

Emergency Number **General Emergencies** (☎ *911*).

Hospitals **Hospital de la Concepción** (✉ *41 Calle Luna, San Germán* ☎ *787/892–1860*). **Hospital de Damas** (✉ *2213 Ponce Bypass Rd., Villa Grillasca, Ponce* ☎ *787/840–8686*).

Pharmacies **Walgreens** (✉ *1 Calle Marginal, Guayama* ☎ *787/864–5355* ✉ *13 Av. Fagot, Ponce Centro, Ponce* ☎ *787/841–2135* ✉ *64 Calle Luna, San Germán* ☎ *787/892–1170*).

INTERNET, MAIL & SHIPPING

Internet cafés are few and far between on this part of the island. If you'll need to be wired on your trip, make sure your hotel has an Internet connection.

There are branches of the U.S. Post Office throughout the region. You can buy stamps in Pueblo Supermarkets and in many gift shops.

Post Offices **Guayama Post Office** (✉ *151 Calle Ashford, Guayama* ☎ *787/864–1150*). **Ponce Post Office** (✉ *94 Calle Atocha, Ponce Centro, Ponce* ☎ *787/842–2997*).

OVERNIGHT SERVICES Express delivery services are available at the U.S. Post Office. Some shops are authorized to handle Federal Express (FedEx) packages, and there are FedEx stations in Ponce and Guayama. Note that there's no Saturday pick-up service in the area. You can drop off packages and U.S. mail at area PostNet stores, which also sell envelopes and boxes.

Information **FedEx** (✉ *Plaza Guayama, Rte. 3, Km 134.9, Guayama* ☎ *877/838–7834* ✉ *Mercedita Airport, Ponce* ☎ *877/838–7834*).

TOUR OPTIONS

Alelí Tours and Encantos Ecotours Southwest in La Parguera offer ecological tours of the southwestern area, including two- or three-hour kayak trips that cost about $25.

Information **Alelí Tours** (✉ *Rte. 304, Km 3.2, La Parguera* ☎ *787/863–5153*). **Encantos Ecotours Southwest** (✉ *El Muelle Shopping Center, Av. Pescadores, La Parguera* ☎ *787/808–0005*).

VISITOR INFORMATION

In Ponce the municipal tourist office is open weekdays from 8 to 4:30, as is the small information desk in the Parque de Bombas. The Puerto Rico Tourism Company's office in the Paseo del Sur plaza is open weekdays from 8 to 5. Smaller cities generally have a tourism office in the city hall that's open weekdays from 8 to noon and 1 to 4.

Information **Ponce Municipal Tourist Office** (✉ *2nd fl. of Citibank, Plaza las Delicias, Ponce Centro, Ponce* ☎ *787/841–8160 or 787/841–8044*). **Puerto Rico Tourism Company** (✉ *291 Av. Los Caobos, Sector Vallas Torres, Ponce* ☎ *787/843–0465* 🌐 *welcome.topuertorico.org*).

Rincón & the Porta del Sol

WORD OF MOUTH

"Rincón has several nice calm beaches with good snorkeling and others with big waves for the surfing crowd."

–bexrob

"The village of Boquerón has a few restaurants and bars and can get quite lively, especially on summer weekends."

–Prnative

www.fodors.com/forums

Revised and Updated by Mark Sullivan

THE "GATEWAY TO THE SUN" is how tourism officials describe the island's western coast. Although the name calls to mind well-developed, well-traveled vacations spots like Spain's Costa de Sol, the Porta del Sol is neither. Unlike the area around San Juan, the Porta del Sol is relatively undiscovered. Even around Rincón, which has the lion's share of the lodgings, the beaches are delightfully deserted. And in places like Aguadilla and Isabela, two sleepy towns on the northwestern corner of the island, it's easy to find a stretch of shoreline all to yourself.

Adventurers since the time of Christopher Columbus have been drawn to the jagged coastline of northwestern Puerto Rico. Columbus made his first stop here on his second voyage to the Americas in 1493. His exact landing point is the subject of ongoing dispute: both Aguadilla on the northernmost tip of the coast and Aguada, just south of Aguadilla, claim the historic landing, and both have monuments honoring the explorer.

Less than a century ago, western Puerto Rico was still overwhelmingly rural. Some large fruit plantations dotted the coast, while farther inland coffee was grown on hillside *fincas* (farms). The slow pace of rural life began to change during the mid-20th century. New roads brought development to the once-isolated towns. They also brought surfers, who were amazed to find some of the best waves in the Caribbean and long beaches of golden sand. Now there are top-notch hotels, interesting natural areas to explore, and almost every kind of water sport imaginable.

EXPLORING RINCÓN & THE PORTA DEL SOL

The speedy Highway 22 and the more meandering Highway 2 head west from San Juan and swing around the northwestern part of the island, skirting the beaches of the northern coast. A short 45 minutes from the capital, you'll pass through the resort town of Dorado; after Arecibo, Highway 2 continues along the coast, where the ragged shoreline holds some of the island's best surfing beaches, and a steady contingent of surfers in Aguadilla and Rincón gives the area a laid-back atmosphere. Past Mayagüez, Highway 100 leads to an area known as Cabo Rojo, where you'll find seaside communities like Joyuda, Boquerón, and El Combate.

ABOUT THE RESTAURANTS

Throughout northwestern Puerto Rico you'll find wonderful *criollo* (creole) cuisine, interspersed with international restaurants ranging from French to Japanese. You can enjoy five-course meals in elegant surroundings at night, then sip coffee on an outdoor balcony the next morning. Tips, normally 15% to 20%, are usually not included in the bill, but it's always wise to double-check.

WHAT IT COSTS IN U.S. DOLLARS

	$$$$	$$$	$$	$	¢
AT DINNER	over $30	$20–$30	$12–$20	$8–$12	under $8

Prices are per person for a main course at dinner.

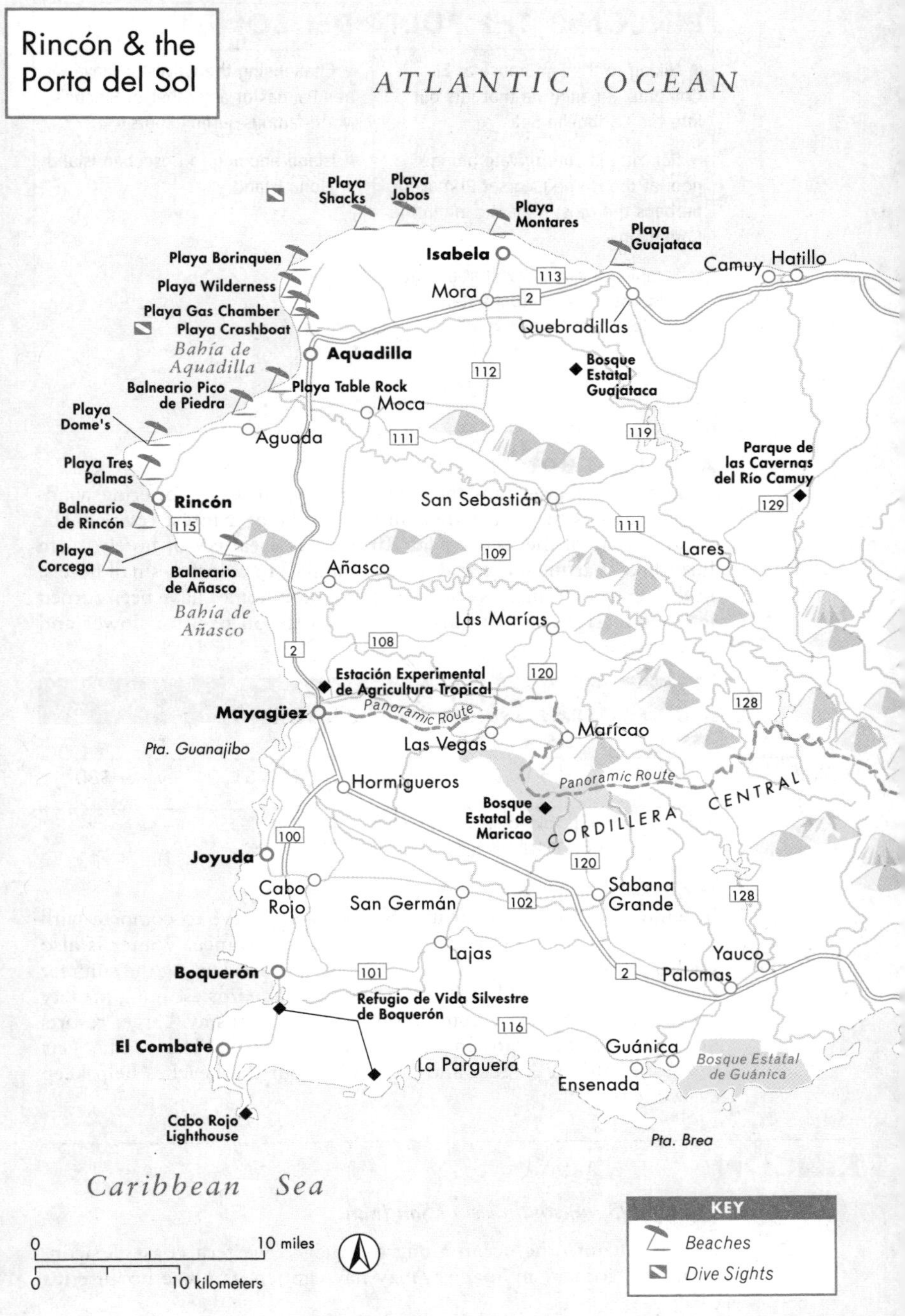

Rincón & the Porta del Sol
ATLANTIC OCEAN
Playa Shacks
Playa Jobos
Playa Montares
Playa Guajataca
Isabela
Camuy
Hatillo
Playa Borinquen
Playa Wilderness
Playa Gas Chamber
Playa Crashboat
Mora
113
2
Quebradillas
Bahía de Aquadilla
Aquadilla
112
Bosque Estatal Guajataca
Balneario Pico de Piedra
Playa Table Rock
Moca
Playa Dome's
Aguada
111
119
Parque de las Cavernas del Río Camuy
Playa Tres Palmas
Rincón
San Sebastián
129
Balneario de Rincón
115
111
Playa Corcega
Balneario de Añasco
Añasco
109
Lares
Bahía de Añasco
Las Marías
108
2
120
Estación Experimental de Agricultura Tropical
128
Mayagüez
Panoramic Route
Las Vegas
Marícao
Pta. Guanajibo
Hormigueros
Panoramic Route
CENTRAL
Bosque Estatal de Maricao
CORDILLERA
100
Joyuda
120
Cabo Rojo
San Germán
102
Sabana Grande
128
Lajas
Yauco
Boquerón
101
2
Palomas
Refugio de Vida Silvestre de Boquerón
116
El Combate
Guánica
La Parguera
Ensenada
Bosque Estatal de Guánica
Cabo Rojo Lighthouse
Pta. Brea
Caribbean Sea
0
10 miles
0
10 kilometers
KEY
Beaches
Dive Sights

RINCÓN & THE PORTA DEL SOL TOP 5

- Hiking to the lighthouse at El Combate, a peninsula that juts out into the Caribbean Sea.
- Relaxing in your private plunge pool at the Horned Dorset Primavera, perhaps the most romantic inn in the Caribbean.
- Sampling fresh seafood at any of the dozens of oceanfront eateries along Joyuda's "Golden Mile."
- Challenging the waves at Playa Tres Palmas or any other of Rincón's world-famous surfing spots.
- Island-hopping to Desecheo Island or Mona Island.

ABOUT THE HOTELS

Lodging in the area runs the gamut from posh resorts offering windsurfing lessons to rustic cabins in the middle of a forest reserve. The western part of the island near Rincón has a variety of hotels, from furnished apartments geared toward families to colorful, small hotels. In the central mountains a few old plantation homes have been turned into wonderful country inns that transport you back to slower and quieter times.

WHAT IT COSTS IN U.S. DOLLARS

	$$$$	$$$	$$	$	¢
FOR 2 PEOPLE	over $350	$250–$350	$150–$250	$80–$150	under $80

Prices are for a double room in high season, excluding 9% tax (11% for hotels with casinos, 7% for paradores) and 5%–12% service charge.

TIMING

In winter the weather is at its best, but you'll have to compete with other visitors for hotel rooms; book well in advance. Winter is also the height of the surfing season on the west coast. During the summer many family-oriented hotels fill up with *sanjuaneros* escaping the city for the weekend—some hotels require a two-night stay. Larger resorts normally drop their rates in summer by at least 10%. The weather gets hot, especially in August and September, but the beaches help keep everyone cool.

RINCÓN

150 km (93 mi) southwest of San Juan.

Jutting out into the ocean along the rugged western coast, Rincón, meaning "corner" in Spanish, may have gotten its name because it's

IF YOU LIKE

EATING WELL

If you like seafood, you're in the right place. Simply stop at one of the seafood shacks in Joyuda—a place so well-known for its fresh fish that people come here from as far away as Ponce and San Juan. You'll do no better anywhere else on the island. In Boquerón people line up at push-carts where vendors sell oysters on the half shell. (Hot sauce is optional.) If you're in Rincón, the Horned Dorset Primavera has one of the most elegant eateries in the Caribbean.

ECOTOURISM

Ecotourism is catching on in Puerto Rico. Not surprisingly, many outfits are based in Rincón and center around trips to Mona Island. This protected island has world-class diving as well as a series of trails that wind their way along the edge of steep cliffs.

SURFING

The waves of northwestern Puerto Rico have long served as a siren song for traveling surfers. Spared the trade winds that can limit surf in other areas, the northwest's beaches have some of the best waves in the world, especially in winter. Rincón first drew international attention when it hosted the World Surfing Championship in 1968. Other areas on the north coast, such as Aguadilla, have impressive waves as well. The area around Isabela has some well-known breaks but this stretch of coast also can reveal some hidden gems to those willing to explore a little.

tucked into a bend of the coastline. Some, however, trace the town's name to Gonzalo Rincón, a 16th-century landowner who let poor families live on his land. Whatever the history, the name suits the town, which is like a little world unto itself.

The most famous hotel in the region is the Horned Dorset Primavera—the only Relais & Chateaux property in Puerto Rico. It's one of the most luxurious resorts on the island, not to mention in the Caribbean. A couple of larger hotels, including the Rincón of the Seas and Rincón Beach Resort, have been built, but Rincón remains a laid-back place. The town is still a mecca for wave-seekers, particularly surfers from the East Coast of the United States, who often prefer the relatively quick flight to Aguadilla airport direct from New York–area airports instead of the long haul to the Pacific. The town continues to cater to all sorts of travelers, from budget-conscious surfers to families to honeymooners seeking romance.

The beat pace picks up from October through April, when the waves are the best, but tourists can be found here year-round, and many American mainlanders have settled here.

Surrounding the Punta Higuera Lighthouse, **Parque Pasivo El Faro** has small kiosks at the water's edge with telescopes you can use to look for whales. (Have patience, though, even during the "season," from December through February; it could take days to spot one.) You can also glimpse the rusting dome of the defunct Bonus Thermonuclear Energy Plant from here; it has been closed since 1974, but is being resurrected as a nuclear-energy museum. The park—complete with benches, a shop, and a refreshment stand—is a nice place to take in sunsets. The lighthouse is closed to the public, but it's hard to walk away without taking a photo of the stately white structure. ✉ *End of Calle 4413, off Rte. 413* 🎫 *Free* ⏲ *Daily 8* AM*–midnight.*

WORD OF MOUTH

"Main thing to report: Steps Beach (or Escalera) is the absolutely best beach in the area. Little tidal pools great for the kiddies, best snorkeling offshore." –KGates

For divers, **Desecheo Island,** about 20 km (13 mi) off the coast of Rincón, has abundant reef and fish life. A rocky bottom sloping to 120 feet rims the island; long tunnels and caverns covered with purple hydrocoral distinguish one formation known as Yellow Reef. There are other sites with plentiful fish and coral in the shallower water just off Rincón's shores.

BEACHES

The best beaches north of Rincón are lined up along Route 413 and Route 4413 (the road to the lighthouse). South of town the only beach worth noting is Playa Córcega, off Route 115. The beaches below are in geographical order, north to south.

Balneario de Rincón. Swimmers can enjoy the tranquil waters at this beach. The beautiful facility has a playground, changing areas, restrooms, and a clubhouse. It's within walking distance of the center of town. Parking is $2. ✉ *Rte. 115.*

Domes. Named for the eerie green domes on a nearby power plant, this beach is extremely popular with surfers. It's also a great whale-watching spot in winter. To get here, head north on Route 4413. The beach is just north of the lighthouse. ✉ *Rte. 4413, north of the lighthouse.*

Maria's. This surf spot, south of Domes, can get crowded when the waves are high. It's popular with locals, as much for its breakers as for its proximity to the Calypso Café. To get here, look for the street sign reading SURFER CROSSING. ✉ *Rte. 4413, south of the lighthouse.*

Playa Córcega. The long stretch of yellow sand in front of Villa Cofresí is considered one of the best swimming beaches in Rincón. ✉ *Rte. 115, Km 12.0.*

Steps. A set of concrete steps sitting mysteriously at the water's edge gives this beach its name. The waves here can get huge. It's hard to find—look for the turnoff at a whale-shaped sign indicating PLAYA ESCALERA. ✉ *Rte. 413, north of turnoff for Black Eagle Marina.*

Tres Palmas. When the surf is on here—which may be only a handful of days each year, at best—this epic wave spot is one of the world's best. At other times, it's an excellent snorkeling spot. It is on the same road as Steps. ✉ *Rte. 413, north of turnoff for Black Eagle Marina.*

WHERE TO EAT

In addition to the restaurants recommended below, the Villa Confresí and the Lazy Parrot hotels also have good restaurants serving fresh seafood.

> **CAUTION**
>
> The waves in the Rincón area range from gentle, low waves suitable for novice surfers to expert-only breaks. It's a good idea to talk with other surfers about which beaches would be suitable for your skill level.

$$$$ Fodor's Choice ★ ✕**Horned Dorset Primavera.** People come from all over the island for a meal at the Horned Dorset Primavera, and it's easy to see why. A pair of stone stairways carries you up to the elegant dining room, with black-and-white marble floors and chandeliers with ruby-red shades. From the terrace you'll hear the constant crash of the waves. The 10-course tasting menu, an extravagant meal with an extravagant price tag of $110, might include pan-seared scallops with asparagus risotto or roasted grouper with pumpkin puree. Or select from the á la carte menu, which includes wahoo in a pistachio crust with a passion fruit vinaigrette. Dress is formal by island standards, meaning that no shorts are allowed. One disappointment: the wine list is well traveled, but not to budget destinations. ✉*Rte. 429, Km 3, Box 1132, Rincón* ☎*787/823–4030* *Reservations essential* ▭*AE, MC, V.*

$–$$$ ✕**Smilin' Joe's.** This open-air terrace restaurant highlights the impossibly lush greenery that draws so many people to Rincón. On the second floor of the Lazy Parrot, it catches a breeze even when the rest of the island is stifling in the heat. It's a convenient stop for lunch if you're on your way to or from the beach. The wonderful wraps are filled with chicken cutlet and garlic-lime sauce or mahimahi and cilantro sour cream. For dinner there are tropical entrées like sesame-ginger steak and pineapple-coconut shrimp. There's also a surprisingly large wine list. This is one of the few places in Rincón with a children's menu. ✉*The Lazy Parrot, Rte. 413, Km 4.1, Rincón* ☎*787823–5654 or 800/294–1752* ▭*AE, MC, V.*

$–$$ ✕**Rincón Tropical.** Don't be scared off by the cheap plastic tables and chairs. What you should notice is that they are almost always full of locals enjoying the area's freshest seafood. The kitchen keeps it simple, preparing dishes with the lightest touch. Highlights include mahimahi with onions and peppers, or fried red snapper with beans and rice. Fried plantains make a nice accompaniment to almost anything. ✉*Rte. 115, Km 12, Rincón* ☎*787/823–2017* ▭*AE, MC, V.*

$–$$ ✕**Shipwreck Bar & Grill.** This open-air restaurant has been voted the most popular restaurant in town, and it's easy to see why. It has a laid-back vibe and a friendly staff that's always ready with a smile or a joke. The food is good, too. Look for four specials a night, including steak with guava sauce and mahimahi in a butter-and-white wine sauce. There are also plenty of wraps (we liked the marinated pork) and other light fare. Don't miss the Sunday afternoon pig roast. ✉*Black Eagle Marina, Black Eagle Rd., off Rte. 413, Rincón* ☎*787/823–0578* ▭*AE, MC, V.*

GREAT ITINERARIES

IF YOU HAVE 1 DAY

If you have only a day to spend in the Porta del Sol, make the drive to **Joyuda** for some of Puerto Rico's freshest seafood. You probably won't be the only ones driving from San Juan for this feast.

IF YOU HAVE 3 DAYS

If you have a few days to explore the region, start in **Rincón,** where you'll find accommodations for every taste, from compact inns to sprawling resorts. There isn't too much to see, other than the lighthouse at Parque Pasivo El Faro, but you will see plenty of beautiful beaches. Most have been discovered, however. If you crave complete solitude, you're more likely to find empty beaches in the communities of **Aguadilla** or **Isabela.** On Day 2 drive south to the coastal communities in the Cabo Rojo. Your first stop should be **Joyuda,** where you can choose from dozens of seaside restaurants. After lunch, continue past **Boquerón** to **El Combate.** This is the end of the line, quite literally. The road ends at the lighthouse that once warned sea captains about the treacherous waters around the island's southwestern tip. On Day 3 you can explore more of this windswept landscape, or head offshore for a look at Mona Island.

IF YOU HAVE 5 DAYS

After spending three days along the western coast, you may be tempted to set sail to one of the islands off the coast. On Day 4, head out on an overnight trip to **Mona Island,** a 14,000-acre paradise known as the "Galápagos of the Caribbean." You'll have to camp on this deserted island, but the view from the 200-foot cliffs on the northern shore makes it all worth it.

\$–\$\$ ✕**Tamboo.** Here is a bar and grill that doesn't fall too much into either category. The open-air kitchen prepares any number of unusual items, from king-crab sandwiches to chicken-and-basil wraps. The bar, also open to the elements, serves a mean margarita. Happy hour sometimes starts dangerously early—at 10 AM on Saturday. The deck is a great place to watch the novice surfers wipe out on the nearby beach. A 2007 renovation made the place look great, and every table has a million-dollar view of the ocean. ✉*Beside the Point, Rte. 413, Km 4.7, Rincón* ☎*787/823–3210* 💳*AE, MC, V.*

WHERE TO STAY

\$\$\$\$ Fodor's Choice ★ **Horned Dorset Primavera.** This is, without a doubt, the most luxurious hotel in Puerto Rico. The 40 whitewashed villas scattered throughout the tropical gardens are designed so you have complete privacy whether you are relaxing in your private plunge pool or admiring the sunset from one of your balconies. The furnishings in each of the two-story suites are impeccable, from the hand-carved mahogany table in the downstairs dining room to the four-poster beds in the upstairs bedroom. The marble bathroom has a footed porcelain tub that's big enough for two. (There's a second bath downstairs that's perfect for rinsing off after a walk on the beach.) Breakfast is served in your room, and lunch is available on a terrace overlooking the ocean. Dinner in the elegant restaurant is included in the rate. A place to unplug from the rest of the world, the hotel has no radios or televisions, and does not allow children younger than 12. **Pros:** Unabashed luxury, unmatched meals, lovely setting. **Cons:** On a very slender beach, staff is sometimes haughty. ✉*Rte. 429, Km 3, Box 1132, Rincón* ☎*787/823–4030 or 800/633–1857* 🌐*www.horneddorset.com* *22 villas* *In-room: safe, kitchen, no TV. In-hotel: restaurant, bar, pools, gym, beachfront, no kids under 12* 💳*AE, MC, V* 🍽*MAP.*

WORD OF MOUTH

Horned Dorset Primavera

"If you want an amazing beach, entertainment or nightlife, I'd seek elsewhere. If you want fabulous accomodations, excellent service, and amazing dining, seek no further." –Ben

5

$$–$$$ **Rincón Beach Resort.** It's a bit off the beaten path, but that's part of the allure of this oceanfront hotel. The South Seas–style decor begins in the high-ceilinged lobby, where hand-carved chaises invite you to enjoy the view through the almond trees. The rooms continue the theme with rich fabrics and dark-wood furnishings. A variety of activities are available, including whale- and turtle-watching in season. At the end of the infinity pool, a boardwalk leads down to the sand. Unlike many of the beaches just a few miles north, the waters here are calm—not great for surfing, but perfect for a dip if you're staying here. The resort is tucked away in Añasco, about halfway between Rincón to the north and Mayagüez to the south. **Pros:** Beautiful setting, gorgeous pool area, laid-back vibe. **Cons:** Far from dining options, lacks a Puerto Rican flavor. ✉*Rte. 115, Km 5.8, Añasco* ☎*787/589–9000* 🌐*www.rinconbeach.com* *112 rooms* *In-room: safe, kitchen (some), refrigerator, dial-up. In-hotel: restaurant, room service, bars, pool, gym, beachfront, diving, water sports, laundry service, parking (no fee)* 💳*AE, D, DC, MC, V* 🍽*EP.*

$$–$$$ **Rincón of the Seas.** Tucked at the end of a palm-lined drive, this high-rise hotel feels like it could be in Miami Beach. The gentle curve of the facade and the elegant railings on the balconies give it a vaguely Art Deco feel. (The lobby and some of the suites echo this with streamlined furnishings.) Of course, the free-form pool has a swim-up bar where you can order drinks with umbrellas. The open-air lobby takes full advantage of the lush foliage in the courtyard. A U-shaped design gives every room a wall of windows facing the beach. **Pros:** Lush gardens, gorgeous pool area, professional staff. **Cons:** On a slender beach, building has an institutional feel. ✉*Rte. 115, Km 12.2 Rincón* ☎*787/823–7500* 🌐*www.rinconoftheseas.com* *109 rooms* *In-room: safe, Ethernet. In-hotel: 2 restaurants, room service, bars, pool, beachfront, public Internet* 💳*AE, MC, V* 🍽*EP.*

$–$$ **Beside the Pointe.** This perennial favorite sits right on Sandy Beach, where the waves are big, but not too large for novice surfers. After a complete renovation, the tropical-themed rooms—ranging from studios to two-bedroom apartments with full kitchens—now dazzle you with gorgeous furnishings and brilliant fabrics. All of the tables downstairs, at the popular bar and grill Tamboo, have a view of the ocean. Sometimes you can spot a whale from the sun deck. **Pros:** Social atmosphere, popular restaurant, great views. **Cons:** Noise from restaurant, not all rooms have ocean views. ✉ *Rte. 413, Km 4.7, Rincón* ☎ *787/823–8550* 🌐 *www.besidethepointe.com* *4 rooms, 4 apartments* *In-room: kitchen (some), refrigerator. In-hotel: restaurant, bar, no elevator, public Wi-Fi* *AE, MC, V* *CP.*

$–$$ ★ **Casa Isleña.** With its barrel-tiled roofs, wall-enclosed gardens, and open-air dining room, Casa Isleña might remind well-traveled souls of a villa on the coast of Mexico. The secret of its charm is that this little inn retains a simplicity without compromising the romantic flavor of its setting. Several of the terra-cotta–floored rooms have balconies overlooking the pool and the palm-shaded stretch of beach. Others have terraces facing the courtyard. There's also a hot tub and an indoor patio with a soothing, burbling fountain. If it's booked solid—which happens frequently during high season—there's a second building a few minutes away. **Pros:** Secluded setting, beautiful beach, eye-catching architecture. **Cons:** A bit hard to find, books up quickly. ✉ *Rte. 413, Km 4.8, Barrio Puntas* ☎ *787/823–1525 or 888/289–7750* 🌐 *www.casa-islena.com* *9 rooms* *In-room: refrigerator (some). In-hotel: restaurant, bar, pool, beachfront, water sports, parking (no fee)* *AE, MC, V* *EP.*

$–$$ ★ **Lazy Parrot.** Painted in eye-popping tropical hues, this mountainside hotel doesn't take itself too seriously. Colorful murals of the eponymous bird brighten the open, airy lobby. The accommodations are a bit more subdued, though they continue the tropical theme. Several have colorful fish swimming across the walls, and the family-themed Dolphin Room has—what else?—a stuffed dolphin. Each room has a balcony, but if you want to enjoy the view ask for one upstairs. Smilin' Joe's restaurant serves red snapper and other excellent seafood dishes. You can sample a parrot-themed concoction at the bar, or browse through the "parrotphernalia" at the small gift shop. An annex with a dozen more rooms opened at end of 2007. **Pros:** Whimsical design, lush setting, friendly staff. **Cons:** Not on the beach, stairs to climb. ✉ *Rte. 413, Km 4.1 Rincón* ☎ *787/823–5654 or 800/294–1752* 🌐 *www.lazyparrot.com* *23 rooms* *In-room: refrigerator, Wi-Fi. In-hotel: 2 restaurants, bars, pool, no elevator, public Wi-Fi* *AE, D, MC, V* *CP.*

¢–$$ **Blue Boy Inn.** A walled garden that surrounds this little inn makes you think you're miles away from civilization. But the Blue Boy Inn is within walking distance of several bars and restaurants. The rooms are individually decorated in a style that might be called plantation modern, including elegant wooden sleigh beds as well as flat-screen televisions. The best—we liked Number 3 and Number 6—have private terraces. The pool area is wonderful, especially at night when it's lit with the inn's trademark blue. A delicious breakfast is included in the rate. **Pros:** Gorgeous gardens, pretty pool, lots of privacy. **Cons:** Not on beach, some noise from nearby restaurant. ✉ *556 Black Eagle Rd., off Rte. 413, Rincón* ☎ *787/823–2593* 🌐 *www.blueboyinn.com* *6* *rooms* ♁*In-room: refrigerator. In-hotel: pool, public Internet, public Wi-Fi* ▭*AE, MC, V* ⦾*BP.*

$ **Lemontree Oceanfront Cottages.** Sitting right on the beach, this pair of lemon-yellow buildings holds six apartments of various sizes. Choose from one three-bedroom unit, one two-bedroom unit, two one-bedroom units, or two studios. No matter which one you pick, each sleek option has a full kitchen, dining area, and private balcony with views of the coastline. Ted and Jane Davis, who bought the place in 2005, have added uncommon amenities for this price range, such as plasma televisions, DVD players, and free Wi-Fi. There is a dive shop on the premises and a massage therapist on call. This is one of the few gay-friendly places in Rincón. **Pros:** Far from the crowds, friendly on-site owners. **Cons:** Beach is very narrow, must drive to shops and restaurants. ✉*Rte. 429, Km 4.1, Box 200, Rincón* ☎*787/823–6452* ⊕*www.lemontreepr.com* *6 apartments* ♁*In-room: kitchen, DVD, Wi-Fi. In-hotel: beachfront, diving, public Wi-Fi, no elevator* ▭*MC, V* ⦾*EP.*

5

$ **Villa Cofresí.** On one of the best swimming beaches in Rincón, Villa Cofresí is extremely popular with families. Parents can keep an eye on the kids while they enjoy the beachfront bar or restaurant. The guest rooms are more spacious than most, especially those that have kitchenettes. Rooms on the second floor are preferable, as those surrounding the pool can get a bit noisy; second-floor rooms have better views, too. The weekend breakfast buffet draws locals who love the omelet bar. The hotel can arrange a host of water sports. **Pros:** Good on-site restaurants, family-friendly environment. **Cons:** Standard rooms lack ocean views, not enough parking, lots of noise from pool area. ✉*Rte. 115, Km 12.0, Rincón* ☎*787/823–2450* ⊕*www.villacofresi.com* *51 rooms* ♁*In-room: kitchen (some), refrigerator. In-hotel: restaurants, bar, pool, beachfront, public Wi-Fi* ▭*AE, D, MC, V* ⦾*CP.*

¢–$ **Rincón Surf & Board.** All the rooms here have surfboard racks, which should give you a clue about the customers this out-of-the-way guesthouse attracts. Two hostel-type rooms with bunk beds—remains of the original lodging concept—are available at $20 per person. One- to three-bed private rooms are ample size and have a clean and fresh feel; some are like small apartments. Common areas are fun and friendly, but are not conducive to late-night partying, as the best surfing is for the early birds. **Pros:** Great for outdoorsy types, congenial crowd. **Cons:** Younger crowd, a bit hard to find. ✉*Off Rte. 413, Barrio Puntas, Rincón* ☎*787/823–0610* ⊕*www.surfandboard.com* *13 rooms, 2 hostel rooms* ♁*In-room: refrigerator (some). In-hotel: restaurant, pool, beachfront, water sports, parking (no fee)* ▭*AE, MC, V* ⦾*EP.*

VILLA RENTALS

Villa rentals are becoming more and more popular in Rincón. Because many people come here for a week or more to surf, find a secluded spot on the beach, or just hang out, renting a villa makes perfect sense. They can make the place their own, without worrying about the noise from the kids bothering the people in the next room or leaving sandy shoes outside the door.

A few things to keep in mind. If you're looking for a secluded location, you won't find it on this crowded part of the coast. It's likely that your neighbor will be within shouting distance. In addition, few villas are actually on the ocean, and the ones that are go for a premium price. Many are within walking distance of the water, but some will require that you drive to reach the shore. If a beachfront location is important to you, make sure to specify. And where you stay will depend on whether or not you're a surfer. Those who like to ride the waves favor the northern coast, while those who want to snorkel, scuba dive, or swim prefer the calmer southern shore.

Island West Properties & Beach Rentals (✉*Rte. 413, Km 1.3, Box 700, Rincón* ☎*787/823–2323* 🌐*www.islandwestrentals.com*) can help you rent villas in Rincón by the day, week, or month. The company has been around for years, so it corners the market.

$$$$ **Villa Tres Palmas.** Not all beach houses are created equal, as Villas Tres Palmas makes clear. The hand-hewn columns and railings on this gorgeous three-story house might make you think you're in the South Seas. The exotic decor continues inside, where wooden headboards and other furnishings are carved with intricate patterns. The enormous house has six bedrooms that look out toward the tropical gardens surrounding the kidney-shaped pool. Beyond the pool, at the foot of the property, is the palm-lined beach. This is Tres Palmas, which has a break that makes it popular with surfers. There's a full kitchen, and the location is near many good restaurants. Only the bedrooms have air conditioning. ✉*Off Rte. 413, Playa Tres Palmas* ☎*787/823–2323* 🌐*www.islandwestrentals.com* *6 bedrooms, 5 bathrooms* *No a/c (some rooms), DVD, pool, beachfront, laundry facilities.* *D, MC, V.*

$$$ **Caribbean Paradise.** This two-story house would be great for two families traveling together, as each floor has plenty of room. There are two bedrooms and one bathroom upstairs, and two bedrooms and two bathrooms downstairs. A spacious dining area is off the full kitchen, but most people prefer taking their meals at the table on the upstairs balcony. From here you can scan the horizon for passing whales (very easy to see from this part of the coast). There's no pool, but just beyond the picket fence is Corsega Beach, one of the area's best swimming beaches. You can cook dinner in the kitchen, outside on the gas grill, or let someone else do the cooking by taking advantage of one of the hotel restaurants down the beach. The air-conditioning is only in the bedrooms. ✉*Calle 8, Corsega Beach* ☎*787/823–2323* 🌐*www.islandwestrentals.com* *4 bedrooms, 3 bathrooms* *No a/c (some), beachfront, laundry facilities.* *D, MC, V.*

$$$ **Casa Grande.** Part of a small complex, this two-story villa doesn't give you complete privacy; for example, you share the pretty pool area with renters in the other two buildings. The trade-off, however, is that it's one of the area's more affordable options. Four bedrooms can accommodate up to a dozen people, making this place perfect for an extended family. The bedrooms have French doors leading out to a pair of wide terraces, where you can catch a glimpse of the ocean above the palm trees. The villa isn't on the beach, but you can walk there

in a few minutes. Full-size appliances in the kitchen make it easy to cook for a crowd, and a couple of restaurants are within walking distance. Only the master bedroom has an air conditioner; the others have fans. The villa is in Puntas, on the northern shore. ✉ *Rte. 413, Puntas* ☎ *787/823–2323* 🌐 *www.islandwestrentals.com* *4 bedrooms, 2 bathrooms* *No a/c (some rooms), pool, laundry facilities.* 💳 *D, MC, V.*

WHALE-WATCHING

If you visit between December and February, you might get a glimpse of the humpback whales that winter off the Puerto Rico coast.

NIGHTLIFE

Rincón attracts a younger crowd, so there are plenty of options for fun after dark. On weekends the **Calypso Café** (✉ *Rte. 4413, Maria's Beach* ☎ *787/823–4151*) often has live rock-and-roll bands. The open-air establishment, more bar than grill, is also a good place to go after you've had your fill of the beach.

5

SPORTS & THE OUTDOORS

DIVING & SNORKELING

Most of the region's dive operators also run fishing charters around Desecheo Island and whale-watching trips in season.

Taíno Divers (✉ *Black Eagle Marina, Black Eagle Rd., off Rte. 413* ☎ *787/823–6429* 🌐 *www.tainodivers.com*) has daily snorkeling and diving trips that cost $75 and $109, including lunch. It also has daily trips to Desecheo Island, charters to Mona Island, and scuba PADI certification courses.

HORSEBACK RIDING

Pintos R Us (✉ *Rte. 413, Km. 4.7* ☎ *787/823–8614*) has daily riding along the beach to the lighthouse. The horses are spirited, but gentle enough for newcomers.

SURFING

Desecheo Surf & Dive Shop (✉ *Rte. 413, Km 2.5* ☎ *787/823–0390* 🌐 *innsurfanddiveshop.com*) rents snorkeling equipment ($10 a day), boogie boards ($20 a day), and a variety of short and long surfboards ($25 to $30 a day). The company also organizes diving and snorkeling trips and rents Jet Skis.

★ **Rincón Surf School** (✉ *Rincón Surf & Board, Rte. 413* ☎ *787/823–0610* 🌐 *www.surfandboard.com*) offers full-day lessons for $89, which includes board rental and transportation. You can also arrange two-, three-, and five-day surfing seminars for $169 to $369. There is also a special five-day surf and yoga school taught by and for women that takes place several times throughout the year.

SAILING

Set sail in the morning for a day in the sun, or in the late afternoon for unobstructed sunset views, with **Katarina Sail Charters** (✉ *Black Eagle Marina, off Rte. 413* ☎ *787/823–7245* 🌐 *www.sailrinconpuertorico.com*). The catamaran sails from Black Eagle Marina.

MAYAGÜEZ

24 km (15 mi) southeast of Rincón.

"Me encanta" is what most people from Puerto Rico say when you ask them about Mayagüez. But you are likely to be less than enchanted by the city. With more charming communities in every direction, there's no real reason to stop in this traffic-clogged city. But if you have some spare time, the city known as the "Sultan of the West" has some worthwhile attractions. Its tree-lined main square, called Plaza Colón, is dominated by a large statue of Christopher Columbus. On the surrounding streets you'll find the domed Teatro Yagüez, which dates from 1902, and a mishmash of buildings that run the gamut from neoclassical to baroque to Art Deco.

Puerto Rico's only zoo, the 35-acre **Zoológico de Puerto Rico,** is just north of downtown. After $13 million in renovations, it's looking pretty spiffy. New on the scene is a 45-foot-tall aviary, which allows you to walk through a rain forest environment as tropical birds fly freely above your head. There's also a new butterfly park where you can let brilliant blue morphos land on your hand, and an arthropodarium where you can get up close and personal with spiders and their kin. Video monitors are built into the floor to show off the bugs that normally get trampled underfoot. The older section of the park has undergone an extensive renovation, so most of the cages have been replaced by fairly natural-looking environments. One of the most popular residents is Mundi, a female elephant who arrived as a baby more than two decades ago. There are also plenty of lions, tigers—and even bears. There is a $2 charge for parking. ✉ *Rte. 108, north of Rte. 65* ☎ *787/622–6330* 🌐 *www.parquesnacionalespr.com* 🎫 *$6* ⏲ *Wed.–Sun. 8:30–4.*

Founded in 1901 on a 235-acre farm on the outskirts of Mayagüez, the **Estación Experimental de Agricultura Tropical** *(Tropical Agriculture Research Station)* is run by the U.S. Department of Agriculture and contains a tropical plant collection that has been nurtured for more than a half century. More than 2,000 plant species from all over the tropical world are found here, including teak, mahogany, cinnamon, nutmeg, rubber, and numerous exotic flowers. Free maps are available for self-guided tours. ✉ *Hwy. 2 and Rte. 108* ☎ *787/831–3435* 🎫 *Free* ⏲ *Weekdays 7–4.*

The **Teatro Yagüez** is an extravagant yellow-and-white theater dating from 1902 that's famed throughout the island for its lavish, columned facade and domed roof. The structure, a little over the top, is still the main venue for theater in Mayagüez. As this writing, it was closed for renovations until sometime in 2008. ✉ *Calle McKinley at Calle Dr. Basora* ☎ *787/834–0523* 🎫 *Free* ⏲ *Daily, except when rehearsals are scheduled.*

BEACHES

Balneario de Añasco. Mayagüez isn't famous for its beaches—you'll find better stretches in Rincón, about 25 minutes north—but this sandy stretch, also called Tres Hermanos Beach, is 10 minutes north of town via Highway 2 and Routes 115 and 401. Dotted with palm trees, it's good for swimming and has changing facilities and restrooms.

WHERE TO EAT

$$–$$$ ✕**El Estoril.** The elegantly tiled dining room calls to mind the old world, while the friendly, relaxed service is all about the new one. Seafood is the specialty: order a traditional paella, or the unusual lobster wrapped in mozzarella and bacon and flambéed. If you're in the mood for something lighter, you can order tapas in the wood-and-brick bar. Call ahead, as the place occasionally closes for private parties. ✉*100 Calle Méndez Vigo* ☎*787/834–2288* ▭*AE, MC, V* ⊙*Closed Sun.*

¢ ✕**Ricomini Bakery.** This popular bakery, open daily from 6 AM to midnight, is a good spot to try one of the city's trademark delicacies, a *brazo gitano* (literally "gypsy arm"). These gigantic jellyrolls are filled with anything from guava to lemon to sweet cheese. You can also find another famous local product here, Fido's Sangría, made from the closely guarded secret recipe of Mayagüez resident Wilfredo Aponte Hernández. There are also tasty pastries, freshly baked bread, and a selection of sandwiches. ✉*202 Calle Méndez Vigo* ☎*787/832–0565* ▭*AE, MC, V.*

WHERE TO STAY

$$ **Holiday Inn Mayagüez & Tropical Casino.** Everything seems shoehorned into this big box on the northern edge of Mayagüez. The sound of slot machines is impossible to escape in the extremely popular casino, which is adjacent to the lobby, as well as the bar and restaurant. The rooms are a bit larger than usual, but otherwise are nothing special. Holly's Restaurant serves Caribbean cuisine with a Sunday "South American" brunch. The casino is popular with locals, but could use a new paint job. The easy-to-reach location is about 10 minutes from the downtown historic district and five minutes from the airport. **Pros:** Great staff, pretty pool area. **Cons:** Not on the beach, motel-style rooms. ✉*2701 Hwy. 2, Km 149.9* ☎*787/833–1100* 🌐*www.hidpr.com* *141 rooms* *In-room: Wi-Fi. In-hotel: restaurant, room service, bar, pools, gym, laundry facilities, laundry service, public Internet, public Wi-Fi, parking (free)* ▭*AE, D, MC, V* *CP.*

$$ **Mayagüez Resort & Casino.** The center of the city's social life, this old-fashioned hotel is packed with elegantly dressed men and women all weekend. Some are trying their luck in the casino, some are dancing the tango in the lounge, and some are sipping cocktails on the long, sweeping terrace. The nicely decorated guest rooms look out onto 20 acres of lush gardens. El Castillo specializes in seafood. The public beach in Añasco is 10 minutes away. **Pros:** Lovely pool area, best casino on this coast. **Cons:** Not on the beach, must pay parking even to visit

the casino. ✉ *Rte. 104, Km 0.3, off Hwy. 2, Box 3781* ☎ *787/832–3030 or 888/689–3030* 🌐 *www.mayaguezresort.com* *140 rooms* *In-room: Wi-Fi. In-hotel: restaurant, bar, tennis courts, pool, gym, public Internet, parking (fee)* *AE, D, DC, MC, V* *EP.*

$ **Howard Johnson Downtown Mayagüez.** Set in a former monastery, this downtown hotel still has stained-glass windows in some rooms and a stone cross on the roof. The rooms are mostly small (they were originally for monks, after all), but more stylish than those in your standard chain hotel. The best are the extremely colorful accommodations designed for families with kids. A Continental breakfast is included in the rate. **Pros:** Interesting building, rooms designed for families and businesspeople. **Cons:** Far from the beach, on an uninteresting block. ✉ *70 Calle Méndez Vigo* ☎ *787/832–9191* 🌐 *www.hojo.com* *39 rooms* *In-room: refrigerator (some), Ethernet (some). In-hotel: pool* *AE, D, MC, V* *CP.*

NIGHTLIFE & THE ARTS

A block from Plaza Colón, **Dom Pepe** (✉ *56 Calle Méndez Vigo* ☎ *787/834–4941*) has live eclectic music upstairs.

SHOPPING

Small stores and pharmacies dot downtown Mayagüez. For heavy-duty shopping, the **Mayagüez Mall** (✉ *Hwy. 2, Km 159.4* ☎ *787/834–2760*) has local stores, a food court, and stateside chains such as JCPenney.

CABO ROJO

Named for its pinkish cliffs, "Red Cape" was used in the late 18th century as a port for merchant vessels—and for the smugglers and pirates who inevitably accompanied ocean-going trade. Today the miles of coastline to the west and north of this tiny curl of land jutting into the Atlantic Ocean are a destination for families. Many small, inexpensive hotels can be found in the small communities of Joyuda, Boquerón, and El Combate. (There's also a town with the name of Cabo Rojo, but there's little of interest here.) Outdoor activities are quite popular, from sailing out of Boquerón to hiking to the lighthouse near El Combate.

JOYUDA

21 km (14 mi) south of Mayagüez.

Known as the *Milla de Oro* (Golden Mile) because of its string of more than 30 seaside restaurants, the community of Joyuda is a must for seafood lovers. The same can't be said for those in search of a beautiful beach, as erosion has taken a terrible toll, leaving in some places only a sliver of sand. But that doesn't stop hordes of local families from making a beeline to the bit of beach that is left.

★ About 50 mi off the coast of Cabo Rojo, **Mona Island** sits brooding in the Atlantic Ocean. Known as the Galápagos of the Caribbean, the 14,000-acre island has long been a destination for adventurous travelers. It's said to have been settled by the Taíno and visited by both Christopher Columbus and Juan Ponce de León. Pirates were known to use the small island as a hideout, and legend has it that there is still buried treasure to be found here. Today, however, Mona's biggest lure is its distinctive ecosystem. It is home to a number of endangered species, such as the Mona iguana and leatherback sea turtle. A number of seabirds, including red-footed boobies, also inhabit the island. Off its coast are reefs filled with 270 species of tropical fish, black coral, and purple seafans. There are plenty of places to explore, such as the 200-foot cliffs on the north side of the island or the abandoned lighthouse that once protected ships off the southern coast. Travelers must reach the island by boat—planes aren't permitted to land. Several tour operators in Joyuda and Boquerón, as well as companies in Mayagüez and Rincón, offer overnight camping trips to the island; they will help you with the camping permits from the Department of Natural and Environmental Resources. You need to reserve at least a few weeks ahead for an overnight stay. ☎ *787/724–3724 for Department of Natural and Environmental Resources.*

5

WHERE TO EAT

$$–$$$ ★ ✕ **Tino's.** The colorful neon sign outside this restaurant touts its signature dish: AN EARTHENWARE GOBLET OVERFLOWING WITH MASHED PLANTAINS AND SEAFOOD. It comes in two sizes, but the smaller one is usually enough to satisfy all but the biggest appetites. There are plenty of other dishes on the menu, from red snapper in a spicy sauce to lobster with butter. There's no ocean view, but the elegant dining makes up for it. ✉ *Rte. 102, Km 13.6* ☎ *787/851–2976* ▭ *AE, DC, MC, V.*

$$ ✕ **El Bohío.** Watch seagulls dive for their dinner while you dine on a covered deck extending out into the bay. The long list of seafood is prepared in a variety of ways: shrimp comes breaded, stewed, or skewered; conch is served as a salad or cooked in a butter-and-garlic sauce; and the lobster can be prepared in just about any way you can imagine. ✉ *Rte. 102, Km 9.7* ☎ *787/851–2755* ▭ *AE, DC, MC, V.*

WHERE TO STAY

$ **Parador Joyuda Beach.** Talk about truth in advertising: the beach in question is so close to this place that the water laps against the seawall. Rooms here are spic and span, with terra-cotta tile floors. Ask for one of the sunset suites, which have ocean views. There's an open-air restaurant by the beach and a snack bar by the pool. **Pros:** Waterfront location, friendly staff. **Cons:** Motel-style rooms; ugly white plastic chairs in pool area, bar, and restaurant. ✉ *Rte. 102, Km 11.7* 📫 *Box 18410, 00623* ☎ *787/851–5650 or 800/981–5464* 🌐 *www.joyudabeach.com* *41 rooms* *In-hotel: restaurant, bar, pool, beachfront, no elevator* ▭ *AE, MC, V* *EP.*

¢ **Joyuda Plaza.** Across the road from the beach, this three-story hotel is one of the best deals in Joyuda. You don't come here for the ambience—the building is little more than a box, and the rooms make only a vague attempt at decor. But if you're on a budget, this place has nice touches you don't always get in this price range, like a pair of kidney-shaped pools sitting side by side in a pretty courtyard. A dozen or so bars and restaurants are within walking distance. **Pros:** Good value, located in the middle of the action. **Cons:** Not much atmosphere, noise from other rooms can be a problem. ✉*Rte. 102, Km 14.7* *Box 18410, Joyuda 00623* ☎*787/851–8800* *55 rooms* *In-hotel: 2 restaurants, room service, bar, pool, no elevator* *AE, MC, V.*

SPORTS & THE OUTDOORS

DIVING & SNORKELING

Several reef-bordered cays lie off the Cabo Rojo area near walls that drop to 100 feet. A mile-long reef along Las Coronas, better known as Cayo Ron, has a variety of hard and soft coral, reef fish, and lobster. You can arrange snorkeling and scuba-diving trips with Captain Elick Hernández Garciá, who runs **Tour Marine Adventures** (✉*Rte. 101, Km 14.1* ☎*787/375–2625* *www.tourmarinepr.com*). They cost between $35 and $75 per person. He'll also arrange trips out to Mona Island for $115 per person.

GOLF

Get in 18 holes at the **Club Deportivo del Oeste** (✉*Rte. 102, Km 15.4* ☎*787/851–8880*). Jack Bender incorporated the region's rolling hills in his design to provide golfers with panoramic views. The nicely tended course is open daily; greens fees are $30.

BOQUERÓN

5 km (3 mi) south of Joyuda.

Once a quiet fishing village, Boquerón still has its share of seaside shanties. Its narrow streets are quiet during the week but come alive on the weekend, when vendors appear with carts full of clams and oysters you can slurp down on the spot—wedges of lemon are provided, of course. Bars and restaurants throw open their doors—if they have any, that is. Many of the establishments here are open to the breeze. Boquerón is also a water-sports center; many companies operate from or near the docks of the imposing Club Nautico de Boquerón, which is easy to find at the end of Route 100.

The **Refugio de Vida Silvestre de Boquerón** *(Boquerón Wildlife Refuge)* encompasses three tracts of land at the island's southern tip. The first is about 1 mi (2 km) south of Boquerón. There is a trail that leads through three different types of mangroves to picnic areas and a dock where you can launch a canoe or kayak. Note: hunting is allowed in the reserve between November and January. ✉*Rte. 101, Km 1.1* ☎*787/851–4795* *Free* *Weekdays 7:30–4.*

BEACHES

Balneario Boquerón. The long stretch of sand at this beach off Route 101 is a favorite with islanders, especially on weekends. You'll find changing facilities, cabins, showers, restrooms, and picnic tables; it costs $3 to enter with a car. ✉*Off Rte. 101.*

Playa Buyé. The white-sand beach has swaying palm trees and crystal clear water. ✉ *Rte. 307, north of Boquerón.*

WHERE TO EAT

$$–$$$ ✕ **Galloway's.** From a covered deck overlooking Bahía Boquerón, you can catch the sunset while enjoying some seafood—caught fresh from local waters, of course. There's a lively happy hour and occasional live music. This place is along the main drag, but is set back from the street so you don't have to be a part of the passing parade. One major plus in this traffic-choked town: there's a large free parking lot. ✉ *12 Calle José de Diego* ☎ *787/254–3302* ▭ *AE, MC, V* ⊙ *Closed Mon.–Wed.*

WHERE TO STAY

$ **Cofresí Beach Hotel.** A favorite with families, this place puts you a few blocks from the hustle and bustle of Boquerón. Its four floors—practically a high-rise in these parts—are filled with one-, two-, and three-bedroom apartments complete with full kitchens. The owners didn't forget a thing, as the cupboards are even stocked with nice china and flatware. The pool is small, but very much appreciated on hot afternoons. **Pros:** Best value in the area, family-friendly environment, walking distance to many restaurants. **Cons:** Not on the beach, some traffic noise. ✉ *57 Calle Muñoz Rivera* *Box 1209, Boquerón 00622* ☎ *787/254–3000* ⊕ *www.cofresibeach.com* *12 apartments* *In-room: kitchen, refrigerator. In-hotel: restaurant, pool* ▭ *AE, D, DC, MC, V.*

$ **Parador Boquemar.** Even though it's a hike from Balneario Boquerón, families flock to this friendly parador on weekends. Rooms on the first floor are so cramped that people tend to leave their doors open; for enough room to breathe, ask for a third-floor room with a balcony overlooking the water. The seafood restaurant, La Cascada, has an actual waterfall along one wall. On weekends the lounge is filled with live music. **Pros:** Near plenty of dining and nightlife options, family-friendly environment. **Cons:** Ugly building, can get very noisy ✉ *Calle Gill Buyé* *Box 133, Boquerón 00622* ☎ *787/851–2158* ⊕ *www.boquemar.com* *75 rooms* *In-room: refrigerator. In-hotel: restaurant, bar, pool, bicycles* ▭ *AE, D, DC, MC, V* *EP.*

NIGHTLIFE

A curvy bar distinguishes **Boquerón Bay** (✉ *Calle Jose de Diego* ☎ *787/640–3820*) from its straightforward neighbors. The open-air establishment has a second floor where you can catch a glimpse of the sunset.

SPORTS & THE OUTDOORS

DIVING & SNORKELING Snorkeling and scuba-diving trips are the specialty at **Mona Aquatics** (✉ *Calle Jose de Diego* ☎ *787/851–2185* ⊕ *www.monaaquatics.com*). Night dives are available as well.

WORD OF MOUTH

"Boquerón and El Combate are some of the best beaches to see but in the far southwest part of the island. I particularly liked Cabo Rojo with its wide & calm beach and bay. Swimming there is very good and calm, but not for snorkeling. There is a lighthouse there, but I found the salt flats there even more visually interesting."
–netmd

You'll find the crew in a wooden shack painted an eye-popping shade of blue next to the Club Nautico de Boquerón. The company has weekly trips to Mona Island.

FISHING You can arrange fishing trips with Captain Francisco "Pochy" Rosario, who runs **Light Tackle Adventure** (☎*787/849–1430* 🌐*www.lighttackleadventure.8k.com*). His specialty is tarpon, which are plentiful in these waters.

EL COMBATE

3 km (2 mi) south of Boquerón.

This is the end of the earth—or the end of the island, anyway. El Combate sits on the southwest corner of Puerto Rico, a bit removed from everything. The travel industry hasn't figured out how to market this place, so they've left it mostly to the locals, who have built small but elaborate weekend homes—some with grandiose touches like fountains—along the narrow streets. On the road closest to the beach, which for some reason is called Calle 3, is a cluster of seafood shacks. The more prosperous ones have added second stories.

If you're wondering about the town's odd name, which literally means "The Combat," it seems that long ago some unscrupulous characters were eyeing the salt flats just outside town. But they were repelled by machete-wielding villagers who were to live forever in local lore. Is it a true story? Residents of El Combate swear it is.

The **Refugio de Vida Silvestre de Cabo Rojo** *(Cabo Rojo Wildlife Refuge)* has an interpretive center with exhibits of live freshwater fish and sea turtles. You can see as many as 100 species of birds along the trails, even the elusive yellow-shouldered blackbird. The entrance is about 1 mi north of the turnoff for El Combate. ✉*Rte. 301, Km 1.2* ☎*787/851–7260* 🎫*Free* ⏲*Weekdays 8–4.*

The **Centro Interpretativo Las Salinas de Cabo Rojo** *(Cabo Rojo Sal Flats Interpretive Center)* has a small display about the salt flats and their importance to the local economy. (Remember that the name of the town comes from a battle over control of the salt flats.) The best part of the center is a massive observation tower that lets you scan the outline of Cabo Rojo itself. The last time we checked, a new audio-visual center was set to open next door to the main building. ✉*End of Rte. 301* ☎*787/851–2999* 🌐*proambientepr.org* 🎫*Free* ⏲*Wed.–Sat. 8:30–4:30, Sun. 9:30–5:30.*

★ The area's most popular attraction is the neoclassical **Cabo Rojo Lighthouse,** dating from 1881. The magnificent structure is not open to the public, but you are free to hike around the rugged terrain or relax on La Playuela or one of the other pink-sand beaches nearby. ✉*End of Rte. 301, El Combate* ☎*787/851–7260* 🎫*Free* ⏲*24 hrs.*

BEACHES

El Combate Beach. This great beach draws college students to its rustic waterfront eateries. You can rent small boats and kayaks here, and in summer there are often concerts and festivals. ✉*At the end of Rte. 3301.*

> **CAUTION**
>
> It's a good idea to rent a four-wheel-drive vehicle if you are heading to Cabo Rojo Lighthouse, as it is reached via a truly terrible dirt road.

La Playuela. The crescent-shaped strand is the most secluded of the area's beaches. There are no amenities, so bring everything you need. ✉*Rte. 301, past the vast salt flats.*

WHERE TO EAT

$$–$$$ ✕**Annie's.** A dining room with windows facing the ocean is a fitting place to try some of the southwest coast's best seafood. You can snack on *empanadillas* (deep-fried fritters), then move on to red snapper with rice and beans or plantains stuffed with seafood. This place, in an unmistakable orange building on the main drag, is casual and friendly. ✉*Calle 3* ☎*787/254–2553* ▭*AE, MC, V* ⊙*Closed Mon.–Wed.*

¢–$ ✕**Los Chapines.** This rustic seaside shack—painted, like Annie's, a vivid shade of orange—sells a variety of fish and chicken dishes. Be sure to try one of the specialty sandwiches, which are made with deep-fried plantains instead of bread. (Our favorite was conch, but several locals swore by the octopus.) The dinky deck in back is a perfect place to catch the breeze. ✉*Calle 3* ☎*787/254–4005* ▭*MC, V.*

WHERE TO STAY

$$ ★ **Bahía Salinas Beach Hotel.** The Cabo Rojo Lighthouse is this resort's closest neighbor. You can wander along the boardwalk or down the garden paths, bask in the sun on a deck or terrace, or relax in the beachfront pool. Another option is the spa, which offers a wide range of massages and other treatments. The hotel's pair of restaurants serve freshly caught seafood. The guest rooms are spacious and have nice wood furnishings. Note that on weekends a two-night stay is required. **Pros:** Near interesting sites, good dining options. **Cons:** Beach at hotel is extremely narrow, staff often seems overworked. ✉*End of Rte. 301* *Box 2356, El Combate 00622* ☎*787/254–1212 or 877/205–7507* *www.bahiasalinas.com* *22 rooms* *In-room: no phone. In-hotel: restaurant, bar, pool, gym, spa, no elevator* ▭*MC, V* *BP.*

¢ **Combate Beach Hotel.** On a quiet side street, this little hotel puts you within walking distance of the main drag. It's not right on the beach, but the second-floor rooms all have views of the water through the palm trees. The downstairs restaurant serves seafood, including tasty *mofongo.* **Pros:** Good value, quiet neighborhood. **Cons:** Not much atmosphere, isolated location. ✉*Rte. 3301* *Box 1138, El Combate 00622* ☎*787/254–2358* *20 rooms* *In-room: no phone, refrigerator. In-hotel: restaurant, bar, pool, no elevator* ▭*MC, V* *EP.*

NIGHTLIFE

Check in at **Tropicoro Sports Bar** (✉*Calle 3* ☎*787/254–2466*), a lively spot with billiard tables, to see whether there's a band playing.

5

THE NORTHWESTERN COAST

North of Rincón you'll find a string of beaches that have yet to be discovered. You won't find much large-scale development along this stretch of shoreline. Instead, the area is populated with modest hotels that cater to local families. Many surfers say the waves here are better than those in Rincón itself.

WORD OF MOUTH

"I lived for three years in Rincón, and as far as surfing I would recommend Wilderness Beach in Aguadilla. Take note, though, it is for advanced surfers. I have seen Wilderness go off at 40-foot ground swells before." –caribedon

AGUADILLA

18 km (12 mi) north of Rincón.

Resembling a fishing village, downtown Aguadilla has narrow streets lined with small wooden homes. Weathered but lovely, the faded facades recall the city's long and turbulent past. Officially incorporated as a town in 1775, Aguadilla subsequently suffered a series of catastrophes, including a devastating earthquake in 1918 and strong hurricanes in 1928 and 1932. Determined to survive, the town rebuilt after each disaster, and by World War II it became known for the sprawling Ramey Air Force Base. The base was an important link in the U.S. defense system throughout the Cold War. Ramey was decommissioned in 1973; today the former base has an airport, a golf course, and some small businesses, although many structures stand empty.

Along Route 107—an unmarked road crossing through a golf course—you'll find the ruins of **La Ponderosa,** an old Spanish lighthouse, as well as its replacement Punta Borinquen at Puerto Rico's northwest point. The original was built in 1889 and destroyed by an earthquake in 1918. The U.S. Coast Guard rebuilt the structure in 1920. ✉ *Rte. 107.*

Parque Acuático las Cascadas has a large wave pool, giant slides, and the "Crazy River," a long, free-flowing river pool. Strictly kid stuff. ✉ *Hwy. 2, Km 126.5* ☎ *787/819–1030* ⏲ *Mar.–Aug., weekdays 10–5, weekends 10–6.*

BEACHES

Fodor's Choice ★ **Playa Crashboat.** This is where you'll find the colorful fishing boats that are portrayed on postcards all over the island. The sand here is soft and sugary, and the water is as smooth as glass. Named after rescue boats used when Ramey Air Force Base was in operation, this *balneario* has picnic huts, showers, parking, and restrooms. There's a modest food stand run by local fishermen where the catch of the day is served with cold beer. ✉ *Off Rte. 458.*

Playa Gas Chamber. This beach with crashing waves is favored by surfers. ✉ *Rte. 107, north of Playa Crashboat.*

Playa Wilderness. This undeveloped beach north of Playa Gas Chamber is recommended only for experienced surfers, as it can have dangerous breaks. ✉*Rte. 107, north of Playa Gas Chamber.*

WHERE TO STAY & EAT

$ **Hotel Cielo Mar.** Just north of the town of Aguadilla, this hotel is perched on a bluff high above the water. The good news is that nearly every room has a jaw-dropping view of the coastline; the bad news is that the beach is far, far away. The accommodations are comfortable, if a bit old-fashioned. The hotel's restaurant, El Bohío ($–$$), specializes in lobster, as well as other types of seafood. The open-air dining room is extremely pleasant, especially in the evening, and it often has live music on weekends. **Pros:** Reasonable rates, great views. **Cons:** No beach, far from other dining options, noise from the game room off the lobby ✉*84 Av. Montemar, off Rte. 111* ☎*787/882–5959 or 787/882–5961* *www.cielomar.com* *72 rooms* *In-room: refrigerator, Ethernet. In-hotel: restaurant, bar, pool, no elevator* *AE, MC, V* *EP.*

5

$ **El Faro.** This family-friendly resort isn't very close to the lighthouse from which it takes its name, or to any of the beaches. But it's a good place to keep in mind if you're driving along the coast and need a place to stop for the night. (Keep a sharp eye out for the PARADOR sign on Route 107, as it's easy to miss.) Cheerfully decorated rooms surround a pair of pools. There are two restaurants on the premises, including the popular Tres Amigos, one of the most highly regarded in the area. Its specialty is steaks and other meats that come sizzling from the grill. **Pros:** Reasonable rates, pretty pool areas. **Cons:** No beach, rather secluded location. ✉*Rte. 107, Km 2.1, Box 5148* ☎*787/882–8000 or 866/321–9191* *www.farohotels.net* *70 rooms, 5 suites* *In-hotel: 2 restaurants, tennis court, pool, laundry facilities, public Wi-Fi, airport shuttle* *AE, D, DC, MC, V* *EP.*

$ **El Pedregal.** Located in what looks like a tropical forest, El Pedregal is a great place to stay on the island's northwestern tip. There's no beach, but several of the best are only a short drive away. In the meantime, the pool can be a refreshing oasis. The rooms, in several two-story buildings, are simple but comfortable. The Spanish-style architecture is a refreshing change in a region where everything looks like it was built in 1970. **Pros:** Family-friendly environment, helpful staff. **Cons:** Noise from nearby housing development, not on beach. ✉*Rte. 111, Km. 0.1* ☎*787/891–6068* *www.hotelelpedregal.com* *29 rooms* *In-hotel: restaurant, bar, pool* *AE, MC, V* *EP.*

$ **JB Hidden Village.** This family-friendly hotel is in Aguada, about halfway between Aguadilla and Rincón. There's plenty here to keep the kids occupied. If you have your heart set on the beach, however, the landlocked location won't be ideal. The modern rooms and suites all have balconies, most of which overlook the sparkling pool. A well-regarded restaurant and bar are on the premises. **Pros:** Close to several beaches, good base for exploring the area. **Cons:** No beach, bland architecture. ✉*Rte. 4416, Km 9.5, Aguada* ☎*787/868–8686* *787/868–8701* *45 rooms* *In-hotel: restaurant, bar, pool* *MC, V* *EP.*

SPORTS & THE OUTDOORS

DIVING & SNORKELING

Near Gate 5 of the old Ramey Air Force Base, **Aquatica** (✉ *Rte. 110, Km 10* ☎ *787/890–6071*) offers scuba-diving certification courses, as well as snorkeling and surfing trips. It also rents bikes.

GOLF

The 18-hole **Punta Borinquen Golf Club** (✉ *Rte. 107, Km 2* ☎ *787/890–2987* 🌐 *www.puntaborinquengolfclub.com*), on the former Ramey Air Force Base, was a favorite of President Dwight D. Eisenhower's. Now a public course, the beachfront course is known for its tough sand traps and strong crosswinds. The course is open daily.

ISABELA

20 km (13 mi) east of Aguadilla.

Founded in 1819 and named for Spain's Queen Isabella, this small, whitewashed town on the northwesternmost part of the island skirts tall cliffs that overlook the rocky shoreline. Locals have long known of the area's natural beauty, and lately more and more offshore tourists have begun coming to this niche, which offers secluded hotels, fantastic beaches, and, just inland, hiking through one of the island's forest reserves.

Explore karst topography and subtropical vegetation at the 2,357-acre **Bosque Estatal Guajataca** *(Guajataca State Forest)* between the towns of Quebradillas and Isabela. On more than 46 walking trails you can see 186 species of trees, including the royal palm and ironwood, and 45 species of birds—watch for red-tailed hawks and Puerto Rican woodpeckers. Bring a flashlight and descend into the **Cueva del Viento** to find stalagmites, stalactites, and other strange formations. At the entrance to the forest there's a small ranger station where you can pick up a decent hiking map. (Get here early, as the rangers don't always stay until the official closing time.) A little farther down the road is a recreational area with picnic tables and an observation tower. ✉ *Rte. 446, Km 10* ☎ *787/872–1045* 🎫 *Free* ⏲ *Ranger station weekdays 8–5.*

OFF THE BEATEN PATH

Palacete Los Moreau. In the fields south of Isabela toward the town of Moca, a French family settled on a coffee and sugar plantation in the 1800s. The grand two-story house, trimmed with gables, columns, and stained-glass windows, was immortalized in the novel *La Llamarada,* written in 1935 by Puerto Rican novelist Enrique A. Laguerre. In Laguerre's novel about conditions in the sugarcane industry, the house belonged to his fictional family, the Moreaus. Although it doesn't have many furnishings, you can walk through the house and also visit Laguerre's personal library in the mansion's basement. On the grounds is an old steam engine once used to transport surgarcane. ✉ *Hwy. 2, Km 115.9* ☎ *787/877–3390* 🎫 *Free* ⏲ *Tues.–Sat. 8–4:30.*

BEACHES

Playa de Guajataca. Stretching by what is called El Tunel—part of an old tunnel used by a passenger and cargo train that ran from San Juan to Ponce from the early to mid-1900s—this beach is lined with kiosks selling local snacks and souvenirs. On weekends you'll hear live music

CLOSE UP

The Abominable Chupacabra

The Himalayas have their Yeti, Britain has its crop circles, New Jersey has its legendary Jersey Devil . . . and Puerto Rico has its Chupacabra. This "goat sucker" (as its name translates) has been credited with strange attacks on goats, sheep, rabbits, horses, and chickens since the mid-1970s. The attacks happen mostly at night, leaving the animals devoid of blood, with oddly vampirelike punctures in their necks.

Though the first references to these attacks were in the 1970s, the biggest surge of reports dates to the mid-1990s, when the mayor of Canóvanas received international attention and support from local police for his weekly search parties equipped with a caged goat as bait. The police stopped short of fulfilling the mayor's request for a special unit devoted to the creature's capture.

Sightings offer widely differing versions of the Chupacabra; it has gray, scraggly hair and resembles a kangaroo or wolf, or walks upright on three-toed feet. Some swear it hops from tree branch to tree branch, and even flies, leaving behind, in the tradition of old Lucifer, the acrid stench of sulphur. It peers through large, oval, sometimes red eyes, and "smells like a wet dog" as its reptilian tongue flicks the night air. It has, according to some, attacked humans, ripped through window screens, and jumped family dogs at picnics.

According to a 1995 article in the *San Juan Star,* island lore abounds with monsters predating the Chupacabra. The *comecogollo* was a version of bigfoot—but smaller and a vegetarian. It was particularly sweet on *cogollo,* a baby plantain that springs up near its parent plant. In the early 1970s the Moca vampire also attacked small animals, but opinion differed on whether it was alien, animal, or really a vampire. The *garadiablo,* a swamp creature that emerged from the ooze at night to wreak havoc on the populace also struck fear in the early 1970s. This "sea demon" was described as having the face of a bat, the skin of a shark, and a humanlike body.

The Chupacabra has also been active in other spots with large Hispanic communities—Mexico, southern Texas, and Miami—and its scope is pretty wide. The list of reported sightings at 🌐 *www.elchupacabra.com* includes such unlikely locales as Maine and Missouri. And the Chupa's coverage on the Web isn't limited to sci-fi fan sites: Princeton University maintains a Web site meant to be a clearinghouse for Chupa information.

What to make of Chupa? Above the clamor of the fringe elements, one hears the more skeptical voice of reason. Zoologists have suggested that the alleged condition of some Chupacabra victims may actually be the result of exaggerated retelling of the work of less mysterious animals, such as a tropical species of bat known to feed on the blood of small mammals. Even some bird species are known to eat warm-blooded animals. Skeletal remains of an alleged Chupacabra found in Chile were determined to be those of a wild dog. This, however, doesn't explain the sightings of the hairy, ravenous beast. Then again, there's no accounting for the Loch Ness monster either.

–Karl Luntta

playing around the area. Just before El Tunel is El Merendero de Guajataca, a picnic area with cliffside trails that have a spectacular view of the coastline. ✉ *Off Rte. 113.*

> **WORD OF MOUTH**
>
> "I love [Isabela]. It is quiet, very nicely kept. The beach has quite a strong current (this is a surfing area), but it is great to walk and lay around. There is a great swimming beach a few minutes away."
>
> –marigross

Playa de Jobos. This beach is famous for surfing, but it can have dangerous breaks. On the same stretch there are a couple of restaurants with oceanfront decks serving light fare and drinks. Down the road, the dunes and long stretches of golden sand are gorgeous for walks or running. Route 466 runs parallel, and there are narrow accesses to the beach scattered all along the road. ✉ *Rte. 466.*

Playa Montones. Not far from Playa de Jobos on Route 466, this is a beautiful beach for swimming and frolicking in the sand; it has a protected natural pool where children can splash safely. An outcropping of coral creates a huge wave spray on the ocean side. ✉ *Rte. 466.*

Playa de Shacks is known for its surfing and horseback riding. It also has an area called the Blue Hole that is popular with divers. ✉ *Rte. 4446.*

WHERE TO EAT

In addition to the restaurant listed below, the restaurants at Villa Montaña and Villas del Mar Hau are known for having good food.

$–$$$ ✕ **Happy Belly's.** If you're in the mood for a hamburger or club sandwich, this laid-back restaurant is a good choice. The seating is in comfortable wooden booths that overlook Playa de Jobos—the wind that whips up the waves may also blow away your napkin. In the evening the menu changes to more substantial fare, including everything from shrimp scampi to baby back ribs. But many people come just to socialize and watch the sunset. ✉ *Rte. 4466, Km 7.5* ☎ *787/872–6566* 💳 *AE, MC, V.*

WHERE TO STAY

$$–$$$ **Villa Montaña.** This secluded cluster of villas, situated on a deserted stretch of beach between Isabela and Aguadilla, feels like a little town. You can pull your car into your own garage, then head upstairs to your airy studio or one-, two-, or three-bedroom suite with hand-carved mahogany furniture and canopy beds. Studios have kitchenettes, while the larger suites have full-size kitchens and laundry rooms. Eclipse, the open-air bar and restaurant, serves Caribbean-Asian fusion cuisine. Playa de Shacks, a very popular surfer beach, is nearby. **Pros:** An away-from-it-all feel, on a secluded beach, great food. **Cons:** A bit pricey, far from other dining options. ✉ *Rte. 466, Km 1.9, Box 530,Isabela* ☎ *787/872–9554 or 888/780–9195* 🌐 *www.villamontana.com* *38 rooms, 41 apartments* *In-room: DVD. In-hotel: restaurant, tennis courts, pools, gym, laundry facilities* 💳 *AE, D, MC, V* *EP.*

$$ **Villas de Costa Dorada.** Painted cheerful shades of pink, blue, and yellow, this cluster of buildings certainly gets your attention. The studios

and one- and two-bedroom apartments, all with spacious balconies overlooking the ocean, have a homey feel. The complex has a pool and hot tub, but shares most of its facilities with the older hotel next door. **Pros:** Large accommodations, shared amenities with neighboring hotel. **Cons:** Cookie-cutter buildings, some unfortunate fabric selections. ✉ *Rte. 466, Km 0.1* ☎ *787/830–0303 or 800/981–5693* 🌐 *www.costadoradabeach.com/villas.html* *24 rooms* *In-hotel: restaurant, room service, bar, tennis courts, pools* *AE, MC, V* *EP.*

$–$$ ★ **Villas del Mar Hau.** One-, two-, and three-bedroom cottages—painted in cheery pastels and trimmed with gingerbread—are the heart of this beachfront resort. The accommodations aren't luxurious, but if you're looking for an unpretentious atmosphere, you'll have a hard time doing better. If you are planning on cooking, you should consider one of the studios, all of which have full kitchens. The open-air restaurant Olas y Arena is known for its excellent fish and shellfish; the paella is especially good. The hotel also has a stable of horses reserved for guests. **Pros:** Laid-back vibe, calm beach, good restaurant. **Cons:** Very basic rooms, may be too kitschy for some. ✉ *Rte. 466, Km 8.9, Box 510* ☎ *787/872–2045 or 787/872–2627* 🌐 *www.hauhotelvillas.com* *40 cottages* *In-room: kitchen (some). In-hotel: restaurant, tennis court, pool, laundry facilities* *AE, MC, V* *EP.*

5

$ **Pelican Reef.** This is one of the best deals on the coast: studio and one-bedroom apartments for less than you'd pay for a cramped hotel room. The five studios are almost as big as the seven one-bedroom apartments, making them a slightly better value. What they lack, however, are the private balconies overlooking beautiful Playa de Jobos. All have full kitchens and dining areas, and there are plenty of restaurants within walking distance. **Pros:** Great location, good value. **Cons:** Some traffic noise, musty smell in a few of the units. ✉ *Rte. 4466, Km 0* ☎ *787/866–9818* 🌐 *www.pelicanreefapartments.com* *12 apartments* *In-room: kitchen. In-hotel: beachfront* *AE, MC, V* *EP.*

SPORTS & THE OUTDOORS

HORSEBACK RIDING

Tropical Trail Rides (✉ *Rte. 4466, Km 1.9* ☎ *787/872–9256* 🌐 *www.tropicaltrailrides.com*) has two-hour morning and afternoon rides along the beach and through a forest of almond trees. Groups leave from Playa de Shacks, one of the region's prettiest beaches. At the end you—and your horse—have a chance to take a dip.

DIVING & SNORKELING

Beginning and advanced divers can explore the submerged caves off Playa de Shacks through **La Cueva Submarina Dive Shop** (✉ *Rte. 466, Km 6.3* ☎ *787/872–1390* 🌐 *www.cuevasubmarina.com*), which also offers certification courses and snorkeling trips.

SURFING

You won't find a friendlier group of people than at **Alamar Surf School** (✉ *Rte. 4466, Km 7.5* ☎ *787/379–1990*), which is so close to Playa de Jobos that you can hear the surfers hooting and hollering as they ride the waves. Surf lessons are an affordable $50 an hour. If all you need is a board, it is only $20 for three hours. Afterward, head back to the shop for a fresh fruit smoothie.

RINCÓN & THE PORTA DEL SOL ESSENTIALS

To research prices, get advice from other travelers, and book travel arrangements, visit www.fodors.com.

TRANSPORTATION

BY AIR

Aguadilla is a convenient gateway to western Puerto Rico, thanks to several daily international flights. Continental Airlines flies from Newark to Aguadilla, and JetBlue has daily service from Orlando or New York–JFK to Aguadilla. American Eagle and Cape Air fly between San Juan and Mayagüez.

Information **American Eagle** (☎ *787/749–1747* 🌐 *www.aa.com*). **Cape Air** (☎ *800/525–0280* 🌐 *www.flycapeair.com*). **Continental** (☎ *800/433–7300* 🌐 *www.continental.com*). **JetBlue** (☎ *800/538–2583* 🌐 *www.jetblue.com*).

AIRPORTS & TRANSFERS Aguadilla's Aeropuerto Internacional Rafael Hernández (BQN) is on the old Ramey Air Force Base. The renovated structure, as modern as any on the island, has a tourist information office, car-rental agencies, and a handy ATM. Tiny Aeropuerto Eugenio María de Hostos (MAZ), just north of Mayagüez on Highway 2, looks a bit like a strip mall. There's little inside besides the car-rental counters and an ATM machine. There are no airport shuttles in either Aguadilla or Mayagüez. A taxi from either airport into town is about $6 to $10, but if you are going any farther, you should rent a car.

Information **Aeropuerto Eugenio María de Hostos** (✉ *Hwy. 2, Km 148.7, Mayagüez* ☎ *787/833–0148 or 787/265–7065*). **Aeropuerto Internacional Rafael Hernández** (✉ *Hwy. 2, Km 148.7, Aguadilla* ☎ *787/891–2286*).

BY BOAT & FERRY

Ferry service, by Ferries del Caribe, shuttles between Mayagüez and Santo Domingo. Trips are overnight leaving at 8 PM and arriving at 8 AM. Small cabins with sleeping accommodations for two, three, and four persons are provided. Tickets are usually available, but reserve well in advance if you're bringing your car. Ships leave from the Zona Portuaria, past the Holiday Inn on Route 2.

Information **Ferry Reservations** (☎ *787/832–4800* 🌐 *www.ferriesdelcaribe.com*).

BY BUS & VAN

No easy network of buses links the towns in the Porta del Sol region of northwestern Puerto Rico. Some municipalities and private companies operate buses and large shared vans *(públicos)* that travel from one city to another, but schedules are loose. It's not wise to count on them as your primary means of transportation. That said, if you're adventurous and not easily frustrated, it's possible to arrange for cheap transportation from San Juan to Aguadilla, Rincón, and Mayagüez, among other towns. Prices from terminal to terminal are set, but drivers may go to another destination if arranged beforehand.

Choferes Unidos travels from San Juan to Aguadilla for about $10 per person. Linea Sultana has vans from San Juan to Mayagüez that also drop off passengers along Highway 2 in Aguada, Quebradillas, and Isabela; the price is about $12 per person. Línea Caborrojeña travels between San Juan and Cabo Rojo.

Information **Choferes Unidos** (☎ *787/751-7622*). **Linea Sultana** (☎ *787/765-9377*). **Línea Caborrojeña** (☎ *787/723-9155*).

BY CAR

You really need a car to see northwestern Puerto Rico, especially the mountain area. The toll road, Highway 22, makes it easy to reach Arecibo from San Juan. Highway 22 turns into Highway 2 just after Arecibo, swings by the northwestern tip of the island, then heads south to Mayagüez.

If you are not flying into San Juan, you can rent a car in Aguadilla or Mayagüez. Prices vary from $35 to $65 per day.

Information **Avis** (☎ *787/890-3311 in Aguadilla, 787/832-0406 in Mayagüez*). **Budget** (☎ *787/890-1110 in Aguadilla, 787/823-4570 in Mayagüez*). **Hertz** (☎ *787/890-5650 in Aguadilla, 787/832-3314 in Mayagüez*). **L & M Rent a Car** (☎ *787/890-3010 in Aguadilla*). **Leaseway of Puerto Rico** (☎ *787/833-1140 in Mayagüez*). **Thrifty** (☎ *787/834-1590 in Mayagüez*).

GASOLINE Prices are measured in liters instead of gallons and are not terribly different from those in the United States. The chain gas stations, Esso and Shell, are open 24 hours. Locally owned stations in small towns generally close before 6 PM.

PARKING Parking is usually available on the street, though downtown Mayagüez can become congested, especially in the historic district, where streets are narrower. At tourist or commercial sites, parking is normally provided.

ROAD CONDITIONS The major highways throughout the northwest region, Highways 22 and 2, are well maintained. The Ruta Panorámica throughout the central mountains is also in good condition and has amazing vistas, but its twists and turns should be driven with caution. Road signs in the mountains may be missing—some have been blown down by storms or hurricanes and have yet to be replaced.

BY TAXI

Taxis can be hailed near the main plaza in Mayagüez, but in the smaller towns they may be hard to come by. Check with your hotel or restaurant, and they may be able to call one for you. In Mayagüez, White Taxi is reliable and charges flat rates—no meters—by location. Fares to or from San Juan are steep: for example, service is $120 from Mayagüez.

Information **Arecibo Taxi Cab** (☎ *787/878-2929*).

CONTACTS & RESOURCES

BANKS & EXCHANGE SERVICES

Banks are plentiful in larger cities, and smaller towns usually have at least one; they are occasionally attached to grocery stores. All banks have ATMs (called ATHs), and many businesses accept ATM cards. If you need to change money into U.S. dollars, you can do so in banks in Aguadilla or Mayagüez.

Information **Banco Popular** (*✉ Calle Mercedes Moreno, corner of Muñoz Rivera, Aguadilla ☎ 787/891–2085 ✉ Mayagüez Mall, Hwy. 2, Km 159.4, Mayagüez ☎ 787/834–4750 ✉ 13 Av. Agustín Ramos Calero, Isabela ☎ 787/872–3100 ✉ 1 Calle Commercio, Rincón ☎ 787/823–2055*).

EMERGENCIES

Contacts **General emergencies** (*☎ 911*).

Hospitals **General Hospital Dr. Ramón Emeterio Betances** (*✉ Hwy. 2, Km 157, Mayagüez ☎ 787/834–8686*). **Hospital Bellavista** (*✉ Rte. 349, Km 2.7, Mayagüez ☎ 787/831–2048*). **Hospital Subregional Dr. Pedro J. Zamora** (*✉ Hwy. 2, Km 141.1, Aguadilla ☎ 787/791–3000*).

24-hour Pharmacies **Walgreens** (*✉ Hwy. 2, Km 129.7, Aguadilla ☎ 787/882–8005 ✉ Mayagüez Mall, Hwy. 2, Km 159.4, Mayagüez ☎ 787/831–9249 ✉ Plaza Universitaria, Mayagüez ☎ 787/805–4005*).

INTERNET, MAIL & SHIPPING

Getting connected is a bit difficult in this part of the island. We didn't run across a single Internet café, and most lodgings don't have any online access. If you're desperate, sit in the restaurant or the lobby of one of the larger hotels with wireless connections.

Larger towns like Arecibo and Mayagüez have a main post office with smaller branches throughout the city. You can often buy stamps in grocery and drug stores. Generally, post offices are open weekdays from 7 or 8 AM until 5 or 6 PM and for a few hours Saturday morning.

Post Offices **Cabo Rojo Post Office** (*✉ 64 Calle Carbonell, Cabo Rojo ☎ 787/851–1095*). **Mayagüez Main Office** (*✉ 60 Calle McKinley W, Mayagüez ☎ 787/265–3138*). **Rincón Main Office** (*✉ 100 Rte. 115, Rincón ☎ 787/823–2625*).

OVERNIGHT SERVICES

Express Mail, overnight, and two-day service is available at all main post offices. FedEx has offices in Aguadilla at the Borinquen Airport (Hangar 404) and in Arecibo (Rte. 10, Km 83.2). There are drop boxes at the Holiday Inn Mayagüez and the Mayagüez Resort & Casino. UPS has a branch in Mayagüez at Airport El Maní, which closes at 5 PM.

Information **FedEx** (*☎ 877/838–7834*). **UPS** (*☎ 800/742–5877 or 787/253–2877*).

SAFETY

Unless you're camping in a recreational area, it's best to go to forest reserves during daylight hours only. Outside metro areas there's little crime, but you should take normal precautions: remember to lock your car and don't leave valuables unattended.

TOUR OPTIONS

The Mayagüez-based AdvenTours offers bird-watching, biking, and kayaking trips.

Information **AdvenTours** (✉ *17 Calle Uroyán, Mayagüez* ☎ *787/831-6447* 🌐 *www.adventourspr.com*).

VISITOR INFORMATION

The Puerto Rico Tourism Company has an office at the Rafael Hernández Airport in Aguadilla. The Cabo Rojo branch is open Monday through Saturday from 8 to 4:30. The town of Rincón has a tourism office on Route 115; it's open weekdays from 9 to 4. Mayagüez has a tourism office in city hall.

Information **Mayagüez City Hall** (✉ *8 McKinley St., Mayagüez* ☎ *787/834-8585*). **Puerto Rico Tourism Company** (✉ *Rafael Hernández Airport, Aguadilla* ☎ *787/890-3315*). **Rincón Tourism Office** (✉ *Rte. 115, Rincón* ☎ *787/823-5024*).

The Cordillera Central

6

WORD OF MOUTH

"If you want a nice beach; check out Playa [Cerro] Gordo. It's very close to Hyatt [Hacienda del Mar]. [It has l]ocal flavor, w/lots of Puerto Rican food, beer, fries, etc. The people are great."

–EJC

www.fodors.com/forums

Revised and Updated by Mark Sullivan

THERE'S MORE TO PUERTO RICO than beautiful beaches, as anyone who lives on the island will tell you. When islanders want to escape the heat, they head to the Cordillera Central. This mountain range, which runs most of the length of the island, seems impossibly lush. Towering trees lean over the narrow roadways that crisscross the region, often brushing branches with those across the pavement. In the shade below, impatiens in shades of pink and purple bloom in profusion.

Agriculture is very important to the economy of the Cordillera Central. Bananas, pineapples, and plantains are grown throughout the region. Coffee was once a dominant crop along hillsides between Utuado and Maricao, and it can still be seen growing in small plots today. A few of the old plantation homes have been turned into quaint country inns, all of them stocked with plenty of blankets for cool evenings, when temperatures—especially in higher elevations—can drop into the 40s.

In the east you'll find several attractive colonial towns, such as Aibonito and Barranquitas. Farther west is karst country—terrain built up by limestone deposits in which erosion has produced fissures, sinkholes, and underground streams and rivers. The peaks above are often astounding. It's in the Bosque Estatal de Toro Negro that the island's highest peak, Cerro de Punta, rises 4,398 feet above sea level. It may not measure up to many around the world, but on this island it seems as tall as Mount Everest.

Visitors to the Cordillera Central often arrive via the island's northern coast. There's little to keep you in Arecibo, but the dusty little town makes a perfect gateway to such unmissable attractions as the Observatorio de Arecibo and Parque de las Cavernas del Río Camuy. And if you want your trip to combine hiking in the mountains with walking on the beach, you couldn't do better than to stop in the cozy coastal town of Dorado.

EXPLORING THE NORTHERN COAST & CORDILLERA CENTRAL

The speedy Highway 22 and the more meandering Highway 2 head west from San Juan and swing around the northwestern part of the island, skirting the beaches of the northern coast. Only 45 minutes from the capital are the resort town of Dorado and, shortly thereafter, Arecibo. From the north, Route 10 speeds you from Arecibo to the mountain town of Utuado and the Cordillera Central, at an elevation of 3,000 feet.

If you want to get anywhere else in the Cordillera Central, you're going to have to take the narrow roads that traverse the rugged mountain range. Driving here takes patience; some roads aren't clearly marked, and others twist and turn for what seems an eternity. Towns such as Aibonito and Barranquitas can be reached on these twisting roads between Highway 10 and Highway 52, the other main route down from San Juan.

CORDILLERA CENTRAL TOP 5

- Hiking in the Bosque Estatal de Toro Negro, home to the island's highest lake and tallest mountain.
- Feasting on roasted suckling pig at one of the roadside *lechoneras* near Cayey.
- Reliving scenes from the movie *Contact* at the Observatorio de Arecibo, the world's largest radar-radio telescope.
- Bird-watching in the Bosque Estatal de Maricao, where you can see more species than anywhere else on the island.
- Looking for blue-eyed river crabs and long-legged tarantulas in the Parque de las Cavernas del Río Camuy.

The Ruta Panorámica, which runs horizontally across the island, passes through this area. The grandiose name may lead you to think that the Ruta Panorámica is a highway. Don't be fooled. It's a network of mountain roads that snakes through the region. Some are nicely maintained, others are little more than gravel. But the Panoramic Route does live up to its name, providing eye-catching vistas around every bend of the road.

ABOUT THE RESTAURANTS

Traditional Puerto Rican cooking is the norm in this part of the island. But that's not to say you won't find anything memorable. Along Route 184, look for restaurants serving slow-roasted *lechón* (suckling pig), a local delicacy cooked outdoors over coals.

WHAT IT COSTS IN U.S. DOLLARS

	$$$$	$$$	$$	$	¢
AT DINNER	over $30	$20–$30	$12–$20	$8–$12	under $8
FOR 2 PEOPLE	over $350	$250–$350	$150–$250	$80–$150	under $80

Prices are per person for a main course at dinner.

Prices are for a double room in high season, excluding 9% tax (11% for hotels with casinos, 7% for paradores) and 5%–12% service charge.

ABOUT THE HOTELS

In this part of the island there are seldom more than two or three options in any given town. Sometimes there's one hotel—take it or leave it. You'd better take it, especially if you're traveling on a weekend. The best lodgings, rustic retreats set beside a river or on acres of lush forest, are often booked solid. Make sure to call ahead, as it's a long way between towns.

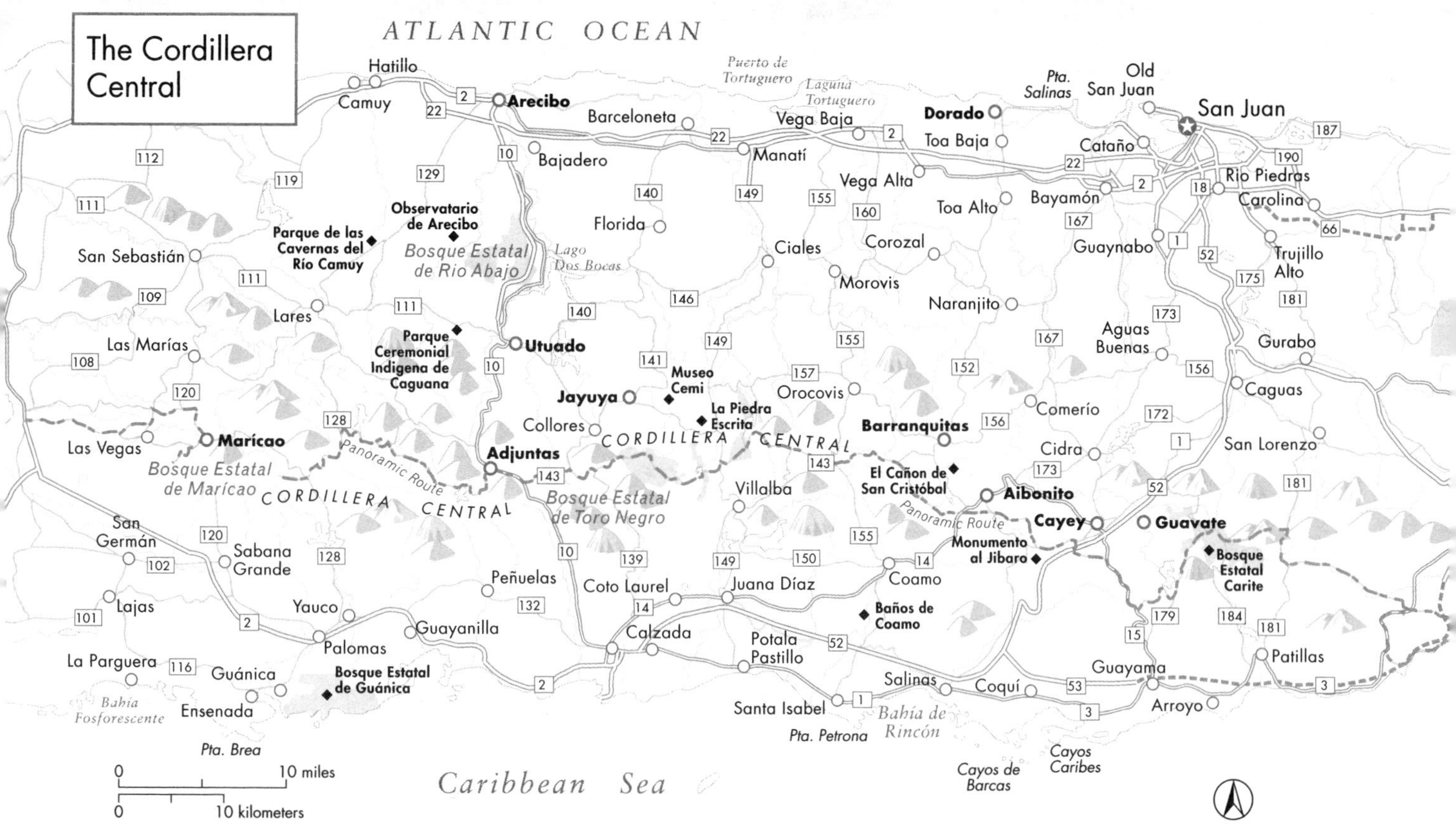
The Cordillera Central
ATLANTIC OCEAN
Caribbean Sea
Hatillo
Camuy
Arecibo
Barceloneta
Puerto de Tortuguero
Laguna Tortuguero
Vega Baja
Dorado
Pta. Salinas
Old San Juan
San Juan
Toa Baja
Cataño
Bajadero
Manatí
Vega Alta
Río Piedras
Carolina
Toa Alto
Bayamón
Guaynabo
Trujillo Alto
Observatorio de Arecibo
Parque de las Cavernas del Río Camuy
Bosque Estatal de Río Abajo
Lago Dos Bocas
Florida
Ciales
Corozal
Morovis
Naranjito
San Sebastián
Lares
Las Marías
Parque Ceremonial Indigena de Caguana
Utuado
Aguas Buenas
Gurabo
Caguas
Museo Cemi
Jayuya
La Piedra Escrita
Orocovis
Comerío
Collores
Barranquitas
San Lorenzo
Cidra
Las Vegas
Maricao
Bosque Estatal de Maricao
Adjuntas
CORDILLERA CENTRAL
Panoramic Route
El Cañon de San Cristóbal
Villalba
Bosque Estatal de Toro Negro
Aibonito
Cayey
Guavate
Bosque Estatal Carite
Monumento al Jibaro
San Germán
Sabana Grande
Peñuelas
Coto Laurel
Juana Díaz
Coamo
Baños de Coamo
Lajas
Yauco
Guayanilla
Calzada
Potala Pastillo
Palomas
La Parguera
Guánica
Bosque Estatal de Guánica
Ensenada
Bahía Fosforescente
Pta. Brea
Santa Isabel
Pta. Petrona
Salinas
Bahía de Rincón
Coquí
Guayama
Patillas
Arroyo
Cayos de Barcas
Cayos Caribes
0
10 miles
0
10 kilometers

TIMING

The temperate climate of the mountainous central zone makes it a pleasure to visit year-round. Locals especially like to head up to this area in summer, when Aibonito holds its Flower Festival (late June or July) and Barranquitas hosts its Artisans Fair (July). The weather gets hot in August and September, but the north-coast beaches help everyone stay cool. Note that during busy times some hotels require a minimum two- or three-night stay on weekends.

THE NORTH COAST

West of San Juan, large tracts of coconut palms silhouette Dorado and its environs, the scenic remnants of large coconut and fruit plantations. Farther west, near Arecibo, the island's limestone karst country is distinguished by haystack-shaped hills (called *mogotes* by locals) and underground rivers and caves. One of the island's most fascinating geological wonders is the Río Camuy cave system, one of the largest such systems in the Western Hemisphere. Nearby, science takes center stage at the Arecibo Observatory, the largest radar–radio telescope in the world.

DORADO

27 km (17 mi) west of San Juan.

This small and tidy town has a definite festive air about it, even though more and more it's turning into a suburb for San Juan's workers. It's one of the oldest vacation spots on the island, having gotten a boost in 1955 when Laurance Rockefeller bought the pineapple, coconut, and grapefruit plantation of Dr. Alfred Livingston and his daughter Clara, and built a resort on the property. Sadly, the Hyatt Dorado Beach Resort & Country Club closed in May 2005. But its excellent golf courses—among the best-known in Puerto Rico—are still open. The town of Dorado itself is fun to visit; its winding road leads across a bridge to a main square, with small bars, restaurants, and shops nearby. Most visitors, however, don't stray too far from the beach.

BEACHES

Playa Breñas. The exceptional stretch of beachfront near the Hyatt resort is known for its surfing; adventurous swimmers also enjoy the waves. ⊠*Rte. 693, Km 10.8.*

Playa Cerro Gordo. The 2,500-foot-long beach at the end of Route 690 is lined with cliffs. It's very popular and can get crowded on weekends. ⊠*At the end Rte. 690.*

Playa Los Tubos. This beach is popular for both swimming and surfing. It holds a summer festival with live music and water-sports competitions, normally the first week of July. ⊠*Rte. 687, Vega Baja.*

Playa Sardinera. This Dorado beach is suitable for swimming and has shade trees, changing rooms, and restrooms. ⊠*At the end of Rte. 697.*

GREAT ITINERARIES

IF YOU HAVE 1 DAY

If you feel like escaping from San Juan for a day, head to one of the resorts in **Dorado.** Because so many *sanjuaneros* do just that, this pretty little town has some good restaurants.

IF YOU HAVE 2 DAYS

If you have another day, you can still make your home base by the lovely Dorado beaches. If you tire of beach-bumming and feel like having a feast, head to **Guavate.** Along Route 184 you will find a string of open-air eateries serving suckling pig. On weekends the roads are jammed with people from San Juan and Ponce sampling the Puerto Rican version of comfort food. To burn off a few calories, you might go for a stroll in the 7,000-acre Bosque Estatal Carite. If you're spending the night, head to **Aibonito** or **Barranquitas.**

IF YOU HAVE 3 DAYS

Set up base camp at one of the converted coffee plantations near **Utuado.** Make sure to explore the area's sights, such as Parque Ceremonial Indígena de Caguana. If it's a weekend, take a boat ride across Lago Dos Bocas. On Day 2 explore the trails that crisscross Bosque Estatal de Toro Negro, a state forest near **Jayuya.** On Day 3 head to **Maricao,** where you'll find the spectacular Bosque Estatal de Maricao. This state forest is one of the island's most important bird-watching destinations.

WHERE TO EAT

$$$–$$$$ ✕ **El Ladrillo.** This cozy spot covers its brick walls (*ladrillo* means "brick") from floor to ceiling with original paintings. Many of the dishes on the menu are Spanish, which might account for the numerous portraits of Don Quixote. There's a wide selection of seafood—try the *zarzuela,* a combination of lobster, squid, octopus, and clams. Lobster is a specialty, and you can order it *a la criolla* (in a spicy stew), *a la parrilla* (from the grill), or *ajillo* (with a garlic sauce). The steaks are also good, especially the filet mignon. The red-jacketed waiters really know their stuff. ✉ *Calle Méndez Vigo 334* ☎ *787/796–2120* ▭ *AE, MC, V.*

WHERE TO STAY

$$$ **Hyatt Hacienda del Mar.** Formerly called the Hyatt Regency Cerromar, this well-known property has been converted into a vacation club with studio, one- and two-bedroom condos. Don't worry, you can still arrange to stay in one of these brightly colored rooms for about what you'd pay at another nearby hotel. On the plus side, you may feel like you have the place to yourself; on the other hand, it sometimes feels deserted. The beach here is gorgeous, the lazy river pool is one of the loveliest on the island, and the legendary East and West golf courses have hosted many a tournament. There are two on-site restaurants, the poolside Bohio Bar & Grill and the more formal Zen Garden. **Pros:** Lots of peace and quiet, beachfront setting, great golf. **Cons:** A bit too isolated, need to drive to other dining options. ✉ *301 Rte. 693* ☎ *787/796–3000* 🌐 *hyatthaciendadelmar.hyatt.com* *64 rooms*

In-room: safe, refrigerator, kitchens (some), dial-up, Wi-Fi. In-hotel: restaurant, pool AE, D, MC, V EP.

$$–$$$ **Embassy Suites Dorado del Mar Beach & Golf Resort.** Kids love the free-form pool that shimmers in the courtyard of this beachfront resort. All the suites have separate bedrooms and living rooms but are otherwise uninteresting. Golfers can take in the mountains and the sea at the same time while playing a course designed by the legendary Chi Chi Rodríguez. The Paradise Café serves Caribbean favorites such as crusted sea bass with mango butter. **Pros:** On a gorgeous beach, family-friendly environment. **Cons:** Chain-hotel feel, noisy common areas, parking lot is crowded and has confusing signs. *201 Dorado del Mar Blvd. 787/796–6125 www.embassysuitesdorado.com 174 suites, 35 condos In-room: kitchen, Wi-Fi. In-hotel: 2 restaurants, room service, bar, golf course, tennis courts, pool, gym, laundry facilities, laundry service, no elevator AE, D, DC, MC, V BP.*

SPORTS & THE OUTDOORS

GOLF ★ Originally sketched out by Robert Trent Jones, Sr., the four 18-hole golf courses at the **Hyatt Hacienda del Mar** (*301 Rte. 693 787/796–1234*) are looking better than ever. Six new holes and six redesigned holes mean that the **Pineapple** and the **Sugar Cane** courses feel completely different. Jack Nicklaus has said that the 4th hole at the **East Course** is one of the top-10 holes in the world. The **West Course,** buffeted by constant breezes off the Atlantic, is tough to negotiate. All golfers can use the Plantation Club, a 45,000-square-foot pro shop.

The 7,100-yard **Dorado del Mar** (*Rte. 693, west of Dorado city center 787/796–3065*) is a Chi Chi Rodríguez signature course with narrow fairways that can be a challenge to hit when the wind picks up.

SHOPPING

About 20 minutes from Dorado via Highway 22 at Exit 55 is Puerto Rico's first factory outlet mall. **Prime Outlets Puerto Rico** (*Hwy. 2, Km 54.8, Barceloneta 787/846–9011*) is a pastel village of more than 40 stores selling discounted merchandise from such familiar names as Liz Claiborne, Polo, Calvin Klein, Brooks Brothers, the Gap, Reebok, and Tommy Hilfiger.

ARECIBO

60 km (38 mi) west of Dorado.

As you approach Arecibo on Highway 22, you see its white buildings glistening in the sun against an ocean backdrop. The town was founded in 1515 and is known as the "Villa of Captain Correa" because of a battle fought here by Captain Antonio Correa and a handful of Spanish soldiers to repel a British sea invasion in 1702. Today it's a busy manufacturing center, and serves as a link for visits to two of the island's most fascinating sights—the Parque de las Cavernas del Río Camuy and the Observatorio de Arecibo, both south of the city—and for deeper exploration of the central mountain region. For one of the best ocean drives on the island, get off the main road at Barceloneta and take Route 681 through Arecibo's waterfront district.

A beautiful example of Spanish colonial architecture, the **Faro de Arecibo** *(Arecibo Lighthouse)* is among the loveliest on the island. Dating from 1897, it sits on a bluff high above Arecibo. Although the museum inside the lighthouse has maritime treasure that will interest everyone in your group, the rest of the park is strictly kid stuff. There are scaled-down replicas of Christopher Columbus's *Niña,Pinta,* and *Santa María* and replicas of the huts used by the island's original inhabitants, the Taíno Indians. On weekends, groups in traditional costumes play live music; you can watch the revelry from the sitting area of the café. Follow the signs from Highway 2. ✉*End of Rte. 655, off Rte. 681* ☎*787/817–1936* *$9* *Weekdays 9–6, weekends 10–7.*

Fodor's Choice ★ Hidden among pine-covered hills is the **Observatorio de Arecibo,** the world's largest radar–radio telescope. Operated by the National Astronomy and Ionosphere Center of Cornell University, the 20-acre dish lies in a 563-foot-deep sinkhole in the karst landscape. If the 600-ton platform hovering eerily over the dish looks familiar, it may be because it can be glimpsed in scenes from the movie *Contact.* (And yes, the dish has been used to search for extraterrestrial life.) You can walk around the viewing platform and explore two levels of interactive exhibits on planetary systems, meteors, and weather phenomena in the visitor center. ✉*Rte. 625, Km 3.0* ☎*787/878–2612* *www.naic.edu* *$5* *June–July and mid-Dec.–mid-Jan., daily 9–4; mid-Jan.–May and Aug.–mid-Dec., Wed.–Fri. noon–4, weekends 9–4.*

Fodor's Choice ★ The 268-acre **Parque de las Cavernas del Río Camuy** contains one of the world's largest cave networks. A tram takes you down a trail shaded by bamboo and banana trees to Cueva Clara, where the stalactites and stalagmites turn the entrance into a toothy grin. Hour-long guided tours in English and Spanish lead you on foot through the 180-foot-high cave, which is teeming with wildlife. You're likely to see blue-eyed river crabs and long-legged tarantulas. More elusive are the more than 100,000 bats that make their home in the cave. They don't come out until dark, but you can feel the heat they generate at the cave's entrance. The visit ends with a tram ride to Tres Pueblos sinkhole, where you can see the third-longest underground river in the world passing from one cave to another. Tours are first-come, first-served; plan to arrive early on weekends, when local families join the crowds. Tours are sometimes canceled if it is raining, as the steep walkways can get slippery. There's a picnic area, cafeteria, and gift shop. ✉*Rte. 129, Km 18.9* ☎*787/898–3100* *$10* *Wed.–Sun. 8–4; last tour at 3:45.*

CAUTION

If it's rainy, call ahead before making the long drive to Parque de las Cavernas del Río Camuy. The caves are sometimes closed during wet weather, when the paths can get slippery.

CLOSE UP

Modern Day Taínos?

Puerto Rico's first inhabitants—today known as *Arcaicos* (Archaics)—appear to have traveled on rafts from Florida around AD 500. These hunter-gatherers lived near the shore and subsisted on fish and fruit. By AD 1000, the Arawak, who came from South America by canoe, were replacing the Arcaicos. The agrarian Taíno (a subgroup of the Arawak) established thatched villages on the island, which they called Boriquén.

In his journal Columbus describes the Taíno as "beautiful and tall, with a gentle, laughing language." Although this language was unwritten, it still echoes in some island place names and in everyday items such as *casabe* (a kind of bread). Many Taíno folktales have also survived, as have some art and artifacts. They were adept at wood, shell, and stone carving, and the small figures they made of people and animals had great significance. Known as *cemí* (or *zemí*), the diminutive statues were believed to have the power to protect villages and families.

Studies suggest that there are still islanders with Taíno genes. In some isolated communities in the mountains of Maricao, around 70% of subjects with dark skin and straight black hair had traces of Amerindian DNA. A study in Mayagüez found that 50% of the subjects had such traces. Although it's been long thought the Taíno died out after their 1493 encounter with Columbus, it's possible the Taíno survived much longer or were more numerous than previously believed.

–Karen English and John Marino

6

WHERE TO EAT

$–$$ ✕ **El Buen Café.** Halfway between Arecibo and Hatillo, this diner is packed with locals, especially on weekends. You can sit at the curvy counter or at one of the cozy booths. A favorite dish on the long menu is *carne mechada* (stuffed pot roast). Breakfast is also served starting at 5 AM. ✉*381 Hwy. 2, Km 84, Hatillo* ☎*787/898–3495* ▭*AE, MC, V.*

WHERE TO STAY

¢ **Hotel Villa Real.** Near the eastern edge of Arecibo, the Hotel Villa Real is a good choice if you're heading to any of the attractions in the mountains or along the coast. It's nothing fancy, but it's one of the few options in the area. The rooms are clean and spacious; for a few dollars more you can get one with a hot tub. The restaurant serves local fare. **Pros:** Only hotel in the area, good value. **Cons:** Very basic furnishings, noise from adjoining rooms. ✉*Hwy. 2, Km 67.2, Box 344, Arecibo* ☎*787/881–4134* *787/881–1992* *40 rooms, 4 villas, 13 apartments* *In-hotel: restaurant, pool, no elevator* ▭*AE, MC, V* *EP.*

THE CORDILLERA CENTRAL

The Cordillera Central is for those who like to get off the well-traveled roads and spend time exploring small towns, rural areas, and unspoiled nature. It's here, in several large forest reserves, that Puerto Rico has its greatest ecotourism potential. The area's natural beauty has attracted people for centuries, including pre-Columbian Indians, who have left behind remnants of earlier civilizations. You can explore these artifacts at the Parque Ceremonial Indígena de Caguana, near Utuado. There are also some forests that rival El Yunque: Bosque Estatal de Toro Negro in Jayuya and Bosque Estatal de Río Abajo in Utuado.

CAUTION

Give yourself plenty of time when navigating the Ruta Panorámica, the so-called Panoramic Route that runs through the Cordillera Central. Almost all parts of the route are marked by hairpin curves and bridges originally built for horsedrawn carts.

UTUADO

32 km (20 mi) south of Arecibo, 24 km (15 mi) northwest of Jayuya.

Utuado was named after a local Taíno chief, Otoao. Surrounded by mountains and dotted with blue lakes, the town of Utuado sits in the middle of lush, natural beauty. Driving on Route 10 between Arecibo and Utuado is an experience—imposing brown limestone cliffs flank the road, and clouds often hover around the tops of the surrounding hills. Utuado's narrow and sometimes busy streets lead to a double-steepled church on the main plaza. The best sights, however, are outside town along the winding side roads.

In the middle of karst country, the **Bosque Estatal de Río Abajo** *(Río Abajo State Forest)* spans some 5,000 acres and includes huge bamboo stands and native silk-cotton trees. It also has several plantations of Asian teaks, Dominican and Honduran mahogany, and Australian pines, which are part of a government tree management program that supplies wood for the local economy (primarily for artisans and fence building). Walking trails wind through the forest, which is one of the habitats of the rare Puerto Rican parrot. An information office is near the entrance, and a recreation area with picnic tables is farther down the road. ✉ *Rte. 621, Km 4.4* ☎ *787/817–0984* 🎫 *Free* ⏲ *Daily dawn–dusk.*

East of Bosque Estatal de Río Abajo is **Lago Dos Bocas,** one of several man-made lakes near Utuado. Government-operated boats take you around the U-shaped lake from a dock, called El Embarcadero, near the intersection of Routes 123 and 146. Although the boats are used primarily as a means of public transit for residents, the 45-minute ride around the lake is pleasant and scenic, and gets you to four shoreline restaurants known for criollo cuisine and seafood. The boats are free and leave daily between 7 and 5. Trips after 3 PM are usually reserved for residents and returning passengers. The lake is stocked with sunfish, bass, and catfish; you can also fish from the shore. ✉ *Off Rte. 10, accessed via Rtes. 621, 123, 146, and 612* ☎ *787/879–1838 for El Embarcadero* 🎫 *Free* ⏲ *Boats daily 7–5.*

The 13 acres of **Parque Ceremonial Indígena de Caguana** were used more than 800 years ago by the Taíno tribes for worship and recreation, including a game—thought to have religious significance—that

IF YOU LIKE

BOATING
On any weekend, people from all over Puerto Rico make a beeline for Lago Dos Bocas, a beautiful reservoir north of Utuado. Take the ferry leaving from the main dock to any of the seafood shacks on the opposite shore. These boats, which are used as public transportation for the locals, have spectacular views of the mountains.

COLONIAL TOWNS
Although the island's southern edge has the best-known colonial capitals, the Cordillera Central has several little-known gems. Towns such as Aibonito and Barranquitas have lovely central squares. And don't miss Jayuya, which has Casa Canales, a replica of a 19th-century coffee plantation.

HIKING
The Cordillera Central has a number of forest reserves that rival the better-known El Yunque. The Bosque Estatal de Río Abajo has trails in the island's "karst country." The cloud-covered Bosque Estatal de Toro Negro has waterfalls, natural pools, and the island's tallest mountain peak, Cerro de Punta, which rises to 4,398 feet. The drier Bosque Estatal de Maricao is known for its numerous species of birds, including many on the endangered list.

resembled modern-day soccer. Today you can see a dozen *bateyes* (ball courts) of various sizes, as well as some large stone monoliths carved with petroglyphs. Archaeologists believe this may have been one of the most important ceremonial sites for the Taíno people. ✉*Rte. 111, Km 12.3* ☎*787/894–7325* *$2* *Daily 8:30–4:30.*

WHERE TO EAT

$–$$$ **El Fogón de Abuela.** This rustic restaurant on the edge of Dos Bocas Lake would make any Puerto Rican grandmother envious. The menu features stews, red snapper (whole or filleted), and fricassees, including pork chop, goat, and rabbit. You arrive either by taking the public boat from El Embarcadero on Route 612, by calling the restaurant from the dock and requesting a boat be sent to pick you up (free of charge), or by driving to the south side of the lake. From Utuado, take Route 111 to Route 140 to Route 612 and follow that to its end. The restaurant is open weekends only. ✉*Lago Dos Bocas* ☎*787/894–0470* *MC, V* *Closed Mon.–Thurs.*

WHERE TO STAY

$ **Casa Grande Mountain Retreat.** This place is about as close as you'll get to sleeping in a tree house. The guest rooms on this 107-acre ranch are in five wooden buildings that sit on platforms high above the varied vegetation. When you lie in the hammock on your private porch, all you can see is mountains in every direction. The furnishings couldn't be simpler—little more than a bed and a dresser—but that's part of the rustic charm. Leave the windows open at night to hear the chorus of tiny tree frogs sing cantatas. One of the best views is from the pool, which looks great after a renovation in 2007. Even people who are staying elsewhere stop to dine on Puerto Rican specialties on the

Fodor's Choice ★

terrace at Jungle Jane's restaurant. **Pros:** Unspoiled setting, great food. **Cons:** Long drive to other dining options, tin roofs are noisy in the rain. ✉*Rte. 612, Km 0.3, Box 1499, Utuado* ☎*787/894–3939 or 800/343–2272* 🌐*www.hotelcasagrande.com* *20 rooms* *In-room: no a/c, no phone, no TV. In-hotel: restaurant, pool, no elevator, no-smoking rooms* 💳*AE, MC, V* *EP.*

SPORTS & THE OUTDOORS

HIKING **Expediciones Tanamá** (✉*Rte 111, Km 14.5, Barrio Angeles* ☎*787/894–7685*) leads half-day or full-day excursions into the Río Tanamá underground-cave system. Guides speak limited English but are friendly and eager. Lunch is included. There's a free camping site adjacent to the office, which provides electricity and bathrooms.

HORSEBACK RIDING Across from Casa Grande Mountain Retreat, **Rancho de Caballos** (✉*Rte. 612, Km 0.3* ☎*787/894–0240*) offers three- to four-hour horse rides through mountain forests.

KAYAKING Jenaro Colón at **Locura Arecibeña** (✉*End of Rte. 612* ☎*787/878–1809*) can arrange for rentals and guided tours of Lago Dos Bocas.

JAYUYA

24 km (15 mi) southeast of Utuado.

This small town of 15,000 is in the foothills of the Cordillera Central, Puerto Rico's tallest mountain range. Cerro de Punta, the island's highest peak, looms to the south of the town center. Named after the Indian chief Hauyua, Jayuya is known for preserving its Indian heritage and draws people from all over the island for its yearly Indigenous Festival in November, which features crafts, exhibits, parades, music, and dancing. Coffee is still grown in the area—look for the locally produced Tres Picachos.

★ The main attraction of the 7,000-acre **Bosque Estatal de Toro Negro** *(Toro Negro State Forest)* is the island's crowning glory: 4,398-foot Cerro de Punta. The Black Bull State Forest also has the island's highest lake, Lago Guineo, and one of the most impressive waterfalls, 200-foot Doña Juana Falls). The best place to start exploring this vast park is at the ranger station on Route 143. Make sure to ask the friendly staffers for a trail map, although it's certain to be a copy of a copy of a copy. The trails, such as one from the ranger station that leads to an observation tower with views of the northern and southern sides of the island, are not always well marked. There are more trails east of the ranger station, at the Doña Juana Recreational Area. Keep an eye out for exotic birds such as the Guadalupe woodpecker. The reserve also contains a huge, but often out-of-service, swimming pool built into the side of a mountain. ✉*Rte. 143, Km 32.4* ☎*787/867–3040* *Free* *Ranger station daily 6–6.*

You'll want to relax on the front porch of the charming **Casa Canales,** a re-creation of the home of Jayuya's first mayor, Rosario Canales. Like the original building, dating from the late 19th century, it has tiny bed-

CLOSE UP

Hit That Perfect Beat

Music is the heart and soul of Puerto Rico. Take the instruments from the days of the Taíno Indians—the *guiro* (scratch gourd) and the *fotuto* (conch shell)—and blend them with the drums and rhythms of Africa that took root on the island's sugarcane-lined coasts. To this mixture, stir in the Spanish-Moorish-influenced music of the inland farmers and mountain folk—the *trovadores*, who still perform their improvised songs accompanied by the *cuatro* (10-string Puerto Rican guitar). Let all this simmer for a couple of centuries, and there you have it.

The island's brash Latin sound is best exemplified by the highly danceable salsa, especially as interpreted by such entertainers as the late, great Tito Puente and pop sensation Ricky Martin. Salsa, Spanish for "sauce" (as in the sauce that energizes the party), is a fusion of West African percussion and jazz with a swing beat. Two of its predecessors, *bomba* and *plena*, can still be heard today. Bomba is African-based drum and dance music in which a lead singer often leads a chorus of singers in a call-and-response interplay, similar to Cuba's rumba music. Plena is a more melodic country music that makes use of the cuatro as well as scratch gourds.

Other Latin beats heard on the island—with origins in the Caribbean, Latin America, and Spain—are mambo, merengue, flamenco, cha-cha, and rumba. Increasingly, young musicians are experimenting with new musical forms. Salsón and reggaetón, high-energy versions of salsa and reggae, are the newest beats of the island. You hear them everywhere, from bars to beaches.

rooms surrounding a central parlor. Windows on all sides can be flung open to catch the breeze. There are lots of period furnishings, such as the hand-carved wooden chairs. Even the china on the dining room table belonged to the family. ✉ *Rte. 144, Km 9.3* ☎ *787/828–4094* 🎫 *$1* 🕒 *Weekdays 12:30–4, weekends noon–4.*

This is definitely the weirdest building in Puerto Rico. The tiny **Museo Cemí** *(Cemí Museum)* is named for a Taíno artifact believed to have religious significance. This structure resembles the snail-like cemí, and you enter through its mouth. The collection, however, is pretty dull. On display are religious and ceremonial objects found on the island. ✉ *Rte. 144, Km 9.3* ☎ *787/828–1241* 🎫 *Free* 🕒 *Weekdays 8–4:30, weekends 10–3:30.*

La Piedra Escrita *(Enscribed Rock)* is a huge boulder with a handful of highly visible Taíno petroglyphs, located in a stream among several other large rocks. The area has been completely renovated, so now there are several viewing areas and a shady spot for a picnic lunch. Don't worry, the boulder in the parking lot painted a lurid shade of blue is *not* La Piedra Escrita. ✉ *Rte. 144, Km 7.8* 🎫 *Free.*

WHERE TO STAY & EAT

$ Fodor'sChoice ★ ✕🏨 **Parador Hacienda Gripiñas.** Built on the grounds of a coffee plantation, this 19th-century inn is surrounded on all sides by mountain peaks. Several of the clapboard-walled rooms in the red-roofed manor house

> **WORD OF MOUTH**
>
> "My parents, who are in their 60s and not the rustic type of traveler at all, have stayed at [Parador] Hacienda Gripiñas and enjoyed it."
>
> –PRnative

have private balconies overlooking lush gardens and the spring-fed pool; the nicest are Numbers 4 and 5. There are plenty of small parlors where you can relax with a drink from the bar. Breakfast and dinner are included in the room rates. The dining area, which meanders through three different rooms, serves criollo fare such as chicken with rice and beans. Nonguests are welcome for dinner, too. One hiking trail near the property leads to Cerro de Punta, about a 2½-hour climb. **Pros:** Set in the coffee fields, interesting old building, good meals. **Cons:** Isolated location ✉*Rte. 152, Km 1.7, Box 387* ☎*787/828–1717* 🌐*www.haciendagripinas.com* *19 rooms* *In-hotel: restaurant, bar, pools, no elevator* 💳*AE, MC, V* *MAP.*

ADJUNTAS

27 km (17 mi) southwest of Jayuya.

The coffee-growing town of Adjuntas sits north of Puerto Rico's Ruta Panorámica. Although known for its coffee, it's also the world's leading producer of citron, a fruit whose rind is processed here and then shipped for use in sweets, especially fruitcakes. Few tourists do more than drive through the town itself, but it has a quaint central plaza and a sporadic trolley used mostly by locals and schoolchildren.

Hiking trails, surrounded by wild-growing impatiens, lead up to the 3,900-foot Pico Guilarte and into other areas of **Bosque Estatal de Guilarte** *(Guilarte State Forest).* Bird-watchers have 26 different species to look for, including the carpenter bird. Or if your interest is botany, you can find a variety of trees, including candlewood, trumpet, Honduran mahogany, and Honduran pine. There's a pleasant picnic area near a eucalyptus grove. ✉*Rte. 518 at Rte. 131* ☎*787/829–5767* *Free* *Information center weekdays 7–3:30, weekends 9–5:30.*

WHERE TO STAY & EAT

$ **Villas de Sotomayor.** Covering more than 14 acres, this complex of modern villas has a summer-camp atmosphere. The focus is on horseback riding, and there are stables on the premises. You can also take horse-and-carriage rides around the grounds. Freestanding villas range in size from one bedroom with a refrigerator only to two bedrooms with a kitchenette. The on-site restaurant ($$) is open daily and serves international and criollo cuisine—it's known for its *mofongo relleno* (stuffed mashed plantains). **Pros:** Family-friendly environment, lots of space for kids to run around, nice pool area. **Cons:** Basic rooms, rather noisy ✉*Rte. 123, Km 36.8, Box 28* ☎*787/829–1717* 🌐*www.paradorvillassotomayor.com* *35 villas* *In-room: kitchen (some), refrigerator (some). In-hotel: restaurant, tennis courts, pools, no elevator* 💳*AE, D, MC, V* *EP.*

MARICAO

59 km (37 mi) west of Adjuntas; 43 km (27 mi) east of Mayagüez.

Puerto Rico's smallest municipality (pop. 6,200), Maricao is part of the island's coffee country and hosts a well-known Coffee Harvest Festival each February. Although not far from Mayagüez—the third-largest urban area on the island—Maricao feels completely isolated.

> **WORD OF MOUTH**
>
> "If you are looking for a beautiful, lush, clean, quiet, uncrowded place, but not too far from active society, Maricao is just perfect. It is not the typical tourist destination, kind [of] off the beaten path . . ." –Armando

★ Drier than other forest reserves found near the central mountains, **Bosque Estatal de Maricao** *(Maricao State Forest)* is known as one of the island's most important bird-watching destinations. The 60 species found here—29 of which are endangered—include the Puerto Rican vireo and the elfin woods warbler. You'll find an information center and a stone observation tower about ½ mi beyond the forest entrance. The Centro Vacacional Monte de Estado has rustic cabins for rent. ✉*Rte. 120 at Rte. 366* ☎*787/838–1040* *Free* *Park daily dawn–dusk.*

6

Part of the Bosque Estatal de Maricao is the **Vivero de Peces de Maricao.** The Maricao Fish Hatchery contains a collection of ponds and tanks where fish are raised to stock the island's lakes and streams. The carefully tended grounds are better groomed than most golf courses. ✉*Rte. 410, Km 1.7* ☎*787/838–3710* *Free* *Thurs.–Sun., 8:30–11:30 and 1–3:30.*

WHERE TO STAY & EAT

$ ★ **Parador La Hacienda Juanita.** Part of a coffee plantation dating from the 1800s, the hotel exudes the slower pace of days gone by. Rooms are in four wooden buildings, some of which have four-poster beds and antiques from the coffee industry's heyday. The accommodations are rustic—most have classic wooden shutters instead of glass windows. La Casona de Juanita ($$–$$$) serves up criollo cuisine, including *sancocho,* a hearty soup made of meat and root vegetables. Meals are served on a sweeping balcony where you can reach up and pull fruit off the trees. The Hernández-Cánovas family runs the place, and they treat you like one of their own. **Pros:** Gorgeous location, off-the-beaten-track feel, kids under 12 stay free. **Cons:** Far from other dining options, metals roofs are noisy in the rain. ✉*Rte. 105, Km 23.5* ☎*787/838–2550* *www.haciendajuanita.com* *21 rooms* *In-room: no a/c, Wi-Fi. In-hotel: restaurant, tennis court, pool, tennis, no elevator, public Wi-Fi* *AE, MC, V* *MAP.*

BARRANQUITAS

66 km (41 mi) east of Adjuntas, 15 km (9 mi) northwest of Aibonito.

Founded in 1804, the small mountain town of Barranquitas appears to have changed little over the years. Its steep streets and quaint plaza seem light years away from the frenetic energy of Puerto Rico's larger cities. Its tranquillity has made Barranquitas a popular location for summer homes. One of the most beautiful, **El Cortijo** (on Route 162 at Km 9.9), was built in 1938 and is said to be haunted by a former servant. Although it's closed to the public, consider stopping to admire the sprawling white structure from the road. You *can* visit the former home and mausoleum of two of Barranquitas' most famous residents: Luis Muñoz Rivera, a politician and newspaperman, and his son, Luis Muñoz Marín, the island's first elected governor. In July craftspeople gather in Barranquitas for the annual Feria Nacional de Artesanías (National Artisans Fair), one of the most popular such events on the island.

Museo Luis Muñoz Rivera, one block west of the main square, occupies the house where Luis Muñoz Rivera—a politician, poet, and journalist famous for his support of Puerto Rican autonomy—was born in 1859. Many personal belongings and the manuscripts of his political writings and poems are housed here. There's also a friend's car—a 1912 Pierce Arrow—that transported Muñoz to political events. The small wooden house is considered a superb example of 19th-century rural architecture. It's wise to call in advance; the museum doesn't always stick to its posted hours. ✉ *10 Calle Muñoz Rivera, at Calle Padre Berríos* ☎ *787/857–0230* 🎫 *Free* ⏲ *Tues.–Sat. 8–noon and 1–4:30.*

Steps away from Luis Muñoz Rivera's birthplace you'll find the **Mausoleo de la Familia Muñoz** (✉ *Calle Padre Berríos, 2 blocks west of main plaza*), where Muñoz Rivera and his son, Luis Muñoz Marín, are buried with other members of their family. It's in a small, parklike area.

WHERE TO EAT

$–$$$ ✕ **Casa Bavaria.** Enjoy a bit of Germany at this out-of-the-way eatery outside the town of Morovis, about 16 km (10 mi) northwest of Barranquitas. Casa Bavaria is a kitschy blend of biergarten and casual country restaurant. Choose bratwurst and sauerkraut or chicken with rice and beans. On weekends, patrons spend a good part of the day enjoying the view from the terrace, singing along with the jukebox, and joking with the waiters, some of whom speak German as well as English and Spanish. ✉ *Rte. 155, Km 38.3* ☎ *787/862–7818* 💳 *AE, MC, V* ⏲ *Closed Mon.–Wed.*

AIBONITO

15 km (9 mi) southeast of Barranquitas, 20 km (12 mi) northwest of Cayey.

Legend has it that Aibonito got its name when a Spaniard exclaimed "*¡Ay, que bonito!*" ("Oh, how pretty!") upon seeing the valley where the town now stands. At 1,896 feet above sea level, it's Puerto Rico's highest city. Aibonito is known as "The Queen of Flowers" because flowering plants thrive in its temperate climate. The city hosts a flower festival every year, usually in late June or July, and gives awards for blossoms and garden design. Live music and craft

CLOSE UP

Puerto Rico's Black Gold

When the late island poet Tomás Blanco wrote that coffee should be "black as the devil, hot as hell, and sweet as sin," he may well have had Puerto Rican brews in mind. Cultivated at high altitudes in a swirl of cool, moist air and mineral-rich soil, the island's beans are like gold—the black and aromatic sort.

Introduced in the mid–18th century from nearby Martinique, coffee started its life in Puerto Rico as a minor cash crop, cultivated mainly for consumption. But by the end of the 1700s Puerto Rico was producing more than a million pounds of coffee a year, and by the late 19th century, the island was the world's seventh largest producer of coffee.

Puerto Rican coffee benefited from the labors and experimentation of immigrants experienced in coffee production, and it was highly respected by connoisseurs in Europe and the Americas. Its status grew, yet Puerto Rican coffee suffered after Spain ceded the island to the United States in 1898, and after several major hurricanes. Today, Puerto Rican beans have once again taken their place next to the Jamaica Blue Mountain and Hawaiian Kona varieties as one of the world's premium coffees.

The secret is in the coffee bean itself (called "cherry"). The island's dominant bean is the *arabica*; it has a more delicate and lower-yielding cherry and produces half the caffeine of the prolific *robusta* bean found on the mega-plantations of Central and South America. The arabica cherry, in the proper conditions, is known as the richest and most flavorful among the coffee varieties. Cloud cover, tree shade, soil composition, and the altitude at which the coffee bushes are grown—higher than 3,000 feet above sea level—combine to produce a slow-ripening bean that stays on the bush at least two months longer than at lower elevations. This lengthy ripening process acts as a sort of "pre-brew," imbuing the bean with a rich flavor and a slightly sweet aftertaste.

As the beans ripen, they turn from green to yellow to red, and the trees produce a white flower with a pleasant aroma similar to jasmine. Coffee-picking season starts in August and continues through February. The process is slow and delicate because workers pick through bushes manually to collect only the cherries that are fully ripe. Small, family-run pulperies are the norm. The ripened beans are pulped (shelled) to remove the outer covering and then fermented to remove a thin layer that covers the bean, called the *mucilago*. The beans are then dried, roasted, and packed. The main coffee-growing areas of the island lie in the wet, mountainous regions of Yauco, Lares, and Las Marís, where the limited suitable terrain makes large-scale production impossible, making the coffee all the more precious a commodity.

Look for local brands: Yauco Selecto, Rioja, Yaucono, Cafe Rico, Crema, Adjuntas, Coqui, and Alto Grande Super Premium. Alto Grande, guaranteed to have been grown at high altitudes, has gained the most fame off the island. It's best consumed straight up as espresso, though many prefer to cut it with hot milk, the traditional *café con leche*, a local equivalent of café au lait.

–Karl Luntta

stalls add to the festivities. A double-steepled cathedral graces the charming town square, which is surrounded by shops and restaurants. Local guides organize outings to nearby Cañon de San Cristóbal.

> **WORD OF MOUTH**
>
> "If you get a chance to hike the Cañon San Cristóbal by Aibonito, arrange it in advance with a guide, but we only saw it from a distance and it's very steep and beautiful." –lilipad

Mirador Piedra Degetau *(Degetau Lookout Rock)* is a scenic point near Aibonito. From the tower, use the telescope to get a closer look at the surrounding mountains. You'll find picnic tables under gazebos and a playground nearby. ✉*Rte. 7718, Km 0.7* ☎*787/735–3880* *Free* *Wed.–Sun. 9–6.*

★ The **Cañon de San Cristóbal** is difficult to find, but it's well worth the effort. Trails of tropical vegetation lead to a breathtaking waterfall. Félix Rivera, a local guide, heads expeditions to the canyon *(see Tour Options in Northern Coast & Cordillera Central Essentials, below).* ✉*Rte. 725, Km 5.1* ☎*787/857–2065* *Free* *Daily.*

WHERE TO STAY & EAT

$–$$$ ✕ **La Piedra.** Near the Mirador Piedra Degetau, this hilltop restaurant has a panoramic view of Aibonito. At night you can see the lights of the city through the floor-to-ceiling windows. The food is abundant, from the *pechuga de pollo en salsa tamarindo* (chicken breast with tamarind sauce) to the *filete encebollado* (beef topped with sautéed onions). Even the side dishes, including the tender fried plantains, are memorable. If you're in the area on Sunday, drop by for the excellent buffet. ✉*Rte. 7718, Km 0.8* ☎*787/735–1034* *D, MC, V* *Closed Mon. and Tues. No dinner Wed. and Thurs.*

$ **El Coquí.** This shoebox-size hotel is much better than you'd expect in this out-of-the-way town. The rooms are spacious and have kitchenettes with more cabinet space than most people have at home. There are even small private balconies. **Pros:** Reasonable rates, plenty of rooms for families. **Cons:** Bland decor, rooms are above a fast-food restaurant. ✉*Rte. 722, Km 7.3* ☎*787/735–3150* *787/735–2225* *13 rooms* *In-room: kitchen, refrigerator. In-hotel: restaurant* *AE, D, MC, V* *CP.*

GUAVATE

25 km (17 mi) east of Aibonito, 45 km (30 mi) south of San Juan.

If you're headed east on Route 184, you might be surprised at how many people are on the road toward the Bosque Estatal Carite. Most of them won't get that far, as the stretch of the road just outside the state forest is lined with dozens of *lechonerías,* or restaurants specializing in mouthwatering pork, slow-roasted over open pits. Did we mention that these are whole pigs? And that they are slowly turning on enormous spits? There are sometimes also chicken and sausages. Traffic jams are legendary on Sundays, when locals gather here along the strip to spend the day eating and listening to local bands.

In the 7,000-acre **Bosque Estatal Carite,** 40 km (25 mi) of trails run through stands of palms, Honduras mahogany, and Spanish cedars—many of which host orchids. One trail leads to the cool waters of Charco Azul (Blue Pond), which often appeals to overheated hikers. Before setting out, get hiking information at the park manager's office near the entrance on Route 184. If you'd like a space in one of the two campgrounds, be sure to get a permit in advance from the Puerto Rico Department of Natural Resources in San Juan. Picnic tables are scattered throughout the forest, and bathroom facilities are available near the campgrounds. ✉ *Rte. 184, Km 27.5* ☎ *787/747–4545* *Free* *Office open weekdays 7–3.*

WHERE TO EAT

¢ ✕ **Los Pinos.** There are dozens of *lechonerías* along Route 184, but this pleasant place happens to be one of the few that serves seven days a week. (Most others open only for the weekend rush.) There's always a big pig in the front window, with festive garlands of link sausages hanging on either side. A large platter will set you back less than $6. The open-air dining room is never empty, even on a weekday afternoon. But on weekends, things really get hopping, as musicians jam on the small stage in the corner and customers dance in the aisles. The serious drinking takes place in the bar in back. ✉ *Rte. 184, Km 27* ☎ *787/286-1917* *No credit cards.*

6

THE CORDILLERA CENTRAL ESSENTIALS

To research prices, get advice from other travelers, and book travel arrangements, visit www.fodors.com.

TRANSPORTATION

BY AIR

Arecibo has a small airport for charter planes but no regularly scheduled service. There are no airports in the Cordillera Central. Depending on your destination, you can fly into the airports in San Juan, Fajardo, Ponce, Mayagüez, or Aguadilla.

BY BUS

No easy network of buses links the towns in the Cordillera Central. You'll have to depend on *públicos* (usually large vans) that make many stops. These vans usually stop near a town's main square. Linea de Utuado travels between San Juan and Utuado daily. Prices are $12 per person. Trips to nearby Jayuya and Lares are also possible.

Information **Linea Utuado** (☎ *787/765–1908*).

BY CAR

The well-maintained and scenic Route 10, which can be accessed in Arecibo, is a main link to the central mountain region. The Ruta Panorámica runs east–west across the island and near some of the central mountain towns. It's made up of a number of small roads, many of which can be hilly and curving. With few public transportation options, a car is essential if you want to see this area.

A road map is a must in the Cordillera Central. Most signs in the region give a route number, rather than the name of a town. You'll also need patience in navigating the twisting mountain roads.

Your best bet is to arrange for a rental car in one of the large cities on the coast, as there are only a handful of agencies in the Cordillera Central itself. If you are coming from the northern coast, you could rent a car from one of the major agencies in Arecibo or Dorado. If you arrive here and find you need a rental car, try Barranquitas Car Rental in Barranquitas or Payless Car Rental in Utuado.

Major Agencies **Avis** (☎ *787/796–7243 in Dorado*). **Hertz** (☎ *787/879–1132 in Arecibo*).

Local Agencies **Barranquitas Car Rental** (✉ *Barranquitas* ☎ *787/857–7283*). **Leaseway of Puerto Rico** (☎ *787/878–1606 in Arecibo*). **Payless Car Rental** (✉ *Utuado* ☎ *787/894–5015*).

GASOLINE Except for on major highways such as Route 52 (which runs past Guavate) and Route 10 (which leads from Arecibo to Utuado), gas stations are rare. Most towns will have at least one, but they are sometimes difficult to find. Locals are glad to point you in the right direction.

ROAD CONDITIONS Major highways in the Cordillera Central are well maintained. Watch out for potholes on secondary roads, especially after heavy rains.

BY TAXI

In Arecibo, try Arecibo Taxi Cab, but note that they close at midnight. Fares to or from San Juan are steep: for example, service is $50 from Arecibo.

Information **Arecibo Taxi Cab** (☎ *787/878–2929*).

CONTACTS & RESOURCES

BANKS & EXCHANGE SERVICES

You'll find few banks in the region, although many supermarkets, drug stores, and gas stations have ATMs (or ATHs, as they are often called here). Banks are normally open weekdays from 9 AM to 3 PM or 4 PM.

Information **Banco Popular** (✉ *55 Calle Degetau, Aibonito* ☎ *787/735–6191* ✉ *Rte. 156, Km 7.1, Barranquitas* ☎ *787/857–4380* ✉ *84 Guillermo Esteves, Jayuya* ☎ *787/828–4120* ✉ *Calle Zuzuaregui at Calle Baldorioty, Maricao* ☎ *787/838–3660* ✉ *59 Calle Cueto, Utuado* ☎ *787/894–2700*).

EMERGENCIES

Contacts **General emergencies** (☎ *911*).

Hospitals Centro de Salud (*✉ Calle Isaac González Martínez, Utuado ☎ 787/894-2875*). **Hospital Regional Dr. C. Coll y Toste** (*✉ Rte. 129, Km 0.7, Arecibo ☎ 787/878-7272*).

24-hour Pharmacies Walgreens (*✉ Rte. 123, Bldg. 940, Utuado ☎ 787/894-0100 ✉ 4210 Rte. 693, Dorado ☎ 787/728-5800 ✉ Calle del Mar 547, Hatillo ☎ 787/880-0290*).

INTERNET, MAIL & SHIPPING

There are no Internet cafés in this part of the island. If you need to be wired, make sure that your hotel has a connection.

Branches of the U.S. Post Office are located throughout the region. Generally, post offices are open weekdays from 7 or 8 AM until 5 or 6 PM and for a few hours Saturday morning.

Post Offices Arecibo Main Office (*✉ 10 Av. San Patricio, Arecibo ☎ 787/878-2775*). **Dorado Main Office** (*✉ 100 Rte. 698, Dorado ☎ 787/796-1052*). **Utuado Main Office** (*✉ 41 Av. Fernando L. Ribas, Utuado ☎ 787/894-2940*).

TOUR OPTIONS

Atlantic Sun San Juan Tours has several different tours of the region. It has an office in Utuado. Félix Rivera, a local guide, heads expeditions to the Cañón de San Cristóbal.

Information Atlantic San Juan Tours (*Box 215, Utuado 00611 ☎ 787/644-9841 www.puertoricoexcursions.com*). **Felix Rivera** (*✉ Aibonito ☎ 787/644-5122*).

VISITOR INFORMATION

Arecibo, Jayuya, Maricao, and Utuado have tourism offices in their town halls. All are open weekdays during normal business hours.

Information Arecibo City Hall (*☎ 787/879-2232*). **Jayuya** (*☎ 787/282-5010*). **Maricao** (*☎ 787/838-2290*). **Utuado** (*☎ 787/894-3505*).

UNDERSTANDING PUERTO RICO

COCINA CRIOLLA

PUERTO RICO'S *cocina criolla*—literally, the creole kitchen—is a relative of other Caribbean cuisines, sharing basic ingredients common to Cuban, Dominican, and to some extent even Brazilian culinary traditions. Still, it has its own distinct flavorings.

The origins of contemporary Puerto Rican cuisine can be traced to the Taíno people, who inhabited the island in the 15th century. Taíno staples still used today include yucca, peppers, and corn. The Taíno used yucca to make *casabe*, a flat bread, and also a variety of vinegar that they used for seasoning instead of salt. The Taíno also are believed to have grown guava, pineapple, and soursop.

When the Spaniards arrived on the island, they brought other ingredients, including olives, eggplant, onion, garlic, rice, and cilantro. Wheat would not grow on the island, so yucca remained a staple, as did rice. Regional culinary specialties from Spain, such as paellas, came out of the Spanish-influenced kitchen. These specialties played an important role in the development of Puerto Rican recipes, recognizable today in such dishes as *arroz con pollo*. Lacking olive oil, early Puerto Ricans often used lard as a fat. Back in those days, shortly after the Spanish arrived in the late 15th century, the bubbling cauldron of a hungry soldier welcomed any ingredient that was available. So a typical Spanish recipe might be transformed with yucca and pumpkin and colored with the red of achiote.

African slaves brought by the Spanish from Guinea and the Gold Coast of Africa during the 16th century to toil in the sugar fields also left their marks on the Puerto Rican table. The slaves brought plantains, bananas, pigeon peas, okra, and yams. The Taíno used corn husks to wrap foods, but the Africans replaced them with plantain leaves. The African population developed a variety of coconut-based dishes and preferred frying foods to stewing them.

Other important ingredients were the result of Spanish exploration of the world. For example, breadfruit was brought in from Tahiti and has remained a staple. But Puerto Ricans have also adopted the mango from South Asia and oranges from China.

A wooden *pilón*, which the Taínos used to mash ingredients and paints, is still used today, particularly in the preparation of *mofongo* (mashed plantains with garlic and olive oil), which is of both African and Spanish origin.

Puerto Rican cookery constantly reveals a rich, historical blend. Dishes often feature pepper, lime rind, cinnamon, cloves, fresh ginger, garlic, and the juice of the sour orange. Two popular herb seasonings are cilantro (coriander) and oregano. These ingredients, along with small sweet peppers, are commonly used to flavor soups and meats. The conventional wisdom says that the real secret of the cocina criolla depends on the use of sofrito (a sauce that may include tomatoes, onion, garlic, peppers, and coriander), achiote, lard, and the *caldero* (cooking pot).

Plátanos, or plantains, are related to bananas but are larger and starchier. They are served mostly as side dishes and may be eaten green (as *tostones*, which are salty) or ripe (as *amarillos*, which are sweet). They can be fried, baked, boiled, or roasted and served either whole or in slices. Sometimes whole amarillos are served with cinnamon as a dessert. *Pasteles*, boiled plantain leaves wrapped around fillings, tamale-style, are a Christmas specialty but can be eaten anytime.

Rice is omnipresent on the Puerto Rican plate. It can be served "white" with kidney beans, or prepared with *gandules* (pigeon peas) or garbanzos (chickpeas); most often rice is simply served with *hab-*

ichuelas (red beans). Whatever the case, the accompaniment for rice is almost always some kind of bean, always richly seasoned. Rice stuck to the pot, known as *pegao,* is the most highly prized, full of all the ingredients that have sunk to the bottom.

Popular soups include the *sopón de pollo con arroz* (chicken soup with rice), *sopón de pescado* (fish soup), and *sopón de garbanzos con patas de cerdo* (chickpea soup with pig's feet). More than a soup, but maybe less than a stew, is the *asopao. Asopao de pollo,* the most popular variety, is made with a whole chicken, flavored with spices such as garlic, paprika, and oregano, as well with salt pork, cured ham, green peppers, chili peppers, onions, tomatoes, chorizo, and pimentos. A remarkable number of ingredients go into the *sancocho,* a hearty soup that includes vegetables, plantains, meats, and anything a poor man could find.

The *lechón asado* (a roasted or barbecued pig) is the quintessential Puerto Rican Christmas tradition. The whole pig is roasted in an open pit, a process that takes several hours. It's basted with sour orange juice and achiote coloring. The lechón asado is best when the pig's skin is golden and absolutely crisp. The traditional dressing served with the dish is the *aji-li-mojili,* a combination of garlic, sweet seeded chili peppers, vinegar, lime juice, salt, and olive oil.

Snacks—particularly different kinds of fritters—are an important part of the Puerto Rican diet. All-time favorite street snacks include *bacalaítos fritos* (deep-fried codfish fritters), *pastelillos* (deep-fried cheese and meat turnovers), and *alcapurrias* (green plantain croquettes stuffed with beef or pork). *Piononos,* made from ripe bananas, are also high-ranking fritters.

Tropical fruits often wind up at the table in the form of delicious juices. A local favorite is pineapple juice from crops grown in the north of the island. Coconut, mango, papaya, lime, and tamarind are other local favorites. Puerto Rico is home to lesser known fruits that are worth trying if you find them; these include the *caimito* (which is also called a star apple and has a mild, grapelike flavor), *quenepa* (also called a Spanish lime, which has yellow sweet-tart pulp surrounded by a tight, thin skin), and *zapote* (a plum-size fruit that tastes like a combination of peach, avocado, and vanilla). The Plaza del Mercado in the Santurce sector of San Juan is a good place to look for the unusual.

Popular Puerto Rican desserts include the custard flan and the coconut tembleque, or pudding. Guava paste or papaya cubes cooked in sugar and cinnamon must be accompanied by *queso blanco* (white cheese). *Arroz con dulce* is made of cooked rice, coconut cream, sugar, and cinnamon.

Until the 19th century, sugar and coffee were the most important of the island's crops and the backbone of the economy. Puerto Rican coffee is still the source of pride for many; Pope John Paul II was said to like Puerto Rican coffee. A sip's worth of strong black coffee in a small cup is known as *puya*; when mixed with hot milk, it's *café con leche.*

Likewise a source of pride is a by-product of the sugar industry: rum. Puerto Rico makes first-rate rum, including the most popular, Bacardí. The best rums can be sipped like a fine cognac, but lesser white and golden rums make great mixed drinks. The piña colada is a well-known Puerto Rican invention—a blend of coconut cream, pineapple juice, and rum. A lesser-known but potent local rum specialty is *bilí,* made from quenepas (similar to lychee fruit) soaked in rum and marinated in the bottle for weeks. *Coquito* is the Puerto Rican version of Christmas rum eggnog.

Puerto Rican cuisine has been experiencing a boom of sorts, with innovative, gourmet restaurants opening around the island. Today, more chefs and restaurateurs are developing menus in the line of a Nuevo Latino cuisine. Joyfully departing from traditional continental and Puerto Rican recipes, these chefs nevertheless include traditional ingredients and update old favorites. Traditional meats like chicken, fish, and lamb are given an added zest by sauces made from such tropical fruits as tamarind, mango, or guava. Take your palate out for a few adventures. Puerto Rican cuisine may surprise and delight you with both new and old tastes.

—Isabel Abislaimán

THE STATE OF THE ARTS IN PUERTO RICO

ALTHOUGH SPANIARDS LANDED IN PUERTO RICO in the late 15th century (Columbus was guided to the island by the Taíno Indians of Guadeloupe in 1493), several hundred years passed before what could be considered an authentically Puerto Rican art movement was born on the island in the 18th century. Notwithstanding the Taíno and their pre-Columbian works of art that are now highly prized among collectors, most of the existing paintings that came after the Spanish were part of the larger European tradition of Renaissance painting and sculpture.

A 16th-century religious mural, discovered in 1978 in Old San Juan's Iglesia de San José, is among the oldest artworks—aside from those by the Taíno, of course—to have been discovered in Puerto Rico. It is, however, widely considered insignificant in the development of the fine arts on the island. According to art historian Osiris Delgado, this anonymous repertoire of religious images continued uneventfully throughout the 17th century. In the 18th century, sculptor Tiburcio Espada (1798–1852), along with his father Felipe (c. 1754–1818), created some of the oldest surviving *santos* in the San Germán tradition.

With them, and with portrait painter José Campeche (1752–1809), an indigenous tradition of Puerto Rican art, separate from the traditions of Europe of the time, began to emerge.

Another turning point for Puerto Rican artists occurred in the 19th century with the paintings of Francisco Oller (1833–1917). Oller, who was educated in Europe in the company of Gustave Courbet, Camille Pissarro, and Paul Cézanne, may be the first truly modern painter in Puerto Rico. (Oller's *El estudiante* is in the permanent collection of the Musée d'Orsay in Paris.) Unlike his peers, Oller painted realistic scenes of island life, though his use of light and color was heavily influenced by the impressionists. His most important work, *El velorio,* is the cornerstone of the collection in the Museo de la Universidad de Puerto Rico. Depicting a scene of mourning in a rural setting, the painting is one of the first attempts to create a Puerto Rican cultural identity. Such was his commitment to promoting the arts on the island that, around 1870, Oller personally opened the first art gallery in Old San Juan, which exhibited his own works and those of his friends and pupils, all of whom were island natives.

Throughout the first half of the 20th century, most Puerto Rican artists followed Oller's aesthetic and grounded their works in the love of the rural landscape and lifestyle. The *jìbaro* (a poor, usually illiterate, mountain man) and the ideal of the lone house on the mountain became the affirmation of the Puerto Rican identity.

In the 1940s the government started to support the arts by providing artists with studio spaces. Shortly after, art institutions began to flourish, with the Museo de la Universidad de Puerto Rico opening in 1946. Also around this time, carvings of wooden saints (*santos de palo*) became cherished collectors items.

During the 1950s artists began to shift their interests from the agrarian ideal toward social justice and the urban proletariat, and artists of this period focused their eyes on slums, poverty, and hardships of the city. You can see this contrast in the work Ramón Frade's *Nuestro pan* (a celebration of rural life) and Rafael Tufino's *Goyita* (focusing on dignified urban poverty). The artists of the 1950s made art with social impact and wide distribution. Murals were widely commissioned during the 1950s and '60s for government buildings and factories. One example is *La Plena,* a mural by Rafael Tufino celebrating the African roots of

Puerto Rican folk music in the Centro de Bellas Artes.

The 1950s also saw two specific developments. The Instituto de Cultura Puertorriquena (ICP) was established in 1955 to promote Puerto Rican artists; today the agency oversees many museums and art programs all over the island. And in 1959 the Museo de Arte de Ponce (MAP) was founded by former governor and philanthropist Luis A. Ferré. MAP houses a private collection of more than 2,400 cataloged works from the 14th through 19th centuries, including paintings by El Greco, Goya, Rubens, Cranach, Murillo, and Delacroix. The collection is particularly strong in Italian baroque and Pre-Raphaelite works, with good representation by Latin American and Puerto Rican artists from the 18th century to the present. Myrna Baez, Julio Rosado del Valle, and Antonio Martorell are included in the collection.

In the 1960s, as the art world moved away from socially committed art, Puerto Rican artists still struggled with nationalism and identity issues. Locally, this struggle resulted in a battle between abstraction and avant-garde expression (with artists such as Julio Rosado Del Valle, Olga Albizu, and Luis Hernández Cruz) on the one hand, and figurative and socially minded art considered "genuinely" Puerto Rican on the other.

Finally, in the 1980s, abstract expressionists and other stylistic experimenters were granted a place at the table of Puerto Rican identity. These years opened art to the irreverent humor of Carmelo Sobrino, to the environmental activism of Carlos Marcial, and to aspects of the fantastic, as in the works of Marta Pérez, Jorge Zeno, and Rafi Trelles. Also, in the early 1980s the Puerto Rican landscape was deemed to include El Barrio in New York City and issues related to migration, poverty, colonialism, and crime. Broadening their geographic horizons also prompted Puerto Rican artists to use the self-portrait as a means of exploring politics, race, the psyche, sexuality, and gender, as seen in the works of Arnaldo Roche and Mari Mater O'Neill.

By 1988 a group of artists, professors, critics, collectors, and art lovers had come together to establish the Museo de Arte Contemporáneo de Puerto Rico. The museum's collection comprises mostly works donated by the artists themselves. The museum finally moved to its own new building in 2003. By 1989 even the Puerto Rico Tourism Company recognized that art can be an important way to present Puerto Rico to the world, so it began acquiring its own collection.

In the 1990s sculpture started playing a more significant role. The most visible evidence were the large investments in public art in the city of San Juan and the Sculpture Symposium of the Universidad de Puerto Rico, whose works are permanently exhibited at the Botanical Garden.

Although the government has done a lot to promote the arts in Puerto Rico, it was only in 2000 that the Museo de Arte de Puerto Rico opened, the island's first government-sponsored museum of international caliber. Since it has relatively few pieces in its permanent collection—relying largely on loans from other institutions—the museum is primarily a collection of collections.

The state of the arts is looking up. Puerto Rico's Public Art Project promises to make the whole island an indoor and outdoor showcase of international and Puerto Rican art. The project consists of works in various urban and rural settings around the island—from the stations of the new Urban Train in the San Juan metropolitan area to beach benches in the shape of surfboard-petals by Aaron Salabarrias in Rincón to festive mosaic murals by Daniel Lind in Loíza.

—Isabel Abislaimán

A GAMBLING PRIMER

CASINOS ARE NO LONGER as large a part of the tourism experience in Puerto Rico as they once were—but that's due more to growth in other areas than to a decline in the casinos themselves. If gambling is your thing, or if you're feeling yourself drawn to the "action" for the first time, Puerto Rico's resort-based casinos provide an attractive setting for trying your luck.

The most popular games have their rules, etiquette, odds, and strategies. If you're new to gambling, take a reconnaissance stroll through the casino, read up on the games here, and choose the one that best suits your style. If you take the time to learn the basics and fine points thoroughly, you'll be adequately prepared to play with as much of an edge as the game allows.

Baccarat

The most "glamorous" game in the casino, baccarat (pronounced bah-kuh-rah) is a version of chemin de fer, popular in European gambling halls. The Italian word baccara means "zero"; this refers to the point value of 10s and picture cards. The game is run by four pit personnel. Two dealers sit side by side at the middle of the table; they handle the winning and losing bets and keep track of each player's "commission" (explained below). The "caller" stands at the middle of the other side of the table and dictates the action. A pit boss supervises the game and acts as final judge if any disputes arise.

How to Play. Baccarat is played with eight decks of cards dealt from a large "shoe" (or card holder). Each player is offered a turn at handling the shoe and dealing the cards. Two two-card hands are dealt: the "player" and the "bank" hands. The player who deals the cards is called the banker, though the house, of course, banks both hands. The players bet, before the deal, on which hand, player or banker, will come closer to adding up to 9 (a "natural"). The cards are totaled as follows: Ace through 9 retain face value, and 10s and picture cards are worth zero. If a hand adds up to more than 10, the number 10 is subtracted from the total. For example, if one hand contains a 10 and a 4, the hand adds up to 4. If a hand holds an ace and 6, it adds up to 7. If a hand has a 7 and 9, it adds up to 6.

Depending on the two hands, the caller either declares a winner and loser (if either hand actually adds up to 8 or 9), or calls for another card for the player hand (if it totals 1, 2, 3, 4, 5, or 10). The bank hand then either stands pat or draws a card, determined by a complex series of rules depending on what the player's total is and dictated by the caller. When one or the other hand is declared a winner, the dealers go into action to pay off the winning wagers, collect the losing wagers, and add up the commission (usually 5%) that the house collects on the bank hand. Both bets have a house advantage of slightly more than 1%.

The player-dealer (or banker) continues to hold the shoe as long as the bank hand wins. As soon as the player hand wins, the shoe moves counterclockwise around the table. Players are not required to deal; they can refuse the shoe and pass it to the next player. Most players bet on the bank hand when they deal, since they "represent" the bank, and to do otherwise would seem as if they were betting "against" themselves. This isn't really the case.

Baccarat Strategy. Making a bet at baccarat is very simple. All you have to do is place your money in either the bank, player, or tie box on the layout, which appears directly in front of where you sit at the table. If you're betting that the bank hand will win, you put your chips in the bank box; bets for the player hand go in the player box. (Betting on a tie is a sucker bet.)

Because the caller dictates the action, the player's responsibilities are minimal. It's not necessary to know any of the card-drawing rules, even if you're the banker. Playing baccarat is a simple matter of guessing whether the player or banker hand will come closer to 9, and deciding how much to bet on the outcome.

Blackjack

Blackjack is the most popular table game in the casino. It's easy to learn, it's fun to play, and it involves skill, and therefore rewards those who learn its nuances. Blackjack also has one of the lowest house advantages. Because blackjack is the only table game in the casino in which players can gain a long-term advantage over the house, it's the only table game in the casino (other than poker) that can be played professionally. And because blackjack can be played professionally, it's the most written-about and discussed casino game. Dozens of how-to books, trade journals, magazines, newsletters, computer programs, videos, theses, and novels are available on every aspect of blackjack, from how to add to 21 to how to play against a variety of shuffles, from when to stand or hit to the Level-Two Zen Count. Of course, training someone to play blackjack professionally is beyond the scope of this guide. Contact the **Gambler's Book Club** (☎ *800/552—1777*) for a catalog of gambling books, software, and videotapes, including the largest selection on blackjack around.

The Rules. Basically, here's how it works: You play blackjack against a dealer, and whichever one of you comes closest to a card total of 21 without going over is the winner. Number cards are worth their face value, picture cards count as 10, and aces are worth either 1 or 11. (Hands with aces in them are known as "soft" hands. Always count the ace first as an 11; if you also have a 10, your total will be 21, not 11.) If the dealer has a 17 and you have a 16, you lose. If you have an 18 against a dealer's 17, you win (even money). If both you and the dealer have a 17, it's a tie (or "push") and no money changes hands. If you go over a total of 21 (or "bust"), you lose immediately, even if the dealer also busts later in the hand. If your first two cards add up to 21 (a "natural"), you're paid 3 to 2. However, if the dealer also has a natural, it's a push. A natural beats a total of 21 achieved with more than two cards.

You're dealt two cards, either face down or face up, depending on the custom of the particular casino. Two cards go to the dealer—one face down and one face up. Depending on your first two cards and the dealer's up card, you can:

- stand, or refuse to take another card.
- hit, or take as many cards as you need until you stand or bust.
- double down, or double your bet and take one card.
- split a like pair; if you're dealt two 8s, for example, you can double your bet and play the 8s as if they're two hands.
- buy insurance if the dealer is showing an ace. Here you're wagering half your initial bet that the dealer does have a natural; if so, you lose your initial bet but are paid 2 to 1 on the insurance (which means the whole thing is a push).
- surrender half your initial bet if you're holding a bad hand (known as a "stiff") such as a 15 or 16 against a high-up card like a 9 or 10.

Blackjack Strategy. Playing blackjack is not only about knowing the rules—it's also about knowing how to play. Many people devote a great deal of time to learning strategies based on complicated statistical schemes. However, if you don't have the time, energy, or inclination to get that seriously involved, the following basic strategies, which cover more than half the situations you'll face, should allow you to play the game with a modicum of skill and a paucity of humiliation:

- When your hand is a stiff (a total of 12, 13, 14, 15, or 16) and the dealer shows 2, 3, 4, 5, or 6, always stand.
- When your hand is a stiff and the dealer shows a 7, 8, 9, 10, or ace, always hit.
- When you hold 17, 18, 19, or 20, always stand.
- When you hold a 10 or 11 and the dealer shows a 2, 3, 4, 5, 6, 7, 8, or 9, always double down.
- When you hold a pair of aces or a pair of 8s, always split.
- Never buy insurance.

Caribbean Stud

Caribbean Stud is played on a blackjack-size table. It's a poker-based game, so you need to know the ranking of hands. You are playing against the dealer, and your hand must beat the dealer's hand. You do not have to worry about beating the other players' hands.

The game starts with each player making an ante bet equal to the table minimum. This is placed in the circle marked "ante" in front of the player. At this time the player also has the option of making an additional dollar side bet for the bonus jackpot. An automatic shuffler is used, and the dealer distributes a five-card hand to each player face down. The dealer retains a hand and turns one card face up.

Players look at their cards and decide to fold and forfeit their ante bet or call by making an additional bet, which is twice the size of the ante. For example, at a $5 table your ante bet would be $5 and your call bet would be $10.

After the players have made their decision to fold or call, the dealer's hand is turned over. The dealer must qualify by having a hand with ace plus king or better. If the dealer does not qualify, the players are paid even money for their original ante bet and the second call bet is a "push," which means it does not win or lose.

If the dealer qualifies and the player wins the hand, he or she is paid even money for the ante bet, and the call bet is paid based on the winning hand on a predetermined schedule.

The player must act before the dealer. This means there will be times when you fold a hand only to have the dealer not qualify. This does not mean you should play every hand. A simple strategy is to play your hand if it contains ace-king or better, and fold anything else.

The house edge for the main game is about 5%, but the pace of the game is fairly slow. Because of this the house edge won't hurt your bankroll too much if you play for smaller stakes.

The same is not true of the side bet for the progressive jackpot. As with all so-called bonus bets, the bonus jackpot has a high house edge. You need a flush or higher to qualify for one of the bonus payouts, and the money you win when you receive one of these hands is not close to the odds of doing so.

If for some reason you decide to make the side bet, you should know that you are eligible for the jackpot even if the dealer's hand does not qualify. You must inform the dealer immediately before they pick up the cards. Normally the dealer will pick up all the cards without turning them over. Make sure you speak up.

That is about all you need to know to play Caribbean Stud. Give it a try, but stay away from the side bet.

Craps

Craps is a dice game played at a large rectangular table with rounded corners. Up to 12 players can crowd around the table, all standing. The layout is mounted at the bottom of a surrounding "rail," which prevents the dice from being thrown off the table and provides an opposite wall against which to bounce the dice. It's important, when you're the "shooter," to roll the dice hard enough so that they bounce off the end wall of the table; this ensures a random bounce and shows that you're not trying to control the dice with a "soft roll." The layout grid is duplicated on the right and left side of the table, so players on either end will see exactly the same design. The top of the railing is grooved to hold the bettors' chips; as always, keep a close eye on your stash to prevent victimization by rail thieves.

It can require up to four pit personnel to run an action-packed, fast-paced game of craps. Two dealers handle the bets made on either side of the layout. A "stickman" wields the long wooden stick, curved at one end, which is used to move the dice around the table; the stickman also calls the number that's rolled and books the proposition bets (⇨below) made in the middle of the layout. The "boxman" sits between the two dealers and oversees the game; he settles any disputes about rules, payoffs, mistakes, etc. A slow crap game is often handled by a single employee, who performs stick, box, and dealer functions. A portable end wall can be placed near the middle of the table so that only one side is functional.

How to Play. To play, just join in, standing at the table wherever you can find an open space. You can start betting casino chips immediately, but you have to wait your turn to be the shooter. The dice move around the table in a clockwise fashion: The person to your right shoots before you, the one to the left after. (The stickman will give you the dice at the appropriate time.) If you don't want to roll the bones, motion your refusal to the stickman and he'll skip you.

Playing craps is fairly straightforward; it's betting on it that's complicated. The basic concepts are as follows: If the first roll turns up a 7 or 11, that's called a "natural"—an automatic win. If a 2, 3, or 12 comes up on the first throw (called the "come-out roll"), that's termed "crapping out"—an automatic loss. Any other total on a first roll is known as a "point": The shooter keeps rolling the dice until the point comes up again. If a 7 turns up before the point does, the shooter loses. When either the point (the original number thrown) or a 7 is rolled, this is known as a "decision"; one is made on average every 3.3 rolls.

But "winning" and "losing" rolls of the dice are entirely relative in this game, depending on how you bet. There are two ways you can bet at craps: "for" the shooter or "against" the shooter. Betting for means that the shooter will "make his point" (win). Betting against means that the shooter will "seven out" (lose). (Either way, you're actually betting against the house, which books all wagers.) If you're betting "for" on the come-out, you place your chips on the layout's "pass line." If a 7 or 11 is rolled, you win even money. If a 2, 3, or 12 (craps) is rolled, you lose your bet. If you're betting "against" on the come-out, you place your chips in the "don't pass bar." A 7 or 11 loses; a 2 or 3 wins (a 12 is a push). A shooter can bet for or against himself or herself.

At the same time, you can make roughly two dozen wagers on any single roll of the dice. Besides the "for" and "against" (pass and don't pass) bets, you can also make the following wagers at craps:

Come/Don't Come: After a pass-line point is established, the come bet renders every subsequent roll of the dice a come-out roll. When you place your chips in the come box, it's the same as a pass-line bet. If a 7 or 11 is rolled, you win even money. If a 2, 3, or 12 is rolled, you've crapped out. If a 4, 5, 6, 8, 9, or 10 is rolled, it becomes another point, and the dealer moves your chips into the corresponding box on the layout. Now if that number comes up before the 7, you win the come bet. The opposite (almost) is true for the don't come box: 7 and 11 lose, 2 and 3 win (12 is a push), and if 7 is rolled before the point, you win.

Odds: The house allows you to take odds on whether or not the shooter will make his or her point, once it's established. Since the house pays off these bets at "true odds," rather than withholding a unit or two to its advantage, these are the best bets in a crap game. Odds on the 6 and 8 pay off at 6 to 5, on the 5 and 9 at 3 to 2, and on the 4 and 10 at 2 to 1. "Back up" your pass-line bets with single, double, triple, or up to 109 times odds (depending on the house rules) by placing your chips behind your line bet. For example, if the point is a 10 and your bet is $5, backing up your bet with single odds ($5) returns $25 ($5 + $5 on the line and $5 + $10 single odds); taking triple odds returns $55 ($5 + $5 on the line and $15 + $30). To take the odds on a come bet, toss your chips onto the layout and tell the dealer, "Odds on the come."

Place: Instead of waiting for a point to be rolled on the come, you can simply lay your bet on the point of your choice. Drop your chips on the layout in front of you and tell the dealer to "place" your number. The dealer puts your chips on the point; when it's rolled you win. The 6 and 8 pay 7 to 6, the 5 and 9 pay 7 to 5, and the 4 and 10 pay 9 to 5. In other words, if you place $6 on the 8 and it hits, you win $7. Place bets don't pay off at true odds, which is how the house maintains its edge (1.51% on the 6 and 8, 4% on the 5 and 9, and 6.66% on the 4 and 10). You can "call your place bet down" (take it back) at any time; otherwise the place bet will "stay up" until a 7 is rolled.

Buy: Buy bets are the same as place bets, except that the house pays off at true odds and takes a 5% commission if it wins. Since buy bets have an edge of 4.7%, you should only buy the 4 and 10 (rather than place them at a 6.6% disadvantage).

Big 6 and 8: Place your own chips in these boxes; you win if the 6 or 8 comes up, and lose on the 7. Since they pay off at even money, rather than true odds, the house edge is large—9.09%.

Field: This is a "one-roll" bet (a bet that's decided with each roll). Numbers 3, 4, 9, 10, and 11 pay even money, whereas 2 and 12 pay 2 to 1. The house edge on the field is 5.5%.

Proposition Bets: All proposition bets are booked in the grid in the middle of the layout by the stickman. "Hardways" means a matching pair of numbers on the dice (two 3s for a hardways 6, two 4s for a hardways 8, etc.). A hardways 4 or 10 pays 7 to 1 (11.1% edge), and 6 or 8 pays 9 to 1 (9.09%). If a 7 or a 4, 6, 8, or 10 is rolled the "easy way," hardways bets lose. "Any seven" is a one-roll wager on the 7, paying 4 to 1 with a whopping 16.6% edge. "Yo'leven" is also a one-roll wonder paying 14 to 1 with a 16.6% edge. "Any craps" is a one-roll bet on the 2, 3, or 12, paying 7 to 1 (11.1%). Other bad proposition bets include the "horn" (one-roll bet on 2, 3, 11, or 12 separately; 16.6%), and "c and e" (craps or 11; 11.1%).

Note: The players place their own pass line, field, Big 6 and 8, and come line bets. Players must drop their chips on the table in front of the dealers and instruct them to make their place and buy bets, and to take or lay the odds on their come bets. Chips are tossed to the stickman, who makes the hardways, any craps, any seven, and c and e bets in the middle of the layout.

Roulette

Roulette is a casino game that utilizes a perfectly balanced wheel with 38 numbers (0, 00, and 1 through 36), a small white ball, a large layout with 11 different betting options, and special "wheel chips." The layout organizes the 11 different bets into six "inside bets" (the single numbers, or those closest to the dealer) and five "outside bets" (the grouped bets, or those closest to the players).

The dealer stands between the layout and the roulette wheel, and chairs for five or six players are set around the roulette table. At crowded times, players also stand among and behind those seated, reaching over and around to place their bets. Always keep a close eye on your chips at these times to guard against "rack thieves," clever sleight-of-hand artists who can steal from your pile of chips right from under your nose.

To buy in, place your cash on the layout near the wheel. Inform the dealer of the denomination of the individual unit you intend to play (usually 25¢ or $1, but it can go up as high as $500). Know the table limits (displayed on a sign in the dealer area); don't ask for a 25¢ denomination if the minimum is $1. The dealer gives you a stack of wheel chips of a different color from those of all the other players and places a chip marker atop one of your wheel chips on the rim of the wheel to identify its denomination. Note that you must cash in your wheel chips at the roulette table before you leave the game. Only the dealer can verify how much they're worth.

The dealer spins the wheel clockwise and the ball counterclockwise. When the ball slows, the dealer announces, "No more bets." The ball drops from the "back track" to the "bottom track," caroming off built-in brass barriers and bouncing in and out of the different cups in the wheel before settling into the cup of the winning number. Then the dealer, who knows the winning bettors by the color of their wheel chips, places a marker on the number and scoops all the losing chips into his or her corner. Depending on how crowded the game is, the casino can count on roughly 50 spins of the wheel per hour.

How to Place Inside Bets. You can lay any number of chips (depending on the table limits) on a single number, 1 through 36 or 0 or 00. If the number hits, your payoff is 35 to 1, for a return of $36 on a $1 bet. You could, conceivably, place a $1 chip on all 38 numbers, but the return of $36 would leave you $2 short, which divides out to 5.26%, the house advantage.

If you place a $1 chip on the line between two numbers and one of those numbers hits, you're paid 17 to 1 for a return of $18 (again, $2 short of the true odds).

Betting on three numbers returns 11 to 1, four numbers returns 8 to 1, five numbers pays 6 to 1 (this is the worst bet at roulette, with a 7.89% disadvantage), and six numbers pays 5 to 1.

How to Place Outside Bets. Lay a chip on one of three "columns" at the lower end of the layout next to numbers 34, 35, and 36; if the winning number falls in the column you've chosen, the payoff is 2 to 1. A bet placed in the first 12, second 12, or third 12 boxes also pays 2 to 1. A bet on red or black, odd or even, and 1 through 18 or 19 through 36 pays off at even money, 1 to 1. If you think you can bet on red and black, or odd and even, in order to play roulette and drink for free all night, think again: The green 0 or 00, which fall outside these two basic categories, will come up on average once every 19 spins of the wheel.

Slot Machines

At the beginning of the 20th century, Charlie Fey built the first mechanical slot in his San Francisco basement. Slot-machine technology has exploded in the past 20 years, and now there are hundreds of different models, which accept everything from pennies to specially minted $500 tokens. Electronically operated machines known as "multipliers" accept more than one coin (usually three to five, maximum) and have flashing lights, bells, and whistles, and spin, credit, and cash-out buttons. Multipliers frequently have a variety of pay lines:

three horizontal for example, or five horizontal and diagonal.

The major advance in the game, however, is the progressive jackpot. Banks of slots within a particular casino are connected by computer, and the jackpot total is displayed on a digital meter above the machines. Generally, the total increases by 5% of the wager. If you're playing a dollar machine, each time you pull the handle (or press the spin button), a nickel is added to the jackpot.

How to Play. To play, insert your penny, nickel, quarter, silver dollar, or dollar token into the slot at the far right edge of the machine. Pull the handle or press the spin button; then wait for the reels to spin and stop one by one, and for the machine to determine whether you're a winner (occasionally) or a loser (the rest of the time). It's pretty simple—but because there are so many different types of machines nowadays, be sure you know exactly how the one you're playing operates.

The house advantage on slots varies widely from machine to machine, between 3% and 25%. Casinos that advertise a 97% payback are telling you that at least one of their slot machines has a house advantage of 3%. Which one? There's really no way of knowing. Generally, $1 machines pay back at a higher percentage than quarter or nickel machines. On the other hand, machines with smaller jackpots pay back more money more frequently, meaning that you'll be playing with more of your winnings.

One of the all-time great myths about slot machines is that they're "due" for a jackpot. Slots, like roulette, craps, keno, and the big six, are subject to the Law of Independent Trials, which means the odds are permanently and unalterably fixed. If the odds of lining up three sevens on a 25¢ slot machine have been set by the casino at 1 in 10,000, then those odds remain 1 in 10,000 whether the three 7s have been hit three times in a row or not hit for 90,000 plays. Don't waste a lot of time playing a machine that you suspect is "ready," and don't think that if someone hits a jackpot on a particular machine only minutes after you've finished playing on it that it was "yours."

Video Poker

Like blackjack, video poker is a game of strategy and skill, and at select times on select machines, the player actually holds the advantage, however slight, over the house. Unlike with slot machines, you can determine the exact edge of video-poker machines (or in gambler's lingo, "handicap" the machine). Like slots, however, video-poker machines are often tied into a progressive meter; when the jackpot total reaches high enough, you can beat the casino at its own game.

The variety of video-poker machines is already large, and it's growing steadily larger. All of the different machines are played in a similar fashion, but the strategies are different. This section deals only with straight-draw video poker.

How to Play. The schedule for the payback on winning hands is posted on the machine, usually above the screen. It lists the returns for a high pair (generally jacks or better), two pair, three of a kind, a straight, flush, full house, straight flush, four of a kind, and royal flush, depending on the number of coins played—usually 1, 2, 3, 4, or 5. (The machine assumes you're familiar with poker and its terminology.) Look for machines that pay, with a single coin played, 1 coin for "jacks or better" (meaning a pair of jacks, queens, kings, or aces; any other pair is a stiff), 2 coins for two pairs, 3 for three of a kind, 4 for a straight, 6 for a flush, 9 for a full house, 25 for four of a kind, 50 for a straight flush, and 250 for a royal flush. This is known as a 9/6 machine: one that gives a nine-coin payback for the full house and a six-coin payback for the flush with one coin played. Other machines are known as 8/5 (8 for the full house, 5 for the flush), 7/5, and 6/5.

You want a 9/6 machine because it gives you the best odds: The return from a standard 9/6 straight-draw machine is 99.5%; you give up a half percent to the house. An 8/5 machine returns 97.3%. On 6/5 machines, the figure drops to 95.1%, slightly better than roulette. Machines with varying paybacks are scattered throughout the casinos. In some you'll see an 8/5 machine right next to a 9/6, and someone will be blithely playing the 8/5 machine!

As with slot machines, it's always optimal to play the maximum number of coins in order to qualify for the jackpot. You insert five coins into the slot and press the "deal" button. Five cards appear on the screen—say, 5, J, Q, 5, 9. To hold the pair of 5s, you press the "hold" buttons under the first and fourth cards. The word "hold" appears underneath the two 5s. You then press the "draw" button (often the same button as "deal") and three new cards appear on the screen—say, 10, J, 5. You have three 5s; with five coins bet, the machine will give you 15 credits. If you want to continue playing, press the "max bet" button: Five units will be removed from your number of credits, and five new cards will appear on the screen. You repeat the hold and draw process; if you hit a winning hand, the proper payback will be added to your credits. Those who want coins rather than credit can hit the "cash out" button at any time. Some older machines don't have credit counters and automatically dispense coins for a winning hand.

Video-Poker Strategy. Like blackjack, video poker has a basic strategy that's been formulated by the computer simulation of hundreds of millions of hands. The most effective way to learn it is with a video poker–computer program that deals the cards on your screen, then tutors you in how to play each hand properly. If you don't want to devote that much time to the study of video poker, memorizing these six rules will help you make the right decision for more than half the hands you'll be dealt:

- If you're dealt a completely "stiff" hand (no like cards and no picture cards), draw five new cards.
- If you're dealt a hand with no like cards but with one jack, queen, king, or ace, always hold on to the picture card; if you're dealt two different picture cards, hold both. But if you're dealt three different picture cards, only hold two (the two of the same suit, if that's an option.)
- If you're dealt a pair, always hold it, no matter what the face value.
- Never hold a picture card ("kicker") with a pair of 2s through 10s.
- Never draw two cards to try for a straight or flush.
- Never draw one card to try for an inside straight.

MENU GUIDE

SPANISH	ENGLISH
GENERAL DINING	
Arroz	Rice
Carne	Meat (beef)
Cazuela	Stew
Cena	Dinner
Comida	Lunch
Desayuno	Breakfast
Ensalada	Salad
Mariscos	Seafood
Menu del día	Menu of the Day
Pescado	Fish
Pollo	Chicken
Puerco	Pork
Servicio	Service (tip)
Sopa	Soup
ESPECIALIDADES (SPECIALTIES)	
A la criolla	Onion and tomato creole sauce that meat and seafood are sautéed in
Arroz con pollo	Sautéed chicken mixed into rice
Atún	Tuna
Camarones	Shrimp
Cambute	Conch
Cazuela de mariscos	Seafood stew
Ceviche	Fish marinated in lime juice, served with chopped onion and garlic
Chuleta	Pork chop
Dorado	Mahimahi (dolphin)
Empanadas	Pastry turnovers filled with meat, or fruit
Langosta	Lobster
Langostinos	Prawns
Palmitos	Hearts of palm

Platanos	Fried sweet plaintains
Ropa Vieja	Stringy stewed beef in a red sauce
Sancocho	Chicken soup with tropical tubers
Tostones	Mashed and fried green plantains
Yucca	Cassava (a tropical tuber), served boiled or deep fried

POSTRES (DESSERTS) & DULCES (SWEETS)

Cajeta	Molasses-flavored fudge
Dulce de leche	Thick syrup of boiled milk and sugar
Flan	Crème caramel
Tres leches	Sponge cake soaked in condensed, evaporated, and fresh milk

FRUTAS (FRUITS)

Aguacate	Avocado
Fresa	Strawberry
Granadilla	Passion fruit
Guanábana	Soursop; large green fruit with sweet white pulp
Guayaba	Guava
Melón	Cantaloupe
Piña	Pineapple
Pipa	Green coconut, for drinking
Sandia	Watermelon

BEBIDAS (BEVERAGES)

Batido	Fruit shake made with milk (con leche) or water (con agua)
Café con leche	Coffee with milk
Café negro	Black coffee
Cerveza	Beer
Vino (blanco, tinto)	Wine (white, red)

Puerto Rico Essentials

PLANNING TOOLS, EXPERT INSIGHT, GREAT CONTACTS

There are planners and there are those who, excuse the pun, fly by the seat of their pants. We happily place ourselves among the planners. Our writers and editors try to anticipate all the issues you may face before and during any journey, and then they do their research. This section is the product of their efforts. Use it to get excited about your trip to Puerto Rico, to inform your travel planning, or to guide you on the road should the seat of your pants start to feel threadbare.

GETTING STARTED

We're proud of our Web site: Fodors.com is a great place to begin any journey. Scan Travel Wire for suggested itineraries, travel deals, restaurant and hotel openings, and other up-to-the-minute info. Check out Booking to research prices and book plane tickets, hotel rooms, rental cars, and vacation packages. Head to Talk for on-the-ground pointers from travelers who frequent our message boards. You can also link to loads of other travel-related resources.

WORD OF MOUTH

After your trip, be sure to rate the places you visited and share your experiences and travel tips with us and other Fodorites in Travel Ratings and Talk on www.fodors.com.

RESOURCES

ONLINE TRAVEL TOOLS

ALL ABOUT PUERTO RICO

You can get basic information about Puerto Rico from *www.puertoricowow.com* and *www.gotopuertorico.com*. Maps are available at *www.travelmaps.com*. For information on conferences and conventions, see the Puerto Rico Convention Center Web site at *www.prconvention.com* or the Puerto Rico Convention Bureau at *www.meetpuertorico.com*.

Time Zones **Timeanddate.com** (www.timeanddate.com/worldclock) can help you figure out the correct time anywhere.

Weather **Accuweather.com** (www.accuweather.com) is an independent weather-forecasting service with good coverage of hurricanes. **Weather.com** (www.weather.com) is the Web site for the Weather Channel.

VISITOR INFORMATION

In addition to the Puerto Rico Tourism Company's *Qué Pasa,* pick up the Puerto Rico Hotel and Tourism Association's *Bienvenidos* and *Places to Go*. Among them you can find a wealth of information about the island and its activities. All are free and available at tourism offices and hotel desks. The Puerto Rico Tourism Company has information centers at the airport, Old San Juan, Ponce, Aguadilla, and Cabo Rojo. Most island towns also have a tourism office, usually in the city hall.

Contacts **Puerto Rico Tourism Company** (Box 902-3960, Old San Juan Station, San Juan 00902-3960 787/721-2400 or 800/866-7827 666 5th Ave., 15th fl., New York, N Y10103 212/586-6262 or 800/223-6530 3575 W. Cahuenga Blvd., Suite 560, Los Angeles, CA 90068 323/874-5991 or 800/874-1230 901 Ponce de León Blvd., Suite 101, Coral Gables, FL 33134 305/445-9112 or 800/815-7391 www.gotopuertorico.com).

THINGS TO CONSIDER

GEAR

Although "casual" is the operative word for vacation clothes, wearing resort attire outside the hotel or at the casino will peg you as a tourist. Puerto Ricans, particularly in the cities, dress up to go out. Pack some dressy-casual slacks and shirts, summer skirts for women, casual clothes for the resort, at least two bathing suits (to avoid having to wear that wet one from yesterday), and sturdy shoes for walking. A light sweater or jacket isn't a bad idea either.

PASSPORTS & VISAS

U.S. citizens don't need passports to visit Puerto Rico; any government-issued photo ID will do. Nor is there passport control either to or from Puerto Rico; in this respect, flying here is just like traveling on any domestic flight. Nevertheless, it's always wise to carry some form of identification that proves your citizen-

Trip Insurance Resources

INSURANCE COMPARISON SITES		
InsureMyTrip.com	800/487-4722	www.insuremytrip.com
SquareMouth.com	800/240-0369 or 727/490-5169	www.squaremouth.com
COMPREHENSIVE TRAVEL INSURERS		
Access America	800/729-6021	www.accessamerica.com
CSA Travel Protection	800/873-9855	www.csatravelprotection.com
HTH Worldwide	610/254-8700 or 888/243-2358	www.hthworldwide.com
Travelex Insurance	800/228-9792	www.travelex-insurance.com
Travel Guard International	715/345-0505 or 800/826-4919	www.travelguard.com
Travel Insured International	800/243-3174	www.travelinsured.com
MEDICAL-ONLY INSURERS		
International Medical Group	800/628-4664	www.imglobal.com
International SOS		www.internationalsos.com
Wallach & Company	800/237-6615 or 540/687-3166	www.wallach.com

ship, and we still recommend that you carry a valid passport when traveling to Puerto Rico; it's a necessity if you're making any other trips around the Caribbean, except to the U.S. Virgin Islands, where you will pass through customs but not passport control.

TRIP INSURANCE

What kind of coverage do you honestly need? Do you need trip insurance at all? Take a deep breath and read on.

We believe that comprehensive trip insurance is especially valuable if you're booking a very expensive or complicated trip (particularly to an isolated region) or if you're booking far in advance. Who knows what could happen six months down the road? But whether you get insurance has more to do with how comfortable you are assuming all that risk yourself.

Comprehensive travel policies typically cover trip-cancellation and interruption, letting you cancel or cut your trip short because of a personal emergency, illness, or, in some cases, acts of terrorism in your destination. Such policies also cover evacuation and medical care. Some also cover you for trip delays because of bad weather or mechanical problems as well as for lost or delayed baggage. Another type of coverage to look for is financial default—that is, when your trip is disrupted because a tour operator, airline, or cruise line goes out of business. Generally you must buy this when you book your trip or shortly thereafter, and it's only available to you if your operator isn't on a list of excluded companies.

If you're going abroad, consider buying medical-only coverage at the very least. Neither Medicare nor some private insurers cover medical expenses anywhere outside of the United States (including time aboard a cruise ship, even if it leaves from a U.S. port). Medical-only policies typically reimburse you for medical care (excluding that related to preexisting conditions) and hospitalization abroad, and provide for evacuation. You still have to pay the bills and await reimbursement from the insurer, though.

Expect comprehensive travel insurance policies to cost about 4% to 7% or 8% of the total price of your trip (it's more like 8%–12% if you're over age 70). A medical-only policy may or may not be cheaper than a comprehensive policy. Always read the fine print of your policy to make sure that you're covered for the risks that are of most concern to you. Compare several policies to make sure you're getting the best price and range of coverage available.

■ TIP→ OK. You know you can save a bundle on trips to warm-weather destinations by traveling in rainy season. But there's also a chance that a severe storm will disrupt your plans. The solution? Look for hotels and resorts that offer storm/hurricane guarantees. Although they rarely allow refunds, most guarantees do let you rebook later if a storm strikes.

BOOKING YOUR TRIP

Unless your cousin is a travel agent, you're probably among the millions of people who make most of their travel arrangements online.

But have you ever wondered just what the differences are between an online travel agent (a Web site through which you make reservations instead of going directly to the airline, hotel, or car-rental company), a discounter (a firm that does a high volume of business with a hotel chain or airline and accordingly gets good prices), a wholesaler (one that makes cheap reservations in bulk and then resells them to people like you), and an aggregator (one that compares all the offerings so you don't have to)?

Is it truly better to book directly on an airline or hotel Web site? And when does a real live travel agent come in handy?

ONLINE

You really have to shop around. A travel wholesaler such as Hotels.com or HotelClub.net can be a source of good rates, as can discounters such as Hotwire or Priceline, particularly if you can bid for your hotel room or airfare. Indeed, such sites sometimes have deals that are unavailable elsewhere. They do, however, tend to work only with hotel chains (which makes them just plain useless for getting hotel reservations outside of major cities) or big airlines (so that often leaves out upstarts like JetBlue and some foreign carriers like Air India).

Also, with discounters and wholesalers you must generally prepay, and everything is nonrefundable. And before you fork over the dough, be sure to check the terms and conditions, so you know what a given company will do for you if there's a problem and what you'll have to deal with on your own.

TIP→ To be absolutely sure everything was processed correctly, confirm reservations made through online travel agents, discounters, and wholesalers directly with your hotel before leaving home.

Booking engines like Expedia, Travelocity, and Orbitz are actually travel agents, albeit high-volume, online ones. And airline travel packagers like American Airlines Vacations and Virgin Vacations—well, they're travel agents, too. But they may still not work with all the world's hotels.

An aggregator site will search many sites and pull the best prices for airfares, hotels, and rental cars from them. Most aggregators compare the major travel-booking sites such as Expedia, Travelocity, and Orbitz; some also look at airline Web sites, though rarely the sites of smaller budget airlines. Some aggregators also compare other travel products, including complex packages—a good thing, as you can sometimes get the best overall deal by booking an air-and-hotel package.

WITH A TRAVEL AGENT

If you use an agent—brick-and-mortar or virtual—you'll pay a fee for the service. And know that the service you get from some online agents isn't comprehensive. For example Expedia and Travelocity don't search for prices on budget airlines like JetBlue, Southwest, or small foreign carriers. That said, some agents (online or not) *do* have access to fares that are difficult to find otherwise, and the savings can more than make up for any surcharge.

A knowledgeable brick-and-mortar travel agent can be a godsend if you're booking a cruise, a package trip that's not available to you directly, an air pass, or a complicated itinerary including several overseas flights. What's more, travel agents that specialize in a destination may have exclusive access

Online Booking Resources

AGGREGATORS		
Kayak	www.kayak.com	looks at cruises and vacation packages
Mobissimo	www.mobissimo.com	examines airfare, hotels, cars, and tons of activities
Qixo	www.qixo.com	compares cruises, vacation packages, and even travel insurance
Sidestep	www.sidestep.com	compares vacation packages and lists travel deals and some activities
Travelgrove	www.travelgrove.com	compares cruises and vacation packages and lets you search by themes
BOOKING ENGINES		
Cheap Tickets	www.cheaptickets.com	discounter
Expedia	www.expedia.com	large online agency that charges a booking fee for airline tickets
Hotwire	www.hotwire.com	discounter
lastminute.com	www.lastminute.com	specializes in last-minute travel; the main site is for the U.K., but it has a link to a U.S. site
Luxury Link	www.luxurylink.com	has auctions (surprisingly good deals) as well as offers on the high-end side of travel
Onetravel.com	www.onetravel.com	discounter for hotels, car rentals, airfares, and packages
Orbitz	www.orbitz.com	charges a booking fee for airline tickets but gives a clear breakdown of fees and taxes before you book
Priceline.com	www.priceline.com	discounter that also allows bidding
Travel.com	www.travel.com	allows you to compare its rates with those of other booking engines
Travelocity	www.travelocity.com	charges a booking fee for airline tickets but promises good problem resolution
ONLINE ACCOMMODATIONS		
Hotelbook.com	www.hotelbook.com	focuses on independent hotels worldwide
Hotel Club	www.hotelclub.net	good for major cities and some resort areas
Hotels.com	www.hotels.com	big Expedia-owned wholesaler that offers rooms in hotels all over the world
Quikbook	www.quikbook.com	offers "pay when you stay" reservations that allow you to settle your bill when you check out, not when you book; best for trips to U.S. and Canadian cities

to certain deals and insider information on things such as charter flights. Agents who specialize in types of travelers (senior citizens, gays and lesbians, naturists) or types of trips (cruises, luxury travel, safaris) can also be invaluable.

TIP→ Remember that Expedia, Travelocity, and Orbitz are travel agents, not just booking engines. To resolve any problems with a reservation made through these companies, contact them first.

A top-notch agent planning your trip to Russia will make sure you get the correct visa application and complete it on time; the one booking your cruise may get you a cabin upgrade or arrange to have a bottle of champagne chilling in your cabin when you embark. And complain about the surcharges all you like, but when things don't work out the way you'd hoped, it's nice to have an agent to put things right.

Agent Resources **American Society of Travel Agents** (☎703/739–2782 🌐www.travelsense.org).

ACCOMMODATIONS

San Juan's high-rise hotels on the Condado and Isla Verde beach strips cater primarily to the cruise-ship and casino crowd, though some also target business travelers. Outside San Juan, particularly on the east coast, you'll find self-contained luxury resorts that cover hundreds of acres. In the west, southwest, and south—as well as on the islands of Vieques and Culebra—smaller inns, villas, condominiums, and government-sponsored *paradores* are the norm.

CATEGORY	COST
$$$$	over $350
$$$	$250–$350
$$	$150–$250
$	$80–$150
¢	under $80

All prices are for a standard double room in high season, based on the European Plan (EP) and excluding tax and service charges.

Most hotels and other lodgings require you to give your credit-card details before they will confirm your reservation. If you don't feel comfortable e-mailing this information, ask if you can fax it (some places even prefer faxes). However you book, get confirmation in writing and have a copy of it handy when you check in.

Be sure you understand the hotel's cancellation policy. Some places allow you to cancel without any kind of penalty—even if you prepaid to secure a discounted rate—if you cancel at least 24 hours in advance. Others require you to cancel a week in advance or penalize you the cost of one night. Small inns and B&Bs are most likely to require you to cancel far in advance. Most hotels allow children under a certain age to stay in their parents' room at no extra charge, but others charge for them as extra adults; find out the cutoff age for discounts.

TIP→ Assume that hotels operate on the European Plan (EP, no meals) unless we specify that they use the Breakfast Plan (BP, with full breakfast), Continental Plan (CP, Continental breakfast), Full American Plan (FAP, all meals), Modified American Plan (MAP, breakfast and dinner) or are all-inclusive (AI, all meals and most activities).

APARTMENT & HOUSE RENTALS

Local Agents **Island West Properties** (✉Rte. 413, Km 1.3, Box 700, Rincón ☎787/823–2323 🌐www.islandwestrentals.com) can help you rent condos in Rincón by the week or the month. **Puerto Rico**

Vacation Apartments (✉Calle Marbella del Caribe Oeste S-5, Isla Verde ☎787/727-1591 or 800/266-3639 🌐www.sanjuanvacations.com) represents some 200 properties in Condado and Isla Verde. **Rainbow Realty** (✉Rte. 996, Esperanza, Vieques ☎787/741-4312 🌐www.enchanted-isle.com/rainbow) rents condos and villas on Vieques.

HOTELS

In the most expensive hotels your room will be large enough for two to move around comfortably, with two double beds (*camas matrimoniales*) or one queen- or king-size bed, air-conditioning (*aire acondicionado*), a phone (*teléfono*), a private bath (*baño particular*), an in-room safe, cable TV, a hair dryer, iron and ironing board, room service (*servicio de habitación*), shampoo and toiletries, and possibly a view of the water (*vista al mar*). There will be a concierge and at least one hotel restaurant and lounge, a pool, a shop, and an exercise room or spa. In Puerto Rico's smaller inns, rooms will have private baths with hot water (*agua caliente*), air-conditioning or fans, a double to king-size bed, possibly room service, and breakfast (Continental or full) included in the rates. In some smaller hotels, several rooms share baths—it's a good idea to ask before booking. All hotels listed in this guide have private baths unless otherwise noted.

PARADORES

Some paradores are rural inns offering no-frills apartments, and others are large hotels; all must meet certain standards, such as proximity to an attraction or beach. Most have a small restaurant that serves local cuisine. They're great bargains (usually from $65 to $125 for a double room). You can make reservations by contacting the Puerto Rico Tourism Company. Small Inns of Puerto Rico, a branch of the Puerto Rico Hotel & Tourism Association, is a marketing arm for some 25 small hotels island-wide. The organization occasionally has package deals including casino coupons and LeLoLai (a cultural show) tickets.

Contacts **Puerto Rico Tourism Company** (☎787/721-2400 or 800/866-7827 🌐www.gotoparadores.com). **Small Inns of Puerto Rico** (☎787/725-2901 🌐www.prhtasmallhotels.com).

AIRLINE TICKETS

Most domestic airline tickets are electronic; international tickets may be either electronic or paper. With an e-ticket the only thing you receive is an e-mailed receipt citing your itinerary and reservation and ticket numbers.

The greatest advantage of an e-ticket is that if you lose your receipt, you can simply print out another copy or ask the airline to do it for you at check-in. You usually pay a surcharge (up to $50) to get a paper ticket, if you can get one at all.

The sole advantage of a paper ticket is that it may be easier to endorse over to another airline if your flight is canceled and the airline with which you booked can't accommodate you on another flight.

TIP→ Discount air passes that let you travel economically in a country or region must often be purchased before you leave home. In some cases you can only get them through a travel agent.

RENTAL CARS

When you reserve a car, ask about cancellation penalties, taxes, drop-off charges (if you're planning to pick up the car in one city and leave it in another), and surcharges (for being under or over a certain age, for additional drivers, or for driving across state or country borders or beyond a specific distance from your point of rental). All these things can add substantially to your costs. Request car seats and extras such as GPS when you book.

Online Booking Resources

Contacts		
At Home Abroad	212/421-9165	www.athomeabroadinc.com.
Barclay International Group	516/364-0064 or 800/845-6636	www.barclayweb.com
Vacation Home Rentals Worldwide	201/767-9393 or 800/633-3284	www.vhrww.com
Villanet	206/417-3444 or 800/964-1891	www.rentavilla.com
Villas & Apartments Abroad	212/213-6435 or 800/433-3020	www.vaanyc.com
Villas International	415/499-9490 or 800/221-2260	www.villasintl.com
Villas of Distinction	707/778-1800 or 800/289-0900	www.villasofdistinction.com
Wimco	800/449-1553	www.wimco.com

Rates are sometimes—but not always—better if you book in advance or reserve through a rental agency's Web site. There are other reasons to book ahead, though: for popular destinations, during busy times of the year, or to ensure that you get certain types of cars (vans, SUVs, exotic sports cars).

■ TIP→ Make sure that a confirmed reservation guarantees you a car. Agencies sometimes overbook, particularly for busy weekends and holiday periods.

Rates start as low as $35 a day (not including insurance), with unlimited mileage. Discounts are often offered for long-term rentals, for cars that are booked more than 72 hours in advance, and to automobile association members. All major U.S. car-rental agencies are represented on the island, but not in some areas, such as the smaller islands of Vieques and Culebra. Here you'll have to go with local companies. Most are reliable and some offer competitive rates.

If you're visiting during peak season or over holiday weekends, reserve your car before arriving on the island—not only because of possible discounts but also to ensure that you get a car and that it's a reliable one. Faced with high demand, the agencies may be forced to drag out the worst of their fleet; waiting until the last minute could leave you stranded without a car or stranded with one on the side of the road.

You can find offices for dozens of agencies at San Juan's Aeropuerto Internacional Luis Muñoz Marín, and a majority of them have shuttle service to and from the airport and the pickup point. Most rental cars are available with a choice of automatic or standard transmission. Four-wheel-drive vehicles aren't necessary unless you plan to go way off the beaten path or along the steep, rocky roads of Culebra or Vieques; in most cases a standard compact car will do the trick. If you're given a choice, always opt for air-conditioning. You'll be glad you did when it's high noon and you're in a San Juan traffic jam. Don't rent a car on mainland Puerto Rico and expect to take it to Culebra or Vieques.

CAR-RENTAL INSURANCE

Everyone who rents a car wonders whether the insurance that the rental companies offer is worth the expense. No one—including us—has a simple

Car Rental Resources

AUTOMOBILE ASSOCIATIONS		
U.S.: American Automobile Association (AAA)	315/797-5000	www.aaa.com; most contact with the organization is through state and regional members.
National Automobile Club	650/294-7000	www.thenac.com; membership is open to California residents only.
LOCAL AGENCIES		
AAA Car Rental	787/726-7355 in San Juan	www.aaacarrentalpr.com
Carlos Jeep Rental	787/742-3514 in Culebra	www.carlosjeeprental.com
Charlie Car Rental	787/728-2418 in San Juan	www.charliecars.com
Martineau Car Rental	787/741-0087 in Vieques	www.martineaucarrental.com
MAJOR AGENCIES		
Alamo	800/522-9696	www.alamo.com
Avis	800/331-1084	www.avis.com
Budget	800/472-3325	www.budget.com
Hertz	800/654-3001	www.hertz.com
National Car Rental	800/227-7368	www.nationalcar.com

answer. It all depends on how much regular insurance you have, how comfortable you are with risk, and whether money is an issue.

If you own a car and carry comprehensive car insurance for both collision and liability, your personal auto insurance will probably cover a rental, but read your policy's fine print to be sure. If you don't have auto insurance, then you should probably buy the collision- or loss-damage waiver (CDW or LDW) from the rental company. This eliminates your liability for damage to the car.

Some credit cards offer CDW coverage, but it's usually supplemental to your own insurance and rarely covers SUVs, minivans, luxury models, and the like. If your coverage is secondary, you may still be liable for loss-of-use costs from the car-rental company (again, read the fine print). But no credit-card insurance is valid unless you use that card for *all* transactions, from reserving to paying the final bill.

TIP→ Diners Club offers primary CDW coverage on all rentals reserved and paid for with the card. This means that Diners Club's company—not your own car insurance—pays in case of an accident. It doesn't mean that your car-insurance company won't raise your rates once it discovers you had an accident.

You may also be offered supplemental liability coverage; the car-rental company is required to carry a minimal level of liability coverage insuring all renters, but it's rarely enough to cover claims in a really serious accident if you're at fault. Your own auto-insurance policy will protect you if you own a car; if you don't, you have to decide whether you are willing to take the risk.

U.S. rental companies sell CDWs and LDWs for about $15 to $25 a day; supplemental liability is usually more than

$10 a day. The car-rental company may offer you all sorts of other policies, but they're rarely worth the cost. Personal accident insurance, which is basic hospitalization coverage, is an especially egregious rip-off if you already have health insurance.

TIP→ You can decline the insurance from the rental company and purchase it through a third-party provider such as Travel Guard (www.travelguard.com)—$9 per day for $35,000 of coverage. That's sometimes just under half the price of the CDW offered by some car-rental companies.

VACATION PACKAGES

Packages *are not* guided excursions. Packages combine airfare, accommodations, and perhaps a rental car or other extras (theater tickets, guided excursions, boat trips, reserved entry to popular museums, transit passes), but they let you do your own thing. During busy periods packages may be your only option, as flights and rooms may be sold out otherwise.

Packages will definitely save you time. They can also save you money, particularly in peak seasons, but—and this is a really big "but"—you should price each part of the package separately to be sure. And be aware that prices advertised on Web sites and in newspapers rarely include service charges or taxes, which can up your costs by hundreds of dollars.

TIP→ Some packages and cruises are sold only through travel agents. Don't always assume that you can get the best deal by booking everything yourself.

Each year consumers are stranded or lose their money when packagers—even large ones with excellent reputations—go out of business. How can you protect yourself?

First, always pay with a credit card; if you have a problem, your credit-card company may help you resolve it. Second, buy trip insurance that covers default. Third, choose a company that belongs to the United States Tour Operators Association, whose members must set aside funds to cover defaults. Finally, choose a company that also participates in the Tour Operator Program of the American Society of Travel Agents (ASTA), which will act as mediator in any disputes.

You can also check on the tour operator's reputation among travelers by posting an inquiry on one of the Fodors.com forums.

Organizations **American Society of Travel Agents** (ASTA ☎703/739–2782 or 800/965–2782 www.astanet.com). **United States Tour Operators Association** (USTOA ☎212/599–6599 www.ustoa.com).

TRANSPORTATION

TIP→ Ask the local tourist board about hotel and local transportation packages that include tickets to major museum exhibits or other special events.

BY AIR

Nonstop flights to San Juan from New York are 3¾ hours; from Miami, 2½ hours; from Atlanta, 3½ hours; from Boston, 4 hours; from Chicago, 4¾ hours; from Los Angeles, 8 hours; from the United Kingdom, 5 hours; from Germany, 9¾ hours.

There are dozens of daily flights to Puerto Rico from the United States, and connections are particularly good from the East Coast, although there are a few nonstop flights from the Midwest as well. San Juan's international airport is a major regional hub, so many travelers headed elsewhere in the Caribbean make connections here. Because of the number of flights, fares to San Juan are among the most reasonably priced to the region.

Airlines & Airports **Airline and Airport Links.com** (www.airlineandairportlinks.com) has links to many of the world's airlines and airports.

Airline Security Issues **Transportation Security Administration** (www.tsa.gov) has answers for almost every question that might come up.

AIRPORTS

The island's main airport is Aeropuerto Internacional Luis Muñoz Marín (SJU), 20 minutes east of Old San Juan in the neighborhood of Isla Verde. San Juan's secondary airport is the small Fernando L. Rivas Dominici Airport (SIG), also called Isla Grande, near the city's Miramar section. From either airport you can catch flights to Culebra, Vieques, and other destinations on Puerto Rico and throughout the Caribbean. (Note that although the Dominici airport was still operating at this writing, its future was uncertain.)

Other Puerto Rican airports include Aeropuerto Internacional Rafael Hernández (BQN) in the northwestern town of Aguadilla, Aeropuerto Eugenio María de Hostos (MAZ) in the west coast community of Mayagüez, Mercedita (PSE) in the south coast town of Ponce, Aeropuerto Diego Jiménez Torres (FAJ) in the east coast city of Fajardo, Antonio Rivera Rodríguez (VQS) on Vieques, and Aeropuerto Benjamin Rivera Noriega (CPX) on Culebra.

Airport Information **Aeropuerto Antonio Rivera Rodríguez** (✉Vieques ☎787/741-8358). **Aeropuerto Benjamin Rivera Noriega** (✉Culebra ☎787/742-0022). **Aeropuerto Diego Jiménez Torres** (✉Fajardo ☎787/860-3110). **Aeropuerto Eugenio María de Hostos** (✉Mayagüez ☎787/833-0148). **Aeropuerto Fernando L. Rivas Dominici** (✉Isla Grande, San Juan ☎787/729-8711). **Aeropuerto Internacional Luis Muñoz Marín** (✉Isla Verde, San Juan ☎787/791-3840). **Aeropuerto Mercedita** (✉Ponce ☎787/842-6292). **Aeropuerto Rafael Hernández** (✉Aguadilla ☎787/891-2286).

GROUND TRANSPORTATION

Before arriving, check with your hotel about transfers: some hotels and resorts provide transport from the airport—free or for a fee—to their guests; some larger resorts run regular shuttles. Otherwise, your best bets are *taxis turísticos* (tourist taxis). Uniformed officials at the airport can help you make arrangements. They will give you a slip with your exact fare to hand to the driver. Rates are based on your destination. A taxi turíistico to Isla Verde costs $10. It's $14 to Condado and $19 to Old San Juan. There's a 50¢ charge for each bag handled by the driver.

FLIGHTS

San Juan's busy Aeropuerto Internacional Luis Muñoz Marín is the Caribbean hub of American Airlines, which flies nonstop from Boston, Chicago, Dallas, Hartford, Miami, Newark, New York–JFK, and Philadelphia. Continental Airlines flies nonstop from Houston and Newark. Delta flies nonstop from Atlanta, Orlando, New York–LGA, and New York–JFK. JetBlue flies nonstop from Boston, Orlando, and New York–JFK. Spirit Air flies nonstop from Fort Lauderdale and Orlando. United flies nonstop from Chicago, New York–JFK, Philadelphia, and Washington, D.C.–Dulles. US Airways flies nonstop from Baltimore, Boston, Charlotte, Pittsburgh, Philadelphia, and Washington, D.C.–Dulles.

It used to be that travelers arriving at San Juan's international airport had to transfer to nearby Aeropuerto Fernando L. Rivas Dominici (close to Old San Juan and Condado) to take a flight to Vieques or Culebra. This is no longer the case, as all the carriers servicing the islands also have flights from the international airport. Air Flamenco, Isla Nena Air Service, and Vieques Air Link offer daily flights from both airports in San Juan to Vieques and Culebra. Cape Air flies between the international airport and Vieques.

Puerto Rico is also a good spot from which to hop to other Caribbean islands. American Eagle serves many islands in the Caribbean from San Juan; Cape Air connects San Juan to St. Thomas and St. Croix. Seaborne Airlines has seaplanes departing from San Juan Piers 6 and 7 to St. Thomas and St. Croix.

San Juan is no longer the only gateway into Puerto Rico. If you're headed to the western part of the island, you can fly directly into Aguadilla. Continental flies here from Newark, and JetBlue flies here from New York–JFK. If the southern coast is your goal, JetBlue and Continental fly to Ponce from Newark.

Airline Contacts **American Airlines** (☎800/433–7300 🌐www.aa.com). **Continental Airlines** (☎800/523–3273 for U.S. and Mexico reservations, 800/231–0856 for international reservations 🌐www.continental.com). **Delta Airlines** (☎800/221–1212 for U.S. reservations, 800/241–4141 for international reservations 🌐www.delta.com). **JetBlue** (☎800/538–2583 🌐www.jetblue.com). **Northwest Airlines** (☎800/225–2525 🌐www.nwa.com). **Spirit Airlines** (☎800/772–7117 or 586/791–7300 🌐www.spiritair.com). **United Airlines** (☎800/864–8331 for U.S. reservations, 800/538–2929 for international reservations 🌐www.united.com). **USAirways** (☎800/428–4322 for U.S. and Canada reservations, 800/622–1015 for international reservations 🌐www.usairways.com).

Regional Airlines **Air Flamenco** (☎787/724–1818 🌐www.airflamenco.net). **Cape Air** (☎800/525–0714 🌐www.flycapeair.com). **Isla Nena Air Service** (☎787/741–6362 or 877/812–5144 🌐www.islanena.8m.com). **Seaborne Airlines** (☎888/359–8687 🌐www.seaborneairlines.com). **Vieques Air Link** (☎787/741–8331 or 888/901–9247 🌐www.vieques-island.com/val).

BY BOAT

The Puerto Rico Ports Authority runs passenger ferries from Fajardo to Culebra and Vieques. Service is from the ferry terminal in Fajardo, about a 90-minute drive from San Juan. Advance reservations are not accepted. There are a limited number of seats on the ferries, so get to the terminal in plenty of time. This means arriving an hour or more ahead of the departure time in Fajardo, somewhat less in Vieques and Culebra. In Fajardo, the ticket counter is in the small building across the street from the actual terminal. In Vieques and Culebra, the ticket counters are at the entrance to the terminals. There are food kiosks at Fajardo and Vieques that are open even for the early morning departures. Culebra doesn't have any eateries nearby.

The Fajardo–Vieques passenger ferry departs from Vieques weekdays at 9 am, 1 pm, 3 pm, 4:30 pm, and 8 pm, returning at 6:30 am, 11 am, 3 pm, and 6 pm. On weekends ferries depart from Vieques at 9 am, 3 pm, and 6 pm, returning at 6:30 am, 1 pm, and 4:30 pm. Tickets for the 90-minute journey are $2 each way. The Fajardo-Culebra ferry leaves Culebra daily at 9 am, 3 pm, and 7 pm, returning at 6:30 am, 1 pm, and 5 pm. The 90-minute trip is $2.25.

Information **Puerto Rico Ports Authority** (☎787/863–0705).

BY BUS

The Autoridad Metropolitana de Autobuses (AMA) operates buses that thread through San Juan, running in exclusive lanes on major thoroughfares and stopping at signs marked parada. Destinations are indicated above the windshield. Bus B-21 runs through Condado all the way to Plaza Las Américas in Hato Rey. Bus A-5 runs from San Juan through Santurce and the beach area of Isla Verde. Service starts at around 6 am and generally continues until 9 pm. Fares are 75¢, and are paid in exact change upon entering the bus. Most buses are air-conditioned and have wheelchair lifts and lock-downs.

There's no bus system covering the rest of the island. If you do not have a rental car, your best bet is to travel by *públicos,* which are usually shared 17-passenger vans. They have yellow license plates ending in "P" or "PD," and they scoot to towns throughout the island, stopping in each community's main plaza. They operate primarily during the day; routes and fares are fixed by the Public Service Commission, but schedules aren't set, so you have to call ahead.

Bus Information **Autoridad Metropolitana de Autobuses** (☎787/767–7979).

BY CAR

Several well-marked, multilane highways link population centers. Route 26 is the main artery through San Juan, connecting Condado and Old San Juan to Isla Verde and the airport. Route 22, which runs east–west between San Juan and Camuy, and Route 52, which runs north–south between San Juan and Ponce, are toll roads. Route 2, a smaller highway, travels west from San Juan toward Rincón, and Route 3 traverses east toward Fajardo. Route 3 can be mind-numbingly slow, so consider taking Route 66, a toll road that bypasses the worst of the traffic.

Five highways are particularly noteworthy for their scenery and vistas. The island's tourism authorities have even given them special names. Ruta Panorámica (Panoramic Route) runs east–west through the central mountains. Ruta Cotorra (Puerto Rican Parrot Route) travels along the north coast. Ruta Paso Fino (Paso Fino Horse Route, after a horse breed) takes you north–south and west along the south coast. Ruta Coquí, named for the famous Puerto Rican tree frog, runs along the east coast. Ruta Flamboyán, named after the island tree, goes from San Juan through the mountains to the east coast.

GASOLINE

All types of fuel—unleaded regular, unleaded super-premium, and diesel—are available by the liter. Most stations have both full- and self-service. Hours vary, but stations generally operate daily from early in the morning until 10 or 11 pm; in metro areas many are open 24 hours. Stations are few and far between in the Cordillera Central and other rural areas, so plan accordingly. In cities you can pay with cash and bank or credit cards; in the hinterlands cash is often your only option.

ROAD CONDITIONS

Puerto Rico has some of the Caribbean's best roads. That said, potholes, sharp turns, speed bumps, sudden gradient changes, and poor lighting can sometimes make driving difficult. Be especially cautious when driving after heavy rains or hurricanes; roads and bridges might be washed out or damaged. Many of the mountain roads are very narrow and steep, with unmarked curves and cliffs. Locals are familiar with such roads and often drive at high speeds, which can give you quite a scare. When traveling on a narrow, curving road, it's best to honk your horn as you take any sharp turn.

Traffic around cities—particularly San Juan, Ponce, and Mayagüez—is heavy at rush hours (weekdays from 7 am to 10 am and 4 pm to 7 pm).

FROM	TO	RTE./ DISTANCE
San Juan	Aguadilla	Rte. 22 130 km/81 mi
San Juan	El Yunque	Rte. 3 55 km/35 mi
San Juan	Fajardo	Rte. 3 54 km/34 mi
San Juan	Mayagüez	Rte. 22 160 km/98 mi
San Juan	Ponce	Rte. 52 112 km/70 mi

ROADSIDE EMERGENCIES

In an emergency, dial 911. If your car breaks down, call the rental company for a replacement. Before renting, make sure you investigate the company's policy regarding replacement vehicles and repairs out on the island, and ask about surcharges that might be incurred if you break down in a rural area and need a new car.

RULES OF THE ROAD

U.S. driving laws apply in Puerto Rico, and you'll find no problem with signage or directionals. Street and highway signs are most often in Spanish but use international symbols; brushing up on a few key Spanish terms before your trip will help. The following words and phrases are especially useful: *calle sin salida* (dead-end street), *cruce de peatones* (pedestrian crossing), *cuidado* (caution), *desvío* (detour), *estación de peaje* (tollbooth), *no entre* (do not enter), *prohibido adelantar* (no passing), *salida* (exit), *tránsito* (one way), *zona escolar* (school zone).

Distances are posted in kilometers (1.6 km to 1 mi), whereas speed limits are posted in miles per hour. Speeding and drunk-driving penalties are much the same here as on the mainland. Police cars often travel with their lights flashing, so it's difficult to know when they're trying to pull you over. If the siren is on, move to the right lane to get out of the way. If the lights are on, it's best to pull over—but make sure that the vehicle is a *marked* police car before doing so.

ON THE GROUND

ADDRESSES

Addresses in Puerto Rico, especially in and around San Juan, can be confusing because Spanish terms like *avenida* and *calle* are used interchangeably with English terms like avenue and street. This means that the shopping strip in Old San Juan may be called Calle Cristo or Cristo Street. (And it might just be called Cristo, as it is on many maps.) A highway is often called an *expreso,* and an alley or pedestrian-only street is labeled a *paseo.*

Outside a metropolitan area, addresses are most often given by the kilometer mark along the road. That means that the address for Parque de las Cavernas del Río Camuy, south of Arecibo, is given as Route 129, Kilometer 18.9.

COMMUNICATIONS

INTERNET

Internet cafés are more common than they once were, but are still few and far between. As if that weren't bad enough, many hotels have yet to install high-speed Internet access in their rooms. Your best bet is to use your hotel business center.

Contacts **Cyber Net** (✉1128 Av. Ashford, Condado ☎787/724-4033 ✉5980 Av. Isla Verde, Isla Verde ☎787/728-4195).

Cybercafes (🌐www.cybercafes.com) lists more than 4,000 Internet cafés worldwide.

PHONES

The good news is that you can now make a direct-dial telephone call from virtually any point on earth. The bad news? You can't always do so cheaply. Calling from a hotel is almost always the most expensive option; hotels usually add huge surcharges to all calls, particularly international ones. In some countries you can phone from call centers or even the post office. Calling cards usually keep costs to a minimum, but only if you purchase them locally. And then there are mobile phones (⇨ *below*), which are sometimes more prevalent—particularly in the developing world—than landlines; as expensive as mobile phone calls can be, they are still usually a much cheaper option than calling from your hotel.

All Puerto Rican phone numbers—like those throughout the United States—consist of a three-digit area code and a seven-digit local number. Puerto Rico's area codes are 787 and 939. Toll-free numbers (prefix 800, 888, or 877) are widely used in Puerto Rico, and many can be accessed from North America. You can also access many North American toll-free numbers from the island.

CALLING WITHIN PUERTO RICO

Pay phones, which are abundant in tourist areas, use coins or prepaid phone cards; some accept credit cards. Local calls are 25¢, and on-island, long-distance calls cost about 50¢.

CALLING OUTSIDE PUERTO RICO

The country code for the United States is 1.

Access Codes **AT&T Direct** (☎787/725-0300). **Cellular One** (☎787/505-2273 or 787/505-4636). **MCI WorldPhone** (☎787/782-6244 or 800/939-7624). **Sprint International Access** (☎800/473-3037 or 800/298-3266).

CALLING CARDS

Phone cards are widely available. The Puerto Rico Telephone Company sells its "Ring Card" in various denominations that can be used for both local and international calls. They're available in shops, supermarkets, and drugstores as well as from the phone company.

Information **Ring Cards** (☎800/981-9105 🌐www.telefonicapr.com).

MOBILE PHONES

If you have a multiband phone (some countries use different frequencies than what's used in the United States) and your service provider uses the world-standard GSM network (as do T-Mobile, Cingular, and Verizon), you can probably use your phone abroad. Roaming fees can be steep, however: 99¢ a minute is considered reasonable. And overseas you normally pay the toll charges for incoming calls. It's almost always cheaper to send a text message than to make a call, since text messages have a very low set fee (often less than 5¢).

If you just want to make local calls, consider buying a new SIM card (note that your provider may have to unlock your phone for you to use a different SIM card) and a prepaid service plan in the destination. You'll then have a local number and can make local calls at local rates. If your trip is extensive, you could also simply buy a new cell phone in your destination, as the initial cost will be offset over time.

TIP→ If you travel internationally frequently, save one of your old mobile phones or buy a cheap one on the Internet; ask your cell phone company to unlock it for you, and take it with you as a travel phone, buying a new SIM card with pay-as-you-go service in each destination.

Cell phones are a viable alternative to using local service if you need to keep records of your bills. Call your cell-phone company before departing to get information about activation and roaming charges. Companies that have service on the island include Cellular One, Cingular, and Sprint.Puerto Rico is considered part of the regular nationwide calling area for many cell-phone users; it's considered international for others.

Contacts **Cellular Abroad** (☎800/287–5072 🌐www.cellularabroad.com) rents and sells GMS phones and sells SIM cards that work in many countries. **Mobal** (☎888/888–9162 🌐www.mobalrental.com) rents mobiles and sells GSM phones (starting at $49) that will operate in 140 countries. Per-call rates vary throughout the world. **Planet Fone** (☎888/988–4777 🌐www.planetfone.com) rents cell phones, but the per-minute rates are expensive.

CUSTOMS & DUTIES

Puerto Rico is considered to be a part of the U.S. for customs purposes, so you will not pass through customs on arrival if you're coming from the United States. When leaving Puerto Rico for the mainland, you must pass your bag through a checkpoint of the U.S. Department of Agriculture's (USDA) Animal and Plant Health Inspection Service (APHIS). The list of organic products that can be transported from Puerto Rico to the States includes avocados, bananas, breadfruits, citrus fruits, ginger, papayas, and plantains.

U.S. Information **U.S. Customs and Border Protection** (🌐www.cbp.gov).

EATING OUT

Throughout the island you can find everything from haute French cuisine to sushi bars, as well as superb local eateries serving *comidas criollas*, traditional Caribbean-creole meals. Note that the *mesón gastronómico* label is used by the government to recognize restaurants that preserve culinary traditions. *For information on food-related health issues see Health, below.* The restaurants we list are the cream of the crop in each price category. Properties indicated by a ✕🏨 are lodging establishments whose restaurants warrant a special trip.

For information on food-related health issues, see Health below.

MEALS & MEALTIMES

Puerto Ricans' eating habits mirror those of their counterparts on the mainland United States: they eat breakfast, lunch, and dinner, though they don't tend to down coffee all day long. Instead, islanders like a steaming, high-test cup in the morning and another between 2 and 4 pm. They may finish a meal with coffee, but they never drink coffee *during* a meal.

People tend to eat dinner late in Puerto Rico; you may find yourself alone in the restaurant if you eat at 5 pm; at 6, business will pick up a little, and from 7 to 10, it may be quite busy.

Unless otherwise noted, the restaurants listed in this guide are open daily for lunch and dinner.

RESERVATIONS & DRESS

Regardless of where you are, it's a good idea to make a reservation if you can. In some places, it's expected. We only mention them specifically when reservations are essential (there's no other way you'll ever get a table) or when they are not accepted. For popular restaurants, book as far ahead as you can (often 30 days), and reconfirm as soon as you arrive. (Large parties should always call ahead to check the reservations policy.) We mention dress only when men are required to wear a jacket or a jacket and tie.

Puerto Ricans generally dress up to go out, particularly in the evening. And always remember: beach attire is only for the beach.

WINES, BEER & SPIRITS

Puerto Rico isn't a notable producer of wine, but it does make several well-crafted local beers. Legends trace the birthplace of the piña colada to any number of San Juan establishments. Puerto Rican rum is popular mixed with cola (known as a *cuba libre*), soda, tonic, juices, or water, or served on the rocks or even straight up. Rums range from light mixers to dark, aged sipping liqueurs. Look for Bacardí, Don Q, Ron Rico, Palo Viejo, and Barrilito. The drinking age in Puerto Rico is 18.

WORD OF MOUTH

Was the service stellar or not up to snuff? Did the food give you shivers of delight or leave you cold? Did the prices and portions make you happy or sad? Rate restaurants and write your own reviews in Travel Ratings or start a discussion about your favorite places in Travel Talk on www.fodors.com. Your comments might even appear in our books. Yes, you, too, can be a correspondent!

ELECTRICITY

Puerto Rico uses the same 110-volt AC (60-cycle), two-prong-outlet electrical system as in North America. Plugs have two flat pins set parallel to each other. European visitors should bring adapters and converters, or call ahead to see whether their hotel has them on hand.

Consider making a small investment in a universal adapter, which has several types of plugs in one lightweight, compact unit. Most laptops and mobile phone chargers are dual voltage (i.e., they operate equally well on 110 and 220 volts), so require only an adapter. These days the same is true of small appliances such as hair dryers. Always check labels and manufacturer instructions to be sure. Don't use 110-volt outlets marked for shavers only for high-wattage appliances such as hair-dryers.

EMERGENCIES

Emergencies are handled by dialing 911. You can expect a quick response by police, fire, and medical personnel, most of whom speak at least some English. San Juan's Tourist Zone Police are particularly helpful to visitors.

General Emergency Contacts **Ambulance, police, and fire** (☎911). **Air Ambulance Service** (☎787/756–3424). **Fire Department** (☎787/343–2330). **Medical Emergency** (☎787/754–2222). **Police** (☎787/343–2020). **Tourist Zone Police** (☎787/726–7015 for Condado, 787/728–4770 for Isla Verde).

GAY & LESBIAN TRAVEL

In sophisticated San Juan, gays and lesbians will find it easy to mingle. Many gay-friendly hotels, restaurants, and clubs are scattered throughout the city, and the beaches at Condado and Ocean Park tend to attract a gay crowd. On the first Sunday in June a gay pride parade takes place in Condado and is preceded by a week of events. The bohemian Old San Juan crowd is particularly friendly and—just as in Ocean Park and Condado—many businesses there are owned by gays or lesbians. Some clubs and bars also host a weekly "gay night." Other welcoming areas include Ponce in the south, Rincón in the west, and the out-islands of Vieques and Culebra in the east.

Frank Fournier of Connections Travel, which is a member of the International Gay & Lesbian Travel Association, is a reliable local travel agent for gay and lesbian travelers.

Information Connections Travel (☎787/721-7090).

HEALTH

The most common types of illnesses are caused by contaminated food and water. Especially in developing countries, drink only bottled, boiled, or purified water and drinks; don't drink from public fountains or use ice. You should even consider using bottled water to brush your teeth. Make sure food has been thoroughly cooked and is served to you fresh and hot; avoid vegetables and fruits that you haven't washed (in bottled or purified water) or peeled yourself. If you have problems, mild cases of traveler's diarrhea may respond to Imodium (known generically as loperamide) or Pepto-Bismol. Be sure to drink plenty of fluids; if you can't keep fluids down, seek medical help immediately.

Infectious diseases can be airborne or passed via mosquitoes and ticks and through direct or indirect physical contact with animals or people. Some, including Norwalk-like viruses that affect your digestive tract, can be passed along through contaminated food. If you are traveling in an area where malaria is prevalent, use a repellant containing DEET and take malaria-prevention medication before, during, and after your trip as directed by your physician. Condoms can help prevent most sexually transmitted diseases, but they aren't absolutely reliable and their quality varies from country to country. Speak with your physician and/or check the CDC or World Health Organization Web sites for health alerts, particularly if you're pregnant, traveling with children, or have a chronic illness.

SPECIFIC ISSUES IN PUERTO RICO

An outbreak of dengue fever, a mosquito-borne disease, hit the island in 2007. Virulent forms of the virus can cause high fever, joint pain, nausea, rashes, and occasionally death, but the strain that spread through the island's urban areas was mild, causing mostly flu-like symptoms. Most cases were reported in urban areas far from the usual tourist destinations. As a precaution, the U.S. Centers for Disease Control and Prevention advises the use of an insect repellent with DEET and clothing that covers the arms and legs.

Health care in Puerto Rico is among the best in the Caribbean, but expect long waits and often a less-than-pleasant bedside manner. At all hospitals and medical centers you can find English-speaking medical staff, and many large hotels have an English-speaking doctor on call.

Tap water on the island is generally fine for drinking, but avoid drinking it after storms (when the water supply can become mixed with sewage). Thoroughly wash or peel produce you buy in markets before eating it.

Do not fly within 24 hours of scuba diving.

OVER-THE-COUNTER REMEDIES

All the U.S. brands of sunscreen and over-the-counter medicines (for example, Tylenol, Advil, Robitussin, and Nyquil) are available in pharmacies, supermarkets, and convenience stores.

HOURS OF OPERATION

Bank hours are generally weekdays from 9 to 5, though a few branches are also open Saturday from 9 to noon or 1. Post offices are open weekdays from 7:30 to 4:30 and Saturday from 8 to noon. Government offices are open weekdays from 9 to 5.

Most gas stations are open daily from early in the morning until 10 or 11 pm. Numerous stations in urban areas are open 24 hours.

As a rule, San Juan–area museums are closed on Monday, and in some cases, Sunday. Hours otherwise are 9 or 10 am to 5 pm, often with an hour off for lunch between noon and 2. Sights managed by the National Parks Service, such as Fuerte San Felipe del Morro and San Cristóbal, are open daily from 9 to 5.

In cities, pharmacies are generally open weekdays and on Saturday from 9 to 6 or 7. Walgreens operates numerous pharmacies around the island; some are open 24 hours.

Street shops are open Monday through Saturday from 9 am to 6 pm; mall stores tend to stay open to 9 or sometimes even later. Count on convenience stores staying open late into the night, seven days a week. Supermarkets are often closed on Sunday, although some remain open 24 hours, seven days a week.

HOLIDAYS

Puerto Rico observes all U.S. federal holidays, as well as many local holidays. Public holidays in Puerto Rico include: New Year's Day, Three Kings Day (Jan. 6), Eugenio María de Hostos Day (Jan. 8), Dr. Martin Luther King Jr. Day (3rd Mon. in Jan.), Presidents' Day (3rd Mon. in Feb.), Palm Sunday, Good Friday, Easter Sunday, Memorial Day (last Mon. in May), Independence Day (July 4), Luis Muñoz Rivera Day (July 16), Constitution Day (July 25), José Celso Barbosa Day (July 27), Labor Day (1st Mon. in Sept.), Columbus Day (2nd Mon. in Oct.), Veterans' Day (Nov. 11), Puerto Rico Discovery Day (Nov. 19), Thanksgiving Day, and Christmas.

MAIL

Puerto Rico uses the U.S. postal system, and all addresses on the island have zip codes. The rates to send letters and postcards from Puerto Rico are the same as those everywhere else in the United States. However, mail between Puerto Rico and the U.S. mainland can take more than a week.

Main Branches U.S. Post Office (✉100 Paseo Colón, Old San Juan, San Juan ✉102 Calle Garrido Morales, Fajardo ✉60 Calle McKinley, Mayagüez ✉94 Calle Atocha, Ponce).

SHIPPING PACKAGES

Many shops—particularly those in Old San Juan and Condado—will ship purchases for you. Shipping services are especially common at art galleries. Pay by credit card, and save your receipts. Make sure the proprietor insures the package against loss or damage, and ships it first-class or by courier. Grab a business card with the proprietor's name and phone number so you can readily follow up with him or her if needed.

Post offices in major Puerto Rican cities offer express mail (next-day) service to the U.S. mainland and to Puerto Rican destinations. In addition, you can send packages via FedEx or UPS. Ask at the concierge desk of your hotel; most have regular courier pickups or can call for one. Hotels that offer business services will take care of the entire ordeal for you. Caveat emptor: courier delivery and pickup is not available on Saturday, and even "overnight" packages often take two to three days to reach the U.S. mainland.

Express Services FedEx (☎787/793–9300). UPS (☎787/253–2877).

MONEY

Puerto Rico, which is a commonwealth of the United States, uses the U.S. dollar as its official currency. Prices for most items are stable and comparable to those in the States, and that includes restaurants and hotel rates. As in many places, city prices tend to be higher than those in rural areas, but you're not going to go broke staying in the city: soft drinks or a cup of coffee run about $1; a local beer in a bar, $3; museum admission, $2.

Prices throughout this guide are given for adults. Substantially reduced fees are almost always available for children, students, and senior citizens.

ATMS & BANKS

Your own bank will probably charge a fee for using ATMs abroad; the foreign bank you use may also charge a fee. Nevertheless, you'll usually get a better rate of exchange at an ATM than you will at a currency-exchange office or even when changing money in a bank. And extracting funds as you need them is a safer option than carrying around a large amount of cash.

TIP→ PIN numbers with more than four digits are not recognized at ATMs in many countries. If yours has five or more, remember to change it before you leave.

Automated Teller Machines (or ATMs, known here as ATHs) are readily available and reliable in the cities; many are attached to banks, but you can also find them in gas stations, drugstores, supermarkets, and larger hotels. Just about every casino has one—to keep people in the game—but these can carry large surcharges, so check the fee before withdrawing money. ATMs are found less frequently in rural areas, but there's usually at least one in even the smallest village. Look to local banks, such as Banco Popular.

CREDIT CARDS

Throughout this guide, the following abbreviations are used: **AE,** American Express; **D,** Discover; **DC,** Diners Club; **MC,** MasterCard; and **V,** Visa.

It's a good idea to inform your credit-card company before you travel, especially if you're going abroad and don't travel internationally very often. Otherwise, the credit-card company might put a hold on your card owing to unusual activity—not a good thing halfway through your trip. Record all your credit-card numbers—as well as the phone numbers to call if your cards are lost or stolen—in a safe place, so you're prepared should something go wrong. Both MasterCard and Visa have general numbers you can call (collect if you're abroad) if your card is lost, but you're better off calling the number of your issuing bank, since MasterCard and Visa usually just transfer you to your bank; your bank's number is usually printed on your card.

Reporting Lost Cards **American Express** (☎800/528–4800 in U.S., 336/393–1111 collect from abroad 🌐www.americanexpress.com). **Diners Club** (☎800/234–6377 in U.S., 303/799–1504 collect from abroad 🌐www.dinersclub.com). **Discover** (☎800/347–2683 in U.S., 801/902–3100 collect from abroad 🌐www.discovercard.com). **MasterCard** (☎800/627–8372 in U.S., 636/722–7111 collect from abroad 🌐www.mastercard.com). **Visa** (☎800/847–2911 in U.S., 410/581–9994 collect from abroad 🌐www.visa.com).

TRAVELER'S CHECKS

Some consider this the currency of the caveman, and it's true that fewer establishments accept traveler's checks these days. Nevertheless, they're a cheap and secure way to carry extra money, particularly on trips to urban areas. Both Citibank (under the Visa brand) and American Express issue traveler's checks in the United States, but Amex is better known and more widely accepted; you can also avoid hefty surcharges by cashing Amex checks at Amex offices. Whatever you do, keep track of all the serial numbers in case the checks are lost or stolen.

Contacts **American Express** (☎888/412–6945 in U.S., 801/945–9450 collect outside of the U.S. to add value or speak to customer service 🌐www.americanexpress.com).

SAFETY

San Juan, Mayagüez, and Ponce, like most big cities, have their share of crime, so guard your wallet or purse in markets, on buses, and in other crowded areas. Avoid beaches at night, when muggings have been known to occur even in Condado and Isla Verde. Don't leave anything unattended on the beach. If you must keep valuables in your vehicle, put them in the trunk. Always lock your car. The exception is at the beaches of Vieques, where rental-car agencies advise you to leave the car unlocked so thieves don't break the windows to search for valuables. This happens extremely rarely, but it does happen.

We recommend that women carry only a handbag that closes completely and wear it bandolier style (across one shoulder and your chest). Open-style bags and those allowed to simply dangle from one shoulder are prime targets for pickpockets and purse snatchers. Avoid walking anywhere alone at night.

TIP→ Distribute your cash, credit cards, IDs, and other valuables between a deep front pocket, an inside jacket or vest pocket, and a hidden money pouch. Don't reach for the money pouch once you're in public.

TAXES

You must pay a tax on your hotel room rate: for hotels with casinos it's 11%, for other hotels it's 9%, and for government-approved paradores it's 7%. Ask your hotel before booking. The tax, in addition to each hotel's discretionary service charge (which usually ranges from 5% to 12%), can add a hefty 12% to 23% to your bill. There's a 5.5% sales tax in Puerto Rico.

TIME

Puerto Rico operates on Atlantic Standard Time, which is one hour later than the U.S. Eastern Standard Time in winter. The island does not keep U.S. daylight saving time. This means that when it's noon on a winter day in New York, it's 1 pm in Puerto Rico. In summer Puerto Rico and the East Coast of the United States are on the same time, and three hours ahead of the West Coast. Sydney is 14 hours ahead of Puerto Rico, Auckland is 16 hours ahead, and London is 4 hours ahead.

TIPPING

Some hotels automatically add a 5% to 12% service charge to your bill. Check ahead to confirm whether this charge is built into the room rate or will be tacked on at checkout. Tips are expected, and appreciated, by restaurant waitstaff (15% to 20% if a service charge isn't included), hotel porters ($1 per bag), maids ($1 to $2 a day), and taxi drivers (10% to 15%).

INDEX

A

B

C

D

Photo Credits: 6, *Joe Viesti/viestiphoto*. 7 (left), *Greg Vaughn/Alamy*. 7 (right), *Lucid Images/age fotostock*. 10, *Envision/Corbis*. 11, *Ricardo Ordóñez/age fotostock*. 12, *Marty Cooper/viestiphoto.com*. 13 (left), *Atlantide S.N.C./age fotostock*. 13 (right), *Philip Coblentz/Medioimages*. 20, *David Sanger Photography/Alamy*. 21 (left), *Joe Viesti/viestiphoto.com*. 21 (right), *Nicholas Pitt/Alamy*. 22, *David R. Frazier Photolibrary, Inc./Alamy*. 23 (left), *Doug Scott/age fotostock*. 23 (right), *Kim Karpeles/Alamy*.

NOTES

NOTES

NOTES

ABOUT OUR WRITER

It was a trip to Bahía Mosquito that convinced **Mark Sullivan** that Puerto Rico was not just another spot in the Caribbean. Diving into the bioluminescent bay—and watching the trail of blue-green sparks he left in his wake—made him realize that this is truly an *isla encantada*. Since that time he's explored every nook and cranny, from the bat-filled caverns of the Parque de las Cavernas del Río Camuy to the cactus-lined trails of the Bosque Estatal de Guánica. What were a few of his favorite pastimes? Trying the lechón (suckling pig roasted on a spit) at roadside stands near Guavate was an experience, as was eating the mofongo (mashed plantains stuffed with lobster and other delicacies) in several of the seafood shacks at Joyuda. He has written or edited dozens of travel guides, including *Fodor's Central America, Fodor's South America,* and *Fodor's Pocket Aruba*. His cultural reporting has also appeared in many magazines, including *Billboard, InStyle,* and *Interview.* When not on the road, he splits his time between a shoebox apartment in New York City and a rambling Victorian in the Catskills.